What people are saying about the *Key Word Study*:

Inductive Bible Study students know that understanding the author's intended meaning is vital to proper interpretation of the Word of God. *The Bible Knowledge Key Word Study* is a welcome addition to the library of those who seek to understand the use and meanings of words as the biblical authors used them, in context, book by book. We look forward to using this valuable new tool in the years ahead.

—Kay Arthur
Co-founder/CEO,
Precept Ministries International

The Bible Knowledge Key Word Study has the potential of becoming one of the most useful quick reference tools for students and teachers of the Bible in the church. The principles of sound word study are explained and followed, including close attention to the fact that meaning is found not in the isolated words but in the way they are used with other words in clauses, sentences, and paragraphs. Moreover, the authors clarify the connections between passages and the testaments that are so important to theological understanding, reflection, and application of the Bible in the lives of people today.

—Richard E. Averbeck
Professor of Old Testament and Semitic Languages,
Trinity Evangelical Divinity School

I wish this tool had been available for my ministry over the last 25 years. This *Bible Knowledge Key Word Study* series will save the serious student or communicator of God's Word much time and protect from many errors of interpretation. The introductory prefaces alone are worth special attention, as they teach the method of term analysis practiced throughout the volumes. I highly commend this new tool for the accurate interpretation and proclamation of the Scriptures.

—Dr. Mark L. Bailey
President,
Dallas Theological Seminary

The Bible Knowledge Key Word Study belongs on one's desktop—open, next to an open Bible and an open volume of *The Bible Knowledge Commentary*. Arranged by book, chapter, and verse, it is convenient and practical. Its selective analysis of key words within their contexts keeps the focus where it belongs: on the biblical propositions themselves. For the serious student and expositor, this resource series bridges the gap between linguistic/exegetical keys and theological dictionaries.

—Dr. William D. Barrick
Professor of Old Testament,
Director of Doctoral Studies,
The Master's Seminary

The study of biblical words is both a science and an art. Bock is a master of both. For ministers and Bible teachers who want quick access to responsible but concise word studies, this volume fits the bill.

————Dr. Daniel I. Block
Associate Dean
John R. Sampey Professor of Old Testament Interpretation
The Southern Baptist Theological Seminary

While comments tied merely to individual words do not replace a full-fledged commentary on a biblical book, if one is looking for concise, accurate insights on biblical words in the specific contexts in which they appear, the method and contents of this work can hardly be bettered. What is more, Darrell Bock is American evangelicalism's leading expert on Luke; he'll not lead you astray.

—Dr. Craig Blomberg
Professor of New Testament Studies,
Denver Seminary

Drs. Darrell Bock and Eugene Merrill (KWS OT editor) have opened the windows, and a fresh breeze has blown across my Bible study. This morning I learned the fascinating history behind the word translated "idle tales," which were attributed to the women running from the empty tomb. I'm reading through my Bible with this easy-to-use tool.

—Dee Brestin,
Author, *A Woman's Journey* series, and
The Friendships of Women

Effective communication requires careful definition, clear illustration, and convincing application. The communication of the ancient Scriptures to modern audiences necessitates great skill in all these areas. The *Key Word Study* will help immeasurably.

—Stuart and Jill Briscoe
Authors and ministers at large,
Elmbrook Church (Brookfield, WI)

This volume is a gold mine of valuable information that will wonderfully illuminate the biblical text. It is written in a clear style, which makes the lexical and background material easily accessible and useful for a wide audience. What is more, the editor prefaces this book with a concise introduction on how to do word studies. Take out your Bible, open *The Bible Knowledge Key Word Study*, and let the journey into a deeper knowledge of God's truth begin!

—Dr. M. Daniel Carroll R.
Professor of Old Testament,
Denver Seminary

I predict that *The Bible Knowledge Key Word Study*, aside from the Bible itself, will become the single most helpful tool for anyone whose serious desire is to be "rightly dividing the word of truth." It holds a prominent place on my study desk. Read it and reap.

—Dr. O. S. Hawkins
President,
Southern Baptist Convention Annuity Board

If a student of the Scriptures wants the most accurate and scholarly word study available, here it is. My colleagues, Drs. Bock and Merrill, have teamed up to produce a truly reliable reference that is a treasure chest full of usable insights from the living Word, ready for searching minds. I recommend it without reservation.

—Howard G. Hendricks
Distinguished Professor and Chairman,
Center for Christian Leadership,
Dallas Theological Seminary

For busy people, discovering *The Bible Knowledge Key Word Studies* is like a carpenter discovering the complete tool kit. It's all there—lexical analysis, original language transliterations, translation comparisons, pointed commentary, biblical references, and best of all, each entry explains the best contextual meaning of the word. With the Key Word Studies, teaching God's Word with accuracy and authority just got a lot easier.

—Woodrow Kroll
President,
Back to the Bible

What Drs. Bock and Merrill have given us wonderfully captures the sense and meaning verse by verse in an elegantly simple fashion. What a useful tool to help gain a greater relationship with the Word, whether from the pulpit or the pew!

—J. Otis Ledbetter
Pastor, Author, and
Co-founder of the Heritage Builders Association

What a great tool for the Christian worker on the fast track! Because it addresses the vocabulary of the text, the *Key Word Study* will go a long way towards getting at the text's meaning. It's like hearing a good teacher in staccato fashion bringing insight upon insight. The cross-referencing is especially valuable, as is the statistical information. A very handy tool for teachers and pastors, and a decidedly helpful resource to nourish any Bible reader's curiosity.

—Elmer A. Martens
Professor Emeritus of Old Testament,
Mennonite Brethren Biblical Seminary

The Bible Knowledge Key Word Study volumes will seriously enhance the ministry of the layperson and pastor in personal Bible study, and in teaching and preaching. Its accurate and clear presentations of meaning, based on sound and learned judgment by esteemed scholars, assures that the series will take a prized place among Bible study resources. At last top-rate scholarship has provided the Church a clear and certain path through the maze of Hebrew and Greek words that have been an obstacle to a richer understanding of God's Word.

—Kenneth Mathews
Professor of Divinity,
Beeson Divinity School,
Samford University

Serious students of the New Testament have found everything Darrell Bock writes to be worth reading. This reference work is no exception. It is a full and empty book: amazingly full of helpful data and insight and surprisingly free of the tangential, idiosyncratic and insignificant material that fills too many commentaries.

—Dr. Al Mawhinney
Professor of NT/Academic Dean,
Reformed Theological Seminary–Orlando

What a wealth of knowledge at one's fingertips! The *Key Word Study* is a powerful resource that I not only intend to use, but I'll recommend that any serious Bible students use it.

—Josh McDowell
Author and Speaker

I'm very excited and grateful to have this tremendous resource available to augment the use of my favorite commentary, *The Bible Knowledge Commentary*. I love to learn the meaning behind words, and these volumes will give me greater understanding for my speaking, teaching, and writing. I appreciate the way the words are explained with simple yet powerful ideas that make the biblical text come alive.

—Kathy Collard Miller
Author of the *Daughters of the King* Bible study series,
Princess to Princess, and a popular women's conference speaker

These *Key Word Study* volumes will be in my library! What a great tool!

—Beth Moore
Author and popular speaker,
Living Proof Ministries

The Bible Knowledge Key Word Study is a tool useful to any who read, study, or reflect on God's Word. Hats off to editors Darrell Bock and Eugene Merrill (KWS, OT) for these companion volumes, which will add to the excitement that always accompanies Scripture intake. Knowing the significant meanings of key words in each passage will add real biblical meat to one's daily or weekly diet of the Word, all to the ultimate improvement and strengthening of faith and practice.

—Tom Phillips
Vice President,
Billy Graham Evangelistic Association

The Bible Knowledge Key Word Study is another fine resource from Victor Books, known for its commitment to providing books that bring insight and depth to Bible study for young and mature Christians alike.

—Dr. Larry Richards,
Author of the *Home Bible Study Library* series

Preachers need all the help they can muster to understand the Bible themselves and then communicate its message to others. *The Bible Knowledge Key Word Study* is a good investment in your budget for books.

—Dr. Haddon W. Robinson
Harold John Ockenga Professor of Preaching,
Gordon-Conwell Theological Seminary

This is a well-conceived work occupying a special place between a full commentary and a traditional Bible word study. By providing the meaning of key words in their contextual setting, often with helpful background, this unusual work provides a ready tool for the understanding of Scripture. Written for the lay person as well as the pastor, the reading of Scripture will be greatly enriched with this work open alongside.

—Robert L. Saucy
Distinguished Professor of Systematic Theology,
Talbot School of Theology

Some of my best friends are books, especially when they take me to deeper levels of understanding God's Word. I'm adding the *Key Word Study* to my 'best friends' list.

—Dr. Joseph M. Stowell
President,
Moody Bible Institute

Any tool that helps us dig more effectively into God's infallible Truth is worth owning. This series—*The Bible Knowledge Key Word Study*—is just such a tool. It helps people like you and me find hidden treasures in God's Word.

—Luci Swindoll
Author and Speaker,
Women of Faith

A great tool to open the student of Scripture to its vocabulary, through mentors who are steeped in the language of Scripture. Dr. Bock's contribution is a good example of an outstanding commentator who guides the serious student in the text of the Gospel of Luke.

—Dr. Willem A. VanGemeren
Professor of Old Testament,
Director of the Ph.D. in Theological Studies,
Trinity Evangelical Divinity School

A valuable tool for all serious students of the Bible. The newest believer and most seasoned veteran teacher will be helped by using these volumes. The studies are marked by clarity, brevity, orthodoxy, and practicality. How fortunate we are to have this new tool available to us!

—Dr. Warren W. Wiersbe,
Author and conference speaker

The verbal inspiration of the Bible means that God the Holy Spirit inspired not just the concepts of Scripture but their very words. Thus to understand what God has communicated to us in the Bible, we need to comprehend its very words—their origins, uses, and meanings. *The Bible Knowledge Key Word Study* is an excellent resource for Bible students who want to know the backgrounds of important Bible words and the meanings of those words in their contexts. Here is a helpful tool for all who seek to understand and communicate the Bible accurately.

—Dr. Roy B. Zuck
Senior Professor Emeritus of Bible Exposition,
Dallas Theological Seminary
Author, and Editor, *Bibliotheca Sacra*

THE
BIBLE
KNOWLEDGE
KEY WORD
STUDY

THE GOSPELS

THE
BIBLE
KNOWLEDGE
KEY WORD
STUDY

THE GOSPELS

EDITOR
Darrell L. Bock

Run So That You May Win
ivictor.com

Victor is an imprint of
Cook Communications Ministries, Colorado Springs, Colorado 80918
Cook Communications, Paris, Ontario
Kingsway Communications, Eastbourne, England

THE BIBLE KNOWLEDGE KEY WORD STUDY: THE GOSPELS
© 2002 by Cook Communications Ministries

First Printing, 2002
Printed in the United States of America

1 2 3 4 5 6 7 8 9 10 11 12 Printing/Year 12 11 10 09 08 07 06 05 04 03 02

Editor: Darrell L. Bock, General Editor; Craig A. Bubeck, Sr. Editor
Interior Design: Pat Miller

Library of Congress Cataloging-in-Publication Data

The Gospels / editor, Darrell L. Bock.
    p. cm. -- (The Bible knowledge key word study)
Includes indexes.
 ISBN 0-7814-3444-0
 1. Bible. N.T. Gospels--Language, style. I. Bock, Darrell L. II.
Series.
 BS2385 .G67 2002
 226'.04047--dc21

                 2002002872

CONTENTS

PREFACE

Darrell L. Bock

I. Introduction to the *Bible Knowledge Key Word Study*

Watching a building under construction fascinates people. After the edifice has been constructed piece by piece, it eventually reveals a master plan. Similarly, words—the building blocks of Scripture—reveal mind-changing concepts about God and his world. The construction of words determines not only the meaning of the parts but also shapes the concepts of the whole. Studying the words of the New Testament (NT) involves investigating the most basic components that lead to exegetical and theological discovery. When one examines the words in the NT, one is looking at the units that form the starting point for exegetical and theological meaning. There is something exciting about understanding not only what is before the student of Scripture but in determining how that understanding is present.

The *Bible Knowledge Key Word Study* (KWS) volumes are designed for lay people and pastors who want a ready reference to the basic meaning of certain key words in their individual context. They also seek in spots to give some relevant information on the background to the word's use that may inform its particular use in a specific context. As such this tool is not a "word study book" or lexicon because a given entry is not intended to give an exhaustive look at a given term. Other tools, such as lexicons or word dictionaries, give a comprehensive look at a term. Rather the individual entries in KWS highlight the use of the word in a specific passage and help to explain why it has that meaning in that given locale. Thus, the KWS is designed as a tool that can be kept to one side and used for reference as one reads through Scripture. This is also why the work proceeds in the order of Scripture itself. This essay serves also to introduce the reader to the common abbreviations found in the NT volumes.

The relationship of these volumes to *The Bible Knowledge Commentary* (BKC) is also important for the reader to appreciate. The NT contributors were selected because they have taught the book and written about it with expertise in the Greek. All the contributors teach in NT studies departments. Each contributor to the *Key Word Study* volumes was allowed to treat the book and its terms as he saw fit. This means that in some locations there will be differences in how the text is read between these volumes and the BKC. These differences reflect the range of possibilities that often are a part of interpretation. Thus there has been no effort to "match" interpretations between the volumes. In the case of a few individual biblical books, this difference would influence how the book as a whole is being read. In some cases these differences, as they touch on lexical questions specifically, are noted in terms of a discussion of interpretive options.

Each contributor to the series was asked to focus on a few key concerns, establishing why a given term was discussed:

1. Contributors might discuss those words where debate exists about how the term should be translated in a given context. In such cases the possibilities for meaning are noted in the entry by the notation of how various English translations have handled the term in question in that passage. Among the translations consulted are the *King James Version* (KJV), the *New King James Version* (NKJV), the *Revised Standard Version* (RSV), the *New Revised Standard Version* (NRSV), the *NET Bible* (NET), the *New American Standard Bible* (NASB), the *New International Version* (NIV), and the *New LIving Translation* (NLT), the *New English Bible* (NEB), the *Revised English Bible* (REB), and the *Contemporary English Version* (CEV). Then there is an attempt to explain why a particular rendering is a better one or where the decision is uncertain.

2. Certain words possess a significance specific to the meaning of a passage, making discussion of their meaning important for an understanding of the larger passage. This is precisely what makes that particular term a "key" one to discuss.

3. Other texts have a particularly significant background to their meaning in Greek and so the entry makes explicit what that background is for those who do not know or work with Greek or for those whose Greek is not polished.

4. Some entries possess all of these qualities. All discussions of foreign language are transliterated, so the student not knowing Greek [or Hebrew or Aramaic in the OT] can recognize how the form of the term is pronounced. At the end of each discussion entry, the basic lexical form of the term appears so it can be easily looked up in a more detailed lexical source. Those who know Greek will have to convert the transliterated form into the proper Greek.

The contributors were asked to discuss the key information about a term concisely, noting key supportive resources (like lexical tools) briefly so that if readers wished to look up more information about a term they would be directed to additional discussion. The significance of the choice is also often developed in a sentence or two. The goal was to be explanatory and concise with a view to showing how a given term contributes to the larger passage.

Each entry was to be concise and describe the term using everyday language. The goal of this tool is to make the Greek linguistic background and the theological-interpretive point of the term clear in its context. Additional descriptions of the term's use in the Bible or NT might be supplied but was not a requirement for a given discussion of a term. Since the work is not a commentary, not every term possible was discussed. Choices were made either because the term has a key role in the verse or the Greek background enhances understanding. In general, only one or two words in a verse receive treatment. A few verses are not discussed and a few verses treat more than one word. If the same word is used several times significantly in one book with the same basic force, the contributor has selected where to discuss that word in detail and then referred back or forward to that full discussion. This helped us to avoid needless repetition.

The entries possess the following form:

1:33 The one who <u>baptizes</u> (*baptizōn*)—Like the Synoptic Gospels, John presents Jesus as the one who would "baptize" people with the Holy Spirit (Matt. 3:11; Mark 1:8; Luke 3:16). See also 1:25. [*baptizō*].

The verse is indicated first, unless the entry is a second or subsequent entry in that verse, then it begins with the phrase in bold. The bold is the contributor's translation of the word or phrase under discussion. If a word in a phrase is the point of the discussion, then the English term focused on is underlined. Then the term is transliterated in the form it has in the verse. This allows the English-only student to know the pronunciation of the Greek in context. Sometimes a slight difference between the student's English translation and that of the entry may mean the student will need to figure which term in his translation is referred to in the bold. Since people use a wide variety of translations, it was thought best to let the contributor select his translation and explain it. For several entries, translation alternatives have been noted for the student. The discussion of the term follows. At the end of the entry the term in brackets is the transliterated lexical form of the term, in case the student with some knowledge of the language wishes to find out more information on the word in a lexicon. This form will allow the student to know the base form listed in a lexicon and how the base term is pronounced. In some cases more than one word is listed in these brackets. This indicates that the discussion covers more than one lexical term.

Our prayer is that this tool proves useful to many as they engage in quiet times, Bible study, or preparation for teaching.

II. About Method in Word Studies

Anyone who studies the Bible for very long knows that interpretation is often not a straightforward matter of immediate agreement about what the Bible teaches. Like any other deep and complex work, disagreement can emerge about what a text exactly teaches. Obviously, the terms of Scripture are an important part of such discussions. What can get in the way of agreement? How is the interpreter to hurdle the obstacles that lead to such disagreement? How do we proceed with the possibilities of what the biblical text might and does mean? How sensitive should we be to the types of disagreements that arise? Are some differences more important than others? The rest of this introductory essay will attempt to explain what hinders our understanding of the meaning of words and how words should be handled interpretively. In thinking through word analysis, one should first consider several fundamental questions: What are the basic rules of word study? What obstacles impede an understanding of the meaning of words? These two questions form the next two sub-sections of this essay.

In a third sub-section we will overview the two important approaches to word study, the diachronic approach (or "through time," comprehensive word study) and the synchronic (or "at a given time," more focused word study) approach. The fourth and final sub-section will detail the stages of word analysis, including a list of common errors that often accompany the study of words. A proper method may not remove all the ambiguity and debate—after all, humans are finite creatures—but it should allow exegetes to understand why a passage speaks as it does and to articulate clearly one's own understanding to others so that together they can discuss and benefit from each other's insights and observations on the Scriptures.

A. Fundamental Rules of Word Study

In thinking about words and interpretation, there are three fundamental rules that should have general assent:

1. *The exegete must initially pursue the meaning intended by the author for his original audience.*[1] Communication fundamentally involves the transfer of an idea from one mind to another. In biblical study the interpreter's goal is to understand what the original author said through the terms he used. One needs to recognize that words do not automatically have meaning. They receive their meaning from the author who produced the words. Most of the entries in the KWS deal with meaning at this level, because it is the starting point for all reflection about what a passage teaches.

Another point emerges from this consideration. To communicate, the message must be potentially sharable with the audience. It must relate to a category of meaning that the writer's audience can perceive—or else the message is incomprehensible. This observation does not deny that an author can communicate new sense in the words that he uses. It does suggest, however, that when the author intends new meaning, he will signal it so that the audience can grasp the new force of the term.[2]

2. *To establish the precise meaning of a word, one must recognize its possible range of meanings.* Often an interpreter simply assumes that a word has a certain meaning. However, the meaning of terms can change—from situation to situation, from person to person, most importantly, from context to context. Therefore, the exegete must exercise care in studying the words that compose the message of Scripture to be most sensitive to the context of a given usage. This is why the KWS works with words in a given context as it discusses their meaning. Words do not have an "automatic" general meaning. They have a range of meanings, which yields a specific sense in a specific context.

3. *Words operate in a context and receive meaning from that context.* This point is crucial. Words as separate, isolated entities do not provide the key to the meaning of Scripture. Instead, words *in relationship* to other words form the basis of the concepts that represent the message of a text. Thus the major concern of the interpreter in determining the meaning of a word is the setting of the word in its verse, paragraph, and book. In other words, words are like chess pieces on a chess board. Their importance and force is determined by their relationship to other pieces in the sentence and paragraph.

These three fundamentals provide a solid foundation for lexical analysis—a crucial discipline that the interpreter must appreciate in order to interpret the Word of God correctly.

B. The Complexities of Meaning
i. The Meanings of Meaning

Part of what makes meaning so difficult to ascertain is its very complexity. Most of us do not think about how many levels of meaning we interact with in dealing with words and trying to interpret them. Formally speaking, meaning and the study of words are bound together with the formal and broader academic discipline called semantics.[3] Semantics is the study of "signification" or "meaning." It can offer to the interpreter many insights regarding the issue of method in studying words. The goal of this discipline at the lexical level is to examine how meaning is communicated through words.

In semantics one of the problems of lexical meaning is, in fact, determining what one means by speaking about a word's meaning![4] Semanticists have produced as many as 25 possible senses for meaning, but a few distinctions are extremely significant for exegesis and indicate the need for careful analysis. A list of these distinctions follows.

1. *Entailment meaning* pertains to a word or idea that implies some type of conclusion or

implication not explicit in the term or context. For example, a passage that shows Jesus engaged in an activity that only God can perform entails the idea that Jesus is divine, even though the specific theological assertion that Jesus is God is not explicitly made in the text (e.g., Mark 2:1-12).

2. *Emotive meaning* applies to the use of a term that carries emotional force. So when James calls his readers adulterous people for their poor behavior (4:4), he is picking a term with emotive meaning to purposely shame them. A sensitive interpreter will note this emotive force to the term.

3. *Significance meaning* refers to a term or concept that takes on new meaning when brought into a context different from the original one (e.g., the NT use of the OT may bring additional force to an earlier text). So when Jews are seen as enemies of Messiah in Acts 4:25-27, using an appeal to Psalm 2, the category of enemy has expanded from the general expectation of a Psalm that used to be read by the nation of Israel about those who opposed God's chosen ruler. The switch in who is referred to shows how much things have changed with Jesus' coming and the rejection of him by many Jews. A text that used to express Jewish hope now surfaces their position as currently opposed to the gospel.

4. *Encyclopedic meaning* denotes all the possible meaning that a term may have. One generates such a full list from a dictionary, lexicon, or exhaustive word study tool.[5] This range of possible meanings allows for a variety of possible interpretations, as well as misinterpretation. The goal of an interpreter is to take these possibilities for meaning and determine which particular meaning fits in a given context.

5. *Grammatical meaning* refers to the grammatical role of a term, such as the categories that one learns in an intermediate Greek grammar course. Some interpreters use this limited area of meaning to secure meaning, when in fact often all it does is limit the possible meaning. Just as words have possible meanings, so grammatical categories often have a variety of possible forces or uses, with the exact force being determined by contextual factors.

6. *Figurative meaning* indicates the use of a term because of the association it makes, not because the term's sense and referent are directly applied to what the term describes. For example, when Jesus speaks of faith that can "move mountains," he is not referring to the use of earth-moving equipment but to faith that can do marvelous things. Many exegetical debates turn on whether a term is literal or figurative, which is always an appropriate question to consider. Usually an understanding of genre, idiom, and authorial style can help in interpreting figures.

These senses of meaning can be significant in assessing the force of a given term, and must receive attention in thinking through the study of a term. However, they are not as central to the study of a term as the three basic elements of a word.

ii. The Three Elements of a Word

Considered most abstractly, words are made up of three basic elements that contribute most directly to their intended meaning: sign, sense, and referent. In reality a word is a symbol that communicates meaning within a given culture or subculture.[6] A word does not have meaning; it is assigned meaning through cultural convention and usage.

The first element of a word is *the sign*, the collection of symbols that comprise a word. For example, the English word "p-a-r-a-c-l-e-t-e" is made up of nine alphabetic symbols. These symbols allow us to identify and pronounce the word. If we know the symbols and the coding patterns of the language, then we can understand the meaning. Sometimes a word is obscure because we do not know the symbols that comprise it. If one went to Israel and tried to read Hebrew without having studied the language, that person could not even get started in working with meaning because he or she would not even be able to read the symbols that make up the words. Without translation or explanation, the reader would be unable to work with the text. The contributors to the *KWS* are rendering a service to readers by applying their knowledge of Greek and experience with the language in interacting with the text of the original language. The same is true of contributors to the Old Testament (OT) volumes with their knowledge of Hebrew and Aramaic. This kind of interpretation of a document in its original language is technically known as exegesis.

The second element of a word is *sense*, which is the content associated with the symbol.[7] The sense of a word is closely related to the lexical "definition" of the word. However, the concept referred to by the sense of the term need not precisely identify what a text is actually referring to with a given term. For example, the Greek term for paraclete means "comforter," which by itself is ambiguous in English, since it could refer specifically either to an object similar to a quilt or to a sympathetic encourager. The ambiguity results in part from an ambiguity the "receptor" language (in this case English) possesses. In addition, one must identify what exactly is referred to as a comforter. In this case, the sense of the term is really a description of an attribute as opposed to making an identification of what exactly is being described. So the sense often gets one closer to the meaning of a text, but it does not always specify or identify clearly what exactly is being referred to by the sense meaning. Interpretation requires that we inquire into what exactly is being described. The context in which the word appears will help us not only to determine the term's sense, but also, hopefully, its referent (what it actually refers to). Nonetheless, once the general content of the term is clear, one begins to know the general direction of the passage in terms of its meaning.

The third element of a word is the *referent*. The referent is the actual thing denoted by a term in a specific context. In John 14–16, for example, the referent of "paraclete" is clearly neither a human sympathetic figure nor a blanket; rather the term refers to the one Jesus will send after his resurrection to be with believers. This is specifically a reference to the Holy Spirit. It is the identification of the referent, where that is possible, that produces specificity and clarity in interpretation.

The complex nature of a word's meaning and its various elements require that the interpreter exercise great care in approaching the study of words. Once the biblical student has grasped the fundamentals of word study, the meaning of meaning, and the basic elements of a word, then he or she can proceed with care and precision in the actual procedure of word analysis.

III. Diachronic and Synchronic Word Analysis

Word meanings can be examined in two ways. First, words can be studied historically by examining how they have been used in the past and how they have changed in meaning through time. This is called *diachronic word analysis,* the approach of the technical word study tools like *TDNT* and *NIDNTT*.[8] These two reference tools examine a word's use beginning with the classical Greek period and continuing through the NT or even the patristic period (that is, the time of the church "fathers"). Examining words in this way indicates the possible senses that a term may have.

Second, words can also be studied within a given period (e.g., the intertestamental period, or pre-A.D. 70), or within the writings of a specific author (e.g., Paul, John, Matthew, Philo, or Josephus). This is called *synchronic word analysis*. This is perhaps the most crucial phase of lexical analysis since the meaning of a word in its specific context, either temporal or literary, is the major concern of the interpreter.

The following sections present an example of both the diachronic and synchronic processes used for NT word analysis. Assumed in the work of the contributors are various levels of such a process of word study. The *KWS* is merely the result of a process like the method described here. The following section will be of value to anyone who has worked in Greek and has access to a wide range of tools in Greek. Those who do not have Greek should proceed to the discussion of word study method in the NT itself and to the discussion of common errors made in word studies.

A. Basic Procedure for NT Word Analysis: Getting Ready

Getting ready to examine words and their usage on our own requires various tools. These tools come in two forms, book resources and computer tools. Basic book resources include major lexicons, like *Liddell-Scott-Jones* (LSJ) for general Greek usage, or *Moulton and Milligan* (MM) for Koine Greek usage, and *Bauer-Arndt-Gingrich-Danker* (BAGD) or its recent update, *Bauer-Danker-Arndt-Gingrich* (BDAG). They might include concordances like *Hatch-Redpath* for the Greek Old Testament (LXX) or a solid concordance of the Greek NT or secondarily of a solid NT translation. Computer programs can help accomplish the same thing as a concordance. In fact, for the LXX and other tools, a computer concordance may be the most effective tool to use, if the text the computer tool uses is an up-to-date edition of the text in question. Here for the PC, we have found the *Logos Library* computer system to be most helpful for such study, while the search program *Accordance* has proven most helpful for the Macintosh platform. Both come with individual modules of selected key ancient works in their "scholarly" collections that allow you to search a range of ancient materials for information. For computer help with classical Greek, there is the *Thesarus Linguae Graecae* (TLG) and online there is the *Perseus* project (www.perseus.tufts.edu). These last two tools require a detailed acquaintance with Greek. Other tools that can be used for reference by advanced students include the ten-volume *Theological Dictionary of the New Testament* (TDNT), the four-volume, *The New International Dictionary of New Testament Theology* (NIDNTT), and the three-volume *Exegetical Dictionary of the New Testament* (EDNT).[9] Unfortunately there are no solid one-volume lexical tools that are up-to-date and readily accessible to the English based student. This is another reason we have produced the *KWS* volumes. For personal diachronic word study, the above noted tools are part of a basic resource library.

Several options exist as to which terms to select for closer analysis. First, one could choose to study any words whose English definitions are unclear. Second, words that have apparent synonyms and antonyms in the context make good candidates. Third, words that are used rarely or only once (*hapax legomenon* [used only once]) are also good candidates, especially if they appear to carry conceptual weight in a passage. Fourth, figures make a good choice, since their precise meaning is often not transparent. The most crucial words, however, are those terms that are either repeated or that appear to bear the conceptual weight of a passage. One must understand these to ascertain the meaning of a passage.

An expositor should learn how to spot the key terms in a given passage. If a personal reading of the text does not reveal these key terms, then the use of lexically sensitive commentaries on the Greek text or solid commentaries working from an interaction with the Greek behind an English translation can often help to locate them. Another way to discover these key terms is by comparing different English translations. If the translations render the original Greek text with clearly distinct English terms, then perhaps the term behind the differences merits closer examination.

B. Word Study Method: Four Stages of Diachronic Word Study and Two Stages of Synchronic Usage

i. Diachronic 1: Examining for Classical Uses

A diachronic word study includes four distinct stages, each of which utilizes a certain tool or set of tools.[10] The examination of terms used during the classical Greek period (900 B.C.–330 B.C.) requires the use of the Liddell-Scott-Jones lexicon.[11] Next, one enters the Hellenistic or Koine period (330 B.C.–A.D. 330). Here one will consider three groups of material: the LXX, popular nonbiblical sources, and the NT. A study of the Septuagint (LXX) will involve the use of the concordance of Hatch and Redpath.[12] An examination of terms in nonbiblical sources of the Koine period involves using both LSJ and the volume of Moulton and Milligan.[13] The study of terms in the NT will involve the use of a NT concordance, the most up-to-date being the work produced by Bachmann and Slaby or computer programs tied to the Nestle-Aland 27th edition or the UBS 4th edition of the Greek New Testament.[14]

Practically speaking, the best way to proceed is to use some sheets of paper and record the results of the study in these four periods, which will ultimately help to organize one's thoughts and formulate one's conclusions about the data. Such study can also be recorded in a computer word processing format. For exegesis, the most significant results will emerge as one moves closer to the text in question, with primary consideration being given to context and authorial intention.[15]

The following sections illustrate the four stages of a word study, using the Greek noun ἀρραβών (transliterated and pronounced *arrabōn*), the possible definitions based upon usage are: (1) earnest-money, caution-money; (2) pledge, earnest; and (3) present, bribe.[16] The examples in the writings of Isaeus[17] and Aristotle show that ἀρραβών is a commercial term that refers to the initial payment in a series of payments. Classical sources to which LSJ refers may be checked in *The Loeb Classical Library* (LCL).[18]

The study of a word's usage in the classical period yields a base from which to draw possible meanings. Only in the case of rarely used words, however, does it have significant importance, though the examples may illustrate the force of the term.

ii. Diachronic 2: Examining for Hellenistic Biblical Uses. (LXX)

In this particular step, one studies the use of Greek terms in the LXX, the Greek translation of the Hebrew Old Testament.[19] Here the study becomes more interesting and complicated: more interesting, because one of the objectives of this step is to determine possible religious or theological meaning for terms in the LXX; more complicated, because this step involves a knowledge of Hebrew.

This particular step, however, is not free from potential errors. One common error is simply to discover the Hebrew word behind the Greek translation in the LXX, and then determine the translation of the Hebrew word to get the Greek idea. This procedure ignores three important facts. First, words in languages do not overlap exactly in meaning.[20] Second, the LXX is often a paraphrase and not a word-for-word rendering of the Hebrew.[21] In fact, in some places the exact wording behind the LXX is very uncertain. Third, often a particular Greek term was chosen not because the translator was attempting to render a specific Hebrew term but because of the way the passage had been traditionally read and translated. These facts should warn the exegete against hastily concluding that a term has picked up its Greek sense from the Hebrew or that a term indicates technical Hebraic usage. The words may be used in a similar manner, but that does not mean they carry exactly the same sense.

Once the exegete has generated a list of Hebrew words that the Greek LXX terms translate, then he should study the meanings of those Hebrew terms in a Hebrew lexicon and, if possible, a theological dictionary for biblical Hebrew words.[22]

Looking up ἀρραβών in the LXX reveals that this term occurs only in Genesis 38:17, 18 and 20,[23] the passage about Tamar and Judah. In these verses the meaning of ἀρραβών clearly is "pledge," since an object was given to Tamar as a guarantee. The term as used here indicates a "business" deal; though no money was exchanged, a family seal, cord, and staff were. A glance at the Hebrew term עֵרָבוֹן (which is translated "pledge," NIV), shows that the LXX term is merely a transliteration of the Hebrew term. It is a "loanword," that is, a borrowed word.

iii. Diachronic 3 and Synchronic 1: Examining for Hellenistic Nonbiblical (or Koine) Uses

When we move to this period, we begin to cross from diachronic analysis to synchronic analysis. The objective in this phase of study is to trace the variety of meanings a given term has within the time period of 330 B.C. to A.D. 100. Actually, the Koine period extends beyond this later date, but when studying NT usage the student need not move beyond the period of the NT writings.

A significant resource for the study of Hellenistic Greek words in nonbiblical sources is the volume by Moulton and Milligan.[24] This tool illustrates the use of Koine Greek words as found in papyri and epigraphical remains. Some examples are left untranslated, but fortunately, most examples are translated or summarized, as well as dated. Some examples postdate the NT period and should be excluded. However, many excellent examples occur that vividly illustrate the everyday usage of many terms.[25]

A quick look at ἀρραβών in Moulton and Milligan discloses several important items.[26] First, the entry notes that the term is a Semitic loanword, an observation we made earlier after comparing the LXX term with the Hebrew term that it translated. Second, the entry gives alternate spellings of the term. Third, according to several helpful examples, ἀρραβών is used for a deposit of 1,000 drachmae for the purchase of a cow, a deposit of 160 drachmae for a land purchase, and a downpayment of eight drachmae for the services of a mouse catcher. These examples clearly indicate the use of ἀρραβών as a commercial term. A note to the entry says, "The above vernacular usage amply confirms the NT sense of an 'earnest,' or a part given in advance of what will be bestowed fully afterwards, in 2 Cor. 1:22, 5:5, Eph. 1:14."[27] In this entry, they have not only defined the NT term with "earnest" but have also paraphrased it with "a part given in advance of what will be bestowed fully afterwards."[28]

In some cases, the study of terms in the Koine period will surface new meanings. Usually, however, the Koine sources will supply information about the common understanding of terms in the period contemporary to the NT writings.

iv. Diachronic 4 and Synchronic 2: Examining for Biblical Uses (NT)

The objective of this phase of word study is to determine the meaning of a term in the NT. There are a variety of ways to do this. First, one can study the use of a term author by author, creating lists for each writer of the NT material. This approach allows the student to make valuable biblical-theological observations by observing each author's distinctive treatment of terms. Second, the use of a term can be studied within a specific genre (i.e., within the Gospels, Pauline Epistles, Apocalypse, etc.). The value of this division is that one can examine how genre may affect the use of certain terms and images. Third, one can also study the use of a term by proceeding through the text in chronological order. This process is perhaps less helpful in the Gospels, since these documents in their final written form portray events that occurred considerably earlier. But in Paul or in the general Epistles this third approach can help trace the development of a writer's theology or the theology of the early church. (Here, "development" may simply mean the introduction of a new topic that naturally produced new associations.)

Now what does one find about ἀρραβών?[29] It occurs only three times in the NT, all in Pauline letters. Its use in 2 Corinthians 1:22; 5:5; and Ephesians 1:14 shows that it is related both to the Holy Spirit and to the idea of sealing. According to 2 Corinthians 1:22, God "put his Spirit in our hearts as a deposit [ἀρραβών], guaranteeing what is to come." In 2 Corinthians 5:5 Paul states that God "has given us the Spirit as a deposit [ἀρραβών], guaranteeing what is to come." Ephesians 1:13–14 says that believers "were marked in him with a seal, the promised Holy Spirit, who is a deposit [ἀρραβών] guaranteeing our inheritance until the redemption of those who are God's possession. . . ." Thus the gift of God's Spirit to believers not only indicates God's ownership (seal) of them, but also a pledge of his future inheritance for them. Clearly, for Paul the Spirit is a pledge, a promise of more to come.

This concludes the basic four-step process. A question that the exegete might now ask, however, is "Which tools should I own?" Ideally, all the tools that have been mentioned should be owned. But at a minimum, one should own the Bauer lexicon, a Greek NT concordance, and either *TDNT* or *NIDNTT*. The advantages of *TDNT* are that its articles offer a full array of ancient references, often cite portions of the pertinent ancient texts, and frequently include notes about the exegetical possibilities in a given passage. *NIDNTT* has the advantage of examining concepts, of being more up-to-date in its discussion and method, and of being more succinct. Also, the one-volume abridgement of *TDNT* (often referred to as "little Kittel") is helpful as a quick reference guide and gateway to the larger *TDNT*.[30] Another helpful tool that presents compact discussion of key data is the *Exegetical Dictionary of the New Testament* (EDNT).[31] All such tools also need to be evaluated for their own method and approach, especially as they relate to certain historical judgments about the date and authorship of NT books or the relevance of issues tied to debates about relevant historical background to certain key terms. Thus such tools are for advanced students who understand how they work and are aware of the limitations and suppositions.

IV. Avoiding Errors: Common Fallacies Made in Word Analysis

Before turning to the final step of the procedure, one additional issue needs attention: to note the common fallacies made in the word-study process.[32] Several of the most common fallacies are listed in the following paragraphs.

1. The *etymological fallacy*, also known as the "root fallacy," assumes that the meaning of a word is governed by the meaning of its root or roots.[33] Also, it may assume that what a word originally meant is what a later author meant by the term. Though the sense may be related, it is not certain that an author cites a term with a knowledge of the meaning of its component parts. Thus it is best not to appeal to etymology unless contextual factors make it clear the author is aware of this meaning.

2. *Illegitimate totality transfer* assumes that a word carries all of its senses in any one passage. It could be called "meaning overload." However, linguists agree that the "correct meaning of any term is that which contributes the least to the total context."[34] One of the implications of this error is that technical meaning or unusual meaning for terms need to be determined contextually rather than imported from other contexts. It is best not to give a term added nuance in a given context unless double entendre or some type of technical meaning is clearly signaled by context, authorial style, or genre.

3. Another error is the problem of *semantic anachronism*, in which a late meaning of a word is read back into an earlier term. What often contributes to this error is the way the church today uses biblical terminology. Often a meaning develops that differs from ancient usage. A simple example of this is "salvation," which in the popular modern church almost always means justification-sanctification-glorification. Today the term refers broadly to the whole package, rather than to any one of these specific elements, as was possible in earlier usage. In other words, later meaning should not be read back into earlier usage. Another example of this problem is when appeal is made to later Jewish or Greek materials to support a first-century meaning for a term that lacks attestation for that sense in earlier sources. Obviously keeping a careful eye on the dates of sources guards against this error.

4. *Semantic obsolescence* is when one assigns to a term an early meaning that is no longer used. In NT word study this would be the same as giving a classical Greek meaning to a first-century Koine Greek term. An English illustration can suffice. One reason why the KJV is difficult to read in places is because some meanings of its terms have fallen out of use since A.D. 1611. A term may exist but it no longer carries the meaning it once had.

5. The *prescriptive fallacy* argues that a word has only one meaning and means the same thing in every passage. For example, if a word has the meaning "X" in 13 out of 14 occurrences, then it must mean "X" in the disputed case. But word meanings are determined by context, not word counts.[35]

6. The *word-idea fallacy* assumes that the study of a term is the study of an idea. But the study of a concept is broader than word study, and many terms can be related to a single concept. For example, if one studies the concept of Jesus as King, one is not limited to those texts where the term "king" *(basileus)* appears. Other relevant terms for study might include "rule," "reign," "kingdom," etc.

7. The *referential fallacy* limits meaning only to a specific referent. However, in contexts where principles are given, where commands are offered, where figures are used, or where abstractions are expressed, it is faulty to limit the meaning to a single referent. In such cases, the specific referent of a term is not the only object to which the passage can be related.[36]

When the OT prophets, for example, characterized the return from exile as a "new exodus," they applied an earlier image of the OT to their own experience. When the NT authors cited OT passages that originally referred to *Yahweh* and applied them to Jesus, they interpreted the OT in light of activities that Jesus performed that matched the text. They were not confined to relegating their understanding of such passages only to God in heaven. It should be noted, however, that as one moves beyond the author's original referents, the interpreter is moving beyond the technical realm of exegesis—whose goal is to recover the original intention of the author—and into application.

8. *Verbal parallelomania* refers to the practice of some biblical exegetes who claim that the presence of the same term in several different contexts automatically indicates conceptual parallelism, borrowing of terms, or literary dependency. Admittedly, many ancient cultures used similar terms in vaguely similar contexts, and the Greek religious world used terms that also appear in the NT. However, Philo's use of the term *logos* does not mean that it has the same sense for him as it does for the apostle John. Only careful, comparative study of all relevant texts will establish the veracity of possible parallels, borrowings, or literary dependencies.

9. Perhaps the most serious error is the *selective evidence fallacy* wherein one cites only the evidence that favors the interpretation one wants to defend. Certainly, unintentional errors in judgment do occur sometimes. However, the intentional avoidance of certain facts will always result in inaccurate and biased conclusions.

These nine fallacies present a cross section of some of the obstacles that can hinder the exegete in determining the meaning of words. At one time or another every exegete trips over one or more of these obstacles while engaged in the enterprise of interpretation. This is why dialogue with other reference works is an essential part of the process. Thus we include one final step in the analysis of words: comparing the results of our study with the results obtained by other biblical scholars.

V. Checking other Authorities: BAGD,[37] BDAG, TDNT, NIDNTT

A check of these sources shows that our analysis of ἀρραβών agrees with that of others. For example, the *TDNT* article says the word "always implies an act which engages to something bigger."[38] Thus the Spirit is "the guarantee of their full future possession of salvation,"[39] an excellent description of the contextual force of the term ἀρραβών. *NIDNTT* agrees with this description but also notes that since the Spirit is a gracious gift from God, one should not speak of God as our debtor.[40] This is one instance in which the image differs from its daily use. *BAGD* defines ἀρραβών as a "first installment," "deposit," "down payment," and "pledge." It is a commercial or legal term that denotes "pay[ing] part of the purchase price in advance, and so secur[ing] a legal claim to the article in question, or mak[ing] a contract valid."[41]

This concludes the final step of the process of word analysis. Thus the use of a term has been traced through various periods (diachronic word analysis), as well as the NT period (synchronic word analysis).

Preface

Lexical analysis is demanding but necessary. Through lexical study the barriers that hinder one's understanding of the meaning of terms are often overcome or significantly lowered. The exegete who strives to understand the basic rules of word study, who grasps the complexities of meaning, who appropriates and implements sound methodology, and who avoids the common fallacies made in word study will be able to achieve a high level of accuracy in interpreting words, the building blocks of Scripture.

Conclusion: Welcome to the *Key Word Study* Volumes

The contributors to the *KWS* volumes offer their study with the hope that the meaning and key lexical details of the Bible are made accessible to a larger public. This essay, though technical in spots, presents the underlying method that informs proper, careful lexical study for those who have some background in the study of Greek. A parallel essay as it applies to the OT will introduce those volumes. It is our prayer that the user of the *KWS* will find instruction and personal edification through the use of these volumes.

Darrell L. Bock

---

1 This is the *initial* goal of the exegete. The exegete is preoccupied with the message of the human author. Initially the goal is to understand the message as set forth in the setting in which the author operated. The process of correlating that message with other biblical texts, either earlier or later ones, is the task of a subsequent theological process. In this latter phase one wrestles with concepts like the "progress of revelation," the "fuller sense" that God intended, the use and application of the OT in the NT, and the personal application of the text. All of these involve subsequent reflection beyond the initial exegetical concern with the message of a given document in a given setting. E. D. Hirsch presents a fine discussion and defense of authorial intention in *Validity in Interpretation* (New Haven: Yale University Press, 1967). For a fine caveat in regard to authorial intention, see J. P. Louw, *Semantics of New Testament Greek* (Philadelphia/Chico: Fortress/Scholars, 1982), 48. The complex issue of *sensus plenior* is handled nicely by D. J. Moo, "The Problem of Sensus Plenior," in *Hermeneutics, Authority, and Canon*, ed. D. A. Carson and J. Woodbridge (Grand Rapids: Zondervan, 1986), 179-211, 397-405.

In speaking of authorial intention, one does not try to reproduce what the author must have been thinking at a given point or why he wrote. Rather, the interpreter's goal is to ascertain what the writer wanted to communicate through the terms he chose for his message. Speaking about an author's intention is more appropriate than speaking about the meaning of the text, since words do not carry meaning autonomously and their meaning can be variously construed when detached from their original setting. The concern of the exegete is the meaning that emerged from the author's choice of expression, the sense he gave to the words in presenting them.

2 This means that in historically sensitive interpretation one will not use later NT passages to determine the referents of OT passages. Since meaning can emerge in a variety of ways when one introduces the factor of the passage of time, going to later revelation at this stage of the exegetical-interpretive process would possibly cloud the force of the original message, if not obscure it altogether. For this complex area see D. L. Bock, "Evangelicals and the Use of the Old Testament in the New," *Bibliotheca Sacra* 142 (1985): 209-23, 306-18, which surveys and evaluates four models offered by evangelicals to deal with this particularly difficult issue and more recently my "The Use of the Old Testament in the New," in *Foundation for Biblical Interpretation*. David S. Dockery, Kenneth A. Mathews and Robert B. Sloan, eds. (Nashville: Broadman & Holman, 1994), 97-114.

Preface

3 See J. Barr, *The Semantics of Biblical Language* (Oxford: Oxford University Press, 1961), 1; A. Thiselton, "Semantics and New Testament Interpretation," in *New Testament Interpretation*, ed. I. H. Marshall (Grand Rapids: Eerdmans, 1977), 75-104, esp. 75; M. Silva, *Biblical Words and Their Meaning: An Introduction to Lexical Semantics* (Grand Rapids: Zondervan, 1983). For an excellent study of all aspects of semantics as it applies to NT Word Studies, see J. P. Louw, *Semantics of New Testament Greek*. This study addresses meaning as it is related to words, sentences, and paragraphs. For the broader discipline of semantics, see S. Ullmann, *The Principles of Semantics*, 2d ed. (Oxford: Blackwells, 1957), 1-137, 197-258; idem, *Semantics: An Introduction to the Science of Meaning* (Oxford: Blackwells, 1962).

4 G. B. Caird, *The Language and Imagery of the Bible* (Philadelphia: Westminster, 1980), 37-61.

5 In a normal lexicon the meanings of a word are simply listed along with passages that reflect a particular meaning. They can also be charted semantically in relation to the term's "field of meaning," where the senses are charted as categories of meaning that a word may have and are placed alongside other terms that can be associated with that category of meaning (see Thiselton, "Semantics," 91, where he charts out the word *pneuma*; see also Louw, *Semantics*, 60–66). Words that address the same conceptual area are said to share the same semantic domain. A semantic domain lexicon examines words according to conceptual groupings. See J. P. Louw and E. A. Nida, eds., *Greek-English Lexicon of the New Testament Based on Semantic Domains* (New York: United Bible Societies, 1988). The abbreviation for this work in these volumes is LN. For another excellent treatment of the various relationships among words, see Silva, *Biblical Words*, 118–35.

6 This point is illustrated by the existence of different languages and alphabets, which are simply different symbolic systems for representing concepts in words.

7 Silva, *Biblical Words*, 101–3.

8 *Theological Dictionary of the New Testament*, ed. E. Kittel and G. Friedrich, trans. G. W. Bromiley, 10 vols. (Grand Rapids: Eerdmans, 1964–76), abbrev. *TDNT*, and *The New International Dictionary of New Testament Theology*, ed. E. Brown, 4 vols. (Grand Rapids: Zondervan, 1975–85), abbrev. *NIDNTT*. The difference in these tools is that *TDNT* lists individual lexical terms tied to a specific root form, while *NIDNTT* organizes words according to concepts, groups of similar lexical terms, or synonyms that may not necessarily share the same root form. While *TDNT* provides fuller historical information, *NIDNTT* traces concepts better since it explicitly associates related terms. For a critique of *TDNT*, see J. Barr, *Semantics*, 21–45, 206–62.

9 These tools are for advanced students because sometimes these tools make critical assumptions about date and the authorship of biblical works or about issues tied to historical background that require significant historical knowledge by the student who uses these tools. Key bibliographic information for these tools follows in the discussion of the individual sub-sections to which the tool applies.

10 A fifth step could be added that studies the use of NT terms in Christian patristic literature. For this latter step, use G. W. H. Lampe, *A Patristic Greek Lexicon* (Oxford: Clarendon, 1961–68), which gives one access to the use of terms in the writings of the church fathers. The most complete collection of Greek patristic texts is J.P. Migne, *Patrologia Graeca*, 161 vols. (New York: Adlers, 1965–1971). Many of these texts have been translated and can be located in other series. A possible sixth step could examine the use of related terms in Jewish or rabbinic literature (e.g., Hebrew or Aramaic equivalents). For this step, judiciously use H. L. Strack and P. Billerbeck, *Kommentar zum Neuen Testament aus Talmud und Midrasch*, 6 vols. (München: Beck, 1921–61). See also M. Jastrow, *A Dictionary of the Targumim, the Talmud Babli and Yerushalmi, and the Midrashic Literature* (London: Judaica, 1971).

11 H. G. Liddell and R. Scott, *A Greek-English Lexicon: A New Edition Revised and Augmented Throughout with Supplement*, rev. H. S. Jones and R. McKenzie, 9th ed. (Oxford: Oxford University Press, 1924–40; Supplement, 1968). Hereafter abbreviated as LSJ. The intermediate lexicon by Liddell-Scott is abbreviated as LS.

12 E. Hatch and H. A. Redpath, *A Concordance to the Septuagint and the Other Greek Versions of the Old Testament (Including the Apocryphal Books)*, 2 vols. (1897; reprint, Graz: Akademische Drückü. Verlagsanstalt, 1975; reprint Grand Rapids: Baker, 1983).

13 J. H. Moulton and G. Milligan, *The Vocabulary of the Greek New Testament* (Grand Rapids: Eerdmans, 1974).

14 H. Bachmann and H. Slaby, eds., *Computer-Konkordanz zum Novum Testamentum Graece* (New York: W. de Gruyter, 1980). Another concordance that could be used is that by W. F. Moulton and A. S. Geden, *Concordance to the Greek Testament*, 5th ed. (Edinburgh: T. & T. Clark, 1897; supplement, 1977), a work based on the 1881 text of Westcott and Hort. Major advantages of the *Computer-Konkordanz* include not only its use of the most recent Greek text but also the larger context it provides for each word it cites. Advanced students will profit by using the *Vollständige Konkordanz zum griechischen Neuen Testament*, ed. K. Aland, 2 vols. (Berlin: Walter de Gruyter, 1978, 1983), a multivolume tool that offers complete word statistics. Most popularly circulating concordances on the NT, such as Strong's and Young's, work with the King James. Other concordances are specific to a given English translation. Though these concordances are adequate for the pursuit of the basic meanings of terms, the best concordances are those grounded in Greek and tied to more recent editions of the text. Some argue that the best form of the NT text is that which underlies the *King James Version*. However, this claim ignores the fact that our manuscript base for the Greek NT has improved since the time of the production of the *King James Version* in the 17th century.

15 It should be stressed that in lexical matters evidence for usage is weighed, not counted. Thus a word whose meaning is uncertain will not necessarily reflect the most popular sense; and the context will always be the most important factor.

16 LSJ, 246.

17 LSJ cites Isaeus 8.20; however, the term of the entry is not found in this section but in 8.23. This example illustrates the value of looking up references, for then errors and typos can be discovered and removed.

18 *The Loeb Classical Library* (Cambridge, Mass.: Harvard University Press) is an extensive collection (approx. 450 vols.) of both Greek and Latin texts with English translations.

19 For a helpful presentation on the value of the LXX for biblical studies, see F. W. Danker, "The Use of the Septuagint," in his *Multipurpose Tools for Bible Study*, 3d ed. (St. Louis: Concordia, 1970), 81–95 and Karen H. Jobes and Moises Silva, *Invitation to the Septuagint* (Grand Rapids: Baker, 2000).

20 For example, English has one word for "history," while German has two, *Geschichte* and *Historie*. To equate either of the German words with the English is to lose some of the precision in the German terminology. The problems in this area are detailed by Silva, *Biblical Words*, 52–73.

21 In fact, the translation quality of the LXX varies from book to book. For details, see J. Roberts, *The Old Testament Text and the History of the Ancient Versions* (Cardiff: University of Wales Press, 1951), 172–87. For a recent overview of Septuagintal studies, see E. Tov, "Jewish Greek Scriptures," in *Early Judaism and its Modern Interpreters*, ed. R. Kraft and G. W. E. Nickelsburg (Philadelphia: Fortress, 1986), 223–37.

22 F. Brown, S. R. Driver, and C. A. Briggs, eds., *A Hebrew and English Lexicon of the Old Testament* (Oxford: Clarendon Press, 1907); L. Koehler and W. Baumgartner, eds., *Lexicon in Veteris Testamenti Libros*, 2d ed. (Leiden: Brill, 1958). The latter volume is undergoing a complete revision under a new name (*Hebräisches und aramäisches Lexikon zum Alten Testament*, 3 vols. [Leiden: Brill, 1967, 1974, 1983]). The student should also consult the ongoing work of G. J. Botterweck and H. Ringgren, eds., *Theological Dictionary of the Old Testament*, (Grand Rapids: Eerdmans, 1974–), of which several volumes have been published (12 volumes are projected).

23 Hatch and Redpath, *Concordance to the Septuagint*, 160.

24 See n. 13. This work is somewhat dated (1932); however, it is in the process of being updated by

a working group of the Society of Biblical Literature (SBL), but it is uncertain when the update will be produced. For very advanced students, there is a series of papyri collections that can be referred to that updates information available in Mouton and Milligan.

25 Moulton and Milligan contains only a small sampling of all of the occurrences of a given word, so it should not be regarded as providing an exhaustive treatment of terms in this period. Exhaustive treatments of this material do not exist in a single collected form. However, some papyri updates are available online on the Perseus project site at www.perseus.tufts.edu.

26 Moulton and Milligan, *Vocabulary*, 79.

27 Ibid.

28 The entry includes several intriguing later examples. One example relates ἀρραβών to "purchasing a wife." A second example speaks of the engagement ring as an ἀρραβών. Again, the picture of an object as a pledge is very clear here.

29 Bachmann and Slaby, *Computer-Konkordanz*, 222.

30 "Little Kittel" (Grand Rapids: Eerdmans, 1985), prepared by G. Bromiley, is the one-volume abridged edition of *TDNT*.

31 Horst Balz and Gerhard Schneider, eds. *Exegetical Dictionary of the New Testament*. 3 vols. (Grand Rapids: Wm. B. Eerdmans, 1990-93). Another word tool, C. Spicq, *Theological Lexicon of the New Testament*. 3 vols. (Peabody, Mass: Hendrickson Publishers, 1994), is helpful but very selective in the words it covers. When this work is cited it is abbreviated as Spicq.

32 For a more comprehensive discussion of fallacies, see D. A. Carson, *Exegetical Fallacies* (Grand Rapids: Baker, 1984), 25-66. He notes 16 such fallacies. This essay shall note only the more common errors.

33 See Louw, *Semantics*, 23–31; Silva, *Biblical Words*, 35–51; Barr, *Semantics*, 107–60.

34 E. A. Nida, "The Implications of Contemporary Linguistics for Biblical Scholarship," *Journal of Biblical Literature* 91 (1972): 86; Louw, *Semantics*, 51–52.

35 This raises a key issue that often complicates exegesis, especially for the beginning student. One does not establish a meaning merely by showing that a term's sense is contextually possible. Often commentators think their work is done when they have shown that a context could support the defended sense. However, the sense that should be chosen is the one that is the most likely among the options. Often a context can support a variety of senses, but the meaning is the one that fits the context the most naturally and with the least amount of contextual strain.

36 This fallacy is the most abstract of the ones mentioned and is difficult to explain briefly. For a more detailed discussion, see Silva, *Biblical Words*, 103–8.

37 *BAGD* is the abbreviation for W. Bauer, *A Greek-English Lexicon of the New Testament and Other Christian Literature*, trans. W. F. Arndt and F. W. Gingrich, rev. Ed. F. W. Gingrich and F. W. Danker (Chicago: University of Chicago Press, 1979). The revised third edition of this lexicon was released in 2000 and is abbreviated as *BDAG* as Danker's role warranted an elevation in the noting of his contribution to the lexicon. The earlier version of the lexicon is cited for the example here.

38 *TDNT*, 1:475.

39 Ibid.

40 *NIDNNT*, 2:39–40.

41 *BAGD*, 109.

Darrell L. Bock, B.A., Th.M., Ph.D., University of Aberdeen
   Research Professor
   Dallas Theological Seminary
   General Editor, *Preface, and Luke*

W. Hall Harris, B.A., Th.M., Ph.D., University of Scheffield
   Professor of New Testament Studies
   Dallas Theological Seminary
   John

David K. Lowery, B.A., Th.M., Ph.D., University of Aberdeen
   Professor of New Testament Studies
   Dallas Theological Seminary
   Matthew

Joel F. Williams, B.A., Th.M., Ph.D., Marquette University
   Associate Professor of Biblical Studies
   Columbia International University
   Mark

ABBREVIATIONS
AND
ANCIENT SOURCES

For extra-biblical sources, standard abbreviations are used. They can be found in a comprehensive list in *The SBL Handbook of Style: For Ancient Near Eastern, Biblical and Early Christian Studies*. Edited by Patrick H. Alexander, John F. Kutsko, James D. Ernest, Shirley A. Decker-Lucke, and for the Society of Biblical Literature David L. Petersen. Peabody, Mass: Hendrickson, 1999. Only a few of the more prevalent, but less well known abbreviations appear in the list below. Cross referenced commentaries are cited by the author's last name (Matthew: Allison/Davies, Keener; Mark: Cranfield, Evans, Guelich, Gundry, Hooker, Marcus, Taylor; Luke: Bock, Green, Marshall, Fitzmyer; John: Barrett, Bernard, Brown, Carson). Commentaries are on the book being covered. Abbreviations for biblical books are standard and self-evident. Other sources in the list are authors of given books.

Ant.   *The Antiquities of the Jews.* Josephus (first-century A.D. Jewish historian).

Apocryhpha   A collection of Jewish works from the period between the Testaments that gives us insight into Jewish life and practice of this period. These were respected works in Judaism though they never clearly attained canonical status.

Athenaeus   Third-century A.D. Greek writer.

b   This abbreviation refers to the *Babylonian Talmud,* the rabbinic commentary on the *Mishnah* (see the abbreviation *m* below). This commentary dates to about the fifth century A.D. The abbreviation is followed by the tractate name of the book referred to within the *Talmud.*

BAGD   Bauer-Arndt-Gingrich-Danker, *A Greek-English Lexicon of the New Testament and Other Early Christian Literature.* 2nd ed., 1979.

BDAG   Bauer-Danker-Arndt-Gingrich, *A Greek-English Lexicon of the New Testament and Other Early Christian Literature.* 3rd ed., 2000.

Abbreviations and Ancient Sources

BDF   F. Blass and A. Debrunner, *A Greek Grammar of the New Testament and Other Early Christian Literature*, translated and revised by R. W. Funk, 1961.

Bock   Bock, Darrell L. *Blasphemy and Exaltation in Judaism and the Jewish Examination of Jesus.*

CEV   *Contemporary English Version*

Dead Sea Scrolls   A library of a Jewish separatist community covering the period of the mid-second century B.C. to circa A.D. 70.

DJG   *Dictionary of Jesus and the Gospels* (Items are cited by article writer).

EDNT   *Exegetical Dictionary of the New Testament.* 3 vols., 1978-80, 1990 English edition.

Eng.   This indicates a differing versification in English versions from the Greek or Hebrew texts, with chapter and verse noted.

Epictetus   First- and second-century A.D. Greek writer.

ESV   *English Standard Version*

Eusebius   Fourth-century A.D. church historian.

Howard   W. F. Howard, *Accidence and Word Formation*, 1929 (Vol. 2 of J. H. Moulton, *A Grammar of the Greek New Testament*).

Irenaeus   Church Father, second century A.D.

Jerome   Late fourth-century, early fifth-century A.D. Church Father.

Josephus   A first-century Jewish historian who lived in Israel. His four works (*Antiquities, Jewish Wars, Life, and Against Apion*) are among the most important ancient sources for Jewish life, practice, and belief that we have.

Justin Martyr Church Father, second-century A.D.

Juvenal   Late first-century, early second century A.D. Roman writer.

JW   *The Wars of the Jews,* Josephus.

KJV   *King James Version*

LS   Liddell and Scott, *Intermediate Greek-English Lexicon.*

LSJ	Liddell, Scott, Jones, and McKenzie, *English-Greek Lexicon*.
LN	Johannes P. Louw and Eugene Nida, *Greek-English Lexicon of the New Testament Based on Semantic Domains*. 2 vols., 1988.
m	This abbreviation refers to the *Mishnah*, the Jewish codification of the oral law made in the second century A.D. It is followed by the tractate name of the book as the *Mishnah* consists of many books covering a wide array of topics relevant to Judaism.
Marshall	Marshall, Christopher D., *Faith as a Theme in Mark's Narrative*, 1989.
MM	Moulton-Milligan, *Vocabulary of the Greek New Testament*, 1930.
NASB	*New American Standard Bible*
NCV	*New Century Version*
NEB	*New English Bible*
NET	*New English Translation*
NIDNTT	*New International Dictionary of New Testament Theology*. 4 vols., 1975-85.
NIV	*New International Version*
NKJV	*New King James Version*
NLT	*New Living Translation*
NRSV	*New Revised Standard Version*
NT	New Testament
OT	Old Testament
Pesiq. Rab Kah	*Pesiqta de Rab Kahana*, a Jewish Rabbinic work of lessons for the Sabbath from the sixth century A.D.
Philo	A Hellenistic Jewish philosopher who lived in Egypt in the late first century B.C. and early first century A.D. His works cover many Jewish biblical books and topics.
Pliny the Elder	First-century Roman writer.

Plutarch First- and second-century A.D. Greek writer.

Pseudepi-
grapha
A collection of Jewish works that range from the intertestamental period to several centuries after the time of Christ that give us insight into Jewish thinking in the period surrounding the New Testament.

Q Part of an abbreviation that usually includes a number before it. It specifies a document from Qumran. The number tells in which cave at Qumran the document was found. These documents are part of the Dead Sea Scrolls.

Qumran The locale of the Dead Sea Scrolls, a library of a Jewish separatist community.

R. Rabbi (is usually followed by the rabbi's name).

Rab. *Rabbah.* This abbreviation is preceded by the biblical book (with its normal abbreviation) covered as part of a larger work of Jewish exposition known as the *Midrash Rabbah,* a work of around the fourth century A.D. The ten biblical books covered are Genesis through Deuteronomy, Lamentations, Ruth, Ecclesiastes, Song of Songs, and Esther.

REB *Revised English Bible*

Robertson A. T. Robertson, *A Grammar of the Greek New Testament in Light of Historical Research,* 1934

RSV *Revised Standard Version*

Schürer *The History of the Jewish People in the Age of Jesus Christ (175 B.C.–A.D. 135).* 3 vols., 1973-87.

Seneca First-century A.D. Roman writer.

Sir. Sirach——a Jewish book from the apocrypha.

Suetonius Early second-century A.D. Roman historian.

Spicq *Theological Lexicon of the New Testament,* 3 vols., 1978-82, 1994 English edition.

T. *Testament* (usually used with a name of one of the sons of Jacob as part of the title of one of the *Testament of the Twelve Patriarchs,* a book in the Old Testament Pseudepigrapha or tied to a *Testament* associated with another Jewish great, like Moses or Abraham).

t	*Tosefta* (After the abbreviation *t* comes the name of the specific tractate that is referred to within the *Tosefta*. This work is a Jewish rabbinic text that supplements the *Mishnah,* so it emerged after the late second century A.D.)
Tacitus	Late first-century and early second-century A.D. Roman historian.
TDNT	*Theological Dictionary of the New Testament,* ed by Gerhard Kittel and Gerhard Friedrich, 10 vols., 1964 English edition.
TEV	*Today's English Version*
Theodotion	Second-century A.D. translator into a version of the Greek Old Testament.
Virgil	First-century B.C. Roman writer.
Wallace	Daniel B. Wallace, *Greek Grammar Beyond the Basics,* 1996.
Wis.	The book of Wisdom—a Jewish book from the apocrypha.
x	Abbreviation for the number of times a word or phrase is used or appears (e.g., 3x = 3 times).
Xenophon	Late fifth- and early fourth-century B.C. Greek writer.

TRANSLITERATIONS

Greek Transliterations

The *Bible Knowledge Key Word Study* uses the standard transliteration system for Greek. Below is a chart of how the letters correspond. This chart can help the reader get back to the Greek lettering.

α	—	a	ν	—	n
β	—	b	ξ	—	x
γ	—	g	ο	—	o
δ	—	d	π	—	p
ζ	—	z	ρ	—	r
η	—	ē	σ, ς	—	s
θ	—	th	τ	—	t
ι	—	i	υ	—	y *
κ	—	k	φ	—	ph
λ	—	l	χ	—	ch
μ	—	m	ψ	—	ps
			ω	—	ō

*Except in diphthong; see below.

The unusual features of the normal transliteration include the following variations.

ῥ	—	rh	αυ	—	au
	—	h	ει	—	ei
γγ	—	ng	ευ	—	eu
γκ	—	nk	ηυ	—	ēu
γξ	—	nx	οι	—	oi
γχ	—	nch	ου	—	ou
αι	—	ai	υι	—	hui

In the index on transliteration we follow the alphabetization of English in rendering the order of words.

MATTHEW

David K. Lowery

1:1 Book (*biblos*)—This word is related to the Egyptian word for the papyrus plant (*byblos*) used in the production of writing material (the word "paper" comes from the Latin name, *papyrus*). Although our oldest copies of the Gospel of Matthew were written on papyrus, the use of the word here does not identify the material on which the Gospel was written (the Jewish community at Qumran, for example, usually wrote on parchment made from the skin of sheep or goats). Rather, it describes either the Gospel as a whole or the genealogy that immediately follows. It could be translated "record" (NASB, NIV) since it is used in the phrase "book of life" (Phil. 4:3; Rev. 3:5) to mean a record or book of accounts, or even simply "account" (NRSV), especially if it refers specifically to the genealogy that follows. However, as an introductory verse, it is more likely used to refer to the Gospel as a whole (BDAG 192-3). In this way the Gospel's account of Jesus' life and ministry serves as a new addition and companion to earlier Scriptures ("the book of the history of Jesus Christ," cf. "the book of Moses" Mark 12:26; "the book of the words of Isaiah," Luke 3:4; "the book of Psalms," Acts 1:20). [*biblos*]

Genealogy (*geneseōs*)—This word can also mean "birth" (v. 18) and in this first use could serve as a heading to the family lineage presented in the following verses (vv. 1-17). In connection with *biblos* it could then mean "the record of the family line" and function as an introduction to verses 1-17 (so NIV, NASB, NRSV). But it probably refers to the entire account of Jesus' life that follows in the Gospel so the translation "the book of the history of Jesus Christ" more accurately reflects the meaning of the phrase here (BDAG, 193). [*genesis*]

Jesus (*Iēsou*)—This personal name is the Greek form of Joshua, meaning "the Lord saves." [*Iēsous*]

Christ (*Christou*)—This is the Greek form of Messiah, meaning "anointed one." This title was applied to those claiming to be Israel's deliverer or redeemer from foreign tyranny. It is so closely linked with Jesus in the Gospels that it is used as a personal name. The title applied to Jesus will be defined clearly for the reader as the Gospel unfolds, although 1:21 shows at the outset that Israel's preeminent need is not deliverance from political tyranny but liberation from sin's tyranny. [*Christos*]

Son of David (*huiou Dauid*)—This phrase evokes the promise of 2 Samuel 7:12-16, and was used as a messianic title. Matthew shows that Jesus is the fulfillment of this promise to David (e.g., 11:4-6). [*Dauid*]

Son of Abraham (*huiou Abraam*)— Matthew also shows that the promise in Genesis 12:1-3, namely that through Abraham all the world would be blessed, is fulfilled in Jesus' life and ministry. God's mercy shown to Gentiles is a theme in this Gospel (e.g., 8:10-13). [*Abraam*]

1:2-16 was the parent of (*egennēsen*)—This word is used in genealogies to describe direct descent but is not limited to immediate parentage, that is, it may describe a grandparent, levirate or legal (not biological) parent. An unusual feature of the genealogy is the mention of four Gentile women: Tamar (1:3), Rahab, Ruth (1:5) and Bathsheba (1:6, identified only as "the wife of Uriah"), a reminder to readers that the line of the Messiah includes Gentiles. Also many of these women shared in suspect events in their past, showing God's grace. Joseph (1:16) is Jesus' legal parent, and in that sense the genealogy ends with him as "the husband of Mary." The last use of the verb *gennaō* in the genealogy is in the passive voice ("was born" rather than "give birth to"). As the following verses make clear (1:18-25), the passive voice points toward the conception brought about by God the Holy Spirit. [*gennaō*]

1:17 Fourteen (*dekatessares*)—The emphasis on 14 (3x) may call attention to the name of David whose three Hebrew consonants (*d w d*) are the fourth, sixth and fourth letters in the alphabet. Their sum would be 14. This kind of enumeration was widely used in the ancient world. Thus, the sum underscores Jesus' messianic lineage. [*dekatessares*]

1:18 birth (*genesis*)—This is the same word used in 1:1, but in this context it means birth (BDAG, 192). [*genesis*]

betrothed (*mnēsteutheisēs*)—Jewish sources suggest that young women like Mary were often engaged in their early teen years (*m Abot* 5.21, 32; *Gen Rab* 95; *Pesiq Rab Kah* 11:6; Keener, p. 88). Engagement usually lasted a year. But though the marriage was not yet consum-

mated ("before they came together," probably refers both to sharing a home and sexual relationship) the woman was regarded as a "wife" and considered a widow if her betrothed died (*m Ketub* 1.2). She also was liable to punishment for adultery in cases of infidelity (2 Enoch 71:6-11; *p Ketub* 1.4 § 4). This possibility intensified Joseph's dilemma. [*mnēsteuō*]

by the Holy Spirit (*ek pneumatos hagiou*)—But Mary's pregnancy is due to the Holy Spirit. The preposition "by" (*ek*) in reference to birth was often used to introduce the male's role. Although the translation suggests agency, the preposition also points toward Jesus' origin as a divine person whose beginning as a human being is mediated by the creative agent of God the Holy Spirit. [*pneuma*]

1:19 righteous (*dikaios*)—A righteous or just person was a person of faith who lived according to God's revelation in the OT (Job 1:1). Joseph intends to follow the law's stipulations, but to do so lovingly and mercifully. [*dikaios*]

divorce (*apolysai*)—Joseph seems to have had two options open to him. According to Deuteronomy 22:23-27, a trial could be held to determine if an engaged woman was involved in a consensual or a forced sexual relationship. (A verdict of guilty called for the death penalty. Whether this was ever carried out in Israel's history is unclear, but in any case Israel was at this time a Roman province, where capital punishment was the prerogative of Rome alone.) The second course of action open to Joseph was to follow Deuteronomy 24:1 and write Mary a certificate of divorce. (The Mishnah required witnesses to the writing of the certificate, *Gittin* 9.4, and even this may not have been necessary in Mary and Joseph's day.) [*apolyō*]

without humiliating (*me . . . deigmatisai*)—This word means "expose, make an example of, disgrace" (BDAG, 214). Joseph determined to do what he believed was right but did not want to bring Mary's pregnancy to public attention. [*deigmatizō*]

1:20 After Joseph had thought about doing this (*tauta de autou enthymēthentos*)—The participle indicates Joseph thought long and hard about his course of action. It was divine revelation that caused him to change his mind. [*enthymeomai*]

Angel (*angelos*)—In this instance the revelation is through an angel (the word *angelos* means "messenger," BDAG, 8) who communicated to Joseph by means of a dream what Matthew had already explained to readers in 1:18: Mary's pregnancy is not due to human but to divine agency. [*angelos*]

do not fear (*mē phobēthēs*)—These consoling words are probably stated not so much in connection with the angel's appearance but with his message: Joseph should not follow the law's precepts concerning divorce but proceed with the marriage. In the NT this term only appears in the passive form of *phobeomai*. [*phobeō*]

1:21 He will save his people (*sosei ton laon autou*)—Jesus' name describes his destiny (see 1:1). Throughout Matthew's Gospel, *the people* refers to the people of Israel. Israel looked forward to a Messiah who would save them. Jesus was this Messiah. Although the Gospel will show that Jesus was rejected by most of the people, this revelation serves as a word of hope that God has not finally rejected Israel. The ending of the Gospel, with the mission to all nations (28:19), shows that salvation is not limited to Israel. [*laos*]

From their sins (*apo tōn hamartiōn autōn*)—Jesus will save people from their sins by means of his death (26:28). Sin is a rejection of God and his revelation. If sin is not forgiven, the consequence is wrath and judgment (3:6,10,12) resulting in banishment from God's presence (7:23; 25:46). [*hamartia*]

1:22 to fulfill (*hina plērōthē*)—Matthew will use similar words about ten times to introduce passages from the OT. Such notes assure the reader that the events of Jesus' life take place in accordance with God's revelation. [*plēroō*]

What was spoken by the Lord through the prophet (*to rhēthen hypo kyriou dia tou prophētou*)—Although the prophet may deliver the message with his own style and words, he does so as the Lord's representative and spokesperson. Matthew reminds his readers regularly that the words of Scripture, though written and spoken by people, ultimately derive from God. In that sense God can be called the author. [*eipon, legō*]

Lord (*kyriou*)—This is the usual designation for God in the Greek OT. It refers primarily to his authority as ruler. [*kyrios*]

1:23 Virgin (*parthenos*)—Isaiah's prophecy (7:14) was likely first fulfilled in the days of King Ahaz by a young woman who would soon marry and give birth to a child as a sign that God would sustain the Davidic line (see Isa. 7:15-16 which gives a time frame that says the king will be deposed before the child reaches an age of discernment). However, the greater fulfillment of this prophecy and the pattern of divine activity it represents is in Mary's life, the young, virgin woman who would soon marry and give birth to Jesus, the one who would culminate the Davidic line, the Messiah. In Isaiah's time, no indication is given that the birth came about other than by natural means. In the case of Mary, it is clear that the birth of Jesus is by supernatural means. Such prophecy where a pattern is intensified in its realization in Jesus is common in the NT (e.g., uses of Ps. 2:1-2 and Ps. 118 in Acts 4). [*parthenos*]

Immanuel (*Emmanouēl*)—God showed his presence with the people of Israel in the days of Ahaz by sustaining them and preserving the Davidic line despite their lack of faith. Though many in Israel similarly lacked faith in Jesus' day, God showed his faithfulness to his Word in Jesus' birth and ministry. In a preeminent way, Jesus manifested God's presence. And as Jesus told his disciples, his presence would be with them continually: "I will be with you always, to the end of the age" (28:20; cf. also 18:20). [*Emmanouēl*]

1:24 Joseph . . . did (*epoiēsen*)—Like his OT namesake, Joseph is a man of dreams who obeys God. (Dreams play a prominent role in Matthew's infancy account [2:13, 19, 22]) Jesus will emphasize that those who have a relationship with God "do" (*poiōn*) his will (7:21). The wise person responds to Jesus by hearing and "doing" (*poiei*) what he says (7:24). Joseph was this sort of person. [*poieō*]

1:25 he did not know her (*ouk eginōsken autēn*)—The word "know" is used as a euphemism for sexual relationship (cf. Gen. 4:1, 17; Luke 1:34), which most translations make explicit: "kept her a virgin" (NASB); "he had no union with her" (NIV); "did not have marital relations with her" (NET). [*ginōskō*]
    until she gave birth (*heōs ou eteken*)—The conjunction "until" is usually used "to denote the end of a period of time" (BDAG, 422; although as Mark 9:1 shows, a change in circumstances may not take place immediately). By this statement Matthew indicates that Joseph and Mary began normal marital relations after Jesus' birth. [*heōs*]

2:1 Bethlehem (*Bēthleem*)—The wise men expect to find the King of the Jews born in the capital city, Jerusalem. Instead, he is born in a small town about seven miles to the south. The contrast between the expected and the actual circumstances of Jesus' birth is part of a theme about his life and ministry that is shown to take place in various ways in the Gospel. For example, instead of joy at the birth of the Messiah, the people of Jerusalem and its leadership are "troubled" (2:3). Thus from the very beginning in Matthew, Jesus' presence introduces tension in Israel. [*Bēthleem*]

Herod (*Hērōdou*)—This king, also known as Herod the Great, reigned from 37-4 B.C. His son, Herod Antipas, extended his bloody legacy by killing John the Baptist (Matt. 14:10) and his grandson, Herod Agrippa, followed his forbears by killing the apostle James, the son of Zebedee (Acts 12:1-2). [*Hērōdēs*]
    Wise men from the east (*magoi apo anatolōn*)—The term first described members of the priestly caste in Persia who practiced astrology and the interpretation of dreams. It was later applied to similar practitioners in Babylon and then to those throughout the ancient world performing magic and occult arts (Acts 13:6, 8). Whether these men came from Persia, Babylon, or Arabia (the gifts of gold and spices are associated with this region, cf. Isa. 60:6), they are presented as Gentiles. Matthew probably sees in their response to natural revelation a positive contrast with the Jews who, despite having special revelation about Messiah and his birthplace in the OT (Mic. 5:1-4), refuse to honor him. This is the first of many indications of Gentile sensitivity to Jesus in Matthew [*magos*]

2:2 Where? (*pou*)—Natural revelation brings the wise men to Israel's capital. The special revelation of the Scripture (2:6) will finally answer their question. [*pou*]
    Jews (*Ioudaiōn*)—Because Jerusalem is in Judea, the region became identified with the people of Israel generally. The wise men literally ask for the "king of the Judeans," the same title given him by the Romans at the crucifixion (27:11, 29). However, this is understood to be a name now applied to the people of Israel wherever they may be living (e.g., the Jews at Corinth, Acts 18:12). (For an argument in support of retaining the translation

"Judean" for every occurrence of this word see, BDAG 477-79). [*Ioudaios*]

worship (*proskynesai*)—The word describes the practice of people like the Greeks and Persians who would prostrate themselves before kings or deities and kiss the ground, feet, or hem of the garment as an expression of submission or dependence (BDAG, 882). [*proskyneō*]

his star (*autou ton astera*)—The context initially points toward a natural phenomenon which the wise men could interpret. Modern astronomers note the convergence of Jupiter (associated with kingship) and Saturn (associated with the Jews) on three different occasions in 7 B.C. (Allison and Davies, 235). However, the function of the star in 2:9 seems to go beyond a natural phenomenon. [*astēr*]

2:4 chief priests (*archiereis*)—Included among the chief priests were former holders of the office of high priest, the current high priest, and probably those involved with the temple's administration. [*archiereus*]

scribes (*grammateis*)—The scribes were the "teachers of the law" (NIV), or "experts in the law" (NET), knowing not only the written Scriptures and especially the Law of Moses (Gen.–Deut.), but also the traditional laws and regulations developed to supplement the written code. They formed the intellectual class in Israel, interpreting the legal code and communicating these interpretations to the people. [*grammateus*]

2:6 ruler (*hēgoumenos*)—Although Herod and the Roman governors occupy positions of rule, Israel's rightful ruler is born in Bethlehem. [*hēgeomai*]

will shepherd (*poimanei*)—The image of shepherd extends the idea of a ruler who cares for those under his authority by looking after their well-being. The image's roots look back to the time of David (2 Sam. 7:7-8). Matthew will later describe the people of

Israel as suffering from poor leadership, "like sheep without a shepherd" (9:36). That description recalls the rebuke of Ezek. 34. Although this prophecy found only limited fulfillment in Jesus' first years of ministry (Jesus is the shepherd of his disciples, cf. 26:31), Matthew believes in God's faithfulness to do what he says. The future tense of this verb looks forward to that day. [*poimainō*]

my people Israel (*ton laon mou ton Israel*)—The word "people" describes the Jewish people throughout the Gospel. The pronoun "my" refers to God and serves to underscore his covenantal relationship. "Israel" also refers only to Jewish people in the Gospel. [*Israēl*]

2:10 they shouted with great joy (*echarēsan charan megalēn sphodra*)—Matthew underscores the joy, "the experience of gladness" (BDAG, 1077), the delight felt by the wise men, with this emphatic string of words. By contrast, the people of Jerusalem were "troubled" (2:3). [*chara*]

2:11 frankincense (*libanon*)—Frankincense is a fragrant resinous gum obtained from trees primarily in Arabia and Somalia. It was used in medicines and for religious purposes (Exod. 30:34-38; Lev. 2:1-2; 24:7) giving a strong, pleasing odor when burned. A related word, *libanōtos*, meant "incense" or the container, "the censer," in which incense was burned (Rev. 8:3,5). [*libanos*]

myrrh (*smyrnan*)—Like frankincense, myrrh is an aromatic gum from trees in Arabia and Somalia. Myrrh was mixed with oil to produce a perfume (Esth. 2:12; S. of S. 5:5), was the main ingredient in anointing oil (Exod. 30:23-25), and was used to prepare a body for burial (John 19:39). It was also mixed with wine (Mark 15:23) to increase the sedative effect. [*smyrna*]

2:15 my son (*huion mou*)—The people of Israel

(Exod. 4:22) and later its kings (2 Sam. 7:14) were often described as the son of God. It communicated their special relationship with God and bore the expectation that they would represent God by being a people who carried out his will. Jesus is the preeminent son with a unique relationship with God the Father (11:27) who perfectly fulfilled the will of God (26:39). As God protected his people from Pharaoh (Exod. 14) so he protected Jesus from Herod. [*huios*]

2:18 Ramah (*Rhama*)—The traditional site of Rachel's grave, who died giving birth to her son, Benjamin, en route to Bethlehem (Gen. 35:16-20), is at Ramah. In the quotation from Jeremiah (31:15), she is a representative mother of Israel mourning the loss of children by death and exile. Also at Ramah, located north of Jerusalem, Jeremiah was released from among those being taken to Babylon (Jer. 40:1-6), and heard the judgment of God upon Israel from the lips of a pagan soldier: "All this happened because you sinned against the Lord and did not obey him" (Jer. 40:3). But despite Israel's pattern of disobedience, evident in Jeremiah and Matthew's day, the same chapter in Jeremiah that portrays Rachel's grief also contains the prophecy of the new covenant (31:31-34), a reminder of God's enduring grace, hope, and mercy. [*Rhama*]

2:23 Nazarene (*Nazōraios*)—The simple reading of this verse is that Jesus is called a Nazarene because his hometown was Nazareth. And this primary point should not be neglected. The point is complicated, however, by the introductory phrase that cites this name as a fulfillment of something said by more than one prophet. But nowhere in the OT is a statement like this found. It seems likely, then, that a play on the word Nazarene is intended, the sort of thing often done with names in the OT and in Judaism. There are several possible plays on Hebrew words, and

the plural "prophets" means Matthew has more than one in mind. Suggested allusions include: a play on the word *nazir* (Nazirite or Nazarite) defined in Judg. 13:5 as one "set apart to God from birth;" a play on the word *neser* (branch), an allusion to Isaiah 11:1 (cf Isa. 53:2); a play on the word *nsyry* (servant) in Isaiah 49:6; a play on the word *nzyr* variously translated as "prince" (NIV) or "distinguished" (NASB) or "set apart" (NRSV) in Genesis 49:26. [*Nazōraios*]

3:1 Proclaiming (*kēryssōn*)—This word is also translated "preaching" (NIV, NASB). It refers to public speaking. John comes as a prophet proclaiming God's message to the people of Israel in preparation for Jesus' ministry. Jesus will follow John and preach the same message (cf. 3:2, 4:17) to show their mutual commitment to declaring faithfully God's Word to the people. [*kēryssō*]

3:2 Repent (*metanoeite*)—John told people to change their way of thinking about God and themselves. The people of Israel needed to see themselves as ones needing God's forgiveness. Instead of presuming upon their relationship with God as descendants of Abraham (3:9), they needed to cast themselves upon God's mercy and seek his forgiveness for their sins. Repentance is an expression of faith in God that leads to living faithfully, expressed initially in baptism. [*metanoeō*]

Kingdom (*basileia*)—This word refers both to the authority to rule and reign and the place where that rule takes place. In the Gospels it is frequently associated with Jesus and his ministry. In Matthew 12:28, for example, the exorcisms Jesus performed by means of the Spirit signify the kingdom's presence. However, most of the references to the kingdom look forward to a future time and place entered by those approved by Jesus (Matt. 7:21-23). [*basileia*]

Heaven (*ouranōn*)—Although heaven is

God's dwelling place, it is frequently used as an indirect way of referring to God, so that the phrase "kingdom of heaven" and "kingdom of God" mean the same thing (see Matt. 19:23-24). Thus the kingdom John is announcing belongs to God and concerns the fulfillment of his will. [*ouranos*]

near (*ēngiken*)—This word can be used with reference to people and events or time. In Matthew 26:45 Jesus says the time of his betrayal is near and in the next verse (26:46) refers to the nearness of the betrayer, Judas, who is described as arriving while Jesus is speaking these words (26:47). John's announcement of the nearness of the kingdom focuses on Jesus' coming ministry. John's ministry was to prepare people to hear and be responsive to Jesus. [*engizō*]

3:3 Prepare (*hetoimasate*)—John's message to the people of Israel is a call to prepare for the Lord's coming. People prepared themselves by confessing their sins and undergoing baptism (3:6) as a sign of their need for God's forgiveness. By doing so, they became ready to hear Jesus and be responsive to his message. [*hetoimazō*]

3:4 Clothing (*endyma*)—John's clothing was like that of the prophet Elijah. In the Greek translation of the OT, the Septuagint, the same words are used to describe Elijah's clothes as Matthew uses to describe John's clothing (see 17:12). [*endyma*]

3:7 Pharisees and Sadducees (*Pharisaiōn kai Saddoukaiōn*)—These were the two major Jewish religious groups of John's and Jesus' day. The Pharisees looked forward to a coming Messiah who would deliver Israel from its enemies. But they refused to believe Jesus was the Messiah. The Sadducees, on the other hand, were the party in control of the temple and sought to maintain their position as members of the ruling class, cooperating with Rome in the process. They did what they could to discourage talk of a Messiah, since he would replace them as Israel's ruler. [*Pharisaios, Saddoukaios*]

wrath (*orgēs*)—God's wrath is his judgment against evildoers. Sometimes it is expressed historically, as in the flood (Gen. 6) and the destruction of Sodom and Gomorrah (Gen. 19), but more often it refers to God's final judgment at the end of the world (3:10). John described the Messiah as God's agent of this judgment (3:12) and his wrath as the burning of an unquenchable fire. [*orgē*]

3:8 fruit (*karpon*)—The fruit John called for was behavior consistent with repentance, that is, a confession of sin and public acknowledgment of that confession in the act of baptism. It is clear for John that this is seen as the first step in a life with God that is characterized by "good fruit" as a manner of life (3:10). [*karpos*]

repentance (*metanoias*)—The Greek words used to express repentance describe a change of mind. Those who think they don't need God and his ways need to think again. Repentance involves a new way of thinking and living rooted in faith in God and obedience to his word. [*metanoia*]

3:9 Abraham (*Abraam*)—Jews regarded Abraham as the father of their people and based their confidence in a relationship with God on their birth (from a Jewish mother) into the family of Israel. But John said that more was required than simple material kinship. A spiritual relationship was necessary, a relationship that began with confession of sin and sought God's mercy. [*Abraam*]

3:10 already (*ēdē*)—John saw his ministry as the first step in the process of God's judgment in which people were separated into one of two categories: those who responded to his message and those who did not. Those who responded to John's message would in turn welcome the Messiah and be received by him. Those who rejected John's message would reject the Messiah and be judged by him. [*ēdē*]

3:11 Holy Spirit (*pneumati hagiō*)—John associates the baptism of the Holy Spirit with Christ's ministry. It seems likely that John saw the Holy Spirit's work as both a cleansing or purifying fire in the life of those who welcomed the Messiah and a fire of wrath for those who rejected him, associating both experiences with God's judgment (v. 12). John does seem to have one baptism in mind. What is clear, however, is that the greater ministry of the Messiah is connected with the Holy Spirit's presence. Jesus will later ascribe the miracles he did to the Holy Spirit (12:28) and the authority he gives to the disciples to perform miracles (10:1) is probably a reference to the Holy Spirit's enabling, an anticipation of the pouring out of the Spirit in the later church. [*pneuma* + *hagios*]

3:12 unquenchable fire (*pyri asbestō*)—The image of unquenchable fire to describe God's judgment refers to the certainty of judgment and the fact that there is no escaping it. The word *asbestos* ("unquenchable") is used to describe "something whose state of being cannot be nullified or stopped" (BDAG, 141). [*pyr* + *asbestos*]

3:15 Proper (*prepon*)—Since John baptized people in relation to confession of sin, he did not think it "fitting" (NASB) or "proper" (NIV, NRSV) that Jesus undergo his baptism (3:14). But Jesus regards baptism as an expression of submission to God's will. It acknowledges God's will for his people as right and true. Thus for Jesus, at the beginning of his public ministry, his desire to be baptized testifies to his wholehearted commitment to fulfilling the work ahead of him and to his acknowledgment of John the Baptist's call to

the nation as being from God. [*prepō*]

Righteousness (*dikaiosynēn*)—Righteousness means doing God's will. Although Paul often speaks of righteousness as a status God gives to people of faith, in Matthew it refers to a manner of life that characterizes people of faith. Jesus preeminently exemplifies the faithful Son who completely fulfills God's will. From the baptism to the crucifixion, from the beginning to the end of his public ministry, Jesus fulfilled all righteousness. He wholly and completely did the will of God. [*dikaiosynē*]

3:16 heaven (*ouranoi*)—Matthew often uses the plural noun, "heavens," to refer to the place where God dwells. The opening of heaven thus refers to a revelation from God. [*ouranos*]

Spirit of God (*to pneuma tou theou*)—The "third person" of the Trinity is vividly connected with the beginning of Jesus' public ministry. Jesus will later attribute his miraculous works to the Spirit's ministry (12:28). It seems that Matthew is presenting Jesus as the Messiah who does not make use of his own power but instead relies upon the Spirit to accomplish the work of God he carried out. In this way Jesus becomes a model for all the faithful as one who depended upon God and witnessed the Spirit's work throughout his ministry. [*pneuma*]

dove (*peristeran*)—The Spirit's appearance being compared to a dove may echo the account of Noah (Gen. 8:8-12), a hopeful era following God's judgment of the world, but more likely it is a reminder of the hovering presence of the Spirit in the account of creation in Genesis 1:2. Thus the Spirit's presence signals the new order that emerges with the ministry of the Messiah (Isa. 42:1-9). [*peristera*]

3:17 My Son (*huios mou*)—The Father's affirmation of the Son combines words of Scripture from Ps. 2 and Isaiah 42. He will faithfully carry out the Father's will as messianic King and Servant following the perilous path that leads to the cross. These same words will be affirmed again on the Mount of Transfiguration (17:5). [*huios*]

4:1 Wilderness (*erēmon*)—This word is applied to uninhabited areas generally. In this context it refers to the dry, barren area away from the Jordan River. Thus the NIV translates it "desert." [*erēmos*]

To be tempted (*peirasthēnai*)—Depending on the context, this word can mean "to test" and thus reveal a person's nature or character to good effect, or "to test" with hostile intent in order to find cause for accusation or condemnation (as depicted by Jesus' opponents, 19:3, 22:18, 35). It can also mean "tempt," to lead someone to act wrongly. This sense of the word is associated with the devil's work, who is also called "the tempter" (4:3). Since the temptation is carried out by the devil, the word primarily has the negative meaning in this verse. However, it is the Spirit who leads Jesus to this setting and the account will also illustrate the positive aspect of the word by the fact that Jesus is shown to be faithful. [*peirazō*]

Devil (*diabolos*)—The word means "one who engages in slander," (BDAG, 226). It was a common translation in the Greek OT (LXX) for the Hebrew word, *Satan*, or "adversary" (Job 2:1; Zech. 3:1). He seeks to lead God's people astray of God and so defame and dishonor God's name. [*diabolos*]

4:2 Fasting (*nēsteusas*)—Going without food was a voluntary practice in ancient Israel. Nationally it was associated with the Day of Atonement (Lev. 16:29-34) to accompany confession of sin (cf. Neh. 9:1-2). But it also accompanied mourning for bereavement (Judg. 20:26; 1 Sam. 31:13) and personal intercessory prayer (2 Sam. 12:16). Jesus' fast should probably be understood as another

illustration of the commitment he expressed in his baptism, namely, his wholehearted submission to God's will. [*nēsteuō*]

Forty (*tesserakonta*)—Readers of the OT might think of Moses (Deut. 9:9) and Elijah (1 Kings 19:8) who underwent forty-day fasts. Forty might also bring to mind the wilderness years of the people of Israel (Deut. 8:2,4), since Jesus responds to the first temptation by citing Deuteronomy 8:3. Whereas Israel was characterized by unfaithfulness, Jesus shows himself to be the faithful Son, dependent on God and submitted to his will. [*tesserakonta*]

4:3 Tempter (*peirazōn*)—This title describes an essential aspect of the devil's behavior (Rev. 2:10). Although it is not used often to refer to the devil (1 Thess. 3:5), temptation is frequently linked to his work as opponent of God's people (1 Cor. 7:5). [*peirazō*]

4:4 It is written (*gegraptai*)—The grammatical voice of this verb (passive) is often used to portray divine agency. The tense (perfect) is used to express the still significant outcome of a past action. In this case the words of Moses to the people of Israel remain just as true in Jesus' day as when they were spoken and then written by Moses in the Scripture of the OT. [*graphō*]

live (*zēsetai*)—While this word can refer to physical life as something requiring food to sustain it, in this verse it refers to life that includes a spiritual dimension, life in relationship with God. That life is possible only for those who receive God's Word and obey it. [*zaō*]

Word (*rhēmati*)—The written word was in this instance originally the spoken word. God spoke through his prophet Moses, who then recorded these words for others who needed to know God's will. In this case, however, the written word is spoken by Jesus to the devil as a testimony to the priority of his life: however necessary food was to sustaining physical life, it was more important for Jesus to fulfill God's will (cf. John 4:34). Much of what Matthew records about Jesus' life is intended to serve as a model for his disciples, including the need to learn and recite Scripture, especially necessary in the midst of trial. [*rhēma*]

4:5 Holy city (*hagian polin*)—Jerusalem is called holy because it is the place where the temple was built and where God manifested his presence in the innermost room, the Most Holy Place. Holiness derives from God, and what is set apart for his use is said to be holy because it belongs to him. [*hagios*]

4:7 Test (*ekpeiraseis*)—To test God is to require him to show himself faithful. It is thus an admission of doubt that God will do what he says he will do. [*ekpeirazō*]

4:10 Satan (*Satanas*)—The name of the arch-enemy of God who also opposes God's people is from a Hebrew word meaning "adversary." The Greek spelling reflects the Hebrew (*satan*) or more commonly spoken Aramaic (*satana*). [*Satan/Satanas*]

Serve (*latreuseis*)—This word is primarily used of religious service, especially those who carried out ministry in the temple (BDAG, 587). [*latreuō*]

4:11 Attended (*diēkonoun*)—This word can also be translated "ministered to" (NASB) or "waited on" (NRSV) and primarily refers to meeting physical needs. The noun form of this word is applied to those who serve the church: deacon (1 Tim. 3:8). [*diakoneō*]

4:15 Galilee of the Gentiles (*Galilaia tōn ethnōn*)—In the years following Israel's exile people from different nations came to live in northern Israel. The word translated "Gentile" was applied to people different from one's own nationality, so in the context

of the Jewish people it described a non-Jew. Though Gentiles were probably never more than a small part of the population, the quotation from Isaiah (9:1) serves to include them within the realm of Jesus' ministry. One of the first people cited as a model of faith will be the Gentile centurion (Matt. 8). But this citation from Isaiah associates the Gentiles with the Jews as an equally needy people to whom Jesus comes. [*ethnos*]

4:16 Darkness (*skotei*)—This is a figurative description of the spiritual and moral condition of people who have no relationship with God. In the 27th psalm David associated light and salvation with God (Ps. 27:1), but these people in darkness have no relationship with God nor do they have the experience of his salvation. [*skotos*]

Light (*phōs*)—As in Ps. 27:1, light can refer to God and the salvation he brings. But light can also refer to God's revelation of the path of life, how those who are related to God can best live. According to the 119th psalm, the revelation of God is a light to our path (Ps. 119:105). In responding to God's revelation we gain life with him and escape the world's darkness. Matthew identifies Jesus as God's revealer and bearer of salvation. [*phōs*]

Shadow of death (*skia thanatou*)—Death is associated with a state of separation from God. In the imagery of this verse death is personified as a tyrant who casts a shadow over his subjects, blocking the light of God from shining on them. [*thanatos*]

Dawned (*aneteilen*)—As the rising of the sun dispels the darkness of the night and scatters the shadows of twilight before it, so the beginning of Jesus' public ministry breaks forth as the light of God upon the people of Israel and the Gentiles living among them (Luke 1:78-79). [*anatellō*]

4:17 Began (*ērxato*)—Jesus began his ministry by preaching the same message as John and in this way confirmed John's ministry (cf. 3:2). This verb, in the midst of an identical series of words in the Greek text ("from that time Jesus began"), will appear again at 16:21, signaling the beginning of the final phase of Jesus' ministry, as he turns toward Jerusalem and confronts the cross. [*archō*]

4:18 Simon (*Simōna*)—Simon was a common name among Greeks (BDAG, 924). Its Hebrew equivalent is Simeon, one of the sons of Jacob and Leah (Gen. 29:33), meaning "God has heard." [*Simōn*]

Peter (*Petron*)—Simon's nickname is from the Aramaic word (*Cephas*) for "rock." The Greek equivalent is *Petros*. According to John 1:42, he was given this name by Jesus. Among NT writers only Paul calls Peter "Cephas" (1 Cor. 3:22, Gal. 1:18). [*Petros*]

Net (*amphiblēstron*)—This was a round net cast on the water which snared fish as it sank (BDAG, 55). Peter and Andrew were busy at their work when Jesus called them to be his disciples. [*amphiblēstron*]

4:20 Followed (*ēkolouthēsan*)—The disciples model a single-minded response to Jesus' call to them ("come after me," 4:19). They leave what they are doing and accompany him, becoming his followers. The call to Matthew is literally "follow me" (9:9). When Jesus later challenges a man to leave his possessions and follow him (19:21), the man declines, in contrast to Peter and the other disciples (19:27). The phrase "you who have followed me" (19:28) defines Jesus' disciples. [*akoloutheō*]

4:23 Teaching (*didaskōn*)—Jesus' teaching is illustrated by Matthew in five major sections in the Gospel on various topics: discipleship (chapters 5-7); mission (10); parables (13); community relationships (18); the end of the age (24-25). But portions of Jesus' teaching appear throughout the Gospel, sometimes

nearly equal in length to the teaching sections. Chapter 23, for example, is an extended warning about hypocrisy and its destructive effects. Drawing a distinction between preaching and teaching is problematic. Preaching tends to describe a wide proclamation concerning what God is doing and what people should do by way of response (e.g., "Repent, for the kingdom of God is near" 4:23). Teaching, on the other hand, defines further what those who have responded to preaching need to know and do about relationship with God and one another. [*didaskō*]

Synagogues (*synagōgais*)—The synagogue was the meeting place of Jews to hear the Scripture read and be instructed in its application to life. Wherever ten men formed a community, a synagogue could be established. It served as a place for prayer, for education of adults and children, for resolution of judicial issues and legal disputes, and even as a place of hospitality for travelers. If the temple was Israel's national place of worship, the synagogues were the center of a local community's religious life. When synagogues began is a matter of debate, but they probably owe their origin to the period of the exile when the temple was no longer available as a place of meeting. The people in Galilee might visit the temple once a year, as Jesus' parents did, but otherwise they would meet each Saturday (Sabbath) from early in the morning until noon in the synagogue for prayer and study of the Scripture. [*synagōgē*]

Gospel (*euangelion*)—The word "gospel" means the announcement of "good news." In this case the "gospel of the kingdom" is the good news that God is at work fulfilling his promise about a Messiah to liberate people from some type of tyranny and bring them under his rule. Most Jews at this time thought this would mean the end of Roman rule. But the destructive tyranny that people need to be delivered from is sin and death, which Jesus would accomplish by his death on the cross. [*euangelion*]

Healing (*therapeuōn*)—Jesus cited his healing ministry as a substantiation of his messiahship (11:3-6). But healing also foreshadowed life under God's rule when death, the consequence of sin, would be banished (cf. Rev. 20:14). [*therapeuō*]

4:24 Syria (*Syrian*)—Syria was the large Roman province to the north of Galilee with its capital at Antioch. Paul was sent out from and returned to the church at Antioch on his first missionary journey (Acts 13-14). Many interpreters think Antioch is a likely setting for the writing of this Gospel and find the mention of Syria in this verse a clue pointing in that direction. [*Syria*]

Pain (*basanois*)—This word was used to describe the pain of torture (BDAG, 168) that later Christians experienced at the hands of pagan persecutors (1 Clement 6:1, 2 Clement 17:7). But here it refers to the severe pain associated with various illnesses from which people were delivered by Jesus' healing. [*basanos*]

Demoniacs (*daimonizomenous*)—The "demon-possessed" (NIV) were afflicted by and under the control of an evil spiritual being. Demons are associated with Satan and serve under his authority (12:24-26). A demon can be defined as "a hostile transcendent being with status between humans and deities" (BDAG, 210), that is, a "fallen" angel. Delivering people from the control of demons demonstrated Jesus' power and authority over Satan and his hosts. Jesus will later point to this power as the Spirit's work in his ministry and the evidence of God's liberating rule (12:28). [*daimonizomai*]

Epileptics (*selēniazomenous*)—The ending of this Greek word is like the word for demoniac. But in this case ancient peoples associated seizures with malign powers of the moon (cf. Ps. 121:6). The word means "afflicted by the moon" (cf. our word "lunacy" based on the Latin word for moon,

luna). Epilepsy (from a Greek word meaning "seizure," *epilepsia*) describes various disorders of the electrical rhythms of the central nervous system that produce convulsions. [*selēniazomai*]

Paralytics (*paralytikous*)—The verb form of this word means "to undo or disable" (BDAG, 768). The noun refers to complete or partial loss of function in a feeling or moving part of the body, sometimes resulting in the loss of the ability to move at all (9:2). Although the word is in the form of an adjective here and elsewhere in the NT, it functions like a noun. [*paralytikos*]

4:25 Crowds (*ochloi*)—Although the crowds follow Jesus and are amazed at his teaching (7:28) they are a distinct group from the disciples. Jesus has compassion on them (9:38) and they are designated as the object of the disciples' mission (9:37-38). Ultimately led astray by the religious leaders, the crowds fail to ask for Jesus' release (27:20). Although they acclaim Jesus when he enters Jerusalem (21:9) and regard him as a prophet (21:11), they ask for the release of Barabbas and so eventually become a party to Jesus' death (27:24). [*ochlos*]

Decapolis (*Dekapoleōs*)—The Decapolis was a region south and east of Galilee. Originally a league of ten (*deka*) cities (*polis*) founded during the time of Alexander the Great and his successors, the region embodied the cosmopolitan features of the Greco-Roman age. In the time of Jesus this area, although partially within the borders of Israel, more closely resembled cities in the wider Roman world with synagogues and pagan temples coexisting along city streets. Its mention here illustrates the diverse nature of the crowds who followed Jesus and heard the call of his message. [*Dekapolis*]

5:1 Mountain (*oros*)—Although the location is uncertain, the mention of a mountain in connection with Jesus' teaching may have reminded readers of God's revelation on Mt Sinai. To do so would invite comparison between the message of the old covenant through Moses and the message of the new covenant through Christ. [*oros*]

Sat down (*kathisantos*)—Sitting is the normal posture for a teacher in Jewish tradition. The Hebrew word for school, *yeshiva*, means "seat." It was apparently the pattern in the synagogue for the reader of Scripture to stand (cf. Luke 4:16) and then to sit down when teaching about the passage (cf. Luke 4:20). So Jesus taking a seat and calling his disciples to him would indicate to readers familiar with Jewish practice that teaching was about to begin. [*kathizō*]

Disciples (*mathētai*)—At this point in Matthew's narrative only four disciples have been called, but they represent the pattern of those who will follow Jesus and learn from him. The word can describe someone who learns through formal instruction as a "pupil" or "apprentice." Or it can describe someone who learns by constant association so that the instruction comes in the form of words and manner of life, a "disciple" or "adherent" (BDAG, 609). This particularly describes the relationship of those who will form the Twelve (10:1-4), and who in turn are directed by Jesus to teach others what they have learned from him (28:19-20). So Matthew sees his Gospel as leading to the development of disciples by including these examples of Jesus' teaching and the manner of his life. The reader who regards himself or herself as a disciple should then find in these words of Jesus a message of continuing relevance for them. [*mathētēs*]

5:2 Blessed (*makarioi*)—This word can mean "happy" (1 Cor. 7:40) in relation to one's circumstances of life or "fortunate" (Acts 26:2) in terms of a particular situation or opportunity. But in this verse it describes the state of someone privileged to experience God's grace in a special way. "Blessed," therefore, describes most importantly those who have a relationship with God (cf. Job 5:17; Ps. 1:1-2) so that secondarily they experience his gracious provision and care in their life. The term "beatitudes" applied to the statements of these verses (from the Latin word *beatitudo*), is defined as "a declaration or ascription of special blessedness" (Oxford English Dictionary, 1:743), a blessedness due to God's grace. [*makarios*]

Poor (*ptōchoi*)—There are two basic definitions connected to this word. As might be expected, it is frequently applied to those who are "economically disadvantaged" (BDAG, 896), people who lack the material necessities of normal life. But it can also be applied to those who are "spiritually disadvantaged," those who are "lacking in spiritual worth" (Cf. Rev. 3:17, BDAG, 896). In this verse it could refer to people generally but more particularly it seems to describe those who have heeded the message of John the Baptist and Jesus. They have acknowledged their need for God's mercy and repented of their confidence in themselves or their descent from Abraham (cf. 3:2-9). They see themselves as spiritually impoverished people in need of God's mercy. [*ptōchos*]

Spirit (*pneumati*)—This word can refer to either the Holy Spirit (cf. 3:11) or the human spirit, the "source and seat of insight, feeling, and will . . . as the representative part of human inner life" (BDAG, 832). If it means the Holy Spirit, it describes people who recognize the lack of the Spirit's presence and ministry in their life. But more likely it describes people who recognize the spiritual poverty of their life and the need of God's provision for them (cf. Isa. 61:1, though the alternative meanings lead to a similar conclusion). [*pneuma*]

The kingdom of heaven (*basileia tōn ouranōn*)—Instead of mentioning the name of God, the people of Israel would sometimes use "heaven" as a reverential replacement (cf. 3:2; BDAG, 739). It is likely that Jesus spoke this way too. God's kingdom referred to his realm of rule and authority. Although God's authority extends over all creation, his kingdom was often associated only with those who acknowledged his authority and then experienced his blessing (cf. 7:21). Subjects of the kingdom of heaven welcomed God's rule in their life and sought to live according to it. Although the kingdom is often viewed as the joyous future prospect of the faithful, this may be a passage that has a present viewpoint as well (cf. following discussion of verb tense). [*basileia*]

Is theirs (*autōn estin*)—Although the kingdom belongs to God and people are subjects in it, the construction of this phrase emphasizes that in some sense the subjects of the kingdom can be said to possess it as well. The point is that the kingdom is the sphere of God's special blessing and to be a subject in it is the greatest thing a person can possess (cf. 13:44-46). The tense of the verb used in this phrase is present. Although the present tense can be used to refer to events yet future (a means of emphasizing the certainty of the event's fulfillment) it normally describes present experience. If that is the case here, then the present tense would stress the current blessings of those who have a relationship with God, a blessing emerging because God's will informs and guides them. It does not replace the hope of the kingdom's future manifestation but views the present as an opportunity to know God and serve him as a foretaste of the blessings to come (cf. Paul's view of salvation as something both past [Eph. 2:8] and future [Rom. 13:11]). [*autos*]

5:4 Mourn (*penthountes*)—The word means "to experience sadness as the result of some condition or circumstance" (BDAG, 795). Mourning may describe repentance for personal sin, part of a faith-response to John's and Jesus' preaching. Those who mourn would then be comforted by the relationship with God that follows repentance. However, it may be best to see those who mourn as disciples generally who suffer the trials and tribulations that come with living in a fallen world hostile to God and his people (cf. 5:11-12; 2:18; Rom. 8:18-25). [*pentheō*]

Comforted (*paraklēthēsontai*)—The word means "call to one's side" (BDAG, 764) in order to instruct, request, encourage, or console. It is this last sense which fits the context here. The grammatical voice of the verb is passive, meaning the subject receives the action of the word. The passive was sometimes used to describe God's work without mentioning his name (cf. the discussion about the word "heaven," 5:3). The tense is future. God's people will be comforted when he sweeps away the ills of the present world and makes "all things new" (Rev. 21:1-5). [*parakaleō*]

5:5 Meek (*praeis*)—As a character trait this word describes a person who is unassuming or self-effacing ("humble") in contrast to a self-aggrandizing or pompous spirit often associated with worldly success (cf. 20:25). In this sense it aptly describes Jesus (11:29; 21:5) who did not come "to be served but to serve" (20:28). It also refers to a gentle spirit, not responding in kind or retaliating aggressively in the face of wrongs suffered. [*praus*]

Inherit (*klēronomēsousin*)—The sense of acquiring or gaining possession of something because of family connections colors this word to some degree. It is those who have a relationship with God who will inherit (in 25:40 the inheritance is a place in the kingdom). God will bring about a reversal of fortunes at the end of this age so that when "God's will is read" those who seem to be last in the eyes of the world end up becoming first in the kingdom of God (cf. 19:29-30). [*klēronomeō*]

Earth (*gēn*)—This verse echoes Ps. 37:11

which refers to the meek inheriting the land of Israel and so raises the question if a similar narrow focus is intended here as well. Although this word has been used to refer to the land of Israel or portions of it in previous verses (2:6, 20; 4:15) it is always modified. It is best, therefore, to see this as a reference to the earth as a whole (cf. 5:18, 35; 6:10,19). [*gē*]

5:6 Righteousness (*dikaiosynēn*)—Righteousness means doing God's will (see discussion of the word at 3:15). The blessed seek daily to live according to God's will. They regard righteousness as a necessary component of life: they "hunger and thirst" for it (cf. Ps. 42:1-2). One is reminded of Jesus' statement about himself: "my food is to do the will of the one sending me and to complete his work" (John 4:34). [*dikaiosynē*]

Will be satisfied (*chortasthēsontai*)—Normally this word is associated with food (14:20, 15:33) but here describes the heartfelt satisfaction of people who can see and experience a life where fulfillment of God's will is routine. The tense of the verb is future. This could describe an immediate future in which God satisfies the longing of his people by enabling them to live righteously (cf. Phil. 1:11). But the other future tenses in these verses seem to look forward to a time when God's kingdom is fully and finally established (cf. Rev. 7:16-17), when God's will is done on earth as it is in heaven (6:10). [*chortazō*]

5:7 Mercy . . . obtain mercy (*eleēmones . . . eleēthēsontai*)—This word first occurs as an adjective in this verse (the other occurrence is in Heb. 2:17 with reference to Christ) and then as a verb. Although this word means, "to be greatly concerned about someone in need," (BDAG, 315), it goes beyond feeling to describe compassionate treatment that addresses the need of others and acts to alleviate it. This is an important character trait in Matthew's Gospel. Hosea 6:6 is quoted twice: more important to God than sacrifice is mercy (9:13, 12:7). People appeal to Jesus for mercy and he responds accordingly (9:27, 15:22, 17:15, 20:30, 31). God acts mercifully towards sinners and forgives their debt. He expects sinners to treat one another with similar compassion (18:33). The lack of mercy in hypocrites defines their damnable state (23:23). Thus mercy is an essential characteristic of the blessed. Disciples can show mercy because God has shown it to them (18:33). The merciful are blessed because they can be assured of God's mercy (the future tense of the verb looks forward to judgment, cf. Jas. 2:13). [*eleēmōn, eleeō*]

5:8 Pure (*katharoi*)—The basic meaning of the word pertains "to being clean or free of adulterating matter" (BDAG, 489). Being pure in relation to one's heart is "being free from moral guilt" (BDAG, 489). It describes the person who is wholehearted in his commitment to God, who is single-minded in fulfilling God's will. Ps. 24:4, which this beatitude echoes, emphasizes truthfulness and integrity as defining characteristics of purity. Jesus will later warn disciples about hypocrisy that seeks the praise of men rather than the approval of God (6:1-18). [*katharos*]

Heart (*kardia*)—The heart often stands for the "center and source of the whole inner life, with its thinking, feeling, and volition," (BDAG, 508). The heart makes it possible to seek God (Ps. 27:8) and experience relationship with Christ (Eph. 3:17). Purity of heart then describes thought, emotion, and will as solely and entirely devoted to God. [*kardia*]

See (*opsontai*)—According to Matthew 18:10, angels enjoy the immediate presence of God since they "always see the face of my Father in heaven." This experience was what the psalmist looked forward to: "The upright will see his face" (Ps. 11:7). It is what the final revelation of the NT describes as the destiny of God's servants: "They will see his face"

(Rev. 22:4). That is the prospect awaiting the pure in heart in the life to come: they will see God and enjoy his presence. [*horaō*]

5:9 Peacemakers (*eirēnopoioi*)—This word occurs only here in the NT, describing someone who "endeavors to reconcile persons who have disagreements" (BDAG, 288). This definition suggests a third party brokering a peace between two antagonists. While this is a significant role, the point of the beatitude may be that disciples who experience God's blessing do all they can to maintain right relationships with others. The first issue taken up later in the sermon emphasizes the importance of making peace with a brother and an opponent (5:23-25). A later discourse is devoted to the subject of forgiveness and reconciliation among disciples (18:1-34). While the word "peacemaker" may occur only here, it is part of an important theme in this Gospel. [*eirēnopoios*]

    <u>Sons</u> of God (*huioi theou*)—Like the word "peacemakers," this is an example of a phrase that occurs only one time, yet is part of an important theme in the Gospel's message: relationship with God as Father (v. 16). The beatitude looks forward to a future declaration (cf. 7:21), here associated with disciples as peacemakers. Later in the sermon, disciples are taught to love their enemies and pray for their persecutors so that they may be sons of their Father (5:44-45), suggesting that the notion of making peace may also apply to the disciples' wider mission (cf. 10:13). [*huios*]

5:10 Persecuted (*dediōgmenoi*)—Persecution entails physical and verbal assault (v. 11) because disciples faithfully do God's will ("on account of righteousness"). Their experience is like faithful prophets before them (v. 12) and they can rejoice (cf. Acts 16:25) because persecution confirms their status as servants of God: they are indeed members of the kingdom of God (v. 3). [*diōkō*]

5:12 Reward (*misthos*)—The disciples' reward is associated with heaven, the dwelling place of God. In 6:1 reward is tied to sharing in God's presence ("with your Father in heaven"). The context of 6:1-18 contrasts seeking and gaining people's praise by showcasing religious behavior with the righteous living of disciples done for God alone. Although nothing is said about the nature of the reward from God, the contrast suggests that it is receiving God's approval and enjoying relationship with him (cf. BDAG, 653, God's reward is "recognition" and "affirmation"). [*misthos*]

5:13 Salt (*halas*)—What meanings might be associated with salt are probably less crucial to understanding this saying than seeing that the sphere of the disciples' influence is to be the whole earth. Salt that loses its savor is salt that in various ways becomes diluted by impurity. So this saying defines the scope of the disciples' mission while carrying a warning about being diluted and distracted from the task. [*halas*]

5:14 Light (*phōs*)—Light as a figure of God's salvation was first mentioned in connection with Jesus' coming in ministry (see 4:16). Now it is disciples who bring light to the world. As in the comparison to salt (v. 13) the mission of the disciples extends to all people. Although they will be sent first to Israel (10:5-6) eventually they will be sent to everyone (28:19). They serve as a light to the world by speaking and acting (5:16) as servants of God (cf. Isa. 49:6; Acts 13:47). [*phōs*]

5:16 Glorify (*doxasōsin*)—The word means "to influence one's opinion about another so as to enhance the latter's reputation" (BDAG, 258). In this case the disciples are to speak and act so that people come to honor and praise God. This implies that people who do not have a relationship with God will respond in faith to the disciples' message and those who do will be moved to greater appreciation of and praise for God's presence in their life. The Gospel shows Jesus to be the model for the disciples in doing this (9:8, 15:31). [*doxazō*]

People (*anthrōpōn*)—Although this word is often translated "men," it is a general word referring to people of all races and genders. When Jesus warns his disciples to "beware of men" in Matthew 10:17, it is the same word—a reminder that disciples are to "let their lights shine" before opponents and enemies as well. [*anthrōpos*]

Father (*patera*)—This is the first reference to God as "Father." It depicts not only a special relationship with God, but links disciples together as brothers and sisters in a spiritual family (12:50). An important theme associated with God as Father is the obedience of the disciples to his will (7:21,12:50). By their "good works" they bring honor and praise to God. [*patēr*]

5:17 The law or the prophets (*ton nomon ē tous prophētas*)—Although the law and the prophets specifically refer to two of the three major sections in the OT (the third part being wisdom literature), it is probable that the whole of the OT Scriptures is intended by this phrase (cf. John 1:45; Rom. 3:21). Jesus, by his life and ministry, fulfilled portions of God's previous revelation to his people and further clarified God's will. [*nomos, prophētēs*]

Fulfill (*plērōsai*)—Matthew's frequent citation of OT passages in connection with various events in Jesus' life illustrates that Jesus' life and ministry fulfills previous revelation. This points toward the trustworthiness of God to his Word and in turn inspires confidence that further revelation from and concerning Jesus will be fulfilled as well. [*plēroō*]

5:18 the smallest letter or stroke (*iōta hen ē mia keraia*)—The *iota* is the smallest letter in the Greek alphabet, corresponding to *yod* in Hebrew or Aramaic. The stroke literally means "horn," and has been translated as "tittle," referring to any "projection" or "hook as part of a letter" (BDAG, 540). This assurance of fulfillment in even the smallest details applies to the written revelation that forms the entire OT. [*iōta, keraia*]

5:19 Commandments (*entolōn*)—A command expresses God's will for his people. Jesus will later sharply warn the Pharisees because although they kept the minor commandments they neglected the major ones concerning justice, mercy, and faithfulness (23:23). [*entolē*]

Does and teaches (*poiēsē kai didaxē*)—Disciples must live in accordance with God's will and teach others to do the same. "Doing" can also be translated "keep" (NASB) or "practice" (NIV). If disciples are to "make" other disciples (28:20) they must teach. But teaching must include the example of obedience. [*poieō, didaskō*]

5:20 Righteousness (*dikaiosynē*)—Jesus will shortly address some of the deficiencies in the Pharisees' righteousness (6:1-18): they lived to gain the approval of their fellow countrymen rather than living to please and honor God. Jesus will later decry their failure to live in light of the faith's great truths (23:23): justice, mercy, and faithfulness. Their "righteousness" is more apparent than real. The life style of Jesus' disciples must go well beyond this, both in terms of integrity of character and faithfulness to the whole of God's will (5:48). Some illustration of what that entails follows in the teaching of Matthew 5:21-48. [*dikaiosynē*]

5:21 It was said (*errethē*)—This verb is in the passive voice, a way of speech often used with reference to God's actions. Here, because passages from the OT are cited, it is likely that God is seen as the speaker. Jesus' teaching for his disciples builds on God's message to the people of Israel. [*eipon, legō*]

5:22 Everyone who is angry (*orgizomenos*)— Anger as a human emotion is here linked to murder and to abusive and demeaning speech. Not only destructive behavior, not only hurtful speech, but even the desire to avenge real or perceived wrongs is condemned by Jesus (cf. Jas. 1:20). [*orgizō*]

Brother (*adelphō*)—This usually refers to a fellow member of the community, in this case, a fellow disciple of Jesus. However, in view of what Jesus says later about loving those outside of the community (5:43-47) it is probably appropriate to see the treatment of a brother as a first step in relating rightly to everyone. [*adelphos*]

5:24 Reconciled (*diallagēthi*)—Reconciliation involves making opponents or adversaries friends. Disciples must understand the importance of establishing and maintaining harmonious relationships in their community. Jesus implies that their worship of God is futile if they are unwilling to right the wrongs in their relationships with one another. [*diallassomai*]

5:26 You will not get out (*ou mē exselthēs*)— The peril of judgment is a theme in Jesus' teaching (cf. 18:34) to stress the fact that what he says is not an option for disciples but an obligation. To neglect or ignore what Jesus says has awful consequences. The Greek words are emphatic, "you will never get out." [*exerchomai*]

Last cent (*eschaton kodrantēn*)—The "last penny" (NIV, NRSV) is the smallest Roman coin (the Latin, *quadrans*), worth 1/64 of the coin paid for a day's wage (BDAG, 550). When Jesus tells his disciples to ask God to

forgive their debts as they have forgiven their debtors (6:12), this saying should come to mind. The forgiveness required for reconciliation applies to even the smallest issue and is to be fully given. [*kodrantēs*]

5:28 Lust (*epithymēsai*)—This word means "to have a strong desire to do or secure something," (BDAG, 371) and can be used in a positive way of a worthy object (cf. 13:17). But this same word means "covet" when the object desired is wrong or forbidden (Exod. 20:17; Deut. 5:21). In this context it is sexual desire for someone other than a spouse. As in the case of anger and murder Jesus here identifies the root cause of adultery and commands his disciples to give no chance for lust to be nurtured in their lives. [*epithymeō*]

5:30 Hell (*geennan*)—The Greek word (*Gehenna*) corresponds to the Hebrew name for the Valley of Hinnom, a ravine south of Jerusalem, associated with the final judgment of God (BDAG, 191). Jesus' graphic language serves to underscore the peril of lust. It is a destroyer of lives and by no means to be trifled with. [*geenna*]

5:31 Certificate of divorce (*apostasion*)— Giving a written document confirming a divorce was a practice in accordance with Moses' command in Deut. 24:1-4. In that passage, remarriage is anticipated (at least two remarriages are mentioned) but not to a previous spouse if another marriage had intervened (to prevent circumstances that amounted to trading wives). Jesus' words must be understood against this backdrop of divorce as an accepted practice. [*apostasion*]

5:32 Immorality (*porneias*)—This is a general word for sexual immorality, variously translated here as "marital unfaithfulness" (NIV) or "unchastity" (NASB, NRSV). Apart from this exception Jesus portrays divorce as a cause of adultery. He is not saying immorality must lead to divorce, only that it may. The immoral person is an adulterer so divorce is not a cause of adultery in this case. Otherwise, given the anticipated consequence of remarriage, divorce is presented as a cause of adultery. By this connection Jesus virtually excludes divorce as an acceptable alternative to resolving a marital problem for his disciples. The earlier word about the importance of reconciliation would apply here as well. [*porneia*]

5:36 Do not swear (*mēte . . . omosēs*)—Jesus warns his disciples against the practice of underscoring statements or promises with oaths, as if apart from such oaths their words are perceived as unreliable. Rather, disciples should be known for integrity of speech. They should say what they mean and do what they say. The fact that oath taking is referred to elsewhere in the NT positively (e.g., Luke 1:73; Heb. 6:13-18) and practiced (e.g., Rom. 1:9; 2 Cor. 1:23; Phil. 1:8) suggests that Jesus was not understood to preclude all oath-taking but rather to underscore for his disciples the importance of truthfulness. [*omnuō*]

5:37 Evil one (*ponērou*)—The form of this word (an adjective) makes possible either the translation "of evil" (NASB) or the translation as a personal reference, "from the evil one" (NIV, NRSV). The word is used to refer to the devil in other passages (13:19, 38) and the devil is elsewhere linked to deceitfulness ("the father of lies," John 8:44). It may be best, therefore, to see here as well a reference to the devil as a master deceiver whose guileful and manipulative speech is by all means to be avoided. [*ponēros*]

5:39 Resist (*antistēnai*)—The word means "oppose" or "resist" (BDAG, 80). It is probably significant that the context of these words concerns disciples as salt and light in the

world, that is, engaged in a missionary task. Jesus himself did not resist those who came to seize him (26:50-54). He did not strike back at those who struck him (26:67-68). Nor did he denounce those who took his garments (27:27-31, 35). When disciples face opposition in the course of their mission they are not told to fight but to flee (10:23; cf. the example of disciples described in Acts). However, this need not preclude disciples resisting evil in order to protect others or in connection with other (e.g., civil) duties. [*anthistēmi*]

5:44 Love (*agapate*)—While love is popularly associated with emotion or feelings, it is primarily a volitional word, describing appropriate action. This is not to suggest that feelings or emotions are not a part of its meaning, but to affirm that what is primarily called for is action that seeks what is best for another person. The prayer offered for the enemy or persecutor is that they may themselves become disciples and come to glorify God as Father (5:16). [*agapaō*]

5:48 Perfect (*teleioi*)—This word refers not so much to the flawless attainment of a standard but to a single-minded or wholehearted commitment to God's will. God himself is undivided in his will. Disciples likewise are to unreservedly follow God's will as it is made known to them by Jesus. In so doing they show themselves to be sons of God who are pure in heart (5:8) seeking first and foremost his kingdom and righteousness (6:33). [*teleios*]

6:1 Seen (*theathēnai*)—This word appears in a phrase that expresses the purpose of the main verbal idea (doing righteous deeds). Jesus warns his disciples about doing the right things for the wrong reason: to receive the praise of their fellow men. They are to live their lives in such a way that others see their good works (5:16). However, the praise should go to God, not themselves. Jesus tells his disciples that those who want to impress their fellow men may achieve this, but by so doing they forfeit God's approval. Jesus warns his disciples about thinking they can have it both ways: gaining the approval of their fellow man and God. The life of a disciple is not a both/and. It is an either/or. [*theaomai*]

6:2 Alms (*eleēmosynēn*)—Jesus encourages his disciples to give what monies they can to help the poor among them. [*eleēmosynē*]

Hypocrites (*hypokritai*)—A hypocrite is an actor in the sense of a "pretender, dissembler" (BDAG, 1038). As an actor may play a part to hear the crowd's applause so the hypocrite performs religious duties to win his fellow man's approval. Jesus does not deny that the hypocrite may achieve his objective. But it is a temporary prize of no lasting value when compared with gaining God's approval. [*hypokritēs*]

6:4 Secret (*kryptō*)—"In secret" describes both the manner of the disciples' giving and the sphere of God's presence: it is a hidden reality. Though present and real, it is spiritual and unknown to most people. Though 6:3 may suggest that an uncalculated spontaneity should mark the disciples' giving (cf. 25:37-38), "secret" more likely refers to an extreme subtlety of giving, as if the giver's opposite hand is unaware of the generous act. This is an exaggerated way for Jesus to tell his disciples that righteousness must be an expression of obedience to God, not a performance done to win the praise of others. [*kryptos*]

6:6 Inner room (*tameion*)—In contrast to the hypocrites who look for the most prominent public place to offer prayer, the disciples ought to retreat to the inner room of a house. There, out of public view, they should offer prayer in accordance with God's will. Jesus is not decrying all public prayer but warning against doing right things for wrong reasons. [*tameion*]

6:7 Meaningless repetition (*battalogēsēte*)—"Do not heap up empty phrases" (NRSV), or "keep on babbling" (NIV), Jesus tells his disciples. He says this to underscore that the mere repetition of formulaic prayer will not induce God to answer. God is not manipulated by a petitioner reciting words in accordance with a set formula. Pagans believed if they called upon the gods with the proper names addressed to their exact locale and with the appropriate words the gods would act in their behalf. Jesus tells his disciples that prayer is not a matter of repetition but of relationship. The One to whom they pray relates to them as a father who knows their need and is willing to answer their request even before they ask him (v. 8). [*battalogeō*]

6:9 Hallowed (*hagiasthētō*)—The first and most encompassing petition in the prayer Jesus gives his disciples as a model concerns God's glory. They are to ask God to make his name something people will treat as holy, and not common or profane. This will ultimately be done after the judgment when the righteous remain (13:41-43). But this petition probably has a present relevance, too, as people become disciples and begin to relate to God as Father. This petition thus becomes a missionary prayer that God would enable Jesus' followers to accomplish their mission of making disciples of all nations, honoring God in the process (28:19-20). [*hagiazō*]

6:10 Your kingdom (*basileia sou*)—Like the previous petition, this probably looks forward to the consummation when "the righteous will shine like the sun in the kingdom of their Father" (13:43). But there is also a present spiritual aspect to God's kingdom as his will is done. The disciples' prayer is a means to making the fulfillment of God's will a reality for them as members of a community of faith. [*basileia*]

6:11 Daily (*epiousion*)—The meaning of this word as it modifies "bread" is debated. Proposals range from "necessary for existence," "for today," "for the following day," to the bread that will be eaten in the future kingdom (BDAG, 376-77). Since Jesus assures disciples of God's provision for them (6:25-34), the translation "daily" seems most reasonable. Once again prayer is set forth as a means by which God fulfills his will (that is, what God says he will do disciples are called to pray for). [*epiousios*]

6:12 Debts (*opheilēmata*)—Here this word refers to "obligation in a moral sense" so that "debt=sin" (BDAG, 743). In this petition disciples ask God's forgiveness for their failure to live according to his will. But they also express the necessity of extending forgiveness to others (and in the context of the general request seek God's aid in doing so). [*opheilēma*]

6:13 Temptation (*peirasmon*)—This word can be translated "time of trial" (NRSV). It would then be a request that God deliver disciples "from the hour of trial that is coming on the whole world to test its inhabitants" (Rev. 3:20), a petition for eschatological deliverance. It is more likely, however, that the word means "temptation," "enticement to sin" (BDAG, 793) since the conclusion of the petition calls to mind Jesus' temptation by the devil (4:1). Acknowledging their weakness, disciples must seek God's aid in escaping temptation (cf. 1 Cor. 10:13). [*peirasmos*]

6:14 Trespasses (*paraptōmata*)—This word is variously translated "transgressions" (NASB), "trespasses" (NRSV), or "sins" (NIV). It is normally used of offenses against God (e.g.,

6:15; cf. Rom. 5:15). It pictures a person making a false step (BDAG, 770), departing from the path of life defined by God's will. Here is another warning about forgiveness (cf. 5:23-24) as a necessary aspect of a right relationship with God. Disciples should not think they are able to ignore a request for forgiveness from another person while asking God to forgive them (cf. v. 12). A similar statement of this theme, emphasizing God's prior forgiveness, is made in a later parable (cf. 18:21-35). [*paraptōma*]

6:16 Fast (*nēsteuēte*)—Fasting consisted of abstinence from food to express dependence on God and submission to his will (cf. 4:1). The fasting Jesus refers to is private fasting, probably done as an aid to prayer (cf. Luke 2:37). Although the early church collectively fasted and prayed (e.g., Acts 13:3, 14:23), it seems to have been done primarily by Jewish Christians. The practice is never mentioned in any of the NT letters and while Jesus is with them the disciples do not fast (9:14). Like alms and prayer, fasting is to be done as an act of devotion to God and not to win the approval of anyone else. [*nēsteuō*]

6:19 Treasure (*thēsaurous*)—Although the treasure is not specifically defined in Jesus' statement, the wider context has contrasted the praise of men with the reward of God (vv. 1-18). Elsewhere the kingdom itself is portrayed as a treasure worth selling everything one has in order to gain it (13:44; cf. 19:21). This suggests that the time and energy and resources disciples expend doing God's will produces something of greater and more lasting worth than the similar effort expended in acquiring and holding on to earthly treasure. [*thēsauros*]

6:21 Heart (*kardia*)—What people pursue by investing time, energy, and resources reveals the disposition of their hearts: what they truly love and value. The either/or nature of these statements functions to compel decisions about priorities and ultimate concerns. This saying is a companion to the following pair that also address the necessity of a disciple's single-minded devotion to fulfilling God's will (cf. 5:8). [*kardia*]

6:22 Clear (*haplous*)—This adjective is variously translated as "good" (NIV) or "healthy" (NRSV) or "clear" (NASB) in relation to the noun it modifies, "eye." BDAG (p. 104) rightly notes that it signifies "singleness of purpose." A person with a clear eye looks with singleness of purpose to fulfilling God's will. A person with an evil eye focuses not on what God wants, but what he wants. He relies upon himself rather than trusting God. Instead of experiencing God's light, he wanders in darkness, seeking his own way rather than God's revelation (cf. 4:16). [*haplous*]

6:23 Evil (*ponēros*)—An "evil eye" was sometimes associated with selfishness (Deut. 15:9; Prov. 23:6) or greediness (Prov. 28:22). The evil eye may thus carry a two-fold nuance in this context: the more general self-centeredness discussed above (6:22) and the particular manifestation of that condition in an unwillingness to give up dependence on personal wealth (cf. 19:21). [*ponēros*]

6:24 Wealth (*mamōna*)—This word can refer to property or wealth or as the NIV translates it, "money." Jesus personifies wealth as an authority opposed to God. While many people may think they possess wealth, Jesus shows that it is more often wealth that owns the person. People end up serving it rather than it serving them. And wealth is a master that holds its subjects firmly in its grasp (cf. 19:21-23). The challenge for disciples is to get their eyes off of the treasures of this world and to focus on the treasures found in serving God (vv. 19-20). [*mamōnas*]

6:25 Anxious (*merimnate*)—Like the word "desire" (5:28) this word can be negative ("to worry, be apprehensive") or positive ("to be concerned about") depending on its object (BDAG, 632). When the object is one's self (e.g., Phil. 4:6), as here, it is negative. When it is centered on others (1 Cor. 7:32, 12:25; Phil. 2:20) it is positive. Anxiety ultimately expresses a lack of trust in God and is a distraction to the important task of fulfilling God's will. Jesus has already spoken about God's care for the world generally (5:45) and told his disciples to pray about their daily food (6:11). These instructions are particularly relevant for disciples who receive hospitality from those to whom they preach (10:9-14) [*merimnaō*]

6:33 Seek first (*zēteite . . . prōton*)—The priority of a disciple's life must be fulfilling God's will. Jesus will tell his followers that the good news about the kingdom must be preached throughout the world (24:14). This aim, to be the light of the world (cf. 5:14), requires disciples who are righteous, who see the fulfillment of God's will as the first and highest calling of their life. Those who "strive for" (NRSV) this objective follow a path of life that leads to ultimate satisfaction (5:6). [*zēteō*]

6:34 trouble (*kakia*)—In every other occurrence of this word it means either "wickedness" or "malice" (BDAG, 500). This is a stark reminder to disciples that they live in a fallen world. Although they serve a good God, they live in a world marked by evil. Though they do not seek trouble, it will find them. This saying serves as a counterbalance to Jesus' encouraging words about God's provision for disciples. They should not imagine that they can escape "hard times." A later disciple, Paul, knew that God sustained him (Phil. 4:11-13), but he also experienced times without adequate food and clothing (2 Cor. 11:27). [*kakia*]

7:1 Judge (*krinete*)—Jesus does not tell his disciples to be uncritical or undiscerning (cf. 7:3-6, 15) or to ignore and overlook sin (18:15). But he does warn them about assuming for themselves a role that belongs to God alone. Judgment is a divine prerogative (cf. Rom. 14:10-12). Only God has all the facts (cf. 6:6). Disciples must be careful to live and act in accordance with God's revelation without alteration, addition, or assuming authority not given to them (cf. 15:1-11). [*krinō*]

7:3 Notice (*katanoeis*)—This word means "observe or consider carefully" (BDAG, 522). A distinct failure of the hypocrite is self-examination. The disciple must consider carefully his own deficiencies and act to address them before he can assist others with their needs. The hypocrite deceives himself by judging others in order to avoid personal examination. By so doing he condemns himself and becomes useless to others (cf. 5:13). [*katanoeō*]

7:6 Dogs (*kysin*)—Usually living as scavengers in the ancient world, to call someone a dog was a word of reproach (1 Sam. 17:43). It was also applied to those who reject God's truth (Prov. 26:11). The saying serves to remind disciples that not all will heed their message. At times they will need to refrain from further ministry and take their message elsewhere (cf. 10:14). [*kuōn*]

7:7 Ask (*aiteite*)—Although God knows what disciples need before they ask (6:8), prayer remains an essential part of life. Prayer is a means God has ordained for the fulfillment of his will and a fundamental way to nurture and sustain relationship with him. A father wants to hear from his children and delights in responding to them (vv. 9-11). [*aiteō*]

7:11 Evil (*ponēroi*)—Although there is a contrast of words in this saying (cf. "give good gifts" / "being evil"), this reference to being evil is also a stark description of the fundamental human condition. When Jesus later speaks of his blood poured out for many (26:28) the disciples are understood to be among those needing forgiveness. [*ponēros*]

7:12 Do (*poieite*)—Jesus had earlier told his followers to love their enemies (5:44). This statement is similar and clearly shows that disciples are to do what is best for all people. Later Jesus will summarize the law in relation to others by saying, "Love your neighbor as yourself" (Lev. 19:18). [*poieō*]

7:13 Way (*hodos*)—The way or "road" (NIV, NRSV) in this saying refers to a "course of behavior" (BDAG, 691) that describes the course of a person's life. Following Jesus is not easy or popular. On the contrary, it is constraining ("narrow," NRSV) and beset with difficulty ("hard," NRSV), but it ends as it began—in life with God. By contrast, the broad, easy way ends where it began—in separation from God. [*hodos*]

7:15 False prophets (*pseudoprophētōn*)—Unlike John the Baptist, the false prophets do not follow the way of righteousness (21:32). Like ravenous wolves they destroy the sheep to satisfy their own appetites. They may sing Ps. 95:7 ("we are the people of his pasture and the sheep of his hand"), but their deeds ultimately betray them as people who do not do God's will (7:21, 23). Jesus' warning implies that where God's people are, false prophets will be as well (cf. 24:11). [*pseudoprophētēs*]

7:16 Fruits (*karpōn*)—Fruit refers to manner of life, what a person does; the word translated "produce" in this saying elsewhere refers to actions (e.g. vv. 12, 24). In a later saying "fruit" will refer to words (12:33-37). Here people may in fact say the right things, but what they do reveals who they are (cf. v. 21) and brings them to judgment (7:19, 23; cf. 3:12). [*karpos*]

7:18 Good tree (*dendron agathon*)—The good tree in this saying, like the good seed in the parable of the weeds (13:37-38), is good because it is planted by God (cf. 15:13) and belongs to him. The good tree is distinguished by doing good things: namely, God's will. [*dendron, agathos*]

7:21 Lord (*kyrie*)—Jesus is depicted here in the role of judge (3:12; 25:31-46). One day all people will acknowledge his authority over them (cf. Phil. 2:10-11). The person who is a member of God's family demonstrates the reality of that bond by doing God's will (cf. 12:50). It is not the publicly spectacular ministry but the private acts of righteousness that reveal a person's relationship with God (6:1-18). Although Judas may have prophesied, cast out demons, and performed miracles (10:4-8), he ultimately showed himself to be a "bad tree" (7:18). [*kyrios*]

7:23 Knew (*egnōn*)—This is not a statement about understanding, but about relationship. Jesus as judge will completely disclose what is thought to be secret (10:26; cf. Rom. 2:16) and will declare that he has had no relationship with those not doing the Father's will (7:21; cf. 25:12). [*ginōskō*]

7:24 Wise man (*andri phronimō*)—A wise man responds to Jesus' message by living according to its commands. He does what Jesus says to do. The "rock" is the message of Jesus. The "house" that is built on the rock is the life lived according to Jesus' teaching (cf. 1 Cor. 3:10-15). [*phronimos*]

7:25 Floods (*potamoi*)—Floods may refer to the trials and tribulations that are part of life in a fallen world (cf. Ps. 66:12) which the wise man will be able to endure by living accord-

ing to Jesus' message. More likely this is a picture of the final judgment (cf. Isa. 30:28), later compared by Jesus to Noah's flood (24:39). The wise man is not destroyed by God's judgment because he has put into practice Jesus' teaching (cf. Rom. 14:10). [*potamos*]

7:26 Foolish man (*andri mōrō*)—The foolish man listens to Jesus' teaching but does not obey it. He builds his life according to his own interests and agenda and is swept away to destruction (cf. 7:13) by God's final judgment. [*anēr, mōros*]

7:29 Authority (*exousian*)—Authority is "the right to control or command" (BDAG, 353). This Jesus had by virtue of his status as God's Son on whom the Spirit rested (3:16-17; 11:27). That this authority is connected to everything Jesus says or does is illustrated in the following chapters as he shows his control over natural (e.g., 8:27; 9:8) and supernatural realms (8:29-32). [*exousia*]

Their scribes (*grammateis autōn*)—Only here does Matthew use a personal pronoun to refer to the Jewish teachers of the law as a distinct group. Their authority exists only to the extent that they indeed teach the truth of the Mosaic Law (cf. 23:2-3). The same is true for Christian teachers of Jesus' message (13:52; 23:34). The authority for their teaching derives from Jesus' message and extends only to the point that their teaching expounds that truth. [*grammateus*]

8:2 Cleanse (*katharisai*)—The leper calls Jesus "Lord" and acknowledges Jesus' authority to cleanse him by curing the leper's disease. Jesus does so willingly in fulfillment of his mission as Messiah (v. 17; cf. 11:5), restoring the leper to worship with God's people (8:4). [*katharizō*]

8:5 Centurion (*hekatontarchos*)—A centurion was a "Roman officer commanding about a hundred men" (BDAG, 299) and formed the backbone of the army as the top enlisted soldier. [*hekatontarchēs*]

8:10 Faith (*pistin*)—Jesus healed the leper with a touch (8:3) and the centurion's servant with a word (8:13). The confidence of this Gentile in Jesus' authority is total. Jesus could simply "say the word and my servant will be healed" (8:8). Such faith provoked Jesus' pronouncement of acclaim (8:10) and warning (8:11). [*pistis*]

8:11 Recline (*anaklithēsontai*)—This word describes the style often associated with banquets in the ancient world where guests would recline on their left side and extend their right hand to eat. BDAG suggests "dine in style" (p. 65) as a suitable translation of this passage since it refers to the Messianic banquet. The "many" include not only Jews scattered around the world but Gentiles like the centurion. [*anaklinō*]

8:12 Sons of the kingdom (*huioi tēs basileias*)—The phrase here refers to the presumptive guests, the people of Israel, who thought their physical connection to the patriarchs would guarantee their part in the messianic kingdom. But Jesus warns that many of those who presume their place in the kingdom will find themselves excluded. Unlike the centurion's faith in Jesus, many of his fellow Jews would reject him and, as a result, condemn themselves. [*huios, basileia*]

Darkness (*skotos*)—Darkness defines "the state of unbelievers and the godless" (BDAG, 932). If light refers to God's presence and his salvation (cf. 4:16), darkness describes the awful circumstances of those separated from God's presence and his salvation. Instead of joyful fellowship with God and his people, those in the darkness experience the anguish of separation and banishment from God's presence. [*skotos*]

8:15 Serve (*diēkonei*)—Peter's mother-in-law is a model for all who have experienced Jesus' healing touch; she used her restoration as an opportunity for service. [*diakoneō*]

8:16 With a word (*logō*)—Although the Gentile centurion is a positive example (8:8) and the spirits afflicting the demon-possessed are a negative example, they testify to the same truth: they know Jesus' authority to be absolute. He has but to speak a word and they obey. [*logos*]

8:17 Isaiah the prophet (*Ēsaiou tou prophētou*)—There are more citations from Isaiah in Matthew than from any other OT book. This quotation is from Isaiah 53:4, identifying Jesus as the Suffering Servant, described later in that passage as the one who "made his life an offering for sin" (53:10). Human mortality (and the sickness and disease that define it) is a consequence of sin and the fall. Jesus' ministry of healing foreshadowed the victory over sin and death he would accomplish by his death as an offering for sin, an offering shown to be sufficient by the resurrection. [*Ēsaias*]

8:20 Son of Man (*huios tou anthrōpou*)—This is Jesus' usual self-designation. It emphasizes his humanity and humility (but the title will also be used to describe his exalted role as judge of all creation [25:31; 26:64; cf. Dan. 7:13]). Here he tells a would-be disciple that following him involves privation and difficulty like the life of a homeless man. [*huios + anthrōpos*]

8:21 Bury (*thapsai*)—Honoring father and mother is an essential duty (cf. 15:4) and stands as the first of the commandments dealing with human relationships (Exod. 20:12; Deut. 5:16). Certainly honoring a parent by proper burial was an important task. But the most important task a person can undertake is following Jesus. By comparison, all other priorities are relegated to secondary status and can be done by others. [*thaptō*]

8:22 Dead (*nekrous*)—The first use of "dead" in this passage describes people who do not yet recognize who Jesus is and how important it is to follow him. They are "so spiritually obtuse as to be in effect dead" (BDAG, 668). [*nekros*]

8:26 You of little faith (*oligopistoi*)—The disciples are not without faith; they are not "dead" (v. 22). They responded with obedience to Jesus' call to follow him. But they hardly have the faith of the Gentile centurion (8:10). They illustrate that the size of one's faith is not nearly so important as the object. The small faith of the disciples was rightly placed in a great Lord. Just how great he was they did not yet understand. They did not grasp that Jesus' authority over disease and demons extended to the whole world. Even the chaos of the natural world submitted to the authority of his word. [*oligopistos*]

8:28 Gadarenes (*Gadarēnōn*)—Gadara was a part of the Decapolis (4:25) touching the southeast shore of the Sea of Galilee. [*Gadarēnos*]

Extremely violent (*chalepoi lian*)—Like the furious storm (8:24) the demoniacs' destructive power strikes fear in the hearts of mortal men. And rightly so, as they demonstrate extraordinary violence. This is frightfully illustrated by Jesus' exorcism. It sends the demons into a herd of swine that rushes headlong into destruction in the sea (8:31-32). So the evil supernatural world's ruinous nature is clearly revealed. [*chalepos*]

8:29 Before the time (*pro kairou*)—The meaning of this phrase is "before the end time and the judgment" (BDAG, 498). The demons understand that God has set a time for judgment, but they protest the fact of its arrival in the course of Jesus' ministry. On this point they were partially right. Jesus' first coming foreshadowed the judgment he would effect and the rule he would establish at his second coming (cf. 19:28). The demons could appeal to his authority, but they could not resist it, even in the present time. [*kairos*]

8:32 Go (*hypagete*)—Matthew had earlier described Jesus as casting out demons with a word (8:16). Here is an example: the simple word "go." Jesus spoke the same word to the centurion, expressing assurance concerning his servant's healing (v. 13). Here the command to "go" serves to deliver the demon-possessed from their tyrants. In his hymn, "A Mighty Fortress," Martin Luther evoked the truth of this passage when he wrote about Satan's demise: "one little word shall fell him." [*hypagō*]

8:34 Leave (*metabē*)—It is a commentary on the folly of humanity that the One who can set right all the ills that befall us is asked to leave. [*metabainō*]

9:1 His own city (*idian polin*)—Capernaum was the place where Peter had a home. This town of a few thousand became the base of Jesus' ministry. [*polis*]

9:2 Their faith (*pistin autōn*)—The paralytic and his friends believe that Jesus can heal. The paralytic shows his faith by asking his friends to bring him to Jesus. The friends show their faith by bringing him. [*pistis*]

9:6 Forgive (*aphienai*)—More important than Jesus' authority to cast out demons and to heal is his authority to forgive sins. Ultimately this is rooted in the work Jesus came to do (26:28). But immediately it is linked to the authority God gave him (11:27) to speak and act in behalf of his Father. [*aphiēmi*]

9:8 Glorified God (*edoxasan ton theon*)—Jesus is the model for the disciples (5:16). By his life he brought honor and praise not to himself (cf. 6:2) but to God. [*doxazō*]

9:9 Matthew (*Maththaion*)—Working for the Roman government, Matthew collected a tax on the goods and produce that passed through his area. Both because they had opportunity to enrich themselves at other's expense and because they worked for a pagan government, tax collectors were associated with the scum of Jewish society. That Matthew's name is linked to this Gospel is good reason to think he is the author. The Gospel was apparently written as an anonymous document. However, the fact that it was linked to Matthew by early church tradition is significant testimony since Matthew was not otherwise a disciple of prominence (Eusebius, *Ecclesiastical History* 3.39; Irenaeus, *Against Heresies* 3.1.1). [*Maththaios*]

Follow me (*akolouthei moi*)—Jesus speaks and Matthew obeys. This is the hallmark of a disciple. Although Matthew and Mark do not make this clear, it is likely that these summons by Jesus to become his disciple follow previous encounters in which disciples have met Jesus and heard his message, as the call to disciples in Luke follows ministry in Capernaum (Luke 4:31–5:11). [*akoloutheō*]

9:11 Eating (*esthiei*)—Eating with someone implied relationship and kinship in the ancient world. One ate with friends. Jesus showed God's love for sinners and his desire to bring these people into relationship with himself, even though they were shunned by more scrupulous Jews. [*esthiō*]

9:13 Mercy (*eleos*)—Mercy is "kindness or concern expressed for someone in need" (BDAG, 316). By quoting Hosea 6:6, Jesus is not saying that sacrifice is unimportant, but

that God values mercy more highly. Mercy epitomizes God's compassion toward guilty sinners, which Jesus displays by eating with them. The self-righteous Pharisees misunderstand Hosea's message because they failed to see themselves as sinners, an essential first step in experiencing God's mercy. [*eleos*]

9:15 Bridegroom (*nymphios*)—A wedding is a time of celebration and rejoicing. Jesus likens his coming and ministry to that event to explain why his disciples do not fast. The writer of Revelation looks forward to celebrating a wedding feast at Christ's return (Rev. 19:7-10). But it is also true that Jesus by his death and resurrection creates a relationship between himself and believers that is compared to a marriage (cf. Eph. 5:22-32; 1 Cor. 6:15-17). Yet the ultimate intimacy of relationship that defines a marriage is seen as something yet future (cf. 1 Cor. 13:12). So the wedding image is something that is applied in the NT both to Jesus' initial ministry and his ministry to come. It is both "now" and "not yet." [*nymphios*]

9:18 Died (*eteleutēsen*)—This word literally means "come to an end" (BDAG, 997). With reference to people, it means "die." These chapters have documented Jesus' authority over sin, sickness, demons, storms, and the chaos of the natural world. Now Matthew shows Jesus' authority over death. Here a leader in a Jewish synagogue places his faith in Jesus to defeat the great consequence of sin, death. [*teleutaō*]

9:22 Well (*sesōken*)—This word means "saved from," and, depending on the object, it describes being delivered from sickness and disease or sin and eternal death (BDAG, 982). Jesus underscores the link between the woman's faith and her experience of deliverance. Touching him (vv. 20-21) expressed her faith. As in the other encounters described in these chapters (8-9), the healing is linked to Jesus' authoritative declaration. [*sōzō*]

9:23 Flute players (*aulētas*)—The flute players of the ancient world played an instrument that more closely resembled a clarinet than a modern flute. Their music helped people express emotions and sing laments at times of mourning (cf. Josephus, *Jewish War* 3.437). [*aulētēs*]

9:24 Asleep (*katheudei*)—Jesus describes the dead child as sleeping in view of the "awakening" about to take place (cf. John 11:11-13). The promise of the resurrection likewise influenced the view that death was not a final state and so could be compared to sleep (cf. Dan. 12:2; 1 Thess.. 5:10). [*katheudō*]

9:27 Son of David (*huios Dauid*)—Though this is a messianic title (cf. 1:1) it is also associated with Jesus' ministry of healing (cf. 12:23; 15:22; 20:30). Jewish tradition identified Solomon as one who healed (*Testament of Solomon*; Josephus, *Antiquities* 8.42-49). This background and connection may have been a factor in these appeals to Jesus for healing. The blind receiving sight begins the list of signs of the Messiah given to John (11:5). [*huios Dauid*]

9:28 Do you believe (*pisteuete*)—Faith in Jesus and the miracle that takes place is a repeated theme in these chapters (8–9) as is the connection to Jesus' authoritative words (v. 29). [*pisteuō*]

9:30 Sternly warned (*enebrimēthē*)—Because Jesus needed to define his role as a suffering Messiah, he sought to limit public acclaim and misunderstanding (illustrated by his disciples [cf. 16:21-22]) by commanding silence. People, however, prove to be the persistent exception when it comes to submitting to Jesus' authority (v. 31). [*embrimaomai*]

9:33 Israel (*Israēl*)—Chapters 8–9 have illustrated Jesus' authority to do miracles by merely speaking. Although a Gentile centurion is acclaimed for his faith (8:10), the main beneficiary of Jesus' miracle-working power has been the people of Israel. Their acclaim brings this section of the Gospel to an appropriate conclusion (cf. the response to Jesus' teaching, 7:28) and provides a contrast to the view of the religious leaders (cf. 7:29) following immediately (v. 34). [*Israēl*]

9:34 Ruler (*archonti*)—The Pharisees attribute Jesus' exorcisms to collusion with the devil, who is described as a "ruler" of the demons. This charge of healing through the prince of demons will be raised again later in the Gospel accompanied by Jesus' rebuttal (12:22-29) and warning about blasphemy against the Holy Spirit (12:30-32). It functions here as an illustration of Jesus' statement earlier in this section that not all Israelites would have a share in the messianic banquet but would instead be banished from the presence of God (8:11-12). It also anticipates Jesus' counsel to the disciples in the next teaching section (10:25). [*archōn*]

9:35 Their synagogues (*synagōgais autōn*)—Jesus continues to teach in the main weekly meeting place of his fellow Jews, the synagogue. Wherever there were ten adult men in a community, a synagogue might be founded and have full worship performed (*m Megillah* 4.3). From early Saturday morning, sometimes until noon, Jews would gather to hear the Scripture read and taught, to offer congregational prayer, and sing psalms. The use of the pronoun "their" might indicate that the writer of the Gospel distinguishes himself and his community from these synagogues primarily influenced by the Pharisees. Or the pronoun might simply refer to the people of Israel, the primary beneficiaries of Jesus' initial ministry (cf. the same pronoun in v. 36, referring to "the crowds"). [*synagōgē, autos*]

9:36 Compassion (*esplanchnisthē*)—This word means to "have pity" for or "feel sympathy" toward (BDAG, 938; BAGD, 762). The noun form of this word referred to the intestines (Acts 1:18), commonly understood to be the seat of emotions (cf. the KJV of Phil. 1:8, "I long after you all in the bowels of Jesus Christ"). Jesus' compassion is shown by his ministry to the people. Jesus became a shepherd to Israel (2:6), despite the fact that the religious leaders hindered and harmed Israel's welfare by opposing him. But the needs of the people are very great and other faithful shepherds are required (10:6). [*splanchnizomai*]

9:37 Harvest (*therismos*)—In the message of John the Baptist the imagery of harvest is linked to the judgment and the division of humanity that will result (3:12; cf.13:39-43). Although harvest is here linked to a wider proclamation of Jesus' message and a greater opportunity to meet people's needs (10:5-15), a division of humanity based on acceptance or rejection of the message is still present (10:13-15). [*therismos*]

9:38 Lord (*kyriou*)—Jesus encourages disciples to pray to God to multiply the workers for the harvest. This is a reminder of the importance of prayer in the fulfillment of God's will (7:7-8) and an acknowledgment that it is God who calls workers for the harvest (cf. 11:25; 20:1-16; 21:33-43). However, readers of the Gospel will also see Jesus as someone with authority to send out workers (10:5; cf. 13:37-43; 28:18-20) and so might also appeal to him for more helpers. [*kyrios*]

10:1 Twelve (*dōdeka*)—The calling of the Twelve formally begins a second section of teaching directed more specifically at the disciples' mission (10:1-42), which the preceding verses (9:35-38) introduced. The 12 corre-

spond to the number of Israel's tribes and signal Jesus' intent to take his message first to all the people of Israel (vv. 5-6). [*dōdeka*]

Authority (*exousian*)—The authority of Jesus, illustrated in chapters 8–9, is now given to the disciples. Jesus had called them to be "fishers of men" (4:19) and that role begins with this mission. Although the precise nature of this authority is never defined, it is reasonable to see it linked to the power of the Spirit (cf. Acts 1:8). As the Spirit came upon Jesus at the outset of his ministry (3:16), so the Spirit enables the disciples to fulfill their task as Jesus' representatives (cf. v. 20; 12:28-32) continuing the work he began (cf. 4:23; 9:35). [*exousia*]

10:2 Apostles (*apostolōn*)—The verb form of this word means "send away . . . for the achievement of some objective" (BDAG, 120; BAGD, 98). Jesus sends out the apostles as his authorized agents proclaiming his message and extending his ministry to the people. [*apostolos*]

10:6 Lost sheep (*probata to apolōlota*)—The people of Israel are described as lost sheep in part because they lack faithful shepherds (cf. 9:36) to bring them back to the fold (cf. 18:12). The adjective "lost" is elsewhere used to describe the destiny of those separated from God (cf. v. 28, "destroy . . . in hell;" v. 39; John 3:16) and points toward the importance of the disciples' mission. They are involved in a task with eternal consequences. [*probaton, apollymi*]

Israel (*Israēl*)—The people of Israel are the sole focus of the disciples' first mission. Although disciples are to be the "light of the world" (5:16) and this teaching section will address ministry to Gentiles (v. 18), the wider mission to all nations does not begin until after Jesus' death and resurrection (28:19). Even then Paul, the apostle to the Gentiles, followed a pattern of preaching "to the Jew first and also to the Greek" (Rom. 1:16). [*Israēl*]

10:9 Gold (*chryson*)—Jesus had previously instructed the disciples not to worry about their daily needs (6:25-34). Now he sends them on a mission without any money in their pocket to buy life's necessities. Instead, they are to depend on the hospitality of those to whom they minister (v. 11). [*chrysos*]

10:11 Worthy (*axios*)—People show themselves to be worthy by their reception of the disciples and their message. In terms of the imagery of the mission to the lost sheep (v. 6), the worthy are the sheep who are found and return to the fold. This adjective distinguishes the person who is in right relationship with God, and thus is worthy, from those who are not (cf. vv. 37-38; 22:8). [*axios*]

10:12 House (*oikian*)—Normally a house is thought of as a structure and to some degree that is true here. The disciples enter a place that will afford them shelter. But more importantly the house represents those who occupy it, from the owners to their children and in some cases their servants (cf. 13:57). The disciples do not greet a building but the people who occupy it. Thus, the expression is a *synedoche*, a figure that in this case associates the container with that which is contained in it. [*oikia*]

10:13 Peace (*eirēnē*)—It is possible that Jesus instructs his disciples to greet the household with a formulaic statement like "may you have good health" (BDAG, 287-88, 2; BAGD, 227, 2). But this is more likely a declaration of salvation (cf. Isa. 52:7) and the resultant peace with God (cf. Rom. 5:1), since the only alternative in the context is God's condemnation and wrath (v. 15). To receive the disciples is to receive their message, an act of faith that brings people into right relationship with God. [*eirēnē*]

10:14 Dust (*koniorton*)—The act of shaking the dust off of feet or garments was a sign of renunciation (cf. Neh. 5:13; Acts 18:6). Jews leaving Gentile territory would do this before entering the land of Israel as a way to signify transition from unholy or common ground to land sanctified by God's presence, therefore holy (cf. *m Ohol* 2.3, 18.6; *m Tohar* 4.5; Josephus, *Apion* 2.203). For the disciples to do this upon leaving a town or village that refused their message depicts the status of that town as unholy, lacking the blessing of God's presence. [*koniortos*]

10:15 Judgment (*kriseōs*)—Rejecting the disciples and their message is perilous. This warning does not imply that people may not later repent of their folly, but does affirm that those who refuse repentance will suffer awful consequences in God's judgment. Sodom and Gomorrah were destroyed by fire (Gen. 19:24-28). The judgment for rejecting the message of salvation is even more severe (cf. 25:46). [*krisis*]

10:16 Wolves (*lykōn*)—A lone wolf can wreak havoc in a flock of sheep. Even worse are a few sheep among a pack of wolves. Jesus describes those to whom the disciples take their message as powerful foes. To withstand their onslaught, the disciples must be prudent ("wise as serpents") yet straightforward ("innocent as doves") in advancing their mission, fully aware that they face fearsome opposition along the way. [*lykos*]

10:17 Councils (*synedria*)—The major governing council in Israel was the Sanhedrin in Jerusalem (cf. Acts 22:30-23:10). But other cities had smaller councils to address local judicial matters, usually connected with a synagogue. Part of their authority included administering punishment. As Jesus was accused of blasphemy (9:3; 26:65), the disciples should expect to be similarly charged (cf. vv. 24-25). [*synedrion*]

Flog (*mastigōsousin*)—A beating with a whip or lash is described in Deut. 25:1-3 as a punishment for certain offenses. A section of the Mishnah, *Makkoth*, called "stripes" to refer to the whipping of punishment, describes the administration of such penalties. Jesus' warning looks ahead to the persecution his followers will experience after the opposition of their fellow Jews solidifies (cf. 23:34; Acts 22:19). [*mastigoō*]

10:18 Gentiles (*ethnesin*)—This word means "nations" and refers to people who are not Jewish. Since Jesus sends his disciples only to the people of Israel on this first mission (10:5-6), this is another indication that his words about later missions to the world (5:14) are incorporated in this teaching section as well. As Jesus was forced to appear before a Gentile governor, (Pilate, 27:2) and a Jewish king (Herod, Luke 23:6-12), so would his followers who carried on his mission (e.g., Paul before Festus [a Gentile governor] and Agrippa [a Jewish king], Acts 25:14-26:32). [*ethnos*]

10:20 Spirit (*pneuma*)—Jesus highlights the ministry of the Spirit which focuses on aid during times of trial when disciples would need to speak in their own defense (e.g., Acts 25:14-36). Rather than be anxious about what they might say in a hostile situation like this (v. 19), they can rely upon God's faithful provision of the Spirit to give them the ability to offer adequate testimony (v. 18) as needed. [*pneuma*]

10:22 Endures (*hypomeinas*)—Jesus assures his disciples that however difficult the situation or perilous the circumstance, they can be confident of ultimate deliverance and vindication. That being so, disciples are called to be steadfast in the face of adversity by persisting in their course of life, remaining faithful to their calling, and fulfilling their ministry, even in the face of death (v. 21). [*hypomenō*]

10:23 Cities of Israel (*poleis tou Israēl*)—This would seem at first glance to refer to cities the disciples will visit in the course of their first missionary journey (v. 6). However, it occurs in a series of verses that address future missions to the wider Gentile world and is linked to the coming of the Son of Man which elsewhere is associated with the end of the age (13:43; 24). For Jesus to tell the disciples that they will not finish going to the cities of Israel until the end of the age means that even though future missions will be extended to all peoples (28:19), the mission to Israel remains an ongoing part of that endeavor (cf. 23:34). [*polis, Israēl*]

10:24 Disciple . . . teacher (*mathētēs . . . didaskalon*)—A disciple is someone who is learning. The teacher referred to here is Jesus. Later the disciples will be told to make disciples of others (28:19) and to do so by teaching them the lessons they have received from Jesus (28:20). Matthew wrote his Gospel in part to assist disciples with this task by giving exemplary portions of Jesus' teaching (e.g., chapters 5–7, 10, 13, 18, 23–24) and by showing how Jesus lived. The teacher instructs by both word and deed. [*mathētēs, didaskalos*]

Slave . . . master (*doulos . . . kyrion*)—A disciple's relationship is also compared to that of a slave and master. The point of this comparison is that a slave does not do what he wants to do but what his master commands. The word "master" may also be translated "Lord." To call Jesus "Lord" is to submit to his authority and to do his will (cf. 7:21). [*doulos, kyrios*]

10:25 Become like (*genētai hōs*)—This is the essence of discipleship, becoming a person who speaks and acts like Jesus. When he was faced with the most awful circumstance anyone ever faced, he said, "Not my will but yours be done" (26:39). [*ginomai*]

Beelzeboul (*Beelzeboul*)—Some ancient translators (e.g., the Coptic, Syriac, and Latin versions) thought this was a reference to the god of Ekron, *Beelzebub*, the "Lord of the flies" (cf. 2 Kings 1:2-3). But it probably is a reference to the ancient Canaanite god, *Baal*, in which *Beelzeboul* means, "the exalted one." In light of the charge made against Jesus noted earlier (9:34) and later (12:24), it probably refers here to Satan. [*Beelzeboul*]

10:26 Hidden (*krypton*)—When this word was used in the first discourse (5–7) it had a positive connotation (6:4, 6). Here it is negative, referring to the harm done to disciples by those who oppose them. Disciples are assured that God will bring to light all wrongs suffered. Just as God will reward disciples for their acts of righteousness done for him (6:4, 6) so, it is implied, he will punish the wrongdoers for their injustices against disciples. [*kryptos*]

10:27 Speak (*eipate*)—Disciples are urged to speak openly and fearlessly the message they have received from Jesus. The references to darkness and whispering in contrast to light and rooftops are likely a comparison of private instruction to public declaration. [*eipon, legō*]

10:28 Soul (*psychēn*)—The disciples' opponents may persecute them even to the point of death, but that only ends their life in an earthly body. The soul is the immaterial and lasting aspect of life that extends beyond mortality. The lives of all people are finally subject to the authority of God alone. [*psychē*]

Destroy (*apolesai*)—Although this word might suggest the idea of annihilation, rendering soul and body nonexistent, it is unlikely. Hell (*Gehenna*) as the place of judgment and destruction refers to the awful con-

dition of those separated from God's presence. Only God has authority to make this determination. The reference to soul and body suggests a continued, corporeal existence for the condemned. [*apollymi*]

10:29 Apart from (*aneu*)—This important preposition means that the death of even the sparrow does not happen "without the knowledge and consent" (BDAG, 78 a; BAGD, 65, 1) of God. The context suggests that just as a sparrow might be snared by a fowler so disciples may be captured by their enemies and put to death. This does not imply that God arranges these events, but it does affirm that God permits suffering and death in this fallen world, affecting even disciples. [*aneu*]

10:30 Numbered (*ērithmēmenai*)—This is probably a proverbial way to affirm both that God's knowledge of us and his care for us exceeds our own. The smallest details, including the grievous moments of life, are known to God and their occurrence does not suggest any lessening of his affection or care. [*arithmeō*]

10:33 I will deny (*arnēsomai*)—To deny Jesus is ultimately to disavow by word or deed relationship with him. The backdrop to this statement is the reality of Jesus as the future judge of all humanity (25:31-46). For Jesus to deny someone is another way for him to say he had no relationship with him (cf. 7:23). Peter's later denial of his relationship with Jesus (26:69-75) is an illustration of what Jesus wants his disciples to avoid. However, it is also a reminder that temporary failure is not necessarily permanent. Restoration can and does occur. Judas, on the other hand, illustrates denial with all of its lasting perilous consequences. [*arneomai*]

10:34 Peace (*eirēnēn*)—Jesus is the Prince of

Peace (Isa. 9:6), but he will not establish this peace universally until his second coming (cf. 13:41-43; 19:28-29; 24:30; 25:31-34). The message of his first coming is a message of peace to those who receive him and his disciples (v. 13), but it is a peace experienced in terms of relationship with God. The experience of disciples, like that of the world generally, may be full of conflict and anguish. Indeed, wars and upheaval characterize the world until the end (24:6-14). [*eirēnē*]

Sword (*machairan*)—The image of the sword fits both the prospect of martyrdom (cf. vv. 28-31; 38-39) and the division involving human bonds that allegiance to Jesus may produce (vv. 21-22, 35-37; cf. 8:21-22). Following Jesus is a perilous enterprise fraught with danger and pain that requires single-minded commitment to reach the end (v. 22). [*machaira*]

10:38 Worthy (*axios*)—Jesus divides response to him into two categories: acceptance or rejection (cf. v. 13). Acceptance of him and his message calls for an allegiance higher than family ties (v. 37) and a devotion that holds nothing in reserve, even self-preservation. This is the response of the worthy person. [*axios*]

10:39 Lose (*apolesei*)—The future tense of this verb probably looks toward the end of a person's life. The individual intent on preserving and enhancing life on his own terms is ultimately involved in a self-defeating course that ends in ruin (cf. 7:26-27). On the other hand, those who follow the path set forth by Jesus may appear to be following a course of personal sacrifice and ruin (v. 38) but ultimately find more than they could ever imagine in terms of relationship and well-being (cf. 19:27, 29). [*apollymi*]

10:40 Receives (*dechetai*)—Welcoming and receiving disciples as guests (BDAG, 221, 3;

BADG, 177, 1) indicates reception of their message (cf. v. 14). Since they are sent out by Jesus to proclaim his message (cf. 4:17; 10:7), those receiving the disciples enter into a relationship with Jesus and God the Father, whom Jesus represents (cf. 11:25-27). [*dechomai*]

10:41 Reward (*misthon*)—The reward of a prophet may refer to the reward belonging to a prophet which the person who receives him will also gain. But more likely it is the reward a prophet bestows on those who receive him (cf. v. 13). Those who receive a prophet and his message receive the blessings associated with that message (cf. 3:2, 6; namely, forgiveness of sins and participation in the kingdom). Those who receive a righteous man follow the teaching he presents and reap the benefits the practice of righteousness brings (cf. 6:1-18). [*misthos*]

10:42 Little ones (*mikrōn*)—This is a general description of Jesus' disciples probably reflecting their reduced social status in the eyes of the wider community (BDAG, 651, 2a; BAGD, 521, 1c; cf. 11:25). The prophet and righteous man (v. 41) are among those so described, their welcome (v. 40) shown by extending even the small kindness of a cup of water (cf. 25:35). [*mikros*]

11:1 Instructing (*diatassōn*)—The words "when Jesus had finished . . ." signal the end of each of the five major teaching sections (cf. 7:28, 13:53; 19:1; 26:1). The qualifying word here points to a focus on mission and means "to give (detailed) instructions as to what must be done" (BDAG, 237, 2; BDAG, 189). Jesus' final words (28:20) underscore the abiding significance of these instructions. [*diatassō*]

11:3 Coming one (*erchomenos*)—John foresaw the Messiah as one who would vindicate the righteous and punish the wicked (cf. 3:11-12). As a righteous man suffering under the control of the wicked, John naturally anticipated vindication. The Baptist shows the importance of paying careful attention to Jesus' words, which assure vindication but also stress patient endurance until the time of the end (10:16-42; 13:24-30; 24:3-25:36). [*erchomai*]

11:6 Offense (*skandalisthē*)—This word is variously translated "fall away" (NIV), "stumble" (NET), or "offend" (NRSV), in relation to causing sin (BDAG, 926). The sin warned about here is unbelief manifested by a rejection of Jesus' words and deeds (v. 5), which in turn witness to his ministry and message. [*skandalizō*]

11:9 Prophet (*prophētēn*)—A prophet is "a proclaimer or expounder of divine matters or concerns that could not ordinarily be known except by special revelation" (BDAG, 890; BAGD, 723). John is greater than others because he himself fulfilled prophecy (v. 10) by introducing the Messiah. The greatness of John (v. 11) is due to this role and his faithfulness in fulfilling it. [*prophētēs*]

11:11 Least (*mikroteros*)—No human could hold a more exalted place in history than that occupied by John as forerunner of the Messiah. Yet human greatness is easily eclipsed by the blessings of divine grace. John's exalted status is compared to that of the most insignificant member of the kingdom of heaven. All who heed John's message (as he himself certainly did, cf. 3:14-15) and welcome Jesus and his disciples (10:40) enjoy a relationship with God that makes all human achievement pale by comparison. [*mikros*]

11:12 Suffers violence (*biazetai*)—This saying could be positive (cf. Luke 16:16) and translated "forcefully advancing, and forceful men lay hold of it" (NIV), positive and negative

("forcefully advancing, and violent people attack it" NLT) or negative (NET, NASB, NRSV, NKJV): "violent men have been trying to take over the kingdom of heaven by force" (CEV). Two reasons lend support to a negative translation. First, in general the word is "most often used in the unfavorable sense of attack or forcible constraint" (BDAG, 175; BAGD, 140-41). Second, the preceding context has warned disciples about fearful opposition (e.g., 10:16-39) which will soon be graphically illustrated in the death of John the Baptist (14:1-12)—the lauded character of the immediate context (vv. 7-19). There is no guarantee the term is used in the same way in Matthew and Luke as the contexts differ. [*biazō*]

11:14 Elijah (*Ēlias*)—The final words of Malachi (4:5-6) predict the coming of Elijah before the day of the Lord. Although John did not see himself as fulfilling Elijah's role (John 1:21), Jesus did (cf. Luke 1:17). Jesus made the equation explicit for his disciples (cf. 17:12). [*Ēlias*]

11:16 Generation (*genean*)—The contemporaries of John and Jesus are described uniformly as people who reject the emissaries of God (vv. 20-24; cf. 10:14-15). Negative adjectives are applied to them: evil and adulterous (12:39; 16:4); evil (12:45); unbelieving and perverted (17:17). The description evokes comparison to the wilderness generation (Deut. 1:35; 32:5, 20). Finally "this generation" is compared to those swept away in judgment in the days of Noah (24:34-44). [*genea*]

11:19 Friend (*philos*)—The tax collectors and sinners are society's "outsiders" (BDAG, 51, see reference there to *hamartōlos*) who end up being "insiders" with Jesus because they welcome him (cf. 9:9-13). These are people whom Jesus loves and who enjoy relationship with him. [*philos*]

Wisdom (*sophia*)—Wisdom is shown by living in accordance with the revelation of God. That "wisdom is vindicated by her works" is thus a proverbial truth, here applied to the "works of Christ" (v. 2) and the welcome accorded Jesus by the "outsiders." All of this shows the wisdom of God's plan. [*sophia*]

11:21 Woe (*ouai*)—The opposite of the pronouncement of blessing (v. 6) is the pronouncement of woe. Like a blessing it looks toward the future only in this case, warning that those who persist in their present course of life are destined for a terrible end (v. 24). Jesus functions here as a prophet, expressing with this warning his disappointment in the hardness of heart of the people living near him. [*ouai*]

11:23 Hades (*Hadou*)—The Greeks named the god of the underworld, the realm of the dead, Hades (BDAG, 19; BAGD, 16). Although it was a neutral term to Greeks, its contrast here with heaven identifies it as the realm of those separated from God's presence and thus a synonym for Gehenna or hell. [*Hadēs*]

11:25 Hidden . . . revealed (*ekrypsas . . . apekalypsas*)—Jesus ties people's response to him and his message ("these things") to the work of God who has authority over all creation. Jesus will later link Peter's confession to God's revelation (16:17). This affirmation of God's sovereignty is placed between passages that affirm human responsibility in either rejecting (vv. 20-24) or accepting (vv. 28-30) Jesus and his message. Jesus affirms both the human responsibility to believe and to live in light of the truth as well as the necessary provision of God to do so (cf. Rom. 9-10; Phil. 2:12-13), he does not explain the relationship between the human and divine elements (however, explanations that diminish either divine responsibility or human responsibil-

ity are certainly incorrect). [*kryptō, apokalyptō*]

Wise . . . infants (*sophōn . . . nēpiois*)—Society's evaluation of wisdom is radically different than God's. The Psalms similarly extol God's grace to the weak and simple (cf. Psalm. 19:7; 119:130) as does Paul (1 Cor. 1:20-21). [*sophos, nēpios*]

11:27 All things (*panta*)—The context concerns God's revelation (v. 25). Jesus is here identified as the agent of that revelation. Whatever anyone needs to know about relationship with God can be learned from Jesus. Only by means of what Jesus says and does can a person have a relationship with God (cf. John 14:6). [*pas*]

11:28 Come . . . all (*deute . . . pantes*)—Jesus' invitation is universal, qualified (if at all) only by recognition of personal need (would the "wise" of v. 25 see themselves as "weary and burdened"?). Seeing such a need requires a response for help, the accepting of the divine invitation to find rest. The plight of those in need is reminiscent of the crowds (cf. 9:36) who followed Jesus. But it is only those who respond to Jesus' invitation who experience the rest he offers. [*deute, pas*]

Rest (*anapausō*)—The rest Jesus provides is the security that relationship with him brings to people. It is membership in the family of God (12:46-50) that brings assurance of care for present needs (6:8, 25-34; 7:11) and the expectation of blessing in the world to come (5:2-12). The disciples are authorized to pronounce God's peace on those who receive them and their message (10:13). It is the assurance of this peace from God that Jesus mediates (v. 27). [*anapauō*]

11:30 Yoke (*zygos*)—A yoke was "a frame used to control working animals" (BDAG 429; BAGD, 339). It serves to clarify Jesus' meaning of "rest" (vv. 28-29). It is not the absence of labor but meaningful duty in following Jesus (cf. 10:38-39) and the assurance of God's presence and provision for the task (cf. 10:19-20; 28:20). [*zygos*]

12:2 Not lawful (*ouk exestin*)—As poor people, the disciples were permitted to gather small amounts of grain (Lev. 19:9-10), but (strictly read) the disciples were in violation of Exodus 34:21 which prohibits sowing and harvesting on the seventh day, a Sabbath. A list of Sabbath violations appears in the Mishnah (*m Shab* 7.2). [*ou, exestin*]

12:7 Innocent (*anaitious*)—Jesus seems to set forth several reasons why the disciples are not guilty of violating the sanctity of the Sabbath, all revolving around the notion that some things are more important than others. Although keeping the law is important, showing mercy takes precedence over perfunctory ritual. Provision for the hungry legitimates the means of supplying food for both David and the disciples. The importance of the priests' service takes precedence over resting on the Sabbath. The disciples are involved in an even greater task than the priests in following Jesus, whose authority is over not only the Sabbath but all things (28:19). [*anaitios*]

12:12 More valuable (*diapherei*)—The theme of the preceding Sabbath controversy is reinforced here as well. Some things are more important than others. Meeting human need by showing mercy takes precedence over perfunctory ritual (v. 7). [*diapherō*]

12:14 Destroy (*apolesōsin*)—The opponents of Jesus show their utter lack of mercy by conspiring to destroy him. To their dismay they will find their zeal for the law fulfilled in one respect, the law of reciprocity. What they intend for Jesus they will bring on themselves (cf. 10:39). [*apollymi*]

12:18 Servant (*pais*)—Although this word can refer to one's own child or children generally (BDAG, 750; BAGD, 604-05), it is also used for a slave or servant (cf. 8:6, 8, 13) "who is committed in total obedience to another" (BDAG, 750). In this quotation from Isaiah 42:1 Jesus is identified as the servant of God (in language evoking the approbation spoken at his baptism [3:17]) who fulfills his role quietly (v. 19) and gently (v. 20), hardly the image of a conquering hero (cf. 11:29). [*pais*]

12:21 Hope (*elpiousin*)—The future tense of this verb looks forward to the mission to the Gentiles (cf. v. 18; 28:19) and the success that mission will enjoy. That the Gentiles will hope in his name makes the point that unlike so many in Israel (cf. the opposition profiled in the verses surrounding this passage), the Gentiles will embrace the Gospel and look forward to the salvation that Jesus will bring (cf. Acts 13:47). Hope is ultimately an expression of trust that God will fulfill his promise of deliverance from the tyranny of sin (cf. Rom. 8:23-25). [*elpizō*]

12:28 Has come (*ephthasen*)—The past tense (aorist) of this verb connects the miracles of Jesus (cf. 11:5) with the power of the Spirit and the presence of God's rule. The authority of Jesus over natural and supernatural powers narrated in chapters 8–9 illustrates God's rule mediated by Jesus. This beginning manifestation of God's rule also shows the kind of kingdom Jesus will establish in the future (19:28; 25:31) when Satan ("the strong man" v. 29) is extensively bound (cf. Rev. 20:2-3). [*phthanō*]

12:32 Will not be forgiven (*ouk aphethēsetai*)—The "unpardonable sin" is rejection of the witness of the Holy Spirit to Jesus as the Christ (v. 23). Though this may be a sin only Jesus' contemporaries could commit, Matthew probably views this rejection as a refusal to repent (cf. 11:20-24), equivalent to the sin of unbelief. It is then a sin that will not be forgiven because the sinner rejects the only means of forgiveness (cf. 11:27-28; 26:28). [*aphiēmi*]

12:36 Judgment day (*hēmera kriseōs*)—God's judgment is a recurring theme in these chapters (10:15; 11:22, 24; 12:41-42). These verses (vv. 33-37) focus on words as the means by which a person expresses faith (e.g., "confessing their sins," 3:6) or unbelief (e.g., "blasphemy against the Spirit," v. 31). The mouth reveals the state of the unseen heart (v. 34; cf. Rom. 10:10), so that words become a testimony to one's status as a good or evil person (v. 35), part of the evidence at the day of judgment that will distinguish the just and the unjust (v. 37). [*hēmera, krisis*]

12:39 Jonah (*Iōna*)—Jonah escaped death by God's intervention and preached successfully to Gentiles (Jonah 3:5). Jesus will be delivered from the grave by God and send disciples on a greater and wider mission to Gentiles (cf. Rom. 15:18). The resurrection is not a sign but a vindication of Jesus' words and works that his kinsmen ignore to their peril (cf. 26:64). The "sign of Jonah" is the mercy of God upon Gentiles (cf. Rom. 11:11). [*Iōnas*]

12:45 Last state (*eschata*)—By telling this story Jesus issues another warning to the people of Israel. His works bring temporary relief from illness, demon possession, and even death (11:5). However, if people do not respond to his message, it would have been better if he had never come. Because he is greater than Jonah or Solomon, rejection of him brings more awful consequences (cf. Heb. 10:28-31). The "last state" (NASB, NRSV) or "final condition" (NIV, NET) of that person is condemnation at the judgment. [*eschatos*]

12:50 Sister (*adelphē*)—Relationship with Jesus is not a matter of physical kinship. The one who responds to his message by living according to it becomes a member of God's family in a relationship that takes precedence over all others (cf. 10:37). This was true for Jesus as well. [*adelphē*]

13:3 Parables (*parabolais*)—Parables are stories or sayings that "illustrate a truth especially through comparison" (BDAG, 759; BAGD, 612). The parables in vv. 3-52 form the third major teaching section in the Gospel (chapters 5–7; 10; 13; 18; 24–25). This is the only teaching section in which portions are specifically addressed to the crowds. Like Jesus' ministry generally, the parables evoke a response of either rejection (vv. 13-15) or a request for further explanation (v. 36; cf. 15:15). [*parabolē*]

13:11 Has been given (*dedotai*)—The form of this verb (passive voice) indicates God as the one revealing the meaning of the parables to people (cf. 11:25-26). The agent of this revelation is Jesus (cf. 11:27) who explains their meaning to the disciples (e.g., vv. 18-23, 36-43; cf. 15:15-20). What they receive goes beyond grasping the point of a particular parable (cf. 21:45) to embracing its message. [*didōmi*]

Secrets (*mystēria*)—God's "secrets" (NIV, NET, NLT) or "mysteries" (NASB, NKJV) refer to truths about God and his ways which can only be known because God reveals them. [*mystērion*]

13:13 Understand (*syniousin*)—The meaning of this word is "to have an intelligent grasp of something that challenges one's thinking or practice" (BDAG, 972; BAGD, 790). More significantly in this chapter, it is a defining characteristic of people. Those who do not understand do not respond to the truth (e.g., vv. 15, 19). Those who understand respond to the truth and are changed by it (v. 23). [*syniēmi*]

13:15 Turn (*epistrepsōsin*)—This word means

"to change one's mind or course of action" (BDAG, 382; BAGD, 301). In this passage it means to repent, to turn away from a futile course of life, and to turn to God. [*epistrephō*]

13:19 The word of the kingdom (*ton logon tēs basileias*)—The word of the kingdom is the message John the Baptist, Jesus, and his disciples have been preaching. It calls people to repentance and faith in God. Those who receive this message enter a relationship with God in which they obey him (cf. 12:50) and see Jesus as the one through whom God's rule will be established throughout the world (vv. 37-43). [*logos*]

13:21 Temporary (*proskairos*)—This word is translated in various ways to communicate the notion that the right response to Jesus and his message is a lasting response: "temporary" (NASB); "lasts only a short time" (NIV); "endures only for a while (NRSV, ESV); "does not endure" (NET). The opposite (and positive) word is "endure" (10:22; 24:13; cf. Luke 8:15). Judas illustrates a temporary disciple, though he corresponds as well to the one deceived by wealth (v. 22; cf. 26:14-16). [*proskairos*]

13:23 Good soil (*kalēn gēn*)—Like the "good tree" (7:17; 12:33) and the "good person" (12:35), the "good soil" represents people who understand the message of Jesus (contrast v. 19), who hold firmly to it (contrast v. 21) and whose lives are changed by it (contrast v. 22). [*kalos*]

13:31 Mustard (*sinapeōs*)—Some mustard plants grow to a height of ten feet. Yet the seeds are "popularly viewed as the smallest of all seeds" (BDAG, 924; BAGD, 751). Jesus likens the great size of the mustard plant and its small beginnings to the work that begins with his ministry and will end with the good news preached and disciples

made throughout the world (24:14; cf. v. 38). [*sinapi*]

13:33 Yeast (*zymē*)—Also translated "leaven" (NASB, NKJV), the preparation process was not like modern baking where a separate product like yeast is mixed with flour. Instead, a portion of fermented dough from a previous batch was used (BDAG, 429; BAGD, 340). The point is the same, however: gradually the small portion effects the whole. The small beginnings of Jesus' ministry will ultimately effect the whole world (vv. 37-43). [*zymē*]

13:35 Hidden (*kekrymmena*)—Jesus is the revealer of God's truth (cf. 11:25-27) and the parables are a part of that revelation. However small and insignificant the beginning of his ministry may appear to be (vv. 31-33), Jesus will ultimately judge and rule the world (vv. 41-43). [*kryptō*]

13:38 Sons (*huioi*)—This is an illustration of a word that normally describes a male but also can be used of females. It refers to the division of humanity into one of two groups: either members of a group belonging to God ("the kingdom") or members belonging to Satan ("the evil one"). The translations "children" (KJV, NCV) or "people" (NLT, NET) unambiguously reflect the word's meaning in this context. [*huios*]

13:41 Lawbreakers (*poiountas tēn anomian*)—This is also translated "evildoers" (NRSV) or "all who do evil" (NIV, NLT), but it more narrowly refers to those who commit or practice lawlessness (NASB, NKJV, NET). A lawbreaker lives contrary to the will of God (cf. 7:21-23). By contrast, the righteous (v. 43) do the will of God (cf. 12:50). When Jesus was asked about the greatest commandment of the law (22:34-40), he cited Deut. 6:5 and Lev. 19:18, the priority of loving God and loving one's neighbor. When Jesus warns his disciples about trials and persecutions to come (24:6-14), he links an increase in lawlessness with a lessening of love (24:13). [*anomia*]

13:44 Sell all (*pōlei panta*)—Participation in the kingdom—a treasure seen for what it is by some (vv. 11, 16-17), but hidden to others (vv. 13-15)—is worth selling all one has to gain (v. 45). Wealth can be a cruel tyrant (cf. 6:24), strangling those serving it (v. 22; cf. 19:21-24). Selling all one has testifies to the incomparable value and unrivaled priority of participation in the kingdom (cf. 6:33; 19:27). [*pōleō*]

13:49 Separate (*aphoriousin*)—The inevitability of judgment and the division of humanity into two categories is a recurring theme in Jesus' teaching (e.g., vv. 12-17; 41-43; cf. 7:19, 23, 26-27; 8:12; 12:37; 24:40-41; 25:32). This word means "to remove one party from other parties so as to distinguish or eliminate contact" (BDAG, 158; BAGD, 127). [*aphorizō*]

13:52 Trained (*mathēteutheis*)—This is the verb form of the word "disciple." It is variously translated "become a disciple" (NASB, NLT), "been instructed" (KJV, NIV), "been taught" (NCV), or "been trained" (NRSV, NET). Those who have been trained by Jesus are sent out by him (23:34) and given the responsibility of training others (28:19-20). [*mathēteuō*]

13:57 Prophet (*prophētēs*)—Jesus' saying applies to himself and John the Baptist. Like other prophets before them, they were persecuted (cf. 5:12) and both died ignominiously at the hands of evil men. Matthew places the account of Jesus' rejection by the unbelieving people of Nazareth together with John's execution as a graphic illustration of this saying. [*prophētēs*]

14:1 Tetrarch (*tetraarchēs*)—This word originally meant "ruler of a fourth" of a region, but gradually came to be used as a "title of a petty prince who ruled by courtesy of Rome" (BDAG, 1000; BAGD, 814). Although he aspired to be a king like his father (2:1) and was sometimes called that in a popular sense (14:9), Herod Antipas died in exile without obtaining his goal (Josephus, *Ant.* 18.240-56). After divorcing his wife, Herod married his niece, Herodias, the divorced wife of his half brother (cf. BDAG, 440; BAGD, 348). Since his brother was still alive, John saw this as a violation of Leviticus 18:16 (cf. 20:21) and condemned it. For this he was imprisoned and killed (vv. 3-12). [*tetraarchēs* (also *tetrarchēs*)]

14:16 You give (*dote*)—Jesus asks the disciples to give food to people and then makes it possible for them to do so (v. 19). This is a vivid example of God's provision (cf. 6:25-34), Jesus' miraculous authority, and an illustration for the disciples that they can do what Jesus commands (cf. John 21:15-17 as a summary of ministry). This meal may also foreshadow the future feast in the kingdom (cf. 8:11; 26:29) enjoyed by followers of Jesus. [*didōmi*]

14:27 Do not be afraid (*mē phobeisthe*)—The human response to supernatural appearances is commonly fear (17:6; 28:4; cf. 27:54), eliciting these words of assurance (17:7; 28:5, 10). This account also illustrates the ability of a disciple to do what Jesus commands (cf. v. 16). Here, however, fear (v. 30) and doubt (v. 31) disrupt the outcome. [*phobeō*]

14:31 Doubt (*edistasas*)—This word, meaning "to be uncertain, to have second thoughts about a matter" (BDAG 252; BAGD, 200), occurs only in Matthew (28:17). A synonym (*diakrinō*) occurs in 21:21 and Jas. 1:6. The latter passage could serve as a summary of Peter's plight. An aspect of faith is single-minded trust that what Jesus invites one to do can be done. "Little faith," on the other hand

(v. 31), is partner to a divided mind. [*distazō*]

14:36 The <u>edge</u> of his cloak (*kraspedou tou himatiou*)—So great is Jesus' authority that even the edge of his cloak conveys healing power (cf. 9:20-22; and compare Acts 19:11-12). In 23:5 the word "edge" refers to the "tassel which an Israelite was obligated to wear on the four corners of his outer garment" (BDAG, 654; BAGD, 448). According to Numbers 15:37-41 the tassels were a reminder to obey the commandments. Jesus denounces those who lengthen these for self-serving aggrandizement (23:5). [*kraspedon*]

15:2 Tradition (*paradosin*)—The word referred to "the content of instruction that has been handed down" (BDAG, 763, 2; BAGD, 615, 2). This was primarily discussion about how the law should be applied, passed down orally, but later included in documents such as the Mishnah (c. A.D. 170) and Talmud (c. 5th Century). Although it was intended to aid the practice of the law, Jesus denounced this instruction as counterproductive to fulfilling the commandments of God (vv. 3, 6). [*paradosis*]

15:3 Commandment (*entolē*)—A commandment is specific instruction about behavior, whether from God (v. 4) or from men (v. 9). Jesus warned his disciples about breaking one of the least of God's commandments (5:19). Here Jesus charges the scribes and Pharisees with breaking one of the most important, the fifth commandment (Exod. 20:12; Deut. 5:16). It stands at the head of those related to human relationships (commands 5-10) and to violate it made one guilty of a capital crime (Exod. 21:17; Lev. 20:9). [*entolē*]

15:11 Defiles (*koinoi*)—This word can also be translated "make (ritually) unclean" (BDAG, 552; BAGD, 438; cf. NIV, NCV, CEV) in rela-tion to the purity laws of Leviticus (e.g., 11:1-47). These purity laws are related to the holiness of God (Lev. 11:44-45), so that ritual uncleanness disrupted relationship with God (cf. Lev. 15:31). Jesus, however, focuses on moral (v. 19) rather than ceremonial (v. 20) uncleanness as the major cause of disruption in relationship with God. He also links this defilement not to matters external to a person but to matters of the heart, the essence of human experience (v. 18). He condemns the foolishness of being scrupulous about minor matters while neglecting the major impediments to relationship with God (cf. 23:23). [*koinoō*]

15:22 Canaanite (*Kananaia*)—As the Roman centurion (8:5-13) embodied not just a Gentile but the enemy of the Jewish people in Jesus' day, so the Canaanite woman represents not only a Gentile but the historic enemy of the people of Israel. Like the centurion (8:12), the woman serves as a model of faith that starkly contrasts with Israel's unbelief. While Jesus' neighbors (13:57) and Pharisees (15:12) were offended by him, the woman pursues Jesus despite the obstacles placed in her path (vv. 23-26). As a result her faith is rewarded (v. 28). [*Kananaios*]

15:26 Dogs (*kynariois*)—This is the "diminutive" (BDAG, 575; BAGD, 457) of the word "dog" at 7:6, so sometimes translated "little dogs" (NKJV). Although Jesus probably spoke Aramaic normally (the common language of Jews in his day), it is likely that he also spoke Greek, particularly with Gentiles, as here. His point seems clear enough: the needs of the children come before those of household pets; his ministry to Israelites has priority over ministry to Gentiles. The woman grants his contention but argues that even those of secondary status deserve some attention, a point to which Jesus yields. [*kynarion*]

15:31 Praised the God of Israel (*edoxasan ton theon Israēl*)—To "praise" (NIV, NLT, NRSV) or "glorify" (KJV, NASB, NKJV) someone means "to influence one's opinion about another so as to enhance the latter's reputation" (BDAG, 258; BAGD, 204). By means of his ministry Jesus caused people to praise and honor God (cf. 5:16). Regrettably, this response seems to have been the exception rather than the rule among the people of Israel. [*doxazō, theos, Israēl*]

15:32 Crowd (*ochlon*)—The crowd describes those who listen willingly to Jesus but refrain from making a decision to become disciples. Jesus loves these people and does what he can to meet their needs. It is the crowd, however, that eventually demands Jesus' death (27:15-26). [*ochlos*]

16:3 Signs of the times (*sēmeia tōn kairōn*)— Jesus earlier had referred the disciples of John to his miracles as testimony to who he was as Messiah (11:5). In addition to these miracles, the consummate sign would be the resurrection (v. 4; cf. 12:38-39), indicating God's acceptance of Jesus' death for forgiveness of sin (cf. 26:28; Rom. 4:25; 1 Cor. 15:17). [*sēmeion, kairos*]

16:12 Teaching of the Pharisees and Sadducees (*didachēs tōn Pharisaiōn kai Saddoukaiōn*)—The way this phrase is written, linking the teaching of the Pharisees and Sadducees, is curious since the views of the parties were quite distinct on important points. The Sadducees were basically defined by what they did not believe in comparison to the Pharisees. They did not believe in a resurrection, a Messiah, his kingdom, angels, or the validity of oral tradition. Only on this last point would Jesus agree with the Sadducees (cf. 15:1-9). What united these otherwise opposed parties was their rejection of Jesus. Their mutual teaching denying his role as the Messiah (cf. 27:65-66; 28:12-15) proved to be destructive for many in Israel. [*didachē, Pharisaios, Saddoukaios*]

16:18 This rock (*tautē tē petra*)—The nearest referent (for the pronoun "this") in the context of Jesus' statement is Peter, forming a word-play on his name, *Petros*. While it is possible Jesus is referring to Peter's confession of him as the Christ (v. 16), it seems more likely that Jesus is describing Peter and the other disciples' future ministry as the foundation of the future church (cf. Eph. 2:20). As representative spokesman for the disciples, Peter was the first to preach to both Jews (Acts 2) and Gentiles (Acts 10) the truth that salvation is through Jesus (cf. Acts 2:36; 10:36). [*petra, houtos*]

Church (*ekklēsian*)—Only this Gospel refers to the church (18:17), what became the assembly of Jews and Gentiles joined together by their mutual faith in Jesus as the Messiah (cf. Eph. 2:11-22). The everyday use of the term simply means an assembly (BDAG, 303; BAGD, 240). Jesus' disciples would become the founding members of the church and would be his agents in bringing others into its membership (28:19-20). [*ekklēsia*]

Gates of Hades (*pylai hadou*)—This is a figure of speech (a part for the whole) in which "gates" as the passageway of a city represents its fortifications and inhabitants. If Hades refers to the realm of the dead (BDAG, 19; BADG, 16-17) the statement becomes a declaration that the power of death will not overcome the church and its people (CEV, New Century Version [=NCV]). If Hades is seen as the realm of condemnation (cf. 11:23), it would describe the evil power of hell (KJV, NLT) as equally unable to overcome the church. On either view the ultimate victory of the church over hostile powers is affirmed. [*pylē, hadēs*]

16:19 Keys (*kleidas*)—The keys given to Peter

refer to the authority given to him and the other disciples in their preaching of the Gospel (cf. 10:13). Peter is singled out because of his representative role as the first disciple to declare the Gospel after Jesus' death and resurrection to both Jews (Acts 2) and Gentiles (Acts 10) in the founding days of the church. He declares to all the prospect of forgiveness of sins and relationship with God. [*kleis*]

Bind . . . loose (*dēsēs . . . lysēs*)—Forgiveness of sins is declared to those who respond to the Gospel (cf. Acts 2:38-42; 10:43). But those who reject this message must bear the consequences of their sins at the judgment (cf. 10:14-15; Acts 10:42). The translation of the second occurrence of these verbs as they apply to God is more problematic. Should the perfect/passive form of the verbs be literally translated, "have been bound . . . have been loosed" (NASB, NET) or should the future form of the associated verb (*estai*), "will be," dominate the translation ("will be bound . . . will be loosed," KJV, NIV, NKJV, NRSV, NLT)? In the first instance the emphasis is on the disciples acting in accordance with the already determined will of God. The second instance emphasizes God's action in accordance with the decision of the disciples. Although the difference may be primarily a matter of emphasis and not an either/or proposition, the theme of God's sovereignty in this Gospel (e.g., 11:25-27; 13:11-17) supports the first translation. [*deō, lyō*]

16:22 God forbid (*hileōs*)—BDAG (474; also BAGD, 376) defines this word as "gracious, merciful." Its expanded sense in this statement would be, "God save you from those things" (NCV) or more simply, "God forbid!" (NASB, NET; cf. NLT, "Heaven forbid"). However, the use of this word in the Greek translation of the OT (e.g., 1 Kings 21:3; 1 Chron. 11:19) indicates the meaning "far be it from you, Lord" (NKJV, KJV; cf.

NIV, "Never, Lord!") may be appropriate here as well. [*hileōs*]

16:23 Satan (*Satanas*)—The name means "adversary" (BDAG, 916; BAGD, 744-45). Satan had offered Jesus a kingdom without the cross (4:8-9) to which Jesus replied, "Go away!" (v. 10). Peter (apparently speaking for the other disciples as well, cf. Mark 8:33) promotes the same idea and unwittingly becomes an ally of Satan. Here, however, the words "behind me" (used again in v. 24, "come after me") are included in Jesus' response. Peter is still a follower (but with much yet to learn). [*Satan/Satanas*]

Stumbling block (*skandalon*)—This word describes "an action or circumstance that leads one to act contrary to a proper course of action" (BDAG, 926; BAGD, 753). It is translated here in a variety of ways: "you are a stumbling block" (NASB, NIV, NRSV, NET); "you are an offense" (KJV, NKJV); "you are a dangerous trap" (NLT); "you are not helping me" (NCV); "you're in my way" (CEV); "you are tempting me to sin" (BDAG, 926, 2; BAGD, 753, 2). [*skandalon*]

17:2 Transfigured (*metemorphōthē*)—The word here means "to change in a manner visible to others" (BDAG, 639; BAGD, 511) and so is sometimes translated "Jesus' appearance changed" (cf. NLT, NCV, CEV). Jesus "took on the form of his heavenly glory" (BDAG, 639, 1; BAGD, 511, 1). [*metamorphoō*]

17:3 Moses and Elijah (*Mōysēs kai Ēlias*)—Both Moses and Elijah experienced theophanies, appearances of God, on a mountain. Now they see Jesus in his heavenly glory, a preview of his future appearance (cf. 16:28) and the future of the righteous (13:43). [*Mōusēs, Ēlias*]

17:4 Shelter (*skēnas*)—This word refers to "a place of shelter, frequently of temporary quarters . . . tent, hut" (BDAG, 928; BAGD, 754). It is translated in a variety of ways: "tabernacles" (KJV, NKJV, NASB); "shelters" (NIV, CEV, NET); "tents" (NCV); "shrines" (NLT); "dwellings" (NRSV). Whether a connection to the OT tabernacle or the yearly feast of tabernacles (suggested by the first translation) is intended is uncertain. Peter's proposal may be a further illustration of the disciples' failure to accept Jesus' path to the cross (cf. 16:22; 17:23) or it may reflect an equal weighting of Moses, Elijah, and Jesus. Either way, the disciples have much to learn. [skēnē]

17:11 Will restore (apokatastēsei)—John the Baptist began the ministry prophesied for Elijah by Malachi (4:5-6). The combination of past ("has come," v. 12) and future tenses ("will restore," v. 11) suggests that the present fulfillment begun by John awaits completion in the future (cf. 19:28, "when all things are renewed"). In this respect Elijah's ministry is similar to Jesus' (cf. 3:11-12). [apokathistēmi/apokathistanō]

17:20 Little faith (oligopistian)—If faith the size of a grain of mustard seed can bring about miracles, one would think even the disciples' "little faith" would be sufficient. But here they seem to be part and parcel with their countrymen (v. 17) as people lacking trust in God. Although Mark's depiction of the disciples is the bleakest of the Gospel writers, this section shows Matthew's outlook to be not much brighter. The disciples' "little faith" appears to be smaller than a grain of mustard seed, so virtually nonexistent. The encouraging lesson for readers is that if God used people like this to establish the church, he can use anyone. [oligopistia]

17:23 Greatly distressed (elypēthēsan spho-dra)—The disciples have progressed from resistance (cf. 16:21-23) at the first mention of

Jesus' passion to feeling profound anguish at the prospect. They seem to grasp the horror of what men will do to Jesus. Whether the idea of God's vindication in raising Jesus is too incomprehensible for them or their grief about his death is too deep for any solace is unclear. [lypeō, sphodra]

17:24 Temple tax (didrachma)—The "temple tax" is an interpretive translation (NCV, CEV, NLT, NET, NRSV NKJV, cf. "two-drachma tax" NASB, NIV) of the word for a two-drachma coin. It was "about equal to a half shekel (two days' wages) among the Jews, and was the sum required of each person annually as the temple tax" (BDAG, 241; BAGD, 192). The practice is based on Exodus 30:11-16. If this support for the temple was not voluntary at the time, Jesus makes it so for his followers, as his example encourages disciples to continue their support by making a payment. [didrachmon]

17:26 Free (eleutheroi)—What makes support of the temple a voluntary act is the disciples' relationship with God. The distinction between "sons" and "others" in this passage reinforces a distinction between disciples and the wider Jewish community (cf. 8:11-12; 12:49-50). However, maintenance of relationship with that community is encouraged by Jesus' payment. [eleutheros]

18:3 Turn (straphēte)—This word describes a person moving in one direction (away from God) and turning to go in the opposite direction (toward him and following a way of life defined by God). Some translations focus on the initial turning and render this word "convert" (KJV, NASB, NKJV). Others offer a more general translation that could also apply to "course corrections" in the path of discipleship as well as to the first step: "change" (NIV, NRSV, NCV) or "turn" (NLT, NET, English Standard Version [= ESV]). One of Jesus' closest disciples had not taken the first step (Judas) and others needed a further lesson in humility (v. 4; cf. 11:29). [*strephō*]

Children (*paidia*)—This word usually describes a person "below the age of puberty" (BDAG, 749; less specifically defined, BAGD, 604). It may be used figuratively here to refer to "one who is open to instruction" (BDAG, 749, 2). As the introduction to the fourth major discourse in this Gospel (chapters 5–7, 10, 13, 18), such a meaning would suit the context well. The idea of becoming like a child also fits the notion of repentance, where one turns away from self-reliance to trust and confidence in God. However, the disciples' opening question about greatness in the kingdom (v. 1) and Jesus' subsequent reference to humility (v. 4) suggest that the issue of status as it related to children is a prominent part of the word's meaning here. Though children may have been accorded a secondary social status in comparison to adults (cf. 19:13), Jesus places them as a model for how disciples should see themselves in relation to one another (cf. Rom. 12:16; Phil. 2:3). [*paidion*]

18:4 Humble (*tapeinōsei*)—This word can mean "to cause to be at a lower point" or "to cause someone to lose prestige or status" (BDAG, 990, 2; less specifically, BAGD, 804-05). Here disciples are to humble themselves by adopting an attitude of respect and regard for others that shows itself in acts of care. This attitude fosters a spirit of self-sacrifice that seeks to restore straying members of the community (vv. 12-15) and extend forgiveness (vv. 21-22) as needed. Humility is an essential character trait for a united community, but it was a virtue the disciples were slow to appreciate (cf. 20:20-28). [*tapeinoō*]

18:6 Cause to sin (*skandalisē*)—The general meaning of this word is "to cause to be brought to a downfall, cause to sin" (BDAG,

926; BAGD, 752). Depending on the context "the sin may consist in a breach of the moral law, in unbelief, or in the acceptance of false teachings" (BDAG, 926, 1). Jesus warns the disciples about the peril of causing spiritual harm to others by disregarding their needs. Sometimes people persist in their sin because they are offended by the truth (cf. 13:57; 15:12). Here, however, the wrong lies with the one who causes another to sin. The context draws particular attention to unwillingness to restore a straying member (vv. 12-14) or offer forgiveness (vv. 32-35). [*skandalizō*]

Little ones (*mikrōn*)—This word contrasts with the word "greatest" in v. 1. The "little ones who believe in me" describe all disciples, but in keeping with the spirit of the passage, especially those whom society generally would regard as people of lesser status. Within the community of the disciples it was important that all members be treated with respect because of their relationship with Jesus (v. 5; cf. Rom. 15:7), regardless of their status (or lack of it) in society at large. [*mikros*]

18:7 Stumbling blocks (*skandalōn*)—This is the noun form of the word translated "cause to sin" (v. 6). It is variously translated as "offenses" (KJV, NKJV), "things that cause sin" (NCV, NIV), "temptations to sin/do wrong" (ESV, NLT), or "stumbling blocks" (NASB, NRSV, NET). It refers to "an action or circumstance that leads one to act contrary to a proper course of action" (BDAG, 926; BAGD, 753). The fact that these will inevitably occur in a fallen world does not provide an excuse for anyone to be indifferent to them. They are life-threatening (vv. 6, 8-9). Disciples are responsible to be vigilant about causes of sin and immediate in eliminating them (vv. 8-9). [*skandalon*]

18:10 Angels (*angeloi*)—An angel is a messenger, "a transcendent power who carries out various missions or tasks" (BDAG, 8, 2; BAGD, 7, 2). This text might be understood to describe the assignment of personal guardian angels. While the pronoun "their" implies a personal ministry of angels to particular individuals, there is no implication that this is anything more than a brief ministry similar to the service Gabriel rendered to Zechariah (Luke 1:11-20) and Mary (Luke 1:26-38). [*angelos*]

Face (*prosōpon*)—To continually see the face of God describes the nearness of these angels to God's presence. Their proximity to God implies their exalted stature (cf. Luke 1:19). The point is that the greatest angels are given ministry concerning the "little ones" (v. 6), an indication of the importance of these people to God and the utter folly of treating them with contempt. [*prosōpon*]

18:12 Go astray (*planēthē*)—The imagery depicts a member leaving the fellowship and way of life that characterize the community. Rather than disdainfully disregarding him (v. 10) with a "good riddance" wave of the hand, the community (or at least its leadership) should do what it can to seek and return the straying member to its fellowship. [*planaō*]

18:14 Perish (*apolētai*)—Although this word can refer to the end of a person's earthly life (8:25; 26:52), it also is used "with reference to eternal destruction" (BDAG, 115; BAGD, 95; cf. 10:6, 39). The meaning here is not certain, but the prospect of leaving the community suggests a temporary association (cf. 13:19-22) lacking commitment that can only result in a perilous end. If the person can be returned, an opportunity for ministry would remain. Like the kindred statement in 2 Pet. 3:9, God is portrayed as unwilling that any should perish. [*apollymi*]

18:15 Against you (*eis se*)—This phrase does not appear in two early and valued manu-

scripts (01, 03) and is considered a scribal addition by some (e.g., NET). However, the edition of the Greek text used by most translators includes it and so it appears in most translations. If it is not original, then the exhortation to confront a fellow member of the community ("brother") about a sin is a general principle and is similar to the depiction of seeking the straying sheep (vv. 12-14). If the more specific phrase is original, then it forms a natural corollary to Peter's question (v. 21) and the following parable (vv. 21-35). [*eis, sy*]

Show a fault (*elenchon*)—The standard lexicon defines this word's meaning here as "express strong disapproval of someone's action" (BDAG, 315, 3; less specifically, BAGD, 249). However, an alternative definition, "to bring a person to the point of recognizing wrongdoing," (BDAG, 315, 2) seems better in this context and is reflected by translations such as "show/point out the fault" (KJV, NASB, NIV, NLT, NKJV, NET). [*elenchō*]

Listens (*akousē*)—This is an illustration of the word "hear" meaning both listen to and act appropriately. The member confronted about his sin "listens" by admitting wrongdoing and seeking forgiveness and restoration of relationship (cf. 13:13-15). [*akouō*]

Regained (*ekerdēsas*)—The goal of constructive confrontation is the restoration of the sinning individual to the fellowship of the community. In this sense the translation "regained" (NRSV, NET) or "won back" (CEV, NLT) brings this out more emphatically than the simple "gain/won" of other translations (KJV, NASB, NIV, NKJV, ESV). [*kerdainō*]

18:16 Witnesses (*martyrōn*)—This word appears in the quotation of Deut. 19:15. In the OT context it seems to refer to those who have direct knowledge of the issue in question. It is not clear that the word is limited to that meaning in this context. Here the witnesses seem to serve, that is, to lend support and weight to the appeal to the sinner to admit his wrong and encourage forgiveness and restoration of relationship. [*martys*]

18:17 Church (*ekklēsias*)—The concerted appeal of every member of the community to the erring brother is finally called upon in the hopes that he will admit his wrong and be restored to fellowship. [*ekklēsia*]

Treat him (*estō soi*)—Literally this phrase is translated "Let him be to you" (KJV, NASB, NKJV, NRSV, ESV), but it basically describes how the church should respond to a member who refuses to admit wrongdoing. The translation "treat him . . ." reflects well the idea expressed by this phrase (NIV, NLT, NCV, CEV, NET). [*eimi, sy*]

Gentile . . . tax collector (*ethnikos . . . telōnēs*)—Within Jewish culture the Gentile and tax collector were regarded as "outsiders" in terms of relationship to the community. That is the idea here, but what that means practically is debated. Stringently interpreted, it could refer to excommunication, the community's severing of all relationships with the sinning member and refusal of admission to any of its gatherings. On the other hand, it may describe the way community members are to relate to this member. He is welcome to attend any and all meetings, but he is treated as a person who needs to acknowledge his status as a sinner, to repent of the error of his way and cast himself on the mercy of God. The latter more closely matches the spirit of Jesus, who associated with tax collectors (cf. 11:19) and reached out to Gentiles as part of his ministry to all people (8:5-13; 15:21-28). On this view, the community would welcome the sinning member to meetings but not acknowledge membership with the community by word (calling him "brother") or deed (excluding him from participation in observance of the Lord's supper; cf. 26:26-29, 1 Cor. 11:23-26). [*ethnikos, telōnēs*]

Bind . . . loose (*dēsēte . . . lysēte*)—This reference to binding and loosing (cf. 16:19) occurs in the context of seeking restoration for a sinning brother (vv. 15-17). Here it appears to be the community (each and every disciple) that is given the authority as a representative of God either to declare forgiveness to those who acknowledge sin and seek restoration or to declare the peril of punishment/discipline of sin to those who refuse repentance. [*deō, lyō*]

18:19 Agree (*symphōnēsōsin*)—This statement affirms the preceding verse and encourages unity among members of the community. In context, the verse looks toward a sinning brother's admission of guilt and expression of repentance as the means for restoration in the community (vv. 15-17). The brother who confronts the sinner (v. 15) and finds willing repentance is authorized to extend the forgiveness and restoration it brings. In this case, the two agree about the reality of sin and the solution to dealing with it. This is a good illustration of the importance of interpreting a verse in its context as a variety of bizarre interpretations could be connected to this verse if it is taken out of context. [*sympōneō*]

18:20 I am there (*ekei eimi*)—This statement illustrates the forward-looking orientation of Jesus' teaching in this passage. Jesus affirms his spiritual presence in the future church for those seeking the restoration of the sinning brother. This is similar to the general affirmation to disciples who are carrying out the mission to all nations (28:20) and is expressed specifically here with regard to the important ministry of restoration. [*ekei, eimi*]

18:22 Seventy-seven times (*hebdomēkontakis hepta*)—Whether this phrase should be translated "seventy-seven" (NIV, NLT, NCV, CEV, NRSV, NET; cf. BDAG, 269; BAGD, 213) or "seventy times seven" (KJV, NASB, NKJV, ESV) the point is the same (cf. Gen. 4:24). No limitations must be placed on forgiveness. No one would count this high. [*hebdomēkontakis, hepta*]

18:23 Settle accounts (*synarai logon*)—This phrase occurs only in Matthew (cf. 25:19) but evokes similar statements about personal accountability to God at the judgment (cf. Rom. 14:12). Here God is portrayed as a king who graciously forgives huge debts (vv. 24-27; cf. 6:12) but expects a similar willingness to forgive among his servants (vv. 32-35; cf. 6:14-15). [*synairō, logos*]

18:27 compassion (*splanchnistheis*)—In the context of this parable, the first master has compassion on the plight of the servant, unlike what the servant will do for his debtors. It is this inconsistency and hypocrisy about forgiveness that the parable condemns. If God can forgive, then one should be willing to forgive others (Eph. 4:32). [*splanchnizomai*]

18:33 mercy (*eleēsai*)—Both this attribute of mercy and the compassion mentioned in 18:27 describe God in his dealings with humanity (cf. Jesus, 9:27-29, 36). In his compassion and mercy he forgives. But he expects those who have experienced this forgiveness and mercy to extend it to others (vv. 15-22). [*eleeō*]

You should (*edei*)—Although expressed in the context of a rhetorical question ("should you not?"), the idea is that forgiveness is not an option but an obligation. The verb is used of "something that should happen" (BDAG, 214, 2d; BAGD, 172, 6b). The fact that it is ethically obligated becomes clear in 18:34-35, which gives a serious warning to listeners about the consequences of not being forgiving after one experiences God's forgiveness. [*dei*]

18:34 Anger (*orgistheis*)—The noun form of this verb is used to describe God's future judgment (*orgē*, cf. 3:7; Rom. 2:5). There is a similar orientation in this passage, depicting the awful judgment that comes to those who nominally—instead of genuinely—receive God's forgiveness. Those who receive it truly extend it in turn to others. The peril of disregarding others or being unforgiving toward them runs like a fearsome thread through this chapter (vv. 6-9, 14, 18, 32-35). [*orgizō*]

19:3 Cause (*aitian*)—This word means "that which is responsible for a condition" (BDAG, 31; cf. BAGD, 26) here referring to grounds for divorce. With the adjective (*pasan*) it means "for any and every cause" (ibid). The focus of the debate about divorce is the meaning of the phrase "something objectionable" in Deuteronomy 24:1. The popular interpretation, allowing for something as minor as a poorly prepared meal (i.e, "for any and every cause"), is presented as a middle position in the collection of Jewish oral law, the Mishnah (*Gittin 9.10*). Two alternative minority views are that a divorce may be initiated for no other reason than to marry a more appealing spouse (a "no fault" divorce) and the more stringent view that immorality is the primary (though not necessarily the only one, cf. Exod. 21:10-11) ground (*m Gittin 9.10*). [*aitia*]

19:5 One flesh (*sapka mian*)—Jesus moves the discussion from what separates people in marriage to what should keep them together. He quotes Gen. 2:24, a statement that focuses on a man and woman in marriage forming a union distinct from their former family connections. "One flesh" emphasizes the intimacy and interconnectedness of two people fulfilling God's will by their formation of a new family relationship (v. 6). [*sarx, heis/hen*]

19:6 Joined together (*synezeuxen*)—The word means "to make a pair" and can be translated "join together, pair" (BDAG, 954; cf. BAGD, 775). Jesus here provides further commentary on the model of marriage depicted in Genesis

2. As God joined together Adam and Eve, he provided an illustration of the lasting union that should characterize the marriage relationship. [*syzeugnymi*]

19:7 a scroll of certificate of divorce (*biblion apostasiou*)—The certificate of divorce, based on the admonitions in Deut. 24:1-3, consisted of a brief written notice (e.g. *m Gittin* 9.1-3). One example is, "I ___ divorce and release of my own free will today you ___ who had been my wife before this time. You are free on your part to go and become the wife of any Jewish man you wish. This is for you a writ of release and bill of divorce . . ." (*Discoveries in the Judean Desert*, 2.19, in D. Instone-Brewer, "1 Corinthians 7 in the Light of Jewish Greek and Aramaic Marriage and Divorce Papyri," *Tyndale Bulletin* 52.2 (2001):237). Note how the divorce writ includes explicit mention of the right to remarry. [*apostasion*]

19:8 Hardness of heart (*sklērokardian*)—The word refers to "an unyielding frame of mind" (BDAG, 930; cf. BAGD, 756) that manifests itself in obstinacy toward God and a stubborn refusal to follow the course of life set forth by him. It is a basic description of the human condition since the entrance of sin has oriented the experience of all people toward evil (cf. 7:11; Mark 10:5; Rom. 3:9-18; 5:12). [*sklērokardia*]

19:9 Except for immorality (*mē epi porneia*)—This exception clause is similar in meaning to the parallel statement at 5:32. The word for immorality is a general word applied to "unlawful sexual intercourse" (BDAG, 854; cf. BAGD, 693) of various kinds. Given the emphasis Jesus put on the preservation of the family unit (vv. 5-6) and the importance of forgiveness (18:21-35) this permission to divorce is probably not meant to be applied automatically. Rather, it recognizes that unrepentant immorality breaks the marriage

bond and makes the "one flesh" relationship impossible to sustain. Both Jewish and Gentile culture viewed remarriage as the norm after divorce (see the writ of divorce in Matthew 19:7). [*porneia*]

19:10 Better not to marry (*sympherei gamēsai*)—Given Jesus' constraint on divorce some disciples apparently wondered if celibacy might not be a more preferable state than marriage (presumably not the married ones like Peter). How serious the disciples were in making this statement may be questioned given the fact that Jews generally were expected to marry (cf. Gen. 1:28, the first commandment in the OT). Jesus, however, accepts it as a statement that is true for some, with the qualification given in v. 11. [*sympherō, gameō*]

19:11 To whom it is given (*hois dedotai*)—The passive voice of this verb suggests that God is the unnamed one who gives the capacity to some to live as a single person. On this understanding celibacy is a gift given to certain individuals in accordance with God's determination (cf. 1 Cor. 7:7). They would be the exceptions to the normal tendency to be married. [*didōmi*]

19:12 Eunuchs (*eunouchoi*)—This word is applied to the situation of three different individuals in this statement. The first is "a castrated male," a person whose testes were surgically removed to render him sexually impotent. Eunuchs often served in royal households, sometimes in high government position, such as the treasurer to the Ethiopian queen (Acts 8:27). The second is "a human male who, without a physical operation, is by nature incapable of begetting children" (BDAG 409; cf. BAGD, 323), in other words, a person who is naturally impotent. The third is "a human male who abstains from marriage, without being impotent, a celibate" (ibid). Jesus holds open the prospect that certain people are given the ability to remain single so as to devote themselves fully to God's service (cf. 1 Cor. 7:32-35). To those given the capacity to be celibate, Jesus encourages adoption of this lifestyle. [*eunouchos*]

Kingdom of heaven (*basileian tōn ouranōn*)—This phrase has various nuances of meaning revolving around the basic idea of God's rule. Here the focus is on serving God in the present time without the constraints of family responsibilities. One can readily see how those involved in itinerant missionary activity would find it easier to carry out their responsibilities without concern for the well-being of family members left behind (10:5-25; cf. 1 Cor. 7:32-35). This was the lifestyle of both Paul (1 Cor. 7:7) and Timothy (cf. Phil. 2:19-21) among others (cf. 27:55). [*basileia, ouranos*]

19:13 Lay hands on (*cheiras epithē*)—Placing a hand on a person was a traditional accompaniment of prayer requesting God's blessing (e.g., Gen. 48:14-20). Jesus had previously addressed the importance of children, going so far as to identify himself with them (18:2-5). But the disciples illustrate the difficulty of understanding and putting into practice Jesus' teaching. As Jesus previously had emphasized the permanence of marriage as fundamental to the family (vv. 4-6), here he extends his blessing to family life as it involves children. The different lifestyles of celibacy (vv. 10-12) and marriage (including having children) are both ways of life approved by God. [*cheir, epitithēmi*]

19:16 Eternal life (*zōēn aiōnion*)—Basic to the meaning of eternal life is the notion of relationship with God. As God is eternal, so relationship with him will involve a life without end. Although this life with God has a present dimension, most of the references look toward the future. In this passage a variety of related terms are used to carry forward the discussion between the first (v. 16) and last (v. 29) references to eternal life: "life" (v. 17); "kingdom of heaven" (v. 23); "kingdom of God" (v. 24); "saved" (v. 25). [*zōē, aiōnios*]

19:21 Perfect (*teleios*)—As at 5:48, this word does not refer to sinless behavior, but to wholehearted or single-minded devotion to God. Although the young man presents himself as someone devoted to God, he is shown to be at best a person of divided loyalty. Jesus had warned about the impossibility of serving two masters (6:24) and that truth is sadly illustrated in the life of this man. Although he is said to own many things (v. 22), it is also the case that his possessions owned him and effectively choked his ability to serve God by following Jesus (cf. 13:22). [*teleios*]

19:24 Kingdom of God (*basileian tou theou*)—That the "kingdom of heaven" (v. 23) and "kingdom of God" are synonyms is illustrated by their use in complementary statements in these verses. Here the phrases refer to a realm populated by "saved" people (v. 25) who have been delivered from the tyrannies of this world (like wealth) to a life under God's rule and reign. This deliverance is not something people can accomplish themselves (vv. 23-24); only God can do it (v. 26). [*basileia, theos*]

19:27 Left (*aphēkamen*)—Peter here directs attention to the disciples' obedience of Jesus' call. He and Andrew left their livelihood as fishermen (4:20; cf. 9:9). James and John did the same, leaving their business and family (4:22). Jesus had assured the young man of treasure in heaven (v. 21). Peter is wondering what that might look like. He is told the disciples' recompense will be 100 times greater than what they left (v. 29) and most importantly they will gain what the young man sought (v. 16), what they otherwise could never have achieved—everlasting life with God (v. 29). [*aphiēmi*]

19:28 Renewal (*palingenesia*)—This word

appears twice in the NT. At Titus 3:5 it refers to the personal experience of regeneration, the capacity to have a relationship with God. Here it refers to the "renewing of the world in the time of the Messiah" (BDAG, 752; cf. BAGD, 606). The depiction of Jesus seated upon a throne portrays his rule in the messianic kingdom. That the disciples will share his authority to rule (cf. Rev. 20:4) answers in part Peter's question about what the future might hold for those like himself who left everything to follow Jesus (v. 27; cf. Rev. 3:21). [*palingenesia*]

Throne (*thronou*)—A throne is a "chair set aside for one of high status" (BDAG, 460; cf. BAGD, 364). Here it belongs to "Christ, who occupies the throne of his ancestor David" (ibid). Disciples are promised a share of different aspects of Jesus' experience (cf. Rom. 8:29; 1 Cor. 15:20) which in this statement focuses on sharing his rule. Jesus also will illustrate a dramatic reversal of status in his personal circumstances: the one treated as "last," a person of no importance, by men (16:21, 17:22-23, 20:17-19), will be exalted to "first" (v. 30), as the ruler over all people (25:31, 26:64; cf. Phil. 2:6-11). [*thronos*]

Twelve (*dōdeka*)—The repetition of this number with reference to thrones and tribes is a form of emphasis. The mention of the 12 tribes calls to mind the whole people of Israel. The imagery depicts the fulfillment of a hope expressed at 2:6. [*dōdeka*]

Judging (*krinontes*)—Although this word might refer to the act of dispensing justice at a final judgment, it more likely describes a ruling or governing role for disciples like that carried out in the period of Israel's judges (cf. Judg. 8:22-23). The depictions of judgment in Matthew focus on Jesus alone as the judge (e.g., 7:21-23; 25:31-46) whereas references to ruling hold open the prospect of a place for disciples (e.g., 20:20-28). [*krinō*]

20:1 Vineyard (*ampelōna*)—Reference to a vineyard appears in several of Jesus' parables (21:28, 33). In the OT Israel was often depicted as God's vineyard (Isa. 5; Jer. 12). In this parable the vineyard portrays a field of ministry into which disciples are sent by God. [*ampelōn*]

20:2 Denarius (*dēnariou*)—The denarius was the usual daily wage for laborers in the Roman empire (BDAG, 223; cf. BAGD, 179) and so is sometimes translated "normal" (NLT), "usual" (NRSV), or "standard daily wage" (NET). [*dēnarion*]

20:3 Third <u>hour</u> (*tritēn hōran*)—The day was broken into 12 hours from dawn (around 6 A.M. to dusk (around 6 P.M.). The first workers were sent into the vineyard at dawn and the last workers during the 11th hour (v. 6). Several translations (NCV, CEV, NLT, NRSV, NET) replace the references to hours with the approximate times: 9 A.M. (v. 3); noon (v. 5); 3 P.M. (v. 5); and 5 P.M. (v. 6). [*hōra*]

20:4 Right (*dikaion*)—The workers in the parable can count on the owner to do the right thing and pay them a just or fair wage. What he agreed to pay the first workers (v. 2), he is faithful to do (vv. 10, 13). The later workers trust his justice. So rather than negotiating a wage, they go to work. They will be glad they did since they will discover that it is even better to experience the owner's generosity than to guarantee a fair wage (vv. 8-9, 15). [*dikaios*]

20:8 Last . . . first (*eschatōn . . . prōtōn*)—In addition to its placement in the middle of the parable this saying also functions like a bookend, appearing just before (19:30) and in the conclusion (20:16). The effect of these bookends is to link the message of the parable to the preceding discussion (19:16-29) about treasure in heaven (19:21). The parable serves as a warning to disciples like Peter

(19:27), or James and John (20:20-21). They might be tempted to become presumptive or calculating about their future recompense (19:28-29) given their personal sacrifices or length of service in ministry. [*eschatos, prōtos*]

Pay (*misthon*)—This word in the parable refers to the workers' pay or wages. But it is also used to refer to reward (e.g., 6:1, 2, 4). The discussion with Peter and the disciples about treasure in heaven (19:27-29) is also about reward and forms the backdrop to understanding this parable. [*misthos*]

20:14 I want (*thelō*)—This verb means "to have a desire for something" (BDAG, 447; cf. BAGD, 355) and describes the exercise of a person's will. The word "benevolence" is composed of two Latin words meaning "good will" and in this case aptly describes the desire of the owner (v. 15). He has a generous disposition and is free to act accordingly. [*thelō*]

20:15 Generous (*agathos*)—This word is usually translated "good" as it is at 19:17 where it refers to God. It is another point of contact between the events narrated in the previous chapter and this parable (though the connection is clearest in those versions that translate the word "good" here, e.g, KJV, NKJV). In this context the translation "kind" or "generous" (NASB, NIV, NRSV, NET) expresses well this aspect of the owner's character (BDAG, 4; cf. BAGD, 3). [*agathos*]

Envious (*ophthalmos . . . ponēros*)—The words are literally translated "evil eye" (KJV, NKJV) with the meaning "one that looks with envy or jealousy upon other people" (BDAG, 744; cf. BAGD, 599). For this reason most translations render this phrase "envious" (NIV, NRSV, NET) or "jealous" (NCV, CEV). [*ophthalmos, ponēros*]

20:18 Son of Man (*huios tou anthrōpou*)—In Jesus' third foretelling of his death (16:21-23; 17:22-23; cf. 26:2) he refers to himself with this preferred self-designation. Jesus, in the fullness of his humanity, is destined to be treated mercilessly by both Jews (v. 18) and Gentiles (v. 19). After the experience of being humiliated by his fellow men and condemned by them to death, he will be vindicated by God and raised from the dead. [*huios, anthrōpos*]

20:21 Your kingdom (*basileia sou*)—While the disciples may not have understood the suffering aspect of Jesus' messiahship, they seem to have believed in Jesus' eventual vindication and triumph. This request for places of prominence beside Jesus when he rules as king shows two things. First, they took seriously Jesus' promise about sharing in his future rule (19:28). Second, the point of the parable about the workers in the vineyard escaped them entirely. Instead of trusting the generosity of God, they seek to negotiate a prized position in the messianic kingdom for themselves. [*basileia*]

20:23 Prepared (*hētoimastai*)—Like the owner of the vineyard, God will do what he wants with what belongs to him (v. 15). That includes assigning people to places of honor in Messiah's kingdom. The tense of this verb (perfect) depicts a sure and settled thing, showing God already knows when the kingdom will come and who will occupy its places of honor. [*etoimazō*]

20:25 Rulers . . . those in high position (*archontes . . . megaloi*)—The first word refers to "one who has eminence in a ruling capacity" and may be translated as "ruler," "lord," or "prince" (BDAG, 140; cf. BAGD, 113). The second word is a general word for rulers meaning "the great ones" or "those in high position" (BDAG, 624; cf. BAGD, 498). The corresponding verbs refer to having governing authority or power over others. These two depictions of rule are contrasted with two positions of servitude (vv. 26-27). [*archōn, megas*]

20:26 Servant (*diakonos*)—This word describes someone "who gets something done at the behest of a superior" (BDAG, 230; cf. BAGD, 184). The standard lexicon suggests "assistant" (cf. KJV, "minister") as an equivalent term, but almost all translations use the word "servant." In contrast to those in positions of power and authority (v. 25) who gave orders, the servant was a person without status who carried out the wishes of a superior. Though the role of a servant was without esteem in world society, it became an honorable term applied to leaders in the church (cf. Phil. 1:1). [*diakonos*]

20:27 Slave (*doulos*)—This word described "one who is solely committed to another" (BDAG, 260; cf. BAGD, 205). The standard lexicon suggests "subject" as an alternative term (cf. KJV, "servant"), but almost all translations use "slave" in this verse. Like the servant (v. 26), the slave was a person without social status who existed to carry out the will of his master. By urging disciples to think of themselves as servants and slaves, Jesus clarifies the nature of ministry for them in the present time. The time for ruling and reigning (19:28; 20:20-21) is still future. In the present age disciples must see themselves as humble people whose mission is to fulfill God's will. That Jesus spoke approvingly of this role and modeled it in his life (v. 28; cf. 11:29) led subsequent disciples to identify themselves as "slaves of Christ" (cf. Phil. 1:1). [*doulos*]

20:28 Ransom (*lytron*)—This word means "the price of release" (BDAG, 605; cf. BAGD, 482) and was often used for "the ransom money for the manumission of slaves" (ibid). After foretelling his death three times (16:21; 17:22-23; 20:17-19), Jesus now explains its purpose: he will give his life so that others can be free. A later statement by Jesus (26:28) clarifies the meaning of this freedom: the reader understands that Jesus' death gains for them

freedom from sin. Later writers, like Paul, will elaborate on this freedom by depicting salvation as a release from sin's ruinous power over human life (e.g., Rom. 6:20-23). [*lytron*]

20:34 Compassion (*splangnistheis*)—This is a favorite verb of Matthew to describe Jesus' emotions of pity or sympathy for people's painful circumstances of life (9:36; 14:14; 15:32; 18:27). It describes the emotional counterpart associated with an act of mercy, behavior equally lauded as a distinguishing mark of a disciple in this Gospel (5:7; 9:13; 12:7; 15:22; 17:15; 18:33; 23:23). [*splanchnizomai*]

21:1 Mount of Olives (*oros tōn elaiōn*)—This might also be called a hill or a ridge, since it is only about 17 meters higher than the city of Jerusalem to its west (BDAG, 725; cf. BAGD, 582). It is about two miles in length and was planted with olive trees. From its summit (actually a series of three summits), Jerusalem and the temple mount are easily visible and accessible (cf. Zech. 14:4). [*oros, elaia*]

21:5 King (*basileus*)—Jesus is indeed the King of the Jews (cf. 2:2; 27:37). But he comes as a humble Messiah destined to die for his people (20:28). This quotation from Zechariah 9:9 fits the pattern of Jesus' fulfillment of the messianic role: he begins in his first coming what he will complete in his second (Zech. 9:9 is here fulfilled; Zech. 9:10 will be fulfilled). [*basileus*]

21:7 He sat on them (*epekathisen epanō autōn*)—It is possible that Matthew intends the reader to see the antecedent of the pronoun "them" as the just mentioned garments the disciples placed on the animals. But most interpreters think the antecedent is the donkey and her colt. According to the Hebrew text (Zech. 9:9) the foal is ridden. Jesus may have ridden the colt while placing a hand on the accompanying mare. [*epikathizō*]

21:9 Hosanna (*hōsanna*)—This expression appears in the psalms of praise (Psalms 113–118) as an appeal to God for help or salvation. By this time, however, it seems to have become a word of praise or acclamation (cf. v. 16; Luke 19:37-38) that was "familiar to everyone in Israel" (BDAG, 1106; cf. BAGD, 899). Ps. 118 (v. 26 is cited) celebrates the faithfulness of God. Here the crowd acclaims Jesus as the Son of David voicing a truth few among them will firmly embrace (cf. 27:20). [*hōsanna*]

21:13 House of prayer (*oikos proseuchēs*)—Previously Jesus had warned his disciples about hypocrites who used prayer as a means to gain the praise of their fellow men (6:5-6). Here he censures those who turn a place intended for prayer into a means of making a profit. Jesus had warned his disciples that they could not serve God and money (6:24). The temple leaders show their allegiance to money by permitting this disruption. The people had rightly hailed Jesus as a prophet (v. 11) and this cleansing is an act of prophetic censure. [*oikos, proseuchē*]

21:16 Read (*anegnōte*)—Jesus meets the objections of his opponents by referring to Scripture. He has done this before with the Pharisees (12:5; 19:4). He will do it later with the Sadducees (22:31). Here it is the chief priests and scribes (cf. 21:42). These references show the Scriptures as a guide to truth. They also show that a right response to Scripture requires the grace of God. This passage illustrates what Jesus had said earlier: God's truth is often hidden from the wise and learned but revealed to babes (11:25). [*anaginōskō*]

21:19 Fig tree (*sykē*)—The withering of the fig tree ominously illustrates Jesus' authority. John the Baptist had warned about the coming judgment saying that God will cut down trees that do not bear good fruit (3:10). The religious leaders had rejected John and his message (cf. vv. 25-26; 32), and they would like to suppress Jesus (vv. 45-46). They will in fact succeed in doing this, resulting in judgment for themselves (v. 43) and the eventual destruction of the temple (23:37-38). Situated as it is between these confrontations with the leaders of the temple, the withering of the fig tree likely illustrates their coming doom. [*sykē*]

21:22 Prayer (*proseuchē*)—What connects this saying to the withering of the fig tree is the notion that words can be powerful. In Jesus' case, it is a matter of the authority given him by God (cf. 11:27). In the disciples' case it is a matter of availing themselves of God's power through prayer. The religious leaders may have frustrated the role of the temple as a house of prayer (v. 13), but they could not suppress the work of God through people who pray. Those who trust God can be confident that the one who prays can do his will, however impossible it might seem (cf. 17:19-20; 19:26). [*proseuchē*]

21:27 Authority (*exousia*)—The fact of Jesus' right to speak and act in behalf of God has been repeatedly noted in this Gospel (7:29; 8:9; 9:6,8). He even confers authority on his disciples (10:1). Jesus' status as God's authoritative representative is implicitly stated at 11:27 (as revealer of truth) and made explicit at 28:18 (as ruler over all). Those who reject Jesus' authority also rejected John's ministry (vv. 25, 32; cf. 3:7-10) and find themselves in peril of judgment (3:10). [*exousia*]

21:31 Go into (*proagousin*)—This parable shows the connection between faith and behavior in this parable of workers in the vineyard. The tax collectors and prostitutes may have refused to believe God's message at first. But they repented at the preaching of

John and responded with obedience to God's will. The religious leaders said they believed God but showed their unbelief by refusing to work. Whether the present tense of the verb "go into" refers to entry into the kingdom of God now (KJV, NIV, NKJV, NIV, NRSV) or in the future (NASB, NLT, CEV, NET, NCV) may be debated, though the following parable portrays a kingdom of God already present (v. 43). [*proagō*]

21:33 Tenants (*geōrgois*)—This word describes "one who does agricultural work on a contractual basis" (BDAG, 196; cf. BAGD, 157). In the parable it refers to the leaders of Israel (v. 45) who are to work among the people of Israel. They were supposed to be faithful to God, living according to his will and encouraging the people to do the same. [*geōrgos*]

21:34 Fruit (*karpous*)—The fruit God sought was a faithful people who lived according to his will as tenants should. The righteousness of the people of Israel was the expected fruit (5:20; 6:33; cf. Phil. 1:11). [*karpos*]

21:35 Slaves (*doulous*)—Although frequently translated as "servants" (KJV, NKJV, NIV, NLT, NCV, CEV, ESV), this word refers to slaves (NASB, NET, NRSV, BDAG, 260). It is a term applied, as here, to both OT (Jer. 25:4; Amos 3:7; Dan. 9:6) and NT prophets (Rev. 10:7; 11:18). As the OT prophets of God were rejected by the leaders of Israel, so was John (cf. 11:12; 17:12), who died a martyr's death (cf. 14:10-12). [*doulos*]

21:38 Heir (*klēronomos*)—The heir is the "one who receives something as a possession" (BDAG, 548; cf. BAGD, 435). In the parable the inheritance is Israel. Jesus is born "King of the Jews" (2:2), but the religious leaders persuade the people to reject and ultimately kill him (27:20-23). In fact, Christ will ultimately rule over not only Israel (19:28) but all

creation (28:18; cf. 1 Cor. 15:23-28). The writer of Hebrews (1:2) rightly describes Christ as the one "whom God has appointed heir of all things." [*klēronomos*]

21:41 Evil men (*kakous*)—This is an adjective "pertaining to being socially or morally reprehensible" (BDAG, 501; cf. BAGD, 397) and is variously translated "wicked men" (KJV, NKJV, NLT), "wretches" (NASB, NIV, ESV), or "evil men" (NCV, NRSV, NET). The irony here is that the religious leaders correctly describe themselves (v. 45) and accurately predict their end with the related adverb (*kakōs*): "miserably destroy" (KJV, NKJV); "miserable death" (NRSV, ESV, NET, BDAG, 116; cf. BAGD, 95); "wretched end" (NASB, NIV); "horrible death" (NLT, CEV). Although this may foretell the destruction of Jerusalem by the Romans in A.D. 70, it more likely refers to final judgment (cf. 10:28). [*kakos*]

21:42 Stone (*lithon*)—The stone refers to Christ. Although rejected by the leaders of Israel, he will become the foundation stone of the church (Eph. 2:20). Because they reject him, the leaders of Israel will eventually founder and fall (v. 44). [*lithos*]

21:43 Kingdom of God (*basileia tou theou*)—Removing the kingdom from one group (Israel) and giving it to another (the church) signifies a transfer of responsibilities so that the church becomes the tenant of God in the present era. The church must assume responsibility to declare God's truth and encourage faith and righteousness among those who hear and obey the Gospel. In this way the church will give back to God the "fruit" due him (v. 34). [*basileia, theos*]

People (*ethnei*)—This word refers to "a body of persons united by a kinship, culture, and common traditions" (BDAG, 276; cf. BAGD, 218). In this case what unites these people is their allegiance to Jesus. Those who hear his words and obey him, regardless of their ethnicity, become members of a community of people called to proclaim the Gospel and make disciples for him (28:19-20). The followers of Jesus have become the tenants of the kingdom in the present era seeking to bring forth the fruit of faith and righteousness among many nations (cf. Rom. 1:13-15). [*ethnos*]

22:2 Son (*huiō*)—As in the Parable of the Tenants (21:33-41), the son here is Jesus. He is also compared to a bridegroom in other texts (9:15; 25:1-13; cf. Eph. 5:25-27; Rev. 19:7-9). Like the previous parable as well, the servants of God (including John the Baptist [3:2] and later the disciples [10:17] and other associates [23:34]) are treated shamefully by the people of Israel (v. 6). [*huios*]

22:3 Invited (*keklēmenous*)—This word means "to request the presence of someone at a social gathering" (BDAG, 503; cf. BAGD, 399). In the context of the parable, those invited are the people of Israel. John the Baptist (3:2) and Jesus (4:17) called people to enter the kingdom, but for the most part the people refused to respond (vv. 3, 5; cf. 11:16-19). As in the Parable of the Tenants (21:33-41), those privileged to be a part of the people of Israel responded to God's graciousness with shameful behavior, killing his representatives (v. 6) and by so doing rejecting him. [*kaleō*]

22:7 Burned their **city** (*polin autōn eneprēsen*)—The destruction of Jerusalem is depicted in similar fashion to OT descriptions of cities conquered and set aflame (Josh. 6:24; Judg. 1:8; 18:27; 20:48). Josephus describes the burning of the temple and Jerusalem by the Romans in the A.D. 66-70 rebellion (*Jewish War* 6.353-5, 363, 406-8). The rejection of Jesus is the beginning of the end for Jerusalem and the temple (23:37-38). [*empimprēmi, polis*]

22:8 Not worthy (*ouk . . . axioi*)—The unworthy reveal themselves by rejecting the message that comes to them (cf. 10:13; Rev. 16:6). [*axios*]

22:9 Everyone (*hosous ean*)—Normally this correlative means "as many as" (BDAG, 729; cf. BAGD, 586; so KJV, NASB, NKJV, ESV). But with the particle (*ean*) it means "everyone" (ibid. cf. NCV, CEV, NLT, NRSV, NET). The imagery foreshadows the mission to all nations (28:19-20), including responsive Jews (cf. 21:31). [*hosos, ean*]

22:10 Bad and good (*ponērous te kai agathous*)—This parable is like the parable of the net thrown into the sea that drew in all kinds of fish (13:47). Those who respond to the invitation to the wedding are both bad and good. As even the company of Jesus' disciples was composed of good and bad (Judas), so those who respond to the wedding invitation are a mixed assembly. As the fish in the net were eventually sorted out (13:48-49; cf. 13:24-30), so the guests at the wedding will be also (vv. 11-14). [*ponēros, agathos*]

22:11 Wedding garment (*endyma gamou*)—The fate of the guest without the wedding garment (v. 13) is like the destiny described for the weeds in an earlier parable (cf. 13:42). The similarity suggests that the wedding garment might be compared to the glorious destiny depicted for the righteous in that parable as well, a "shining like the sun" (cf. 13:43; Rev. 3:5). But this Gospel routinely points to obedience to the will of God as a distinguishing feature of genuine disciples (e.g., 5:16, 20; 6:1, 33; 7:21; 12:50). Since texts elsewhere link ethical behavior with clothing imagery (e.g., Rom. 13:12; Eph. 4:24), a text like Rev. 19:8 may be an apt comparison here: the garment represents "the righteous deeds" of the guests. [*endyma, gamos*]

22:14 Chosen (*eklektoi*)—This word refers to "those whom God has chosen from the generality of mankind and drawn to himself" (BDAG, 306; cf. BAGD, 242). If the garment portrays human responsibility (cf. v. 13), then this is a reminder of God's role as sovereign (cf. 11:25-27). As elsewhere in this Gospel, this makes it clear that not all those who answer the call will enter the kingdom (e.g., 7:21-23; cf. 25:31-46). [*eklektos*]

22:15 Entrap (*pagideusōsin*)—The use of this hunting term (cf. Eccl. 9:12) aptly describes the intent of Jesus' opponents. They can find no fault with his manner of life, so they seek by what he says to find a way to condemn him (cf. 26:63-66). They probably hope he will declare himself and his followers free from taxation (as he did with the temple tax, 17:25-26) and so give them grounds to accuse him of sedition to the Roman authorities. [*pagideuō*]

22:17 Caesar (*Kaisari*)—This Greek word is a transliteration of the Latin word *Caesar*. It was the family name of the first Roman emperor, Julius (his full name was Gaius Julius Caesar), and subsequently came to be used as a title. The emperor is named here as the representative head of the Roman government and its system of taxation so translations like "Emperor" (CEV), or "Roman government" (NLT), instead of "Caesar" are accurate. [*Kaisar*]

Tax (*kēnson*)—This Greek word is a transliteration of the Latin word *census*. It was a personal property tax collected annually by the Romans on the basis of a registration of the populace, a census (Luke 2:1-5). [*kēnsos*]

22:19 Denarius (*dēnarion*)—This Greek word is a transliteration of the Latin word *denarious*. It was a silver coin, about the size of a dime, equal in value to a laborer's daily wage. Payment of a denarius usually suf-

ficed for the property tax due most people during this time. A profile of the emperor's face and head appeared on the front of the coin with pagan deities commonly adorning the back. The fact that they had the coins meant they already participated in the commerce of the nation. [*dēnarion*]

22:21 Give (*apodote*)—This word sometimes has the meaning "give back, return" as, for example, when used of the repayment of a debt (e.g., 5:26, 18:25, 34). Here it means "to meet a contractual or other obligation" (BDAG, 109; cf. BAGD, 90). With reference to God, the reader should probably think back to the Parable of the Tenants (21:33-46). The people of Israel belong to God, and the religious leaders should have led them to worship and honor him. They need to give back to God because they had failed to do so. Jesus' words are a further indictment of their failure to fulfill this trust. [*apodidōmi*]

22:23 Resurrection (*anastasin*)—The first five books of the OT (the Pentateuch) were the authoritative source for the Sadducees' system of belief. Since there is no clear reference to resurrection in those books (Dan. 12:2 is probably the only undisputed text in the OT), it was not a part of Sadducean dogma. They probably believed, like the Greeks and Romans, that the dead continued to exist in an underworld realm (Jews called it *Sheol*; to others it was *Hades*). [*anastasis*]

22:24 For his brother (*adelphō autou*)—This phrase is part of the quotation combining Deut. 25:5 (the statement of the law) with Gen. 38:8 (an example). A brother-in-law (the Latin term is *levir*, hence the name "levirate" marriage) was to marry his brother's widow and produce a child to carry on his brother's line. While this may have been discussed in the first century (cf. Mishna, *Yebamoth*), there is no evidence that this was anything but a theoretical question. The ludicrous example really seeks to poke fun at the belief, suggesting a dilemma of a woman having seven husbands in heaven. The implication is that God would not create a situation like that, so resurrection must not be. [*adelphos*]

22:30 Angels (*angeloi*)—Jesus' argument seems based on the conviction (related to the levirate question) that marriage enabled people to fulfill the first commandment (Gen. 1:28) by having children. Since angels were created immortal beings, their numbers did not need to be increased. As marriage was unnecessary for angels, so it will be for those who also have immortal bodies in the resurrection (cf. 13:43; 1 Cor. 15:42-49; Phil. 3:21). [*angelos*]

22:32 Living (*zōntōn*)—Jesus takes a text the Sadducees would find authoritative (from Exod. 3:6) and argues from it that God's description of himself to Moses must be understood as verifying the life of Abraham, Isaac, and Jacob. While not yet resurrected, their life with God suggests a relationship with him not unlike that of angels presently. The appearance of Moses at the transfiguration would be a further indication of that existence for readers of the Gospel. [*zaō*]

22:35 Lawyer (*nomikos*)—A lawyer in Israel was an expert in the interpretation and application of the Law of Moses, the first five books of the OT. Though associated with the Pharisees, this question continues the focus on the Pentateuch and seeks to test Jesus about his understanding. [*nomikos*]

22:36 Greatest (*megalē*)—The form of this adjective is in the first degree (positive) and so could be translated "great" (KJV, NASB, NKJV). However, the meaning of adjectives

during this time is primarily a matter of context, and here the superlative, "greatest" (NIV, NRSV, NET) or even the translation "most important" (NCV, CEV, NLT) seems best. The question is: if only one commandment could be fulfilled, what should it be? [*megas*]

22:37 Love (*agapēseis*)—Although this word includes a person's emotions in its meaning, it is a verb primarily describing behavior. It means acting with regard to the best interests of another. To love God means to be wholly devoted to him and to do all one can to please and honor him. [*agapaō*]

22:39 Neighbor (*plēsion*)—This word is an adjective meaning "nearby, near, close" (BDAG, 830; cf. BAGD, 672). It is most commonly used as a noun, however. Because this word appears in the quotation of Leviticus 19:18, it is usually translated "neighbor." In addition, it can simply mean "fellow human being" (ibid). Given what Jesus had taught about loving one's enemies (5:43-45), the rendering of the CEV is neatly unambiguous: "Love others." [*plēsion*]

22:42 Son (*huios*)—Jesus asks the final question in this series of discussions with opponents (vv. 15-46): whose son is Christ? The Pharisees answer rightly (but partially) that he is a descendant of David. Matthew has shown this to be true as well through his genealogy (1:1-16). But he is more than David's son, as Ps. 110:1 will indicate. He is also uniquely God's son (3:17), so that David calls him "Lord" (v. 43). [*huios*]

22:43 Spirit (*pneumati*)—This is a reference to "the Spirit of God as exhibited in the character or activity of God's people or selected agents" (BDAG, 835; cf. BAGD, 677). As a writer of Scripture, David is God's agent, an example of how "the Spirit inspires certain people . . . in their capacity as proclaimers of divine revelation" (ibid). [*pneuma*]

22:44 Lord (*kyrios*)—The basic meaning of "lord" concerns authority over others. The first reference to "Lord" in this verse is to God. The second is to another "Lord" whom David acknowledges as greater than he and under whose authority he exists. If someone other than David had written this Psalm, the second reference might have been to Israel's reigning king. But as king, David had no one above him but God—and this heir under whose authority he would one day come. So what is unusual here is that the Messiah as a Son of David has a position of authority over David, his ancestor. In a patriarchal culture, this is most unusual. So the point is that David's recognition of such authority not only identifies the Messiah as "Lord" but in a surprising way, pointing to a unique situation. [*kyrios*]

23:2 Moses' seat (*Mōuseōs kathedras*)—Those who sit in Moses' seat serve as his interpreters. Some synagogues actually have a separate seat near the front of the synagogue carved in stone (e.g., *Chorazin*), though the examples all postdate the first century. Jesus does not deny that when the Law of Moses is interpreted (by scribes and others), it is often done so accurately. The primary problem is that although they know the truth, his opponents do not act upon it (v. 3; cf. 2:5). By their failure to do so, they end up leading many astray (15:14). [*Mōusēs, kathedra*]

23:5 Seen (*theathēnai*)—This recalls the failing of the hypocrites described in the first sermon (6:1, 5, 16). They try to win the approval of others by what they do. For self-serving reasons they exaggerate the things they should be doing to call greater attention to themselves. The echo of the first sermon is probably an indicator that these words too are primarily for the instruction of disciples, namely, what not to do. They also serve as a

warning to those depicted to turn from the error of their ways. [*theaomai*]

Phylacteries (*phylaktēria*)—Pious Jews wore two black leather boxes containing copies of particular Scriptures. One was worn on the upper left arm and the other on the forehead in accordance with a literal interpretation of Exod. 13:9, 16; Deut. 6:8; 11:18. The straps holding the boxes in place may have been widened for greater visibility. Phylacteries are still worn today by some Jews during times of prayer. [*phylaktērion*]

Tassels (*kraspeda*)—Fringes made of blue and white thread were attached to the four corners of an outer garment in accordance with Num. 15:38-39 and Deut. 22:12. These Scriptures do not specify a size or length. It is probably the exaggerated lengthening of these to call attention to one's piety that Jesus deplores. Otherwise he seems to have worn tassels himself (cf. 9:20; 14:36). [*kraspedon*]

23:7 Rabbi (*rabbi*)—This form of address, literally meaning "my lord, master," became "an honorary title for outstanding teachers of the law" (BDAG, 902; cf. BAGD, 733). The use of titles serves to distinguish and separate members of a community rather than bring them together. Probably for this reason Jesus encouraged his disciples to think of themselves as equal members of a family with different roles and areas of service. No one of them should think himself more important than another (v. 8). [*rabbi*]

23:10 Teacher (*kathēgētai*)—This word may be translated "master" (KJV, NLT, NCV), "leader" (NASB), "instructor" (NRSV) or "teacher" (NIV, CEV, NKJV, NET, BDAG, 490; cf. BAGD, 389). Making more disciples was the defining task of Jesus' followers (28:19) and essential to that end is the role of teaching (28:20). What the disciples are to teach, however, has continuity with what they were taught by Christ (28:20). Whatever authority they may wield as teachers is ultimately rooted in their relationship with him, a fact that should bring them together rather than separate them. [*kathēgētēs*]

23:13 Woe (*ouai*)—This word is an "interjection denoting pain or displeasure" (BDAG, 734; cf. BAGD, 591). As a beatitude (5:3-11) encourages certain behavior and holds out the promise of blessing so in the opposite way these woes warn about certain behavior and the fate that awaits those doing these things. As such they are a pronouncement of foreboding only to those who ignore their warning, while being a means of instructing others about the error of these ways. [*ouai*]

Enter (*eiserchesthe*)—By opposing John the Baptist and Jesus (cf. also the experiences of Paul and his associates, e.g., Acts 13:45,50; 14:2), the religious leaders not only harm themselves but the many following them (cf. 15:14). The tense of this verb and accompanying participle ("trying to enter") point toward the present possibility of entering into relationship with God by responding to his messengers. [*eiserchomai*]

23:15 Convert (*prosēlyton*)—In this context this word describes a Gentile who leaves pagan belief and practices to embrace the faith and life of Judaism. Some versions simply transliterate the word here: "proselyte" (KJV, NASB, NKJV). Synagogues outside the land of Israel were often places where Gentiles were converted or simply embraced the faith without undergoing all the ordinances (such as circumcision). These latter were called "God-fearers" (e.g., Acts 13:50; 16:14; 18:7). [*prosēlytos*]

23:16 Swear (*omosē*)—Jesus had instructed his disciples to dispense with swearing oaths altogether and be a people known for stating the simple truth (5:33-37). Here he notes their refinement into binding and non-binding

oaths. Non-binding oaths meant that what was said in effect was "nothing." This extra category serves as an illustration of how the hypocrites' charade with words fails to reckon with the fact that God is the ever-present witness (cf. 12:33-37). [*omnuō*]

23:17 Fools (*mōroi*)—Jesus' seems to be acting contrary to what he told the disciples (5:22) by using this expression. There are differences, however. In the sermon Jesus was instructing disciples about words spoken in anger with the intent to hurt others. Jesus is here functioning like a prophet, warning as pointedly as he can that a particular way of life can only end in God's judgment (cf. 7:26-27). The intent here is to turn people from the error of their way or at the very least prevent others from following their example (v. 3). [*mōros*]

23:21 Dwells (*katoikounti*)—The present tense of this word connects God's presence with the temple (cf. Psalm. 135:21). This is a particularly poignant affirmation given the prophecy of the temple's destruction that concludes this chapter (v. 38). [*katoikeō*]

23:23 Tithe (*apodekatoute*)—The word means "to give one tenth" and is usually translated that way in modern versions (otherwise KJV, NASB, NKJV, NLT use "tithe"). The tithing of small seeds is discussed in the *Mishnah* (*Masseroth*, esp. 4.5). Jesus does not suggest that tithing is invalid, only that it is no substitute for the more important aspects of life that become marks of character: justice, mercy, faithfulness. A tithe cannot buy character (cf. the unjustified tither, Luke 18:12). [*apodekatoō*]

23:28 Inside (*esōthen*)—The essence of a person is within. That is why the greatest commandment concerns the heart, soul, and mind (22:37). Purity of heart (5:8) and singleness of mind (6:33) define the person, because it is what issues from the heart that ultimately affects one's life (15:18-20). Like the false prophets (7:15), the hypocrites' appearance belies reality: they are in fact hypocrites at heart. [esōthen]

23:31 Sons (huioi)—Two related meanings are connected with this description of the hypocrites. They are physically descended from their ancestors and members of the same family. More importantly, they share the disposition of their ancestors, they think and act like them and continue their hostility to God and his servants (cf. 21:34-39; 22:6). [huios]

23:32 Fill up (plērōsate)—This verb is an imperative, used here in the sense of prophetic resignation that judgment is inevitable (cf. Jer. 7:21; Amos 4:4). It develops an OT notion that refers to the filling up or completion of transgression (Cf. Dan. 8:23; Gen. 15:16) that inevitably precedes God's wrath (cf. v. 35). [plēroō]

23:33 Vipers (echidnōn)—Although this is a general term for "snake," it is usually construed as a poisonous snake. The viper is a common example in this region (BDAG, 419; cf. BAGD, 331). The epithet echoes John the Baptist's denunciation (3:7; cf. 12:34) and suggests that the hardness of heart of the religious leaders against the servants of God remains unchanged. [echidna]

23:34 Sending (apostellō)—This statement echoes and reaffirms the mission to Israel (10:16-23). The verb is present tense, implying continuing action. The earlier warning (10:17), including the prospect of martyrdom (10:28), is now stated explicitly. As Jesus remained faithful to the end, so must his disciples (cf. 24:14). [apostellō]

23:35 Zechariah (Zachariou)—The final

work in the Jewish canon is 2 Chronicles, which contains an account of the death of the priest Zechariah in the temple (2 Chron. 24:20-22). That account identifies his father as Jehoiada (v. 20). Barachiah could be a grandfather (cf. Ezra 5:1; Zech 1:1), or the prophet Zechariah may be alluded to by conflation in order to bring a message of hope (cf. Zech. 14:9) to this otherwise grim prospect for Israel. [Zacharias]

23:36 This generation (genean tautēn)—There is both a temporal and a moral aspect to the meaning of this phrase. Just as these contemporaries of Jesus are closely tied to their forebears physically and sinfully (vv. 31-32, 37), in the same way it will be true of their descendants at the end of the age (24:34). [genea, outos]

23:38 Desolate (erēmos)—This adjective describes a place that is "unfrequented, abandoned, empty, desolate" (BDAG, 391; cf. BAGD, 309). This is a summary description of the temple complex after its destruction by the Romans in A.D. 70 (cf. 24:1-2). [erēmos]

23:39 Until you say (heōs an eipēte)—One could read this as a hopeless farewell since Israel's rejection of Jesus and consequent guilt seems so clear in these verses. Yet the quoted verse is from Ps. 118:26, which celebrates the faithfulness of God to Israel. Though Israel may have rejected God, he has not rejected them. The translation of the NCV expresses this hopeful nuance: "until that time when you will say." The disciples' subsequent question about the time of his return (24:3) is consistent with the idea that Jesus will come again to be received with acclamation by the people of Israel. [eipon]

24:3 Sitting (kathēmenou)—The final teaching section (24:3–26:1) begins like the first with Jesus sitting on a mountain (5:1) and concludes with a similar ending (7:28; 26:1). This final discourse addresses the disciples' questions about the destruction of Jerusalem and Jesus' coming. But the main theme of these final words is a message of encouragement to disciples to remain faithful. [*kathēmai*]

Coming (*parousias*)—In light of Jesus' parting lament over Jerusalem (23:37-39) the disciples wonder about the timing of his return (actually, "arrival," as it relates to Jesus' presence again in Jerusalem more accurately expresses the meaning of *parousia*). They associate his return with the end of the present order and the establishment of the messianic kingdom (cf. 19:28). [*parousia*]

24:4 Lead astray (*planēsē*)—This word means "to cause to go astray from a specific way" (BDAG, 821; cf. BAGD, 665). Jesus' first words are a warning to the disciples about those who falsely present themselves as God's servants (vv. 5, 11, 24). There will be no shortage of charlatans looking for people who will serve their interests rather than God's. This echoes a warning from the first sermon (7:15-23; cf. 18:12-14). [*planaō*]

24:6 Must happen (*dei . . . genesthai*)—The world is a chaotic place. It is the (necessary) consequence of living in a fallen world. Disciples should not think that human or natural disasters, however tragic, signal the end. These are but the prelude (v. 8) to a truly catastrophic finale (v. 21). Disciples must keep their balance and stay faithful. [*dei*]

24:9 All nations (*pantōn tōn ethnōn*)—The disciples' mission is to all the world (v. 14; cf. 10:18; 28:19). But they should not think it will be accomplished easily. No, the mission will go forward in the teeth of adversity (cf. 10:16-22). Disciples will die. Opponents will flourish (v. 11). Faith will seem rare (v. 12; cf. 13:19-22). But all nations will finally hear the message (v. 14). [*pas, ethnos*]

24:12 Lawlessness (*anomian*)—Jesus previously summarized the law as love of God and love of neighbor (22:34-40). It follows that lawlessness is essentially behavior without regard for God or concern for neighbor. It is behavior that basically focuses on serving oneself. [*anomia*]

24:13 Endures (*hypomeinas*)—Disciples are called to patient endurance, "to maintain a belief or course of action in the face of difficulty" (BDAG, 1039; cf. BAGD, 845). This is the essence of discipleship until Jesus' returns: faithful service in his behalf. In various ways this theme is echoed in this closing message. [*hypomenō*]

24:14 Will be preached (*kērychthēsetai*)—There is a note of certainty in this future tense verb. Despite awful opposition and calamity, the message will go forth to all nations. When this is finally achieved, Jesus will return. In one sense this is the answer to the disciples' question about the end of the age (v. 3): the end will come when the mission is completed. [*kēryssō*]

24:15 Abomination (*bdelygma*)—This word refers to what is "totally defiling" and the phrase "to what defiles a sacred place and causes it to be left desolate" (BDAG, 172; cf. BAGD, 138). The word occurs four times in Daniel (8:13; 9:27; 11:31; 12:11). It could describe a defiling image or action, but it probably refers to a person ("standing"). Although this could refer to the Roman general, Titus, the man described in 2 Thess.. 2:3-4 is the likeliest candidate. [*bdelygma*]

Let the reader understand (*anaginōskōn noeitō*)—This is a parenthetical statement that may come from the Gospel writer. But it is not unreasonable to think Jesus is urging a careful reading of Daniel (cf. *The Message*: "If you've read Daniel, you'll know what I'm talking about"). The reader of the last chapters of

Daniel (7–12) will find numerous points of similarity to the circumstances described in vv. 3-30. [*anaginōskō, noeō*]

24:21 Tribulation (*thlipsis*)—This word can be variously translated "distress" (NIV), "trouble" (NCV), "suffering" (CEV, NRSV), or "tribulation" (KJV, NASB, NKJV). The adjective "great" calls to mind Daniel 12:1 (cf. Rev. 7:14). While the destruction of Jerusalem in A.D. 70 was horrific, it appears to be a foreshadowing of a more awful event yet to come. [*thlipsis*]

24:22 Cut short (*kolobōthēsontai*)—The necessity for God's intervention underscores the destructive effect of those days. If left unchecked, these destructive forces would consume everyone before they were finished. Daniel 12:1 describes God's intervention for his people also. [*koloboō*]

24:27 Coming (*parousia*)—Here is a partial answer to the disciples' question about a sign (v. 3). Jesus will come suddenly and dramatically. As visible as lightning in the sky or birds of prey around a corpse on a plain (v. 28), there will be no mistaking and no escaping his coming (vv. 29-30). Daniel's vision (7:13-14) will be fulfilled. [*parousia*]

24:32 Fig tree (*sykēs*)—Here is a further answer to the disciples' question (v. 3). The phrase "when you see" (v. 33) echoes the beginning of v. 15. The appearance of the abomination signals the nearness of the end. Though far from clear, the fig tree may represent Israel and portend the responsiveness of its people to the Gospel (v. 14). [*sykē*]

24:34 This generation (*genea hautē*)—There is again (cf. 23:36) a temporal and a moral dimension to this phrase (i.e., this evil generation). The contemporaries of Jesus will reap the awful consequence of their rejection of him. And some of their descendants at the end of the age will witness even more horrific events, yet be no more responsive to Jesus as Messiah than their forbears. [*genea, outos*]

24:36 Father (*patēr*)—The exact time of the end is known to God alone. If the phrase "nor the Son" is original (it is not included in the KJV, NKJV, NET in Matthew, but is in Mark 13:32), then it discloses an aspect of Jesus' incarnation (a self-limitation of knowledge). But the point of the statement is to underscore for disciples the priority of faithfulness in the present rather than preoccupation with speculation about the future (cf. 6:34). The best preparation for the future is obedience in the present time. [*patēr*]

24:35 My words (*logoi mou*)—In Matthew 5:18 Jesus said that everything in the law will be fulfilled before the world passes away. Here Jesus notes that even when something as seemingly permanent as the world passes away, Jesus' words will endure. The rhetorical remark stresses the abiding quality of Jesus' teaching. So the wise should both hear and obey (vv. 45-46; cf. 7:24-27). [*logos*]

24:39 They did not know (*ouk egnōsan*)—Two lessons are drawn from the account of Noah and the flood (Gen. 6:9–7:24): the people were unprepared, and the judgment was final. These two themes will be repeated in the remainder of the discourse: the necessity of faithfulness and the certainty of judgment. [*ginōskō*]

24:40 Taken (*paralambanetai*)—Judgment will separate people. Whether the verb here is positive (i.e., "rescued," cf. vv. 31, 38) or negative (i.e., "destroyed," cf. v. 39) is unclear. However, it is often a positive term in the Gospel (e.g., 1:20,24; 2:13,14,20,21; 17:1; 26:37; but cf. 4:5,8; 27:27). [*paralambanō*]

24:42 Alert (*grēgoreite*)—This is a repeated warning in these next chapters (25:13; 26:38-41), often contrasted with sleepiness as an illustration of unfaithfulness (v. 43; 25:5; 26:40). The alert are spiritually prepared (vv. 43-44) and diligent in their service (vv. 45-51). [*grēgoreō*]

24:44 Expect (*dokeite*)—Because its time is known only to God (v. 36), the sudden unexpected fact of Jesus' coming is associated with an array of images: the flood (v. 39); a thief at night (v. 43); a returning master (v. 50); and a bridegroom at night (25:5-6). Faithful endurance will prove to be the best course of action (cf. v. 13). [*dokeō*]

24:47 Put in charge (*katastēsei*)—This verb means "to assign someone a position of authority" (BDAG, 492; cf. BAGD, 390). The faithful slaves are similarly rewarded in the Parable of the Talents (25:21, 23) and picture God's rewarding of the faithful. As such, the account is an incentive to be faithful. [*kathistēmi*]

24:48 Is staying away a long time (*chronizei*)—This word means "to extend a state or activity beyond an expected time" (BDAG, 1092; cf. BAGD, 887). This idea is repeated in The Parable of the Ten Virgins (25:5) and The Parable of the Talents (25:19). It contributes to the unexpected nature of Jesus' coming. But it is also a reminder to the disciples of the importance of patient endurance (v. 13). [*chronizō*]

24:51 Hypocrites (*hypokritōn*)—The evil slave (v. 48) feigned a role temporarily that was ultimately revealed by his self-serving ways (v. 49). One is reminded of the warning about false prophets (7:15-23). There may be some irony in the "two-faced" slave being cut in two, but there is no mistaking the awful fact that the imagery depicts and warns that some of Jesus' followers will find themselves condemned with the hypocrites (cf. 23:15). [*hypokritēs*]

25:2 Foolish . . . (*mōrai*)—Here is another echo of a theme from the first sermon (7:24-27). The wise and foolish are separated by an event. In the first sermon it was a great storm (cf. 24:38-40). In this parable it is the bridegroom's return (v. 10). As the house of the foolish could not endure the storm (7:26-27), here their lamps cannot endure the bridegroom's delay (v. 10; cf. 13:20-21). [*mōros*]

25:4 Wise (*phronimoi*)—In the preceding account (24:45-51) the wise slave is also described as faithful (v. 45). In the following parable the two commended slaves are also described as faithful (vv. 21, 23). Wisdom reveals itself in behavior (cf. 11:19). What seems to characterize the wise virgins in this parable is their faithful endurance. They are prepared to remain steadfast despite the bridegroom's delay (v. 5). So they are ready when he comes (v. 10). [*phronimos*]

25:5 Delayed (*chronizontos*)—Although this is the same word used at 24:48, it serves to reveal a different failing. There it revealed the evil slave's hypocrisy for what it was. Here it reveals the foolish virgins' folly for what it is: presumption about the time of the end. Though only God knows when the bridegroom will come (24:36), the foolish do not take this word seriously and act like they know the time will be short. They ignore these words to their peril. The warning is to remain faithful no matter how long it takes for vindication to come. [*chronizō*]

25:8 Oil (*elaiou*)—The oil in the parable is a commodity, derived from olives. But it represents a behavioral characteristic. Whether it is regarded as faithful endurance or simple acceptance of Jesus' message, it is not something that can be shared. It requires individual acquisition. [*elaion*]

25:12 Know (*oida*)—This word is part of another echo from the first sermon (7:23). In the first discourse Jesus is the judge, but the basic failure is the same in both scenes: a failure to do what needed to be done. Although this is a different word than the verb at 7:23 (*ginōskō*), the meaning is the same. Although they call him "Lord" (v. 11; cf. 7:21), Jesus declares that he has no relationship with them. He does not know them. There are no "second chances" at this judgment (v. 11). [*oida*]

25:14 Entrusted (*paredōken*)—This word means to "convey something in which one has a relatively strong personal interest" (BDAG, 761; cf. BAGD, 614). Here it is property in the form of wealth that has been placed in the servants' care. The noun form of this word means "tradition." [*paradidōmi*]

25:15 Talents (*talanta*)—A talent was equal to about 6,000 denarii (BDAG, 988; cf. BAGD, 803). The average wage for a day laborer was one denarius, so one talent is roughly equivalent to what a laborer might earn in 20 years. The variation in distribution suggests that the talents represent different responsibilities or opportunities for service given to disciples. [*talanton*]

25:19 Time (*chronon*)—This parable too discourages speculation about the time of the end, saying only that a long time elapsed between the master's departure (v. 26) and his return. Attention is focused on what people have done with the opportunities afforded them in the meantime. So the call is to be faithful in the interim. [*chronos*]

25:21 Little . . . much (*oliga . . . pollōn*)—The master's generosity calls to mind Jesus'

words to disciples about recompense in the kingdom (19:29). The slave's stewardship of the "little" would give most readers pause since to most people it represents an enormous sum. The combined lifetime wages of three laborers is about equal to the "little" amount (five talents) the first slave was given. What the slave received in trust or as a loan is now given back to him many times over (cf. 24:47). [*oligos, polys*]

25:23 Joy (*charan*)—This word means "the experience of gladness" and here is a figure of speech for "a state of joyfulness" (BDAG, 1077; cf. BAGD, 875). This is probably intended to convey the opposite experience of those shut out of the kingdom: the anguish of separation ("weeping and gnashing of teeth," v. 30; cf. 24:51). The joy described here is the experience of God's approval for faithful service (cf. 6:1). It will be shared by all who enter the kingdom (v. 21; cf. 20:15). [*chara*]

25:25 Hid (*ekrypsa*)—By hiding the talent, the slave made it clear he wanted nothing to do with what he was given. He refused the opportunity extended him by his master and avoided any responsibility associated with being a steward of it by burying it in the ground (v. 18). But responsibility cannot be so easily avoided or inconsequentially discharged. He will be held accountable for what was given him, whether he wanted it or not (cf. 10:26). The example is a negative one to be avoided. [*kryptō*]

25:26 Lazy (*oknēre*)—This word is usually translated "lazy" (NASB, NIV, NKJV, NRSV, NET) or "slothful" (KJV, ESV), but the verb form of this adjective means "to hold back from doing something" (BDAG, 702; cf. BAGD, 563) without reference to a particular cause. In fact, the slave's professed fear (v. 25) should probably be taken at face value.

"Cowardly" might more accurately describe (though not excuse) the inaction of this slave. [oknēros]

25:28 Take (arate)—The slave had reasonable grounds for fearing his master (vv. 26-27). In fact, rather than causing him to shrink back, fear should have driven him to deliberate activity. Now he will receive the consequence of refusing what was given him. His opportunity to act is over. By the decree of the master it is taken from him. He allowed fear to make him useless (v. 30) and as a result finds himself condemned (cf. 10:26-33). There had been no real relationship to the master. [airō]

25:32 Separate (aphorisei)—This word literally means "to mark off or set apart as if by a line or boundary" (BDAG, 158; cf. BAGD, 127). John the Baptist had proclaimed Jesus as the one who would separate the wheat from the chaff (3:12). The division of humanity that John prophesied is now depicted. The judgment of Jesus effects eternal destiny (v. 46). [aphorizō]

Nations (ethnē)—Since this word (as a plural) commonly refers to Gentiles rather than Jews, this scene may portray the judgment of the nations only. But this is the only extended depiction of judgment in Matthew. Since it appears at the climax of the eschatological discourse, it seems unlikely that any group of people is excluded. The adjective "all" (panta) seems intended to signal the inclusion of Jews and Gentiles (cf. 24:14; although occasionally "all nations" means "all Gentiles," e.g., Rom. 15:11). [ethnos]

25:34 Blessed (eulogēmenoi)—This word describes the righteous (vv. 37, 46). The form of the word (perfect passive) implies a past pronouncement of blessing by God on these people. It serves to balance the focus on human responsibility in the passage and points toward the priority of God's grace and mercy (cf. 11:25-30). [eulogeō]

25:37 Righteous (dikaioi)—Righteousness was set forth as a distinguishing mark of disciples in the first sermon (e.g., 5:20; 6:1; 6:33). Those called "righteous" have followed this way of life. The focus of these verses, however, concerns simple acts of charity and hospitality given to those preaching the Gospel (24:14) as representatives of Jesus (10:40-42). By their response to these messengers the righteous show their reception and acceptance of the Gospel (10:11-13). By their indifference to them, the cursed show their rejection of this same message (cf. 10:14-15) [dikaios]

25:40 Least (elachistōn)—Although much debated (and often understood to be anyone in need), the clue to identifying these people seems to go back to the missionary discourse (10:5-42) especially 10:42. Related to that passage is the statement in this discourse (24:14) that the end will not come until the Gospel is preached to "all nations." That the end has arrived (with Jesus' return and the judgment) means that the mission has been completed. What marks out the righteous (v. 37) is their reception, care for, and identification with these missionary disciples (cf. 10:11), regarded as "least" by the world but as the emissaries of Jesus by those who believe (10:40-42). [elachistos]

25:41 Fire (pyr)—The destiny of the cursed is described as an eternal fire "prepared from the foundation of the world." The same phrase about preparation describes the destiny of the righteous (v. 34). The language probably serves to affirm the sure and certain existence of both realms. Jesus has regularly warned about this punishment (v. 46; e.g., 5:12; 13:50; 23:13). [pyr]

Devil and his angels (diabolō kai tois

angelois autou)—The judgment of the devil and his angels (demons) is a certain reality. The word *diabolos* describes "one who engages in slander" (BDAG, 226; cf. BAGD, 182). The one who lies about God and his people will one day be silenced. His work to disrupt the reception of the Gospel (13:19) and to send forth false members of the kingdom (13:38-39; cf. 24:4-5, 11, 24) will come to an end. Demons also will finally fulfill their destiny (cf. 8:29). Those for whom the fire is prepared will meet their doom. [*diabolos, angelos*]

26:2 Crucified (*staurōthēnai*)—For a fourth time (16:21; 17:22-23; 20:17-19) Jesus speaks of his impending death but now indicates the time of its arrival. This shows that the plan (vv. 3-5) of his opponents is known. Crucifixion was a form of execution used by the Romans, so although Jesus will be condemned by a Jewish court, he will be put to death by Gentiles. [*stauroō*]

26:3 High priest (*archiereōs*)—The office of high priest at this time was primarily a political role. As presiding officer of the Sanhedrin, the chief governing body in Israel, the chief priest was the principal representative of the Jewish people to the Roman authorities. What the chief priest wanted was preservation of the status quo (cf. John 11:47-49), which best served his interests and those aligned with him. [*archiereus*]

26:7 Perfumed oil (*myrou*)—Anointing with a perfumed oil may have been customary at banquets of the wealthy (cf. Psalm. 23:5). The disciples regard it, however, as a wasteful indulgence (v. 8) that could have been turned to better use in the service of the poor (v. 9). They may have in mind putting to practice Jesus' words to the rich man (19:21). [*myron*]

26:10 Good service (*ergon . . . kalon*)—The woman's act is literally described as a "good work" done out of devotion to Jesus. The first words of this final section to the Gospel are about his impending death (v. 2). It is the theme of this chapter, and this woman's act is interpreted in light of it. The disciples' reaction shows their failure to grasp the overwhelming significance of Jesus' death. By means of this woman's act of devotion Jesus calls attention to it once again. [*ergon, kalos*]

26:13 Gospel (*euangelion*)—The content of the gospel is shaped and molded by the progress of revelation. After Jesus' death and resurrection what he has done will be at the heart of the good news (cf. 1 Cor. 15:1-4), even as it presently forms the climax to Matthew's portrait of his life (cf.1:1). That the woman's act will be remembered (as it is here, in Matthew's account) points forward to the abiding significance of the events about to unfold that she commemorates because of the one she honors. [*euangelion*]

26:16 Betray (*parado*)—In contrast to the woman who anoints Jesus for burial, Judas betrays him ("hands him over") to death. Both play a part in the unfolding events— one to her honor, the other to his shame. Her act cost her much (v. 9), while Judas sells Jesus for the price of a slave (Exod. 21:32; cf. Phil. 2:6, "taking the form of a slave"). [*paradidōmi*]

26:19 Passover (*pascha*)—The Passover is an annual festival in memory of Israel's deliverance from bondage in Egypt. It is celebrated the day before (Nisan 14) the Feast of Unleavened Bread (Nisan 15-21). Whether this Last Supper of Jesus with the disciples was the Passover meal is debated (it does not seem to be in John 13:1-4; 19:18, while Luke 22:8 suggests it is). Still a connection (at least in terms of meaning) is evident (cf. 1 Cor. 5:7). This is because an association with the Passover is hard to miss given the proximity of the feast. [*pascha*]

26:24 As it is written (*gegraptai*)—This form (perfect passive) of the verb "write" always appears this way in the Gospel (9x) in reference to the OT Scriptures. It makes the point that the events of Jesus' life, including those leading to his death, are a part of the revealed plan of God. [*graphō*]

26:25 You have said it yourself (*sy eipas*)—This is an indirect "yes." By means of it Jesus emphasizes (with the pronoun) Judas's responsibility for what he said (cf. v. 24). The form of Judas's question (the same as the other disciples, v. 22) anticipates a negative response. But both he and Jesus know the truth. Both the high priest (v. 64) and the Roman governor (27:11) will be given similar answers to their questions as a means of emphasizing their responsibility for the actions they take. All three are guilty of self-serving behavior. [*sy, eipon*]

26:28 Covenant (*diathēkēs*)—Jesus describes the "blood of the covenant" as his own. The words echo the institution of the Mosaic covenant (Exod. 24:8). As the sprinkling of blood on the people secured the covenant between God and Israel (cf. Zech. 9:11), so here Jesus' blood will secure the relationship between God and the followers of Jesus. Luke (22:20), Paul (1 Cor. 11:25) and the writer of Hebrews (9:15-22) view this as the establishment of the new covenant (Jer. 31:31). [*diathēkē*]
   Forgiveness (*aphesin*)—The first statement recorded about Jesus was that he would save people from sin (1:21). Here Jesus shows the means by which he will do that. He will die so that people's sins can be forgiven. As the Passover recalled freedom from slavery in Egypt, so the Last Supper will recall freedom from the awful effects of

sin. The imagery of his blood poured out for many recalls the work predicted for the Servant in Isaiah 53:12. [*aphesis*]

26:31 I will strike (*pataxō*)—The verb refers to striking "a blow that kills" (BDAG, 786; cf. BAGD, 634). Although the main point of this citation of Zech. 13:7 is the scattering of the disciples, the clear reference to God as the subject of this verb also serves to show the sovereign hand of God in connection with Jesus' death. It calls to mind another passage from Isaiah that describes the Servant as "stricken, smitten of God" (Isa. 53:4). It also sets the context for Jesus' prayer in Gethsemane that he might be spared this destiny. [*patassō*]

26:34 Deny (*aparnēsē*)—Jesus had warned his disciples about the peril of denying him before men (10:33). But here he declares that Peter will do just that, not once but three times. It is a reminder that despite the lack of qualification in Jesus' earlier words, there remains grace and forgiveness for the penitent. Jesus' death "for the forgiveness of sins" (v. 28) will also cover Peter's sin of denial. [*aparneomai*]

26:36 Gethsemane (*Gethsēmani*)—The word means "oil press," a name connected with an olive grove on the slope of the Mount of Olives. Although there is presently a small garden with ancient olive trees located next to the modern Church of All Nations, the exact site of Gethsemane is unknown. It nonetheless afforded Jesus a secluded place for prayer (cf. 14:23). As Peter, James, and John saw his glory (17:1-2), they now see his agony (v. 37). [*Gethsēmani*]

26:39 As you will (*hōs sy*)—At the heart of Jesus as Son of God is obedience. His prayer in Gethsemane is probably a further illustration of the self-limitation of knowledge that marked his incarnation (cf. 24:36). He did not know if God might intervene at the 11th hour, as he did for Isaac (Gen. 22:11-14), and provide a way other than the path to the cross. He asks that he might be delivered from the hands of evil men (cf. 6:13) or otherwise strengthened to face what will come (cf. 6:10). Despite the suffering awaiting him, he maintained his disposition of submission to God's will. [*hōs, sy*]

26:40 With me (*met emou*)—In a reversal of the usual circumstance, Jesus here asks for the disciples' support. He wants and needs their prayer on his behalf. The depth of his emotions threaten to overwhelm him (v. 38), and he wants the presence and encouragement of those closest to him. But despite the passion in their recent profession of support for him (cf. 35), they fail to grasp the importance of the hour. The weakness of their frame overcomes them, and they sleep (vv. 40-43). [*meta, egō*]

26:45 Approaching (*ēngiken*)—Here is an instance with this word of where the usually distinct meanings of nearness in space or nearness in time converge. The approaching hour (v. 45) marks the beginning of the period of suffering at the hands of sinners. It will end in his crucifixion. It begins with the approach of the betrayer (v. 46). The near is in fact here, with Judas arriving even as these words are on his lips (v. 47). [*engizō*]

26:50 Do what you are here to do (*eph ho parei*)—This colloquial phrase is either an ironic question ("Why have you come?" cf. KJV, CEV, NKJV) or a statement (NASB, NIV, NRSV, NLT, NCV, NET, as above). Given the depiction of Jesus taking the initiative in going toward Judas (v. 46), the statement fits a scene in which Jesus does not shrink back from what awaits him but steadfastly advances to fulfill his destiny (vv. 54, 56). [*epi, pareimi*]

26:51-52 Sword (*machairan*)—This is a relatively short sword, though more than sufficient for landing a fatal blow. The Gospel of John says the one delivering this inexact stroke was Peter (John 18:10). That a disciple would carry a sword like this seems unusual. Peter may have recently acquired it to demonstrate the seriousness of his commitment to remain loyal (cf. v. 35). Jesus may be quoting a proverbial statement that, given the disciple's lack of prowess with a sword, seems readily applicable (cf. Rev. 13:10). Further, Jesus' response is consistent with his earlier message to disciples about a ministry that refused retaliation (5:38-39). [*machaira*]

26:56 Fled (*ephygon*)—For Matthew there was no misunderstanding the significance of the progress of the events beginning Jesus' passion. So in a narrative note, Matthew declared a second time that what was happening was a fulfillment of the prophets' writings (cf. vv. 54, 56). The flight of the disciples is then recorded, calling to mind the citation of Zechariah 13:7 (v. 31) and confirming its fulfillment. [*pheugō*]

26:59 Sanhedrin (*synedrion*)—The Sanhedrin was the main governing body of the Jews. It was composed of representatives of the major parties (Pharisees and Sadducees) and leading citizens. It decided not only legal and governmental issues but handled religious rulings as well. Though it might decide someone was guilty of a capital crime, it could carry out executions only with the permission of the Roman authorities. Sometimes this word is translated "council" (KJV, NASB, NKJV, CEV, NRSV), "high council" (NLT) or simply transliterated "Sanhedrin" (NIV, NET). [*synedrion*]

False testimony (*pseudomartyrian*)—Jesus told his disciples to expect that lies would be spoken against them (5:11). It was also to be his experience, as one who went before them and showed the way of faithful obedience (cf. 5:12; 10:16-25; 23:29-36). [*pseudomartyria*]

26:61 Temple (*naon*)—Jesus had predicted the destruction of the Jerusalem temple (24:2). But the reference to three days echoes the predictions of his own death and resurrection (16:21; 17:22-23; 20:17-19; cf. John 2:19). The false testimony ironically testifies to Jesus' voluntary death and resurrection as the basis of a new center of worship. Paul in particular will make the connection to Christ as the foundation of a new temple composed of his followers (1 Cor. 3:16; 6:19; Eph. 2:20-22). [*naos*]

26:64 You will see (*opsesthe*)—These words (citing Dan. 7:13 and alluding to Psalm. 110:1) evoke the image of Jesus' coming described at 24:30. The scene here also brings to mind the judgment described in that final discourse (25:31). Jesus now stands before the Sanhedrin with a sentence of judgment soon to be passed upon him. But when he comes again, the scene will be reversed. The judges will be standing before him as he declares the destiny of all people. [*horaō*]

26:65 Blasphemy (*blasphēmian*)—Blasphemy is "speech that denigrates or defames" (BDAG, 178; cf. BAGD, 142). The high priest does not identify the part or parts of Jesus' words that he judges blasphemous, but it probably applies to two things he has said. First is Jesus' identification with God and assumption of God's authority (the application of Dan. 7:14 and Psalm. 110:1 to himself). Second is the implication that he will condemn them when he comes as judge, implying their present guilt (cf. Exod. 22:28). [*blasphēmia*]

26:68 Prophesy (*prophēteuson*)—Jesus has just prophesied the awesome event of his coming judgment (v. 64). Now his accusers humiliate

him by challenging him to identify them. In due time he will (cf. 25:31-32), but for now he remains silent (cf. Isa. 53:7; 50:6). While this goes on the narration shifts to his prophecy about Peter (vv. 34, 75) that is in the process of being fulfilled (vv. 69-75). [*prophēteuō*]

26:70 Deny (*ērnēsato*)—As if to underscore Peter's scandalous defection, the intensity of his denials increases from the first instance to the third. He begins with a straightforward denial of association with Jesus (v. 70), proceeds to denying with an oath (v. 72) and finally denies by cursing and swearing (v. 74). Jesus had warned about the peril of denying him in his missionary message to disciples (10:33). With these words as a backdrop, Peter's anguish must be all the more abject. [*arneomai*]

26:75 Wept bitterly (*eklausen pikrōs*)—Peter's remorse is a sign his denials do not express what he truly believes (cf. v. 41). While it is possible Jesus' words in 10:33 are tempered by what he says at 12:32, it is more likely that hope for Peter is bound up with Jesus' earlier prophecy (vv. 31-32). The disciples' fall (including Peter's) is predicted along with a prediction of their gathering again (including Peter) with Jesus in Galilee (v. 32; cf. 28:10). [*klaiō, pikrōs*]

27:2 Governor (*hēgemoni*)—The "head imperial provincial administrator" (BDAG, 433; cf. BAGD, 343) in Judea at this time was Pilate (governing from A.D. 26-36/37). Although his Roman title (according to a Latin inscription naming him, BDAG, 813; cf. BAGD, 657) was *prefect*, the more general title of "governor" is used in the Gospel accounts. The Romans controlled the application of the death penalty in the provinces (in part to avoid its use against people sympathetic to them). If the Jewish leaders are to carry out their plan to put Jesus to death

(v. 1), they must enlist the Roman governor's aid. [*hēgemōn*]

27:3 Regretted (*metamelētheis*)—This word means "to have regrets about something, in the sense one wishes it could be undone" (BDAG, 639; cf. BAGD, 511). Most versions translate the word as "remorse" (NASB, NIV, NLT, CEV, NKJV), avoiding the KJV rendering "repent" (but cf. NRSV), though the word can mean "to change one's mind" (e.g., 21:29, 32). Genuine repentance (e.g., 3:2; *metanoeō*), however, involves a change of life leading to obedience to God. Instead, Judas experiences profound pain that leads him to suicide (v. 5), unlike the bitter weeping of Peter (26:75) that leads him to return to the company of the other disciples and to a reunion with Jesus (cf. 26:33; 28:10,16-17). [*metamelomai*]

27:6 Blood (*haimatos*)—The word is used figuratively here (so too at vv. 4, 24) with the meaning "blood as constituting the life of an individual" (BDAG, 26; cf. BAGD, 23). In this construction it refers to "the money paid for a bloody deed" (ibid, 1005; cf. BAGD, 817), an acknowledgment of the impending death of Christ. Judas (v. 4), the religious leaders (v. 6), and Pilate (v. 24) attempt to distance themselves from the guilt of Jesus' blood. But none of them can avoid complicity in his death even as they act to fulfill prophecy (cf. 26:24, 54; 27:8-10). [*haima*]

27:11 You say so yourself (*sy legeis*)—Jesus' answer recalls his reply to Judas (26:25) and the high priest (26:64). All three are given affirmative answers to their questions (the pronoun is emphatic). All three state what they wish to deny. Judas is the betrayer (26:25), Jesus is the Christ, the Son of God (26:63), and he is also the King of the Jews (v. 11). [*sy, legō*]

27:16 Barabbas (*Barabban*)—The name "Barabbas" means "son of Abba." Additionally, "abba" means "father" (cf. Rom. 8:15), so his name could be translated "son of the father." Also noteworthy is the fact that Matthew seems to have supplied his given name, "Jesus." This name appears in several manuscripts and is inexplicable apart from the fact that it was original to Matthew but deleted for reasons of clarity or respect by later copyists. The choice was then between two men named Jesus (cf. CEV, NRSV, NET): Jesus Barabbas or Jesus the Christ. One, a notorious criminal (v. 16), was called "son of the father." The other, a righteous man (v. 19), was truly Son of the Father. [*Barabbas*]

27:19 Innocent (*dikaiō*)—This word can be translated "just" (KJV), "righteous" (NASB, NKJV), or "innocent" (NIV, NLT, NCV, CEV). Since the word basically refers to being in accord with the law, the notion of "innocent" fits this judicial context well. What is interesting is that this declaration comes from a Gentile woman who came to this conclusion through a dream (cf. 2:12). Like the other Gentile woman who encountered Jesus (15:21-28), she is correct in her judgment about him. [*dikaios*]

27:24 Innocent (*athōos*)—Pilate's attempt to act without guilt in the wrong he is about to do to Jesus is futile. If he wanted to be innocent, he should have released him. However, his declaration and depiction of innocence by hand-washing (cf. Deut. 21:6-9) serve to provoke the response of the crowd (v. 25). [*athōos*]

27:25 People (*laos*)—If Pilate would like to escape responsibility for Jesus' death, this group of Jewish people claim to assume it for him. In the Greek OT, this noun routinely identifies the people of Israel from the nations around them (e.g., 2:6; cf. Rom. 15:10-11). Jesus' lament over Jerusalem (23:37-39) gains added poignancy against the backdrop of this scene. [*laos*]

27:29 Crown (*stephanon*)—This word is translated "crown" because Jesus is being mocked as a king (cf. the Gentile magi who worship him as king, 2:1-12). But the word can also refer to a wreath given to both athletes and citizens as "an award or prize for exceptional service or conduct" (BDAG, 944; cf. BAGD, 767). It was often a symbol of victory (cf. 1 Cor. 9:25). There may be irony in the soldiers' placing this crown preliminarily on Jesus. Although his race is not yet over, the finish line is near. He will endure and gain the crown (cf. Rev. 14:14). [*stephanos*]

27:34 Gall (*cholēs*)—This word describes "a substance with an unpleasant taste" (BDAG, 1086; cf. BAGD, 883). It is used to translate four different words in the OT, two referring to bitter flavors and two to poison (ibid). While it is possible that the soldiers are offering a wine laced with poison to end Jesus' life, it is more consistent with their behavior that they simply offer bitter wine as a further indignity. To this point they (and Pilate) have shown a heartless inhumanity deserving of condemnation. They are no less guilty than the Jews. Jesus will drink the cup of wrath (cf. 20:22; 26:39) from God's hand but not the soldier's. [*cholē*]

27:37 Charge (*aitian*)—The Roman charge against Jesus (This is Jesus, the King of the Jews) could be construed as sedition, but it amounts to a form of mockery of him and the Jews. The placement of the charge on a plaque above his head suggests that the traditional depiction of Jesus crucified on a cross in the form of a lowercase "t" is correct. [*aitia*]

27:38 Robbers (*lēstai*)—The picture of Jesus crucified with robbers on either side recalls his question to those who seized him in Gethsemane (26:55): have they come to arrest him like a robber? They had, and he here suffers the further indignity of being associated with criminals in his death. This picture also calls to mind the testimony of James and John that they would share the cup of God's wrath with him (20:22). Instead, two robbers take their place. Rather than sharing his suffering, these two criminals amplify it with insults of their own (v. 44). [*lēstēs*]

27:42 Save (*sōsai*)—The mockery of the people, meant to be sarcastic, ends up ironical. He could not rescue others if he brought about deliverance just for himself here. There is no reservation that God could deliver him if necessary (26:53). But if Jesus is to be the messianic deliverer, then he must first deny himself and bear his cross (16:24; cf. 10:38-39). Only by losing himself will he be able to save others. [*sōzō*]

27:46 Forsaken (*enkatelipes*)—A quotation from Ps. 22 is the only record of Jesus' words from the cross in this Gospel. These are the last words of his mortal life that Matthew records. In the words of the psalmist the reality of Jesus' death for the forgiveness of sins (26:28) is expressed. Bearing the sin of many, he is forsaken by God. The word means "to separate connection with someone" (BDAG, 273; cf. BAGD, 215). He drinks the cup of wrath that he prayed might be taken from him (26:39-44), the penalty for sin that ransoms many (20:28), and by so doing endures a separation from God. No other pain in his passion stands comparison. [*enkataleipō*]

27:50 Spirit (*pneuma*)—The meaning of "spirit" here is "that which animates or gives life to the body" (BDAG, 832; cf. BAGD, 674). The verb "gave" signifies the voluntary nature of Jesus' death, extending to the final breath. He had drunk the bitter cup of God's wrath against sin and could now quit this life. [*pneuma*]

27:51 Torn (*eschisthē*)—The death of Christ has several immediate consequences. Matthew records first the tearing of the curtain in the temple. Although this could be a reference to the curtain before the Holy of Holies (2 Chron. 3:14), it more likely refers to the great curtain that separated the sanctuary from the Court of Israel. Josephus describes this curtain (*Jewish War* 5.212-14) which would have been visible to those bringing sacrifices to the great altar in the forecourt. Jesus has been accused (26:61) and mocked (v. 40) for his prediction of the temple's destruction (24:2). This sign portends its eventual demise and serves as his preliminary vindication. [*schizō*]

27:52 Tombs (*mnēmeia*)—This description of raised saints in connection with Jesus' death and resurrection is peculiar to Matthew. The statements in vv. 51-53 are connected by a repeated conjunction (*kai*, "and") and have presented problems for interpreters in sorting out the timing of the events narrated. It seems best to take v. 52 as a summary statement that tombs were opened (in conjunction with the earthquake) and saints raised (probably like Lazarus in mortal bodies). Verse 53 then explains the time of the raising (after Jesus' resurrection) and appearance to the people of Jerusalem. To clarify the function of v. 53, it could be set off by parentheses (cf. NET). Or vv. 51-53 could be punctuated like the NLT (ignoring the verse divisions): "The earth shook, rocks split apart, and tombs opened. The bodies of many godly men and women who had died were raised from the dead after Jesus' resurrection." [*mnēmeion*]

27:55 Supported (*diakonousai*)—In the previous occurrence of this word in Matthew (25:44), it referred to provision of basic needs of life like food and clothing (cf. 4:11; 8:15). Elsewhere it can refer to monetary support (Rom. 15:25; cf. Acts 11:29). Luke refers to a number of women who followed Jesus and the disciples and used their resources to provide occasional support (8:3). This seems to be Matthew's account of these same women who, unlike the disciples, follow him not only to the cross but also to the tomb (v. 61). [*diakoneō*]

27:60 Tomb (*mnēmeiō*)—A family tomb might be cut in a cavern with several niches where bodies could be laid. After a time (usually a year), the family would return to the tomb, gather the bones of the deceased, and place them in a box. In this way a tomb could be used repeatedly for generations. Joseph's tomb is new, and Jesus' body is its first (brief) occupant. [*mnēmeion*]

27:63 Deceiver (*planos*)—The religious leaders label Jesus a deceiver or impostor who led people astray. Here is a final bit of irony, since Matthew will show it is they who concoct a lie to explain the resurrection (28:13-15). [*planos*]

27:66 Guard (*koustōdias*)—This word comes from the Latin, *custodia*, "a group of soldiers doing guard duty" (BDAG, 563; cf. BAGD, 447). The translation "you have a guard" (NASB, NKJV) could be understood to mean Pilate approves the religious leaders' request to use their own guards from the ranks of the temple police to secure the tomb. The CEV expresses this view: "All right, take some of your soldiers and guard the tomb. . . ." But it is much more likely that the guards are Roman soldiers. Pilate, after all, is being asked to do this, and the term applied to them at 28:12 (*stratiōtēs*) also appears at 27:27, where it is clearly a reference to Roman soldiers at Pilate's headquarters. [*koustōdia*]

28:3 Lightning (*astrapē*)—The brilliant appearance of the angel identifies him as a supernatural being, seen by both the women (v. 1) and also the guards (v. 4). Lightning elsewhere in Matthew is associated with

Jesus' coming from heaven at the end of the age (24:27). The resurrection is the harbinger and guarantee of that event. The angel's presence is an example of the many like him who will participate in Christ's return (cf. 16:27; 25:31). The resurrection is a further vindication of Jesus before his opponents (cf. 26:64) that will finally be manifested in a visible reign (cf. 19:28; 1 Cor. 15:23-28). [*astrapē*]

28:6 As he said (*kathōs eipen*)—Despite the fact that Jesus' words about his death and resurrection (cf. 12:40; 16:21; 17:23; 20:19) had seemed incomprehensible even to his disciples, what he said would happen did. The "one who was crucified" (v. 5) "has been raised" (v. 6). God's words to the disciples at the transfiguration come to mind: "Listen to him" (17:5). This also applies to the other half of the prophecy about their falling away from him (26:31). After he was raised he said he would go before them to Galilee (26:32). This he is doing (v. 7), and they must meet him there (v. 16). [*kathōs, eipon*]

28:9 Worshiped (*prosekynēsan*)—The women are the first to encounter the risen Jesus (cf. John 20:11-18), and they respond appropriately. This word means "to express in attitude or gesture one's complete dependence on or submission to a high authority figure" (BDAG, 882; cf. BAGD, 717). It is composed of a verb, "kiss" (*kyneō*) and a preposition, "towards" (*pros*) and reflects a custom of bowing down and kissing the feet or hem of someone. [*proskyneō*]

28:10 My brothers (*adelphois mou*)—Jesus refers to the disciples (including Peter) as his brothers. However miserably they may have failed to support him in his time of need they remain his brothers, implying his forgiveness of them (cf. 18:17). [*adelphos*]

28:13 Stole (*eklepsan*)—What the religious leaders wanted so desperately to avoid (27:63-64) has happened: Jesus' body is no longer in the tomb. But it was not stolen by the disciples (27:64), as the leaders well know, having been told everything by the guards (v. 11). When Jesus was on the cross, they had taunted him. They said that if God would deliver him, they would believe (27:42-43). Now God has delivered him, but it seems to have only hardened their unbelief (cf. 23:31). They thus continue the treachery that characterized their plot against him in the first place (26:4). So they perpetrate a lie. They called him a deceiver (27:63), but it is they who foster deceit. [*kleptō*]

28:15 Jews (*Ioudaiois*)—This word means "Judeans" and is generally used by Gentiles (and Jews, e.g., Rom. 2:17,28) to describe the Jewish people. Before Roman rule, the last independent government in Israel was the Judean kingdom of the Hasmonean dynasty. It lasted 100 years (164-63 B.C.) until the conquest of the Roman general, Pompey, made Israel a province. The name Judean subsequently became descriptive of all Jews. Although CEV translates this word "the people of Judea" here and the standard lexicon suggests it should always be translated this way (BDAG, 478-79), most will find the translation "Jews" acceptable. [*Ioudaios*]

28:16 Mountain (*oros*)—There has been no previous indication that the disciples are to meet Jesus on a mountain in Galilee. Still the location of the first discourse (5:1-7:29) is a logical meeting site. There a preliminary commission was given to them (5:14-16) that will now be amplified. [*oros*]

28:17 Doubted (*edistasan*)—Unlike the women (v. 9), some among the disciples are afflicted by doubt even as they worship Jesus. In the only other use of this word it described Peter in his encounter with Jesus on the sea

(14:31). In fact the disciples who might be expected to approach Jesus hesitantly in this scene, given their failure to support him in Gethsemane (26:37-44), would be Peter, James, and John. Whoever they were, and they go unnamed, they serve to show that those sent out remained a very human lot, fraught with common failings, but enabled even so to fulfill Jesus' commission. [*distazō*]

28:18 All authority (*pasa exousia*)—Jesus is indeed the Lord of heaven and earth. It is an authority given him by God. The echo of Daniel 7:14 is in these words that substantiate Jesus' promise concerning his fulfillment of Daniel 7:13 (cf. 26:64). The Son of Man is about to send his disciples into the world in anticipation of the eventual harvest (13:37-43). When that time comes, everyone will acknowledge what the disciples know to be true: every knee will bow and every tongue will confess that Jesus Christ is Lord (Phil. 2:9-11; cf. 7:22; 24:30; 25:44). [*pas, exousia*]

28:19 Make disciples (*mathēteusate*)—The disciples' task is to reproduce themselves: to call others to become followers of Christ—others who will hear his words and do them (7:24-25). The object of this mission is all nations, both Jews and Gentiles (cf. 10:16-20). In summary it involves bringing other people into relationship with God and teaching them all they have seen and heard from Jesus. No doubt Matthew wrote his Gospel as an aid to completing this task. [*mathēteuō*]

Baptizing (*baptizontes*)—As baptism marked the beginning of Jesus' public ministry (3:15), so baptism is to mark the beginning of a disciple's public following of Christ. Baptism testifies to the beginning of a relationship with God as Father, Son, and Holy Spirit. Matthew's Gospel serves as an exposition in part of what that relationship means for disciples and how they are to live in light of it. [*baptizō*]

28:20 Obey (*tērein*)—This word means "to persist in obedience" (BDAG, 1002; cf. BAGD, 815). As Jesus was concerned that people not just hear his words but put them into practice (7:24-27), so his disciples must make it clear as they teach these words of Jesus that it will not do only to hear his instructions. A disciple must hear and obey. [*tēreō*]

Everything (*panta*)—What Jesus told his first disciples (Jews) is relevant and applicable for later disciples as well (Jews and Gentiles). It is not only some of Jesus' instructions that new disciples should be taught to obey but all of them. If there was any question that Matthew thought his Gospel was for all people, this statement should answer it with a clear affirmative. This is a Gospel to be heard, believed, and obeyed. [*pas*]

MARK

Joel F. Williams

1:1 Good news (*euangeliou*)—Although the word *euangelion* is often rendered in English as "gospel," the translation "good news" (NRSV, NLT) perhaps communicates more clearly that the word is used in the NT for the announcement of the good news concerning Jesus (BAGD, 317-18; BDAG, 402-3). The word *euangelion* appears most often in Paul's writings (60 out of the 76 uses in the NT). For the apostle Paul, the gospel was the message about the life, death, and resurrection of Jesus, a message that brings salvation from sin and from judgment to those who believe by God's power (Rom. 1:1-6, 16-17; 1 Cor. 15:1-11; 1 Thess.. 1:5-10; 4:14). Paul spoke this message of good news to those who would listen (e.g., Rom. 15:19; 1 Cor. 15:1; Gal. 1:11; 2:2; 1 Thess.. 2:9). Mark's use of the term *euangelion* is similar to that of Paul. For Mark, the good news is the message about Jesus (1:1), one which is verbally proclaimed (1:14; 13:10; 14:9). Mark's use of "gospel" in 1:1 is somewhat unique in that it refers to the following written account of Jesus' ministry rather than to a spoken proclamation of the good news. This use of "gospel" for a written proclamation of the good news apparently led Christians in the 2nd century A.D. to begin referring to written accounts of the life of Jesus as "Gospels" (Justin, *1 Apol.* 66.3; Irenaeus, *Haer.* 3.11.8). Therefore, the term "Gospel" became used for a type of litera-ture, and four Gospels were included in the NT canon. For Mark, however, there would have only been one gospel, one message of good news concerning the life, death, and resurrection of Jesus, a message that brings life and an entrance into the kingdom of God to all who repent and believe (1:14-15; 8:35). This one gospel was, of course, to be proclaimed many times and in many places, eventually reaching the whole world (13:10; 14:9). On the "good news" in Mark, see also 8:35. [*euangelion*]

Christ (*Chistou*)—Mark immediately designates Jesus as both "Christ" and "Son of God." The title "Christ," which means "someone who has been ceremonially anointed for an office," is the Greek equivalent for the Hebrew word "Messiah" (K. H. Rengstorf, *NIDNTT* 2:334; cf. John 1:41; 4:25). Mark regarded Jesus as the Messiah, the promised deliverer from the line of David, who would rule as king over the people of Israel (12:35; 14:61; 15:32). Mark's Gospel narrates how people came to recognize the identity of Jesus as both Christ and Son of God by including two important confessions (cf. Lane, 45). At the culmination of the first half of the narrative, Peter confesses that Jesus is the Christ (8:29). In response, Jesus instructs his disciples that, as the Son of Man, he must suffer, die, and rise again (8:31). Jesus is the Messiah, but not apart from the cross. The second half of the narrative reaches a climax when the centurion sees Jesus die and confesses him to be the Son of God (15:39). [*Christos*]

Son of God (*huiou theou*)—Like the title "Christ," "Son of God" is a messianic name. It has its roots in the OT, where the king, the descendant of David, is described as God's Son (2 Sam. 7:8-16; Ps. 2:1-12; 89:19-29; cf. also 4QFlor I, 10-13 in the Qumran literature). However, "Son of God" is more than just a synonym for "Christ," because it is a title that emphasizes the close relationship between the anointed king and God himself (O. Michel, *NIDNTT* 3:607). Mark's Gospel describes a unique relationship between Jesus and God the Father, one that goes beyond common expectations concerning the Messiah (12:35-37). Jesus speaks God's Word (1:14; 9:7), and always does the Father's will (14:36). Jesus has the authority, like God, to forgive sins (2:5-12), and his unique authority will be on display when he is exalted to the right hand of God, a position of Lordship (12:36; 14:62). In Mark's Gospel, Jesus' identity as the Son of God is declared by God (1:11; 9:7) and acknowledged by spirit beings (3:11; 5:7; cf. 1:24). [*huios + theos*]

1:2 It is written (*gegraptai*)—In Mark's Gospel, "it is written" (or "it stands written") is a formula for introducing a quotation or a teaching from the OT Scriptures (1:2; 7:6; 9:12-13; 11:17; 14:21, 27). Mark himself uses the formula in 1:2, while the remaining instances occur in Jesus' teaching. The use of the Greek perfect tense, which expresses a completed action with abiding results, is particularly appropriate in such a formula, since it communicates the present authority of what was written in the past (H. Hübner, *EDNT* 1:261; Marcus, 147). [*graphō*]

1:4 Wilderness (*erēmō*)—The wilderness is a deserted or uninhabited region (BAGD, 309;

BDAG, 391-392). In the introduction to Mark's Gospel, "wilderness" (*erēmos*) functions as a noun to describe the setting for the initial events of the narrative: John's ministry as well as Jesus' baptism and temptation (1:4, 1:12-13). This setting connects John's ministry with the promise of Isa. 40:3 referred to in Mark 1:3, a promise concerning a preparation in the wilderness for the coming of the Lord to deliver his people. Elsewhere in Mark, *erēmos* is always an adjective used to modify "place" (*topos*; 1:35, 45; 6:31, 32, 35). Jesus seeks out deserted places for privacy, rest, and time with God, but the demands of the crowd reach him even there. [*erēmos*]

Repentance (*metanoias*)—In the LXX, particularly in the OT prophets, the verb meaning "to repent, to change one's mind" (*metanoeō*) occurs in connection with verbs meaning "to turn" (*apostrephō, epistrephō*; cf. Isa. 46:8; Jer. 4:28; 18:8; 38:18-19 [31:18-19 Eng]; Joel 2:13-14; Jonah 3:9-10). As a result, the two concepts, "to repent" and "to turn," became related in meaning. In intertestamental Jewish literature and in later Greek translations of the OT after the LXX, "to repent" and "repentance" became common words for expressing the idea of conversion, for turning away from sin and turning toward God and his ways (J. Behm, *TDNT* 4:989-92). A baptism of repentance, therefore, is an outward expression of an inward turning away from rebellion against God and his commands and a turning toward him in surrender. In Mark's Gospel, John the Baptist (1:4), Jesus (1:15), and Jesus' disciples (6:12) all preach a message of repentance. On preaching, see 1:38. [*metanoia*]

Forgiveness (*aphesin*)—Outside the NT, the word used here for forgiveness (*aphesis*) commonly means "release" (LSJ, 288), often in the legal sense of release from office, marriage, obligation, debt, or punishment (R. Bultmann, *TDNT* 1:509). In the NT, however, the word is consistently used for divine forgiveness of sins, for release from the guilt and punishment for sins (e.g., Matt. 26:28; Mark 3:29; Luke 1:77; Acts 2:38; Eph. 1:7; Heb. 9:22). For the use of the related verb *aphiēmi* in Mark with the meaning "to forgive," see 2:5, 7, 9-10; 3:28; 4:12; 11:25. [*aphesis*]

1:6 Camel's hair (*trichas kamēlou*)—Mark probably is referring here to a rough garment, woven with camel's hair (Taylor, 155-56). Zech. 13:4 presents a "garment of hair" (NIV) as the appropriate dress for a prophet in Israel, so that this detail serves to describe John as a prophet (Cranfield, 47). [*thrix + kamēlos*]

  Leather belt (*zōnēn dermatinēn*)—The reference to John's leather belt recalls the description of Elijah in 2 Kings 1:8. The details of John's clothing, therefore, identify him with the prophet Elijah (Hooker, 37), an identification which becomes more explicit in Mark 9:11-13. For Mark, John fulfills the prophecy concerning Elijah's coming, as foretold by Malachi. John is the one who "will prepare the way" before the day of the Lord's coming (Mal. 3:1-2; Mark 1:2). He functions as "Elijah the prophet" who is sent by God "before the great and terrible day of the Lord" in order to "restore all things" (Mal. 4:5-6; Mark 9:12). [*zōnē + dermatinos*]

1:7 Not worthy (*ouk . . . hikanos*)—In this context, the word for "worthy" (*hikanos*) conveys the idea of meeting a standard which identifies someone as sufficient, qualified, or simply good enough to perform a particular task (cf. Matt. 8:8; 1 Cor. 15:9; BAGD 374; BDAG 472). John did not regard himself as sufficiently worthy to stoop down and loosen the leather strap on Jesus' sandals. In rabbinic literature, untying the master's shoes was a task for slaves but beneath the dignity of disciples. In *b. Ketub.* 96a, R. Joshua b. Levi states that "all service that a slave must render to his master a student must render to his teacher, except untying his shoe" (cf. Marcus,

152). John lowered himself to a level below the status of a slave when he compared himself to Jesus, the stronger one who was yet to come. See "sandals," Luke 3:16. [*hikanos*]

1:8 Holy Spirit (*pneumati hagiō*)—The Gospel of Mark has relatively little to say about the Holy Spirit's ministry, especially after the Spirit comes upon Jesus at his baptism (1:10) and leads him out into the wilderness to be tempted (1:12). Mark mentions the Holy Spirit on only three other occasions. In the past, the Spirit spoke through the writers of the Scriptures (12:36); during the time of Jesus' earthly ministry, he gives Jesus authority over demons (3:22, 29-30); and in the future, he will communicate his message through believers (13:11). Therefore, Mark offers little guidance on the meaning of the baptism of the Holy Spirit (1:8). However, the OT background, which Mark considers crucial for understanding John's ministry, sheds light on the meaning of John's promise concerning the baptism of the Spirit through Jesus. The OT anticipated the outpouring of the Spirit on God's people in the last days (Isa. 32:15; 44:3; Ezek. 11:19; 36:25-27; 37:14; 39:29; Joel 2:28-32), and John points to Jesus as the one who will bring about this gift of the Spirit. [*pneuma + hagios*]

1:10 Immediately (*euthys*)—This is the first instance of one of Mark's favorite words; his Gospel accounts for 41 out of the 51 times it occurs in the NT. English translations have made various attempts to express the word's meaning. For example, in the NIV, the following translations appear: "at once," "without delay," "just then," "quickly," "as soon as," "immediately," "then," "right," "at this," "just," "shortly," "very." Sometimes the NIV omits translating the word entirely (cf. 1:10, 21, 30; 2:12; 5:2; 8:10). The NASB uses "immediately" for *euthys* consistently throughout Mark, except in 1:23 where it translates the adverb as "just then." Sometimes the word *euthys* has a temporal function, indicating that one action took place shortly after another event. Sometimes the word simply has a stylistic function, focusing attention on a particular event, so that it means something similar to "Look!" (Guelich, 30). [*euthys*]

Torn apart (*schizomenous*)—The verb *schizō* means "to divide something by force, to split or tear apart" (BAGD, 797; BDAG, 981). After his baptism, Jesus saw the heavens being "torn apart" (NRSV) and the Spirit coming down. The only other use of the verb *schizō* in Mark's Gospel is in 15:38, for the tearing of the temple's veil from top to bottom, an event that takes place at the moment of Christ's death. After the tearing of the heavens, a heavenly voice identifies Jesus as the Son of God (1:11), and then later after the tearing of the temple's veil, the centurion declares Jesus to be the Son of God (15:39). Mark 10:38-39 further strengthens the connection between Jesus' baptism and his crucifixion, since in that passage Jesus refers to his death as a baptism. [*schizō*]

1:11 Beloved (*agapētos*)—Although the primary use for this adjective is to express love and affection for an object, when it modifies "son" it can also imply that this is an "only" or "uniquely special" son (BAGD, 6; BDAG, 7; Guelich, 34; Gundry, 49). For example, the LXX uses "beloved" (*agapētos*) to communicate that Isaac was Abraham's "only" or "unique" son (Gen. 22:2, 12, 16). The NET seeks to communicate both connotations with its translation, "You are my one dear Son" (1:11; cf. 9:7; 12:6). [*agapētos*]

1:12 Compelled (*ekballei*)—Mark chooses a forceful word for the Spirit's act of guiding Jesus into the wilderness. The word appears elsewhere in Mark's Gospel in passages where Jesus "casts out" demons (e.g., 1:34, 39) or "drives out" those who are buying and

selling in the temple (11:15). After coming upon Jesus at his baptism (1:11), the Spirit "compelled" (NLT) Jesus to go into the wilderness (1:12). The term's forcefulness suggests that Jesus stands under the Spirit's powerful control during his earthly ministry (F. Annen, *EDNT* 1:406). [*ekballō*]

1:13 Satan (*Satana*)—The name "Satan" is a Greek transliteration of an Aramaic word that literally means "adversary" (BAGD, 744-45; BDAG, 916-17; MM, 570). In the Gospel of Mark, Satan is the supernatural ruler of a demonic kingdom (3:22-26), who opposes God's work in the world (4:15). In Mark 8:33, Jesus calls his disciple Peter by the name "Satan," apparently because he tried to turn Jesus away from his God-appointed mission to suffer and die. Jesus sees behind the words of Peter a temptation from Satan himself who sought to oppose God's plan by distracting Jesus from the way of the cross. Mark includes only a short account of Satan's temptation of Jesus at the beginning of his ministry (1:12-13), without detailing the nature of the temptation. Jesus' later conversation with Peter helps to fill in the gap. Satan sought to divert Jesus from his mission, a mission that included suffering, death, and giving his life as a ransom for many. [*Satan/Satanas*]

1:15 The kingdom of God (*ē basileia tou theou*)—In the Gospel of Mark, the kingdom of God is God's royal reign, his kingly authority or rule (BAGD, 134-35; BDAG, 168-169) and yet also his royal realm, in the sense of a place in which someone can eventually live (14:25; cf. Matt. 8:11-12; 11:11) or into which someone can enter (9:47; 10:15, 25; U. Luz, *EDNT* 1:202). At times, the Gospel of Mark presents the kingdom of God as a future reality that will come in power (9:1; 14:25; 15:43). In a similar way, Jesus teaches about the Son of Man's visible coming in great power and glory in order to judge the wicked and to gather the elect (8:38; 13:26-27; 14:62). Yet, Jesus also teaches privately about a form of the kingdom that is a secret, a mystery able to be understood only by his own followers (4:10-12). This hidden form of the kingdom begins small like a seed but then grows, not by human effort but by God's work (4:22, 26-29; 30-32). It grows when people hear God's word, accept it, and bear fruit (4:20). When Jesus publicly proclaims that the kingdom of God has drawn near, he apparently means that the visible coming of God's kingdom in power is now imminent (1:15). The threat and promise of its sudden appearance demands repentance and faith. On repentance, see 1:4, on faith, see 2:5, and on entering the kingdom of God, see 9:47. [*basileia*]

Is near (*ēngiken*)—The verb *engizō* can communicate "drawing near" in either a spatial or a temporal sense (BAGD, 213; BDAG, 270). Since later the kingdom is described as coming (9:1), Mark 1:15 apparently means that the event of the coming of the kingdom is ready to happen at any time. When the verb *engizō* appears in the NT in this temporal sense, it indicates not that an event has already arrived but that it is imminent, ready to take place at any moment (Matt. 21:34; 26:45; Luke 21:20, 28; 22:1; Acts 7:17; Rom. 13:12; Heb. 10:25; Jas 5:8; 1 Pet. 4:7). The same is true for the related adverb *engys* in statements expressing nearness in time (Matt. 26:18; Mark 13:28; John 2:13; 7:2; Rom. 13:11; Rev. 1:3; 22:10). The coming of the Messiah is the decisive moment in God's redemptive plan, after which the coming of the kingdom can happen at any time. [*engizō*]

1:18 Left (*aphentes*)—In Mark's Gospel, those called by Jesus inevitably leave something behind in order to follow him. In Mark 1:18, Simon and Andrew abandon their nets, and with them their old lives and livelihood. Others who walk away from their occupations to go with Jesus include James and John (1:20)

and Levi (2:14). Jesus commands the rich man to sell all his possessions and give away what he has to the poor in order to follow (10:21). In light of the rich man's failure, Peter points out that the disciples have left everything to be with Jesus (10:28). Following Jesus involves cost but also reward, since those who sacrifice for the sake of Jesus receive back an abundance in the present age and eternal life in the age to come (10:29-30). [*aphiēmi*]

Followed (*ēkolouthēsan*)—While the verb "to follow" sometimes means literally to walk behind someone who is taking the lead (3:7; 5:24; 14:13), it often bears the idea in Mark's Gospel of accompanying Jesus as a disciple (e.g., 1:18; 2:14-15; 8:34; 10:21, 28; 15:41; cf. G. Schneider, *EDNT* 1:49). Following Jesus, therefore, involves being with him (3:13-14), participating in his ministry (1:17; 3:14-15), learning to think the way he thinks (8:31-33), and accepting the pattern of his life as one's own (8:34). Jesus was different from other Jewish rabbis at the time, in that he commanded prospective disciples to follow him and share in his work. The accepted custom was for disciples themselves to choose a rabbi, so that they might study the Law under him and pass on his teachings (Guelich, 50-51). [*akoloutheō*]

1:21 Synagogue (*synagōgēn*)—In Mark's Gospel, a "synagogue" always refers to a building, a meeting place for Jews. The synagogue's primary purpose was to serve as a location for the reading and teaching of the Mosaic Law, but it could also be used as a place for prayer, for education of children, and for community meetings and events (W. Schrage, *TDNT* 7:821-28; Schürer, *History* 2:424-27; cf. Acts 15:21). During Jesus' time, every significant Jewish community in Galilee had a synagogue, and larger cities had more than one (W. Schrage, *TDNT* 7:812). The Sabbath worship service consisted of prayers, readings from the Law and from the prophets together with a rendering of the Hebrew Scripture into Aramaic, a sermon, and a priestly blessing or a benediction (Schürer, *History* 2:447-54). Teaching in the Sabbath service was not the regular responsibility of any one person; rather the synagogue ruler assigned the task to different worthy individuals. Mark presents Jesus as receiving opportunities to teach and preach in synagogues throughout Galilee (1:21-22, 39; 6:2). On the Sabbath, see 2:24, and on synagogue rulers, see 5:22. [*synagōgē*]

1:22 Authority (*exousian*)—Authority involves both the power to act and the right to exercise that power (W. Foerster, TDNT 2:562-63). Therefore, "authority" (*exousia*) is somewhat different than "power" (*dynamis*), which emphasizes an overwhelming force, though not necessarily one that is linked to an authoritative position or mandate (O. Betz, *NIDNTT* 2:607). On power in Mark, see 5:30. Jesus' teaching is authoritative, that is, his words are powerful, God-given, and so clearly true that they display his inherent right to proclaim his message. References to Jesus' authority in Mark's Gospel always appear in contexts in which Jesus stands in opposition to the scribes (1:21-27; 2:5-12; 11:27-33). Jesus has the right to teach and act in ways that the scribes do not, but the scribes themselves will not accept his authority. [*exousia*]

Scribes (*grammateis*)—The scribes were ordained teachers of the Mosaic Law. Becoming a scribe involved intensive study at the feet of a famous teacher and memorization of the rabbi's teaching. Successful completion of the course of study led to ordination. The scribes focused on three professional activities: (1) They studied and interpreted the Mosaic Law, especially seeking to determine its application to daily life. (2) They taught disciples to understand the Law, their own interpretations, and the traditions of other important scribes. (3) They

served as trial judges, administering justice based on their study of the Law (G. Baumbach, *EDNT* 1:259-60; Schürer, *History* 2:322-36). Mark presents the scribes as Jesus' opponents. They object when Jesus teaches and acts with direct divine authority (2:5-11; 11:27-33), and they criticize him for refusing to accept their traditions (2:16-17; 7:1-5). In turn, Jesus condemns the scribes for their hypocrisy, since they desire honor and privileges based on their outward religious activities, while at the same time keeping their hearts far from God (7:6-7; 12:38-40). They cleverly devise traditions that allow them to neglect the commands of God while still appearing religious (7:8-13). Nevertheless, Mark does not make the antagonism between Jesus and the scribes absolute. He also presents an exceptional scribe who is not far from the kingdom of God because he agrees with Jesus on the priority of love for God and for one's neighbor (12:28-34). [*grammateus*]

1:23 Unclean spirit (*pneumati akathartō*)—"Unclean" was a common, Jewish descriptive term for demons, evil and hostile spirit beings (e.g., Jub. 10:1; T. Benj. 5:2; 1QM XIII, 5). Mark uses "unclean spirit" (*pneuma akatharton*) and "demon" (*daimonion*) with equal frequency, both 11 times. In addition, he uses the verb *daimonizomai* ("to be possessed by a demon") four times. The adjective "unclean," a term indicating ritual impurity, communicates that demon possession exposes individuals to a pollution that makes them unfit for worship or fellowship with God (Taylor, 174). In Mark's Gospel, unclean spirits take control of people ultimately for the purpose of destroying them, through sickness or self-inflicted wounds (5:2-13; 9:17-27). When they see Jesus, they cry out for they know that Jesus is the Son of God and that he has authority over them (1:23-27, 34; 3:11-12; 5:6-8). [*pneuma + akathartos*]

1:26 Shook him violently (*sparaxan auton*)— Just before coming out, the unclean spirit threw the man into convulsions (NASB; NLT) or, perhaps better, shook the man violently (NIV). The verb *sparassō* occurs only three times in the NT, always in the context of a demon doing harm to a human victim (1:26; 9:26; Luke 9:39). In classical Greek, the verb was used for tearing or rending by an animal such as a dog (LSJ, 1624). Second Samuel 22:8 LXX, using the verb with a meaning closer to that found in Mark 1:26, refers to the violent shaking of the foundations of heaven. [*sparassō*]

1:31 She was waiting on them (*diēkonei autois*)—Later in Mark's Gospel, Jesus uses this verb (*diakoneō*) to explain the nature of his mission and the implications of that mission for the demands of discipleship (10:43-45; cf. 9:35). Jesus came to serve (*diakonēsai*), that is, to take care of the needs of others and not his own, and he expects the same attitude from his followers. Jesus' use of *diakoneō* illustrates the verb's more general meaning. However, it also has the more basic meaning of "waiting on people as they sit around a table at mealtime" (A. Weiser, *EDNT* 1:302; cf. Luke 17:8; John 12:2). Peter's mother-in-law waits on her guests, proving through this action that she is completely healed by Jesus. [*diakoneō*]

1:35 He was praying (*prosēucheto*)—Mark's Gospel mentions Jesus' praying, that is, his spending time to speak with God, on three occasions: at the beginning (1:35), middle (6:46), and end (14:35-39) of his earthly ministry. Each time, he is alone in a solitary setting at night. Jesus' private practice of prayer stands in contrast to the long, public prayers of the scribes who want to be noticed and honored by others (12:38-40). [*proseuchomai*]

1:38 I may preach (*kēryxō*)—In the vocabulary of the early church, the verb "to preach" (*kēryssō*) fits not within the context of church instruction but rather in the setting of missionary proclamation (Guelich, 43). Preaching involves the public declaration of a message or important news. The message that Jesus proclaimed was the gospel of God, the good news of the coming kingdom (1:14-15). In Mark's Gospel, John the Baptist (1:4, 7), Jesus (1:14, 38-39), and the disciples (3:14; 6:12) all take up the missionary task of preaching a message from God. According to Mark 13:10 and 14:9, the gospel will eventually be proclaimed to all the nations (13:10; 14:9). In addition, those who observe Jesus' miracles proclaim the news concerning him, even though Jesus orders them not to tell anyone (7:36-37; cf. 1:44-45; 5:19-20). [*kēryssō*]

1:40 Leper (*lepros*)—A leper was an individual with a serious skin disease. The biblical term "leprosy" covered a variety of chronic skin disorders, probably including but not limited to what is known today as leprosy or Hansen's disease (BAGD, 471; BDAG, 592; R. K. Harrison, *NIDNTT* 2:463-64). Since leprosy brought ritual impurity, the afflicted individual faced not only physical anguish but also social isolation. According to the book of Leviticus, "the person with such an infectious disease must wear torn clothes, let his hair be unkempt, cover the lower part of his face and cry out, 'Unclean! Unclean!' As long as he has the infection he remains unclean. He must live alone; he must live outside the camp" (Lev. 13:45-46 NIV). Jesus responds to the suffering of this leper with compassion. On feeling compassion, see 6:34. [*lepros*]

1:43 After he sternly warned him (*embrimēsamenos autō*)—In describing how Jesus sent out the healed leper, Mark employs a strongly emotional word that implies an attitude of anger or displeasure (MM, 206; cf. Dan. 11:30 LXX; Mark 14:5). Jesus moves from compassion to harshness toward the man. In Mark 1:45, the healed leper, in direct disobedience to Jesus' command, goes out and spreads the message concerning Jesus' miraculous power. Apparently, Jesus was able to foresee the likely disregard of his instructions by the healed leper, and his harsh warning was an attempt to impress upon the man the seriousness of his command (Lane, 87). [*embrimaomai*]

1:44 For a testimony against them (*eis martyrion autois*)—Elsewhere in Mark's Gospel, this same phrase appears in contexts where someone is giving a testimony against those who reject the message about Jesus (6:11; 13:9). This testimony mentioned in Mark 1:45 also has a negative function, expressing the idea of incriminating evidence, a witness that exposes the guilt of others (H. Strathmann, *TDNT* 4:502-3; Lane, 87-88; cf. Jas 5:3). The witness is presumably against the priests, since one of them would find it necessary to acknowledge the healing and to accept the appropriate sacrifice. If the priests later reject the person who performed this healing, their own official pronouncement will stand as evidence against their unbelief. [*martyrion*]

2:3 A paralyzed man (*paralytikon*)—Since "paralytic" (NASB; NIV) is an uncommon word in English, the translation "paralyzed man" (NRSV; NLT) probably communicates more clearly the nature of the man's disability. Mark's general description of the man's problem makes it difficult to be more specific about his medical condition beyond simply noting his inability to walk (M. Rissi, *EDNT* 3:31; Lane, 93). [*paralytikos*]

2:4 After they dug out an opening (*exoryxantes*)—The four friends who carried the paralyzed man removed the roof (literally, "unroofed the roof") by digging out an opening. Common people in Israel made roofs for their homes by placing wooden beams across stone or mudbrick walls and then covering the beams with reeds, layers of thorns, and several inches of clay. Typically, an outside, wooden ladder provided access to the roof (Marcus, 216). This method for constructing a roof shows why it was necessary to dig out an opening in order to lower the paralyzed man down to Jesus. [*exoryssō*]

Mat (*krabatton*)—Mark describes the man as lying on a "mat" (NIV; NLT) or a "pallet" (NASB; RSV), which was a poor man's bed (BAGD, 447; BDAG, 563; MM, 357). The more common word for bed was *klinē* (cf. 4:21; 7:30). [*krabattos*]

2:5 Faith (*pistin*)—In Mark's Gospel, the noun "faith" (*pistis*) and the verb "to believe" (*pisteuō*) are used interchangeably (5:34-36; 11:22-24), so that together they express Mark's understanding of faith. For Mark, faith involves both belief and trust (cf., Marshall, *Faith* 228-40). Faith is rooted in belief, in a mental conviction concerning the truth of the Gospel, that is, an acceptance of Jesus' kingdom message and an acknowledgment of his place in God's kingdom plan (1:15; 9:42). Those who will not believe in Jesus cannot be saved (15:31-32). Although faith is an inner attitude, it reveals itself in outward actions, since, according to Mark, faith is something that can be seen (2:5). In other words, faith is sufficiently a matter of the will that it changes not only our thinking but also our behavior. Faith also includes trust, a persistent sense of confidence that God will work through Jesus to meet the needs of the powerless (e.g., 5:34, 36; 10:52; 11:24). Mark illustrates trust in Jesus through the persistent efforts of people of faith to overcome obstacles and reach Jesus, in order that they might find healing through his power. For example, the paralyzed man and his friends demonstrate their faith by seeking out Jesus and by overcoming the press of the crowd to reach him (2:3-5). Trust also expresses itself in petitionary prayer; God answers the prayers of those who believe in him (9:29; 11:22-24). In Mark's Gospel, individuals can have more or less trust in Jesus. The disciples follow Jesus, but they can also have an insufficient faith (4:40), and the man with a demon-possessed boy believes in Jesus but struggles with unbelief at the same time (9:24). [*pistis, pisteuō*]

2:7 He is blaspheming (*blasphēmei*)—The verb "to blaspheme" (*blasphēmeō*) and the related noun "blasphemy" (*blasphēmia*) are used in Mark predominantly for arrogantly disrespectful speech against God, speech that insults him or demeans his uniqueness or majesty (cf. BAGD, 142-43; BDAG, 178). Blasphemy was a serious charge because the penalty prescribed for it in Lev. 24:16 was death: "The one who blasphemes the name of the Lord shall surely be put to death." In Mark's Gospel, there is a pattern of alternating accusations of blasphemy (Bock, *Blasphemy* 188-89). In Mark 2:7, some of the scribes regard Jesus' claim to forgive sins as blasphemy (on the scribes, see 1:22). Shortly after this, when other scribes argue that Jesus' power over demons comes from Satan (3:22), Jesus calls their accusation a blasphemy against the Holy Spirit (3:29-30). Later in the narrative, the high priest charges Jesus with blasphemy, and the whole council condemns him as worthy of death (14:63-64). At the crucifixion, when people mock Jesus as incapable of saving himself, Mark describes their words as a blasphemy against Jesus (15:29-30). This is the final statement on the subject in Mark. It is not Jesus who blasphemes but those who reject him as Savior. [*blasphēmeō*]

2:10 The Son of Man (*ho huios tou anthrōpou*)—The most frequent messianic title for Jesus in Mark's Gospel is not "Christ" (six times in Mark) or "Son of God" (seven times) but rather "Son of Man" (14 times). In Mark, only

Jesus refers to himself as "the Son of Man;" other people never use the title. In addition, Jesus seems to have preferred this title to other possibilities, since when others call him the Christ or the Son of God, he identifies himself as the Son of Man in his answer to them (8:29-31; 14:61-62; cf. 13:21-26). The reasons for this preference are never fully clarified in Mark, but apparently the regular use of a more explicit messianic title like "Christ" would have created expectations that did not match Jesus' own understanding of his mission. Jesus uses the title "Son of Man" in three different contexts: in sayings that emphasize his present authority on earth (2:10, 28; on authority, see 1:22), in those that predict his rejection, death, and resurrection (8:31; 9:9, 12, 31; 10:33, 45; 14:21, 41), and in those that focus on his future coming in power and glory (8:38; 13:26; 14:62). The sayings in this last category clearly allude to the Son of Man figure in Daniel 7, so that the use of this title serves to portray Jesus as a heavenly figure who appears before God to receive an everlasting dominion over all the nations (Dan. 7:13-14). Yet Jesus' use of this title in other contexts shows that this exalted picture remains an incomplete expression of his identity unless it is also connected with his suffering, death, and resurrection. [*huios + anthrōpos*]

2:14 Tax booth (*telōnion*)—In the first century A.D., taxation involved both "direct taxes," such as land taxes on farm production or head taxes paid in connection with a census, and "indirect taxes," such as customs on the transportation of goods or payments at various tolls. The former were under the direct control of the ruling authorities and their representatives, but the government leased to individuals the business of collecting the latter (Guelich, 100-101). Each year, the privilege of collecting indirect taxes went to the highest bidder, who then employed tax collectors to gather the customs or toll payments. The system was open to abuse, since a healthy profit was possible only if tax collectors took in considerably more than what was necessary for payment to the government (O. Michel, *TDNT* 8:89, 99-101). The tax booth at Capernaum, where Levi worked, probably charged customs on goods being transported into the territory of the tetrarch Herod Antipas (N. Hillyer, *NIDNTT* 3:757). [*telōnion*]

2:15 Tax collectors (*telōnai*)—Because of their reputation for greed and dishonesty, tax collectors were outcasts from Jewish society. A tax collector was disqualified from the office of judge or even as a witness in court. He was excommunicated from the synagogue, and in the eyes of the community, his disgrace extended also to his family (N. Hillyer, *NIDNTT* 3:756; Lane, 101-2). [*telōnēs*]

Sinners (*hamartōloi*)—In this context, the term "sinners" designates people who lived an immoral lifestyle, who openly violated the commands of the Mosaic Law. The Pharisees as well as many other respectable people in the community would have distanced themselves from such people (Cranfield, 103). These sinners were not simply those who ignored the many traditions and rules of the Pharisees, since Jesus and his disciples also disregarded them (2:23-24; 7:1-5) and could hardly be faulted for eating with similar people (Guelich, 101-2). [*hamartōlos*]

Disciples (*mathētais*)—A disciple is both a learner who studies under a teacher or religious leader and an adherent who supports the teacher's ideas or cause (cf. BAGD, 485-86; BDAG, 609-10). This is the first of 46 uses in Mark's Gospel of the term "disciples" to refer to those who were called by Jesus to follow him, learn from him, and share in his ministry. On following, see 1:18. At this point in the narrative, the exact number of Jesus' disciples is unclear, but in 3:13-19 Jesus appoints 12 men to be with him and from

then on the "disciples" and "the twelve" seem to be terms that function interchangeably. In Mark's Gospel, the disciples' incomprehension stands out. They struggle to understand Jesus' identity and the extent of his power to care for them (4:35-41; 6:45-52; 8:14-21). Even after they realize that Jesus is the Messiah (8:29), they have difficulty grasping the sacrificial nature of his mission and the cost of following him (8:31-33; 9:30-34; 10:32-41). [*mathētēs*]

2:16 Pharisees (*Pharisaiōn*)—The Pharisees ("separated ones") formed one of the major Jewish religious parties of Jesus' day, along with the Sadducees and the Essenes. Although the number of official members was relatively small (around 6,000 according to Josephus, *Ant.* 17.2.4 § 42), the Pharisees exerted a considerable influence on the common people within the Jewish community (Josephus, *Ant.* 13.10.6 § 298; 18.1.3 § 15). They sought to live in careful obedience not only to the written Law of Moses but also to the oral Law, that is, to the traditions and interpretations passed on by important teachers concerning the proper application of the written Law (cf. Josephus, *Ant.* 13.10.6 § 297; Schürer, *History* 2:388-403; Marcus, 519-23). In Mark's Gospel, the Pharisees appear as Jesus' opponents, especially during his ministry in Galilee. They dispute with Jesus concerning his social interaction with sinners (2:15-17), fasting (2:18-20), Sabbath observance (2:23-28), tradition (7:1-13), divorce (10:2-9), and taxes (12:13-17). On the scribes, see 1:22. [*Pharisaios*]

2:18 Fasting (*nēsteuontes*)—In the Bible, fasting is an act of religious devotion in which someone refrains from eating for a period of time as a sign of grief or as a preparation for prayer (BAGD, 538; BDAG, 672). It was common for Pharisees to fast voluntarily twice a week, on Mondays and Thursdays (Luke

18:12; *Did.* 8:1). As to the way in which John's disciples practiced fasting, Mark's Gospel offers no details. In Mark 2:18-19, Jesus teaches that because of his presence his disciples cannot help but rejoice, and an act of mourning such as fasting is inappropriate. The time for grief will come. [*nēsteuō*]

2:24 Sabbath (*sabbasin*)—The seventh day of the week, or Sabbath, was a day set aside for rest from work and for worship (Exod. 20:8-11; Lev. 23:1-3). In Jesus' day, the matter of what constituted work caused considerable discussion among religious teachers. Eventually, the rabbis specified 39 activities forbidden on the Sabbath, although they continued to debate the exact meaning and extent of each of these actions (*m Sabb.* 7:2; cf. Schürer, *History* 467-75). The third item on the list of forbidden activities was reaping, and when the hungry disciples plucked the heads of grain for a snack, the Pharisees objected, considering the act to be reaping (2:23-24; cf. Philo, *Moses* 2.4 § 22). In the next passage (3:1-6), the Pharisees grow in their hostility toward Jesus because he heals on the Sabbath. Since the man's condition was not life-threatening, treatment should have waited until after the Sabbath was over, at least according to Jesus' opponents (cf. Luke 13:14; *m Sabb.* 14:3-4; *m Yoma* 8:6). [*sabbaton*]

2:26 The sacred bread (*tous artous tēs protheseōs*)—Literally, the phrase means "the loaves of presentation" (BAGD, 706; BDAG, 869), and it refers to 12 loaves of bread that were placed on a table in the holy place of the tabernacle as an offering to the Lord. Every Sabbath, 12 fresh loaves were presented to God, and the old ones were removed and given to the priests to eat (Lev. 24:5-9; cf. Exod. 25:30; Num. 4:7). [*artos + prothesis*]

3:1 Withered (*exērammenēn*)—Mark uses a verb which literally means "to be dried up"

but which in this context carries a more figurative sense and indicates some form of paralysis (P. J. Budd, *NIDNTT* 1:515-16). Therefore, this series of conflict stories, stretching from Mark 2:1 to 3:6, begins and ends with Jesus healing a paralyzed man. In addition, Jesus responds in both situations to a silent objection from the religious leaders with a question. "What is easier, to say to the paralyzed man, 'Your sins are forgiven' or to say, 'Arise and take up your mat and walk?'" (2:9). "Is it lawful on the Sabbath to do good or to do wrong, to save a life or to kill?" (3:4). In the initial healing, Jesus confronts the religious leaders because of what they were reasoning in their *hearts* (2:6). In the later healing, he responds with anger and grief at their hardness of *heart* (3:5). [*xērainō*]

3:5 Hardness (*pōrōsei*)—The noun *pōrōsis* indicates a condition in which something has become hard or dull (BAGD, 732; BDAG, 900). The related verb *pōroō* could be used with the meaning "to become hard, to petrify, to form a callous" (LSJ, 1561). In Mark's Gospel, the noun appears only in 3:5, but the related verb occurs twice, in 6:52 and 8:17. In both verses that use the verb, the disciples are demonstrating their lack of understanding, an incomprehension that results from a hardened heart. In other words, hardness of heart in Mark reveals an intellectual problem more than a lack of compassion. Jesus grieves that the religious leaders are so close-minded, unable to understand or accept the truth. [*pōrōsis*]

3:6 Herodians (*Hērōdianōn*)—The Herodians were influential people who were partisans or political supporters of the Herodian dynasty and consequently of the Roman authority which stood behind it (H. W. Hoehner, *DJG* 325). At the time of Jesus, Galilee was under the rule of Herod Antipas (6:14-29; 8:15), the son of Herod the Great, the king who had died shortly after Jesus' birth. Although the Pharisees and the Herodians had little in common, they were willing to work together to oppose Jesus (3:6; 12:13-15), since the kingdom Jesus was introducing stood as a threat to both of them. [*Hērōdianoi*]

3:11 The Son of God (*ho huios tou theou*)—In the first half of Mark's Gospel, the recognition of Jesus' identity by spirit beings (1:24, 34; 3:11-12; 5:7) stands in contrast with human expressions of confusion concerning who Jesus is (1:27; 2:6-7; 4:41; 6:2-3, 14-16; 8:27-28). For more on Jesus as the Son of God, see 1:1. On unclean spirits, see 1:23. [*huios + theos*]

3:14 Twelve (*dōdeka*)—Mark mentions two purposes for which Jesus appointed the Twelve, in order that they might be with him and in order that he might send them out. Mark uses the title "the twelve" for the disciples especially when he is emphasizing their close relationship with Jesus. The 12 withdraw with Jesus and receive instruction from him that is unavailable to the wider public (4:10; 9:35; 10:32; 11:11; 14:17). The tragedy of Judas is that the betrayer was one of the Twelve, one from among the close associates of Jesus (14:10, 20, 43). Mark also uses "the twelve" in describing how Jesus sent the disciples out on a mission to preach repentance and to have authority over demons and sickness (6:7-13). [*dōdeka*]

3:17 Boanerges (*Boanērges*)—This name apparently is a combination of Hebrew or Aramaic words transliterated into Greek, but the question of which Hebrew or Aramaic words lie behind *Boanerges* has never received a satisfactory answer. Mark translates the word as "sons of thunder," a name that probably characterizes the brothers as hot-tempered, prone to outbursts of anger (Marcus, 269; Lane, 135; cf. 9:38; Luke 9:54). In the list of the twelve disciples, the first three (Peter, James, and John)

receive special names from Jesus and then later in the narrative a unique place in his ministry (5:37; 9:2; 14:33; cf. 13:3). [*Boanērges*]

3:19 Betrayed (*paredōken*)—The verb *paradidōmi* commonly occurs in the Gospels with the meaning "to hand over" or "to deliver up" someone to judgment and death (H. Beck, *NIDNTT* 2:368; MM, 482-83). On several occasions, Mark describes Judas as handing Jesus over to the religious authorities who intend to bring about his death (3:19; 14:10, 11, 18, 21, 41-44; cf. 9:31; 10:33). As a treacherous act done by a close follower of Jesus, this handing over was a betrayal (Spicq, 3:21-22). One difficulty, however, with using "betrayed" for Judas's action is that it obscures possible parallels within Mark's Gospel, since the same verb appears in connection with other events such as John the Baptist's arrest (1:14) and the persecution of believers (13:9, 11-12). In addition, Judas is not alone in delivering up Jesus. The religious authorities hand Jesus over to Pilate (15:1, 10), who hands Jesus over to the soldiers for execution (15:15). [*paradidōmi*]

3:21 His relatives (*hoi par' autou*)—Translations such as "his own people," (NASB), "his family" (NIV; NRSV), and "his relatives" (Marcus, 269-70) are all attempts to express the meaning of the phrase "those from him." The most reasonable assumption from the context is that the phrase refers to the same people mentioned later in 3:31 who come to the house where Jesus is teaching and call for him, in other words, to Jesus' mother and his brothers. In the LXX and other writings of the Hellenistic period, the phrase can point to someone's family or relatives (e.g., Prov.. 31:21; Sus 33; Josephus, *Ant.* 1.10.5 § 93; MM, 479; cf. Taylor, 236-37). Members of Jesus' own family worried that he had lost his mind. In Mark's narrative, the controversies of Mark 2:1–3:6 seem to be the cause for concern. [para]

3:22 Beelzebul (*Beelzeboul*)—The term "Beelzebul" apparently originated as a name for the Canaanite god Baal, meaning "lord of the household" (Marcus, 272). This same name may stand behind the reference to Baal-zebub, the god of Ekron, mentioned in 2 Kings 1:2-6, since the name Baal-zebub ("lord of the flies") appears to be a deliberate distortion of the real name, used to ridicule the pagan god. In Mark's Gospel, "Beelzebul" serves as an alternate name for Satan, the ruler of the demons (3:22-23). On Satan, see 1:13. At the time, various names were given to Satan, including "Asmodeus" (e.g., Tob 3:8), "Beliar" or "Belial" (e.g., *Jub* 1:20; 2 Cor. 6:15), and "Mastema" (e.g., *Jub* 10:8), and apparently "Beelzebul" was another such name. [*Beelzeboul*]

3:23 Parables (*parabolais*)—Mark uses "parables" in this context for proverbial speech and allegorical comparisons (Lane, 142). For more on parables, see 4:2. [*parabolē*]

3:28 Truly (*amēn*)—Mark 3:28 provides the first of 13 instances in Mark of the introductory formula, "truly, I say to you." The Gospel of Mark includes the word "truly" (literally, "amen") only in Jesus' sayings. Jesus begins with "amen" and then expresses his knowledge of the future (e.g., 9:1; 14:9, 30) or his supernatural insight into a recent event (12:43). Normally, "amen" is used to affirm the truth of another person's statement (e.g., Deut. 27:15-26; 1 Chr 16:36; Jer. 11:5; 1 Cor. 14:16). In some churches today, members of the congregation use the word in a similar way when they say "amen" to acknowledge and embrace the truth of the pastor's message. By way of contrast, Jesus introduces his sayings with "amen." He endorses his own words and affirms their reliability and truth even before

he says them (cf. H. Schlier, *TDNT* 1:335-38; Lane, 144). [*amēn*]

3:29 Eternal sin (*aiōniou hamartēmatos*)—The phrase "will never have forgiveness" helps to define what Jesus meant by an eternal sin. It is a rejection of God's ways that is so serious and so final as to have permanent consequences (Gundry, 177). The truth of God's work in Jesus revealed itself clearly through the Holy Spirit's authenticating power. Like at no other time in history, the bright light of God's revelation confronted people through the Spirit's work in Jesus. Whoever could look at this light and call it darkness, whoever could actually observe Jesus' works and call them Satan's works was in danger of making a complete and final rejection of God's offer of salvation in Jesus. Mark never directly states that the scribes had indeed committed this eternal sin, but Jesus definitely was warning them of the peril in which they stood (Taylor, 244). Mark 3:29-30 includes several other words that have already been discussed: blaspheme (see 2:7), Holy Spirit (see 1:8), forgiveness (see 1:4), and unclean spirit (see 1:23). [*hamartēma + aiōnios*]

3:35 The will of God (*to thelēma tou theou*)—In this verse, "the will of God" is simply what God wants people to do (BAGD, 354; BDAG, 447), but this passage by itself does little to clarify the content of God's demands. The noun *thelēma* occurs only once in Mark's Gospel, here in 3:35. The related verb *thelō* appears 25 times in Mark, but only once in connection with God's will (14:36). In Gethsemane, Jesus reveals further the nature of God's will when he submits to his Father's plan concerning the hour of suffering (14:35-36). When God's will involves suffering, the follower of Jesus says to God, "Not what I want, but what you want." [*thelēma + theos*]

4:1 Boat (*ploion*)—A boat on the Sea of Galilee

would have been a relatively small fishing vessel, propelled by oars, though perhaps also by a sail (cf. 1:16-20; 6:48; BAGD, 673; BDAG, 831; R. Kratz, *EDNT* 3:113). Beginning in 4:1 and ending in 8:22, Jesus is in and out of a boat a number of times, traveling back and forth across the Sea of Galilee. These references to Jesus' boat journeys across the Sea of Galilee help to set apart chapters 4–8 as a distinct unit within the overall narrative. In Mark 4–8, three prominent scenes take place in which Jesus is with his disciples in the boat on the Sea of Galilee: the stilling of the storm (4:35-41), the walking on the water (6:45-52), and the conversation concerning leaven (8:14-21). In each of these passages, either Jesus or Mark himself criticizes the disciples for their lack of faith and understanding (4:40; 6:52; 8:17-18). [*ploion*]

4:2 Parables (*parabolais*)—In the Synoptic Gospels, "parables" refer to illustrations of varying lengths used by Jesus, when teaching, to express his message through comparisons or similes (BAGD, 612; BDAG, 759). Jesus draws these illustrations from the daily world of his audience, using observations concerning nature and common social relationships (F. Hauck, *TDNT* 5:752). His parables present typical, ordinary events such as the planting of seeds (4:1-9), as well as exceptional situations such as the revolt of renters who would rather kill the owner's messengers than pay their rent (12:1-12). In Mark's Gospel, Jesus teaches with parables most often in public settings, directing them to the crowds or his opponents. Later, in private, Jesus explains his parables to his disciples and to others who are prepared to follow him (4:10-12; 33-34; 7:17-23). [*parabolē*]

4:10 Those around him (*hoi peri auton*)—The immediately preceding context of Mark's Gospel serves to clarify the identity of the group referred to as "those around him" (*hoi peri auton*). Mark 3:31-35 makes note of a crowd that is sitting around Jesus (3:32: *peri auton*). Jesus looks at those around him (3:34: *peri auton*) and refers to them as his family because they are doing God's will. Although the scene and the audience changes in chapter 4, the motif remains the same. The group of people who hear Jesus' private instructions concerning the parables includes both the twelve disciples and others around him. Those "others" listen to Jesus' public teaching and stay after the rest of the crowd in order to learn more, because they are receptive to God's will (Guelich, 204). On the Twelve, see 3:14. [*peri*]

4:11 Secret (*mystērion*)—The word translated here as "secret" (NIV; NRSV; NLT) or "mystery" (KJV; NASB) refers to the revealed thoughts and plans of God. They are mysterious in the sense that they are too profound for human ingenuity, and they are secretive in the sense that they were at one time hidden but are now revealed by Jesus and available to all who have ears to hear (BAGD, 530; BDAG, 662; Cranfield, 152-53). The term *mystērion* occurs only this one time in Mark's Gospel. It appears more frequently in Paul's epistles where it describes divine wisdom that goes beyond human understanding (Rom. 11:25; 1 Cor. 2:6-9) and the previously hidden thoughts of God that are now being made known (Rom. 16:25-26; Eph. 3:4-5, 9-10; Col. 1:26-27). On the kingdom of God, see 1:15. [*mystērion*]

To those who are outside (*ekeinois . . . tois exō*)—After speaking to a large crowd in 4:2-9, Jesus meets with a smaller group consisting of his disciples and others who stay to learn more from him. The group referred to as "those who are outside" seems, therefore, to include those who have just been left behind, that is, the people in the crowd who have listened to Jesus but have shown no further interest in what he has to say. In addition, the reference to "outside" is reminiscent of the preceding passage in Mark's Gospel (Guelich, 208; Marcus, 299). Mark labels Jesus' relatives who question his sanity as those who are outside (3:31-32: *exō*) in contrast to those who are around Jesus (3:32, 34: *peri auton*). Inserted within this account concerning Jesus' relatives (3:20-21, 31-35) is Jesus' response to the scribes' charge that he is empowered by Satan (3:22-30). Jesus speaks to the scribes in parables (3:23), in other words, in a manner of teaching that is appropriate for outsiders (4:11). Therefore, those who reject Jesus as out of his mind or under Satan's control take their place among "those who are outside" along with the unreceptive members of the crowd. [*exō*]

4:12 In order that (*hina*)—The conjunction *hina* commonly introduces a purpose clause (Wallace, *Greek Grammar* 676), and it functions in this way repeatedly in Mark's Gospel (e.g., 1:38; 2:10; 3:14; 7:9; 10:13; 12:2; 14:10; 16:1). No solid reason exists for rejecting this use of *hina* in 4:12, even though the resulting sense indicates a severe judgment against those who are outside (Cranfield, 155-58; Gundry, 198, 202; Marcus, 299-300). After all, the promise that the secret of the kingdom of God has been given to some implies that it has not been given to others (4:11). Jesus teaches in parables in order that some may remain in their blindness and therefore not turn to God for forgiveness. Jesus directs this judgment toward those who are outside, that is, to those who have already rejected him and his message. Jesus' intention is to keep them in their spiritual blindness and therefore to ratify a process that they themselves have already initiated. [*hina*]

While hearing (*akouontes*)—The use of the verb *akouō* in this verse points to physically hearing a message without understanding. Its use here contrasts with the use of the same verb at the beginning and end of the preced-

ing parable (4:3, 9). Jesus starts and ends the parable of the soils with a command to hear, but this is a call both to listen and to understand the parable's significance (BDAG, 38; Marcus, 300-301). According to 4:12, those who reject Jesus are able to physically see his works and hear his teaching, but their perceptions never move them beyond a superficial insight into his identity and message. This description of Jesus' opponents fits with their characterization in the broader narrative. They see and hear Jesus, but their response is to condemn him and seek his death (2:16; 3:2; 7:2-5; 11:18; 14:58, 64). They demonstrate a shallow level of understanding when Jesus speaks to them in parables, since their understanding only makes them want to arrest him (12:1, 12). [*akouō*]

4:14 The word (*ton logon*)—Elsewhere in his Gospel, Mark makes reference to "the word," without any other qualification, for the public message of Jesus (2:2; 4:33). In this way, "the word" is similar to "the Gospel of God," another expression that Mark uses for Jesus' general proclamation (1:14). In other NT writings as well, "the word" occurs without any other modification to indicate the Christian message proclaimed in a public setting (e.g., Acts 8:4; 14:25; 17:11; 18:5; Col. 4:3; 1 Thess.. 1:6; 2 Tim. 4:2; 1 Pet. 3:1; cf. BAGD, 478; BDAG, 599-600). [*logos*]

4:17 Temporary (*proskairoi*)—The opposite of *proskairos*, which means "lasting only for a time" or "temporary," is *aiōnios*, "eternal" (BAGD, 715; BDAG, 880-81). For example, Paul contrasts the visible and temporary with the invisible and eternal in 2 Cor. 4:18 (cf. 4 Macc. 15:2-3; *Jos. Asen.* 12:12). Mark's Gospel also notes the difference between "this time" and "the coming age," in which those who follow Jesus receive eternal life (10:30). In his interpretation of the parable of the soils, Jesus is making a contrast between those who hear and understand and those who listen without true comprehension. Some may appear to hear in more than a superficial manner but in reality they do not understand, and so when persecution comes they fall away. Since they last only for a time, they will neither receive eternal life nor participate in the coming age. [*proskairos*]

Fall away (*skandalizontai*)—The verb *skandalizō* occurs only in the LXX, the NT, and other Jewish and Christian literature influenced by the Bible. Often the verb means "to cause to sin," with the sin consisting of a failure to obey or to believe (BAGD, 752; BDAG, 926; cf. 9:42, 43, 45 47). In 4:17, the passive form of the verb appears and indicates some people allow themselves to be led astray into sin and unbelief in the midst of persecution or, in other words, they fall away from following Jesus (cf. 14:27, 29). The verb can also be used for causing offense as in 6:3, where Jesus disturbs and offends the people of his hometown. [*skandalizō*]

4:19 Worries (*merimnai*)—The noun *merimna* appears only this one time in Mark's Gospel, although a related verb *promerimnaō* occurs in Mark 13:11. Elsewhere in Jesus' teaching, "worry" is an anxious fear about material needs, inappropriately monopolizing the heart's concern (J. Goetzmann, *NIDNTT* 1:276-77; D. Zeller, *EDNT* 2:408; cf. Matt. 6:25-34; Luke 12:22-31; 21:34). Therefore, the worries of this age, the cares that can choke out the word, involve a preoccupation with what we will eat and drink and with what we will wear for clothing. [*merimna*]

4:21 Bushel (*modion*)—Like the word "bushel" (KJV; RSV), *modios* can refer either to a unit of dry measure (in this case, about two gallons) or to the container that holds that amount (Guelich, 226). A lamp belongs in a place where it can provide light and certainly not underneath a container. [*modios*]

4:26 The kingdom of God (*hē basileia tou theou*)—In Mark 4:1-34, Jesus presents a series of parables that describe the secret of the kingdom of God (cf. 4:11, 26, 30). The parable of the growing seed (4:26-29), a passage found only in Mark's Gospel, teaches that the growth of the kingdom cannot be explained in terms of human effort or ingenuity. For more on the kingdom of God, see 1:15. [*basileia*]

4:31 Mustard seed (*kokkō sinapeōs*)—The small size of the mustard seed among all seeds of garden plants was proverbial (cf. Matt. 17:20; Luke 17:6). For example, one saying in the Mishnah indicates that even the slightest amount of uncleanness defiles, "even though it be like to a grain of mustard" (*m Nid* 5:2). The contrast between the size of the mustard seed and the full-grown mustard plant is dramatic, since in that region the plant grows to a height of 10-12 feet (C. H. Hunzinger, *TDNT* 7:288). The future size of the kingdom of God will stand in sharp contrast to its apparently insignificant beginnings in Jesus' ministry among his followers. [*sinapi* + *kokkos*]

4:39 Be still (*pephimōso*)—Literally, the verb *phimoō* means "to shut a mouth with a muzzle" (e.g., Deut. 25:4 LXX; 1 Tim. 5:18), but the use in Mark 4:39, as in other places in the NT, is figurative, meaning "to silence" (BAGD, 861-62; BDAG, 1060; Cf. Matt. 22:12, 34; Luke 4:35; 1 Pet. 2:15). Jesus' command to the sea is reminiscent of his earlier rebuke to the demon-possessed man in Mark 1:25, since the same verb appears in both commands, except with a change in the verb tense. The perfect passive imperative form in 4:39 ("be silent and remain so") is more rare and more emphatic than the aorist passive imperative form in 1:25 (Cranfield, 174; BDF, 177). [*phimoō*]

4:40 Timid (*deiloi*)—The adjective *deilos* describes someone as cowardly or fearful, as having a lack of courage in the face of danger (Spicq, 1:300-302; cf. Deut. 20:8; Judg. 7:3; 1 Macc. 3:56; Josephus, *JW* 3.8.5 § 365). The disciples' fearful attitude grew out of their lack of trust in Jesus, in his care and power. Fear also stands in contrast to faith in Jesus and his provision elsewhere in Mark's Gospel (5:15-17, 36; 6:49-52; 11:18). On faith, see 2:5. [*deilos*]

5:1 Gerasenes (*Gerasēnōn*)—Some confusion exists as to the exact location of the demoniac's healing. The oldest manuscripts of Mark's Gospel read "Gerasenes," while other manuscripts have "Gadarenes" (see also Matt. 8:28) and still others "Gergesenes." Apparently, Mark's Gospel originally referred to the region of the "Gerasenes," indicating that the event took place in the area around Gerasa. Mark may have written with reference to a little-known town named Gerasa on the eastern shore of the Sea of Galilee, which corresponds to the modern site known as Kersa (Cranfield, 176; Lane, 181). The more well-known city of Gerasa, one of the prominent cities of the Decapolis, was some 30 miles away from the Sea of Galilee and as such was an unlikely location for the demoniac's healing. Matthew perhaps sought to clarify the location by referring to the region around the city of Gadara, an important city about six miles southeast of the Sea of Galilee (Matt. 8:28). The main point is that by crossing over to the other side of the sea Jesus has entered Gentile territory. [*Gerasēnos*]

5:3 No one . . . not any longer, not even (*oude . . . ouketi oudeis*)—In Greek, it is possible to combine several negatives for the sake of emphasis (BDF, 223; Robertson, *Grammar* 1164-65). Literally, Mark wrote, "No one was able to bind him, not any longer, not even with a chain." Mark's strong language concerning the demoniac's uncontrollable power is difficult to express clearly in English. The KJV comes close to Mark's emphasis: "no man could bind him, no, not with chains." [*oude, ouketi, oudeis*]

5:7 Son of the Most High God (*huie tou theou tou hypsistou*)—The title "Most High" commonly appears in the LXX when non-Israelites use it to refer to the God of Israel, acknowledging his superiority and authority over heaven and earth (Gen. 14:18-20; Num. 24:16; Isa. 14:14; Dan. 3:26; 4:2 [3:32 LXX]; cf. also 1 Esdr 2:3; 6:31; 8:19, 21; 2 Macc. 3:31; 3 Macc. 7:9). The use of the title by the demon-possessed man highlights his status as a Gentile. A similar use of "Most High" occurs in the words of the possessed servant girl in Acts 16:17. On Jesus as the Son of God, see 1:1. [*hypsistos*]

Do not torment (*mē . . . basanisēs*)—This verb is used sometimes in a narrow sense of torturing prisoners for the sake of interrogation or punishment (BAGD, 134; BDAG, 168; MM, 104). The related noun *basanistēs* carries this more narrow meaning in Matt. 18:34. However, the verb *basanizō* also expresses a general sense, especially in the NT, of "to torment, to cause severe distress or intense physical pain" (Matt. 8:6; Rev. 9:5; 12:2; cf. BAGD, 134; BDAG, 168; W. Mundle, *NIDNTT* 3:856). The possessed man under the influence of unclean spirits begs Jesus not to torment him. The irony of the request is that the man is already living under constant torment. In Mark's Gospel, demons take possession of individuals not to entice them to evil but to inflict pain, distress, and ultimately destruction on their victims (1:26; 5:5; 9:17-18, 20-22, 26). [*basanizō*]

5:9 Legion (*Legiōn*)—The name given by the demoniac is a military term for the largest unit of troops in the Roman army. In the 1st century A.D., a legion at full strength consisted of approximately 6,000 soldiers, and 25 legions formed the core of the Roman army (F. Annen,

EDNT 2:345-46; BAGD, 468; BDAG, 588). The name Legion expresses the large number of demons that inhabit the man, as well as indicating their power and violence. The destruction of approximately 2,000 pigs later in the story once again suggests Jesus' power over a great number of demons (5:13). The use of a single name for many demons implies that although a host of unclean spirits lived in the man, they worked together as one combined force to torment him. On unclean spirits, see 1:23. [*legiōn*]

5:18 In order that he might be with him (*hina met' autou ē*)—The wording of the man's request to be with Jesus corresponds to the expression in Mark 3:14 concerning the 12 disciples. There Jesus appoints the Twelve in order that they might be with him (*hina ōsin met' autou*). Compare also Mark 5:40, where the phrase "those with him" (*tous met' autou*) refers to Peter, James, and John. The implication of the man's request is not simply that he wants to "accompany" Jesus (NASB); he wants to become a disciple and to join the circle of the Twelve (Guelich, 284-85). [*meta*]

5:19 To your family (*pros tous sous*)—Jesus commands the healed man, "Depart to your (*sou*) house" and then also adds "to those who are yours (*sous*)." The proximity of the possessive adjective *sous* to the possessive pronoun *sou* in 5:19 points to a strong relationship between the house that belongs to him and the people to whom he should report his healing. Jesus wants the man to speak to his family, to those who live in his house, so that the NIV translates this phrase properly as "to your family." This corresponds to the common usage of *sos* ("yours") with the article in the papyri to indicate a person's household, agent or friend (MM 581). The healed man proclaims the message not only to his family but more widely, throughout

the region of the Decapolis. [*sos*]

5:22 One of the synagogue rulers (*heis tōn archisynagōgōn*)—A synagogue ruler was an elected official, whose primary responsibilities involved the supervision of the synagogue building and the organization of the synagogue worship services. In the 1st century A.D., no one individual conducted the synagogue worship service by reading Scripture, offering the public prayer, and preaching. The synagogue ruler arranged for congregational members themselves to share these tasks (W. Schrage, *TDNT* 7:844-47; Schürer, *History* 2:433-36). On the nature of the synagogue, see 1:21. Synagogue rulers were held in high esteem, so that Jairus would have been a man of high standing in his community. For references in the NT to synagogue rulers other than Jairus, see Luke 13:14; Acts 13:15; 18:8, 17. [*archisynagōgos*]

5:25 With a hemorrhage (*en rhysei haimatos*)—The woman's ailment was a chronic condition of vaginal bleeding that had lasted for 12 years. Mark's expression that the woman had "a flow of blood" draws on language found in Lev. 15:25 LXX for a condition that rendered a woman ceremonially unclean. In addition, Mark's later reference to "the fountain of her blood" in 5:29 depends on the terminology in Lev. 12:7 LXX, another passage describing ceremonial uncleanness for women. The woman's condition would have made it nearly impossible for her to maintain her participation in the religious community or normal social relationships, because she would be a source of defilement to anyone who had physical contact with her (Marcus, 357-58, 366-68). The woman's ceremonial uncleanness places her in stark contrast to Jairus, the synagogue ruler. [*rhysis* + *haima*]

5:29 Affliction (*mastigos*)—Literally, the word refers to "a whip" (BAGD, 495; BDAG, 620;

Spicq, 2:453-56), a meaning found in Acts 22:24 where Paul faces possible interrogation with a whip and in Heb. 11:36 where scourging with whips appears as one of the trials endured by people of faith. Mark uses the related verb *mastigoō* for the scourging of Jesus (10:34). In addition to this literal sense, the word can also have a figurative meaning as it does in Mark 3:10; 5:29, 34, where it refers to a severe and distressing illness (BAGD, 495; BDAG, 620-21; C. Schneider, *TDNT* 4:518-19). The English word "scourge" is similar in that it can be used literally for a whip and figuratively for a harsh affliction. [*mastix*]

5:30 Power (*dynamin*)—This is the first of 10 uses of the word *dynamis* in Mark's Gospel. It occurs with a variety of meanings in Mark (O. Betz, *NIDNTT* 2:603-4). Power is an attribute of God (12:24) as well as a reverential circumlocution for his name (14:62), a fitting substitution since everything is possible for God (10:27; 14:36). In his eschatological discourse, Jesus refers to the defeat of the "powers" or demonic beings in the supernatural realm (13:25; cf. Rom. 8:38; Eph. 1:21; 1 Pet. 3:22). The Son of Man's coming at the end of the age takes place with power, that is, with an overwhelming display of force (13:26; cf. 9:1). Finally, Mark uses *dynamis* within the context of miracle stories for powerful miraculous events (6:2, 5; 9:39) and for the ability to perform miracles (5:30; 6:14). The reference to power in Mark 5:30 is somewhat unusual in that it describes Jesus' power not only as an ability to work miracles but also as a force that goes out to bring healing to the hemorrhaging woman. The healing apparently takes place apart from any choice on Jesus' part. Yet, in the context of Mark's Gospel, this healing takes place within the context of God's will. God knows this woman and chooses to honor her faith through the power at work in Jesus (Cranfield, 185). [*dynamis*]

5:34 Daughter (*thygatēr*)—In the OT and later Jewish writings, "Daughter" serves as a respectful and affectionate way to address a woman regardless of age or family relationship (e.g., Ruth 2:8; 3:10-11; cf. Marcus, 360; H.-J. Ritz, EDNT 2:159). Jesus' use of "daughter" takes on added significance in this context, because it provides a connecting link to the story of Jairus's daughter (5:23, 35). Jairus's concern for his own daughter becomes a picture of Jesus' attitude toward this suffering woman. [*thygatēr*]

Has made you well (*sesōken se*)—The verb *sōzō* can mean to save from physical danger and disease or to save from eternal judgment (BAGD, 798; BDAG, 982-83). The idea of eternal salvation appears in Mark 10:26, where "being saved" is parallel to "inheriting eternal life" (10:17, 30) and "entering the kingdom of God" (10:23-25). However, the meaning of deliverance from disease is primary in Mark 5:34, where "being saved" is parallel to "being healed from affliction" (cf. 5:23, 28; Guelich, 299). Her faith, expressed in her initiative to touch Jesus' garment, leads to her healing. On faith, see 2:5. [*sōzō*]

5:36 Overhearing (*parakousas*)—English translations are divided over whether Jesus was "overhearing" the report to Jairus concerning his daughter's death (NASB; NRSV) or "ignoring" it (RSV; NIV; NLT; NET). Although either meaning is possible (BAGD, 619; BDAG, 767), Luke's account of the same event supports the idea that Jesus overheard the report (Luke 8:50), and it seems reasonable to follow Luke's guidance on this point (Cranfield, 187). [*parakouō*]

5:39 Sleeping (*katheudei*)—The underlying sense of Jesus' statement is that the girl is not irrevocably dead, since, in light of his presence, her condition is only temporary like sleep (Gundry, 273-74). The NT uses two different verbs for sleep, *katheudō* and *koimaō* (L. Coenen, *NIDNTT* 1:442-43). The verb *katheudō* appears 22 times in the NT (8 of those instances in Mark), most often as a reference to natural sleep and perhaps only in 1 Thess.. 5:10 as a metaphor for death. By way of contrast, the verb *koimaō* appears 18 times in the NT, most often as a euphemism for death and much less frequently as a reference to natural sleep (Matt. 28:13; Luke 22:45; John 11:12; Acts 12:6). In Mark 5:39, Jesus' statement uses the verb *katheudō*, the term more commonly used for natural sleep. In the Bible, sleep is a frequent metaphor for death, but Mark expresses Jesus' statement in a way that could easily be misinterpreted as indicating that the girl was literally asleep. The mourners take Jesus' words in this literal sense and scoff at him. [*katheudō*]

5:42 Twelve years (*etōn dōdeka*)—The reference to the girl's age provides another point of contact with the story of the hemorrhaging woman who endured her affliction for 12 years (5:25; cf. Guelich, 303). Jairus's need is urgent, since his daughter is at the point of death (5:23); the woman's need has been long-standing, since her suffering has covered the entire life-span of the girl. Jesus is sufficient in both situations. [*dōdeka + etos*]

6:1 Hometown (*patrida*)—Luke is more explicit about identifying Nazareth as Jesus' hometown, the place where he was brought up (Luke 4:16, 23-24). In 6:1, Mark only makes reference to Jesus' hometown, although earlier he states that Jesus came from Nazareth (1:9, 24). The close relationship between the word for "hometown" (*patris*) and that for "father" (*patēr*) conveys the idea that a hometown is the place of one's father or forefathers. Yet, when the townspeople refer to Jesus, they identify him as Mary's son, mentioning his mother rather than his father. The people of Nazareth stumble over Jesus' familiarity, and

perhaps they point to Mary because she was more well-known to them (Guelich, 309-10; Gundry, 290-91). On Jesus' teaching in the synagogue on the Sabbath, see 1:21 and 2:24. Concerning the reference to miracles in 6:2, 5, see the discussion on power in 5:30. [*patris*]

6:3 Carpenter (*tektōn*)—The word *tektōn* refers to a builder, especially one who works with wood, that is, a carpenter (BAGD, 809; BDAG, 995; MM, 628-29). According to Matt. 13:55, Jesus was also "the son of the carpenter." Probably both Jesus and Joseph were builders or carpenters, since in Jewish society one of a father's duties was to teach his son a trade (*t Qidd.* 1:11). For more on the verb used to express Jesus' act of offending the townspeople (*skandalizō*), see the reference to "fall away" in 4:17. [*tektōn*]

6:6 Unbelief (*apistian*)—The negative word "unbelief" is largely dependent on the positive term "faith." On faith, see 2:5. In Mark's Gospel, the opposite of faith is a rejection of Jesus' authority and a lack of trust in God's power at work in him. The unbelief of the people of Nazareth expresses itself in a refusal to acknowledge Jesus' supernatural authority, and it results in an unwillingness to seek after his miraculous power to meet their needs (G. Barth, *EDNT* 1:121-23). In a similar way, the wavering faith and persistent unbelief on the part of the man with the demon-possessed boy make it more difficult for him to ask for Jesus' help with any confidence (9:19, 22-24). [*apistia*]

6:7 Authority (*exousian*)—Just as Jesus' public ministry begins in Mark with a display of his authoritative control over unclean spirits (1:21-27), so also the Twelve's initial mission includes a demonstration of this same authority (6:7, 12-13; cf. Guelich, 321). On authority, see 1:22. Other key words in 6:7-13 which have already received comment include: the

Twelve (3:14), unclean spirits (1:23), testimony (1:44), preach (1:38), and repent (1:4). [*exousia*]

6:8 Money (*chalkon*)—Jesus prohibits his disciples from taking provisions normally brought along on a journey. Among the prohibited items was money or, more specifically, "copper coins" (*chalkos*) which were commonly carried in a belt and were much less valuable than gold or silver coins (cf. Matt. 10:9). In other words, Jesus forbids them to take along even "small change" (BAGD, 875; BDAG, 1076). Without bread or a bag for supplies or money, and with only the clothes on their backs, the disciples are totally dependent on God to provide them with food and shelter (Lane, 207-8). [*chalkos*]

6:11 Shake off (*ektinaxate*)—The verb *ektinassō* appears only four times in the NT. It is always in the context of God's messengers symbolically shaking off dust from their feet or their clothes in the presence of those who reject their message (Matt. 10:14; Mark 6:11; Acts 13:51; 18:6; cf. Neh. 5:13). The action symbolizes a desire to break off all association with someone (Marcus, 384). It leads to a warning about God's coming judgment toward those who refuse to believe. They have heard the message, and now they bear the responsibility for the consequences of their response (cf. Acts 18:6). [*ektinassō*]

6:14 King (*basileus*)—"King Herod" was Herod Antipas who ruled over Galilee and also Perea, a region on the east side of the Jordan river, after the death of his father, Herod the Great. Under the authority of Rome, Herod Antipas governed these territories where both John the Baptist and Jesus concentrated their ministries. Mark's Gospel uses the title "king" for Herod Antipas (6:14, 22, 25, 26, 27), even though his official title was "tetrarch," a position of lower rank. In Luke's writings, the title is always "tetrarch"

(Luke 3:19; 9:7; Acts 13:1; cf. Luke 3:1), while Matthew's Gospel includes both "king" and "tetrarch" (Matt. 14:1, 9). Mark apparently used the popular terminology of his day by calling Herod "king," a custom that the ruler may have done little to discourage (Hoehner, *Herod Antipas* 149-50). In contrast to this royal designation, Herod behaved in Mark 6:14-29 not like a king but like a slave to his passions. In A.D. 39, Herod went to Rome at the insistence of his wife Herodias to ask the emperor to receive the title of "king" officially, an act which eventually led to his downfall and banishment (H. W. Hoehner, *DJG* 322-25). [*basileus*]

6:17 Wife (*gynaika*)—Herod Antipas's family relationships were particularly complicated since his father, Herod the Great, had ten wives and numerous offspring, many of whom intermarried with one another. Herodias, Herod the Great's granddaughter, was at first married to Herod Philip (not the same Philip mentioned in Luke 3:1), who was one of Herod the Great's sons and therefore her uncle and Herod Antipas's half brother (H. W. Hoehner, *DJG* 323-24; cf. Josephus, *Ant.* 18.5.1 § 109). While visiting his brother, Herod Antipas fell in love with his niece Herodias who agreed to marry him provided that he divorce his first wife (Josephus, *Ant.* 18.5.1 § 109-10). John the Baptist boldly denounced Herod Antipas's marriage to the wife of his brother. [*gynē*]

6:18 Not lawful (*ouk exestin*)—The verb *exestin* with the negative occurs elsewhere in the NT to designate what was forbidden in the Law of Moses (e.g., Matt. 27:6; Mark 2:24, 26; John 5:10). The Mosaic Law prohibited a man from marrying his brother's wife (Lev. 18:16; 20:21), except when a brother died without leaving any children (Deut. 25:5-10; Mark 12:19). The exception obviously did not apply in this case since Herodias's first husband was still alive. Josephus probably gave the general public's opinion when he commented with disdain that Herodias repudiated the Jewish people's ways by leaving her husband, especially after the birth of their daughter (Ant. 18.5.4 § 136). [*exestin*]

6:21 Important government officials (*megistasin*)—Included among the guests at Herod's banquet were important government officials, literally "the great ones" (MM 393; Hoehner, *Herod Antipas* 102). The title *megistanes* appears in a similar context, in Dan. 5:23 LXX, for the 1,000 nobles invited to the great feast of Belshazzar the king. [*megistan*]

Military commanders (*chiliarchois*)—Next, Mark mentions the presence of *chiliarchoi*, which literally means "those who lead a thousand soldiers." However, the title also occurs more generally for high-ranking military officers, that is, commanders who were roughly equivalent in rank to majors or colonels (BAGD, 881-82; BDAG, 1084). [*chiliarchos*]

The leading men of Galilee (*prōtois tēs Galilaias*)—Finally, the guests at Herod's banquet included the leading men of Galilee, literally "the first ones of Galilee." They were the region's aristocracy (Hoehner, *Herod Antipas* 102; Marcus, 396). Jesus' teaching against a desire for prominence sheds light on Mark's own attitude toward such important citizens: the first will be last (10:31) and faithful disciples must strive to be last, to be slaves, in order to be first in reality (9:35; 10:44). The next passage after Herod's banquet is Jesus' banquet, the feeding of the 5,000 (6:30-44). By way of contrast, the guest list at this event included those who wanted to hear Jesus' teaching, those upon whom Jesus had compassion because they were like sheep without a shepherd (6:34). [*prōtos*]

6:22 Pleased (*ēresen*)—The verb *areskō* describes an action as pleasing or satisfying

(LSJ, 238). In certain passages in the Septuagint, the word takes on connotations of arousing or satisfying sexual interest (Gen. 19:8; Esth. 2:4, 9; Job 31:10; cf. Jdt. 12:14). A similar meaning here is suggested by the make-up of the audience at Herod's banquet and by the king's excessive promise (Marcus, 396). The similarity between Mark 6:22 and Esth. 2:9 is particularly close, since both verses refer to a young woman (*korasion*) pleasing (*ēresen*) a king who promises to give her up to half of his kingdom (Esth. 5:3; Mark 6:23). [*areskō*]

6:27 One of his body guards (*spekoulatora*)—The term *spekoulatōr* does not denote an official executioner but rather a member of a group of body guards who could be called on to do all sorts of "dirty business" for the ruler, including executions (Marcus, 397; Spicq, 3:157-59; cf. Tacitus, *Hist.* 1.24-25, 2.11; Seneca, *Ben.* 3.25; Seneca, *Ira* 1.18.4). [*spekoulatōr*]

6:34 He felt compassion (*esplanchnisthē*)—The verb *splanchnizomai* occurs 12 times in the NT, with all of these uses in the Synoptic Gospels. The related noun *splanchnon* appears 11 times in the NT, with only one occurrence in the Synoptic Gospels (Luke 1:78). In Mark, the verb refers exclusively to the deep feelings of pity that Jesus has for needy people, a heart response that causes him to act on their behalf (1:41; 6:34; 8:2; 9:22). The use of *splanchnizomai* for Jesus' attitude belongs to the portrait of Jesus in Matthew and Luke as well (Matt. 9:36; 14:14; 15:32; 20:34; Luke 7:13). In addition, feelings of compassion influence human characters at important turning points in three of Jesus' parables (cf. H.-H. Esser, *NIDNTT* 2:599). Moved by compassion, the master forgives a slave who cannot repay his debt (Matt. 18:27), the good Samaritan stops to help the man at the roadside (Luke 10:33), and the father runs to welcome his prodigal son home (Luke 15:20). [*splanchnizomai*]

6:37 Denarii (*dēnariōn*)—The denarius was the standard silver coin during Jesus' time and, according to Matt. 20:2, was an acceptable daily wage for a laborer (B. Schwank, *EDNT* 1:296). Therefore, the disciples estimated that it would take an average worker more than half a year to earn enough money to feed the large crowd. Later in Mark's Gospel, Jesus uses a denarius to explain the necessity both of paying taxes to Caesar and of giving devotion to God (12:15), and a woman anoints Jesus with an expensive perfume worth over 300 denarii, that is, close to a year's income (14:5). [*dēnarion*]

6:39 The green grass (*tō chlōrō chortō*)—A few verses earlier in 6:34, Mark describes the great crowd of people as "sheep without a shepherd." The background for this description lies in Num. 27:15-18, a passage in which Moses, at the end of his ministry, asks God to appoint another leader over the people so that they might not be like sheep without a shepherd. God answers this request by directing Moses to a man who has the Spirit, Joshua, or according to the LXX a man named *Iēsoun* (Jesus), the Greek equivalent to "Joshua" (Num. 27:17 LXX). The reference to "green grass" in Mark 6:39 serves to identify Jesus further as the one who will shepherd God's people (Guelich, 341; Marcus, 408). Jesus is the shepherd who makes his sheep lie down in green pastures and feeds them so that they will not be in want (Ps. 23:1-2; cf. Ezek. 34:23). [*chlōros* + *chortos*]

6:43 Baskets (*kophinōn*)—These baskets, which could be of various sizes, were especially associated with Jews (LSJ, 988; MM, 357). The Roman writer Juvenal twice refers to Jewish travelers as carrying this type of basket (*Sat.* 3.14; 6.542). Mark's mention of Jewish baskets fits the context of the feeding

of the 5,000, since this miracle apparently took place on the side of the Sea of Galilee with a predominantly Jewish population (6:45). [*kophinos*]

6:48 Fourth watch (*tetartēn phylakēn*)—Mark follows the Roman custom of dividing the time between 6 P.M. and 6 A.M. into four equal periods or "watches," so-called because individuals responsible for security were assigned the task of watching or standing guard during each period of time (BAGD, 868; BDAG, 1067; cf. 13:35). Since the fourth watch was from 3 A.M. to 6 A.M., the translation "as the night was ending" (NET) communicates the general time in which Jesus came to his disciples, walking on the water. The disciples, who had left on the boat in the late afternoon or evening, had struggled most of the night against the wind. [*phylakē* + *tetartos*]

To pass by (*parelthein*)—The language used for God's revelation of his glory to Moses provides the background for making sense of Jesus' desire to pass by the disciples (Exod. 33:17–34:8; cf. Marcus, 426). In response to Moses' request to see God's glory, the Lord places him in the cleft of a rock and covers him with his hand to protect his life, while his glory passes by (Exod. 33:18-22). The same verb *parerchomai* occurs in both Mark 6:48 and the LXX translation of the Exodus passage (Exod. 33:19, 22; 34:6; cf. 1 Kings 19:11-13; Job 9:8, 11 LXX). For Jesus to desire to pass by the disciples, therefore, does not mean that he wants to go past them to another location but that he wants to reveal his glory to them. [*parerchomai*]

6:52 Hardened (*pepōrōmenē*)—Mark expresses the difficulty that the disciples have in their lack of understanding with the metaphor of hardened hearts. Earlier Mark described Jesus' enemies in a similar way, that they possessed hardness of heart (3:5), so that the condition of Jesus' disciples is dangerously close to that of his opponents. See the discussion on "hardness" in 3:5. [*pōroō*]

6:56 Fringe (*kraspedou*)—This word appears in the plural in the LXX (Num. 15:38-39; Deut. 22:12) and in the NT (Matt. 23:5) for the tassels worn by Jewish men at the four corners of their garments (J. Schneider, *TDNT* 3:904; Marcus, 437). The purpose for the tassels was to remind them to obey God's commandments and set themselves apart as holy for God (Num. 15:40). Apparently, some who were sick believed that if they were able only to touch one of these tassels on Jesus' garment they would find healing. God saw their faith and granted them deliverance through the power available in Jesus (cf. 5:28-30). [*kraspedon*]

7:2 Defiled (*koinais*)—In the NT, the adjective *koinos* means at times "common, shared" as opposed to what is private (e.g., Acts 2:44; 4:32; Titus 1:4; Jude 3) and at other times "ritually unclean" as opposed to what is holy or set apart for God (e.g., Acts 10:14, 28; 11:8; Rom. 14:14; cf. F. G. Untergassmair, *EDNT* 2:302-3; Cranfield, 232). The latter meaning fits the context of Mark 7:1-5. Therefore, the problem was not that the disciples had dirty hands but that they did not follow the Pharisees' teaching concerning the ceremonial washing of the hands before eating, as many other Jews did. [*koinos*]

7:3 In the proper way (*pygmē*)—A literal translation of the word *pygmē* indicates that the Jews washed their hands "in or with a fist," but what such an expression means is difficult to understand. The RSV reveals the extent of the problem by omitting any reference to the word at all, not even attempting to translate it. The Jewish practice may have involved pouring a small amount of water on each hand with the fingers cupped, so that they were neither tightly clenched nor spread wide. This method would have allowed the entire hand to be washed with the least amount of water possible, since water was too valuable to waste (Gundry, 360). The translation "in the proper way" (CEV) is an attempt to convey the probable underlying significance for Mark's use of the word *pygmē*, that the hand washing took place according to a customary pattern (cf. LN, 1:99). [*pygmē*]

Tradition (*paradosin*)—The noun *paradosis* refers to teachings and commandments that have been handed down as authoritative from preceding generations (BAGD, 615-16; BDAG, 763). More specifically, "the tradition of the elders" points to the oral law, the traditional rules that the Pharisees received from former generations which helped to supplement the written Law of Moses (cf. Gal. 1:14; Josephus, *Ant.* 13.10.6 § 297; 13.16.2 § 408). A ceremonial washing of the hands was not a requirement in the written law for the people in general; rather it was for the priests involved in service at the tabernacle (Exod. 30:18-21; 40:30-31; cf. *b Ber.* 52b). The Pharisees' oral law apparently extended this responsibility to everyone, on the theory that every Jew should live as a priest and every Jewish home should be a place of worship (Marcus, 449). According to Mark 7:1-23, Jesus' primary objection to the oral tradition was that the Pharisees and scribes often used it to set aside God's commandments (7:8-9, 13). [*paradosis*]

7:5 The Pharisees and the scribes (*hoi Pharisaioi kai hoi grammateis*)—Debates between Jesus and the religious leaders often revolve around the issue of authority, as in this passage where the Pharisees and scribes take offense because Jesus' disciples do not accept the Jewish teachers' tradition. For more on the Pharisees, see 2:16, and on the scribes, see 1:22. [*Pharisaios, grammateus*]

7:6 Hypocrites (*hypokritōn*)—The noun *hypokritēs* ("hypocrite") occurs 17 times in the NT, most frequently in Matthew's Gospel (13 times). The word appears in Mark's Gospel only this one time, in Mark 7:6, although the related word *hypokrisis* ("hypocrisy") is also used in Mark 12:15. In classical Greek, *hypokritēs* referred to an actor, someone who played a part on the stage (LSJ, 1886). In the NT, the word *hypokritēs* appears in Jesus' sayings in a metaphorical and a negative sense for those who hypocritically perform visible deeds of religious devotion, who create an outward appearance and public impression that conceals their inward lack of righteousness (e.g., Matt. 6:2, 5, 16). Their religious activity is "an act," not a true reflection of their hearts. In Mark 7:6, Jesus illustrates his point with a quotation from Isaiah, a quotation introduced with "it is written" (see the discussion on 1:2). [*hypokritēs*]

7:11 Corban (*Korban*)—Corban, a loan word from Hebrew, was a technical term for a gift or offering set aside for God and therefore no longer available for ordinary use (cf. Lev. 1:2; Josephus, *Ant.* 4.4.4 § 73; *Ag. Ap.* 1.22 § 167; *m Ned.* 8:7). In other words, to declare something as Corban meant to reserve it for God and to prohibit it from being used by others (cf. Cranfield, 237-38; Lane, 250-51). The scribes of Jesus' day considered such a dedication as a binding vow, one that could not be broken even if it resulted in harm to one's parents. [*Korban*]

7:15 Defile (*koinōsai*)—The adjective *koinos*, examined in 7:2, has a related verb *koinoō*, "to make unclean" (cf. Acts 10:15; 21:28). Jesus uses the verb in Mark 7:15 to explain what makes a person unacceptable in God's presence. Unwashed hands do not defile food and in turn the one who eats it. Instead, what makes fellowship with God impossible is the moral pollution that begins in the heart. In Mark 7:17, the disciples refer to this teaching as a parable. On parables, see 4:2. [*koinoō*]

7:19 Thus he declared clean (*katharizōn*)— The writers of the NT use the verb *kartharizō* in three ways (BAGD, 387; BDAG, 488-89): (1) for bringing physical health and ritual cleansing to lepers (e.g., Matt. 11:5; Mark 1:42; Luke 4:27; 17:14), (2) for declaring all food ceremonially clean (e.g., Acts 10:15; 11:9), and (3) for purifying believers from sin (e.g., Acts 15:9; 2 Cor. 7:1; 1 John 1:7). The context of Mark's parenthetical statement at the end of 7:19 matches with the second use listed above. Just as Jesus is Lord over the OT Sabbath laws (2:28), so also he is authoritative with regard to the OT food laws and is able to bring them to an end (7:19). [*kartharizō*]

7:22 Envy (*ophthalmos ponēros*)—Most recent translations (NASB; NIV; NRSV; NET; NLT) render the Greek phrase as "envy," even though a more literal translation would be "an evil eye." The reason for the rendering "envy" lies in the common use of the Jewish expression "evil eye" as a metaphor for a lack of generosity. A person with an evil eye refuses to give to those in need (Deut. 15:9; cf. Sir. 35:8, 10), chases after wealth (Prov.. 28:22), wants what others have (Sir. 14:8-10), and responds with envy when others receive generous gifts (Matt. 20:15). The expression serves to describe the attitude of someone who carefully keeps an eye on his own possessions out of stinginess and an eye on the possessions of others out of a jealous greed. [*ophthalmos + ponēros*]

7:26 Greek (*Hellēnis*)—The term "Greek" may simply be equivalent to "Gentile," that is, someone who is not a Jew (e.g., Rom. 1:16; 2:9-10; 3:9; 10:12; 1 Cor. 1:22-24; 12:13; Gal. 3:28; cf. NASB; NRSV). "Greek" may also imply that the woman is Greek-speaking and therefore also educated and affluent (Marcus, 462). The woman is not Greek as far as her ethnic origin is concerned, since Mark also identifies her as Syrophoenician by way of nationality. Phoenicia was the coastal area of the Roman province of Syria, along the Mediterranean Sea north of the land of Israel. [*Hellēnis*]

7:27 First (*prōton*)—The neuter form *prōton* functions as an adverb, primarily an adverb of time, meaning "first, earlier" (H. Langkammer, *EDNT* 3:187). In Mark's Gospel, this adverbial use always occurs in contexts that describe the ordering of events in God's redemptive plan. For example, Elijah must come first before the Messiah (9:11-12) and the Gospel must go out to all the nations first before the coming of the Son of Man in power (13:10). According to God's plan, the ministry of Jesus to the people of Israel takes place prior to the spread of God's blessings to the Gentiles (cf. Rom. 1:16). [*prōtos*]

Dogs (*kynariois*)—In his apparent refusal to help the Syrophoenician woman, Jesus refers to Gentiles as dogs. It is not good to take bread (God's blessings available in the Messiah) from the children (the people of Israel) and give it to the dogs (Gentiles). Jesus uses a diminutive form which can be translated "little dogs," but this does little to make the term less harsh. It is difficult to imagine that a Gentile would consider it less offensive to be called a "little dog" than simply a "dog" (Hooker, 183). Jesus' words appear to be a test of the woman's faith, one which she passes because of her humility and her trust in the abundance of God's grace in Jesus. She accepts the priority of Israel but believes that just a leftover crumb of attention from Jesus is sufficient to meet her need. In response, Jesus delivers her daughter from the demon. On "demon" and "unclean spirit," see 1:23. [*kynarion*]

7:32 One who spoke with difficulty (*mogilalon*)—"One who spoke with difficulty" renders the rare word *mogilalos*, which occurs only this one time in the NT as well as only

one time in the LXX, in Isa. 35:6. According to Mark, the deaf man could hardly talk, but when Jesus heals him he begins to speak correctly (7:35). The use of *mogilalos* in Isa. 35:6 LXX probably influenced Mark's word choice in his description of the man's problem. The passage in Isaiah predicts a time when God will come to save, and then the blind will see, the deaf will hear, the lame will leap, and those who speak with difficulty will instead speak clearly. [*mogilalos*]

7:34 Ephphatha (*ephphatha*)—The command *ephphatha* means "be opened" or "be released" in Aramaic, a common language at the time of Jesus (Cranfield, 252). Aramaic words turn up at various places in Mark's narrative: *Boanerges* (3:17), *talitha kum* (5:41), *ephphatha* (7:34), *hosanna* (11:9-10), *abba* (14:36), *Golgotha* (15:22), *Eloi, Eloi lama sabachthani* (15:34). Each time, they seem to depict an event, statement, or place as particularly memorable. Mark translates all these Aramaic words or phrases for his readers, with the exception of the word *hosanna*. For more on *hosanna*, see 11:9. [*ephphatha*]

7:35 Bond (*desmos*)—Using a figure of speech, Mark states that Jesus released the "bond" or "fetter" that held the man's tongue, so that he was able to speak correctly. Recent translations, finding the metaphor difficult to express in English, have dropped the reference to the "bond" and have stated simply that "his tongue was loosened" (cf. NIV; NRSV; NET). The NASB takes away the metaphor by referring more literally to "the impediment of his tongue." Possible translations that seek to retain Mark's imagery include "his tongue was unshackled" (Marcus, 475) or "his imprisoned tongue was set free." [*desmos*]

8:2 I feel compassion (*splanchnizomai*)—Jesus' response is reminiscent of his compassion for the crowd prior to the first feeding miracle (6:34). However, the basis for his compassion changes. Earlier Jesus' feelings of pity arose from the crowd's spiritual need, that they were like sheep without a shepherd. In 8:2, he senses their physical need, that they have been without food for so long (Guelich, 404). For more on Jesus' compassion, see 6:34. [*splanchnizomai*]

8:3 From a distance (*apo makrothen*)—A significant number of Gentiles may have belonged to the crowd fed by Jesus in Mark 8:1-9. The passage begins with the phrase "in those days," indicating that Jesus has not changed locations but is still ministering in the Decapolis (7:31), a largely Gentile territory. In addition, Jesus mentions that some in the crowd have come "from a distance" (8:3), another possible clue to the make-up of the crowd. In the LXX, those who have come "from a distant land" (Josh. 9:6, 9: *ek gēs makrothen*) are Gentiles, and elsewhere the NT describes Gentiles as "distant" (*makran*; Acts 2:39; 22:21; Eph. 2:13, 17; Isa. 57:19). [*makrothen*]

8:8 Baskets (*spyridas*)—Unlike *kophinoi*, the baskets mentioned in the feeding of the 5,000 (see note on 6:43), these baskets did not have any special association with Jews (Marcus, 489). However, like *kophinoi*, these baskets referred to in Mark 8:8 could be of various sizes (MM, 357; Spicq, 3:230), large enough to hold Saul during his escape out of Damascus (Acts 9:25) or small enough to serve as a lunch pail (Epictetus, *Diatr.* 4.10.2; Athenaeus, *Deipn.* 8:365a). In other words, it would be difficult to determine which contained more leftovers, the 12 baskets of Mark 6:43 or the seven baskets of Mark 8:8. [*spyris*]

8:11 Sign (*sēmeion*)—The Pharisees' request for a sign is a demand for "an outward compelling proof of divine authority" (Cranfield,

257). The word "sign" (*sēmeion*) appears less often in Mark than in the other NT Gospels (8:11, 12; 13:4, 22). The term occurs in Matthew 13 times, in Luke 11 times, and in John 17 times. In Mark's Gospel, the desire for a sign has negative connotations, since it reveals a stubborn refusal to believe (8:11-12; cf. 1 Cor. 1:21-22) or a dangerous openness to deception (13:4-5, 22; cf. 2 Thess.. 2:9-10). For more on the word "sign," see 13:4. On the Pharisees, see 2:16, and on testing, see 10:2. [*sēmeion*]

8:12 Generation (*genea*)—The primary background for Jesus' reference to "this generation" is in OT descriptions of the rebellious generation during the wilderness wanderings (Num. 32:13; Deut. 2:14; 32:5, 20; Ps. 12:7; 78:8; 95:10). For example, according to Ps. 95, God loathed the wilderness generation, because the people hardened their hearts and tested him, even though they had seen his works (Ps. 95:8-11). Therefore, "this generation" is a pejorative reference in Mark's Gospel to a sinful and unbelieving class of people who are destined for the judgment of God (cf. R. Morgenthaler, *NIDNTT* 2:36). Later in Mark's Gospel, this generation is described as "adulterous and sinful" (8:38) and "faithless" (9:19). In the eschatological discourse, Jesus predicts that this generation, that is, this sinful class of people who oppose God and his messengers, will be present right up to the coming of the Son of Man (13:30). For more on the introductory formula, "truly, I say to you," see the discussion at 3:28. [*genea*]

8:15 Leaven (*zymēs*)—The word for leaven, *zymē*, is not synonymous with yeast, even though some translations render it that way (NIV; NRSV; NLT). It refers to old, fermented dough that was thoroughly mixed into a new batch of dough in order to leaven the bread (G. T. D. Angel, *NIDNTT* 2:461; BDAG, 429). As a metaphor, leaven symbolizes something small that has the power to permeate and to spread its influence throughout, often negatively (1 Cor. 5:6; Gal. 5:9; cf. W. Popkes, *EDNT* 2:104). Mark's Gospel leaves Jesus' reference to the leaven of the Pharisees and Herod as an unexplained riddle, misunderstood by the disciples (8:15-16). In Matthew's Gospel, the leaven represents false teaching (Matt. 16:12), while in Luke's Gospel it points to hypocrisy (Luke 12:1). Several important words in Mark 8:14-21 were examined previously, including "boat" (see 4:1), "Pharisees" (see 2:16), "hardened" (see 3:5; 6:52), "hear" (see 4:12), and "baskets" (see 6:43; 8:8). [*zymē*]

8:24 Having regained his sight (*anablepsas*)—In the NT, the verb *anablepō* is used with two different meanings: (1) to look up at an object or person or (2) to regain or receive sight (BAGD, 50-51; BDAG, 59). When the verb means "to look up," the context involves people with sight directing their eyes toward something: toward heaven (Mark 6:41; 7:34), toward Zacchaeus in the tree (Luke 19:5), toward the rich giving gifts (Luke 21:1), toward the stone rolled away from the empty tomb (Mark 16:4). The verb normally means "to regain or receive sight" in passages that describe the healing of blind men (e.g., Matt. 11:5; Mark 10:51-52; Luke 18:41-43; John 9:11; Acts 9:17-18). Although English translations often express *anablepsas* in Mark 8:24 with "he looked up" (e.g., NASB; NIV; NRSV), a more appropriate translation in this context would be "he regained his sight" (Guelich, 433; Gundry, 417). In other words, the healing gestures of Jesus in Mark 8:23 cause the blind man to regain his sight in 8:24, but the man's report concerning what he sees shows that his healing is incomplete. [*anablepō*]

8:25 He was restored (*apekatestē*)—When used in connection with the healing of the sick, the verb *apokathistēmi* means "to restore to an earlier healthy condition, to heal" (3:5;

Let. Aris. 316; *T. Sim.* 2:13; in the LXX: Exod. 4:7; Lev. 13:16; Job 5:18; cf. H.-G Link, *NIDNTT* 3:147). With a second touch, Jesus restores the man's vision completely, so that he no longer sees in a distorted manner but rather looks at everything clearly. Jesus is able to heal both blindness and inadequate sight, a point that is particularly important since Jesus has just accused the disciples of spiritual blindness (8:18) and will soon rebuke them for their insufficient perception of his identity (8:29-33). The restoration of the blind man in two stages creates the expectation that Jesus can heal both blindness and shortsightedness, whether physical or spiritual. [*apokathistēmi*]

8:27 Way (*hodō*)—In Mark's Gospel, the noun *hodos* functions both literally and metaphorically. For example, the word refers to a literal path or road on which scattered seeds do not survive (4:4, 15) but also, in a metaphorical sense, to the way of God, the manner of life that God demands (12:14). However, it is often difficult to separate the literal from the figurative use, since they can overlap, and this is especially true of the references to *hodos* clustered in the central section of Mark's Gospel, in chapters 8-10 (cf. M. Völkel, *EDNT* 2:491-92). Mark describes Jesus as "on the way" in passages in which either Jesus is explaining to his disciples the nature of his destiny to suffer and die in Jerusalem or in texts which treat the implications of this life mission on those who follow him (8:27; 9:33-34; 10:17, 32, 45, 52). While Jesus may be on a literal road, he is also in a metaphorical sense on God's path, following God's plan for his life, one that includes suffering, death, and resurrection. [*hodos*]

8:29 Christ (*Christos*)—According to Mark's Gospel, Jesus is the Christ or, in other words, the Messiah, the promised deliverer from the line of David, the anointed king of Israel (cf. 1:1; 12:35; 14:61; 15:32). Peter may have regarded the Christ as an earthly, political ruler who would restore righteousness, freedom, and prosperity to Israel, a nation currently under the oppression of wicked, foreign rulers (cf. *Pss. Sol.* 17-18). Jesus qualified Peter's understanding of his identity by explaining that as the Son of Man he has come to suffer (8:31), but Peter, with his more limited view of the mission of the Messiah, found it difficult to accept Jesus' teaching (8:32). For more on the word "Christ," see 1:1. [*Christos*]

8:31 Must (*dei*)—The verb *dei* is a common word in the NT (101 times), especially in Luke's writings (40 times in Luke–Acts). In Mark's Gospel, *dei* emphasizes that certain events must take place because they are part of God's plan for redemption as it has been announced in the Scriptures. In this way, "must" (*dei*) corresponds to "it is written" (*gegraptai*; cf. Lane, 294; W. Popkes, *EDNT* 1:279-80). According to Mark 8:31, the Son of Man "must" suffer and be rejected. In a parallel statement later in Mark's Gospel, Jesus states that the Son of Man will go just as "it is written" concerning him (14:21; cf. 14:49). Elijah "must" come (9:11), and this coming takes place just as "it is written" concerning him (9:13). In addition, Mark's Gospel uses *dei* in the context of apocalyptic events that must occur before the end, events such as wars and the proclamation of the Gospel to all the nations (13:7, 10). For more on the Son of Man, see 2:10. [*dei*]

Be rejected (*apodokimasthēnai*)—The verb *apodokimazō* indicates that someone or something, after testing, has been found to be useless and unworthy by those performing the test (BAGD, 90-91; BDAG, 110; cf. Jer. 6:27-30 LXX). In Mark 8:31, Jesus predicts that the Son of Man will be examined and rejected by the religious leaders. Concerning the elders and the chief priests, see 11:27, and concerning the scribes, see 1:22. The verb *apodokimazō* occurs most often in the NT in references to

Ps. 118:22 (Matt. 21:42; Mark 12:10; Luke 9:22; 17:25; 20:17; 1 Pet. 2:4, 7). The direct citation of Ps. 118:22 in Mark 12:10 supports the idea of an allusion to that same verse in Mark 8:31. In Mark 12:10, Jesus quotes Ps. 118:22 at the end of his parable about the wicked farmers who refuse to pay their rent and who kill the owner's son. Mark indicates that Jesus spoke this parable against the elders, chief priests, and scribes (cf. 11:27; 12:12). Jesus is the stone rejected by the builders, but the Lord has made him the cornerstone. [*apodokimazō*]

8:32 To rebuke (*epitiman*)—Rebuking involves an expression of strong disapproval, given for the purpose of stopping an action or preventing it altogether (BAGD, 303; BDAG, 384). In Mark's Gospel, Jesus effectively rebukes unclean spirits (1:25; 3:12; 9:25), a threatening storm (4:39), and his own disciples (8:30, 33). Whenever anyone other than Jesus takes up the task of rebuking, it is always a misguided attempt to hinder an appropriate action: a prediction of suffering (8:32), a request for Jesus' blessing (10:13), and a cry for mercy (10:48). In each case, Jesus does not allow the rebuke to stand. [*epitimaō*]

8:34 Let him deny (*aparnēsasthō*)—One of the conditions for following Jesus is to deny oneself, that is, to say "no" to the demands of self (Cranfield, 281-82), to refuse to make personal desires and self-interest the central concern of one's life (Hooker, 208). The same verb *aparneomai* appears later in Mark's narrative in reference to the negative example of Peter who refuses to deny himself, choosing rather to deny his relationship with Jesus (cf. 14:30-31, 72). [*aparneomai*]

Cross (*stauron*)—Crucifixion was a particularly cruel and brutal form of execution, a public event that served as a grim reminder to the general population of the cost of opposing the ruling authorities. As part of the punishment, the condemned person carried the cross-beam out to the place of execution. There the outstretched arms of the prisoner were tied or nailed to the cross-beam, and typically the beam was then raised along with the prisoner's body and fastened to an upright post already implanted in the ground (J. Schneider, *TDNT* 7:573-74; J. B. Green, *DJG* 147-48; cf. Plutarch, *Sera* 9.554b). Jesus calls on the one who wants to follow him to take up the cross, that is, to accept the position of someone who is already condemned to death and so to be prepared at any moment to give up one's life for his sake. [*stauros*]

Follow (*akoloutheitō*)—Jesus lays down three requirements for discipleship: deny self, take up the cross, and follow. This third demand involves a sustained loyalty to Jesus and to the pattern of his life, a pattern that includes suffering and sacrifice. The shift to the present tense in expressing the command to follow seems intentional, designed to stress the importance of a persistent faithfulness to Jesus (Taylor, 381). For more on following Jesus, see 1:18. For more on the disciples, see 2:15. [*akoloutheō*]

8:35 Life (*psychēn*)—The word *psychē* is used with a double meaning in Mark 8:35-37, for physical existence in this present age and for eternal existence in the age to come. If you cling to your present life at any cost, you will lose out on the more valuable life of the age to come. If you willingly give up your earthly life for the sake of Jesus and his message, you will find that you have preserved an unending life with God. The word for "life" in verse 35 appears again in verses 36-37 where it is sometimes translated as "soul" (e.g., KJV; NASB; NIV; NLT). In 8:36-37, the word refers to eternal existence, and this eternal life is more valuable than the whole world. [*psychē*]

Good news (*euangeliou*)—Mark uses "good news" or "gospel" somewhat differ-

ently than the other Gospel writers in the NT. Matthew uses the term "gospel" less frequently than Mark (4 times in Matthew compared to seven times in Mark). Matthew always qualifies the word by referring to "this gospel" (Matt. 24:14; 26:13) or "the gospel of the kingdom" (Matt. 4:23; 9:35; cf. 24:14), while Mark assumes that his readers understand what he means simply by "the gospel" (1:15; 8:35; 10:29; 13:10; 14:9). The noun "gospel" (*euangelion*) never appears in the Gospel of Luke or the Gospel of John, although the related verb "preach the gospel" (*euangelizō*) is used 10 times in Luke's Gospel and 15 times in Acts. Of the four Gospel writers, Mark alone includes the idea of suffering for the sake of the good news (8:35; 10:29; cf. Matt. 16:25; 19:29; Luke 9:24; 18:29). On "good news," see also 1:1. [*euangelion*]

8:38 Is ashamed (*epaischynthē*)—In Matt. 10:32-33, Jesus says, "Therefore, everyone who will confess me before men, I will also confess before my Father in heaven, but whoever denies me before men, I will also deny before my Father in heaven" (cf. Luke 12:8-9). In Mark 8:38, the verb *epaischynomai* ("to be ashamed") functions in a similar way to the language of confession and denial in Matt. 10:32-33 (cf. A. Horstmann, *EDNT* 1:42). Those who are ashamed of Jesus renounce or deny him; they refuse to confess or publicly declare any loyalty to him. In turn, Jesus will repudiate them; he will refuse to acknowledge them when he comes in the glory of his Father. By way of comparison, Paul uses the verb *epaischynomai* as part of a confession formula in Rom. 1:16, where not being ashamed of the Gospel means openly acknowledging its truth and power. On other important words in Mark 8:38, see 2:10 (Son of Man) and 8:12 (generation). [*epaischynomai*]

9:1 Taste (*geusōntai*)—The figurative use of

the verb *geuomai* ("taste") means "to experience something, to come to know it through personal exposure" (cf. BAGD, 157; BDAG, 195; J. Behm, *TDNT* 1:675-77). "To taste death" and "to see the kingdom of God" are parallel expressions in Jesus' prediction, since both emphasize experiential knowledge. Before some in Jesus' presence experience death, they will have a direct encounter with the kingdom of God. This parallel between "taste" and "see" is strengthened by the similarity in meaning between "tasting death" (John 8:52; Heb. 2:9; *4 Ezra* 6:26) and "seeing death" (Luke 2:26; John 8:51; Heb. 11:5; cf. Ps. 34:8). Mark presents the fulfillment of Jesus' prediction by narrating how three disciples "tasted" the kingdom of God and its power at the transfiguration of Jesus (9:2-4; cf. Cranfield, 285-88). Other key words in Mark 9:1 include "truly" (see 3:28), "the kingdom of God" (see 1:15), and "power" (see 5:30). [*geuomai*]

9:2 Was transfigured (*metemorphōthē*)—The transfiguration involved an outwardly visible transformation in Jesus' appearance (J. M. Nützel, *EDNT* 2:415). In contrast to Matthew and Luke who note a change in the appearance of Jesus' face (Matt. 17:2; Luke 9:29), Mark refrains from describing the transformation in Jesus himself, choosing instead to speak about the intense brightness of his clothes. Jesus' brilliant clothing in Mark's account is comparable to the white garments worn by those who share in heavenly glory in apocalyptic visions (Dan. 7:9; *1 En.* 14:20; 62:15-16; *Mart. Ascen. Isa.* 9:6-12; Rev. 3:4-5, 18; 4:4; 6:11; 7:9, 13; 19:14; cf. Mark 16:5). [*metamorphoō*]

9:3 Launderer (*gnapheus*)—The noun *gnapheus*, which occurs only here in the NT, refers to an individual involved in the trade of preparing, cleaning, and bleaching cloth (Lane, 315). One difficulty in translating this word is that in our culture those who wish to whiten cloth often turn to a product rather than to a profession. Therefore, another way to communicate Mark's idea is to say that Jesus' garments became radiantly white, much whiter than any bleach or detergent on earth could make them. [*gnapheus*]

9:5 Tabernacles (*skēnas*)—In the LXX, the noun *skēnē* is used at times to refer to the tabernacle, the tent where God met with Moses (e.g., Exod. 33:7-11; 40:34-38; cf. KJV; NASB), and to the temporary shelters made of branches and leaves that belonged to the celebration of the feast of booths (e.g., Lev. 23:33-44; Neh. 8:14-18; cf. RSV; NIV). During this festival, the people commemorated the Exodus by living in temporary shelters for seven days. Why did Peter mention three *skēnas*? Was Peter making an allusion to the tabernacle or to the temporary shelters in the feast of booths? Both possibilities have been suggested by interpreters, but neither suggestion is entirely satisfactory. For example, it is difficult to understand why Peter would want to build three tabernacles instead of one (unless he was equating Moses, Elijah, and Jesus in some unspecified way). It is also hard to determine why he would only think of making temporary shelters for Jesus, Moses, and Elijah and not also for the three disciples in a celebration of the feast of booths. Perhaps interpreters should not attempt to make too much sense out of Peter's reference to three *skēnas*, since Mark immediately inserts that Peter was afraid and did not know what he was saying. [*skēnē*]

9:7 Cloud (*nephelē*)—The primary OT background for Mark's reference to a cloud (*nephelē*) that overshadows (*episkiazousa*) is in Exod. 40:35 LXX where Moses is not able to enter the tabernacle because a cloud (*nephelē*) is overshadowing (*epeskiazen*) it and the glory of the Lord has filled it. Therefore, the cloud of Mark 9:7 serves as a sign of God's presence and glory (cf. BAGD, 536; BDAG, 670). On Jesus as God's beloved Son, see 1:1 and 1:11. [*nephelē*]

9:12 Restores (*apokathistanei*)—The meaning of the verb *apokathistanō* is "to restore or to put things back into their original condition" (cf. P.-G. Müller, *EDNT* 1:129). Jesus grants that the scribes are correct in saying that Elijah will come before the Messiah. By using the verb "restore," Jesus makes his point with an allusion to Mal. 4:5-6 (cf. Sir. 48:10). Elijah will come before the great and glorious day of the Lord and will restore the heart of the father to the son and the heart of a man to his neighbor (Mal. 4:5-6 LXX). In this passage, Malachi draws on the hope expressed earlier in the prophets for a time of restoration in which the people of Israel will return to the land and will come back to the Lord with their whole heart (e.g., Jer. 15:19; 16:15; 24:6-7; 50:19-20 [27:19-20 LXX]; Ezek. 16:55; Hos. 11:8-11). For Jesus, the promise of the forerunner's work of restoration and the prediction of the Messiah's suffering stand in tension with one another and demand further reflection. [*apokathistanō/apokathistēmi*]

Would be treated with contempt (*exoudenēthē*)—The verb *exoudeneō*, which contains within it the word *ouden* ("nothing"), literally means "to make someone out to be nothing" (BDAG, 352; Lane, 322). The KJV seeks to express this idea by stating that the Son of Man would be "set at nought." Other translations use "rejected" (NIV), "despised" (NET), and "treated with contempt" (NASB, NRSV). When Jesus argued that according to the Scriptures the people would despise the Messiah, he may have had in mind passages such as Ps. 22:6 and Isa. 53:3 (cf. Lane 322). [*exoudeneō*]

9:18 Becomes stiff (*xērainetai*)—Mark describes the severe condition of the possessed boy in a number of ways, including that the spirit causes the boy to become stiff or weak. The verb used here, *xērainō*, literally means "to dry up," but it can also indicate, with reference to human beings, some form of paralysis or an inability to move. See the discussion at 3:1 where the same word describes the ailment of the man with a withered hand. Just as Jesus was able to heal the man with the withered hand, he is fully capable of meeting the needs of this possessed boy. Indeed, Jesus has already demonstrated his ability to cope with the cause of the boy's problems, along with the accompanying symptoms. Jesus is able to cast out unclean spirits (9:17; cf. 1:25-26, 34; 5:8, 12-13; 7:29), to cause the deaf to hear and the mute to speak (9:17, 25; cf. 7:35, 37), to restore what has become withered or stiff (9:18; cf. 3:1-5), and even to raise up those who have apparently died (9:26; cf. 5:35, 41-42). On "unclean spirit," see 1:23. For a discussion on the spirit's act of shaking the boy in 9:20, 26, see 1:26. [*xērainō*]

9:22 Have compassion (*splanchnistheis*)—This is the only example in Mark's Gospel of someone asking Jesus to be moved with compassion. Elsewhere, Jesus' attitude of compassion is simply reported (1:41; 6:34; 8:2). For example, the leper says to Jesus, "If you are willing, you are able to cleanse me," after which Mark states that Jesus had compassion on him (1:40-41). By way of contrast, the man with the possessed boy says to Jesus, "If you are able, help us and have compassion on us" (9:22). For more on compassion, see 6:34. [*splanchnizomai*]

9:24 I believe (*pisteuō*)—In Mark's Gospel, believing in Jesus includes trusting that he has the power and the will to meet the needs of the helpless. In Mark 9:24, the father confesses his faith but also pleads for help with his unbelief. Trust and unbelief are not mutually exclusive categories in Mark's narrative, since an individual can experience both at the same time. Those who believe in Jesus may also struggle with doubt in the midst of difficult circumstances. To the man's credit, he is at least aware of his problem and sufficiently repentant to ask for deliverance, in contrast to the people of Nazareth who receive no help in light of their stubborn unbelief (6:1-6). On faith, see 2:5, and on unbelief, see 6:6. [*pisteuō*]

9:29 Prayer (*proseuchē*)—What Jesus meant by "prayer" calls for further explanation, since after all Jesus himself did not offer any specific prayer before casting out the unclean spirit. Mark's Gospel portrays Jesus as regularly finding time early in the morning or late in the evening to meet with God privately in prayer (1:35; 6:46; 14:32-39). According to the model that Jesus provides, the authority to cast out a powerful unclean spirit comes not through a set prayer offered at the moment of conflict, but through a life pattern of prayer and faith (cf. 11:22-24). On prayer, see also 1:35. [*proseuchē*]

9:31 Is betrayed (*paradidotai*)—The central section of Mark's Gospel (8:22-10:52) contains three similar predictions by Jesus concerning his coming death and resurrection (8:31; 9:31; 10:32-34). In each instance, Jesus, while "on the way," predicts that the Son of Man will be killed and raised after three days. In addition, Jesus finds it necessary to teach his disciples repeatedly about the cost of following him, since they fail to grasp the implications of what his death means for them (8:32-28; 9:32-37; 10:35-45). However, each successive prediction also includes new information for the disciples concerning what they should expect to happen. For example, this second prediction adds the idea that Jesus will be betrayed. This act of betrayal is a future event in the narrative, but it is expressed in the present

tense in order to convey the certainty with which it will take place (Taylor, 403; cf. Wallace, *Greek Grammar* 535-36). On betrayed, see 3:19. See also 2:10 for "Son of Man" and 8:27 for "way." [*paradidōmi*]

9:35 Last (*eschatos*)—With regard to space, *eschatos* refers to the place furthest away; with regard to time, the last event of a series; and with regard to rank, the lowest position (H.-G. Link, *NIDNTT* 2:55). In discussing rank in Mark 9:35, Jesus teaches his followers that if they have a concern for their standing, they should seek out the lowest place and the position of a servant. Within that culture, the "first" meant people of authority and influence, and therefore the "last" referred to those without power, privilege, or recognition (Evans, 61). In Mark 10:31, Jesus teaches again about the first and the last, although in the context of a comparison between the present time and the age to come. Those who are willing to serve others now without any thought of status or honor will be held in high esteem in the coming kingdom. On servant, see 10:43. [*eschatos*]

9:42 Little ones (*mikrōn*)—The "little ones" are those who are insignificant according to the standards of the world, those who lack importance, influence, and power (BAGD, 521; BDAG, 651). Although Jesus at times apparently used the term "little ones" to refer to his followers (e.g., Matt. 10:42), in the context of Mark 9 "one of these little ones" refers more naturally to "one of these children" mentioned back in 9:37 (Gundry, 512, 524; cf. Matt. 18:5-6). The disciples must have the humility to welcome and serve children, those who lack personal status. A failure to treat them as worthy of attention and care would encourage them to fall away into disobedience or unbelief. For more on "cause to stumble," see "fall away" in 4:17. [*mikros*]

A heavy millstone (*mylos onikos*)—A

"heavy" millstone (NASB) and a "large" millstone (NIV, NLT) are both attempts to convey the significance of this phrase, which could be translated more literally as a "donkey-driven" millstone (cf. Evans, 70). The process of turning grain into flour involved grinding the grain between two flat stones. Although some such millstones were small enough to be moved by hand, others were so large that turning them around demanded the strength of a donkey (BAGD, 529; BDAG, 661). [*mylos + onikos*]

9:43 Hell (*geennan*)—The Greek word *geenna* (Gehenna) derives from the Hebrew name for the Valley of Hinnom, a ravine south of Jerusalem. The reforming king Josiah desecrated the place (2 Kings 23:10) because it had served as a location for offering child sacrifices to the god Molech in the days of Ahaz and Manasseh (2 Kings 16:3; 21:6; Jer. 7:31; 32:35). Thereafter, the valley became a site for incinerating refuse. Eventually, Gehenna came to be used as a symbolic name for the place of God's final judgment on the wicked, the place of eternal fire (O. Böcher, *EDNT* 1:239-40; Evans, 72; cf. Matt. 10:28; 18:8-9; Jas 3:6; *1 En.* 54:1-6; *4 Ezra* 7:36; *2 Bar.* 85:13; *Sib. Or.* 1:100-103; 2:290-92; 4:184-86). [*geenna*]

9:47 To enter the kingdom of God (*eiselthein eis tēn basileian tou theou*)—When the kingdom of God arrives in power, some will come into God's realm to live under the blessing of his rule, while others will remain outside and face judgment. In his teaching, Jesus emphasizes how difficult it is to enter the kingdom (10:24), especially for those who are wealthy (10:23-25). Only those who will humble themselves before God like children will be able to enter (10:15). Entrance into the kingdom is so difficult that it would be impossible without the intervention of God (10:27). [*eiserchomai + basileia*]

9:49 Will be salted (*halisthēsetai*)—Jesus' statement that everyone will be salted with fire is best understood from the perspective of the OT sacrificial system (Cranfield, 315-16; Lane, 349). Sacrifices offered to God were to be seasoned with salt (Lev. 2:13; Ezek. 43:24). At the present time, all those who offer themselves to God will also be seasoned, though no longer with salt but with fire. The word "fire" probably functions here as a metaphor for difficult trials and persecutions (cf. 1 Pet. 1:7; 4:12). Those who offer themselves to God, and thus escape the fire of hell, should not assume that they will have a life of ease. Instead, they will be salted with fire, that is, they will be made into acceptable offerings to God through the purifying process of trials and persecutions. [*halizō*]

10:2 In order to test (*peirazontes*)—Depending on the intention behind it, the act of testing may be positive, to prove the value or trustworthiness of someone, or negative, to entice someone into failure (cf. W. Popkes, *EDNT* 3:65). In Mark's Gospel, the verb *peirazō* always has negative connotations. The initial use of *peirazō* occurs in Mark's brief temptation account concerning Satan's testing of Jesus (1:13). The remaining instances all refer to attempts by the Pharisees to trap Jesus (8:11; 10:2; 12:15; cf. 12:13). The Pharisees try to catch Jesus in an action or statement that will damage his credibility with the crowds or will put him in jeopardy with the political authorities. The question about divorce was politically dangerous because by crossing over the Jordan River Jesus was under the jurisdiction of the divorced Herod Antipas. Earlier the arrest and execution of John the Baptist came as a result of his condemnation of Herod's decision to leave his first wife and marry Herodias. On the Pharisees, see 2:16. [*peirazō*]

10:4 Permitted (*epetrepsen*)—In Mark 10:3, Jesus raises the question of what Moses commands, but the Pharisees answer with what Moses permits. To some extent, the whole conversation turns on what is meant by permission. Apparently, the Pharisees take it to mean that God allows divorce in the sense that it has his approval and that it will not come under his judgment (Cranfield, 319). Divorce is their lawful right. They support their position with reference to Deut. 24:1-4, a passage that recognizes the practice of divorce and seeks to limit its damaging consequences. In the following verses, Jesus directs the conversation back to what God commands. He accepts that Moses allowed for divorce, but this permission exists not because of God's approval of divorce but because of God's understanding of the stubborn sinfulness of people. What God commands and desires is that a husband and wife become and remain one flesh. [*epitrepō*]

10:5 Hardness of heart (*sklērokardian*)—Hardness of heart points to a persistent lack of receptivity to the will of God (J. Behm, *TDNT* 3:614; Spicq, 3:261; cf. Deut. 10:16; Jer. 4:4; Sir. 16:10). The use of *sklērokardia* in Deut. 10:16 LXX is relevant to Mark's account of Jesus' debate with the Pharisees. In that passage, Moses is calling on the people to love and serve the Lord with a whole heart and to keep the Lord's commandments (Deut. 10:12-13). The people should remove the hardness of their hearts and stop being stubborn against God (Deut. 10:16). The Pharisees' attitude toward divorce betrays an unwillingness on their part to walk in the Lord's ways with a whole heart. [*sklērokardia*]

10:9 Joined together (*synezeuxen*)—The verb *syzeugnymi* literally means "to yoke together" (e.g., Xenophon, *Cyr.* 2.2.26), but it is also used more generally for the joining together of any two items (e.g., Ezek. 1:11), sometimes for the uniting of a husband and wife in mar-

riage (e.g., Josephus, *Ant.* 6.13.8 §309; cf. LSJ, 1669; BAGD, 775; BDAG, 954). The perspective that God himself is the one who unites a man and woman together in marriage changes the way that the issues surrounding divorce are understood. [*syzeugnymi*]

10:15 Like a child (*hōs paidion*)—The noun *paidion* appears earlier in Mark's Gospel for children who receive healing and deliverance from Jesus: the twelve-year-old daughter of Jairus (5:39-41), the daughter of the Syrophoenician woman (7:30), and the possessed son of the man who struggles with faith (9:24). In addition, Jesus uses a *paidion* in Mark 9:36-37 as an object lesson for his status-seeking disciples in order to teach them about the importance of lowly service. Jesus' followers must be willing to welcome children, those who are without power, position, and wealth. The kingdom of God does not belong to those who have high standing and great influence in the world but to those who, like children, appear to be unimportant according to the world's standards (10:14). Therefore, to receive the kingdom as a child means to give up the pursuit for power and prestige in the world and to come to God with a recognition of one's own helplessness (Cranfield, 323-24). Mark emphasizes this same point through the following account of a rich man who will not give up his station in life to enter into the kingdom of God (10:17-22). Other key words in Mark 10:13-16 include "rebuked" (see 8:32), "the kingdom of God" (see 1:15; 9:47), and "truly" (see 3:28). [*paidion*]

10:17 Good (*agathe*)—The rich man and Jesus have different ideas about the meaning of the word "good." The rich man apparently defines goodness in terms of personal piety attained through human achievement (Lane, 365). Since he felt that he had fulfilled God's commandments from his youth, he probably also believed himself to be good. Now he was asking another good man what else he should do to guarantee eternal life. Jesus' question in Mark 10:18 is not a confession of his own sinfulness but rather a challenge to the rich man's notion of goodness. Jesus points the man to the goodness of God. God is good in an unlimited and perfect way, not by achievement but by his eternal character. This perfect standard of God's righteousness complicates the rich man's quest for eternal life. Instead of taking the opportunity to rethink his views, the rich man simply drops the offending word and addresses Jesus as "teacher" (10:20) rather than as "good teacher" (10:17). [*agathos*]

To inherit (*klēronomēsō*)—The NT commonly uses the verb *klēronomeō* for receiving or obtaining the promises and gifts of God (W. Foerster, *TDNT* 3:781). This instance in Mark 10:17 is the only use of the verb "to inherit" in Mark's Gospel, although the related words "heir" and "inheritance" appear in the parable of the vineyard in Mark 12:7. In the context of Mark's Gospel, "inheriting eternal life," "entering life," "entering the kingdom of God," and "being saved" are all synonymous expressions (Hooker, 241; Lane, 370). Note the similarity between Mark 9:43, 45, and 47 and also Mark 10:17, 23, 24, 25, and 26. [*klēronomeō*]

10:19 Do not defraud (*mē aposterēsēs*)—To defraud involves taking what rightfully belongs to another through corrupt means such as underpaying employees (Mal. 3:5; Sir. 29:22; Jas 5:4), refusing to pay back loans (Sir. 29:6-7), and initiating unjust lawsuits (1 Cor. 6:7-8; cf. BAGD, 99; BDAG, 121). Jesus' rough summary of the second half of the ten commandments includes a command against defrauding others. Two unusual features in Jesus' summary are that he moves the fifth commandment on honoring parents to the end of the list and that he apparently omits the tenth commandment against cov-

eting, replacing it with one against defrauding. This prohibition against cheating others appears to be an expansion of the eighth commandment against theft (Gundry, 553). The rich man sincerely claims to have kept all of these laws, but his subsequent refusal to give up his possessions and follow Jesus exposes his failure to obey the first and most important of the ten commandments which prohibits placing anything in the way of one's devotion to God. [*apostereō*]

10:21 He loved (*ēgapēsen*)—This is the only place where Mark directly states that Jesus loved someone, although the idea that love characterized Jesus' life flows naturally from his teaching that love for God and for one's neighbor constitute God's most important commands (12:28-31). Elsewhere, Mark describes Jesus' heart response toward others as involving compassion (1:41; 6:34; cf. 8:2). He probably means something similar here. In his compassion and love, Jesus feels a deep sense of affection for needy people, an emotional response that moves him to care for them. (See 6:34.) In looking at the rich man, Jesus sees a needy sinner and seeks to help the man by jarring him into a recognition of his own lack of repentance. He also offers himself to the man as the way to eternal life. On following Jesus, see 1:18 and 8:34. [*agapaō*]

10:22 He was shocked (*stygnasas*)—This relatively rare verb, sometimes translated as "his face fell" (NASB; cf. RSV; NIV; NLT), is perhaps better rendered as "he was shocked" (NRSV). The word seems to be used in Mark 10:22 not so much for the man's outward appearance as for his intense reaction to Jesus' demands, his sense of dismay, sadness, and shock (cf. the first suggested translation in BAGD, 771; BDAG, 949). The LXX translation of Ezekiel uses the verb with a similar meaning to describe the way in which onlookers are appalled over the fate of those who are under the judgment of God (Ezek. 27:35; 32:10). [*stygnazō*]

10:25 The eye of a needle (*tēs trymalias tēs rhaphidos*)—Jesus is referring to the small hole in a sewing needle (BAGD, 734, 828; BDAG, 904, 1018). A large camel has a better chance of squeezing through the eye of a needle than a rich man has of finding his way into the kingdom of God. Interpretations that reduce the severity of this statement, such as the one in which "the eye of the needle" serves as the name for a small gate in a city wall through which a camel might be able to crawl, distort the meaning of the Greek words involved and more importantly fail to do justice the point of Jesus' comparison. It is completely impossible to fit a rich man through the entrance into the kingdom of God. His only hope lies with the God of the impossible (10:27). [*trymalia + rhaphis*]

10:30 Persecutions (*diōgmōn*)—In the NT, the noun *diōgmos* always refers to religious persecution, the oppression and suffering that comes to those who profess faith in Jesus at the hands of those who oppose this belief (e.g., Acts 8:1; 13:50; 2 Cor. 12:10; 2 Thess.. 1:4; cf. BAGD, 201; BDAG, 253). Following Jesus leads to both reward and suffering in the present time and also to eternal life in the age to come. Earlier in Mark's Gospel, Jesus warns that some who welcome the message of the Gospel will fall away in the midst of persecution (4:16-17). [*diōgmos*]

10:33 Gentiles (*ethnesin*)—Jesus' prediction of his coming death and resurrection in Mark 10:32-34, the third in a series of three similar predictions (8:31; 9:31; 10:32-34), includes a number of details not previously disclosed. For example, Jesus predicts that he will be handed over to the Gentiles who will treat him with cruelty before his execution. In this

context, *ethnesin* refers to non-Jews, those outside of the people of Israel (cf. N. Walter, *EDNT* 1:382). The portrayal of Gentiles in Mark's Gospel is mixed, containing both positive and negative aspects. Although Jesus directs his ministry primarily toward the people of Israel, he also travels outside of Galilee into predominantly Gentile territories and responds positively toward those who come to him for help (5:1-20; 7:24-8:9, 22-26). Jesus anticipates a future mission in which the Gospel will go out to all the nations, and therefore to the Gentiles (7:27; 13:10; 14:9; cf. 11:17). At the crucifixion, the Gentile centurion recognizes the identity of Jesus and declares him to be the Son of God (15:39). However, Jesus suffers at the hands of the Gentile authorities (10:33-34; 15:1-26), setting a pattern for his followers who will face a similar fate (13:9-13). In addition, the rulers of the Gentiles serve as negative examples since they selfishly seek power and authority over their subjects (10:42). [*ethnos*]

10:38 Baptism (*baptisma*)—There is no example of the word *baptisma* in any existing Greek literature prior to its use in the NT (A. Oepke, *TDNT* 1:545; G. R. Beasley-Murray, *NIDNTT* 1:149-50). In other words, *baptisma* first appears in the NT, where it refers primarily to John's baptism of repentance (e.g., Matt. 3:7; Mark 1:4; 11:20; Luke 7:29; Acts 13:24; 19:4) and to the baptism practiced by the early church (Rom. 6:4; Eph. 4:5; 1 Pet. 3:21). In Mark 10:38-39, Jesus uses *baptisma* in a different way, as a metaphor for his suffering and death (cf. Luke 12:50). On the similarities between Mark's account of Jesus' baptism and his description of Jesus' death, see the discussion on "torn apart" in 1:10. Isa. 21:4 LXX employs the related verb *baptizō* in a comparable way as a metaphor for an overwhelming experience of disaster. On the word "cup" see 14:36. [*baptisma*]

10:40 At my right or at my left (*ek dexiōn mou ē ex euōnymōn*)—According to the custom of the day, the place of highest honor was at the right, and the next in honor was at the left (Lane, 379; cf. 2 Sam. 16:6; 1 Kings 2:19; Ps. 45:9; 110:1; 1 Esd 4:29; Sir. 12:12; Mark 12:36; 14:62; Josephus, *Ant.* 6.11.9 §235). Later in the narrative, Mark uses almost the exact same phrase for the two robbers who were crucified with Jesus, one at his right and one at his left (15:27: *hena ek dexiōn kai hena ex euōny mōn autou*). The dramatic irony of this parallel shows that James and John indeed did not know what they were asking for (10:38) nor had they prepared themselves adequately to accept the same fate as Jesus (10:39). [*dexios, euōnymos*]

10:43 Servant (*diakonos*)—At the time of Jesus, a common, concrete sense of the word "servant" was "one who waits on tables, one who serves a meal to others." This more precise meaning appears in the NT both for the noun *diakonos* (John 2:5, 9; cf. Matt. 22:13) and for the related verb *diakoneō* (Mark 1:31; Luke 10:40; 12:37; 17:8; 22:27; John 12:2; Acts 6:2). Important for understanding *diakonos* is that this basic, concrete sense still echoes in the more general and comprehensive uses of the word. A servant, like someone who waits on tables, takes an inferior position in order to meet the needs of others (H. W. Beyer, *TDNT* 2:82-85, 88; cf. Luke 22:26-27). In the context of Mark 10:42-45, the role of a servant receives further clarification through the negative example of the Gentile rulers who selfishly desire to hold authority over others and through the positive example of Jesus who serves by giving his life. [*diakonos*]

10:44 Slave (*doulos*)—Other references to slaves in Mark's Gospel use the word *doulos* literally for laborers who are the property of an owner (12:2, 4; 13:34; 14:47). However, in Mark 10:44, "slave" occurs in a more general way for someone who gives allegiance to another and who therefore is under obligation to this "master" (cf. BAGD, 205-6; BDAG, 260; Rom. 6:17-20). This idea of obligation or compulsion distinguishes the meaning of "slave" from that of "servant" (cf. K. H. Rengstorf, *TDNT* 2:261). Slaves do not serve as a matter of choice, since they are not free. The needs of someone else determine their responsibilities. In addition, slaves do not profit from their own activity, since their labor belongs to the master. Just as the owner of a tree has a right to that tree's fruit, so a master owns the fruit of a slave's labor (Spicq, 1:381-83). Therefore, the position of a slave within the community of believers involves accepting the obligation to work solely for the benefit of others. [*doulos*]

10:45 Ransom (*lytron*)—Outside the NT, the word *lytron* is commonly used for a ransom, for the payment made to bring about release and to buy freedom for those held in bondage, including prisoners of war, slaves, and debtors (MM, 382-83; H. M. Büchsel, *TDNT* 4:340; K. Kertelge, *EDNT* 2:365; Spicq, 425-28). In the NT, *lytron* occurs only in Mark 10:45 and the parallel passage in Matt. 20:28, although 1 Tim. 2:6 contains the related compound word *antilytron*. These NT references all present Jesus as giving his life as a ransom, as paying through his death for the freedom of those held in bondage and slavery. On the Son of Man, see 2:10. [*lytron*]

For (*anti*)—The prevailing sense of the preposition *anti* involves the idea of substitution (M. J. Harris, *NIDNTT* 3:1179-80). For example, Abraham offers up a ram as a burnt offering "instead of" (*anti*) his son Isaac (Gen. 22:13 LXX). David laments for Absalom, wishing that he had died "in place of" (*anti*) his son (2 Kgdms 18:33 LXX). According to Jesus, if a son asks for a fish, his father would never think to give him a snake "instead of" (*anti*) fish (Luke 11:11). The use of *anti* to express substitution fits within the context of Mark 10:45, since the word "ransom" conveys a similar idea, that a payment is received as a substitute in exchange for those who had forfeited their lives or freedom (cf. Josephus, *Ant.* 14.7.1 §107). The life of Jesus, surrendered in a sacrificial death, takes the place for many others who find deliverance through this ransom. [*anti*]

10:47 Son of David (*huie Dauid*)—The name "Son of David" functions as a messianic title, one that highlights the Messiah's status as a descendant of David who inherits God's promises (E. Lohse, *TDNT* 8:480-82). In his covenant with David, God promised that he would establish David's royal lineage so that his house, throne, and kingdom would endure forever (2 Sam. 7:12-16). Therefore, the title "Son of David" expresses the hope that God will soon raise up a descendant of David who will restore the kingdom to Israel and rule over God's people with righteousness (cf. Mark 11:10). The intertestamental writing *Psalms of Solomon* uses the title "Son of David" in a similar way for a king who will throw off the wicked rule of foreign nations and reestablish Israel's glory, reigning over God's holy people with power (*Pss. Sol.* 17:21). Jesus shows by healing the blind man that he accepts the designation "Son of David" as an accurate description of his identity. However, later in Mark's Gospel, Jesus teaches that "Son of David," while correct, is an insufficient title since the Messiah is more than David's son. He is David's Lord (12:35-37). For more on the crowd's response to Bartimaeus, see "rebuke" in 8:32. [*huios + Dauid*]

10:50 Cloak (*himation*)—Although *himation* may refer to clothing in general, the word points more specifically to an outer garment, a mantle or cloak, in contexts where it is laid aside for the sake of pursuing some activity (W. Radl, *EDNT* 2:187; cf. John 13:4; Acts

7:58). It may have been the custom of the day for beggars to spread out a cloak on the ground to receive alms (Taylor, 449; Hooker, 253). Earlier in the narrative, Simon and Andrew left behind their nets (1:18) and Levi his tax booth to respond to the call of Jesus (2:14). In casting aside his cloak, Bartimaeus may have likewise left behind his occupation and means of income to meet Jesus and follow him. [*himation*]

10:51 Teacher (*rhabbouni*)—The title *rhabbouni* is used twice in the NT in reference to Jesus, once by Bartimaeus (10:51) and once by Mary Magdalene (John 20:16). In the second instance, the Gospel writer John translates this Jewish form of address into Greek as *didaskale* ("teacher"). In the NT, the intensified form *rhabbouni* does not differ significantly in meaning from the more common title *rhabbi* ("Rabbi"), a title of respect used most of all by students to address their teacher (E. Lohse, *TDNT* 6:961-65). Elsewhere in Mark's Gospel, "Rabbi" always appears in the words of the disciples as they speak to Jesus (9:5; 11:21; 14:45). [*rhabbouni*]

10:52 He was following (*ēkolouthei*)—Bartimaeus may have chosen to walk behind Jesus in a literal sense as he headed toward Jerusalem, but the verb *akoloutheō* also has a metaphorical significance in Mark's Gospel, indicating a personal allegiance to Jesus and to his teaching. This deeper significance for *akoloutheō* occurs whenever Mark refers to individuals following Jesus (1:18; 2:14; 8:34; 10:21, 28; 14:54; 15:41). Like a disciple, Bartimaeus responds to a call (10:49-50), addresses Jesus as "Teacher" (10:51), and follows him on the way (10:52). [*akoloutheō*]

11:2 Colt (*pōlon*)—Although the noun *pōlos* often refers to the colt of a horse, it also may indicate other kinds of young animals, including the colt of a donkey (O. Michel, *TDNT* 6:959-61; MM, 561; cf. Justin, *1 Apol.* 54.7). Mark's choice of *pōlos* for a young donkey is in keeping with the usage of the word in the LXX (cf. Gen. 32:15; 49:11; Judg. 10:4; 12:14), especially in Zech. 9:9. In that verse, Israel's king comes to Jerusalem riding on a donkey, that is, on a young colt (*pōlon*). Matthew and John are both more explicit about Jesus' fulfillment of this prophecy in Zech. 9:9 and about his use of the colt of a donkey (Matt. 21:1-7; John 12:14-15). [*pōlos*]

11:9 Hosanna (*hōsanna*)—-The word "hosanna" appears six times in the NT, always in connection with Jesus' triumphal entry into Jerusalem (cf. Matt. 21:9, 15; Mark 11:9, 10; John 12:13). The Greek transliteration *hōsanna* ultimately derives from the Hebrew phrase at beginning of Ps. 118:25, which expresses a cry to God for help, "save now" (W. Rebell, *EDNT* 3:509). After shouting "hosanna," those who accompany Jesus into Jerusalem continue their proclamation with the first part of Ps. 118:26, "Blessed is the one who comes in the name of the Lord." The second use of "hosanna" in Mark, appearing in 11:10, is followed by the phrase "in the highest." This is either a petition addressed to God ("save now, you in the highest") or an exhortation to the angels to join in ("cry hosanna, you in the highest"). [*hōsanna*]

11:13 Fig tree (*sykēn*)—-The fig tree sheds its leaves in the fall and sprouts leaves again in the spring, as early as late March. The time of the Passover (14:1) is not the season for ripe figs, not even for the early figs that grow on the old wood of the tree and ripen in June, much less for the late figs that ripen on new shoots from the middle of August until October. Jesus could not expect to find ripe fruit, but he could realistically hope to find the buds which begin to form just before the fig tree puts forth its leaves. Although these buds are of marginal edibility, people did eat them on occasion (Gundry, 635-36; cf. *m Sheb.* 4:7). Yet Jesus does not even find buds; he sees nothing except leaves. Jesus' subsequent cursing of the fig tree functions as a symbolic representation of the judgment awaiting the religious leaders in Jerusalem who had turned the temple into a den of robbers (11:15-18). Like a fig tree with leaves but no fruit of any kind, they put on an outward show of honoring God, but their hearts are far away from him (7:6). [*sykē*]

11:15 Moneychangers (*kollybistōn*)—-Moneychangers were necessary because of the requirements surrounding the annual temple tax (Exod. 30:13-16). Each year, every adult Jewish male gave half a shekel to the temple (cf. Matt. 17:24-27; *m Sheqal.* 1:1-2:5), a tax to be paid in the currency "of the sanctuary" according to Exod. 30:13. In the first century A.D., all temple dues had to be paid in Tyrian currency, since the Tyrian shekel was the closest available equivalent to the old Hebrew shekel. Moneychangers at the temple were permitted to charge for their service of exchanging Tyrian coins for the more common Roman money (Lane, 405). [*kollybistēs*]

11:17 Den of Robbers (*spēlaion lēstōn*)—-The noun *spēlaion* primarily refers to a "cave" (BAGD, 762; BDAG, 938), a place that could serve as a refuge for hiding from danger (e.g., Josh. 10:16; 1 Sam. 13:6; 22:1; 1 Kings 18:4; 2 Macc. 6:11; Rev. 6:15), for example, as a hideout for robbers (Jer. 7:11; Josephus, *Ant.* 14.15.4 §415; 14.15.5 §421). The word for "robber" (*lēstēs*) contrasts with that for "thief" (*kleptēs*), since thieves steal secretly through cunning while robbers steal openly through threats or acts of violence (N. Hillyer, *NIDNTT* 3:377-79; Spicq, 389-90). Judas, who pilfered funds from the money bag, was a thief (John 12:6), while those who beat the traveler in the parable of the good

Samaritan, taking his belongings and leaving him half dead, were robbers (Luke 10:30). At first, it may seem like hyperbole to accuse the temple leadership of armed robbery as a result of the swindling that apparently took place through the sale of sacrificial animals and the exchange of money. Yet in the next verse (11:18), the chief priests and the scribes demonstrate the accuracy of the charge by beginning to plan for Jesus' destruction (cf. 12:3-8). [spēlaion + lēstēs]

11:22 Faith (*pistin*)—In the earlier part of the narrative, references to faith primarily occur in passages concerning those who overcome obstacles to reach Jesus in order to receive healing from him (2:5; 5:34, 36; 9:24; 10:52). A shift takes place in Mark 11:22-24, since there Jesus calls on his followers to direct their faith toward God and to express their trust in him through petitionary prayer. The narrative background of Jesus' healing miracles clarifies the type of faith that God honors. Like those who came to Jesus for healing, people who pray in faith must have a persistent sense of confidence in God's power and compassion toward them. For more on faith, see 2:5. [*pistis*]

11:23 Mountain (*orei*)—Mark's Gospel includes a number of references to the Mount of Olives during Jesus' ministry in the area around Jerusalem (11:1; 13:3; 14:26), and it is the only mountain referred to by name in Mark. When Jesus mentions "this mountain," he seems to be pointing to a specific location, perhaps to the Mount of Olives which stretches from north to south on the east side of Jerusalem (Lane, 394, 410). During his morning journey into Jerusalem, Jesus was able to use the Mount of Olives as an object lesson on faith. The one who has faith in God can move a large mountain such as this one. Jesus' proverbial statement shows that through faith a

person can accomplish tasks that are apparently impossible (9:23), because all things are possible with God (10:27; cf. BAGD, 582; BDAG, 725; Matt. 17:20; 21:21; 1 Cor. 13:2). [*oros*]

11:27 Chief priests (*archiereis*)—The chief priests included the currently presiding high priest as well as his predecessors in the high priestly office. Since the high priest regularly came from a select number of priestly families, the men in these privileged families also functioned as chief priests, even if they never actually held the office of high priest. Under the authority of the Romans, the chief priests directed the internal affairs of the nation through their leadership on the Sanhedrin, the foremost Jewish council (Schürer, *History* 2:227-35; cf. Acts 4:5-6). In Mark's Gospel, the chief priests cooperate with the elders and scribes to plot against Jesus (11:18; 12:12; 14:1, 10-11), bring him to trial (10:33; 14:43, 53-65), and deliver him over to the Romans for punishment (10:33; 15:1-3, 10-11). They are last seen in Mark's Gospel mocking Jesus as he suffers on the cross, claiming that they would believe in him if only he could save himself from his cruel fate (15:31-32). [*archiereus*]

Elders (*presbyteroi*)—At the time of Jesus, the Sanhedrin consisted of chief priests, scribes, and elders (cf. 8:31; 14:43, 53; 15:1). According to Mark 11:27-28 representatives from each of these groups questioned Jesus' authority. The elders were the lay members of the council, distinct from the chief priests in that they did not belong to priestly families and distinct from the scribes in that they were not ordained religious teachers (G. Bornkamm, *TDNT* 6:658-59; Schürer, *History* 2:212-13). Synonymous terms used to describe these elders include "the leading men of the people" (Luke 19:47; cf. Josephus, *Life* 194), "the notables" (Josephus, *JW* 2.15.3 §318; 2.17.2 §410), and "the powerful"

(Josephus, *JW* 2.15.2 §316; 2.17.3 §411). For more on the scribes, see 1:22. [*presbyteros*]

11:28 Authority (*exousia*)—The chief priests, scribes, and elders inquire about the source of Jesus' authority, that is, about the origin of his right to exercise power within the temple. Their question intends to cast doubt on the legitimacy of Jesus' authority, but their subsequent conversation with Jesus serves to support it. Jesus responds to their demand for information with a question followed by a command, "answer me" (11:30). The religious leaders feel obligated to obey him even though they have nothing to say, while Jesus feels free to ignore their inquiry. Jesus acts with authority, even when his authority is under attack (cf. Evans, 205). For more on authority, see 1:22. [*exousia*]

11:32 Prophet (*prophētēs*)—A prophet is one through whom God speaks to reveal his message (1:2-3; cf. BAGD, 723; BDAG, 890). The common identification of John as a prophet is surprising since for hundreds of years, according to many Jews, no true prophet had spoken in Israel (cf. 1 Macc. 4:46; 9:27). At the end of the Maccabean revolt, a lawful assembly of the people of Israel in 140 B.C. agreed that Simon should be their governor and high priest and military commander forever "until a faithful prophet should arise" (1 Macc. 14:41-42). This decision was written on tablets of brass and displayed in a prominent place in the temple (1 Macc. 14:48). The fears of the religious leaders were justified, since the presence of a true prophet would undermine the legitimacy of their own claims to authority. [*prophētēs*]

12:1 Tenant farmers (*geōrgois*)—The translation "tenant farmers" (NET; NLT) communicates that these agricultural workers labor not on their own property but on rented land. Jesus' parable reflects the social back-ground of the time in which large estates often belonged to absentee owners who leased out the property to tenant farmers who actually worked the land. The lease agreement would normally stipulate that a portion of the produce went to the owner as rent payment (Lane, 416-17). On parables, see 4:2. [*geōrgos*]

12:4 They struck him on the head (*ekephaliōsan*)—This word is unusual both in its spelling (*kephalioō* instead of the more common *kephalaioō*) and in its meaning. The expected sense would be "to sum up," but the context demands a rendering such as "to strike on the head" (BAGD, 430; BDAG, 541-42; MM, 342; LSJ, 945). By way of analogy, the Greek verb *gnathoō* means "to hit on the cheek" based on its relationship to the noun *gnathos*, "cheek" (LSJ, 353). Likewise, *kephalioō* may convey the idea of hitting someone on the head based on the meaning of *kephalē*, "head" or *kephalion*, "head" (Gundry, 685; cf. Howard, *Accidence* 395). [*kephalioō*]

12:6 Beloved (*agapēton*)—The adjective *agapētos* occurs only two other times in Mark's Gospel, both of them in reference to Jesus. At the baptism and at the transfiguration, a heavenly voice declares that Jesus is the beloved Son (1:11; 9:7). The parable of the vineyard highlights Jesus' unique position among the messengers sent by God, since he comes not as a slave but as an only son. For more on "beloved," see 1:11. [*agapētos*]

12:10 Cornerstone (*kephalēn gōnias*)—This phrase *kephalēn gōnias*, literally "the head of the corner" (KJV; RSV), occurs five times in the NT (Matt. 21:42; Mark 12:10; Luke 20:17; Acts 4:11; 1 Pet. 2:7), always in quotations of Ps. 118:22. By pointing to the corner at the head, that is, the one at the farthest extremity, this phrase refers to the most important foundation stone, the squared cornerstone that was the first to be laid. It firmly fixed the building's overall site and determined the direction for the rest of the construction (H. Krämer, *EDNT* 1:267-69; W. Mundle, *NID-NTT* 3:388-90; cf. NET; NLT). Although rejected by the religious leaders, Jesus became the essential, decisive part of the foundation in God's building plans. On "rejected," see 8:31. It is less likely that the phrase "the head of the corner" is referring to the "capstone," the final stone in a building, often set over the gate or entrance (cf. NIV; J. Jeremias, *TDNT* 1:792-93). After all, the assumption in both Luke 20:17-18 and 1 Pet. 2:7-8 is that someone could stumble over this stone and fall, which would be impossible with a capstone. [*kephalē* + *gōnia*]

12:13 To trap (*agreusōsin*)—The verb *agreuō* can mean literally "to catch or trap an animal, to hunt" (cf. Xenophon, *Cyn* 12.6; Job 10:16 LXX; MM, 6) or figuratively "to catch or trap a person in an unguarded moment for the purpose of causing harm" (e.g., Prov.. 5:22; 6:26 LXX; cf. LSJ, 14; BAGD, 13; BDAG, 15). The Pharisees and Herodians hope to ensnare Jesus with their question. If Jesus objects to the tax, they can denounce him to the Romans as a political agitator, but if he sides with the government, he risks losing the support of the people. On the Pharisees and the Herodians, see 2:16 and 3:6. [*agreuō*]

12:14 You do not show partiality (*ou . . . blepeis eis prosōpon anthrōpōn*)—Using an idiomatic expression, the Pharisees and Herodians acknowledge Jesus' impartiality by describing him as one who does not look into the face of people. Parallel expressions in the NT for *blepein eis prosōpon* ("to look into a face;" Matt. 22:16; Mark 12:14) include *thaumazein prosōpon* ("to esteem a face;" Jude 16) and *lambanein prosōpon* ("to receive a face;" Luke 20:21; Gal. 2:6; cf. Acts 10:34; Rom. 2:11; Eph. 6:9; Col.

3:25; Jas 2:1, 9; 1 Pet. 1:17; E. Lohse, *TDNT* 6:779-80). In the NT, partiality is always viewed in negative terms. Showing favoritism on the basis of economic level (Jas 2:1-9) or social status (Gal. 2:6) or ethnic background (Acts 10:34-35; Rom. 2:11-12) is out of step with the character of God. [*blepō* + *prosōpon*]

Taxes (*kēnson*)—The word *kēnsos* could indicate (1) a census, that is, an enrollment of names and an assessment of property for the purpose of taxation or (2) the taxes paid out as a result of such a census. These taxes took the forms of a poll tax, a fixed sum for each individual enrolled, and a property tax, a varying amount based on the assessment (K. Weiss, *TDNT* 9:81; LSJ, 947). The latter meaning fits the context of Mark 12:14. This census tax was a requirement for all provinces under the direct rule of the Roman empire. Josephus details such a census that included Judea which was taken in A.D. 6. This Roman census provoked an ill-fated revolt led by Judas the Galilean who urged the people to reject the tax and to rebel against their foreign dictators (Acts 5:37; Josephus, *JW* 2.8.1 §118; *Ant.* 20.5.2 §102). Animosity toward Roman taxation continued on among the people of Judea throughout the time of Jesus' ministry (H. Balz, *EDNT* 2:287; Evans, 246). [*kēnsos*]

12:17 Render (*apodote*)—According to the NIV, the Pharisees and Herodians ask Jesus in Mark 12:14 whether or not it is right to "pay" taxes to Caesar, and Jesus answers them in Mark 12:17 by telling them to "give" to Caesar (cf. NRSV; NET; NLT). In this case, the KJV stays closer to the Greek text by translating *dounai* in verse 14 with "give" and *apodote* in verse 17 with "render." The verb in Jesus' answer, *apodidōmi*, generally implies making a payment that is owed (cf. Rom. 13:7). Elsewhere in the NT, it occurs for paying a debt (Matt. 5:26; 18:25-26, 28-30, 34; Luke 7:42; 12:59), a wage

(Matt. 20:8), a bill of rent (Matt. 21:41; Luke 10:35), and a vow to the Lord (Matt. 5:33). Therefore, Jesus' answer puts his listeners under obligation, not only to Caesar, but more importantly,. to God (A. Sand, *EDNT* 1:128; Cranfield, 372). [*apodidōmi*]

12:18 Sadducees (*Saddoukaioi*)—The Sadducees make their first and only appearance in Mark's Gospel in 12:18-27. They belonged to a religious party of aristocrats who came from the wealthiest and most influential families in Jerusalem (Josephus, *Ant.* 13.10.6 §298; 18.1.4 §17). A close interrelationship existed between the chief priests and the Sadducees; both groups shared similar views, privileged positions, and political connections (Acts 4:1-4; 5:17-18; Josephus, *Ant.* 20.9.1 §199). The Sadducees accepted only the authority of the written Law of Moses and therefore rejected the oral traditions of the Pharisees (Josephus, *Ant.* 13.10.6 §297; 18.1.4 §16). Another teaching of the Pharisees dismissed by the Sadducees was the future resurrection of the body (Acts 23:8; Josephus, *JW* 2.8.14 §165; *Ant.* 18.1.4 §16; cf. Schürer, *History* 2:404-14). In Mark's Gospel, the Sadducees serve as examples of those who cannot understand the Scriptures because they fail to take into account the power of God. On power, see 5:30. [*Saddoukaios*]

12:24 You are mistaken (*planasthe*)—The verb *planaō* can mean "to lead astray" as in Mark 13:5-6 where Jesus warns his followers against false teachers who will seek to mislead them (cf. 2 Tim. 3:13; 1 John 2:26), or it can mean "to go astray." A frequent use of *planaō* occurs in descriptions of sheep that have gone astray, wandering off and becoming lost (Deut. 22:1; Ps. 119:176 [118:176 LXX]; Isa. 53:6; Ezek. 34:4, 16; Matt. 18:12-13; 1 Pet. 2:25). It is also possible to wander away from the truth and therefore to be mistaken in one's judgment (BAGD, 665; BDAG, 822-23; cf. Jas 5:19). Jesus consid-

ers the Sadducees to have gone astray, and at the end of the passage in verse 27 he intensifies his criticism with the addition of an adverb. They are "badly mistaken" (NIV). [*planaō*]

12:28 Scribes (*grammateōn*)—The scribes, ordained teachers of the Law of Moses, figure prominently in Mark 12:28-40. First, Jesus acknowledges the wisdom of one scribe who recognizes the importance of love for God and one's neighbor (12:28-34). This passage is unique in Mark's Gospel in that it presents a scribe positively as an honest seeker after truth. Next, Jesus finds fault with the teaching of the scribes (12:35-37) as well as their hypocritical behavior (12:38-40). For more on the scribes, see 1:22. [*grammateus*]

12:30 Mind (*dianoias*)—The Hebrew text of Deut. 6:5 reads "heart . . . soul . . . might," which is translated in the LXX with *kardia* . . . *psychē . . . dynamis*, although variations exist within the LXX manuscript tradition on this verse. The quotation of Deut. 6:5 in Mark 12:30 differs from the standard LXX translation in adding the phrase "with your whole mind." Apparently, both *kardia* and *dianoia* represent the Hebrew word for heart, since there is evidence that some LXX manuscripts used *dianoia* instead of *kardia* in the translation of Deut. 6:5 (cf. Cranfield, 377; Evans, 264). The implication is that loving God with your heart includes loving him with your mind, that is, at the center of your thought, understanding, and reflection (Behm, *TDNT* 4:963-67; BAGD, 187; BDAG, 234). Other words in this passage that emphasize the importance of the mind are *synesis* ("understanding") in verse 33 and *nounechōs* ("intelligently") in verse 34. [*dianoia*]

12:34 Not far (*ou makran*)—To be "not far" from the kingdom of God is a positive description, a commendation given by Jesus in light of the thoughtful response of the scribe. It should not be taken as a subtle criticism, indicating some continuing deficiency in the scribe. The man accepts Jesus' teaching, and Jesus affirms him. To be "not far" is the same as to be "near" (cf. Deut. 30:11-14 LXX; Acts 17:27-28), but what it means to be near the kingdom of God depends in large part on what Jesus meant by "the kingdom of God." See the discussion at 1:15. If Jesus is referring to the future coming of the kingdom in power, then to be near the kingdom means that the scribe is open to it, prepared to enter at its arrival. If Jesus is speaking of the kingdom in its present, hidden form, then to be near it means that the scribe is like the good earth, ready to receive the message of the kingdom and bear fruit. [*makran*]

12:35 Son of David (*huios Dauid*)—In Mark 12:35-37, Jesus does not deny that the Messiah is the Son of David, but he does show that the title, though correct, is insufficient for understanding the true status of the Messiah. The prophetic Scriptures attest to the descent of the Messiah from the line of David (Isa. 9:2-7; 11:1-10; Jer. 23:5-6; 30:8-9; 33:14-22; Ezek. 34:23-24; 37:24-25; Hos. 3:5; Amos 9:11), and earlier in the narrative Jesus accepts the designation "Son of David" when he heals Bartimaeus (10:47-49). However, the Messiah is more than David's Son, since he is also David's Lord. For more on "Son of David," see 10:47. On "Christ," see 1:1. [*huios Dauid*]

12:38 Long robes (*stolais*)—The *stolai* were long robes, often worn by priests (e.g., Exod. 29:21, 29; 31:10; Philo, *Embassy* 296; Josephus, *Ant.* 3.7.1 §151; 11.4.2 §80) and probably in imitation of the priests by other religious leaders. The scribes liked to walk around in long robes, perhaps in order to associate themselves with the prestigious temple rulers and in this way to draw attention to themselves (Evans, 278). The NT also uses

the same word to refer to the white robes of angels (Mark 16:5; cf. 2 Macc. 5:2) and glorified believers (Rev. 6:11; 7:9-14; 22:14). [*stolē*]

12:39 Most important seats (*prōtokathedrias*)—The seats of honor in the synagogue were reserved for respected guests and learned scholars. Those with the best seats sat on a bench, facing the congregation, in front of the chest containing the Scriptures (Cranfield, 384; Evans, 278). "How did the elders sit in session? It was facing the people, with their backs toward the sanctuary" (*t Meg.* 3:21). The scribes enjoyed the prestige and visibility that these seats of honor provided. On the synagogue, see 1:21. [*prōtokathedria*]

12:42 Two small copper coins (*lepta duo*)—A *lepton*, a small copper coin, was the least valuable piece of money in circulation (MM, 374). As Mark points out, two *lepta* were equal to one *quadrans*, the smallest Roman coin, which in turn was worth one-64th of a denarius (B. Schwank, *EDNT* 2:350). Therefore, the value of each *lepton* was quite small in comparison to a denarius which was a standard daily wage for a manual laborer (cf. Matt. 20:2). Since the poor widow had two coins, she could have easily given one and kept the other (Lane, 443), but instead, as Jesus says, she gave her "whole life" (*holon ton bion*; 12:44). Shortly after emphasizing the priority of loving God with one's whole heart, whole soul, whole mind, and whole strength, Jesus notices and commends a woman who lives out this complete devotion to God. In contrast to the rich man who refused to leave his possessions (10:21-22), the poor widow gave up all she had (12:44). [*lepton*]

13:4 Sign (*sēmeion*)—In this context, the disciples are not asking for a sign in the sense of a compelling proof of the validity of Jesus' teaching. Instead, they are requesting a warning signal that will allow them to recognize the arrival of a future event, the destruction of the temple that Jesus has just predicted (Evans, 304-5; cf. Luke 21:25; Acts 2:19). For more on the word "sign" in Mark, see 8:11. For a discussion of the complexity of this discourse and what it refers to, see the discussion of "sign" in Luke 21:7. The Gospel of Mark consistently puts the desire for signs in a negative light. Jesus refuses to give the Pharisees a sign (8:11-12), and he also fails to offer one to his disciples in Mark 13, choosing instead to warn them about the deception that comes so easily to those who seek signs (13:4-5, 22). In other words, the disciples' request for a sign is misguided. Jesus' teaching in Mark 13 is not a straightforward answer to a discerning question. Instead, Jesus corrects his disciples by telling them what they need to know about the future: that disasters and persecutions do not signal the close of the age, that the complex of events surrounding the end will take place so rapidly that they will leave no time for careful preparations, and that therefore the followers of Jesus must always be alert and ready for the coming of their master. [*sēmeion*]

13:5 Watch out (*blepete*)—The verb *blepō*, a commonly used word in the NT (133 times), often means "to see, to perceive with the eye." However, in certain contexts, the verb takes on the meaning of "to beware, take heed, watch out for something that is hazardous" (BAGD, 143; BDAG, 178-79; cf. 4:24; 8:15; 12:38). Jesus repeats this call for vigilance four times in his message to the disciples (13:5, 9, 23, 33), a repetition sometimes obscured in translations. For example, the NASB renders *blepete* with "see to it" (13:5), "be on your guard" (13:9), and "take heed" (13:23, 33). Mark's Gospel contains two lengthy teaching sections by Jesus, the parables discourse (4:1-34) and the eschatological discourse (13:1-37). In the first, Jesus punctuates his message with commands to hear

(4:3, 9, 23, 24; cf. 4:33) and in the second with commands to watch (13:5, 9, 23, 33; cf. 13:14, 29). In Mark 13:5, Jesus warns the disciples to watch out lest someone mislead them (*planēsē*). On the verb *planaō*, see 12:24. [*blepō*]

13:8 Birth pains (*ōdinōn*)—The pain associated with childbirth is used as a metaphor for times of intense suffering or anguish (R. K. Harrison, *NIDNTT* 3:858). The image of a woman in labor appears in the OT as a picture of the suffering of Israel, a travail that brings with it the hope for a new beginning (Isa. 26:17-19; 66:7-9; Hos. 13:12-14; Mic. 4:9-10; cf. Hooker, 308). Jesus' reference to birth pains communicates that the age to come will arrive after a time of great suffering. Yet in Mark 13:8, Jesus identifies wars, earthquakes, and famines as only the start of sorrows. The phrase "the beginning of birth pains" in verse 8 is parallel to "not yet the end" in verse 9. In other words, these disastrous events are not signs that the end is near; rather they are just a taste of what the last tribulation will be like before the coming of the Son of Man (Lane, 459). [*ōdin*]

13:9 Councils (*synedria*)—References in the NT to the *synedrion* generally point to the Great Sanhedrin in Jerusalem, the highest Jewish court (e.g., 14:55; 15:1). However, other local councils existed outside of Jerusalem, both in the land of Israel and in the diaspora. Any community with at least 120 Jewish men was to have a council made up of 23 members (*m Sanh.* 1:6), and the Romans allowed these councils to exercise a degree of authority over local Jewish affairs (E. Lohse, *TDNT* 7:866-67). Jesus warns that believers will be delivered up to these courts, and in this way they will follow the pattern of their Lord who was also handed over for trial before the Sanhedrin. On being handed over or betrayed, see 3:19. On the Sanhedrin, see 14:55. On synagogues, see 1:21. [*synedrion*]

Governors (*hēgemonōn*)—A governor was a Roman ruler who served as the chief administrator over a province in the Roman empire (BAGD, 343; BDAG, 433; MM, 277). Jesus himself stood trial and gave his testimony before a governor, since Pilate held this position (Matt. 27:2; Josephus, *Ant.* 18.3.1 §55; cf. Acts 23:24; 26:30-32). In Mark 13:9, Jesus made a reasonable distinction between governors and kings. A governor was in charge of maintaining direct Roman rule over a province, while a king was a local leader who served as a client ruler over a kingdom under the authority of Rome and only with its favor (BDAG, 169). On testimony, see 1:44. [*hēgemōn*]

13:10 Nations (*ethnē*)—While *ethnē* can often refer to Gentiles, those outside of the people of Israel (see 10:33), the word can also mean "nations or people" (BAGD, 218; BDAG, 276-77). According to Rev. 5:9, the redeemed of God will come from every tribe, language, people, and nation (cf. Rev. 7:9; 11:9; 14:6). The placement of *ethnos* in this set of parallel terms serves to define a nation as a group of people who have a shared sense of unity based on a common descent, a common language, or a common history and culture (cf. K. L. Schmidt, *TDNT* 2:369). In the context of Mark 13:10, proclaiming the gospel among "all the nations" includes sharing the message among the Jewish people, since the preceding verse describes the testimony of believers within Jewish courts and synagogues. In addition, the context of Mark 13:9-13 shows that communicating the good news to all the nations will take place in the midst of persecution and suffering. Concerning the Holy Spirit, who is mentioned in 13:11, see 1:8. [*ethnos*]

13:13 Will be saved (*sōthēsetai*)—References to salvation in the NT not only point to deliverance from sin and eternal condemnation (e.g., 10:26) but also to other ways of rescuing,

for example, to deliverance from physical death (3:5; 13:20) or disease (5:23, 28, 34; 6:56). Salvation in Mark 13:13 seems to convey the nuance of vindication, deliverance from accusation and shame (Lane, 460, 464). Those who remain faithful to Jesus in the midst of persecution and unjust condemnation will be vindicated. The decisions of human courts will be reversed by God who will confirm the truth of the Gospel and the wisdom of following Jesus no matter what the cost. The related noun *sōtēria* is used in a similar way in Job 13:16 LXX and Phil. 1:19, both passages in which someone who is obedient to God expects to be delivered from false accusations and unjust opposition. [*sōzō*]

13:14 The abomination of desolation (*to bdelygma tēs erēmōseōs*)—The word "abomination" frequently occurs in the OT for that which is repugnant or abhorrent to God, including, above all, idolatry (e.g., Deut. 7:25-26; 1 Kings 14:24; 2 Kings 23:13; 2 Chron. 15:8; Isa. 44:19; Jer. 16:18; Ezek. 5:11; cf. W. Foester, *TDNT* 1:598-600). The phrase "abomination of desolation" derives from the Book of Daniel (cf. Matt. 24:15), which seems to predict the setting up of idol worship in the sanctuary. This act of desecration will make the temple desolate, that is, unusable for true worship and therefore abandoned by the faithful (Dan. 9:27; 11:31; 12:11). Jesus did not believe that the prophecy of Daniel concerning the abomination of desolation was completely fulfilled by Antiochus Epiphanes's desecration of the temple in 167 B.C. (cf. 1 Macc. 1:54, 59; 6:7). He also foresaw a future fulfillment just before the end of the age, an act of sacrilege that will cause God's people to abandon their place of worship (cf. Evans 318-20). In Mark 13:14, the abomination of desolation is further clarified as "one standing where he must not." The masculine participle *estēkota* ("standing") does not agree grammatically with the neuter noun *bdelygma* ("abomination"). In other words, according to Mark 13:14, it is not the abomination that is standing; rather the abomination is a person who is standing where he should not be. The apostle Paul makes a similar prediction in 2 Thess.. 2:3-4, where he refers to a "man of lawlessness" who will take his seat in the temple of God, displaying himself as God. [*bdelygma* + *erēmōsis*]

13:17 Woe (*ouai*)—Jesus uses "woe" as a cry of lament or an expression of pity for the pregnant women and nursing mothers who will be living during the great distress that takes place immediately after the abomination of desolation. They will find it difficult to flee. The abomination of desolation will come unexpectedly, without the type of warning that allows time for making careful preparations and for gathering provisions before an escape. Those who are in Judea must immediately flee. See also the discussion on *ouai* in 14:21, the only other place where the word appears in Mark's Gospel. [*ouai*]

13:19 Tribulation (*thlipsis*)—In a general way, the noun *thlipsis* refers to trouble that brings about distress, oppression, or tribulation (BAGD, 362; BDAG, 457). Related words that appear in the NT in connection with *thlipsis* include: persecution (*diōgmos*; Mark 4:17; 2 Thess.. 1:4), grief (*lypē*; John 16:21), distress (*stenochōria*; Rom. 2:9; 8:35; 2 Cor. 6:4), anguish (*synochē*; 2 Cor. 2:4), hardship (*anankē*; 2 Cor. 6:4; 1 Thess.. 3:7), suffering (*pathēma*; Col. 1:24), reproach (*oneidismos*; Heb. 10:33), and poverty (*ptōcheia*; Rev. 2:9). In Mark 13:19, *thlipsis* refers in particular to a time of great trouble in the last days before the coming of the Son of Man in power (cf. Dan. 12:1; Zeph. 1:14-15; Rev. 7:14). [*thlipsis*]

13:20 The elect (*tous eklektous*)—In Mark 13:20, Jesus immediately clarifies "the elect" as those whom the Lord has chosen, in other

words, those whom God has selected from throughout humanity and drawn to himself (BAGD, 242; BDAG, 306). In the NT, the term *eklektos* applies to Jesus (Luke 23:35; 1 Pet. 2:4, 6), to God's angels (1 Tim. 5:21), and most often to those who believe in Jesus (e.g., Luke 18:7; Rom. 8:33; Col. 3:12; 2 Tim. 2:10; 1 Pet. 1:1-2; Rev. 17:14). Based on this usage in the NT, "the elect" in Mark 13 should be identified as members of the Christian community, those who follow Jesus (Taylor, 514). God will shorten the time of the great tribulation for the sake of his chosen ones and will protect them from the many deceivers in the last days (13:20, 22). When the Son of Man comes in power, he will send his angels to gather them together from throughout the earth (13:26-27). [*eklektos*]

13:26 The Son of Man (*ton huion tou anthrōpou*)—Jesus uses language that points back to Daniel 7, where one like a son of man comes with the clouds of heaven and appears before the Ancient of Days to receive authority over all the nations (7:13-14). Daniel 7 presents a vision of four beasts representing four successive kingdoms that dominate the earth until God steps in and passes judgment on them, giving all authority instead to a heavenly figure, one like a son of man. Then the kingdom of this one extends over all the earth and lasts forever. For more on the Son of Man in Mark, see 2:10. On power, see 5:30. [*huios* + *anthrōpos*]

13:28 Fig tree (*sykēs*)—While most trees in the land of Israel are evergreens, the fig tree sheds its leaves for the winter and then sprouts them again as early as late March. When the fig tree puts forth its leaves, winter is past and summer is imminent. Since Jesus was teaching this parable shortly before the Passover (14:1), the fig trees in the area would have been in the condition Jesus was describing, with tender branches and sprouting leaves (Lane, 479). As the fig tree puts forth its leaves just before summer, so also the events of Mark 13:14-23. There will be the abomination of desolation followed by a severe tribulation and the efforts of false prophets to lead people astray. These take place just before the coming of the Son of Man (13:29; cf. Gundry, 746). For more on the fig tree, see 11:13. On parables, see 4:2. [*sykē*]

13:30 Will certainly not pass away (*ou mē parelthē*)—In Mark 13:30, the verb *parerchomai* takes on the sense of passing away, coming to an end, or perishing (J. Schneider, *TDNT* 2:681-82). This sinful and unbelieving generation will not come to an end before all the events prophesied in Mark 13 take place. For more on the word "generation" in Mark, see 8:12. On "truly," see 3:28. In the following verse (Mark 13:31), the same verb appears twice in Jesus' statement concerning the passing away of creation and the enduring truth of his words. The verb *parerchomai* occurs elsewhere in the NT to describe the destruction of heaven and earth (Matt. 5:18; Luke 16:17; 2 Pet. 3:10; cf. *T. Job* 33:4), as well as the passing away of the old life of the believer (2 Cor. 5:17) and of the fleeting life of the rich man (Jas 1:10; cf. Wis. 2:4; 5:9). Jesus' reference to the permanence of his words indicates that they will never lose their force or become invalid (BAGD, 626; BDAG, 775; cf. Ps. 148:6). [*parerchomai*]

13:33 Keep alert (*agrypneite*)—Literally, the verb *agrypneō* means "to stay awake at night" (LSJ, 16; cf. NET: "stay awake"). The related noun *agrypnia* occurs twice in the NT, both times with reference to the "sleepless nights" that Paul endured among his other difficulties for the sake of the church (2 Cor. 6:5; 11:27). Yet, *agrypneō* also has the more general meaning of "to be alert, vigilant, on guard" (BAGD, 14; BDAG, 16; cf. NRSV: "keep alert"). Like a watchman who stays alert during the darkest

hours of the night to look out for threatening circumstances, the disciple of Jesus must remain vigilant (cf. Ps. 127:1 [126:1 LXX]; 1 Esd 8:59; Luke 21:36). Failure to remain alert could lead to being found asleep when the master returns (13:36). Unfortunately, the disciples do not take Jesus' warning to heart, since in a short while they will fall asleep when Jesus asks them to watch and pray with him in Gethsemane (14:32-41), and therefore they will find themselves ill-prepared for the events that follow. [*agrypneō*]

14:1 Passover (*pascha*)—The Passover was the annual festival in which the Jewish people remembered God's act of deliverance by which he saved them out of their slavery in Egypt (Exod. 12:1-14, 21-51; Lev. 23:4-5; Num. 9:1-14; 28:16; Deut. 16:1-7). The Passover was celebrated on the 14th and 15th of the month of Nisan (March/April) in connection with the Feast of Unleavened Bread on the 15th through the 21st of Nisan (Exod. 12:15-20; 13:6-10; 34:18; Lev. 23:6-8; Num. 28:16-25; Deut. 16:3-4, 8). Since the Passover was one of the three pilgrimage festivals that took place during the year, Jesus and his disciples would have been among many other travelers coming to Jerusalem for the celebration (Exod. 23:14-17; Deut. 16:1-17; Luke 2:41). The word *pascha* can refer to the Passover festival (Mark 14:1), the Passover lamb (14:12), or the Passover meal (14:12, 14, 16; cf. BAGD, 633; BDAG, 784). On the chief priests, see 11:27. On the scribes, see 1:22. [*pascha*]

14:2 Riot (*thorybos*)—The noun *thorybos* describes the uncontrolled noise and confusion of an angry crowd, the type of chaos that has the potential of leading to violence (BAGD, 363; BDAG, 458; MM, 292). For example, the disturbance instigated by Demetrius the silversmith to protest Paul's influence in Ephesus, with its raging mob, loud commotion, general disorder, and threats of violence, is called a *thorybos* (Acts 20:1; cf. Jdt. 6:1; 3 Macc. 5:48; Matt. 27:24; Acts 21:34; Josephus, *JW* 2.21.5 §611). During the Passover festival, the population of Jerusalem swelled with crowds coming to commemorate God's act of redeeming his people from bondage. The concerns of the chief priests and the scribes about a potential riot were certainly legitimate given the size of the gathering and the history of Passover disturbances in the 1st century A.D. (Evans, 355; cf. Josephus, *JW* 2.12.1 §§224-27; *Ant.* 17.9.3 §§213-18; 20.5.3 §§105-12). [*thorybos*]

14:3 Nard (*nardou*)—-The perfume mentioned in Mark 14:3 was made out of nard, an aromatic oil extracted from the root of the nard plant which is native to India (Lane, 492). According to Mark, the nard was "genuine, authentic" (*pistikēs*; cf. Spicq, 3:108-9), and the perfume was "rare and very expensive" (*polytelous*; cf. Spicq, 134-35), the type of perfume one would expect to find in an alabaster flask. Such containers were normally reserved for only the best and most costly perfumes (Pliny the Elder, *Nat.* 13.3.19). In Mark 14:5, the worth of the perfume is estimated at over 300 denarii, close to a year's wages. On denarii, see 6:37. [*nardos*]

    After she broke (*syntripsasa*)—One use of the verb *syntribō* is to describe the act of breaking and destroying an object (5:4; Rev. 2:27; cf. G. Bertram, *TDNT* 7:920). Mark's Gospel presents the picture of the woman snapping off the neck of the alabaster flask and pouring out all of the perfume on Jesus' head. The significance of this action is that it dramatizes the woman's decision to give the entire contents of the bottle to Jesus. She would not save any of the perfume or use the bottle again (Gundry, 802, 813; Evans, 360). [*syntribō*]

14:8 To anoint (*myrisai*)—The verb used for anointing (*myrizō*) in Mark 14:8 occurs only this one time in the NT. The more common word for anointing in the NT is *aleiphō*, which indicates applying an oil or perfume in a variety of circumstances: maintaining personal appearance (Matt. 6:17), healing the sick (Mark 6:13; Jas 5:14), honoring a guest (Luke 7:46), and preparing a corpse for burial (Mark 16:1). Also in the NT are the words *chriō*, always used figuratively for an anointing by God to set apart an individual for divine service (Luke 4:18; Acts 4:27; 10:38; 2 Cor. 1:21; Heb. 1:9), and *epichriō* and *enchriō*, both used for anointing the eyes of the blind (John 9:6, 11; Rev. 3:18; cf. MM, 180, 251). The verb *myrizō* distinguishes itself through its relationship to the noun *myron*, the word for "perfume" in Mark 14:3. The common Jewish practice at the time was to wash and anoint a body before burial (*m Shabb.* 23:5), and Jesus interprets the woman's gift in light of this custom. This is the only reference to the anointing of Jesus' body for burial in Mark's Gospel, apart from the intended anointing by the women who come to the tomb with spices (16:1), a plan they are unable to fulfill because of the resurrection. [*myrizō*]

14:9 **In memory of her** (*eis mnēmosynon autēs*)—On account of her good deed, this woman will be remembered throughout the whole world, wherever the gospel message goes, which implies that she will be regarded with honor by those who hear and accept the good news concerning Jesus. In the LXX, the word *mnēmosynon* is used for those whose memory is honored as significant because of their good works (Sir. 39:9-11; 46:11-12) and for those whose memory is blotted out, forgotten as insignificant, because of their wickedness (Deut. 32:26; Job 18:17; Ps. 34:16 [33:16 LXX]; 109:15 [108:15 LXX]; Sir. 10:17; 44:9; cf. *T. Jos.* 7:5). Because of what she forfeits for the sake of Jesus, this woman gains a place of prominence "in the whole world" (14:9). Therefore she stands in contrast to those who forfeit their souls while seeking to gain "the whole world" (8:26). On the preaching of the good news, see 1:1, 38; 8:35. On "truly," see 3:28. [*mnēmosynon*]

14:10 In order to betray him (*hina auton paradoi*)—In this context, the verb *paradidōmi* has the connotation of betrayal in light of Judas's act of treachery. He used his position as one of the 12 disciples to help the religious leaders arrest Jesus. For more on "betrayed," see 3:19. Judas's act of betrayal involved providing the chief priests with the opportunity of arresting Jesus quietly, away from the crowd (14:43-50). Judas may have also given them incriminating information to help them in their trial. The issues raised before the Sanhedrin, Jesus' teaching concerning the destruction of the temple and his messianic self-understanding (14:57-58, 61), suggest the help of an insider, someone who knew what Jesus was saying to his disciples (8:27-30; 13:1-2; cf. Evans, 365). On the Twelve, see 3:14. [*paradidōmi*]

14:14 Guest room (*katalyma*)—The related verb *katalyō* sometimes means "to halt on a journey to find lodging" (Luke 9:12; 19:7; cf. BAGD, 414; BDAG, 522). In a similar way, the noun *katalyma* refers to a guest room, a place where travelers find rest and lodging (cf. 1 Kgdms 1:18; Jer. 14:8; *Let. Aris.* 181). In response to the disciples' inquiry concerning a guest room, the owner of the house shows them a large upper room where they can prepare for the Passover meal (14:15-16). [*katalyma*]

14:19 I am not the one, am I? (*mēti egō;*)—The word *mēti* functions as a marker in Greek to indicate that the speaker expects the answer "no" to the question that follows (BDF, 220-21, 226). One way to communicate the idiom in English is by making a negative statement followed by a question that

encourages the listener to affirm the negative statement. For example, the NLT renders the disciples' question as "I'm not the one, am I?" One other question begins with *mēti* in Mark's Gospel, in Jesus' parables discourse (4:21). There Jesus asks, "A lamp is not brought in to be put under a bushel or under a bed, is it?" The answer is clearly "no." In Mark 14:19, each disciple, including presumably Judas, expresses his question in a way that shows he expects Jesus to reply, "No, you are not the betrayer." [*mēti*]

14:21 Woe (*ouai*)—The word *ouai* can communicate (1) a lament, an expression of pity that looks forward to a time of intense suffering, or (2) a threat, an expression of displeasure that points to the future judgment of God (cf. H. Balz, *EDNT* 540). Matthew 18:7 illustrates both meanings by using "woe" to convey concern for the world in light of its many problems and also condemnation toward those who have caused them. Jesus' pronouncement concerning Judas is more a statement of judgment against someone who is disobeying God than one of pity toward someone who faces future misery. This woe is therefore parallel to Jesus' denunciation of the unrepentant (Matt. 11:21; Luke 10:13), the hypocritical (Matt. 23:13-32; 11:42-52), and the rich (Luke 6:24-26). Since "woe" is no longer a common English word, recent attempts to translate *ouai* include: "how disastrous it will be" (Louw & Nida, 1:243) and "how terrible it will be" (NLT). [*ouai*]

14:24 Covenant (*diathēkēs*)—In large measure, the word *diathēkē* in the NT draws its meaning from the teaching of the OT on God's covenants. Of the 33 uses of *diathēkē* in the NT, the vast majority involve either direct quotations of the OT or clear allusions to it. In the context of God's relationship with his people, a covenant is not a contract mutually agreed upon by two equal parties. Instead, a covenant takes place on the basis of God's initiative, as a declaration of his will and purposes. It includes the promises to which he binds himself and at times also the obligations that he places on his people (cf. BAGD, 183; BDAG, 228; J. Behm, *TDNT* 2:124-34). The primary background for understanding the phrase "my blood of the covenant" is in Exod. 24:6-8, the passage in which God's covenant with Israel is publicly ratified. In the ratification ceremony, Moses sprinkles blood on the altar and also on the people themselves, while declaring, "Behold the blood of the covenant which the Lord has made with you." In a similar way, Jesus' shed blood establishes and confirms a covenant between God and his people, one that surpasses the agreement that God made with Israel through Moses (cf. Jer. 31:31-34). [*diathēkē*]

14:26 After they sang a song of praise (*hymnēsantes*)—In the NT, the verb *hymneō* refers to expressing praise to God through song (e.g., Acts 16:25; Heb. 2:12; cf. M. Rutenfranz, *EDNT* 3:392). The Passover celebration included the singing of Psalms 113-118, with the first half of these Psalms coming before the actual meal and the second half at the close of the meal (*m Pesah* 10:5-7; cf. Lane, 501-2, 509). For Jesus, the Passover meal probably ended with the singing of Ps. 118, a psalm that describes how God is able to guide the righteous through the midst of distress and the prospect of death. In addition, Ps. 118:22 teaches that the stone which the builders rejected became the cornerstone. Jesus quoted this passage earlier in the narrative to describe his own death (12:10; cf. 8:31). [*hymneō*]

14:27 You will fall away (*skandalisthēsesthe*)—Of the seven other occurrences of the verb *skandalizō* in Mark's Gospel, the use in 4:17 provides the closest parallel to 14:27. In other words, Jesus is comparing his disciples to the rocky soil, to those who receive the message of the Gospel with joy but who fall away into disobedience and disbelief in the midst of persecution. Jesus confirms his prediction concerning the disciples with a quotation from Zech. 13:7 concerning the scattering of the sheep at the death of the shepherd. Yet he also promises that he will meet them in Galilee after his resurrection, presumably to gather together his scattered sheep and to restore them so that they might fulfill their calling (cf. Evans, 400). For more on *skandalizō*, see 4:17. On "it is written," see 1:2. [*skandalizō*]

14:30 You will deny (*aparnēsē*)—To deny Jesus means to refuse to acknowledge a relationship with him, to repudiate any association with him (BAGD, 81, 107-8; BDAG, 97, 132; cf. Wis. 12:27; 16:16). The opposite of the verb *aparneomai* is *homologeō*, "to confess, to publicly profess one's allegiance." For example, in Luke 12:8-9, Jesus states that he will confess before the angels of God those who confess him before men but will deny those who deny him. Earlier in Mark's Gospel, the same verb *aparneomai* occurs in the list of demands that Jesus gives to those who want to come after him (8:34). Followers of Jesus must deny themselves. Peter will head in a different direction, since instead of setting aside his own self-interest he will disclaim any knowledge of Jesus (14:66-72). [*aparneomai*]

14:33 To be deeply distressed (*ekthambeisthai*)—The verb *ekthambeō*, a word unique to Mark's Gospel in the NT (9:15; 14:33; 16:5, 6), serves to intensify the related verb *thambeō*, another word that occurs only in Mark within the NT (1:27; 10:24, 32). Both verbs can indicate the emotion of amazement or distress in response to an unusual event that has just happened or in anticipation of some difficulty that is soon to arrive (cf. BAGD, 240, 350; BDAG, 303, 442). Mark's Gospel further clarifies Jesus' feelings of distress at Gethsemane, by showing that he was troubled (*adēmonein*; 14:33) and deeply grieved (*perilypos*), sad to the point of death, that is, so grief-stricken that it hardly seemed possible to continue living (14:34). [*ekthambeō*]

14:36 Abba (*abba*)—The Aramaic word *abba* developed within the everyday language of families as a term for addressing one's father. Children, but also adult sons and daughters, used *abba* in speaking to their fathers (O. Hofius, *NIDNTT* 1:614). Mark records Jesus as using this family term in addressing God in his prayer in Gethsemane, and then he translates it for his readers with the Greek word for father (*patēr*). The word *abba* appears two other times in the NT, both once again in the context of prayer. In Rom. 8:15 and Gal. 4:6, Paul indicates that believers can cry out to God with the words "Abba! Father!" because the Spirit of God has made it clear to them that they are God's children. In the context of prayer, therefore, *abba* is a family word that communicates a close, personal relationship with God. [*abba*]

    Cup (*potērion*)—The metaphor of drinking a cup from God may simply indicate accepting the fate of suffering and death (10:38-39; cf. *Mart. Ascen. Isa.* 5:13; *Mart. Pol.* 14:2). However, the intensity of Jesus' emotions at Gethsemane (14:33-35) and his loud cry from the cross when forsaken by God (15:34) suggest a deeper significance for the cup metaphor in Mark 14:36. The dominant figurative use of the cup in the OT is for representing the judgment and wrath of God (Ps. 11:6 [10:7 LXX]; 75:8 [74:8 LXX]; Isa. 51:17, 22; Jer. 25:15-17 [32:15-17 LXX]; 49:12 [29:12 LXX]; Lam. 4:21; Ezek. 23:31-35; Hab. 2:16; cf. *Pss Sol* 8:13-14; 1QpHab XI, 14-15; Rev. 14:10; 16:9). Jesus sees his death not only as a time of physical anguish but also as a redemptive suffering that bears for many others the judgment of God (cf. 10:45; 14:24;

L. Goppelt, *TDNT* 6:152-53; Taylor, 553-54). Although he dreads this possibility, Jesus will accept the will of his Father. On the will of God, see 3:35. On Jesus and prayer, see 1:35. [*potērion*]

14:41 Is it far away? (*apechei*)—The translation of *apechei* in Mark 14:41 is difficult because the word has a fairly wide range of meanings and none of them fits the context of the verse easily. Although many English versions render *apechei* in Mark 14:41 as "it is enough" (e.g., RSV; NASB; NET) or "Enough!" (e.g., NIV; NRSV; NLT), the evidence that *apechei* carries this meaning is scant. A more common use of the verb *apechō*, conveys the meaning "to be far away," especially in the LXX (e.g., Gen. 44:4; Deut. 12:21; Ps. 103:12 [102:12 LXX]; Prov.. 15:29; Isa. 55:9; Ezek. 22:5; cf. MM, 57-58). The verb *apechō* only appears one other time in Mark's Gospel, where it follows this same use: "Their heart is far away from me" (7:6). The meaning "to be far away" can also fit the context of Mark 14:41, if *apechei* is translated as a question that continues Jesus' interrogation of the disciples (Evans, 416-17). The words right after *apechei* would then answer this question. The resulting sense of Jesus' remark would be: "Are you still sleeping? And are you resting? Is it far away? No, the hour has come." [*apechō*]

14:44 Under tight security (*asphalōs*)—In Mark 14:44, the adverb *asphalōs*, often translated as "under guard" (e.g., NASB; NIV; NRSV), means "securely" in the sense of guarding a prisoner securely or carefully to prevent any possible escape or rescue (cf. C. Brown, *NIDNTT* 1:663). The same word appears in Acts 16:23 where the Philippian jailer receives the command to guard Paul and Silas securely, and so he throws them into the inner part of the prison and secures (using the verb *asphal-*

izō) their feet in stocks (Acts 16:24). [*asphalōs*]

14:48 Robber (*lēstēn*)—Translations such as "robber" (NASB), "bandit" (NRSV), and "dangerous criminal" (NLT) help to communicate that the noun *lēstēs* refers to someone who steals through threats or acts of violence. See 11:17, for more on *lēstēs*. Earlier in the narrative, Jesus characterized the chief priests as robbers (11:17), and now in turn they treat him as a dangerous robber by sending out a crowd with swords and clubs to arrest him at night (14:43, 48). To interpret *lēstēs* in this context as "revolutionary" or "insurrectionist" (e.g., NIV) misses the ironic parallel between Jesus' charge against the temple leaders in 11:17 and their treatment of him in 14:48. In addition, Mark uses a different word, *stasiastēs*, if he wishes to identify someone as a revolutionary (15:7). [*lēstēs*]

14:51 Linen garment (*sindona*)—Only Mark's Gospel contains this episode concerning the young man with the linen garment who continues to follow Jesus after the disciples have fled. The word *sindōn* was used for fine linen cloth (MM, 757), the type of cloth that Joseph of Arimathea bought to wrap the dead body of Jesus before his burial in a tomb (15:46). In addition, *sindōn* could refer to any item made out of such material, including a garment (LSJ, 1600). Mark's Gospel does not provide enough detail to describe the nature of the garment. [*sindōn*]

14:52 Naked (*gymnos*)—The adjective *gymnos* can indicate that someone is unclothed, completely bare or just not fully clothed, depending on the context (A. Oepke, *TDNT* 1:773-74; Cranfield, 438; cf. John 21:7). When the young man runs away naked, it suggests that he is so overpowered and beaten in an attack that he is almost unable to escape. It serves as an illustration of a complete and humiliating defeat. Using a similar picture, the prophet Amos predicted a time of defeat that would be so overwhelming that even the bravest of warriors would flee naked (Amos 2:16; cf. 2 Macc. 11:12; Acts 19:16). In Mark's narrative, the flight of the young man symbolizes the cowardly actions of the disciples who abandon Jesus at the moment of crisis and run away in shame and utter humiliation. Instead of leaving everything behind in order to follow Jesus, the young man abandons everything in order to flee. In a similar way, the disciples, who claimed to have left everything in order to follow their master (10:28), now instead leave him and run for their lives (14:50). [*gymnos*]

14:53 High priest (*archierea*)—When used in the singular, *archiereus* refers to the high priest, in contrast to the use of the word in the plural for the chief priests. At the time of Jesus, the high priest was not only the religious leader of the people but also the political representative of the nation, although his political power was greatly curtailed under Roman rule (Schürer, *History* 2:227-32). The high priest was appointed by the Roman governor, always from a select number of influential priestly families, and he could also be removed from office by the governor to make way for the next appointment. Most of the high priest's authority derived from his position as the leader of the Sanhedrin, and it is in this leadership role that the high priest makes his appearance in Mark's Gospel (14:53-65). In 14:53, the high priest gathers together the members of the Sanhedrin: the chief priests (see 11:27), the elders (see 11:27), and the scribes (see 1:22). [*archiereus*]

14:55 Sanhedrin (*synedrion*)—The Sanhedrin, situated in Jerusalem, was the supreme governing council that held authority over the Jewish people, especially those in Judea, in legal and administrative matters (Schürer, *History* 2:200-226). The 71 members of the Sanhedrin included the current high priest, who served as the president, and representatives from the chief priests, elders, and scribes, with the greatest power lying in the hands of the priestly leaders. The Sanhedrin made decisions concerning the interpretation and application of the law with regard to religious practice, temple supervision, civil government, and criminal justice. The council had its own police force for making arrests and keeping order. Although highly influential, the Sanhedrin existed under the authority of the Roman rulers who could at any time restrict the power of the council in order to maintain their own interests. In Mark's Gospel, the Sanhedrin seeks out witnesses to testify against Jesus (14:55), condemns him as worthy of death (14:64), and turns him over to Pilate for punishment (15:1). [*synedrion*]

14:61 Of the Blessed One (*tou eulogētou*)— The adjective *eulogētos* ("blessed"), used in the NT only in reference to God (Luke 1:68; Rom. 1:25; 9:5; 2 Cor. 1:3; 11:31; Eph. 1:3; 1 Pet. 1:3), characterizes God as someone who is worthy of praise (BAGD, 322; BDAG, 408). In Mark 14:61, the high priest makes use of the adjective in order to refrain from mentioning God's name out of reverence for him (cf. *1 En* 77:1-2; *m Ber* 7:3). The high priest's words, which show respectful concern for God's name and yet which also lead to the condemnation of God's Son, reveal him as someone who honors God with his lips even though his heart is far from him (cf. 7:6). On Jesus as the Christ, the Son of God, see 1:1. [*eulogētos*]

14:62 Sitting at the right hand (*ek dexiōn kathēmenon*)—After Peter identified him as the Messiah, Jesus began to speak about his future suffering as the Son of Man (8:29-31). After accepting the title of Messiah before the high priest, Jesus immediately describes his future glory as the Son of Man. He further clarifies his status as the Messiah by claiming that the religious leaders will see him "sitting at the right hand," a phrase that comes from Ps. 110:1. In light of the content of Ps. 110 as a whole, for Jesus to sit at the right hand of God means that he will be exalted by God to the highest place of honor in order to judge the nations and rule over his enemies (cf. Mark 12:36). Jesus will judge those who are now sitting in judgment of him. For more on Jesus as the Son of Man, see 2:10 and 13:26. [*dexios* + *kathēmai*]

14:63 Tearing his clothes (*diarrēxas tous chitōnas*)—The gesture of tearing of one's clothes was an emotional response that expressed intense grief or distress. For example, Jacob tore his clothes in sorrow when he thought that his son Joseph had died (Gen. 37:34; cf. Josh. 7:6; 2 Sam. 1:11; Job 1:20), and King Hezekiah did the same in his distress because of the blasphemous threats of Rabshakeh (2 Kings 19:1; cf. Esth. 4:1; *T Jos* 5:2; Acts 14:14; Josephus, *JW* 2.15.2 §316). Eventually, the tearing of one's clothes became a formal judicial act. According to the Mishnah, when judges hear blasphemy they should "stand up on their feet and rend their garments, and they may not mend them again" (*m Sanh* 7:5). By tearing his clothes, the high priest demonstrates that he regards Jesus' claim to be the Messiah and the exalted judge over all as a blasphemous insult against God. For more on blasphemy, see 2:7. [*diarēssō* + *chitōn*]

14:65 Prophesy (*prophēteuson*)—Since Jesus is blindfolded before he is commanded to prophesy, he is apparently being asked to identify his assailants. Therefore, in this verse, the verb *prophēteō* means to reveal by prophetic speech something that is hidden, something outside the normal realm of human knowledge (G. Friedrich, *TDNT* 6:829). The religious leaders may have decided to mock Jesus as a prophet, because he predicted his own future exaltation to them (14:62). In addition, many people regarded Jesus as a prophet like one of the prophets of old (6:15; 8:28). The religious leaders may have been aware of this evaluation, since they were also familiar with the common identification of John the Baptist as a prophet (11:32). By their words the religious leaders treat Jesus as a prophet, calling on him to prophesy, but by their actions they reveal that they believe him to be a fraud. The irony is that his predictions at that very moment are coming to fulfillment, since he foretold that the chief priests, elders, and scribes would reject him, condemning him to death, and also that he would be mocked and spit upon (8:31; 10:33-34). In addition, the accuracy of his predictions concerning Peter will soon be obvious (14:26-31; 66-72). [*prophēteuō*]

14:66 One of the slave girls (*mia tōn paidiskōn*)—The noun *paidiskē* developed from a term used for a "young woman" into one that was frequently used for a "female slave" (e.g., Exod. 21:20-21; Deut. 15:17; Eccl. 2:7; *Jos Asen* 6:8; Luke 12:45; Acts 16:16; cf. MM, 474). Therefore, the translation "one of the slave girls" (NET), which suggests a lack of freedom, is probably more true to life than "one of the servant girls" (e.g., NASB). The presence of the slave girl in this passage serves to heighten the contrast between Jesus and Peter. Jesus answers the question of the high priest with the truth even though it will lead to his condemnation and death. Peter, however, responds to the accusation of the high priest's slave girl with a lie in order to save his life. On Peter's act of denial, see 14:30. [*paidiskē*]

14:71 To curse (*anathematizein*)—Peter curses in the sense that he seeks to establish the truth of his words by calling a curse down on himself if he is lying (Taylor, 575; cf. NIV). A similar use of the verb *anathematizō* occurs in Acts 23:12, 14, 21, where some of Paul's enemies put themselves under a curse if they fail to kill Paul before they eat or drink again. They invoke a curse in order to stress the truth of their vow (cf. 1 Sam. 20:13; 2 Sam. 3:9; 1 Kings 19:2). [*anathematizō*]

15:1 Handed over (*paredōkan*)—Mark uses the verb *paradidōmi* for a series of actions in which Jesus is handed over: from Judas to the religious authorities (14:10-11, 18, 21, 41-44), from the religious authorities to Pilate (15:1, 10), and from Pilate to the soldiers who carry out the execution (15:15-16). For more on *paradidōmi*, see 3:19. On the Sanhedrin or "Council" and the different groups of religious leaders that made up the Sanhedrin, see 1:22; 11:27; 14:55. [*paradidōmi*]

15:2 King of the Jews (*ho basileus tōn Ioudaiōn*)—In comparison with the other Gospels of the NT, the use of the title "King" for Jesus in Mark's Gospel is somewhat unique. In Mark, the title is applied to Jesus exclusively by those who are active in bringing about his execution, by Pilate, the hostile crowd, the soldiers, the chief priests, and the scribes (15:2, 9, 12, 18, 26, 32). In the other Gospels, however, those who are sympathetic to Jesus also use the title "King" in reference to him and even Jesus uses it for himself (Matt. 2:2; 25:34, 40; Luke 19:37-38; John 1:49; 12:12-13; cf. Acts 17:7). Both Matthew and John state that Jesus is the fulfillment of Zechariah's prophecy concerning the coming messianic King (Matt. 21:4-5; John 12:14-15). Perhaps Mark was seeking to show through his manner of presentation that Jesus' viewpoint on what it meant for him to be a ruler was far different from the perspective of his opponents (cf. 10:42-45). For Pilate, the title "King of the Jews" should only belong to someone with an earthly kingdom, political power, and military might. Jesus is not that kind of king, since he is a ruler who came to serve and to give his life. [*basileus* + *Ioudaios*]

You say so (*sy legeis*)—Jesus answers, "You say so," to Pilate's inquiry concerning his identity as the King of the Jews. As a response to a question, this Greek phrase functions as an affirmative but indirect answer, one which implies that such a statement would not have been made had the question not been asked (BDF, 227; cf. Matt. 26:25, 64; 27:11; Luke 22:70; 23:3; John 18:37). In other words, Jesus agrees that he is the King of the Jews, but he gives his answer with reservation since he knows his own conception of kingship is different than that of Pilate (Lane, 551). [*legō*]

15:7 Insurrectionists (*stasiastōn*)—The noun *stasiastēs* derives from the verb *stasiazō*, "to plot an uprising, to revolt" (Jdt. 7:15; 2 Macc. 4:30; 14:6), so that the noun refers to someone who participates in a rebellion or an insurrection in order to overthrow the existing authorities (Spicq, 3:286; cf. Josephus, *JW* 6.2.8 §157). The chief priests are able to stir up the crowd to demand the release of Barabbas, a man in prison because he had joined in a violent revolt, rather than to accept Pilate's offer to free Jesus. [*stasiastēs*]

15:11 Stirred up (*aneseisan*)—The verb *anaseiō* is a synonym of *seiō*, which can mean literally "to shake," for example, in the shaking that causes an earthquake (Matt. 27:51; Heb. 12:26), or figuratively "to stir up," as in inciting a crowd of people to respond with agitation or excitement (Matt. 21:10; cf. BAGD, 60, 746; BDAG, 71, 918). The two occurrences of *anaseiō* in the NT are both in keeping with the figurative use, stirring up the people (15:11; Luke 23:5). The order of events in Mark's Gospel communicates that many in the crowd would have arrived already hoping to see Barabbas released, even before they knew that Jesus was a prisoner. Therefore,

the chief priests stirred up the crowd in the sense that they encouraged the people to continue to clamor for Barabbas and to refuse to be deflected by Pilate's offer of Jesus (Cranfield, 450). [*anaseiō*]

15:13 Crucify (*staurōson*)—The people call out, "Crucify!"—they are asking Pilate to have Jesus executed. Crucifixion was not the only means of execution at the time, but it was perhaps the most brutal and painful. The ordeal began with a flogging, after which the victim carried the crossbeam to the place of crucifixion, often along a crowded road, where the upright post was already implanted into the ground. There soldiers tied or nailed the outstretched arms of the prisoner to the crossbeam, which was then raised up and fastened to the post. A small wooden peg in the middle of the post provided some support for the suspended body. Since crucifixion did not damage vital organs or result in excessive bleeding, death came slowly, through shock or through fatigue in which the muscles necessary for the victim to continue breathing became too tired for use (J. Schneider, *TDNT* 7:573-74; J. B. Green, *DJG* 147-48). Mark's Gospel provides no details at all about the actual nature of Jesus' crucifixion; it simply states "they crucified him" (15:24-25). [*stauroō*]

15:15 After he had him flogged (*phragellōsas*)—Mark mentions the common Roman practice of tying a condemned prisoner to a post and beating him with a whip as a prelude to crucifixion (cf. Josephus, *JW* 2.14.9 §306; 5.11.1 §449). The whip consisted of leather straps with interwoven pieces of bone and bits of metal. The Roman custom of flogging put no limit on the number of strokes, in contrast to the Jewish practice which allowed only 39 lashes. The beating would continue until the flesh hung down in shreds, and sometimes it was so severe that it could expose the bone (Josephus, *JW* 6.5.3 §304). In many cases, the beating itself was fatal (cf. C. Schneider, *TDNT* 4:515-19). [*phragelloō*]

15:16 Palace (*aulēs*)—The noun *aulē* often indicates a courtyard, an open space surrounded by buildings and walls, and Mark uses the word in this way earlier in his Gospel (14:54, 66). However, *aulē* came to refer sometimes to the entire complex, including not only the courtyard but also the surrounding buildings, especially in the case of royal property. Therefore, *aulē* began to mean "palace" as well (1 Macc. 11:46; 3 Macc. 5:46; Josephus, *Life* 12 §66; 57 §295; cf. BAGD, 121; BDAG, 150). The meaning "palace" fits the context of Mark 15:16 since the *aulē* is further clarified as the "Praetorium," which was the Roman governor's residence or headquarters (Cranfield, 452). Pilate normally stayed in Caesarea along the coast of the Mediterranean Sea, but during times of potential unrest, such as at the Passover feast, he traveled to Jerusalem where he also maintained a residence. [*aulē*]

Company of soldiers (*speiran*)—The word *speira* is typically the Greek equivalent for the Roman cohort, a company of soldiers that was one-tenth of a legion or around 600 soldiers, although the number could vary (BAGD, 761; BDAG, 936; cf. Josephus, *JW* 3.4.2 §67). It is difficult to know if Mark intended to use the word as a precise military term or to employ it more loosely for all the soldiers who were available at the governor's headquarters. However, Mark's choice of words ("the whole cohort") leaves the impression of a large number of soldiers involved in the mocking of Jesus with the full participation of all present. [*speira*]

15:17 A purple robe (*porphyran*)—Since purple clothing was an expensive luxury, it was often associated with great wealth (e.g., 1 Macc. 4:23; Luke 16:19; Rev. 18:11-12) and with royalty (e.g., 1 Macc. 10:62; 14:43; Virgil, *Georg.* 2.495; Josephus, *Ant.* 11.6.10 §§256-57; 17.8.3 §§196-97). The soldiers dressed Jesus in a purple robe, that is, one fit for a king. In light of the cruel humor that produced a wreath of thorns for a crown, it is impossible to know from Mark's account what type of cloak or material the soldiers actually used for a royal garment. Matthew's Gospel apparently identifies it as the scarlet cloak of a soldier (Matt. 27:28). [*porphyra*]

15:20 They had mocked (*enepaixan*)—The verb *empaizō* occurs 13 times in the NT with all except two instances (Matt. 2:16; Luke 14:29) used in reference to the mocking of Jesus prior to his death. To mock means to ridicule, to treat someone with derision and scorn whether through words or through actions (BAGD, 255; BDAG, 323). The history of God's people demonstrates that the righteous face the possibility of such suffering at the hands of the wicked (2 Chron. 36:16; 1 Macc. 9:26; 2 Macc. 7:10; cf. the use of the related noun *empaigmos* in Heb. 11:36). In Mark's Gospel, Jesus predicts that he will be mocked (10:34). This prophecy finds its fulfillment in three separate scenes: at the end of his hearing before the Sanhedrin where he is mocked as a false prophet (14:65), at the end of his trial before Pilate where he is ridiculed as a false king (15:16-20), and at his crucifixion where he is rejected as a false Messiah (15:31-32). [*empaizō*]

15:21 To take up his cross (*arē ton stauron autou*)—Mark expresses the action of Simon of Cyrene with words that recall the demand of Jesus on the one who wants to follow him, that he must take up his cross (8:34: *aratō ton stauron autou*; cf. Cranfield, 455; Hooker, 372). While the phrase is the same, the referent of "his" has changed, since now the cross belongs to Jesus himself. This verse serves to highlight the failure of those like the disciples who decided to follow Jesus. Not only did they abandon their responsibility to take up their own cross in order to be ready to give their lives for their master, but now they are completely unavailable to help Jesus with his cross when he is no longer able to continue. The task goes to someone who happens to be passing by at that moment. For more on taking up the cross, see 8:34. [airō + stauros]

15:23 Flavored with myrrh (esmyrnismenon)—Since wine mixed with myrrh was a delicacy (W. Michaelis, TDNT 7:458-59; cf. Pliny the Elder, Nat. 14.15), the soldiers were in effect offering Jesus a drink of an expensive wine. The purpose for this action was probably not to relieve Jesus' suffering but rather to continue mocking him, offering a fine wine to the king (Evans, 500-501). Jesus refuses to take part in the mockery by drinking the wine, just as earlier he refused to participate by remaining silent in the midst of ridicule and injustice. [smyrnizō]

15:29 Shaking their heads (kinountes tas kephalas autōn)—Those who shake their heads do so in order to express their scorn or contempt toward someone, especially toward an individual who is suffering in misery (2 Kings 19:21; Job 16:4; Ps. 22:7 [21:7 LXX]; Jer. 18:16; Lam. 2:15; Sir. 12:18; 13:7; cf. Ps. 109:25 [108:25 LXX]). Mark's choice of words concerning this gesture depends on Ps. 22:7 which describes those who mock the righteous sufferer, the people who sneer at him and shake their head, saying, "Commit yourself to the Lord; let him deliver" (cf. Lam. 2:15). Mark uses the language of Ps. 22 to relate other events in the crucifixion scene as well, the dividing up of Jesus' garments by casting lots (15:24; cf. Ps. 22:18) and Jesus' cry of abandonment (15:34; cf. Ps. 22:1). In 15:29, Mark also portrays those who are passing by as blaspheming against Jesus,

although this act of blasphemy is not clear with translations such as they "hurled insults" (NIV) or they "shouted abuse" (NLT). For more on blasphemy, see 2:7. [kineō + kephalē]

15:32 That we may see (hina idōmen)—The religious leaders claim that they will believe if they see Jesus rescue himself at the end of his life when his death is imminent (cf. Wis. 2:17-18). However, Jesus has already told them when they will see and perceive the truth, at the day of judgment when they see the Son of Man sitting at God's right hand and coming with the clouds of heaven (14:62). Until that time, because they remain outside of faith, they will see but not really see, and they will not be forgiven (4:11-12). Note also the discussion on "Christ" at 1:1, on "King" at 15:2, and on "faith" at 2:5. [eidon/horaō]

15:34 Cried out (eboēsen)—The verb boaō generally points to a cry of strong emotion, often to a pleading call for help on the part of someone who is in distress or anguish, a use especially common in the LXX (e.g., Num. 12:13; 1 Kgdms 12:10; 2 Kgdms 22:7; 4 Kgdms 4:1; Neh. 9:4; Isa. 58:9; Hab. 1:2; 1 Macc. 3:50; cf. BAGD, 144; BDAG, 180; MM, 113). For example, boaō is a fitting word for the constant pleading of God's chosen ones who cry out to him day and night for justice (Luke 18:7; cf. Luke 9:38; 18:38). In a similar way, the verb boaō in 15:34 presents Jesus as calling out to God in anguish, sensing his own helplessness and distress. [boaō]

Have you forsaken (enkatelipes)—Jesus cries out to God with words drawn from Ps. 22:1, "My God, my God, why have you forsaken me?" For Jesus to be forsaken means that he experienced separation or alienation from God, "the unfathomable pain of a real abandonment by the Father" (Lane, 573). The verb enkataleipō ("forsake") can indicate a break in a relationship that comes about as the result of a desertion or abandonment (e.g., Josh. 24:20; Ps. 27:9-10 [26:9-10 LXX]; 2 Tim. 4:10; Heb. 13:5). The difficult decision in Gethsemane to follow the Father's will has led to the suffering of judgment on the cross, abandonment by God. Jesus pays the ransom price by giving his life in the place of many others (10:45), who will now never face rejection from God because Jesus experienced it for them. [*enkataleipō*]

15:36 Sour wine (*oxous*)—The noun *oxos* occurs six times in the NT, always in connection with the crucifixion scene (Matt. 27:48; Mark 15:36; Luke 23:36; John 19:29-30; cf. Ps. 69:21 [68:21 LXX]). Sour wine (*oxos*) was not of the same quality as regular wine (*oinos*), but it was less expensive and therefore common among people of moderate means as a useful drink for quenching thirst. Consequently, the gesture of giving Jesus sour wine in itself was not a hostile action nor a cruel jest (H. W. Heidland, *TDNT* 5:288-89; cf. Ruth 2:14; Plutarch, *Cat. Maj.* 1 §336-37). However, the purpose for giving Jesus a drink was to refresh him in order to keep him alive longer for further mockery. The people standing by the cross want to demonstrate how foolish it is for Jesus to hold out hope that Elijah will come to rescue him. [*oxos*]

15:38 Was torn (*eschisthē*)—Mark uses the verb *schizō* twice in his Gospel, for the tearing apart of the heavens at Jesus' baptism (1:10) and for the tearing of the temple's veil at Jesus' death (15:38). On both occasions, Jesus is declared to be the Son of God (1:11; 15:39). For more on *schizō*, see 1:10. The tearing of the temple's veil from top to bottom is significant for more than one reason. For the religious leaders, it stands as an omen, a sign that the temple will soon be destroyed. Jesus' predictions concerning the fate of the temple will come true (13:1-2). For Gentiles who

believe that Jesus is God's Son, like the centurion at the cross, it repeats the message that the temple was meant to be a house of prayer for all the nations (11:17). Refusing to limit himself, God will also seek out people of faith from among the Gentiles. For those who look to Jesus as the true Messiah, it demonstrates that the mockers at the cross were blind. The divine action at the temple confirms that Jesus did fulfill his mission as God's Son and that he is able to save others because he would not save himself (15:31, 39). [*schizō*]

15:39 Centurion (*kentyriōn*)—Mark is the only writer in the NT to use the Latin loanword *kentyriōn*, since elsewhere in the NT the Greek word for "centurion" appears, spelled as either *hekatontarchēs* or *hekatontarchos* (e.g., Matt. 8:5; 27:54; Luke 7:2; 23:47; Acts 10:1; 21:32; 27:1). A centurion was a Roman officer who presided over a division of around 100 men (F. G. Untergassmair, *EDNT* 1:405). In Mark's Gospel, the centurion is the first human character, other than Jesus himself (14:61-62), to acknowledge that Jesus is the Son of God. He makes this identification based on his observation of the way that Jesus died. On Jesus as the Son of God, see 1:1. The centurion returns later to the story in order to confirm to Pilate that Jesus had indeed already died on the cross (15:44-45). [*kentyriōn*]

15:42 The day of preparation (*paraskeuē*)—The noun *paraskeuē* commonly means "preparation," but in the NT it is always used of the day of preparation before a Sabbath or a festival day (W. Stott, *NIDNTT* 3:408). Mark clarifies the meaning of the word for his readers by further defining it as the day before the Sabbath, which began at sunset. Friday was the time for preparing everything that would be necessary on the Sabbath, since no work was allowed on that day (cf. Josephus, *Ant.* 16.6.2 §163). According to Deut. 21:22-23, the body of an executed criminal that is hanging on a tree must be taken down and buried. Leaving it on the tree all night would defile the land (cf. Josephus, *JW* 4.5.2 §317). Since Jesus died at the ninth hour, or 3:00 P.M. (15:34), Joseph of Arimathea had only a short time to act in accordance with this law by asking Pilate for Jesus' body and burying it before sunset. [*paraskeuē*]

15:43 A member of the council (*bouleutēs*)— Mark refers to Joseph of Arimathea as a *bouleutēs*, a title for a member of a council, in this case, probably a member of the Sanhedrin (Gundry, 984-85; cf. Josephus, *JW* 2.17.1 §405). Mark seems to present Joseph of Arimathea as belonging to this foremost Jewish council in light of the prominence of the Sanhedrin in the events surrounding Jesus' death and the ability of Joseph of Arimathea to gain access to Pilate. Joseph of Arimathea who cares for Jesus' lifeless body is clearly an exceptional member of the Sanhedrin, just as the wise scribe who acknowledged the truth of Jesus' teaching was an exceptional scribe (12:28-34) and the centurion who recognized Jesus' identity was an exceptional soldier (15:39). Like the wise scribe, Joseph of Arimathea is open to the kingdom of God. On the kingdom of God, see 1:15, and on the Sanhedrin, see 14:55 [*bouleutēs*]

15:45 Dead body (*ptōma*)—Mark shifts from the word *sōma* ("body") in 15:43 to *ptōma* ("dead body") in 15:45. In the NT, *ptōma* always refers to a dead body or corpse, either of an animal or a human being (e.g., Matt. 14:12; 24:28; Rev. 11:8-9; cf. Judg. 14:8 LXX; W. Michaelis, *TDNT* 6:166-67). Outside of 15:45, the word *ptōma* occurs only one other time in Mark's Gospel, in 6:29 where the disciples of John the Baptist came and

took his dead body and "laid it in a tomb" (*ethēkan auto en mnēmeiō*). In a similar way, Joseph of Arimathea apparently accepts the role of a disciple, since he came and took down the dead body of Jesus from the cross and "laid him in a tomb" (15:46: *ethēken auton en mnēmeiō*). His actions make the absence of Jesus' own disciples all the more obvious. [*ptōma*]

16:1 Spices (*arōmata*)—In order to anoint the body of Jesus, the women bought *arōmata*, a word for various spices that were considered valuable because of their fragrance (4 Kgdms 20:13; 2 Chron. 9:1, 9; 32:27; S. of S. 4:10; Sir. 24:15; cf. LSJ, 254). The word *arōma* occurs four times in the NT, always in the narration of the Jesus' burial (16:1; Luke 23:56; 24:1; John 19:40; cf. 2 Chron. 16:14). Anointing a body with spices or perfumes in the process of burial was an act of devotion intended to honor the dead and to offset the odor of decomposition (cf. Lane, 585). On anointing Jesus for burial, see also 14:8. [*arōma*]

16:5 Young man (*neaniskon*)—Mark refers to the messenger at the tomb as a "young man," apparently using the term to indicate the presence of an angel (Evans, 535-36). From the perspective of the women at the tomb, the messenger appeared as a young man, which is in keeping with the description of angels elsewhere (e.g., 2 Macc. 3:26, 33; Josephus, *Ant.* 5.8.2 §277; cf. Acts 1:10; 10:30; 2 En 1:3-7). The young man is wearing a white robe, so that his appearance is similar to that of Jesus when he displayed his heavenly glory at the transfiguration (9:3). He also possesses supernatural knowledge, since he reports the resurrection to the women and repeats the message of Jesus to the disciples concerning their predicted meeting in Galilee. [*neaniskos*]

16:8 Fled (*ephygon*)—When used literally as

in Mark 16:8, the verb *pheugō* means to run away from an imminent danger or a perceived threat, sometimes out of prudent caution (Matt. 2:13; 10:23; Mark 13:14; John 10:5; Rev. 12:6) but at other times out of fearful cowardice and neglect of one's duty (Matt. 26:56; Mark 14:50, 52; John 10:12; cf. D. A. Carson, *NIDNTT* 1:558-59). The disciples disregard their responsibility to follow Jesus when they abandon him and flee (*ephygon*) at his arrest (14:50). Immediately after the disciples run away, a young man who is continuing to follow Jesus also flees (*ephygen*), even though he has to leave behind his clothes to do so (14:51-52). Mark seems to portray the women at the tomb negatively as well by using the same verb (*ephygon*) to describe their fearful flight. Mark characterizes the initial reaction of the women to the supernatural events at the tomb, their fleeing in disobedient silence and fear, as a failure on their part. Yet the initial wrong actions of the women do not thwart God's plans because the resurrection reveals that God is able to accomplish his will in the midst of human failure and disobedience. [*pheugō*]

Verses 9-20 in Mark 16 are absent from the oldest manuscripts of Mark's Gospel (namely, Aleph and B), and they were probably added later, sometime after Mark finished writing his Gospel. In addition to the manuscript evidence, this conclusion gains further support from the awkward transition between verse 8 and verse 9 and the distinctive vocabulary and word usage in 16:9-20, as well as the fact that Jerome seems to have known only a few copies of the longer ending. In addition, the various endings that exist for this Gospel also suggest that these later verses were added later. Since the genuineness of verses 9-20 is at least doubtful, this study has not included lexical evidence from this so-called longer ending when making statements about Mark's use of words, including their frequency or significance. Nonetheless, a few of the significant

terms from this longer ending are treated here.

16:14 Rebuked (*ōneidisen*)—The verb *oneidizō* can mean finding fault with someone in a way that is intended to demean or insult them (e.g., Matt. 5:11; Rom. 15:3; 1 Pet. 4:14). For example, the robbers who were crucified along with Jesus joined in the mocking and cast insults (*ōneidizon*) at Jesus (15:32). However, the word can also involve finding fault with someone for justifiable reasons and therefore can mean "to rebuke or reprimand" (e.g., Wis. 2:12; Sir. 8:5; Matt. 11:20; cf. BAGD, 570; BDAG, 710). This second meaning fits the context of Mark 16:14, since Jesus is rebuking his disciples with good reason in light of their continuing unbelief in spite of the reports concerning his resurrection. [*oneidizō*]

16:15 To all creation (*pasē tē ktisei*)—The temporal aspect of the noun *ktisis* stands out in the phrase "from the beginning of creation" in Mark 10:6 and 13:9, pointing to the act of creation at the beginning of time (cf. Rom. 1:20; 2 Pet. 3:4; G. Petzke, *EDNT* 2:326). In Mark 16:15, *ktisis* occurs with a figurative sense in which the creation as a whole stands for one part of creation, that is, the human race (cf. Col. 1:23; W. Foerster, *TDNT* 3:1028-29). In other words, Jesus is commanding his followers to preach the gospel to "everyone, everywhere" (NLT). In order to fulfill this command, it is necessary for believers to go and move from where they are to where people live who have not heard the message in order to tell them the good news concerning Jesus. [*ktisis*]

16:17 Will accompany (*parakolouthēsei*)—The verb *akoloutheō*, a frequent word in Mark's Gospel (18 times), commonly refers to following Jesus, either in the sense of literally walking behind him (e.g., 3:7; 5:24) or with the idea of following him as a disciple (e.g., 1:18; 8:34; 10:21). The related compound form *synakoloutheō* occurs twice in Mark, also for following Jesus (5:37; 14:51). A change in force occurs, however, with the compound form *parakoloutheō* that appears in Jesus' statement in 16:17, where it means "to go along beside, to accompany" (G. Schneider, *EDNT* 1:52; cf. 2 Macc. 8:11). Yet another compound form, *epakoloutheō*, in 16:20, is similar in meaning to *parakoloutheō* in 16:17. Both verses mention miraculous signs that accompany those who believe and preach the gospel. Jesus' statement concerning signs is a prediction of what will happen at some point rather than a promise of what will always take place. As a result, verse 20 is a report that Jesus' words in verse 17 were fulfilled as his people went out proclaiming the good news. Other parts of the NT, as well as other early Christian writings, offer additional confirmation of the miracles mentioned in 16:17-18, including casting out of demons (Acts 8:7; 16:18; 19:12), speaking in new tongues (Acts 2:4; 10:46; 19:6; 1 Cor. 12:10, 28; 14:2-28), being unharmed by serpents (Acts 28:3-6) and deadly poison (Eusebius, *Hist. eccl.* 3.39; *Acts John* XX), and healing the sick by the laying on of hands (Acts 28:8). [*parakoloutheō*]

LUKE

Darrell L. Bock

1:1 Undertaken to compile (*epecheirēsan*). This term in this context means "to set one's hand to something" (Es. 9:25; BAGD, 304; BDAG, 386; MM, 250-51). It suggests some type of written resource material. Luke alludes to narrative about Jesus circulating in the early Christian community. These would not be full Gospels necessarily, but accounts of aspects of his life that would also have an element of preaching application in them. [*epicheireō*]

Things which have been accomplished among us (*peplērophorēmenōn*). These accounts trace the events fulfilled by Jesus. It could well be translated "things fulfilled among us" (NIV; Green, p. 39). The things accomplished are aspects of a program that is part of a divine plan (see 1:20; 9:31; 21:24; 22:16, where this term also appears). [*plērophoreō*]

1:2 Delivered (*paredosan*). This term refers to the passing on of tradition (1 Cor. 11:2, 23; 15:3; Mark 7:13), a tradition in this case rooted in the testimony of those who witnessed what Jesus did and said, something that vouches for its trustworthiness. Luke will call such eyewitnesses simply "witnesses" later (Luke 24:44-48; Acts 1:8). [*paradidōmi*]

1:3 Having followed all things (*parēkolouthēkoti*). This phrase either means "to keep up with something," like following the story of a movement, or perhaps "to investigate" (So NASB; NIV; BAGD, 618-19; BDAG, 767, 4). There is dispute whether the word has the kind of academic feel that the translation "investigate" might suggest. Regardless, the term refers to the acquaintance and careful attention Luke took in preparing his Gospel (Bock, 59-60). [*parakoloutheō*]

An orderly account (*kathexēs*). The question about this term involves what type of order is meant. It is probably not chronological order, as a comparison of the Gospels shows that the evangelists sometimes choose a topical order over a temporal one. More likely, Luke intends a reference to the orderliness of the story and its persuasive, divinely wrought character (Bock, 62-63; Green, 43). [*kathexēs*]

1:4 That you may know . . . assurance (*epignōs . . . tēn asphaleian*). Many translations render Luke's goal as "truth" in this verse ("that you may know the truth concerning the things about which you are instructed," RSV). However, Luke actually uses a term that refers more to a psychological assurance ("to reassure you," NLT; "have certainty," NET; which assumes truthfulness but goes beyond it; Acts 2:36; 21:34; 22:30; 25:26; 2 Macc. 3:22, where it refers to something safe and secure). [*asphaleia*]

177

About which you were instructed (*katēchēthēs*). Though we get our English term "catechism" from this verb, it is not likely that instruction that formal is meant here. Luke is too early for such formalized teaching (Gal. 6:6; Rom. 2:18; 1 Cor. 14:19). Nonetheless, it is clear that Theophilus has received some instruction in the faith, making it likely that the assurance is really reassurance given to a believer facing the pressure of being a Christian in a hostile world rejecting the Gospel and challenging Christians. [*katēcheō*]

1:5 Division (*ephēmerias*). This was one of 24 such divisions in the priesthood according to Josephus (*Life* 1 §2; *Antiquities* 7 §§363-67). First Chronicles 23:6 traces the organization of these divisions to David. In 1 Chronicles 24:10, Abijah is eighth in the priestly order list. The orders were divided into sub-orders and served in the temple for only two one-week periods a year. The term appears only here and in 1:8 in the NT. [*ephēmeria*]

1:6 Walking . . . blameless (*poreuomenoi . . . amemptoi*). These two expressions, walking in the commandments and being blameless, are good OT and Jewish phrases to describe a righteous person who walks faithfully before God (of Job, Job 1:1; see also Wis. 10:5, 15; 18:21), though Luke's expression of it combines concepts that normally appeared separately. So Luke declares the couple to be exceedingly righteous. The barrenness to be described is not the result of a judgment by God. Blameless is what Abraham was commanded by God to be (Gen. 17:1). Following in the commandments or in righteousness describes the pious in Isaiah 33:15; Proverbs 28:18; Daniel 9:10 and Jubilees 7:26. Blameless appears in the NT only in Philippians 2:15; 3:6; 1 Thessalonians 3:13 and Hebrews 8:7. [*amemptos*]

1:7 Advanced (*probebēkotes*). Luke makes it clear that the natural chance for children has passed, since they are literally, "advanced in their days." (See 1:18; 2:36.) [*probainō*]

1:9 Chosen by lot . . . to offer incense (*elache*). This custom of casting lots took place twice a day at the temple for the morning and evening offerings (Exod. 30:7-8; m *Tamid* 1.2; 3.1; 5.2-4. As these texts read, "They cast lots. And whoever won, won"). A priest only received this opportunity once in a lifetime, as only those "new to the preparation of the incense" could participate in the lot casting (m *Yoma* 2.2-4 explains that priests resorted to the innovation of casting lots to select representatives after a broken foot resulted from the earlier decision-making method—a foot race). It was considered the greatest honor of his priesthood as he represented the nation before God. [*lanchanō*]

1:10 The hour of incense (*tē hōra tou thymiamatos*). This time of prayer was shared by the people because the sacrifice was a corporate one for the whole nation. The sacrifice showed the dedication of the people at both the start and finish of the day. A later Jewish tradition records the spirit of the prayer as, "May the mercy of God enter the Holy Place and accept with favor the offering of his people" (*Targum on the Song* 4.16). [*thymiama*]

1:13 Your prayer (*hē deēsis sou*). The term prayer is singular. What Zechariah would be praying for during the sacrifice would be the nation's deliverance. Luke 1:18 shows he had given up on being a father. The angelic announcement shows God honoring the national request while also meeting an old desire and healing an old wound, as Elizabeth's response in 1:25 also indicates. This term for prayer appears rarely in Luke (2:37; 5:33), a topic Luke points to frequently with the use of the verb to pray (*proseu-*

chomai—19 times). The term Luke uses here is usually used to refer to "specific" requests versus general ones (EDNT 1:287; BAGD, 171-72; BDAG, 213). The term is always used in the NT of prayer to God. [*deēsis*]

1:14 Gladness (*agalliasis*). This is one of two terms for joy in the verse (the other, *chara*, appears earlier in the verse). It refers to an all-encompassing joy which emanates from the whole person (Isa. 51:11; EDNT 1:8). This term is limited to the language of the Bible and the church. In Luke it appears in 1:44 of the fetal John the Baptist's joy at Jesus' presence. That is the only other use of the noun in the Gospel. The verb is used in 1:47 and 10:21. [*agalliasis*]

1:15 Great (*megas*). This term appears here and in 1:32 of Jesus. Here it is part of a phrase indicating John's stature as great before God. When it describes Jesus, it is unqualified as simply "great," indicating Jesus' superior status to John. It is a way of saying Jesus is incomparably great. [*megas*]

Strong drink (*sikera*). The only NT use of this term, it is actually transliterated from Aramaic with roots in Akkadian (BAGD, 750; BDAG, 923). It normally refers to drink other than wine like "barley beer" (Lev. 10:9; Num. 6:3; Isa. 29:9). It is not clear if this drink is stronger than wine or not. The restriction shows that John will be exceedingly pious. [*sikera*]

1:16 Will turn (*epistrepsei*). This term is one of two key Lucan terms for repentance (*metanoeō* is the other). It is used 18 times in Luke–Acts out of 36 uses in the NT. It pictures the "change of direction" repentance represents and has its roots in the Hebrew concept of "turning" as reflective of repentance (Deut. 30:2; Luke 24:47). Thus, John's role is to lead Israel to repent before God. In Judaism, this verb is used to describe the work of the end time Elijah in Sirach 48:10, a figure to whom John is compared in the next verse. [*epistrephō*]

1:17 To turn (*epistrepsai*). The infinitival form of the verb used in the previous verse. It gives a second purpose of John's work, to bring reconciliation and wisdom to God's people as a way to prepare them for God's coming through Jesus. As is often the case in the Bible, proper relationship to God yields better relationship to others. [*epistrephō*]

A people __prepared__ (*laon kateskeuasmenon*). John's goal is to get the people of Israel inwardly ready for God's work of salvation. The image of a "prepared people" recalls Isaiah 43:7 and 2 Samuel 7:24 (NASB; NIV in Luke 1:17). It refers to a people that God has drawn to himself for a special work. Whereas normally the people were called upon to prepare for God and his coming (Isa. 40:3-5), here the reference is to a people God makes ready for his coming and special work. In secular usage, it meant to prepare the way for someone's arrival, even the arrival of a god (BAGD, 418; BDAG, 527-27, 1). [*kataskeuazō*]

1:18 Know (*gnōsomai*). Zechariah is really asking for some type of sign or proof this will happen, since he and his wife are so old that he cannot believe they will be parents. He wants to know that this will be by some other indication (BAGD, 160, 1a; BDAG, 199, 1a). [*ginōskō*]

1:19 Good news (*euangelisasthai*). This is a good everyday use of the term for an announcement from which we get our word "gospel" (compare Isa. 52:7; 61:1). Of the 54 uses of this verb in the NT, 25 appear in Luke–Acts. More theologically oriented uses appear in Luke 4:18, 43, 7:22, 8:1 9:6 and 16:16. The noun, gospel, does not appear in Luke and only twice in Acts (15:7: 20:24). [*euangelizō*]

1:20 Silent (*siōpōn*). The "sign" Zechariah gets for his unbelief is "silence," which refers to his being both deaf and dumb (see 1:62). This silence remains until the promise of a child is realized so he will ponder and believe that what God says he will do. The only other NT use of the term is in Matthew 26:63. [*siōpaō*]

1:21 Wondered (*ethaumazon*). This verb is frequent in Luke for the response to an event. Of 43 NT uses, it appears in Luke–Acts 18 times. It does not denote belief but emotional amazement that has drawn one's attention (BAGD, 352, 1ab; BDAG, 444, 1ab). The delay drew their attention. Often it is crowds that are amazed (1:63; 11:14), but the disciples can also be left in wonder (8:25; 24:41). [*thaumazō*]

1:22 Vision (*optasian*). The crowd recognizes that Zechariah had been permitted to see something that usually remains hidden from view and so had left the encounter in a different condition (Dan. 10:1, 7; BAGD, 576; BDAG, 717). A vision is not a "dream," but a kind of divine disclosure of either spiritual realities or the spiritual world. This term is rare in the NT, appearing elsewhere only in Luke 24:23; Acts 26:19 and 2 Cor. 12:1. [*optasia*]

1:25 Reproach (*oneidos*). Elizabeth's remark is a citation of Rachel's remarks when Jacob was born (Gen. 30:23; also Gen. 34:14). This strong word refers to reproach or shame that usually reflects on one's public reputation. The term is used 52 times in the LXX (Joel 2:17; Isa. 25:8). The related verbal term for reproach (*oneidizō*) shows up in the insulting directed at Jesus during the crucifixion (Matt. 27:44; Mark 15:32). Elizabeth's barrenness had been such a mark for her. Graciously, the Lord had now removed it. She knows that what took place was done by God. This is the only use of this word in the NT. [*oneidos*]

1:27 Virgin (*parthenos*). Unlike Matthew, Luke does not cite Isaiah 7:14 to refer to the fulfillment of Scripture in the birth through a virgin. He merely tells the story. [*parthenos*]

Out of the house of David (*ex oikou Dauid*)—As important as Mary's virginity for Luke is Joseph's connection to the house of David, making the child legally a member of a royal house. The word order in Greek suggests that the Davidic connection in this verse is Joseph's. [*Dauid*]

1:28 O favored one (*kecharitōmenē*). The angel's address of Mary marks her out as the recipient of God's special grace (BAGD, 879; BDAG, 1081). For Luke, she is a model of a beneficiary of God's grace (1:48). The only other use of this verb in the NT is in Ephesians 1:6. [*charitoō*]

1:29 Perplexed (*dietarachthē*). This term is used only here in the NT and refers to someone who is confused by something (BAGD, 189; BDAG, 237), "troubled" by it (NIV) or "perplexed" (NASB). Mary was wondering what was going on. [*diatarassō*]

1:31 Will conceive ... call his name (*syllēmpsē ... kaleseis*). This expression is almost a formula for a birth announcement of a child God will use. It appears in three OT texts (Gen. 16:11; Judg. 13:5; Isa. 7:14). [*syllambanō*]

1:32 Son of the Most High (*huios hypsistou*). The expression "Most High" is a round about way to refer to God, so that Jesus is called the "Son of God." The "Son of God" title becomes explicit in 1:35. Luke uses the term "Most High" nine times in Luke–Acts out of 13 NT uses. In 1:35 it is the power of the Most High, rooted in the work of the Holy Spirit, that is responsible for Jesus' birth. In 1:76, John the Baptist will be a prophet of the Most High. [*hypsistos*]

Throne of David (*ton thronon Dauid*). The angel refers to the regal role of Jesus as Messiah, promised Son of David. Jesus will receive the authority of this figure. This is the only verse in the NT where this exact expression occurs, but Luke loves to connect Jesus to the Davidic promise by other expressions involving his connection to David (Luke 1:27, 69; 2:4, 11; 3:31; 18:38-39). [*Dauid*]

1:33 The house of Jacob (*ton oikon Iakōb*). This expression refers to Israel as the people of God, since Jacob is the patriarch of the nation of Israel. Thus this promise is a way to say Jesus will rule over Israel, another way to call him Messiah. This phrase occurs only here and in Acts 7:46. [*Iakōb*]

His **kingdom** (*tēs basileias autou*). This promise is that Jesus' messianic rule will last forever. Thus the exercise of messianic authority, once it is established, will be in place forever. Peter alludes to such an exercise of messianic authority in his speech in Acts 2:30-36. Most texts on the kingdom in Luke refer to the kingdom of God (31 times out of 64 NT uses), but here the passage discusses the kingdom Jesus brings and is given. However, the two ideas are synonymous. Other variations of this expression also occur (Luke 22:29-30; 23:42). The term kingdom involves a complex association of ideas. Sometimes it is the idea of the presence of a functioning rule that is emphasized (Luke 11:20; 17:20-21). In other texts, it is a specific sphere or realm that is in view (Luke 22:30). In this verse, the term is used comprehensively of the kingdom, describing all such elements together. [*basileia*]

1:34 How shall this be? (*pōs estai touto*). This question is slightly different from Zechariah's in 1:18. The priest asked for a sign to prove what was announced (How shall I know . .

.?). Mary recognizes a birth announcement and understands that an immediate birth is anticipated, but wonders how it can be possible given her lack of sexual experience, a point underscored by the fact she "does not know" (*ginōskō*) a man. Whereas Zechariah received a short term judgment of silence, Mary gets an explanation. [*pōs*]

1:35 Son of God (*huios theou*). This expression highlights Jesus' unique relationship to God, though it has roots in Judaism as a reference to the nation's king. In the OT, God describes Himself as a Father to the king (2 Sam. 7:8-16). Luke also stresses the "regal" character of Jesus' person here in 1:32-35. However, the unique element to Jesus' sonship is grounded for Luke in the role of the Spirit in Jesus' birth, which also sets him apart as "holy" (*hagion*). The title Son of God occurs 45 times in the NT, while Luke uses it six times in his Gospel and once in Acts (Luke 4:3, 9; 41; 8:28; 22:70; Acts 9:20). [*huios*]

1:36 Kinsman (*syngenis*). God graciously gives a sign to Mary to indicate his promise will come to pass. It is the unusual conception of John the Baptist in the elderly Elizabeth. She is Mary's relative. Though a tradition exists that they were cousins, the term here is not that specific (BAGD, 772; BDAG, 950). This is the only NT use of this term. [*syngenis*]

1:37-38 Nothing/word (*rhēma*). A word play of sorts takes place in these two verses. They rotate around the double use of the term *rhēma*, which can have various meanings (BAGD, 735; BDAG, 905). In 1:37, the term has its broadest meaning of "thing" or "matter." So the angel affirms that nothing is impossible for God, even such an unusual birth as he has just announced. This idea is the theme of Luke 1–2, what God has promised he can and will do. In 1:38 in total submission to God's will, Mary replies as an exemplary servant that it can be done to her "according to your word" (NASB; NET; i.e., prophecy or utterance). For Mary this would entail charges that the child was illegitimate (John 8:41), but she was willing to face this false charge because God had called her to bear this child. [*rhēma*]

1:41 Leaped (*eskirtēsen*). Here John begins, even from the womb, to fulfill his role of pointing to Jesus (1:15). The verb for leap is associated in the OT with the experience of God's salvation (Mal. 4:2; Green, 95). It is often associated with joy as well (Jer. 50:11). In the LXX, it is used to describe the jostling between Jacob and Esau in the womb (Gen. 25:22). [*skirtaō*]

Was filled with the Holy Spirit (*eplēsthē pneumatos hagiou*). Reference to Spirit filling in Luke–Acts is common (Luke 1:67; Acts 2:4; 4:8, 31; 9:17; 13:9). It often leads to some expression of testifying to what God is doing. In 1:44 the Spirit-filled Elizabeth explains the leaping action of the fetal John. When someone is "filled" with something they are controlled by it, as the negative expression using filled shows. To be filled with anger, rage, jealousy or fear is to be controlled by it (Luke 4:28; 5:26; 6:11; Acts 5:17; 13:45). [*pimplēmi*]

1:42 Blessed (*eulogēmenē*). This word of welcome acknowledges Mary and the baby as recipients of God's gracious presence and power (BAGD, 322. 2a; BDAG, 408, 2a). It is a different term than the one for blessing in 1:45 (*makarios*), which refers to the joy one possesses as a result of receiving such a blessing. [*eulogeō*]

1:43 Lord (*kyriou*). This title of rank shows Elizabeth's insight into the fact that Jesus will carry an important stature that is worthy of this title of respect. This term appears 104 times in Luke. It can be a mere term of respect, can refer to God or to Jesus. In this context, it is likely that Elizabeth uses the term as a sign of her recognition of Jesus' messianic status, as the rest of the infancy narrative seems to indicate this was the category the family understood Jesus to fit into (Luke 1:69, 78-79). [*kyrios*]

1:44 Joy (*agalliasei*). See note on Luke 1:14. [*agalliasis*]

1:45 Fulfillment (*teleiōsis*). This is one of two NT uses of this term (Heb. 7:11). In this context it highlights one of the themes of Luke's infancy narrative (Luke 1–2) that turns around the idea of "fulfillment" (NET) expressed here. Mary is seen as a model believer because she believes what God says "will be accomplished" (NIV). The burden of the infancy narrative is to argue that God keeps his promises. Mary is blessed (*makaria*) because she has such trust. [*teleiōsis*]

1:46 Magnifies (*megalynei*). This term appears five times in the NT with four of them in Luke–Acts (Luke 1:46; Acts 5:13; 10:46; 19:17). This verb is prominent in the Greek OT psalter, appearing 17 times (Ps. 69:30 [68:31 LXX]). Here it introduces Mary's psalm of praise, where 1:46-55 give the reasons for her praise, both personal (46-49) and for Israel (50-55). She "exalts" (NASB) or "glorifies" (NIV) or "magnifies" (NET) the Lord. [*megalynō*]

1:47 Savior (*sōtēri*). God is described as a savior or deliverer. In this psalm, the deliverance is expressed in God's care and concern for Mary and for Israel. In 2:11, Jesus is called a deliverer. These are the only two uses of the term in Luke. Two other uses of the term for Jesus appear in Acts 5:31 and 13:23. In the NT, the term appears 24 times. This interplay between God as savior and Jesus as savior is common in the NT (John 4:42; Eph. 5:23; 1 Tim. 1:1; 2:3; 4:10). In Hellenism, this title was common for the gods (e.g., Asclepius, god of healing), but was also used of Caesar as a kind of divine figure, while the LXX loved to use the term to describe God as the NT does here (Ps. 25:5 [24:5 LXX]; 27:9 [26:9 LXX]; Mic. 7:7; BAGD, 800; BDAG, 985). The term points to someone engaged in the world's affairs for the good of humanity. [*sōtēr*]

1:49 The one who is mighty (*ho dynatos*). This is another title to describe God in terms of his power and authority ("Mighty One," NASB; NIV). It also appears in the LXX for him (Ps. 24:8 [23:8 LXX]). It also is a description or title of regal power in the LXX (44:4, 6 LXX, where the title is used only in the Greek version in v. 6). It can be used of God as here or of prominent people as in Acts 25:5 or 1 Cor. 1:26. [*dynatos*]

From now on (*apo tou nyn*). This phrase is quite common in Luke to suggest that things are different from this point on, usually because of some event (5:10; 12:52; 22:18, 69). [*nyn*]

1:50 Mercy (*eleos*). This term has OT roots, as the Greek word often translated the Hebrew term *hesed*, which refers to God's loyal or covenantal love, a faithful love that was an expression of his mercy and grace (Gen. 24:12, 14; Exod. 20:6; Ps. 103:17 [102:17 LXX]; TDNT, 2:479-85). God's action often was expressed as "doing mercy." This term appears four more times in this chapter to emphasize this point (Luke 1:54, 58, 72, 78). Mary extols the constancy of this faithfulness, noting it extends from one generation of God-fearers to the next. It is at this point Mary's remarks leave her personal situation and become more generalized. This is how God treats his people. [*eleos*]

1:51 Strength (*kratos*). This is the only time this word appears in Luke. This expression when it is combined with the image of God's arm refers to mighty deeds God performs for his children as the phrase alludes to Ps. 118:15 (117:15 LXX). So various renderings give the force of the phrase ("performed mighty deeds with his arm," NIV; "exercised power with his arm," NET). This term for strength was used to describe the power of great kings or gods in everyday Greek (BAGD, 449; BDAG, 565, 2). The anthropomorphism points to the powerful acts coming from God's strong arm. The details follow as the mighty are brought down and the humble are exalted. [*kratos*]

Scattered (*dieskorpisen*). This word in everyday speech was used of scattering a flock of sheep or an army on the field of battle (BAGD, 188; BDAG, 236). The scattering of God's enemies is an OT theme of which this Lucan use seems to be a variation (Num. 10:35; Ps. 68:1 [67:2 LXX]; 89:10 [88:11 LXX]—with a reference to God's arm as well.). [*diaskorpizō*]

Imagination (*dianoia*). This term describes the "impulses" of the heart ("thoughts of their heart," NASB; "innermost thoughts," NIV). It often was used in the LXX to refer to the heart which for the Hebrew was the seat of understanding (Prov.. 2:10). Here it has a decidedly negative nuance (BAGD, 187; BDAG, 234, 2). [*dianoia*]

1:52 Humble (*tapeinous*). This is the first of several references in Luke to God's concern for people of humble social status like Mary (Luke 4:18-19; 6:20; 7:22; 14:13—these texts refer to the poor). The term in this hymn clearly has sociological overtones as it stands in contrast to the powerful whom God brings down. It is parallel to the hungry in 1:53. This is Luke's only use of the noun. The verb shows up in a non-sociological sense in Luke 14:11 and 18:14. [*tapeinos*]

1:53 Empty (*kenous*). This term signifying the humbling of the rich indicates the eventual reversal God will bring in judgment that represents the vindication of the humble who have depended on God. A parable that depicts this reversal is Luke 16:19-31, the Rich Man and Lazarus. [*kenos*]

1:54 Israel (*Israēl*). God has a concern for his promises, because they relate to his faithfulness. This why this verse repeats the idea of God remembering his mercy to Israel. Luke refers to Israel 12 times in his Gospel and 15 times in Acts (out of 68 uses in the NT). On each occasion in Luke–Acts, the term refers to national Israel or people from ethnic Israel. Jesus' ministry was especially directed to them because of God's promises made to them as early as Genesis 12:1-3, a point the hymn alludes to in 1:55 with its mention of Abraham. Other texts in Luke make this clear (2:32; 22:30; 24:21) Whatever God is doing for the world, he also is working as well eventually to keep his promises to the nation. [*Israēl*]

1:55 Posterity (*spermati*). This use of the term "seed" ("descendants;" NIV; NASB; NET) is a corporate reference to the descendants of Abraham, another way to refer to Israel (also Acts 7:5-6). Other texts in Acts interplay the reference of descendants with the particular descent of Jesus from the seed (Acts 3:25-26; 13:23). This moves in the direction of Paul's remarks and the singular-plural interplay of Galatians 3:16-17 (singular), 29 (plural). One other Lucan use of the term uses it in a non-theological setting of a descendant (Luke 20:28), so there are six uses of the term in Luke–Acts. The point of this hymnic reference is to reaffirm that God is acting out of faithfulness in keeping his word. [*sperma*]

1:59 To circumcise (*peritemein*). This custom was a command of the OT to indicate one was a child of the covenant (Gen. 17; Exod. 4:24-25). The passage shows John's parents were law-abiding Jews. [*peritemeō*]

1:63 Writing tablet (*pinakidion*). This would be a wooden tablet covered with wax (Bock, 168). The choice of the name John shows Zechariah following the angelic instruction and not merely following tradition. This is what causes the crowd to marvel. [*pinakidion*]

1:66 Hand of the Lord (*cheir kyriou*). This phrase expresses the presence of God's power (BAGD, 880, 2; BDAG, 2bb). In the LXX, it is used 24 times. Sometimes it is negative, pointing to God's judgment (Exod. 9:3; Judg. 2:15; Ruth 1:13; 1 Sam. 5:6, 9). Often it is positive to indicate enablement from God (1 Kings 18:46; 2 Kings 3:15; 2 Chron. 30:12; Ezra 7:6; Ezek. 1:3; 3:14). [*cheir*]

1:67 Prophesied (*eprophēteusen*). This is the only positive use of this verb in Luke's Gospel (Luke 22:64 uses it of the mockers of Jesus urging him to prophesy). The term is also present Acts (2:17-18; 19:6; 21:9). It is often associated with the presence of the Spirit as here. In this passage the prophecy takes the form of a praise psalm. In Acts 2, it expresses itself in preaching the Gospel (v. 11). The most predominant use of the term is in 1 Cor. 14 (vv. 1, 3, 4, 5, 24, 31). [*prophēteuō*]

1:68 Blessed (*eulogētos*). For this term, see Luke 1:42. Here we have the adjective ("Blessed be," NASB; NET; "Praise be," NIV), not the verb. This is Luke's only use of this term, which appears eight times in the NT. The term is only used of God (7 times) or Christ (Rom. 9:5) in the NT. In this context, the blessing begins a second praise psalm, where Zechariah praises God for his redemptive work through Jesus with John as the forerunner. This exact phrase appears in the LXX in 3 Kgdms 1:48 [1 Kings 1:48]; 2 Chron. 2:11 [2:12 Eng.]; 6:4; Ps.

71:18 [72:18 Eng.]). [*eulogētos*]
Visited (*epeskepsato*). This term is often used to describe God's coming to his people in salvation (BAGD, 298, 3; BDAG, 378, 3; Heb. 2:6). It can have the nuance of making an appearance to help or look after someone. It appears again later in this hymn for the appearance of the Messiah pictured as a morning star (1:78) and in 7:16. Another key use is in Acts 15:14, when salvation is extended to the Gentiles. Luke–Acts has seven of the 11 uses of this term in the NT. The NIV simply translates "has come" but this softens the key imagery too much. [*episkeptomai*]

Redemption (*lytrōsin*). This noun is rarely used in the NT, appearing three times with two of those uses in Luke (Luke 2:38; Heb. 9:12; the NIV has a verbal phrase "has redeemed" in this verse). It refers to bringing about a deliverance (BAGD, 483; BDAG, 606). As a legal or commercial term in everyday use, it described securing someone's release usually with the payment of a redemptive fee. However, the idea of a ransom payment has no role in Luke 1 or 2 as the mere act of delivering is in view (Ps. 110:9 LXX [111:9 Eng.]; EDNT, 2:366). [*lytrōsis*]

1:69 Horn (*keras*). This term in context is a figure for might or power like that of an animal striking its foe with its horns (BAGD, 429; BDAG, 540, 3). It is often used of God in the OT (Ps. 17:3 [18:2 Eng.]; 2 Kgdms 22:3 [2 Sam. 22:3 Eng.]). Here it is the Messiah out of David's house who possesses such victorious strength that yields salvation. Zechariah is thinking of Messiah as a powerful deliverer. Such a thought was common in Judaism (*Psalms of Solomon* 17–18). How that victory precisely comes through Jesus' suffering will prove surprising, even to the disciples. [*keras*]

1:70 Even as he spoke through (*kathōs elalēsen dia*). Zechariah stresses how what

God is doing was announced through the prophets. Thus the theme of God keeping and completing his revealed promises is again raised here. The expression of God speaking through someone using this verb is rare, appearing only three times (Heb. 2:2 [through angels]; Heb. 2:3 [through the Lord]). [*laleō, dia*]

1:71 Salvation (*sōterian*). Salvation in Luke is seen in terms of rescue from enemies as it indicates here and in Luke 1:69 (Ps. 106:10), as well as salvation provided for through a spiritual provision in relationship to forgiveness of sins (Luke 1:77). Salvation can be both material and spiritual, and messianic salvation is both. It basically refers to deliverance or to the well-being that results from deliverance, which can often refer to a healing of some type when it is not referring to a rescue from mortal danger (BAGD, 801; BDAG, 986, 2; EDNT 3:327; Spicq 344-50). Three Lucan uses of the term are found in this hymn. They all refer to rescue from danger. The term only reappears in Luke's Gospel in 19:9 with a reference to Zacchaeus' salvation. Acts uses the term six times (4:12; 7:25; 13:26, 47; 16:17; 27:34). Particularly significant are 4:12 and 13:47. This second Acts passage has its roots in Isaiah 49:6. The noun is rare in the Gospels as it appears only at John 4:22 and in one of Mark's textually disputed endings known as the shorter ending, a variation of Mark 16:9. Thus the term is far more common in the epistles. [*sōteria*]

1:72 Mercy (*eleos*). See Luke 1:50. [*eleos*]
Covenant (*diathēkēs*). This word is singular. Luke 1:73 makes it clear that the fundamental promise to Abraham in Genesis 12:1-3 and reiterated to him is what is in view (see also v. 54). This covenant was a unilateral pact made by God with Abraham and his seed, the nation of Israel and ultimately the promised descendant of Abraham (Gal. 3,

esp. v. 16). The mention of an oath (*horkon*) in v. 73 shows God's initiative. The only other mention of covenant in Luke is of the new covenant at the Last Supper (22:20). Acts 3:25 notes that Jews are the sons of the covenant. Acts 7:8 declares that God gave a covenant of circumcision to Abraham. [*diathēkē*]

1:73 Oath (*horkon*). God's oath indicates how committed God is to his promise. The only other oath mentioned in Luke–Acts is the one God made to David of an heir for his throne in Acts 2:30 (2 Sam. 7:8-16; Ps. 132:11). [*horkos*]

1:74 Enemies (*echthrōn*). This is the only Lucan use of this word, which summarizes one of God's covenant commitments, to rescue his people from their enemies. Zechariah as a pious Jew is probably thinking of deliverance from earthly, worldly enemies like Rome. However, in the development of Luke's Gospel it will become clear that these enemies include spiritual forces and opposition like that represented by Satan. [*echthros*]

To serve (*latreuein*). This term summarizes the purpose of this deliverance, to free God's people up so they can serve God in righteousness and holiness all their days. In the LXX, this term was consistently used to describe religious service to God, especially acts of worship (TDNT, 4:60; Exod. 4:23; 8:16; Deut. 6:13). Zechariah is saying that salvation is designed to free individuals so they can worship God with the service of their lives. [*latreuō*]

1:75 Holiness (*hosiotēti*). This term only appears twice in the NT, both times it is associated with righteousness. In these two uses it refers to a practiced righteousness (*dikaiosynē*) that emerges from the holiness of a personal piety (TDNT, 5:493; Eph. 4:24). In the OT, it is associated with the heart (Deut. 9:5). God, having set apart his people, frees

them to serve him in righteous character. This is what the coming of promised salvation means for Zechariah. [*hosiotēs*]

1:76 Prophet of the Most High (*prophētēs hypsistou*). John is prophet of the Most High in contrast to Jesus (1:32), who is son of the Most High. On this term as a description of God's position, see 1:32. [*hypsistos*]

Lord (*kyrios*). In this context, to go before the Lord refers not to Jesus, but to God the Father who is responsible for salvation. On the term Lord, see 1:43. [*kyrios*]

To prepare his ways (*etoimasai hodous autou*). This idiom comes from Isa. 40:3, where a path is cleared in the creation for the powerful entry of an honorable figure, namely God, who brings deliverance to his people (Luke 3:4; Matt. 3:3; Mark 1:3). [*etoimazō*]

1:77 In the forgiveness of their sins (*en aphesei hamartiōn autōn*). This term pictures a release of some kind, depending on the context (EDNT, 1:181). In the OT, the noun shows up in the context of jubilee or release (Lev. 25:10-12; 27:18; Deut. 15:1-2; 31:10). Here Zechariah is still discussing John's work. He will give the people of Israel knowledge of salvation with respect to making known to them the forgiveness of sins ("by the forgiveness," NASB, NET; "through the forgiveness," NIV). Thus a release from the debt of sin is in view. This will be pictured in the baptism John presides over as Luke 3 makes clear. The term forgiveness appears four times in Luke (3:3; 4:18; 24:47). In each case it surfaces in a key Lucan theological text, with John the Baptist, in Jesus' preaching, and in Jesus' final commission as a summary term for the disciples' preached message to the world. It appears five more times in Acts (2:38; 5:31; 10:43; 13:38; 26:18). Each of those uses is also strategic. The response to Peter at Pentecost, Peter's message to another Jewish audience, Peter before Cornelius, Paul in the synagogue and Paul's defense speech use this term to summarize what God makes available to people through Jesus. Thus, nine of 17 NT uses of this noun are in Luke–Acts. [*aphesis*]

1:78 Tender mercy (*splanchna eleous*). Zechariah describes God's mercy as an expression of God's heartfelt compassion (BAGD, 763, 1b; BDAG, 938, 2). This term describes the seat of a person's emotions as the "bowels," where the English equivalent is the heart. This is the Gospel's only use of this term. [*splanchnon*]

Visited (*episkepsetai*). This verb is repeated from 1:68. See the discussion there. [*episkeptomai*]

"Rising Star" (*anatolē*). This is a reference to the Messiah as the rising morning sun, functioning as light in the midst of darkness, an allusion to Isaiah 9:1-2 (EDNT, 1:93). The term simply means "rising," but in this context it is the rising of the morning light out of darkness that is described ("rising sun," NIV; "Sunrise," NASB; "the dawn," NET). [*anatolē*]

1:79 Death (*thanatov*). Usually this term in Luke refers to physical death, but in this hymn this use refers to people who live in spiritual darkness and thus are subject to spiritual death in judgment, called living in death's shadow. This is similar to the use in Matthew 4:16 and alludes to Isaiah 9:2 (EDNT, 2:132). [*thanatos*]

Way of peace (*hodon eirēnēs*). God's light in Messiah is pictured as a "path" (NIV, NLT) that leads to peace. The Hebrew concept of *shalom* carries with it the idea of well-being (BAGD, 227; BDAG, 287, 1b; Ps. 13:3 LXX; Isa. 59:8, both uses negative). Luke likes the concept of peace, as he uses it 14 times in the Gospel and seven times in Acts out of 92 NT uses. Here the attention is to the harmony of personal relationship between God and peo-

ple. Those who respond to the disciples are called "sons of peace" (Luke 10:6). The birth of Messiah means "peace on earth" (2:14). In Acts 10:36, the message of Jesus is summarized as a message of peace. Salvation means peace with God. [*eirēnē*]

1:80 Israel (*Israēl*). John, like Jesus, focused his ministry on Israel. Only after Jesus' resurrection did the ministry move in a more diverse direction, though hints of this did take place in Jesus' ministry (Luke 4:24-30; 7:1-10). [*Israēl*]

2:1 Enrolled (*apographesthai*). The decree involved a census undertaken for tax purposes ("to register all the empire for taxes," NET). This underscored Rome's control of Israel and was not popular. Joseph is a faithful citizen and enrolls. The historical accuracy of this census is controversial for Josephus, the ancient Jewish historian, records a first census under Quirinius whose date is A.D. 6, too late for Jesus' birth (*Antiquities* 17.342-44, 355; 18.1-10). Luke either refers to an earlier census or to a census that took some time to complete and was finalized under Quirinius (Bock 1:903-09). The journeying to one's own city gives the census a Jewish flavor, making it based in ancestry (2 Sam. 24). [*apographō*]

2:4 City of David . . . Bethlehem (*polin Dauid . . . Bēthleem*). This description of Bethlehem connected to David is interesting. Normally it would be Zion or Jerusalem that would get such a connection (2 Sam. 5:7, 9; 6:10, 12, 16; Marshall, 105). But occasionally Bethlehem carried this description (1 Sam. 20:6 calls it "his" city; in the Hebrew MT only, 1 Sam. 17:12, 58). Bethlehem's association with a future powerful king is rooted in the OT (Mic. 5:1-2 [4:14-5:1 MT]; Matt. 2:5-6). The remark gives Jesus' legal, regal connection through Joseph. David is named 59 times in the NT with 24 of those coming in Luke–Acts. The name appears 13 times in Luke, but six of those take place in Luke 1–2 (1:27, 32, 69; 2:4 [2x], 11). Luke regards this regal Davidic rootage of Jesus as foundational to his identity as God's promised one. [*Dauid*, *Bēthleem*]

2:5 Betrothed (*emnēsteumenē*). This description of Mary makes it clear that the couple has not yet consummated their marriage (Green, 127-28; Matt. 1:21, 25). Betrothal was about a year-long process in Judaism and was not considered technically completed until consummation took place (*m Ketub* 5.2; *m Ned* 10:5). This is one of two NT uses of the term (Luke 1:27). So we get various renderings about Mary ("who was engaged to him," NASB; "who was pledged to be married to him," NIV; "who was promised in marriage to him," NET). [*mnēsteuō*]

2:7 Manger (*phatnē*). This probably describes an animal feeding trough (TDNT, 9:53-54; MM, 665). This means that Jesus was born in an animal stable of some type. [*phatnē*]
   Inn (*katalymati*). This was because there was no public shelter available, either in the form of lodging or a guest room for them. This term may not mean an inn in the formal sense, since Bethlehem was pretty small. It refers to a temporary resting place (Jer. 14:8 LXX; figuratively of Israel as a lodging place for the nations, 1 Macc. 3:45; BAGD, 414; BDAG, 521). [*katalyma*]

2:9 Glory of the Lord (*doxa kyriou*). This refers to the radiance of the Lord, a presence associated with divine majesty (Ezek. 10:4; EDNT, 1:345). God is present as his messenger is about to reveal what is taking place according to his plan. Luke uses this term 13 times out of 166 NT uses. Normally the term refers to giving honor to another as in Luke 2:14, 32. This exact phrase appears in 2 Corinthians 3:18; 8:19; 2 Thessalonians 2:14; and Jas. 2:1. [*doxa*]

2:10 I declare good news (*euangelizomai*). Here is a good example of the use of the verb, to proclaim good news (1 Kings 1:42), from which we get our noun, gospel. It is a declaration of "good news" that the angel gives in announcing this birth. Luke has 10 of the 54 uses of this verb in the NT. Often it is the kingdom of God that is being proclaimed in Luke (4:43; 8:1; 16:16). [*euangelizō*]

2:11 Today (*sēmeron*). This term is important to Luke to highlight the immediacy of what is taking place. Luke–Acts uses the term 20 times out of 41 NT uses. Thus, the announcement to the shepherds took place on the very day of Jesus' birth. In contrast, the Magi of Matthew two visit Jesus sometime later. [*sēmeron*]
   Savior (*sōtēr*). This is the only place in Luke that Jesus is called Savior. Acts will use this description in 5:31 and 13:23. The NT uses the expression 24 times. In this verse, this is one of three titles used to describe Jesus, as Christ and Lord are also used. Christ is the base title Luke has concentrated on in the early chapters, while Lord will become a key title in the last week and in the early chapters of Acts. In the OT, it is used of God (Deut. 32:15) and of men, such as the judges of Israel (Judg. 3:9, 15). It describes a deliverer. [*sōtēr*]

2:14 Glory (*doxa*). Here is an example where glory refers to the giving of praise or honor to one who is worthy as was noted in the note on this term in 2:9. [*doxa*]
   Among men with whom He is pleased (*anthrōpois eudokias*). This is not a reference to all men, but to those God has chosen to be the recipients of his grace ("with whom he is pleased," NASB, NET; "on whom his favor rests," NIV). These people are "men of his good pleasure or will" (EDNT, 2:75-76). This

phrase has shown up at Qumran (1QH col. 4:32-33; col. 11:9), where it describes "sons of his good pleasure" or "sons of his approval." Luke 10:21 is the only other reference to God's "good pleasure" in his choosing of babes and the unwise for salvation. [*eudokia*]

2:19 Pondering (*symballousa*). All six NT uses of this term are in Luke–Acts. Here it refers to reflective contemplation (BAGD, 777; BDAG, 956, 2, "get it all together"). The term can also refers to engaging in a battle like a king going to war (Luke 14:31; 1 Macc. 4:34) or to engaging in a conversation like Acts 17:18. So the word has a give and take feel to it. Mary is still trying to figure out all that is happening because of Jesus. [*symballō*]

2:20 As it had been told (*kathōs elalēthē*). This reference to things happening as God had said is a major theme of Luke 1–2. God will do what he promises. He has a plan. [*laleō*]

2:21 To circumcise (*peritemein*). This practice was commanded in the OT and was to be performed on the eighth day (Gen. 17:10-14; Luke 1:59). The detail shows that Jesus' parents were law-abiding Jews. This verb is only used twice in Luke's Gospel. [*peritemnō*]

2:22 Purification (*katharismou*). The reference to "their" purification probably combines several items tied to Jewish ritual purity. A wife was to be declared pure 40 days after giving birth (Lev. 12:2-6). There also were rites associated with Jesus' being a firstborn (Exod. 13:2, 12, 15; 34:19), as well as rites to dedicate the child (1 Sam. 1–2). It is also possible that Joseph had helped with the birth so that he would require an offering for cleanliness since the contact with blood at the birth would render him unclean (*m Nid* 5.1; 2.5; 1.3-5). [*katharismos*]

2:23 Holy (*hagion*). This use of the term is rooted in the dedication of the first born (Exod. 13:2, 12, 15). It means that the child is set apart for the Lord and service to him (BAGD, 9; BDAG, 11, 1ab;"consecrated," NIV). Once again Jesus was raised in a way that was faithful to Jewish practice. [*hagios*]

2:24 A pair of turtledoves or two young pigeons (*zeugos trygonōn ē duo nossous peristerōn*). This reference to a sacrifice using birds is an indication that Jesus' parents possessed modest financial means, since this was the sacrifice of poorer families. The reference to turtledoves points especially to this background (BAGD, 828; BDAG, 1018). These sacrifices are described in Leviticus 5:11 and 12:8. [*trugōn, peristera*]

2:25 Devout (*eulabēs*). This term refers to someone who is a faithful fearer of God. In this setting, it is of one who is faithful to the Law. In the LXX, it translates terms that describe one who fears God (Deut. 2:4; Isa. 57:11; TDNT 2:752). The term suggests someone who is careful about his or her walk with God. [*eulabēs*]

Consolation of Israel (*paraklēsin tou Israēl*). This phrase describes a person waiting for Israel's promised national deliverance, like the phrase "redemption of Jerusalem" in 2:38. It is an expression looking to messianic deliverance (Isa. 40:1; 61:2; BAGD, 618, 3; BDAG, 766, 3). Later in Judaism, the Messiah was called the comforter, a variation on this expectation, since he brings the comfort (TDNT, 5:792-93). [*paraklēsis*]

2:26 It had been revealed (*kechrēmatismenon*). This verb for revelation often refers to an oracle or divine declaration (Jer. 33:2 LXX; BAGD, 885; BDAG, 1089, 1ba). Thus it refers here to a prophecy. The remark may suggest that Simeon was an old man, just as Anna was an elder woman. How this came to Simeon other than it was by the Spirit is not indicated. [*chrēmatizō*]

2:27 He came in the Spirit (*ēlthen en tō pneumati*). This idiom refers to being directed by the Spirit ("moved by the Spirit," NIV; "directed by the Spirit," NET; "inspired by the Spirit," RSV; BAGD, 677, 5db; BDAG, 835, 5da). [*pneuma*]

2:29 Lord (*despota*). This term appears 10 times in the NT and is not the normal term for Lord (*kyrios*). It is used in three ways: to describe God (Acts 4:24) or Jesus (Jude 1:4; Rev. 6:10) and to describe the master to a slave in a house (1 Tim. 6:1-2; Titus 2:9; 1 Pet. 2:18). The term suggests the right over someone because of ownership. With God, it is because he is the Creator. With Jesus, it is because of his work on the cross, his right to judge, or the authority he has from the Father (Acts 2:30-36). [*despotēs*]

2:30 Salvation (*sōtērion*). Simeon identifies salvation as completely tied to the baby he holds. To see Jesus is to see God's salvation. Luke 2:31-32 explains why this is so, God has prepared this child to be light in a way that benefits both the nations and Israel. [*sōtēria*]

2:31 Peoples (*laōn*). This is a very important term in Luke–Acts. It is used 36 times in Luke and 48 times in Acts, out of 142 NT uses. Often it merely refers to a group of people (Luke 7:1, 29; 20:1). However, in some contexts it is a way to speak of the special people of God, whether they are made up of Israel (Luke 1:68, 77; 24:19; Acts 4:10; 13:17, 24; 26:17-18, 23) or of all nations (Acts 15:14; Spicq, 371-74). It refers to the special people of God here, as the plural term present plus the reference to Israel and the nations in v. 32 makes clear. Thus, Simeon is suggesting that Jesus has come for all humanity. In 2:32, the term reappears in the singular (*laou*) to refer to Israel. God will make a people for Himself from every nation, even though the promise is rooted in Israel. Its use as a term for Israel has its roots in the LXX, where it has this sense about 2,000 times (Deut. 7:6-8; EDNT, 2:340-41). So the inclusion of people from the nations is a fresh emphasis, though not unprecedented. [*laos*]

2:32 Light (*phōs*). This metaphor for Jesus was already noted in the image of the rising sun in Luke 1:78-79. Here Messiah is a light to the nations and to Israel. The image is also important in Acts (13:47), when Paul turns to go to the Gentiles. It points to Jesus as the revealer of the path to God and the way one should go. Those who respond are called "children of light" (Luke 16:8). The Gospel uses the term seven times, but only two uses carry this force. In Acts, this technical use is also rare, appearing in 13:47 and in Paul's defense speech twice in 26:18, 23. Matthew also likes this image (Matt. 4:16), as do John (John 8:12), Paul (2 Cor. 4:6), and Peter (1 Pet. 2:9). [*phōs*]

Revelation (*apokalypsin*). Revelation in this context refers to a disclosure made to the nations about salvation (BAGD, 92; BDAG, 112). The truth about salvation and their inclusion in it is what Simeon refers to here as Acts 13:47 and 26:18, 23 make clear. [*apokalypsis*]

Glory (*doxa*). This term was covered in 2:9. Here is a use that refers to someone receiving honor or being held in esteem (Exod. 28:2; Ps. 8:5; Luke 14:10; Spicq, 1:364, 367, n. 33). The coming of Messiah and the performing of his mission are causes for honor to Israel. It is her Messiah who leads to blessing for the nations. [*doxa*]

2:33 Marveled (*thaumazontes*). This refers to their contemplating what was taking place. This term was discussed in Luke 1:21. [*thaumazō*]

2:34 Falling and rising (*eis ptōsin kai anastasin*). This phrase describes the first hint in Luke that there will be opposition to Jesus, only what it highlights is that he will make a division in Israel, lifting some up and bringing others down, depending on how individuals respond to him (2:35). The term "fall" can also can mean collapse as it does in Matthew 7:27, the only other use of the term *ptōsis* in the NT. However here it refers to a downfall as it contrasts with rising. The term for "rising" is used in this sense of lift up or elevate only here in the NT. [*ptōsis, anastasis*]

Sign (*sēmeion*). In everyday Greek this term described various things like a flag, a signature or an engraving, something that identified (Spicq, 3:249-53). It described something that "marked out" something else. Religiously, the concept in the OT describes an "indicator" of some kind sent by God (Exod. 3:12; 4:9; Isa. 38:7-8). Thus Simeon predicts that Jesus will be an indicator of opposition to God. Jesus' presence will surface who opposes or rejects (*antilegomenon*) God's way. Twenty two of the 77 NT uses are in Luke–Acts. John's Gospel also uses the term frequently (17 times), and speaks specifically of individual miraculous signs that point to Jesus' identity (John 2:18; 3:2; 20:30). [*sēmeion*]

2:35 Sword (*rhomphaia*). This term describes a large and broad sword used by barbarians or enemies (BAGD, 737; BDAG, 907; Ex 5:21; Ezek. 29:8). Simeon uses the term to picture events that will rip through Mary's soul, causing her great pain. In all likelihood, this is a description of her suffering when she sees the child suffer rejection and death in ministry. (For the interpretive options, see Bock, 248-50). [*rhomphaia*]

2:36 Prophetess (*prophētis*). This term appears only twice in the NT, once positively here and once negatively in Revelation 2:20

of Jezebel. Acts 21:9 refers to Philip's four daughters who prophesy using the verbal form of this word. Anna is yet another pious, elder figure who testifies to Jesus as v. 37 shows. [*prophētis*]

2:38 Those looking for the redemption of Jerusalem (*tois prosdechomenois lytrōsin Ierousalēm*). Anna is speaking in very Jewish terms here about the hope of the rescue of Israel, described in terms of the deliverance of Jerusalem. This expression parallels Simeon's "awaiting the consolation of Israel" in 2:25 and is rooted in the hopes of Isaiah 40–66. In fact, the same verb for awaiting is used in both verses. See earlier discussion of redemption in 1:68. [*lytrōsis*]

2:41 Every year (*kat etos*). The background to the custom of annual observance paints a picture about Jesus' roots. Jesus' parents were faithful Jews and obeyed the custom of annually celebrating the Passover in Jerusalem (Exod. 23:14-17; Deut. 16:16). In the OT, three festivals were to be so observed: at unleavened bread, which included Passover, first fruits and weeks, but by the time of the NT many pilgrims only went once a year to Jerusalem, given the longer distances one had to travel for the feasts. [*etos*]

2:42 Twelve years old (*etōn dōdeka*). Jesus' age is one year short of the age when, in later Judaism, Jewish boys were seen to be responsible as adults for religious duties (*m Nid* 5.6; *m Meg* 4.6; *m 'Abot* 5.21). Instruction picked up at 12 for the average Jewish boy. [*dōdeka*]

2:43 Did not know it (*ouk egnōsan*). This term describes both parents' lack of knowledge about Jesus staying behind ("were unaware of it," NASB, NIV; "did not know it," NET). The text does not explain how the parents could have left without Jesus.

Suggestions like men and women traveled separately, so neither parent knew whether Jesus was with the other parent cannot be demonstrated as true for this time period. In fact, v. 44 suggests that they had supposed Jesus was somewhere else in the caravan, when it says he was "in the traveling company" (*synodia*; BAGD, 791; BDAG, 973). The suggestion is that they thought he was with other travellers, not the other parent. [*ginōskō*]

2:47 Amazed (*existanto*). This term refers to amazement mingled with fear or uncertainty created by a set of surprising events (BAGD, 276, 2b; BDAG, 350, 2b). The term appears 17 times in the NT, with 11 uses in Luke–Acts, many of them with this force (Luke 8:56; 24:22; Acts 2:7, 12; 9:21). [*existēmi*]

2:48 Astonished (*exeplagēsan*). This is yet another term for amazement or surprise, but is a strong term suggesting an intensity of emotion, almost being overwhelmed (Gen. 43:33; Ex 23:27; 1 Macc. 15:32; BAGD, 244; BDAG, 308; EDNT, 1:420). In the NT, the term is often used of reaction to Jesus' teaching (Luke 4:32; 9:43), but here it is at Jesus' action to go to the temple. [*ekplēssō*]

2:49 It is necessary (*dei*). This key term highlights God's design or plan (Dan. 2:28 LXX), appearing 18 times in Luke. There are things it is necessary to get done: preach the gospel (Luke 4:43), the Son of Man must suffer (9:22; 17:25; 24:26), all things written about the Christ in Scripture must be accomplished (24:44). Here Jesus must be literally, "in the . . . of the Father." There is no noun here as the clause is an ellipse. Thus, a rendering "about the Father's business" is contextually appropriate. However in the context, it is especially in discussion about the teaching of God in the midst of the place indicative of God's presence that is meant. For the reply is

designed to explain why Jesus is at the temple (Bock 1:269-71). So Jesus must be at God's house teaching about him. [*dei*]

2:51 Was obedient (*hypotassomenos*). This term is the same one used for wives being submissive to husbands and how believers should relate to each other (Eph. 5:21-22 24). Jesus is portrayed as a faithful, obedient child to his parents. The middle voice indicates this is something Jesus chose to do. Luke emphasizes the humanity of Jesus, as v. 52 also shows. [*hypotassō*]

Kept (*dietērei*). This recalls Mary's reaction in 2:19. The intensive form of the verb plus the mention of Mary's heart adds a note that a deep impression was made by these events. The infancy material in Luke 2 is told from Mary's perspective as she tries to comprehend (see v. 50) all that is taking place with Jesus. This is Luke's only use of this verb. Its only other NT use is in Acts 15:29. In the OT, see Genesis 37:11 (BAGD, 189; BDAG, 238— to keep something mentally) [*diatēreō*]

3:1 Tetrarch (*tetraarchountos*). This term makes its only NT appearance three times in this verse to describe Herod, Philip, and Lysanius. They are Roman-appointed, dependent princes, whose rank and position were established and supported by Caesar and his regional governor, Pilate. Herod (Antipas) and Philip were Herod the Great's descendants. Herod the Great had been appointed a regional client king over the entire area in 40 B.C., but did not assume power until 37 B.C. Thus, when Jesus was born, Herod the Great had a higher office than his two sons, mentioned here. When John the Baptist and Jesus began to minister, Herod Antipas was a Roman client king over the region where John and Jesus preached, as Luke 3:1 notes. We know next to nothing else about Lysanius, who had no ties to the Herod family. His rule was divided up when he died in 5–4 B.C. [*tetraarcheō*]

3:3 <u>Baptism</u> of <u>repentance</u> for the <u>forgiveness</u> of sins (*baptisma metanoias eis aphesin hamartiōn*). Virtually every part of this phrase is important, as is the combination of terms. In Judaism, baptisms were acts of cleansing. At Qumran, there were numerous washings to symbolize movement toward purification and cleanliness in preparation for worship (CD 10:10-13; 1QS 3:2-11; 5:13-14, where the heart, not the rite is emphasized; Josephus, *Antiquities* 18.19 about Essene washings). When Gentiles fully converted, they were called to engage in proselyte baptism to denote their being cleansed (*Sibylline Oracles* 4.162-69; TDNT 1:537). Neither of these Jewish washings represents what John's baptism meant, though the image of cleansing is similar. John's baptism was a washing of eschatological preparation expressing a need for the cleansing and forgiveness that would come with the arrival of God's promise. Thus, rather than an act of preparation for worship or of initiation, this baptism was one of preparation and identification with what God would bring.

A baptism related to repentance meant that there was recognition that Israel's unredeemed condition was tied to the presence of sin in the nation's midst. God needed to come, because the nation had been unfaithful. Thus the nation needed to prepare to receive the Lord. This explains the appeal to Isaiah 40 in the following verses, which detail divine consolation coming to a nation ready to receive her promise. Repentance as an OT and Hebrew concept meant to turn, to embrace a change of direction. John, as a prophet like those of the OT, makes such a concrete call to turn (Luke 3:10-14; Rom. 6:1-4).

What repentance yields is forgiveness of sins. It makes one open to receive the approaching grace of God, a reaction which itself yields forgiveness. As the above description makes clear, there are national overtones in this baptism as John presents it. Though it is individually appropriated, it is part of John's call to Israel to prepare for her Messiah, who brings the promise of deliverance. Thus, John's baptism is not the same as Christian baptism. It merely set the stage for it (Luke 3:15-16). [*baptisma, metanoia, aphesis*]

3:4 **Make** (*poieite*). This image from Isaiah 40:3 is part of the introduction of the prophet's declaration about God's approaching salvation. The image is of creation leveling itself out in a "red carpet" style welcome for God's entry. Readiness involves the repentance John calls for in his baptism (Isa. 57:14-15). There is a word play with the verb "make" (*poieō*) that reveals the pictorial nature of the image, for the same verb reappears in 3:8, 10, 12, 13, 14 to raise the question about what shall be done in response to John's call ("What should we do [*poiēsōmen*]," NET; NIV). The answer comes in terms of how others are treated as reflective of a proper response to God, a point Luke already noted in Luke 1:16-17. [*poieō*]

3:6 **Salvation** (*sōtērion*). This key term was treated in Luke 1:71, though the form here is not the noun, but the adjective (BAGD, 801-02; BDAG, 986). It denotes the actions of saving. In the OT, it was used sometimes to describe the "peace offering" (Exod. 24:5; Lev. 6:5). Luke adds a point here that was not in the earlier setting, namely, that salvation is something that will be seen by "all flesh" as opposed to being something just for Israel. When Luke cites Isaiah 40, he includes vv. 4-5 so he can get to the point of the universal scope of the Gospel being for people of every nation. This is an expansion on the citation of Isaiah 40 as it appears in Matthew 3:1-6 and Mark 1:2-6. [*sōtērios*]

3:7 **Vipers** (*echidnōn*). This is a reference usually to a poisonous snake (BAGD, 331; BDAG, 419; Acts 28:3). Here John uses it to shock and rebuke his audience by comparing his audience to venomous snakes coming out of their ground holes to escape a fire. Matthew likes this expression, using it three times (Matt. 3:7; 12:34; 23:33). This is Luke's only use in his Gospel. [*echidna*]

Wrath (*orgēs*). This is one of five uses of this term in the Gospels, but three of those are shared in the parallel accounts of this saying (Matt. 3:7; Mark 3:5; Luke 21:23; John 3:36). The strong term has OT roots (Ps. 59:13). John speaks as one who anticipates that if one does not respond to his message and the approaching salvation he announces, then only the expectation of God's wrath remains. To seek out John and his message means to seek out escape from God's wrath. Thus, John's remark is a warning and an ironic challenge. [*orgē*]

3:8 Abraham (*Abraam*). This reference to the great patriarch of Genesis 12–21 alludes to not making an appeal that assumes one is saved because of genealogical pedigree. Luke has made frequent reference to him as a figure of promise (1:55, 73). [*Abraam*]

3:9 Good fruit (*karpon kalon*). The concept of good fruit as an expression for expressed righteousness is important to both John and Jesus (Luke 6:43-44; 8:8; 13:6, 7, 9; 20:10; in the OT, Hos. 10:12). Twelve of the 66 NT uses of this term appear in Luke. John equates the product of repentance, good fruit, as something that prevents one from being judged and burned. It is something God calls us to possess. Its practical nature is specified in Luke 3:10-14, a text unique to Luke's Gospel. [*karpos*]

Fire (*pyr*). This term is a figure for divine judgment, which is its prevalent use in the OT (TDNT 6:936-37, 941-43; Gen. 19:24; Exod. 9:24; 2 Kings 1:10; Joel 2:30; Isa. 66:15-

16, 24; Mal. 3:1; BAGD, 730; BDAG, 898, b). One of the things Messiah will do is make this separation (Luke 3:16-17). Given the context about fleeing the coming wrath, John describes final divine judgment here. [*pyr*]

3:10 Multitudes (*ochloi*). This term is what Luke uses to refer to the general audience that went out to hear John or Jesus ("crowds," NASB; NIV; NET; "multitudes," RSV). He uses the term 41 times, with over half of those uses in Luke 4–9. [*ochlos*]

3:11 Tunics (*chitōnas*). This term actually refers to the undergarment, made of either wool or linen, which reached either to the ankles or knees, and could be long or short sleeved. It could be worn over the skin or over another garment (Gen. 3:21; 37:3; Lev. 16:4; EDNT 3:468). John's point is that those who have should share with those who do not. Such concern evidences true repentance. [*chitōn*]

3:12 Tax collectors (*telōnai*). These people bid annually for the right to collect official taxes, tolls, and dues and also collected that money (EDNT, 3:349). They were unpopular with the Jewish populace, for they represented Roman power (*m Ned* 3.4 and *m. B. Qam* 10.2 describe them alongside of murderers and robbers). This person got to keep any excess amounts collected and was usually quite wealthy through the surcharges he added. It would be culturally poignant that a tax collector would ask what repentance involves. The term only appears in Matthew (8 times), Mark (3 times), and Luke (10 times). Luke tends to treat them positively as willing to listen to the message (5:32; 7:29-30; 15:1-2). [*telōnēs*]

3:14 Rob no one by violence (*diaseisēte*). This term literally means "to shake someone violently" ("take money from no one by violence," NET; "don't extort money,"

NIV—lacks the violent overtones of the term; "do not take money from anyone by force, NASB). Our slang term to "shake down" someone is very equivalent in force (BAGD, 188; BDAG, 236). This is the only NT use of the verb. Soldiers were not to take unfair advantage of their authority, that is, extort by violence (3 Macc. 7:21). Once again repentance has a relational result. [*diaseiō*]

3:15 The Christ (*ho christos*). This allusion to the possibility that John might be the Christ might seem odd. However, Judaism did not possess a fixed, single view of what the Christ would be. The technical term is rare in the OT, appearing of a future figure only in Daniel 9:25-26. Otherwise it was used of regal figures (Ps. 2:2) and priests (the high priest—Lev. 4:3-5, 16; 6:15) to designate someone "anointed" by God (TDNT 9:496-523). The most famous extra-biblical Jewish messianic text, *Psalms of Solomon* 17–18, sees the Messiah as a great delivering king in line with OT expectation of a golden age ruled by a promised Davidite (Jer. 23:5-6; Ezek. 17:3-4; 37:24-25). However, other expectations did exist that opened up the option, which John rejected, that he might be a potential candidate (See John J. Collins, *The Scepter and the Star: The Messiahs of the Dead Sea Scrolls and Other Ancient Literature*). [*christos*]

3:16 Sandals (*hypodēmatōn*). This detail about sandals may have important cultural background. A later Jewish text explains to Jewish slaves that they should never demean themselves to the point of undoing their masters sandals (*Mekilta, Nezekin* 1 on Exod. 21:2). John is saying in comparison to the coming Messiah, who will baptize with Spirit and fire, he is not worthy of this demeaning task! [*hypodēma*]

Holy Spirit (*pneumati hagiō*). The reference to baptism by the Spirit contrasts what John is doing with water as a preparatory rite with

what Jesus will do that signals the presence of the Christ and the promised era of deliverance. In effect, John is telling the crowd that the way to know the Messiah has come is that he brings the baptism of the Spirit. This is precisely what Peter declares as fulfilled in Acts 2:14-41, especially vv. 29-36. The additional reference to fire is probably a description of the distinction this baptism makes within humanity, where fire is seen as a purging agent as v. 17 also suggests (Isa. 4:4-5; Bock 322-23). [*pneuma*]

3:17 Winnowing fork (*ptuon*). The winnowing fork pictures the judgment authority the coming Christ will possess as he separates people like someone does wheat from chaff. This implement was a fork-like shovel used for such grain separation (BAGD, 727; BDAG, 895; Matt. 3:12 is the only other NT use). [*ptuon*]

Unquenchable fire (*pyri asbestō*). The judgment the Messiah gives is compared to being tossed in an "unquenchable fire" (So NASB; NIV; "inextinguishable fire," NET). It is a judgment without an end. This term as a description of judgment appears in only three NT texts (BAGD, 114; Matt. 3:12; Mark 9:43). John's warning is designed to shake up his audience about the seriousness of the choice they have. [*asbestos*]

3:19 Herodias (*Hērōdiados*). This reference to Herod Antipas' wife surfaces the immoral roots of his marriage to her, as she had been the wife of his half brother, also known as Herod (BAGD, 348; BDAG, 440; Josephus, *Antiquities* 18.110-11). The remarriage led to war as the initial wife of Herod was divorced, angering her father, Aretas IV, king of Nabatea (Nabatea was located east of the Jordan in what was also called Arabia). Both left previous marriages to enter into this union. Thus, John would have complained about the divorce and remarriage, as well as marriage to the spouse of a blood relative (Lev. 18:16; 20:21). Herod did not grow up with a great example, as his father, Herod the Great, had ten wives. These complaints plus other moral challenges resulted in John's imprisonment. [*Hērōdias*]

3:21 Opened (*aneōchthēnai*). This verb is often used in the NT to describe God opening something up in his power, when it is not being used simply as an everyday description of something that is open like a mouth or eyes or a door (EDNT 1:105; Matt. 9:30; Matt. 5:2; Luke 1:64; 12:36; 13:25). Thus, God opens a door of opportunity (1 Cor. 16:9; Acts 14:27). Here the figure describes heaven being opened so God can reveal something, a common OT use (Ezek. 1:1; Isa. 24:18; 64:1; Gen. 7:11; Mal. 3:10). It is often used in an event that involves a vision as in Ezekiel. Luke has six of the 77 NT uses of the term. [*anoigō*]

3:22 Beloved Son (*ho huios mou ho agapētos*). In the response of the baptismal voice, the reference to Son is an allusion to Ps. 2:7, while God's being pleased with Jesus alludes to Isaiah 42:1 ("Son, whom I love" NIV; "beloved Son," NASB; "dear Son," NET). More discussed is the background for the reference to "beloved." Two candidates are possible. One is an allusion Genesis 22:12, 16. If so, it is a reference to Jesus as an "only" son. A second, slightly more likely possibility is Isaiah 41:8. The emphasis is of the Son-Servant as one who is especially loved and chosen. [*agapētos*]

3:23 As was supposed (*hōs enomizeto*). This expression makes it clear that Joseph, though Jesus' legal father, is not his biological father ("so it was thought," NIV). This verb in Luke–Acts is always used of a false or erroneous assumption (Luke 2:44; Acts 7:25; 8:20; 14:19; 16:27; 17:19; 21:29; EDNT 2:470). Nine of the 15 NT uses are Lucan. [*nomizō*]

3:31 Of Nathan (*tou Natham*). This is where a divergence exists between Matthew and Luke, who names Solomon at this point in his genealogy. Why the differences exist have long been discussed. No clear explanation has emerged. Among the options are that Matthew gives Joseph's genealogy and Luke has Mary's. But Mary is not named in this unit at all. Another is that the difference is that one gives the natural descent and the other a legal descent with perhaps the curse on Jeconiah (Jer. 22:30) playing a role. In these approaches which account is legal and which natural is debated. Levirate marriages may also impact the lists (for details on the views, Bock 1;918-23). [*Natham*]

Of David (*tou Dauid*). This is one of the key names in Luke's genealogy. As with all the names except the last the definite article in the genitive *tou* is an article denoting descent. The presence of this name in the list makes Jesus qualified to be Messiah, as it means that he is of the house of David. [*Dauid*]

3:34 Of Abraham (*tou Abraam*). This is the third key name in the genealogy. His presence alludes to the Abrahamic promise that God would bless the world through Abraham's seed (Gen. 12:1-3). This is what leads to the mention of Isaac, Jacob, and Judah. Matthew's genealogy goes back this far, while Luke's proceeds on back to Adam as the one created by God, showing Luke's concern for all humanity. [*Abraam*]

3:38 Of Adam (*tou Adam*). The reference to Adam is significant not only because it shows Luke's concern for all humanity, but because the genealogy's order, running in reverse back to the end places the reference to Adam next to the temptations. So Jesus as Son of Adam, Son of God successfully undergoes the temptations as Son in a way Adam failed to do, making Jesus a worthy second Adam who is able to represent humanity. [*Adam*]

4:1 Full of the Holy Spirit (*plērēs pneumatos hagiou*). This term is used in the NT 16 times, yet 10 of those uses are in Luke–Acts. Often it is in association with the Spirit, indicating a person who operates in and is directed by God's Spirit (Acts 6:3, 5; 7:55; 11:24). A contrastive use is the description that someone is "full of rage" (Acts 19:28). Thus, the temptations occur after Jesus has been guided by the Spirit, a point emphasized in repeating the idea later in the verse. It was no accident he was in the wilderness fasting. [*plērēs*]

4:2 Being tempted (*peirazomenos*). This present participle indicates that Satan's temptations proceeded across the entire 40 day period ("endured temptations by the devil," NET). What Luke summarizes for us is the end of this trial. Seven of the 38 NT uses of this term for trial or temptation are in Luke–Acts. It can mean test or tempt (tested—Luke 11:16; tempted—Acts 5:9). It usually has a negative implication. [*peirazō*]

4:3 Devil (*diabolos*). Five of Luke's six uses in the Gospel occur in this scene (Luke 8:12; Acts 10:38; 13:10 complete the Lucan uses in his two volumes). The term means "slanderer" and is a LXX translation of the Hebrew word *hasatan*, from which we get our word Satan (Job 2:1; BAGD, 182; BDAG, 226, 2). The one who twists truth will fail to ensnare the one filled with the Spirit. [*diabolos*]

4:4 It is written (*gegraptai*). This is one of three uses of this phrase in this scene, two by Jesus, one by the devil. The perfect tense has the force of "it stands written." Scripture is often cited with this formula (14 times in Luke–Acts). Jesus' scriptural replies all come from Deuteronomy and all affirm a loyalty to

God or, as here with the citation of Deuteronomy 8:3, a reminder that there is more to existence than material well-being. That text alludes to the divinely provided manna in the desert (Exod. 16), a symbol that although the nation was living without much in material surroundings, God was providing and caring for them. [*graphō*]

4:5 Moment (*stigmē*). This represents the only NT use of this word which refers to something insignificant as it means "first point" (BAGD, 768; BDAG, 945). Thus when it is applied to time, it describes an instant ("moment," NASB; RSV; "flash," NET; "instant," NIV). The detail tells us that this temptation took place after a "vision-like" moment when the kingdoms were flashed before Jesus. [*stigmē*]

4:6 Authority (*exousian*). This is an important term in the Gospels. Many conflicts in Jesus' life and ministry turn on debates about authority or the idea that Jesus taught with an unparalleled authority (Matt. 7:29; 8:9; 9:6, 8; 21:23-27; 28:18; Mark 1:22, 27; 2:10; 3:15; 11:28-33; Luke 4:32, 36; 5:24; 7:8; 20:2-8). Here the devil claims to have authority over the earth, a claim that ultimately is false ("domain," NASB; "authority," NIV; "whole realm," NET). He is trying to deceive Jesus by claiming he can give him something he does not have the right to give. [*exousia*]

4:7 Worship (*proskynēsēs*). This word refers to the homage paid to one in religious devotion or in honor (Gen. 18:2—Abraham to three visitors; 24:26—to God; 37:9—to Joseph; EDNT, 3:173-75). It was a term often associated with prostrating oneself before the one being worshiped, though it does not always carry this force, as one can merely honor someone with such a bow. In Luke's Gospel, the term appears three times, twice in this scene. Here it is the devil's offer of an inappropriate worship, followed by Jesus' reminder that only God is to receive such honor in v. 8. Significantly, Jesus receives such honor himself after his resurrection (Luke 24:52) and appears to accept it, unlike the reaction of Peter to Cornelius in Acts 10:25. Another example of inappropriate worship appears in Acts 7:43, where idols are worshiped and Israel ends up guilty and penalized with exile. [*proskyneō*]

4:8 Serve (*latreuseis*). This is a second term denoting religious service in the NT. It is so used in the OT (Exod. 3:12; Deut. 6:13, the text Jesus uses here; the noun form—Josh. 22:27; 1 Macc. 2:19). The NT uses the term 21 times, with eight of those in Luke–Acts. It describes true worship and reverence. Note also its use in Luke 1:74 and 2:37, where its more cultic force is evident (EDNT, 2:344-45). [*latreuō*]

4:10 Guard (*diaphylaxai*). This term was often used in magical literature to appeal to a supernatural kind of protection associated with amulets, while in the LXX it was used of God's protection as in Ps. 91:11, which is cited here ("to guard," NIV; NASB; RSV; "to protect you," NET; BAGD, 191; BDAG, 240; MM, 158). This is the only NT use of the term as the Matthean parallel lacks this clause. The devil wants Jesus to rely on special divine protection. [*diaphylassō*]

4:12 Tempt (*ekpeiraseis*). Jesus refuses to test God and put him on the spot forcing him to act ("test," NIV, NASB; NET; "tempt," RSV). The citation is from Deut. 6:16. Such testing in Deuteronomy was seen as disobedience. [*ekpeirazō*]

4:14 Report (*phēmē*). This term occurs only twice in the NT (Matt. 9:26). Though no reason is given for the report ("news," NASB, NIV), events like the ones reported on in Luke 4 seem to be the cause of the attention. [*phēmē*]

4:15 Glorifying (*doxazomenos*). This term means to honor someone or give praise to them ("praised," NIV, NASB; NET; "glorified," RSV). Usually it refers to giving honor to God, as was noted with the noun in Luke 2:14. However, sometimes people are meant (Matt. 6:2; 1 Cor. 12:26). Since it is the populace at large giving the honor, it is this later sense that is intended here. The verb is used nine times in Luke and four times in Acts of 60 NT uses. [*doxazō*]

4:16 Sabbath (*sabbatōn*). This is the first of six key Sabbath day events in Luke (4:31; 6:1-2, 7-9; 13:10-16; 14:1-5). Luke–Acts has 29 of the 68 NT uses. This seventh day of the week was the weekly day of rest and worship for Jews. It with circumcision comprised two of the major distinctive markers of Judaism (clean and unclean food was a third key marker with worship at a single temple as the fourth; EDNT 1:220). The setting apart of the day goes back to the OT (Exod. 23:12; Deut. 5:13-14). The day was held in such high regard in later Judaism, that it was said the day would be observed in hell (*b Sanh* 65b) and that Messiah would come if Israel kept two Sabbaths perfectly (*b Shab* 188b). [*sabbaton*]

4:18 Anointed (*echrisen*). This term comes from a citation Jesus makes of Isaiah 61:1. The reference to Spirit anointing looks back in the Gospel to what took place at the baptism. Acts will also note this act (4:27; 10:38). Jesus is declaring that he fulfills the role Isaiah describes. [*chriō*]

Poor (*ptōchois*). Here is the emphasized audience for Jesus' preaching, the poor. This term has rich OT roots, referring to the persecuted and pious poor as Luke 6:23 also shows (Exod. 22:25-27 [22:24-26 MT]; Ps.

14:6 [13:6 LXX]; 22:24 [21:25 LXX]; 69:29 [68:30 LXX]; Isa. 3:14-15). The term has both religious and sociological meaning as piety and faith are placed together with social standing. It is those who have been marginalized by the world for their faith that are most open to the Gospel. In the context of Judaism, this is a call to free the spiritually exiled and persecuted. Their suffering opens them up to the hope. Luke has 10 of 34 NT uses. [*ptōchos*]

To proclaim (*kēryxai*). This verb is used twice in this citation, alongside another verb (*euangelisasthai*) that speaks of preaching the good news. Luke uses this term nine times in his Gospel. Much of Jesus' role involves his proclaiming release and offering sight to the blind. These descriptions are pictures of what salvation brings. The later line from Isaiah 58:6 at the end of this verse declares that Jesus will actually effect the release he proclaims ("release," NIV; "set free," NASB, NET; "to set at liberty," RSV). Both the proclamation of Jesus and his work refer to release, using the same term *aphesis*. [*kēryssō*]

4:19 Acceptable year of the Lord (*eniauton kyriou dekton*). This expression is an idiom for the year of Jubilee ("year of the Lord's favor," NET; NIV; "acceptable year of the Lord," RSV; "Favorable year of the Lord," NASB). This year was described in the Law as a time every 50 years when all debt was forgiven (Lev. 25:10). This became a figure of spiritual, divine forgiveness in Isaiah 49:8 and 58:5-8. Jesus uses it in this last sense to picture his work as a labor designed to bring divine forgiveness. [*dektos* + *eniautos*]

4:20 Were fixed (*atenizontes*). This verb means to look at someone or something intently ("were fastened," NIV). It is a term which in this context suggests Jesus' citation generated attention and some emotion. Twelve of the NT's 14 uses of this term are in

Luke–Acts. The other use in the Gospel is where a maid stares at Peter during his denials in an effort to figure out if she recognizes him. [*atenizō*]

4:21 Today (*sēmeron*). This term was treated fully in Luke 2:11. In this scene Jesus declares himself to be the figure described in Isaiah 61:1. In other words, the promised new era of deliverance has come. [*sēmeron*]

4:22 Is this not . . .? (*ouchi*). This interrogative particle expects a positive answer. Thus, the crowd, despite being so impressed and perplexed by Jesus' remarks that they marvel, resolve the situation with the realization that this is a carpenter's son. In other words, someone with this common a background cannot be who he claims to be. [*ouchi*]

4:23 Capernaum (*Kapharnaoum*). This Galilean town located on the northwest corner of the Sea of Galilee became Jesus' headquarters (BDAG, 537). Its mention here suggests that this synagogue scene was moved up chronologically by Luke (In Matthew, it appears in Matthew 13:53-58). For Jesus has not yet been in Capernaum in Luke's Gospel. In fact, it is the ministry Luke describes next in Luke 4:31-44. The importance of the literary move is that Luke is indicating that this synagogue scene typifies Jesus' ministry in this period and the reaction to him. It may also reflect how Jesus preached in the synagogue in general. Luke refers to this location in 4:31; 7:1; and 10:15. The NT mentions it 16 times. [*Kapharnaoum*]

4:24 Acceptable (*dektos*). The scene has an ironic word play in it that ties back to v. 19. Jesus declares the acceptable year of the Lord there, but he is not acceptable as the Lord's prophet to them, indicating a major opportunity missed for the people ("acceptable,"

NET; RSV; "accepted," NIV; "welcome," NASB). Jesus explains the historical basis for the remark in v. 24 in the verses that follow. [*dektos*]

4:25 Elijah (*Ēlias*). The incident alluded to here is in 1 Kings 17–18, but in selecting Elijah, Jesus compares himself to the prophet and compares the people to the nation of old. This is a period in Israel's history when the nation was most obstinate in rejecting God's way. Luke mentions this prophet seven times in his Gospel out of 29 NT uses (1:17; 4:26; 9:8, 19, 30, 33). [*Ēlias*]

4:26 Zarephath (*Sarepta*). This widow of Sidon is a Gentile and had her son revived from the dead in 1 Kings 17:8-24. Jesus' point is that the land was so obstinate that only Gentiles received the benefit of ministry. This is the only mention of this figure in the NT. [*Sarepta*]

4:27 Naaman the Syrian (*Naiman ho Syros*). The reference to this incident from 2 Kings 5:8-19 provides a second example of outreach to Gentiles. This is the only mention of Elisha in the NT. [*Naiman*]

4:28 Wrath (*thymou*). In this scene it was not Jesus' claims about himself that made them angry. Rather it was the suggestion that their reaction made them like one of the worst periods of Israel's history along with the implication that Gentiles might be more helped by God than the nation would be. This is the only place in Luke's Gospel where he uses this term for anger. The term's roots refer to something that boils up or wells up (TDNT 3:167). Similar Jewish reactions to the mention of Gentiles appear in Acts (Acts 22:21-22; 26:23-24). [*thymos*]

4:32 Authority (*exousia*). Here is one of the distinguishing characteristics of Jesus' teaching, its authority. The other Gospels note this characteristic as well (Mark 1:22, 27; Matt. 7:29). Luke 4:36 will couple the authority of teaching with the power of exorcism. Luke uses this term 16 times. Among the major uses are Jesus' authority to do things like forgive sin (5:24) and a major confrontation in Jesus' last week over who gave Jesus such authority (20:2-8). [*exousia*]

4:33 Spirit of an unclean demon (*pneuma daimoniou akathartou*). Though Luke refers to demons 23 times in his Gospel, this is the only verse he does so with this combination of terms. Jesus' first work is seen in his confrontation with the spiritual forces of darkness, making a point about where the fundamental battle is as he seeks to deliver humanity. The spirit that controlled this person was an "unclean" demon. This probably refers to a man whose possession caused him to act in evil ways, since no personal habits are described unlike Mark 5:1-10 (BAGD, 29, 2; BDAG, 34, 2). [*pneuma + daimonion + akathartos*]

4:34 What have you to do with us? (*ti hēmin kai soi*). This question is a Semitic idiom. It can mean, "why are you unjustly bothering me" (Judg. 11:12; 2 Chron. 35:21; 1 Kings 17:18) or "Leave us alone" (NET; NASB; "what do you want with us?" NIV; "what have you to do with us?" RSV)? This sense indicates that hostility is present in the expression. It can also mean, "This is not your business" (2 Kings 3:13; Hosea 14:8; John 2:4). The first sense is intended here. The demons are trying to put Jesus off. [*tis*]

I know (*oida*). The demon's naming of Jesus as Holy One is an attempt to gain control of the situation. In ancient texts of exorcism, it was common to name the demon as a way of showing authority in the encounter. The move is a defensive one born from nervousness about Jesus' position and power. [*oida*]

Holy One of God (*ho hagios tou theou*). This title is a recognition by the demon of Jesus' special status as one set apart by God. A connection between this title and Jesus as the Christ appears in 4:41. In Luke, it looks back to 1:31-35 and Jesus' unique relationship to God. It suggests Jesus as a bearer of the divine Spirit (TDNT 1:101-02). [*hagios*]

4:35 Be silent (*phimōthēti*). This verb means to muzzle, and, thus, to silence ("Be quiet!" NASB; NIV; "Be silent!" NET; RSV; BAGD, 861). Jesus sometimes commands demons not to confess who he is (e.g., Mark 1:24-25). It appears that this kind of an endorsement could produce confusion about who Jesus was, as later the Jews suggest it is through the devil's power that Jesus works (Luke 11:14-20). Jesus also silences a raging creation with his word (Mark 4:39). [*phimoō*]

4:36 Amazed (*thambos*). This term is rare, appearing three times in the NT, all in Luke–Acts (Luke 5:9; Acts 3:10). The astonishment shows that these kinds of miracles were not seen as so common, unlike the way some portray the ancient world. What amazes is the power and authority in Jesus' word. [*thambos*]

4:39 Rebuked (*epetimēsen*). This verb is normally reserved for encounters between people (Luke 4:41; 9:42, 55), so that disease here is almost treated like a power that needs to be stopped and over which Jesus has authority. Creation will be treated in a similar way in Luke 8:24. [*epitimaō*]

4:40 Laid hands on them (*tas cheiras epititheis*). This expression occurs 21 times in the NT, ten of which are in Luke–Acts (Luke 13:13; Acts 6:6, 8:17, 19; 9:12, 17; 13:3; 19:6; 28:8). It is associated with healing (Matt. 9:18), commissioning (Acts 13:3), or with the passing on of the Spirit through the apostles (Acts 8:17, 19). In this scene, Jesus' personal contact in healing is stressed. [*epitithēmi + cheir*]

4:41 The Son of God (*ho huios tou theou*). The demons make this confession as Jesus performs exorcisms. As in 4:34-35, Jesus silences the effort. Luke will use this title only twice more in 8:22, when the storm is calmed, and in 22:70, when Jesus is asked at his trial by the High Priest if he is this figure in a context where being Messiah and Son of Man are the points of dispute. [*huios*]

The Christ (*ton Christon*). The presence of this explanation that Jesus is the anointed one and its equation with Son of God in this scene is only noted by Luke. Just as in Luke 1:31-35, the stress is on Jesus as the unique messianic Son. [*Christos*]

4:43 The kingdom of God (*tēn basileian tou theou*). This important phrase is used 64 times in the NT, with 31 uses in Luke and another seven in Acts. It refers to the promised rule of God. Jesus preaches and brings this kingdom. It is both present with Jesus, having been prepared for by John the Baptist (Luke 7:28; 11:20; 16:16; 17:21) and yet to come in fullness in the future (Luke 19:11). In fullness, it is the promised rule of God on the earth with the righteous vindicated and the wicked judged. In the present, it is the arrival of forgiveness and the presence of the Spirit, an arrival that is based on Jesus' authority to defeat the spiritual forces of evil (see the parable in 11:21-23 following the key kingdom remark in 11:20). As this verse makes clear, the kingdom is the topic of Jesus' preaching the good news. He must (*dei*) preach the kingdom, as he was commissioned to do so (see Luke 2:49 for *dei*). [*basileia*]

4:44 Judea (*Ioudaias*). Some critics have charged Luke with a geographical error in speaking of Judea while Jesus is in the North.

However, Luke is using the term in its broadest sense, referring to all of Israel, so there is no error. This use was not unique to Luke (as it appears in the *Iudea capta* on coins of the Roman ruler, Vespasian; EDNT 2:191-92). Luke uses it this way sometimes (1:5; 6:17; 7:17; 23:5; Acts 10:37; 12:19) and more narrowly of just the South in other places (Luke 1:39, 65; 2:4; 3:1; 5:17; 21:21). [*Ioudaia*]

5:1 Gennesaret (*Gennēsaret*). This is simply another name for the Sea of Galilee, a lake eight to 14 miles in size and quite popular for fishing (BDAG, 194). The NT has two other uses of the term (Matt. 14:34; Mark 6:53). [*Gennēsaret*]

5:2 Nets (*diktua*). These were probably "trammel nets," made of linen and visible to fish in the day. This is why it was better normally to fish at night. This is why Jesus' request in v. 4 is unusual and would not lead normally to a productive catch. It also explains Peter's initial response in v. 5a. The nets took two to four men to deploy and would be washed in the morning (Green, 232; Matt. 4:20-21; Mark 1:18-19; John 21:6, 8, 11). [*diktoun*]

5:5 Word (*rhēmati*). This term refers to an utterance ("as you say," NASB; "because you say so," NIV; "at your word," RSV, NET). Luke–Acts has 32 of the NT's 68 uses of this word. Half of the 18 uses in his Gospel take place in Luke 1–2. In many texts it almost has the feel of making a pronouncement. Peter shows his faith by doing what his fishing experience would tell him would not work. [*rhēma*]

5:7 Boat (*ploiō*). If this were a typical Galilean fishing boat, it would be about 20 to 30 feet long and could hold several men. Two passages in Luke describe such a vessel (5:2-7; 8:22, 37). [*ploion*]

5:8 A sinful man (*anēr hamartōlos*). The term sinner is significant in Luke, for Jesus consciously pursues sinners and responds to those who understand their condition as Peter does. This term is used 47 times in the NT with 17 uses in Luke. This is the first use in Luke. Several passages focus on Jesus' different approach to sinners (5:30-32; 7:34-50; 15:1-10; 18:13). Only in Luke 6:33-34 and 24:7 is the term used negatively. Peter thinks his condition as a sinner disqualifies him from being in the presence of a divinely enabled, holy man like Jesus. Jesus' view is that because Peter understands that he is a sinner and respects the presence of holiness, he can be made a fisher of people. [*hamartōlos*]

5:10 Catching men (*anthrōpous esē zōgrōn*). The verb to catch can often mean to capture, to spare from death, or to save in the Greek OT (Num. 31:18; Josh. 2:13; 6:25—of Rahab spared; 2 Chron. 25:15). So sometimes the term has a nuance of capturing as to save, as it does here ("catching people," NET; NASB; "catching men," RSV; "catch men," NIV). [*zōgreō*]

5:12 Leprosy (*lepras*). This disease isolated one from the culture in Judaism as Leviticus 13–14 gives the process of diagnosis, isolation, as well as how to restore one who no longer has the disease. How seriously this process is to be taken is seen in Deuteronomy 24:8. So to have this disease was socially devastating as it cut one off from people and worship. A reference to this term for the disease appears only in Luke 5:12-13, Matthew 8:3; and Mark 1:42. Lepers are mentioned three times in Luke (4:27; 7:22; 17:12) and nine times in the NT. [*lepra*]

5:14 Testimony to them (*martyrion autois*). To go to the priest and offer sacrifices was the normal OT practice when one sought to be declared clean and restored to society. To this

Jesus adds the note that the entire offering would serve as a testimony to them. The healing was a "witness" to what God was doing through Jesus. Who is the "them"? Some translations, like the RSV, suggest it is "for the people," probably because of the remark that the word spread despite Jesus telling the leper not to say anything except to the priests. Jesus often tried to silence such testimony to the masses, because the issue was not his miraculous work by itself, but what it pictured. The audience should better be seen as the priests, as it is appropriate that they should know what God is doing. After this event, Jewish leaders do show up to check out Jesus (Luke 5:17). The Gospel uses the term twice more (9:5; 21:13). [*martyrion*]

5:17 Pharisees (*Pharisaioi*). This group was made up of laymen committed to following the Law fully. Josephus describes their practices in a series of key texts (*Antiquities* 17.41; 18.12-15; *Jewish War* 2.162-63). Luke's Gospel refers to them 27 times out of 99 NT uses. The fact that these Pharisees came from various regions, (Galilee, Judea, and Jerusalem) shows that the movement within the entire nation is concerned about Jesus. [*Pharisaios*]

5:19 Roof (*dōma*). Most homes in this period had two stories with the roof serving as a second story. Steps up to the roof often lay in the open. It was flat and about six feet above the ground. Most structures had clay, reeds, and thorns for a roof. Luke describes this roof as having tile. Luke's Gospel uses this term twice more (12:3; 17:31). [*dōma*]

5:20 Forgiven (*apheōntai*). The phrase to forgive sin occurs 20 times in the NT with Luke using the phrase eight times (5:20, 21, 23, 24; 7:47, 48, 49; 11:4). Two key incidents, both creating controversy, comprise the bulk of the examples. This healing and the anointing by the sinful woman are two scenes where Jesus

shows this authority that was regarded as possessed only by God. [*aphiēmi*]

5:21 Blasphemies (*blasphēmias*). Blasphemy means to speak or act in a way that dishonors God as the fundamental idea of the term is to slander or defame (EDNT, 1:220-21). In Judaism, usually it had to do with something said, but it also could include something done. This is Luke's only use of the term, though it does show up in the trial scene in both Matthew 26:65 and Mark 14:64. The claim to forgive sin "dishonored" God in the Jewish view as Jesus took on a prerogative only God could possess. Again the issue is Jesus' authority. [*blasphēmia*]

5:23 Easier (*eukopōteron*). This comparative term, used three times in Luke (16:17; 18:25), introduces a reflective question. Jesus says on the one hand to forgive sins is easier, since it cannot be seen. On the other hand, to tell someone to rise up and walk is easier, since to really forgive sin one must have such authority. In the subsequent verse, Jesus will link the two, so that the healing evidences his authority as Son of Man, that is as one with the right to judge (Dan. 7:9-14). [*eukopos*]

5:24 Son of Man (*ho huios tou anthrōpou*). This title is Jesus' favorite way to refer to himself. The title appears 82 times in the NT with 24 times in Luke. The phrase in Aramaic is simply a way to speak of a "human being" or "someone." Thus, when Jesus initially used it, its full force would not be clear. Later in his ministry, he connects the term to the imagery of Daniel 7, where it describes a human being who rides the clouds like God and receives judgment authority from the "Ancient of Days," a reference to God. In that text, Son of Man is not a title, but a description. Thus, the phrase uniquely combines human and divine qualities while highlighting one's divinely bestowed authority, making it a perfect choice to describe who Jesus is and what he does. (*huios* + *anthrōpos*)

5:26 Strange things (*paradoxa*). The crowd reaction to Jesus' healing and declaration of forgiveness is that unusual and uncommon things are taking place ("incredible things," NET; "remarkable things," NASB: NIV; "strange things," RSV). Such activity was a shock to the ancient Jewish crowd, just as it might be if it happened today. That is why it caused amazement. This is the only use of this term in the NT. It appears in a few intertestamental texts with a similar force. (Judith 13:13; 2 Macc. 9:24; Wisdom 16:16). [*paradoxos*]

5:27 Tax office (*telōnion*). This is a reference to the customs house, where tax collectors gathered the taxes. They were usually locals hired by the tax collector who actually held the contract to collect the taxes. For the tax collector, see Luke 3:12 (BAGD, 812; BDAG, 999). [*telōnion*]

5:28 Followed (*ēkolouthei*). This verb is the popular NT term to summarize becoming a disciple. It appears 90 times in the NT, with all but 11 of those uses in the Gospels. Luke's Gospel has the term 17 times. A few of those uses mean to follow in a secular sense as the crowd follows Jesus or someone follows a person into a place (7:9; 9:11; 22:10). However most of the references are to following after Jesus, attaching oneself to his way. [*akoloutheō*]

5:30 Murmured (*egongyzon*). This onomatopoetic word is often used of inappropriate grumbling ("complained," NET; NIV; "grumbling," NASB; "murmured," RSV), as it appears of the nation's grumbling in the wilderness (Exod. 17:3; Num. 14:27). It indicates intense displeasure (BAGD, 164; BDAG, 204). The term is used eight times in the NT and this is its only use in Luke (the

noun appears in Acts 6:1). [*gongyzō*]

5:31 Physician (*iatrou*). This term is rare in the NT, appearing seven times. Luke has it twice, both as a figure for Jesus in a type of proverbial use (Luke 4:23; in the OT, 2 Chron. 16:12; Jer. 8:22). It was also used this way of Plato, as a doctor of the soul (BAGD, 368-69; BDAG, 465-66). [*iatros*]

5:32 To call (*kalesai*). This term usually means to call for someone or to invite (EDNT 2:240-41). The nuance of invite may not be far from this use (Luke 14:15-24). Jesus fellowships with tax collectors and sinners in the hope of inviting them into spiritual health through repentance and into his care as a doctor. [*kaleō*]

5:33 Fast (*nēsteuousin*). The Pharisees would fast twice a week (Luke 18:12), beyond special fasts for key holidays. Thus, this remark suggests a lack of piety in Jesus' disciples. The term appears four times in Luke, three of which are in 5:32-34. The NT uses the term 15 times, all of which are in the Gospels and Acts. The noun referring to fasting appears only three more times in Luke–Acts (Luke 2:37; Acts 14:23; 27:9). [*nēsteuō*]

5:34 Bridegroom (*ho nymphios*). This term pictures Jesus as a groom to a bride and describes the time of his ministry as one of celebration because the promise is present (John 3:29). The image of the people of God, whether Israel or the church, as a bride or wife is common (Isa. 62:5; Jer. 2:2; Hosea; Eph. 5:25-27). Luke only uses the term twice, both in this passage. [*nymphios*]

5:35 Is taken away (*aparthē*). This is an allusion to Jesus' death. He suggests that when he is removed, then fasting will become appropriate. The only place this term is used in the NT is in this text and its parallels (Matt. 9:15; Mark 2:20). [*apairō*]

5:36 Parable (*parabolēn*). This use of the term parable reflects a broad Semitic understanding of a wise saying or proverb, a *mashal*. So Jesus is using a proverb to underscore how the old and new cannot be mixed. He compares his ministry to a new garment that will shrink being attached to an old garment that will not shrink, so that the whole thing tears. This kind of a mix Jesus will not do. [*parabolē*]

5:37 Wineskins (*askous*). These wineskins were made of leather and would expand with the fermentation of new wine. However, if they were old, they would not expand when the wine fermented and thus could break open. Jesus will not mix old and new to prevent this result. The four NT uses of the term appear in this text and its parallels (Matt. 9:17; Mark 2:22). [*askos*]

5:39 Good (*chrēstos*). This adjective normally means to be kind, but in this context it means someone has a preference for something that is good ("good enough," NASB; NET; "good," RSV; "better," NIV). This is an allusion to the leadership's preference for the old ways to the new, so that they will not consider Jesus' new way. [*chrēstos*]

6:1 Sabbath (*sabbatō*). For basic information on the Sabbath, which was a day of prescribed rest, see 4:16. The disciples' action in 6:1 is seen as a multiple violation according to Jewish tradition of the "40 less one," where 39 violations are listed (*m Shabbat* 7.2). Plucking, preparing food, and threshing would all be seen as violations, which explains why some Pharisees ask about the violation. The example explains how some of the leadership are attached to "old" wine. For an example of how specific these instructions were, one was prohibited from writing or erasing two alphabetic letters on the Sabbath. An incident of a man who picked up wood on the Sabbath and was executed

for it appears in Numbers 15:32-36. This incident helped fuel this attention to detail. [*sabbaton*]

6:4 Bread of the presence (*artous tēs prothesēōs*). The phrase is literally "bread of the offering" ("bread of the presence," RSV; NET; "consecrated bread," NASB; NIV). This bread was located in the holy place of the temple and was reserved for the priests (Ex 25:30; 35:13; 39:36; Lev. 21:22; Num. 4:7). The incident is described in 1 Samuel 21:6. Jesus is explicit that what took place "was not lawful." His suggestion appears to be that in this case involving David an exceptional circumstance prevented a violation of the Law (Matt. 12:7). At least God did not judge the king for this act. This is the only passage in Luke that mentions this bread. [*artos + prothesis*]

6:5 Lord (*kyrios*). This key term for authority Jesus uses as a second argument after the David example. It, in effect, argues if you do not like my example, I have authority over the Sabbath anyway. This would be a radical claim within a Jewish context, as God had established the Sabbath as a day of rest (Ex 20:8; Deut. 5:12). [*kyrios*]

6:7 Watched (*paretērounto*). This term has a sinister feel. It means "to spy on" or "watch out of the corner of one's eye" (Ps. 37:12; [36:12 LXX]; Dan. 6:12; BAGD, 622, 1ab; BDAG, 771, 1ab). They were looking to get him. It has a similar force in its two other Lucan uses (14:1; 20:20). [*paratēreō*]

6:9 To do evil (*kakopoiēsai*). This is the only Lucan use of this term. (Mark 3:4 is the only other use in a Gospel.) The term shows that Jesus is exposing the leadership's hypocrisy and intent ("to do harm," RSV; NET; NASB; "to do evil," NIV), for in claiming to protect the Sabbath, they are really trying to "destroy" Jesus, as the next phrase of the question shows. [*kakopoieō*]

6:11 Fury (*anoias*). This term is only used twice in the NT (2 Tim. 3:9). It denotes folly in other contexts. Here it describes a senseless, even pathological rage (TDNT 4:963). [*anoia*]

6:13 Apostles (*apostolous*). This term has an everyday use where it means a commissioned messenger. In Judaism, when a messenger was sent and acted with the authority of the sender, he was called a "sent one" (*m Berakot* 5.5; *m Yoma* 1.5). Similar ideas existed in Greek culture (Josephus, *Antiquities* 17.300; MM 70). So the naming of the Twelve indicated they possessed a special authority. Luke uses the term six times (9:10; 11:49; 17:5; 22:14; 24:10). [*apostolos*]

6:20 Poor (*ptōchoi*). This key Lucan term was discussed in 4:18. Here the pious poor are said to already possess the kingdom. This beatitude expresses God's welcome to those the world has rejected, a theme Luke loves to note (7:22; 14:13). [*ptōchos*]

6:22 Cast your name out (*ekbalōsin to onoma hymōn*). This phrase is an allusion in part to being kicked out of the synagogue. It really describes the rejection of persecution ("Reject your name as evil," NET; NIV; "cast out your name as evil," RSV; "scorn your name as evil," NASB). It shows that Jesus' remarks concern the pious. Those who are blessed have made a stand to identify with the Son of Man, Jesus, and lost their place in the Jewish community as a result. Nevertheless, they are the blessed whom God receives. [*ekballō + onoma*]

6:24 Woe (*ouai*). This exclamation of rejec-

tion is really a term of pain and pity for those who face the misfortune of judgment (Num. 21:29; Amos 5:18; BAGD, 591; BDAG, 734). It is a part of a prophetic declaration and warning. It is the rich, who are often insensitive, who are singled out here. James has similar comments in tone (Jas. 2:6-7; 5:1-6). All the rich will receive as consolation is what they have in this life. Luke likes this term, using it 15 out of the 31 uses in the NT. [*ouai*]

6:26 False prophets (*pseudoprophētais*). This is the only use of this term in Luke. It compares the rich who Jesus warns with the false prophets of old who only sought to declare what was comfortable and self-serving. The presence of this comparison is another indication that Jesus has spiritual concerns in mind. This term is used 11 times in the NT, with six uses in the Gospels and Acts (Matt. 7:15; 24:11, 24; Mark 13:22; Acts 13:6). [*pseudoprophētēs*]

6:27 Love (*agapate*). This is the first of 13 uses of this verb in Luke. Six of those uses occur in 6:27-35, while two more appear in 7:42-47. Love for one's enemies is seen as a distinctive of disciples whose love is different from the way the world loves. The other major theological uses in Luke include the call to love God fully (10:27) and the warning that one cannot love God and mammon for one will love one more than the other (16:13). [*agapaō*]

6:28 Abuse (*epēreazontōn*). This term refers to being mistreated ("mistreat," NET; NASB; NIV; "abuse," RSV). In this context, it especially describes religious persecution. It is used only twice in the NT (1 Pet. 3:16). In everyday use, it could refer to spiteful or insolent treatment (MM, 232). [*epēreazō*]

6:29 Shirt (*chitōna*). This is a reference to the

undergarment or tunic worn under an outer garment ("shirt," RSV; NASB; "tunic," NET). It was made of linen or wool, reached to the ankles or knees, and was long or short sleeved (EDNT, 3:468). The text represents but one example of remaining vulnerable to those around you for the sake of reaching out to sinners. [*chitōn*]

6:32-34 Credit (*charis*). Jesus' question in each of these verses is literally, "What grace is that to you?" The idea is, What evidence is there of God's work in the life of one who does not act like a child of God? There is no evidence of any advantage or benefit rooted in God without living in such a gracious way as Jesus describes here (1 Pet. 2:19-20 is similar). The translation of credit is appropriate here (BAGD, 877, 2b; BDAG, 1079, 2b). [*charis*]

6:35 Reward (*misthos*). This term often refers to a wage (Luke 10:7). Here it is more eschatological in meaning. It refers to how God will respond to our showing of his character in loving the enemy, just as earlier it refers to God's rewarding our faithfulness in persecution (Luke 6:23). Luke only uses the term three times. [*misthos*]

Kind (*chrēstos*). This term describes God's gracious character in his relationship to those who are "ungrateful and selfish." It describes someone who is kind and good to another. Out of its seven NT uses, only a few texts describe God (Rom. 2:4; 1 Pet. 2:3, citing Ps. 34:8). [*chrēstos*]

6:36 Merciful (*oiktirmones*). This key term is part of an important refrain discussing God's character in the OT (Exod. 34:6; Ps. 86:15; 103:8; Joel 2:13). Judaism also highlighted this attribute of God (Sir. 2:11—as a forgiver of sin). The term depicts God's mercy and compassion, sometimes in being slow to anger (Ps. 78:38). In the NT, the term is used only here and in Jas. 5:11. [*oiktirmōn*]

6:37 Forgive (*apolyete*). This is not the normal term for forgive. It usually means to release someone from an obligation or from a place or circumstance (Luke 2:29; 8:38—of exorcising a demon; 9:12; 13:12—of release from a sickness; 23:16, 18, 20, 22, 25). So the idea is of releasing someone of a debt produced by an act that requires our forgiveness ("forgive," NET; RSV; NIV; "pardon," NASB). Luke uses the term 12 times out of its 66 NT uses. Only here in Luke does it mean something close to forgive. [*apolyō*]

6:38 Measure (*metron*). This reference pictures a scene in the market where one buys grain and measures it shaking the grain down as it is poured to get an exact volume. The image looks at the favorable way God responds to our being gracious. These two uses are Luke's only uses of the term [*metron*]

6:39 Can/Will (*mēti/ouchi*). Two distinct interrogative Greek particles open each question in this verse ("can/will," RSV: NIV; NASB; "can/won't," NET). In Greek, the particle chosen signals the reply to the question. So the first question is to be answered negatively and the second reply is positive. A blind person cannot guide. He will lead others into the pit. Jesus' point is to watch who you follow. [*mēti, ouchi*]

6:40 Fully taught (*katērtismenos*). This term usually means to prepare or repair something (Matt. 4:21 Mark 1:19; Rom. 9:22). In Luke 6, it refers to how a teacher prepares disciples for life and living ("fully trained," NASB: NIV; NET; "fully taught," RSV). Jesus' point is that like produces like. So watch who your teacher is. This is Luke's only use of the term, which appears 13 times in the NT. [*katartizō*]

6:41 Log (*dokon*). This is a reference to a big log beam, producing a ludicrous image of the log in one's eye, which prevents one from really being able to see. Luke's three uses of the term are in vv 41-42 ("log," NASB; RSV; "beam," NET; "plank," NIV). The other three NT uses are in the parallel of Matthew 7:3-5. [*dokos*]

6:43 Bad fruit (*sapron*). This term refers to rotten or spoiled fruit (Matt. 12:33). In other texts, it refers to dead fish (Matt. 13:48). What spoiled fruit is as a figure is shown in Matthew 7:17-18 and Luke 6:45. It is doing evil. Jesus is saying that true character shows itself in its fruit, including one's speech and teaching. In this context, Jesus has teaching in mind. [*sapros*]

6:46 Not do (*ou poieite*). This final section of the discourse deals with hearing and doing (see vv. 47, 49; Luke 8:21). Here Jesus highlights the hypocrisy of calling Jesus Lord, a title recognizing his position and authority, but not responding with obedience. In the next passage he illustrates the point by comparing the obedient one, who lives in a solid home, to one who ignores Jesus' teaching in his action. That person lives in a home that tragically will be washed away. [*poieō*]

7:2 Centurion (*ekatontarchou*). A Gentile soldier of the Roman military in charge of 100 soldiers. Often these soldiers would be supportive of locals as a way identifying with the community (see v. 5). That he is a Gentile commended by Jews is significant, given their normal antipathy toward each other. This is a detail unique to Luke's account of this healing. [*ekatontarchēs*]

Honored (*entimos*). This term can mean honored or highly esteemed or valuable ("valued highly," NIV; "highly regarded," NASB; "dear," RSV; "esteemed," NET). Here it seems that the term has a note of respect for the slave, not that he is merely property. Luke's only other use of the term is in 14:8,

where it refers to one with a more honored position. [*entimos*]

7:6 Not worthy (*ou . . . hikanos*). In contrast to his Jewish friends, the centurion argues that he is not worthy to have Jesus under his roof. This term speaks of being "qualified" or "fit" for something (BAGD, 374, 2). The humility and sensitivity of the leader is clear, since perhaps he had sensitivity for Jesus being a Jew who might be rendered religiously unclean by coming to a Gentile. In v. 9, Jesus will commend such a humble faith that recognizes Jesus' authority to extend over distances, just based on his word. [*hikanos*]

7:9 Marveled (*ethaumasen*). Of Luke's 13 uses of this term, this is the only place where Jesus is said to marvel at someone else's action ("marvelled," NASB, RSV; "amazed," NIV, NLT; NET; so also Matt. 8:10). Jesus finds such faith unprecedented and unequalled within Israel. This note is a hint that Gentiles are often more responsive to Jesus than Jews. In Mark 6:6, Jesus marvels at the unbelief in the crowd. [*thaumazō*]

7:13 Had compassion (*esplanchnisthē*). This is the only verse in Luke where Jesus is said to have compassion on someone ("had compassion," RSV; NET; "felt compassion," NASB; "his heart went out to her," NIV; "his heart overflowed with compassion," NLT). This idea is more common in the other Gospels (Matt. 9:36; 14:14; 15:32: 18:27; 20:34; Mark 1:41; 8:2). Compassion is requested in one Gospel text (Mark 9:22). Luke's other uses refer to the compassion of the Good Samaritan (Luke 10:33) and of the father's response to the returning prodigal (15:20). These are all 12 of the NT uses of this verb. The noun speaks of a person's "insides" as the seat of their emotions, much like we use the term "heart" (BAGD, 762-63; BDAG, 938). [*splanchnizomai*]

7:14 Bier (*sorou*). This is the only NT use of this word. It refers to a wooden plank on which the corpse was carried ("coffin," NASB; NIV, NLT; "bier," NET, RSV). It is rare in Judaism (Gen. 50:26; *Testament of Reuben* 7:2). It is not a coffin in the modern sense, as it was open, not closed. Burial customs are such in Judaism that the man would have died that day (*m Shabbat* 23.4-5). For Jesus to touch the bier would normally mean that he would contact uncleanliness. However, here Jesus' power overcomes death. He makes the dead man clean. [*soros*]

7:16 Prophet (*prophētēs*). This is the category the people often entertain for Jesus (Luke 7:39; 9:8, 18). Luke later shows that this category is not adequate for Jesus (Luke 9:18-20). The suggestion may have been made because this miracle was like one performed by Elijah (1 Kings 17:17-24). [*prophētēs*]

Visited (*epeskepsato*). This key verb was treated in Luke 1:68. What this remark shows is that the crowd senses God is doing something special and unusual through Jesus. This is the last of three key uses of this verb in Luke. [*episkeptomai*]

7:19 The one who is to come (*ho erchomenos*). This title is a way of referring to the coming promised one ("the Expected One," NASB). It alludes back to the mightier one who comes that John the Baptist announced in Luke 3:16, an allusion which shows Luke intends the question to be about the Messiah. John now wants reassurance that Jesus is that one, for Jesus' style of ministry and the opposition to him has raised questions about whether Jesus is the one. [*erchomai*]

7:22 What you have seen (*ha eidete*). Jesus' reply involves various redemptive activities promised in the sections of Isaiah, which proclaimed God's salvation (Isa. 29:18; 35:5-6; 42:18; 26:19; 61:1). Thus, Jesus does not

answer the question about his identity with a yes or no, but answers positively by pointing to what he does and the period of time it points to as present. They can see the evidence that God is bringing the era of promise. Jesus also repeats the idea that the Gospel is preached to the "pious poor" (see Luke 4:18). [*horaō*]

7:23 No offense (*mē skandalisthē*). Jesus closes his remarks with a beatitude that affirms God's blessing on anyone who does not "trip over" Jesus or is repelled by Jesus ("does not fall away," NIV; takes no offense," NET; NIV, RSV; BAGD, 752, 1b; 926, 1b). The term refers to someone who is not hesitating or offended about Jesus' claims (used with ironic overconfidence by Peter in Mark 14:29). This use has OT roots (Isa. 8:14). [*skandalizō*]

7:27 My messenger (*ton angelon mou*). Jesus describes John the Baptist as a messenger of God, using a passage from Malachi 3:1. This OT text points to the forerunner announcing the way of God that leads to deliverance. John is greater than a prophet because he announces the arrival of the new era. The term messenger is the same word used to describe angels in most other NT texts. The word means "an envoy" (BAGD, 7; BDAG, 8, 1b). [*angelos*]

7:28 Kingdom (*basileia*). This term refers to the promised rule of God, which Jesus brings. John is seen in this verse as the last great of the old era. However, so great is the new era of the kingdom that anyone in it is greater than the greatest of the old era. For more on this term, see 1:33. [*basileia*]

7:29 Justified (*edikaiōsan*). In this context the word justified means to show God to be right ("acknowledged," NET; NASB; NIV; "justified God," RSV). Luke's point is that the response of sinners and tax collectors to John and his call to be baptized revealed God's wisdom in the way his plan worked out (v. 35), even though the Pharisees (v. 30) rejected that way. Luke uses this verb five times, often to indicate someone seeking to justify themselves (Luke 10:29; 16:15). [*dikaiaoō*]

7:32 Piped . . . wailed (*ēulēsamen . . . ethrēnēsamen*). This contrastive combination points to a game children played in the marketplace. They play a tune and the other children are to dance to it, whether a tune of celebration or mourning ("played the flute/wailed," NET; "played the flute/sang a dirge," NASB; NIV; "piped/wailed," RSV; "played wedding songs/played funeral songs," NLT). Jesus uses the game to illustrate how this generation is complaining that John and Jesus do not dance to their tune. They do not follow the crowd's expectations. Both terms are rare, as the verb "to pipe" appears only here in Luke and three times in the NT, while "to wail" appears in Luke 23:27 and only four times in the NT. [*auleō* + *thrēneō*]

7:33 Demon (*daimonion*). Notice how the charge that John is possessed is similar to what will be said about Jesus in Luke 11:15. [*daimonion*]

7:34 Drunkard (*oinopotēs*). This term describes how Jesus associated with the sinner and charges him with not being pious nor a God-fearer (Prov. 23:20). The term appears in the NT only here and in the parallel (Matt. 11:19). See John 2:1-11. [*oinopotēs*]

7:35 Wisdom (*sophia*). In this context, this term is a personified reference to God's wisdom and plan (also Luke 11:49). So Luke's point is that God's way is shown to be right by the response of those children. They show themselves to be associated with God's wisdom and way, a direction associated with response to John and Jesus. It is one of six

uses of this term by Luke, usually it refers to a person's wisdom in Luke's usage. [*sophia*]

7:36 Pharisee (*Pharisaiou*). This detail tells us that this event is not the same as the later anointing in the house of Simon the leper (Matt. 26:6-13; Mark 14:3-9; John 12:1-8), for a Pharisee would not be in such a location. [*Pharisaios*]

7:37 Sinner (*hamartōlos*). This term was treated in Luke 5:8. Here it is important to note that this illustrates the point made in Luke 7:34 and that the female example pairs up with the Levi scene of Luke 5:30, 32, where a male tax collector is present. [*hamartōlos*]

Perfume (*myrou*). This term is a Semitic loan word. This perfume was expensive, as is indicated by its being kept in an alabaster flask, and was often used to embalm a body or to anoint a special locale (Exod. 30:25; 2 Chron. 16:14; Luke 23:56). [*myron*]

7:39 If (*ei*). In Greek there are three kinds of "if . . . then" constructions. A second class condition, like the one here means that the speaker presents the premise as rejected. So the Pharisee is saying, "If this man were a prophet (but he is not), ..." The reason the Pharisee rejects Jesus is because he is allowing the sinner to be so close to him, something this Pharisee believes a pious person would never permit. [*ei*]

7:41 Denarii (*dēnaria*). A denarius was a Roman silver coin worth a single day's wage for an average worker (BAGD, 179; BDAG, 223). So the difference here is 50 versus 500 days of labor. [*dēnarion*]

7:47 Are forgiven (*apheōntai*). The illustration is important to appreciating this remark about forgiveness. Jesus portrays the woman's act as an evidence of her already established love for Jesus. Thus, Jesus' word of forgiveness here is not a new granting of forgiveness as a reward for her act. It is a confirmation of forgiveness that led to her already present attitude of loving Jesus for the grace of forgiveness already given. Of course, Jesus' remark about forgiveness offends the leadership, for Jesus claims to have authority to forgive sin (Luke 7:48-49). For more on this term, see Luke 5:20. [*aphiēmi*]

7:50 Faith (*pistis*). Here Jesus confirms that it is the heart attitude of the woman, her trust rooted in love, that has saved her. Her anointing was motivated by this trust. Luke has used this term twice already (Luke 5:20—those with the paralytic; 7:9—of the centurion). He will use it eight more times, with three of those uses making this same declaration of saving faith (Luke 8:48—woman with the hemorrhage; 17:19—Samaritan leper; 18:42—blind man). In each case it is someone on the fringe of society who is commended for faith. [*pistis*]

8:3 Steward (*epitropou*). Chuza was Herod the tetrarch's "manager" (NIV; NLT-""business manager"; NET; "steward," "NASB; RSV). This means that Jesus' message had reached into the halls of the government. The term is used only here and in Matthew 20:8 and Galatians 4:2 (2 Macc. 11:1; 13:2; 14:2; BAGD, 303; BDAG, 385). [*epitropos*]

Who **provided** for them (*diēkonoun*). These women "ministered" to Jesus and the disciples through their financial support ("who were contributing to their support," NASB; "were helping to support them out of their private means," NIV; "were contributing from their own resources to support," NLT; "who provided for them out of their means," RSV; NET). The verb describing their action is a general term for serving (Luke 10:40; 17:8; 22:26-27). Luke uses the verb seven times out of 37 NT uses. [*diakoneō*]

8:5 Seed (*sporon*). The agricultural imagery fits Galilee, where farming was one of the more common tasks. Usually such sowing would take place in October to December with the crop sprouting in April or May. Sowing was a common figure of expression for God sowing or giving life in Judaism and in the OT (1 Enoch 62:8; Hos. 2:23 Jer. 31:27; Ezek. 36:9; Isa. 55:10-11). Luke's uses the term twice, both in this passage (Luke 8:11). Other NT uses are Mark 4:26-27 and 2 Corinthians 9:10. [*sporos*]

8:7 Thorns (*akanthōn*). This term appears twice in this verse and again in v. 14. It refers to a weed that could grow to up to six feet in height and took all the ground's nutrients. This is why it chokes the seed. As in this verse, thorns are a common negative figure in the NT for bad fruit or something destructive (Matt. 7:16; 13:7, 22; Mark 4:7; Luke 6:44; Heb. 6:8). [*akantha*]

8:8 Hundredfold (*hekatontaplasiona*). One hundred fold ("a hundred times," NET; NIV; NASB; "one hundred times,," NLT; "hundredfold," RSV) represents a high yield as most ancient crops yielded seven to ten fold. [*hekatontaplasiōn*]

8:10 Mysteries (*mystēria*). This term has OT roots in the *raz* of Daniel (Dan. 2:18, 19, 27-30; 47; 4:6). Thus it refers to something otherwise unknown, revealed by God as an act of grace ("secrets," NET; NIV, NLT, RSV; "mysteries," NASB). The content of the mystery gives access to God's mind or plan. Jesus indicates here that what he says about the kingdom is only for disciples, for everyone else its enigmatic character is an indication of judgment. The mystery of the kingdom as Jesus describes it has to do with the unseen way in which it grows. For in the soils parable lots of seed is planted, but only some bears fruit. The almost unseen way in which the kingdom comes is a surprise as the expectation was that the kingdom would come all at once in obvious glory. The Gospels only use the term in reference to these kingdom parables (Matt. 13:11; Mark 4:11). [*mystērion*]

8:11 Word of God (*ho logos tou theou*). In this context the Word of God ("God's message," NLT) is the word of the kingdom (Luke 8:10; 9:2, 6) which contains the Gospel and is able upon acceptance to bear fruit to life (8:15). This phrase appears in Luke four times (Luke 5:1; 8:21; 11:28). It may well have this meaning in each Lucan use. [*logos*]

8:13 Fall away (*aphistantai*). The usual meaning of this verb is simply to leave or go away. (Luke 2:37; 4:13; 13:27—all the other Lucan uses; NLT keeps the figure and renders this "they wilt," but this obscures this verb's force.) But it sometimes means departing from something as in 1 Timothy 4:1 and Hebrews 3:12. That meaning is present here. The faith described is fleeting and has no root to bear fruit. [*aphistēmi*]

8:15 With patience (*en hypomonē*). This term can refer to endurance or persevering ("with perseverance," NASB; "by perseverance," NIV; "cling to it," NLT; "with steadfast endurance," NET; "with patience," RSV). That is the idea here. There is suffering and a series of obstacles like persecution, worries of life, riches, or pleasures that can distract one from fruitfulness as the previous soils show. This soil yields fruit because it hangs in there with enduring faithfulness. Luke 21:19 describes someone who hangs in there like this and notes the reward that comes for this is life. It is Luke's only other use of this term. [*hypomonē*]

8:16 Lamp (*lychnon*). This refers to an oil burning lamp made of metal or clay (Exod. 25:37-38; 27:20; BAGD, 483; BDAG, 606). The term is sometimes used as a figure for the eyes (Luke 11:34) or as a way to express readiness (Luke 12:35). Here the lamp is a means of illumination that enables one to see and journey through life. The lamp is equated with the function of God's Word, which is not hidden but is on public display, so it should be heeded (v 18). [*lychnos*]

8:17 Shall not be made known (*ou mē gnōsthē*). The passive verb here suggests that God will make it known in the future (v 18) as the word exposes and brings all things to light ("will not be revealed," NET; "be brought to light," NLT; "will not be known," NASB; NIV; "shall not be known," RSV). The double negative indicates such revelation will surely be made known. This use of making known is like Luke 12:2. It is a rare referent for this verb in Luke, which appears 28 times, but only twice with this force. [*ginōskō*]

8:18 What he thinks he has (*ho dokei echein*). This verb indicates a misperception. The person thinks they have something worthy of God's approval, but in fact he will lose even that, showing that it was a misperception. The point of this verse is that those who do not heed the word of the kingdom end up with nothing, even if they mistakenly think they had something. This verb appears 10 times in Luke, but only here does it have this nuance. [*dokeō*]

8:21 Do [the Word of God] (*poiountes*). The object, the Word, is understood here. This is yet another text where Jesus highlights the wisdom of someone who hears and also does the Word ("put it into practice," NIV; "obey it," NLT; Luke 6:47; 12:43; 17:10). For the negative of this, see Luke 6:46, 49. [*poieō*]

8:23 The lake (*limnēn*). The Sea of Galilee is referred to here. It is located 700 feet below sea level and is in a depressed area with hills surrounding it. When cool air rushes down through the hills and hits warm air over the lake, the result is such an instant storm. This term for lake appears only five times in the Gospels, all in Luke (5:1, 2; 8:22, 23 33). All other five uses are in Revelation, where each use refers to the lake of fire (Rev. 19:20; 20:10, 14 [2x]; 15: 21:8). [*limnē*]

8:25 Commands the winds and water (*epitassei kai tō hydati*). Jesus' command over creation ("even the winds and the waves obey him," NLT) raises questions about his real identity, showing how the disciples are still trying to appreciate who he is. Though a prophet like Elijah exercised such power (1 Kings 17:1), normally such authority is left to God as Ps. 107:23-27 argues. Perhaps also an allusion to Ps. 89:25 is in view, where the Son of David is in view, a text with messianic implications. This is the second time the issue of Jesus' authority has raised questions (Luke 4:36). [*epitassō*]

8:27 Did not live at home but among the tombs (*en oikia ouk emenen all en tois mnēmasin*). The verb here "to abide" is often used in everyday Greek of where one lives. That this demoniac lived among the tombs was a sign of uncleanness to a Jew. A later text in the Jewish Talmud states that one who lives overnight in a cemetery is unclean and is possessed with unclean spirits and is in real danger (*b Niddah* 17a). [*menō*]

8:28 Do not torment me (*mē me basanisēs*). This is the only place where this verb is used in Luke ("Do not torment me," NASB, NET; RSV; "Do not torture me," NIV, NLT). In this context, it shows that the demons recognize Jesus' power over them. The effort to name Jesus is an attempt to gain some control over the situation (See Luke 4:34). [*basanizō*]

8:30 Legion (*legiōn*). Usually this term referred to a group of about 6,000 troops, excluding auxiliary troops (BAGD, 467-68; BDAG, 587-88). So this man is clearly possessed by multiple demons. [*legiōn*]

8:31 Abyss (*abysson*). This refers to the underworld, which is the abode of the dead and also possesses a dungeon where demons are kept ("the Bottomless Pit," NLT; Ps. 106:26; 1 Enoch 10:4-6; 18:11-16; Rev. 9:1; 20:3; BAGD, 2; BDAG, 2,2; EDNT, 1:4). As the Revelation texts show, God has authority over this place. The demons fear that Jesus can "lock them up." [*abyssos*]

8:32 Swine (*choirōn*). These animals were unclean (Lev. 11:7; Deut. 14:8). The detail signals we are in a Gentile region, as Jews would not raise pigs ("pigs," NIV; NLT; NET; "swine," NASB; RSV). The request shows that the demons did not care about questions of cleanness. They were trying to avoid confinement. Pigs are mentioned four times in Luke, all of the uses imply a bad situation (8:32-33; 15:15-16). [*choiros*]

8:35 Sitting (*kathēmenon*). The contrast between the man sitting at Jesus' feet, much like a disciple would sit at the feet of a teacher, and his previous living among the tombs shows the power of Jesus' healing. But this presence of God's power left this crowd afraid. They wanted nothing to do with someone whose presence meant God was in their midst. [*kathēmai*]

8:39 Jesus (*ho Iēsous*). This reference to Jesus after the man was instructed to speak of what God had done for him shows how this man could not separate what God had done from what Jesus had done. As far as he was concerned, the two had worked in concert to heal him. [*Iēsous*]

8:41 Ruler of the synagogue (*archōn tēs synagōgēs*). This is the chief elder of the synagogue, a major Jewish leader ("official," NASB; "ruler," NIV, RSV; NET; "leader," NLT). He was in charge of arranging services and the progress of worship (TDNT 7:847). (*archōn*)

8:43 Flow of blood (*en rhysei haimatos*). The perpetual "hemorrhage" (NASB; NLT; "hemorrhages," NET; "bleeding," NIV; "flow of blood, RSV) would have rendered her unclean and made it more difficult for her to be in public. Anyone who touched her would be rendered unclean. Thus, she would live an isolated life. The only two uses of the term "flow" occur in 8:43-44, while the only other NT use is in the parallel in Mark 5:25. The term for blood occurs seven times in Luke, usually it is a reference to one slain (11:50-51; 13:1, esp. 22:20—of Jesus' death that inaugurates the New Covenant). [*rhysis + haima*]

8:45 Press upon you (*apothlibousin*). This term refers to being crushed ("pressing in on you," NASB, NIV, NLT, NET—"pressing against;" RSV—"press upon"). It is used of pressing grapes (Josephus, Antiquities 2.64; BAGD, 91; BDAG, 111). [*apothlibō*]

8:49 Is dead (*tethnēken*). This verb is in the perfect tense, stressing that the girl is dead and will remain so in the view of the servant. This verb is only used twice in Luke (Luke 7:12). [*thēnskō*]

8:52 Sleeping (*katheudei*). This use of the term sleep for a death ("asleep," NASB; NIV; NLT; "sleeping," RSV; NET) that ultimately is not permanent appears in some NT texts (Matt. 9:24; Mark 5:39; 1 Thess. 5:10). [*katheudō*]

9:1 Power and authority (*dynamin kai exousian*). This combination of terms occurs in the NT nine times. Three of those are in Luke to describe authority Jesus possesses or gives to others in mission (4:36; 10:19). The combination sometimes refers to heavenly authorities over whom Jesus sits (Eph. 1:21; 1 Pet. 3:22). This distribution of authority indicates how Jesus commenced his mission through the disciples to indicate the breaking in of divine presence in his message of the kingdom. [*dynamis + exousia*]

9:2 To heal (*iasthai*). This dimension of the disciples' testimony placed deed alongside the word, so that the disciples' message was matched with actions underscoring God's presence. This verb appears 11 times in Luke, but is predominant in the early part of the Gospel with eight of the 11 uses coming in Luke 5–9. Only Luke 9:2, 11 refer to the disciples' ability to heal. The rest of Luke's uses cover Jesus' actions. [*iaomai*]

9:3 Take nothing (*mēden airete*). This command to take nothing extra stresses the urgency of the mission. Disciples are to travel light and be dependent on God for provision. This command will be altered in Luke 22:36. [*airō*]

9:5 Dust (*koniorton*). The expression "shake the dust from your feet" occurs four times in the NT (Matt. 10:14; Luke 10:11 Acts 13:51). It is a symbolic way of showing that a city is responsible to God for its lack of response and is culpable before him, having been duly warned by a messenger who now leaves no trace of his visit behind him. The disciples are shaking off the uncleanness behind them and saying "good riddance" (BAGD, 443 and BDAG, 558 with the verb "to shake" [*ektinassō*], BAGD, 246; BDAG, 310). [*koniortos*]

9:6 Preaching the Gospel (*euangelizomenoi*). Note how "to preach the kingdom" of Luke 9:2 is paralleled here by this phrase. To preach the gospel is to preach the kingdom (in v. 6—"proclaiming the good news," NET; "preaching the good news," NLT; "preaching the gospel," NASB; NIV; RSV). In other words, the context of the good news is the kingdom. Jesus has the same kingdom and healing ministry, which pictures the delivering power of God. [*euangelizō*]

9:7 Perplexed (*diēporei*). This term appears four times in the NT, with all other uses in Acts (2:12; 5:24; 10:17). In each case it describes someone confused and pondering a set of circumstances ("worried and puzzled," NLT). So here Herod is seen to ponder who Jesus is and the source of his power. The options are all prophetic in nature. The parallels to this passage in Matthew 14:1 and Mark 6:14-16 show that Herod opted for John raised from the dead, a possible indication of his discomfort for having slain John. [*diaporeō*]

9:16 Blessed them (*eulogēsen autous*). This may be shorthand for blessing God and thanking him for the food ("gave thanks," NIV; "asked God's blessing on the food," NLT). Such blessings were common in Judaism. Blessing can also be done to consecrate things, which also may be what is happening here (Exod. 23:25; 1 Sam. 9:13; BAGD, 322, 2b; BDAG, 408, 2b). A common blessing went, "Blessed are you, O Lord God, King of the universe, who brings forth bread on the earth; and blessed are you . . . who gives us the fruit of the vine." The scene shows Jesus to be the provider of sustenance. This is the only miracle that is in all four Gospels, other than the resurrection. [*eulogeō*]

9:19 Elijah (*Ēlias*). This prophet was expected to show up at the end time (Mal. 3:1; 4:5; Sir. 48:10). The crowds tended to see Jesus as a prophet (Luke 7:39; 9:7-9). Luke mentions this prophet seven times, with four of those uses in Luke 9 (9: 8, 19, 30, 33; also 1:17 4:25-26). [*Ēlias*]

9:20 The <u>Christ</u> of God (*ton christon tou theou*). Peter's answer highlights Jesus as the promised anointed one of God in contrast to the crowd's assessment of him as a prophet. Luke uses this title with some frequency (12 times). However the bulk of the usage appears in Luke 20–24 (7 times; 20:41; 22:67; 23:2, 35, 39; 24:26, 46). Between Luke 4:41 and 20:41, this is the only use of the title in Luke (2:11, 26; 3:15 are the other uses). Peter is not yet to the point of affirming a full understanding of who Jesus is. Still with the recognition of Jesus as Messiah, Jesus can fill out the portrait in the rest of his ministry. [*christos*]

9:21 <u>To tell</u> no one (*mēdeni legein*). This is one of several Gospel texts where Jesus asks for silence about his identity (see Luke 4:35). Here it is because there are still things about the kind of Messiah Jesus will be that the disciples need to learn before they can share about him as the promised one. Jesus' suffering is the major topic needing instruction. [*legō*]

9:22 Must . . . <u>suffer</u> (*dei . . . pathein*). This is the first of six Lucan passion predictions (9:44; 12:50; 13:31-33; 17:25; 18:31-33). The term for divine necessity also appears here (*dei*). Luke often notes that Jesus will suffer or suffered many things (17:25; 24:26, 46). This prediction, including Luke's first use of this verb, is general. Some of the predictions that come later add more specifics. Much of what Jesus teaches the disciples now will prepare them for his death and departure. This verb appears six times in Luke (Luke 13:2; 22:15 are uses not already noted). The related term for Passover appears seven times and always refers to the Passover or the lamb sacrificed on that day. Six of these uses are in Luke 22 where it refers to symbolism paralleling Jesus' work. [*paschō*]

9:23 His cross (*ton strauron*). This is the first note that transfers imagery of Jesus' death to the walk of the disciple. To bear a cross was to experience shame and rejection, like a criminal being crucified ("shoulder his cross," NLT; most translations speak of "taking up his cross"). Thus, to follow Jesus was to be prepared to share in the rejection by the world that he faced. This preparation and reality is something to be faced each day, a detail only Luke notes about this saying. Luke only mentions the cross three times (14:27—in a saying similar to this one; 23:26, where Simon carries the cross for Jesus). [*stauros*]

9:24 Saves. . . loses his life (*sōsai . . . apolesē tēn psychēn autou*). This figurative contrast warns that people who try to preserve ("keep," NLT) their life by seeking acceptance and shunning rejection will end up losing their soul, their spiritual life, while those who are willing even to face rejection and possibly death, will end up alive. [*sōzō, apollymi*]

9:25 Forfeit (*zēmiōtheis*). This verse explains the previous one and speaks of losing and forfeiting oneself in the process of seeking to gain the world. If forfeiting one's life with God is the cost, is this worth it? This is Luke's only use of this verb out of six NT uses (Matt. 16:26; Mark 8:36; 1 Cor. 3:15; 2 Cor. 7:9; Phil. 3:8). [*zēmioō*]

9:26 Ashamed (*epaischynthē*). This verb actually appears twice in this verse in a contrast. One is measured by the standard they set. To be ashamed of Jesus (the Son of Man) by refusing to acknowledge him means that he will respond similarly at the judgment when he comes in glory. These are the only two uses of this verb in Luke. [*epaischynomai*]

9:27 Until they see the kingdom of God (*heōs an idōsin tēn basileian tou theou*). This phrase predicts that some of the Twelve will not experience death before they get a glimpse of Jesus' glory. It is best understood as referring to a preview of kingdom glory when some see Jesus' transfiguration. [*basileia*]

9:29 White (*leukos*). This description of Jesus' garment ("bright," NIV; "dazzling white," NET; RSV) along with his altered countenance indicates he appeared in a glorified state (see v 32) before the disciples (Matt. 28:3; John 20:12; Acts 1:10; Rev. 3:4). The color pictures purity and glory (EDNT, 2:350-51). This usage has roots in the imagery of the priest's clothes on the Day of Atonement (Lev. 16:4). [*leukos*]

9:31 Departure (*exodon*). This word appears only in Luke's version of this event and details the topic of the conversation between Moses, Elijah, and Jesus. It was his coming "exodus." This word, which evokes Israel's salvation experience, looks to Jesus' death and journey to the right hand of God that will come as a result of events in Jerusalem. The disciples are being told of Jesus' approaching suffering which leads into glory. The term is used three times in the NT and only here in Luke (Heb. 11:22; 2 Pet. 1:15). [*exodos*]

9:33 Three booths (*skēnas treis*). The building of three booths ("shelters," NIV, NET; "tabernacles," NASB; "shrines," NLT; "booths," RSV) would replicate the Feast of Booths, which celebrated God's protection and provision in the wilderness (Exod. 23:16; 34:22; Lev. 23:34; Deut. 16:13). It was seen to anticipate God's ultimate deliverance. By asking for three booths, Peter was equating Moses, Elijah, and Jesus, trying to honor each of them. The voice from heaven will correct this understanding. [*skēnē*]

9:34 Cloud (*nephalē*). The cloud indicates the presence of the divine *shekinah* (Lev. 23:43; BAGD, 536; BDAG, 670). Its presence helps to identify the voice that will speak from heaven. [*nephalē*]

9:35 My Chosen (*ho eklelegmenos*). This utterance is very close to what the voice said at Jesus' baptism (Luke 3:22). The naming of Jesus as Son appeals to Ps. 2:7, while the mention of him as elect or chosen points to God's initiative in marking him out for the task of his calling. The perfect participle really means, the one who stands elected. This is yet another way to highlight Jesus as the promised one. Only Luke's version of this event mentions this title in this context. The title may look back to Isaiah 42:1. [*eklegomai*]

9:39 Spirit (*pneuma*). The descriptions that follow clearly indicate an evil spirit and destructive demon possession. The characteristics of destructiveness associated with demons serve to underscore their basic mission and goals with respect to people. [*pneuma*]

9:41 Faithless (*apistos*). This rebuke with "crooked" is unique to this scene (Matt. 17:17; "unbelieving," NIV; NASB; "stubborn," NLT; "faithless," RSV). Jesus decries a lack of faith in the current generation. The expression has OT roots (Num. 14:27; Deut. 32:5, 20; Prov. 6:14; Isa. 59:8). The Deuteronomy text is closest to this utterance. Jesus seeks to restore the crooked. "Faithless" appears only once more in Luke (12:46). [*apistos*]

9:43 Majesty (*megaleiotēti*). This is the only use of this term in Luke (in the NT, only Acts 19:27—of Artemis; 2 Pet. 1:16—referring to Jesus at the transfiguration; "greatness," NASB; NIV; "mighty power," NET; "majesty," RSV; "display of God's power," NLT). It refers to the grandeur of a person, often of divinity. [*megaleiotēs*]

9:44 To be delivered over (*paradidosthai*). The second prediction of Jesus' passion highlights the idea of betrayal ("going to be betrayed," NET; NIV; NLT; "going to be delivered," NASB; "is to be delivered," RSV). He will be handed over to others (Luke 18:32; 20:20; 22:4, 6, 21-22, 48; 24:7, 20). [*paradidōmi*]

9:45 Not perceive (*mē aisthōntai*). This explanatory phrase probably indicates that although the disciples grasped the words Jesus uttered, they did not understand or perceive how Jesus could be betrayed like this ("did not understand," NASB, NIV; NET, RSV; "could not understand," NLT, which says a little too much here). The Messiah in their view at this point was not one who would suffer. Their fear to ask him means that they sensed something ominous, although they did not understand how that could be a part of God's plan. This is the only use of this term in the NT. [*aisthanomai*]

9:46-47 Argument/thoughts (*dialogismos/dialogismon*). The first use of this word (in 9:16) is the rarer use of the term, to mean "argument." The term more often refers to doubts or thoughts (Luke 24:38; BAGD, 186; BDAG, 232, 2). Only in two other locations does the term mean dispute or argument as in 9:46 (Phil. 2:14; 1 Tim. 2:8). In fact, in the next verse, the other meaning for the term shows up, as Jesus perceives their thoughts (*dialogismon*) in the dispute. [*dialogismos*]

9:48 Child (*paidion*). The reference to a child involves a cultural detail unlike our western culture. In ancient culture, children were almost forgotten and often considered as not worthy of attention. So Jesus elevates their status by using them as an example of who is welcome in the kingdom. If a child can be welcome as the least, so can anyone. Even the least are great in the kingdom. [*paidion*]

9:51 Set his <u>face</u> (*to prosōpon estērisen*). This idiom means to be determined to accomplish a task ("set out resolutely," NET; "determined to go," NASB; literally, "set his face," RSV). The idiom's roots are in the OT (Gen. 31:21; Isa. 50:7; Jer. 21:10; 44:12; Ezek. 6:2; 13:17; 14:8; 15:7; Dan. 11:17-18). Here the allusion is to Jesus preparing to meet his death in Jerusalem. [*prosōpon*]

9:54 Fire (*pyr*). The reference to calling down judgment recalls Elijah's calling down fire on two companies of 50 men in 2 Kings 1:10, 12 and 14. It also suggests the imagery of the judgment of Sodom and Gomorrah in Genesis 19:24-28 (BAGD, 729-30, 1b; BDAG, 898, 1b). Jesus rejects this option without comment. [*pyr*]

9:58 Nowhere (*ouk echei*). This description of the Son of Man's homelessness stands in contrast to foxes and birds. It is a warning to the prospective disciple that Jesus will be rejected by the world and so will his followers. So be prepared for this. Jesus "does not have a place to stay" is what the verse says. [*echō*]

9:59 Bury my father (*thapsai ton patera mou*). This practice was considered a fundamental cultural obligation of children to their parents in honoring them (Lev. 21:1-3; Tobit 4:3-4; 12:12). When Jesus refuses the request, he highlights that the call to the kingdom is a priority even over the most important of cultural expectations. [*thaptō*]

9:61 Say farewell (*apotaxasthai*). This request to "say good-bye" (NASB; NIV; NLT) parallels 1 Kings 19:19-21 ("say farewell," NET; RSV). By refusing this request, Jesus signals rhetorically that this current era and mission are more urgent than the time of the prophet Elijah. For something permitted then is not allowed now. [*apotassō*]

9:62 Is fit (*euthetos*). The use of this term issues a warning. The term means to be suitable or usable for something (3 times in NT; Luke 14:35-of usable salt; Heb. 6:7—suitable for burning; BAGD, 320; BDAG, 405). Effective disciples cannot be double-minded. They are not up to the task. The reference to looking back alludes to Lot's wife in Genesis 19. She looked back because she really did not want to leave her old way of life. [*euthetos*]

10:2 Harvest (*ho therismos*). The picture of harvest was used to depict missionary labor of gathering followers, often associated with the final judgment (Matt. 13:36-43). Here it is tied to something ready to happen, even urgent, because the time of fulfillment of promise has come (Luke 10:10-16; John 4:31-38; Rom. 11:16-24; 1 Cor. 3:6-7). There are many ready to come, but laborers are needed, a topic for prayer. There are OT roots to the imagery (Joel 3:13; Hos. 6:11; Isa. 27:11-12). Luke's three uses of the image are all in this verse. [*therismos*]

10:3 Lambs (*arnas*). The only use of the term in Luke—suggests how dangerous the mission could be because of opposition. In Jewish writing usually Israel was the lamb and Gentiles were the wolves (Isa. 40:11; Ezek. 34:11-31; *Psalms of Solomon* 8:23, 30). [*arēn*]

10:5 Peace (*eirēnē*). This term refers to the Hebrew concept of well-being (*shalom*). It is a greeting of "May God be with you." To bless the house was to ask for God's blessing on those in it. [*eirēnē*]

10:7 Wages (*tou misthou*). The disciples are to live from the provisions God provides through those who support their missionary work. Such "pay" (NET; NLT) is only right ("wages," NASB; NIV; RSV). This saying is one of the few to show up in an epistle (1 Tim. 5:18). Paul also likes to make this point

(1 Cor. 9:12-14). The term is often used of heavenly reward, as in its other two Lucan uses (6:23, 35). [*misthos*]

10:9, 11 Has come near (*ēngiken*). This is one of the more important statements about the kingdom in the Gospels. These missionaries are to proclaim the nearness of the kingdom's arrival, something that can be experienced if those who hear them respond. It is debated whether it means "approaches" or "has come so near as to arrive." The preposition used here, *epi*, often suggests "upon" and suggests a note of arrival ("has come on," NET; "has come near," NASB, RSV; "is near," NIV; NLT). In Luke 11:20, Jesus will use another verb (*phthanō*) about the kingdom that does mean to arrive. Taken either way in this verse, the point is that the kingdom is at least very close and has almost come. It is the nearness and the importance of the kingdom that makes preaching the kingdom so important. [*engizō*]

10:11 Dust (*koniorton*). See Luke 9:5, the only other Lucan use of this image. [*koniortos*]

10:12, 14 More tolerable (*anektoteron*). These are the only two uses of this term in Luke. Jesus takes some of the more notorious cities in Israel's history (Sodom, Tyre, and Sidon) and says judgment will be easier on them ("more bearable," NET, NIV; "will be better off," NLT; "more tolerable," NASB; RSV), because they did not reject something as great as the kingdom like Chorazin and Bethsaida and other towns of Israel are doing now. The note shows the rise of opposition and rejection in Israel, but notes tragically that such opposition has a great cost. The other NT uses are Matthew 10:15 and 11:22, 24. [*anektos*]

10:15 Hades (*hadou*). This reference to Capernaum's judgment shows that the entire community is accountable to God for their lack of response. It is a corporate judgment, not just one of individuals. Hades, the great abyss, is the place where the judged dead are left. It is the opposite of heaven (EDNT, 1:30; Gen. 37:35 LXX, often renders *sheol*). It is a place of death in the NT (Rev. 1:18; 20:13-14). [*hadēs*]

10:17 Satan (*Satanas*). The first of five mentions of this figure in Luke (11:18; 13:16; 22:3, 31). The word refers in the OT to the accuser (Job 1:6-12; 2:1-7; EDNT, 3:234). In this passage the ministry of the disciples reflects the defeat of Satan as a result of Jesus' coming and work. [*Satan/Satanas*]

10:20 Names are written in heaven (*ta onomata hymōn engegraptai en tois ouranois*). This phrase is an allusion to the book of life (Exod. 32:32; Ps. 69:28; Isa. 4:3; Dan. 7:10; 12:1; "stand written in heaven," NET; "are recorded in heaven," NASB; "registered as citizens in heaven," NLT). Jesus' point is that the gift of salvation and having a permanent relationship with God is worth more than power over Satan. [*onoma + graphō*]

10:21 Babes (*nēpiois*). This figurative use of babes is a reference to the "simple" as opposed to the wise; God has chosen the simple, the babes for blessing ("infants," NASB; "little children," NIV; "babies," NET). The roots of this use are also found in the OT as the term is used to describe those who receive God's care (Ps. 19:7; 116:6; 119:130). This theme was raised early in Luke (1:51-54). [*nēpios*]

10:22 Son (*ho huios*). This is a rare use of the title Son by itself in the Synoptics (3 times—here plus Mark 13:32). However, this use of Son is common in John (10:15; 17:2; 3:35; 6:65; 13:3; 14:7, 9-11; 17:25). The expression highlights the close and unique relationship between Jesus and God the Father. [*huios*]

10:25 To inherit eternal life (*zōēn aiōnion kleronomēsō*). This is the Jewish way to ask about being saved by gaining life in the world to come ("to receive eternal life," NLT; "to inherit eternal life," NASB; NIV; NET; RSV; Dan. 12:2; 2 Macc. 7:9). [*zōē* + *klēronomeō*]

10:27 Love (*agapēseis*). This combination of commandments, love for God and neighbor, is known as the "great commandment," combining Deuteronomy 6:5 and Leviticus 19:18. In Judaism, this exhortation was expressed in the *Testament of Issachar* 5:1-2 and *Testament of Dan*. 5:3. In effect, the answer, which Jesus commends, looks at a devotion that could equally be seen as the concrete expression of what faith yields relationally. [*agapaō*]

10:29 Neighbor (*plēsion*). The only uses of the term neighbor in Luke appear in this passage (10:27, 29, 36). The scribe's question is really an attempt to see if his obligation to love can be limited only to some people. Perhaps some are "non-neighbors." Jesus' answer makes it clear that the issue is not whether others are neighbors or not, but the call is to be a neighbor as the Samaritan was. [*plēsion*]

10:33 Samaritan (*Samaritēs*). The Samaritans were half-Jewish and half-Gentile, a race created when many Jews in Israel's northern kingdom intermarried (1 Kings 16:21-24, 30-31). They worshiped north of Jerusalem at a distinct locale (Mt. Gerizim; Green, pp. 404-05). Jews in the south wanted next to nothing to do with them, regarding them with disdain. Some texts equated eating with Samaritans like eating pork (*m Shab* 8.10; TDNT 7:88-92). For Jesus to make an example of such a person indicated everyone was a neighbor and would have been a shock to many Jewish ears. [*Samaritēs*]

10:34 Oil and **wine** (*elaion kai oinon*). Oil served to sooth wounds, while wine worked as a disinfectant (Isa. 1:6; *m Shab* 14.4; 19.2; Fitzmyer, pp. 887-88). [*elaion* + *oinos*]

10:37 Mercy (*eleos*). The lawyer could not bring himself to name the Samaritan as the example, so he highlights the attribute the Samaritan practiced. Jesus turns the answer into an exhortation to be a neighbor and show mercy as a character trait. [*eleos*]

10:39 Sitting (*parakathestheisa*). This is the only use of this verb in the NT. It pictures Mary as a disciple learning at Jesus' feet (Luke 8:35; m Abot 1.4). The reflexive form means she took the initiative to sit at his feet. Jesus accepted the action. Culturally this would be surprising as women were generally regarded as being called to serve and not being worthy of instruction (TDNT, 8:328, n. 95). [*parakathezomai*]

10:40 Do you not care (*ou melei*). Martha asks a question that seeks the Lord's intervention to tell Mary to assume her cultural role and help Martha. In Greek this question expects a positive reply, since it uses the interrogative *ou*, which expects the answer of "yes." Jesus' reply surprises Martha. This is Luke's only use of this term. [*melei*]

10:42 Good portion (*agathēn merida*). Jesus commends Mary's choice as being good ("good part," NASB; "what is better," NIV; "the best part," NET; "the good portion," RSV is the most precise rendering, though some claim a comparative is being used as a superlative here). He does not rebuke Martha for her work, but for her attitude toward Mary in doing it. The reference to a "good portion" views Mary's choice like select a good meal, a good portion of food as she hears the Lord's word (Ps. 119:57-64). This is the only place this term appears in Luke. [*meris*]

11:2 Father (*Patēr*). This intimate way to address God was not common in Judaism, though it did sometimes appear (Sir. 23:1, 4; 51:10). The term does not mean "Daddy" as is sometimes claimed, but it does invoke a sense of a familial relationship. Jesus tells disciples they can address God in such intimate terms. [*patēr*]

Hallowed (*hagiasthētō*). To hallow is to set apart, to sanctify ("may your name be regarded as holy," NET; "may your name be honored," NLT; "hallowed," NASB; NIV; RSV). Thus, even though God is addressed as Father, he also is addressed with the note that his person (his name) is set apart. This is the declaration that God is unique. There is no other like him. [*hagiazō*]

Kingdom (*basileia*). This request looks to the future coming of God's full rule and justice. The disciple longs for the day when God completes his promises and expresses his rule without opposition. [*basileia*]

11:4 One who is indebted (*opheilonti*). Sin is pictured as a debt that is owed ("everyone who is indebted to us," NASB, RSV; "everyone who sins against us," NIV; NET; Matt. 18:23-25; Luke 7:41-43; 13:4). Here the petitioner realizes that if one seeks forgiveness from God, then one should be forgiving as well. [*opheilō*]

Temptation (*peirasmon*). This request is really for God to protect the disciple, since God will not lead anyone into temptation. Judaism had a similar request in *b Ber* 60b, "Bring me not into the power of sin, nor the power of guilt, nor into the power of temptation." All the petitions of this prayer are expressed in second person plurals, meaning that the prayer is something that disciples pray for each other, not just for the disciple alone. It is the disciples' prayer as received from the Lord. [*peirasmos*]

11:7 Children (*paidia*). In the ancient world, the entire family slept together in most homes. So to get up would mean one would stir the children. [*paidion*]

11:8 Bold shamelessness (*anaideian*). This word is hard to translate and its meaning in this context is debated ("bold persistence," NET; "persistence," NASB; "boldness," NIV; "so his reputation won't be damaged," NLT). Some holding the term carries its normal meaning associated with shame argue that the point is that the neighbor answers to avoid shame, as in the culture being a good host was a cultural value to be honored. The problem with this reading is that then God is seen to respond out of some type of potential embarrassment. However, the context is about exhorting the disciple to prayer, so with him as the subject, it seems better to read the verse as expressing a kind of shameless boldness, an audacity, in the pursuit of the request to help (EDNT, 1:81; Sir. 25:22; 40:30). Prayer is to be like that. This is the only use of this word in the NT. [*anaideia*]

11:13 How much more (*posō mallon*). This idiom appears nine times in the NT (Matt. 7:11; 10:25; 12:24, 28; Rom. 11:12, 24; Philem. 16; Heb. 9:14). It is a common Jewish argument of comparison, where if one thing is the case, how much more is another. So here Jesus affirms God's goodness in giving the Spirit to those who ask for Him. The Spirit is probably given for guidance. [*posos*]

11:15 Beelzeboul (alternate spellings—Beelzebul, Beelzebub) (*Beelzeboul*). As one can see, this name for Satan is merely a transliteration from Greek. The seven NT uses appear only in the Synoptics and all three of Luke's uses are in this scene (Matt. 10:25; 12:24, 27; Mark 3:22; Luke 11:18-19). The roots of the name may go back to the Hebrew and the deity described in 2 Kings 1:2-6, Baal-Zebub, who was also known as the Philistine god, Ekron (EDNT, 1:211). Jews believed that the gods were demonic, so there arose an association with the prince of the demons. The charge by some is that Jesus works from such power. There is recognition that Jesus' power is supernatural, but to these Jews it is a diabolical power. [*Beelzeboul*]

11:19 Your sons (*hoi huioi hymōn*). The force of this reference to sons is debated. Is Jesus referring to Jewish exorcists and making the point, that if they work by God's power, why do they not see Jesus' authority (made clear in the rendering "your followers," NIV; NLT)? Or is Jesus' point that he is not alone in doing such work, as his disciples, who are also Jews, also perform this work by God's power, so that the testimony extends beyond himself (possible with the more ambiguous rendering "your sons," which is also literally the phrase; NASB; NET; RSV)? Most interpreters, regardless of the translation, prefer the first option, but the second reading has much to commend it since the conclusion looks to these exorcists being judges over the Jews one day. [*huios*]

11:20 Has come upon (*ephthasen*). Here is Jesus' declaration that these miracles evidence the in-breaking of God's promised rule, since it shows Satan's power being reversed ("has come on," NET; "has come upon," NASB, RSV; "has come to," NIV—a little too vague; "has arrived among," NLT). The charge that Jesus is Satan's agent could not be more incorrect. The miracles evidence Jesus' power to defeat Satan and establish God's delivering presence. This verb normally means to arrive, but when combined with the preposition *epi*, it means to reach something (Dan. 4:24, 28 [*Theodotion*]; other uses of the verb, Rom. 9:31; Phil. 3:16; 1 Thess. 2:16). [*phthanō*]

11:22 One stronger (*ischyroteros*). Jesus portrays himself as a stronger man engaged in a battle with a strong man (Satan). The image, coming as it does after the miracle and the discussion about it, shows how one of the key characteristics of Jesus' ministry is to defeat Satan (Luke 1:71-75). His presence means Satan's defeat. [*ischyros*]

11:24 Unclean spirit (*to akatharton pneuma*). The picture of an "unclean" spirit (NET; NASB; RSV) seeking a place to dwell is a Jewish image (Tobit 8:3; Baruch 4:35). Some tie such a search to the idea that demons like barren locales (Isa. 13:21; 34:14). The passage is built around this basic image, where a spirit is cast out of a person, who is pictured as a home. If that person does not fill the space (himself) with God, then the house is empty and vulnerable to reoccupation. Jesus' point in 11:24-26 is that if God's grace is not embraced, then the spirit will return to render even worse damage. This is the last Lucan reference to an unclean spirit ("evil spirit," NIV; NLT; Luke 4:33, 36; 6:18; 8:29; 9:42). [*pneuma + akathartos*]

11:28 Keep (*phylassontes*). Jesus again emphasizes the special place of those who obey God's Word ("obey," NIV; NET; "put it into practice," NLT; "observe," NASB; "keep," RSV). They are blessed. This term for obey means to keep to something (Luke 18:21-claimed wrongly by the rich ruler) or from something (Luke 12:15-of greed). [*phylassō*]

11:29 Sign (*sēmeion*). This term refers to a confirming sign that underscores the authenticity of a claim (EDNT, 3:239; Spicq, 3:249-54; from God—Exod. 3:12; 4:9; Judg. 6:17; 1 Sam. 10:1, 7; Isa. 38:7-8; Josephus on miracles, *Antiquities* 2.274-280). What appears to be sought here is a "sign from heaven" like that requested in Luke 11:16. The only sign Jesus will give is that of "Jonah," which in Luke's context refers to Jonah's preaching or repentance (11:32), which in turn is like Solomon's wisdom (11:31). This is more focused than the parallel in Matthew 12:40, where both Jesus' preaching and three days and three nights in the fish are the points of comparison. [*sēmeion*]

11:33-34, 36 Lamp (*lychnos*). For this term, see Luke 8:16. Here the term has two uses. In 11:33, it refers to the public, displayed and guiding nature of Jesus' teaching, while in 11:34, it refers to the condition of the person in relation to God's Word. To have a body of light is to be full of righteousness as reflective of God's truth. In this context, the source of such light is Jesus' teaching. In 11:34, the eye is seen as the key lens, a pathway to light, while in 11:36, the person is seen as shining out like a light, when they are full of such truth. [*lychnos*]

11:38 Wash (*ebaptisthē*). This practice to wash before a meal is described in the OT but is not commanded there (Gen. 18:4; Judg. 19:21; Josephus, *Jewish War* 2.129; *m Yad* 1; Mark 7:1-5). The concern was contracting ceremonial uncleanness, which the washing prevented. Jesus refused such an approach here. This is the only Lucan use out of nine where the term refers to washing as opposed to a real baptism or a figurative reference to baptism (Luke 3:7, 12, 16 [2 times], 21; 7:29-30; 12:50). [*baptizō*]

11:39 Extortion and immorality (*harpagēs kai ponērias*). Before Jesus lays out six woes, three for the Pharisees and three for the scribes, he gives this strong general charge. The word for extortion is used in the Gospels only here and in a similar scene in Matthew 23:25 (Heb. 10:34 is the only other NT use). It charges the leaders with taking advantage of people. The second term is a broad term for immorality, usually sexual immorality, but here it is of spiritual unfaithfulness, like calling one spiri-

tually an adulteress as the prophets often called Israel (Isa. 1:10-17; 58:4-8; Amos 5:21-24; Mic. 6:6-8). So there is good Jewish precedent in the prophets for such a public rebuke. [*harpagē + ponēria*]

11:41 Give alms (*dote eleēmosynēn*). Jesus uses the act of giving alms to the poor, which was highly regarded in Judaism, as a figure for how to respond and concentrate one's spiritual health (Hos. 6:6). This verse is often read as Jesus exhorting literally to give to the poor as a contrast to the extortion charge of v 39, "give alms inwardly, that is, from the heart." This meaning is possible here. (So the NIV— "give what is inside the dish to the poor" and NLT—"Give to the needy what you greedily possess"). However slightly more likely is the exhortation to give alms "with respect to inside things." Just as giving alms takes intention, so they should act with regard to their inner life, taking care and giving it focused attention. Luke only uses the term here and in 12:33. [*eleēmosynē*]

11:42 Tithe (*apodekatoute*). This practice of giving a tenth of everything shows how much detail went into the Pharisees' practice, as they even tithed a tenth of these tiny herbs (Lev. 27:30; *m Shab* 9.1; *m Ma'as* 4.5; *m Dem* 2.1). In contrast, Jesus charges that they ignored justice and love for God. These two neglects match in opposite terms the charges of extortion and unfaithfulness made in v. 39. Jesus says that they should be tithing and showing such relational concern. This verb is only used here and in 18:12 in Luke (also only in Matt. 23:23 and Heb. 7:5 in the NT). [*apodekatoō*]

11:44 Graves (*ta mnēmeia*). This third woe to the Pharisees is stinging, for it charges that these leaders bring uncleanness to others and really represent the spread of a type of stealth death. For others walk over their graves unaware ("graves," NIV, NET, NLT, RSV; "tombs," NASB). Death in the OT brought uncleanness for a week (Num. 19:16; Lev. 21:1-4). This effect is the exact opposite of how the Pharisees saw themselves—in their own thinking, they taught to bring life and wisdom. This is the only figurative use of the term grave in Luke. All the other seven uses refer to a grave either of the prophets (11:47) or of Jesus (23:55; 24:2, 9, 12, 22, 24). [*mnēmeion*]

11:45 Insult (*hybrizeis*). This term means "to insult" or "to shame" ("reproach," RSV; BAGD, 831; BDAG, 1022). When words are used, the idea is the giving of an insult. The scribe so identifies with the Pharisees that whatever is said about them is true for the scribes as well. So Jesus addresses them next. Luke 18:32 is the only other Lucan use of this term in his Gospel (Acts 14:5). [*hybrizō*]

11:46 You load men (*phortizete*). This term means to place a burden on someone or to bear a load ("load," NET, NIV, RSV; "weigh men down," NASB; "crush people," NLT; BAGD, 865; BDAG, 1064). The related noun, which is also used in the verse, is used of cargo placed on a ship. Jesus' complaint is that legal burdens are placed on others by these scribes and no aid is given to help others with the load. [*phortizō*]

11:47-48 Build (*oikodomeite*). Jesus uses the term build here with sarcasm. The leaders build and care for the tombs out of respect for the prophets, but Jesus accuses the activity of being an endorsement of the rejection of the prophets. This argues that they really have not respected the message of the prophets. [*oikodomeō*]

11:49 Wisdom of God (*hē sophia tou theou*). This expression occurs seven times in the NT (Rom. 11:33; 1 Cor. 1:21, 24, 30; 2:7; Eph. 3:10).

It is used either as a way to express the will and plan of God or to refer to Jesus. Here it is God's plan that is revealed. Jesus' point is that God will send Israel more prophets and commissioned messengers (apostles), whom they will also slay, proving their desecration of the prophets' tombs of old. [*sophia*]

11:50 Blood . . . required (*ekzētēthē to haima*). This phrase involves the justice and judgment of God ("held accountable," NET; "be required," RSV; "be charged against," NASB, "will be held responsible," NIV; "will surely be charged against you," NLT). Just as the blood of Abel's murder cries out for justice from God, so too will the blood of those slain in this era. In fact, they will be responsible for every death, as their slaying shows their support of those other slayings. Their unrighteous deaths will be avenged (BAGD, 22, 2a; 240; BDAG, 26, 2a; 302, 4). The idea has OT roots (Gen. 9:5; 42:22; 2 Kgdms [= 2 Sam] 4:11; Ezek. 3:18). [*haima + ekzēteō*]

11:52 Key of knowledge (*tēn kleida tēs gnōseōs*). This is a figurative use of the term key (BAGD, 433-34; BDAG, 546, 2). It refers to the idea that these leaders think of themselves as the "gatekeepers" of knowledge. In fact, Jesus claims that they prevent people from being able to pass through that door, as well as not entering in themselves. In other words, they not only fail to accomplish their mission; they do the opposite! [*kleis*]

11:54 To lie in wait (*enedreuontes*). This word is the language of a pending attack, an ambush (Acts 23:21). It is variously translated in this verse ("plotting against," NET, NASB; "waiting to catch," NIV; "trying to trap," NLT; "lying in wait," RSV). [*enedreuō*]

To catch (*thēreusai*). This term is only used here in the NT. It is a term used for hunting

(BAGD, 360). Jesus is like prey. [*thēreuō*]

12:1 Hypocrisy (*hypokrisis*). This is Luke's only use of this word, which is used six times in the NT (Spicq, 3:409-10; Matt. 23:28; Mark 12:15; Gal. 2:13; 1 Tim. 4:2; 1 Pet. 2:1). The warning, in the face of seeming popularity, is not to be a hypocrite to falsely court popularity and acceptance like the Pharisees. [*hypokrisis*]

12:4-5 Afraid/Fear (*phobēthēte*). The repeated use of this term forms a contrast between those people who can kill the body and God, who judges for eternity. Jesus' call is to respond to God and pursue his acceptance. His authority and the damage he can do is far greater than what man can do. So fear God. This verb appears only in its passive form (*phobeomai*) in the NT. [*phobeō*]

12:6 Assraria (*assariōn*). The term, often translated as penny, refers to the smallest of copper coins at the time. It was worth one-sixteenth of a denarius, or 30 minutes basic wage (Matt. 10:29: BAGD, 117; BDAG, 144-45). Jesus' point is that people are worth far more than a cheap sparrow. If God cares for them, he will also care for you. [*assarion*]

12:10 Blasphemes against the Holy Spirit (*to hagion pneuma blasphēmēsanti*). To blaspheme means to slander someone (2 Kings 19:4, 6, 22; BAGD, 142-43; BDAG, 178, bd). Jesus underscores here that failure to confess him as sent by God and witnessed to by the Spirit will result in judgment. To speak against the Son of Man is a rhetorical way to say that someone speaks out at one point against Jesus, but to blaspheme the Spirit is to make a permanent judgment that Jesus is not sent from God, but has another origin. This rejects the testimony of the Spirit and is blasphemy against this divine witness. Mark 3:28-30 makes this distinction the clearest as blas-

phemy against the Spirit is explained as having claimed that Jesus possesses and heals by an unclean spirit. [*blasphēmeō*]

12:13 Teacher (*didaskale*). Here Jesus is addressed as a rabbi—a title whose cultural function might have included settling a personal dispute. However, Jesus refuses to get involved. Luke likes to use this title for Jesus (Luke 7:40; 8:49; 9:38; 10:25; 11:45; 18:18; 19:39; 20:21, 28, 39; 21:7; 22:11). It is meant to communicate respect. [*didaskalos*]

12:15 Covetousness (*pleonexias*). This is the only use of this word in Luke that the NT uses 10 times. Jesus warns the petitioner and the crowd to beware of longing for things others have. Luke has much to say about possessions that will shield one from covetousness (12:13-21, 33-34; 16:1-13, 19-31; 18:9-14, 18-30; 19:1-10). One other saying of Jesus uses the term (Mark 7:22). Most of the other uses are by Paul (Rom. 1:29; 2 Cor. 6:5; Eph. 4:19; 5:3; Col. 3:5; 1 Thess. 2:5; 2 Pet. 2:3, 14). [*pleonexia*]

12:17-19 My (*mou*). The possessive first person pronoun and the first person pronoun show up 11 times in these verses, showing the intense self focus that Jesus condemns here as it has led to a misuse of possessions. Interestingly, our word for "ego" comes from the Greek word for "I." [*egō*]

12:20 Fool (*aphrōn*). The use of this term represents an intense rebuke for lacking wisdom. It appears only here and in one other Gospel text, also in Luke (11:40). [*aphrōn*]

12:22 Life (*psychē*). The Greek term "soul" is often used in the NT as a metonomy (part for whole) that refers to one's life by pointing to the inner person. That is what is happening in this verse as the context shows by referring to eating and clothing. [*psychē*]

12:25 Cubit (*hēlikian*). This term normally refers to growth in height or stature as it is a measure of length (so Luke 2:52; 19:3). However, it can also refer to maturity, being "of age" (John 9:21, 23). The difference has led to discussion about whether Jesus is saying worry cannot add to your height, a remark with a touch of humor to show how worry is worthless, or whether it refers to adding to the length of one's life ("hour," NASB, NIV, NET; "single moment," NLT; "cubit," RSV). Either meaning is possible here, though time is slightly more likely. The choice does not alter the key point about worrying accomplishing nothing. [*hēlikia*]

12:28 How much more (*posō mallon*). See Luke 11:13 and 12:24. Once again Jesus uses the common Jewish "how much more" argument. If God cares for them, how much more will he care for you. [*posos*]

12:31 Seek (*zēteite*). In this context, Jesus is making a powerful comparison. The world seeks with great worry after food, clothing, and other provisions. Such energy the disciple should give to seeking the kingdom, to the pursuit of God's rule, will and blessing ("pursue," NET). [*zēteō*]

12:32 Flock (*poimnion*). All five NT uses of this term are a figure for the members of the believing community who are compared to sheep under God's or a leader's (elder or pastor's) care (Acts 20:28-29; 1 Pet. 5:2-3). Sheep are vulnerable. They need to be guided, provided for, and protected as Ps. 23 also declares. On this image, also see Ezek. 34. [*poimnion*]

12:33 Sell all your possessions (*pōlēsate ta hyparchonta*). The exhortation Jesus gives here is similar to the test Jesus gave to the rich young ruler concerning his trust of God (Luke 18:22). Luke also notes how the community was generous to each other in Acts 4:34, 37, and 5:1. These are the only narrative texts where this idea of selling all is presented. A similar idea also appears in one parable that argues the pursuit of the kingdom is worth everything (Matt. 13:44). Zacchaeus in Luke 19:1-10 is a commended example of how a wealthy person should live, as is Barnabas in Acts 4. [*pōleō*]

12:35 Let your loins be girded (*estōsan hymōn hai osphues periezōsmenai*). This idiom, also appearing in Ephesians 6:14 is a figure for being prepared to act ("get dressed for service," NET; "be dressed in readiness," NASB; "be dressed ready for service," NIV; "be dressed for service," NLT; literally, "let your loins be girded," RSV). It pictures tucking the toga in around the waist so one can move quickly. So Jesus is calling on people to be prepared to be accountable to God and the one he appoints, Jesus. This is Luke's only reference to loins (but see Acts 2:30; Heb. 7:5, 10, where it alludes to issues of one's descent, another common use of the term). [*osphys*]

12:36 Marriage feast (*gamōn*). In the ancient world, a wedding feast could last for up to a week, making it uncertain when the guests would return home. Luke refers to the scene here and in 14:8. The bulk of NT uses comes in Matthew 22, where eight of the 16 uses appear (Matt. 22:2, 3, 4, 8, 9, 10, 11, 12; 25:10; John 2:1, 2; Heb. 13:4; Rev. 19:7, 9—the great wedding feast of the lamb with his own). [*gamos*]

12:38 Watch (*phylakē*). The night was divided into three or four watches, depending on whether one was counting as a Roman or Jew. So the second or third watch would be late into the night either way, a time when one would be less likely to be ready. In 12:40 Jesus compares the time of his coming as unknown like a thief coming in the night. We cannot figure out when it will be, so we must always be ready. [*phylakē*]

12:42 Wise (*phronimos*). The combination of faithful and wise points to a steward (disciple) who is obedient while the Lord is away ("wise," NET; NIV; RSV; "sensible," NASB; NLT). It pictures a person who is faithful in his care of others, which is why Peter was curious if the parable was about the Twelve or all. Jesus never answers his question. He just calls for faithfulness. This is one of two Lucan uses of this term (16:8). [*phronimos*]

12:43, 45, 47 That servant (*ho doulos ekeinos*). This parable goes through a cycle of four possibilities for "that" servant: faithful, totally unfaithful, disobedient with knowledge, disobedient with ignorance. The reward or punishment on the master's return is related to which of the categories "that" servant met. [*ekeinos*]

12:46 Punish/cut him to pieces (*dichotomēsei*). The RSV renders this verse "punish," while the NIV and NASB has "cut to pieces," which is exactly what the term means ("cut him in two," NET; "tear the servant apart," NLT). The image is of a severe judgment that places one with "unbelievers," making this category the "odd one out." Jesus argues that complete unfaithfulness will be judged. Such judgment is evidence of no faith being present. [*dichotomeō*]

12:47-48 Shall receive a beating (*darēsetai*). The difference in vv 47-48 between a severe beating (NET; "many blows," NIV; many lashes," NASB) and a light beating is one's knowledge in failing to do the master's will. The punishments also stand in contrast to v. 46 and the "cutting to pieces" the totally disobedient one receives. So three different categories are likely covered in these verses. Three other uses of this term

occur in Luke (20:10-11; 22:63). [*derō*]

12:49 Fire (*pyr*). This term can refer to judgment (Luke 3:9, 17; 9:54; 17:29) or to the work of the Spirit (Luke 3:16, where it suggests a purging). Jesus appears to be speaking of his purging judgment here. However, that cannot happen until his baptism of death. The fact that purging is intended is seen in vv. 51-53, where division even between families results from Jesus' work. [*pyr*]

12:56 Interpret (*dokimazein*). This term speaks of discernment or making judgments ("analyze," NASB, NET; "interpret," NIV; NLT; RSV). In vv. 54-55, Jesus used examples of the weather in Israel, where a cloud coming from the west from the Mediterranean means rain and wind from the south off of the desert means heat. Jesus chastises the audience for being able to discern the weather, but not what Jesus is doing in the present. [*dokimazō*]

12:58 Magistrate (*archonta*). This term is a general one for a ruler or official (BAGD, 113-14; BDAG, 140,2a). In this case, given the legal setting it pictures a magistrate in a debtor's court, to which Jesus compares one's debt through sin. The exhortation is to settle with the divine representative and God before a decisive judgment comes. The text is not used in the same way as imagery from Matthew 5:25-26, which looks at relationships. [*archōn*]

12:59 Last copper (*lepton*). This is a reference to a small copper coin, much like a penny ("penny," NIV; NLT; NET; "cent," NASB; literally, "copper," RSV). The term appears in Luke 21:2 and Mark 12:42 of the widow's mite. The point is that every portion of one's debt to God will be paid if judgment comes and forgiveness is not sought. [*lepton*]

13:1 Mingled (*emixen*). The mixing (NASB, NIV, NET) of Galilean blood and sacrifices ("mingled," RSV) refers to some unspecified police action that Pilate took at the temple where some were killed. The question is whether the act was a judgment by God, a conclusion Jesus does not make. [*mignymi*]

13:3, 5 Perish (*apoleisthe*). Jesus' point in both the Galilean incident and in the natural disaster noted in 13:4 at Siloam is that it points to an accountability everyone has before God because of the reality of death. More important than the timing of death is whether we will "perish" before God as a result of death and the failure to repent. [*apollymi*]

13:6 Fig tree (*sykēn*). The reference to the vineyard recalls Isaiah 5:1-6 and is a figurative way to describe Israel. Thus, while 13:1-5 looks to individual repentance, 13:6-9 takes on the national repentance that Israel needs. [*sykē*]

13:7 Three years (*tria etē*). In the background of the parable is the fact that a fig tree grows for three years before one seeks its fruit (Bock, 1208-09). So a six year investment was already present, even though only the three unyielding years are mentioned. [*etos*]

13:9 If not (*ei de mē*). There is an important, small grammatical touch in this verse. The earlier "if" in v. 9, looking to the possibility of fruit, is a third class Greek condition, so the "if" is presented with no expectation. However, this "if," which looks to no production, is a first class condition, indicating that it is the more likely outcome. Thus, though the chances are not good of success, the effort is still requested. [*ei*]

13:14 Sabbath (*sabbatō*). The repetition of a set of Sabbath healings in Luke 13–14 shows that despite all of Jesus' protestations for repentance and his offer to wait on the fig tree for response, nothing has changed. The leadership still complains about acts of mercy on the Sabbath. [*sabbaton*]

13:15 Untie (*ou luei*). Jesus alludes here to Jewish Sabbath practice involving basic Sabbath care for animals, such as leading them to water if they do not have a load (*m Shab* 5; 15.2; *m 'Erub* 2.1-4). At Qumran, animals were allowed to travel 2,000 cubits (3,000 feet; CD 11.5-6). [*luō*]

13:16 Be loosed (*lythēnai*). Jesus makes a word play and comparison here using the same verb as was used with the animals in the previous verse. Jesus' view is that it is most appropriate to free her on this day that honors God ("be set free," NIV; "have been released," NASB, NET; "to free," NLT). [*luō*]

13:19 Made nests (*kateskēnōsen*). This verb means "to dwell" or, in the case of birds, "to nest" ("perched in its branches," NIV; "made nests," NET, RSV; BAGD, 418, 2). The image has OT roots (Dan. 4:10-15, where it describes the kingdom of Nebuchadnezzar; Ezek. 17:22-24, where it describes what the rebuilt Davidic house will one day provide). The Ezekiel passage is probably in the background here. Jesus' involvement with the kingdom will one day result in shelter for many. There may even be an implication of Gentile inclusion here. [*kataskēnoō*]

13:21 Three measures (*sata tria*). A measure is 13.13 liters or 4.75 gallons, so this is nearly 50 pounds of flour (BDAG, 917; "three pecks," NASB; "three measures," NET; RSV). Just a little leaven will eventually fill the whole huge, loaf, which pictures the world. The kingdom is the leaven which one day will fill the earth. [*saton*]

13:24 Narrow door (*stenēs thyras*). Jesus responds to the question about many being saved by noting that the entrance is narrow. The word "narrow" was used in everyday Greek to describe things like the entrance to a grave like that of Cyrus the Great or to narrow passes in the mountains (M/M, 588; of mountain passes, *Aristeas* 118; entrance to a grave, Arrian, *Ananbasis* 6.29.5; BAGD, 766; BDAG, 942). Jesus is saying that the way to salvation is very defined and specific. Luke 13:25-27 makes it clear that the issue is knowing the Lord. [*stenos*]

13:28 Weep and gnash teeth (*ho klauthmos kai ho brygmos tōn odontōn*). This idiom expresses the sadness and frustration of experiencing rejection by God (Matt. 8:12; 13:42, 50; 22:13; 24:51; 25:30). This is Luke's only use of the idiom. Jesus is warning the audience that the issue is not how many will be saved, but being sure one is not caught on the outside. [*klauthmos* + *brygmos*]

13:29 Recline (*anaklithēsontai*). This term means to "recline at a meal" as was common in the ancient world ("take their place," NIV; BAGD, 56; BDAG, 65, 2). The image is one of table fellowship and acceptance in the kingdom for people from every direction of the map (also Matt. 8:11; 14:19; Mark 6:39). [*anaklinō*]

13:32 That fox (*alōpeki tautē*). The term fox as a figure can mean several things: (1) an insignificant person (Neh. 4:3), (2) a deceiver (*Midrash Rabbah on Song of Sol.* 2.15.1 on 2:15) or (3) a destroyer (Ezek. 13:4; Lam. 5:18). The Greeks often used the second meaning, but here either of the last two senses is possible, especially given how Herod handled John the Baptist. [*alōpēx*]

13:34 Children (*tekna*). This verse is full of tender imagery. God often called those of

Jerusalem his children (Zech. 9:13; in Judaism—Bar 4:19, 21, 25; 1 Macc. 1:38; also Matt. 23:37; Luke 19:44; TDNT 5:639). [*teknon*]

Hen (*ornis*). The second tender image of the verse. The only use of this term is here and in the parallel in Matthew 23:37. The picture is of the protective care of a hen (BAGD, 582; BDAG, 724) [*ornis*]

13:35 Forsaken (*aphietai*). This is the prophetic language of judgment and exile ("desolate," NASB; NIV; "empty," NLT; "forsaken," RSV; NET; Jer. 12:7; 22:5). They have rejected God's way and care, so that is what they will face. A desolate house is one that is laid waste and is emptied of its goods. They are left exposed. [*aphiēmi*]

The one who comes (*ho erchomenos*). This title comes from Ps. 118:26, where a king comes in the Lord's name to the temple and is welcomed. So Jesus says until they recognize God's chosen king, their house will be desolate. Jesus holds out some hope for Israel's future here, despite their "exile" now. [*erchomai*]

14:1 Watching (*paratēroumenoi*). This term means "to watch lurkingly" ("being carefully watched," NIV; "watching him closely," NASB, NLT; NET; "watching," RSV; TDNT, 8:147). They want to catch any misstep. Positively in other contexts it is used of guarding gates (BAGD, 622; BDAG, 771). [*paratēreō*]

14:2 Dropsy (*hydrōpikos*). This is a condition in which one suffers from swollen limbs because of excess fluids ("dropsy," RSV; NASB; NIV; NET; "whose arms and legs were swollen," NLT). It can be caused by all kinds of conditions. Such a disease was often seen as a result of God's judgment in later Judaism (*b Shab* 33a; *b Ber* 25a). This is the only NT use of this term. [*hydrōpikos*]

14:5 Ox (*bous*). Jesus repeats his point from

Luke 13:15 about Sabbath practice. The ox was a common animal to illustrate the point. [*bous*]

14:8 Seat of honor (*prōtoklisian*). This term literally means the "first chair at the meal." It would be next to the host (BAGD, 725; BDAG, 892). [*prōtoklisia*]

14:11 The one who humbles himself (*ho tapeinōn*). Jesus makes this point twice in Luke (18:14). The contrast is also typical in the NT (Luke 1:51-53; Jas. 4:10). [*tapeinoō*]

14:12 Dinner or banquet (*ariston ē deipnon*). These terms refer to different meals. The first is the late morning meal (BAGD, 106; BDAG, 131), while the second is the main late afternoon meal (BAGD, 173; BDAG, 215). So really Jesus is speaking of either lunch or dinner ("luncheon or dinner," NASB; NIV; "dinner or banquet," RSV; NET). Yet a third term appears in the next verse making Jesus' overall point about hospitality more emphatic. The term for dinner shows up again in 14:16-17. [*ariston, deipnon*]

14:13 Feast (*dochēn*). The third term for a meal in this passage refers to a large banquet, a meal larger than the previous two mentioned in v. 12 ("reception," NASB; "banquet," NIV; "feast," RSV; "an elaborate meal," NET; BAGD, 206; BDAG, 260; Gen. 21:8; 26:30 Esth 1:3; Dan. 5). Jesus argues that the outcast should be included at major events, because they cannot reciprocate and God sees and is pleased. Note how the list of the fringe of society is similar to Luke 14:21. [*dochē*]

14:16 Invited (*ekalesen*). The process of invitation to a meal in the ancient world is important to appreciate for this parable. Invitations went out ahead of time and asked for a preliminary response so the person could plan the size and arrangements, much like an R.S.V.P. would work. When the precise time to begin came, the servant would be sent out to have the guests gather. So those who refuse had previously said that they would come. A meal stood prepared for them. [*kaleō*]

14:18 Alike (*apo mias*). This phrase is actually an idiom meaning "with one mind." Jesus is portraying those asking to be excused as working in unconscious concert (BAGD, 88, VI; BDAG, 107, 6). The effect of the multiple declines is potentially devastating to the meal. This pictures how in Israel many different reasons for not responding to Jesus existed, but they all had the same result, a mass refusal to share in the offered blessing. All three examples stress the greater importance of other earthly commitments. [*apo + heis*]

14:21 Poor (*ptōchous*). The concern for the poor matches what Jesus said in Luke 4:18 and 14:13. The list also recalls Luke 6:20-23 and 7:22. Jesus' disciples will include many of those who the world finds insignificant. [*ptōchos*]

14:23 Compel (*anankason*). In this context the verb does not mean to force someone to come, but to urge them to come (BAGD, 52; BDAG, 60,2). By going outside the city, as the hedges refer to the vineyards outside of town, the imagery may imply the inclusion of Gentiles. [*anagkazō*]

14:26 Hate (*ou misei*). This is a rhetorical use of the verb to hate ("love more than," NLT). It means to love less (Gen. 29:30-31; Deut. 21:15-17; Judg. 14:16). An example of the force is found in the Jewish saying, "If they hated their beauty, they would be more learned." (*b Ta'an* 7b). In the first century setting, Jesus' point is that if one loves family acceptance more than God's way then one will not choose to be a disciple because he will not want the potential family rejection.

This is to love family more. [*miseō*]

14:27 Bear (*bastazei*). In contrast to Luke 9:23 where one takes up a cross daily, here one bears it or carries it along ("carry," NET; NASB; NIV; NLT; "bear," RSV). Luke 9 looks at initiating each day with an understanding of carrying a cross, while Luke 14 looks at the process itself. Beyond the decision to take up a cross is the actual carrying it and bearing its burden (TDNT 1:596; Luke 7:14). [*bastazō*]

14:28 Tower (*pyrgon*). This is a watchtower that goes over a vineyard or that protects a home or city (BAGD, 730; BDAG, 899). [*pyrgos*]

    Count (*psēphizei*). This term is very graphic as it often means "to count with pebbles" as a way of underscoring the process ("calculate," NASB; "estimate," NIV' "compute," NET; "count," RSV; MM, 698). [*psēphizō*]

14:29 Mock (*empaizein*). This is a strong term, as it will show up three times in Luke's Passion narrative ("ridicule," NASB; NIV; "laugh at," NLT; "to make fun of," NET; "mock," RSV; Luke 22:63; 23:11, 36). [*empaizō*]

14:32 Ask terms for peace (*ta pros eirēnēn*). This is the secular use of the term for peace. The image portrays someone facing a stronger army and deciding not to go to war. It is a different image than the first illustration, where one fails to complete a task by poor foresight. Here the enemy who is stronger is probably to be seen as God. Better to negotiate your peace with him than to face him in battle. [*eirēnē*]

14:33 Renounce (*apotassetai*). This verse states positively what Luke 14:26 stated negatively. A disciple's first attachment is to God and his way. The renunciation is of all attachments to the world in terms of priority

("does not give up," NASB, NIV; "renounce," NET; RSV; TDNT 8:33; BAGD, 100, 2; BDAG, 123,2). [*apotassō*]

14:34 Salt (*halas*). Ancient salt was used for three things: seasoning, fertilizer, or as a preservative. The reference to land and the dunghill show that its use as a preservative is present here. However, if the salt has lost its function, it is good for nothing and is tossed away. In other words, be effective in the role God gave you, or else risk being tossed away by him, no longer to be used by him. [*halas*]

15:4 One hundred sheep (*ekaton probata*). This is a modest flock, as a flock of 300 was considered large by ancient standards (Gen. 32:14). Luke's only other use of this term is in 15:6. By contrast, Matthew uses the term 11 times. [*probaton*]

15:7 One sinner who repents (*epi heni hamartōlō metanoounti*). Jesus' priority is reaching out to the lost. They may well repent. As was also argued in Luke 5:27-32, it is the pursuit of the lost, even to the point of taking the initiative, that is in view here. Their lostness demands taking the initiative. The same idea reappears in 15:10. [*metanoeō*]

15:8 Drachma (*drachmas*). This is a modest sum of money. It equals a denarius or one's day's wage for the average market worker ("silver coins," NIV, NET, NASB, NLT, RSV). [*drachmē*]

15:12 His living (*ton bion*). This expression describes the giving over of an inheritance ("the share of the estate," NASB, NET, NIV; "share of the property," RSV). The choice to give the son his inheritance early is advised against in Jewish materials (Sir. 33:19-23). This pictures God's choice to permit a person to go his own independent way, as destructive as that can be. [*bios*]

15:15 Swine (*choirous*). Pigs are unclean animals ("pigs," NET; NIV; NLT; "swine," NASB; RSV; Lev. 11:7; Deut. 14:8). So this was about as low as the son could go. [*choiros*]

15:20 Embraced (*epepesen epi ton trachēlon*). The expression here is "to fall upon the neck" ("hugged," NET; "embraced," NASB, NLT, RSV; "threw his arms around him," NIV). Given what the son had done, the father's reaction is decidedly generous and gracious. [*trachēlos*]

15:22 Ring (*daktylion*). The reference to a ring probably refers to a ring with a family seal. At the least it shows the son is still a son. [*daktylios*]

15:27 Fattened calf (*ton moschon ton siteuton*). This kind of an animal was reserved for such grand occasions as the Day of Atonement (TDNT 4:760-61), so it generally would have been prepared only for special events. It was rare to eat meat in Israel. [*moschos*]

15:30 Your son (*ho huios sou*). Note how the older brother has not received the brother back as a member of the family ("this son of yours," NET; NASB; NIV; NLT; RSV). He will not call him his own brother, a remark the father corrects in v. 32 by explaining that his brother had been found. [*huios*]

16:1 Wasting (*diaskorpizōn*). This term means to scatter, whether it be a flock (Matt. 26:31) or the proud (Luke 1:51) or seed (Ezek. 5:2). Here it means to scatter resources, thus wasting them ("squandering," NASB; "wasting," NIV; NET; RSV; "thoroughly dishonest," NLT—renders the figure's force assuming the dishonesty is in the initial reckoning; BAGD, 188; BDAG, 236,2). The steward was charged with being incompetent or even dishonest (depending on how one reads vv. 5 and 8, see below). [*diaskorpizō*]

16:2 Your stewardship (*tēs oikonomias sou*). A steward was a slave who grew up in the house and was trained for the role of managing the house ("management," NASB, NIV; "stewardship," RSV; "administration," NET; BAGD, 560, 1a; BDAG, 697, 1a). The owner often did not live on the estate that the steward managed. [*oikonomia*]

16:6 Bath (*batous*). A bath is 8.75 gallons or 33.1 liters ("measures," NASB, NET, RSV; "gallons," NIV; NLT; BAGD, 137; BDAG, 171, II). [*batos*]

Fifty (*pentēkonta*). It is debated what halving the bill here meant ("four hundred," —rendering gallons, NIV, NLT; "fifty,"— rendering baths, NASB, NET, RSV). Did the steward slyly reduce the price, cheating his master, but causing those in debt to be grateful to him? This is the traditional view, making the steward dishonest at this point. Or did he cut out his commission, thus reducing the bill in order to find grace later? Then the illegality came before in the exorbitant amount charged earlier. This is the other option. It is hard to be certain which was intended. Either way, he was now thinking ahead, which is the point of the parable. [*pentēkonta*]

16:7 Cor. (*korous*). A cor is 10 ephahs, 30 seahs, 10-12 bushels, or nearly 400 liters of grain. The same discussion applies to the reduction of this bill as in the previous verse ("measures," NASB, NET, RSV; "bushels," NIV; NLT). [*koros*]

16:8 Unrighteous (*adikias*). The steward is called unrighteous (NASB) or dishonest (NIV, NLT, NET, RSV), either because of what he did to lose his job or what he did to get himself commended to others. What the parable commends ultimately is the shrewdness he showed. The term also provides a link word to the point about being generous with "unrighteous" mammon in v. 9. [*adikia*]

16:9, 11, 13 Mammon (*mamōna*). This term comes from Aramaic and refers to property or any form of wealth, not just money ("wealth," NASB, NIV, NET; "resources," NLT; "mammon," RSV; BAGD, 490; BDAG, 614). [*mamōnas*]

16:11 True (*alēthinon*). This contrast of the "true" looks back to "unrighteous mammon," so the reference is to true wealth, a reference to spiritual responsibility. Faithfulness in the lesser things indicates readiness for greater things. [*alēthinos*]

16:15 Abomination (*bdelygma*). An abomination is something that is detestable to someone ("detestable," NASB, NET, NIV, "abomination," NLT, RSV; BAGD, 137; BDAG, 172,1). It is something that brings his displeasure. This is Luke's only use of this strong term. [*bdelygma*]

16:16 Until (*mechri*). Note how John the Baptist's appearance brings the break in eras. This is this Gospel's only use of this preposition. [*mechri*]

Violently (*biazetai*). This term is often translated violently ("forcing his way," NASB, NIV; "enters it violently," RSV), because of the parallel in Matthew 11:12. If the text has this meaning, then the point is that there is much conflict surrounding the kingdom's coming and people's entry into it. The "every one" mentioned here would be all who enter it, not every person. However, this term can also mean "be urged" in a passive voice ("urged to enter in," NET; Gen. 33:11; Judg. 13:15-16; 19:7; MM 109-110). This meaning is quite possible here. Jesus has been exhorting others concerning their response to the kingdom. Jesus may well have made the point that

all are urged to enter into the kingdom. [*biazō*]

16:17 Dot (*keraian*). This is actually a reference to the serif that adorns some ancient letters ("one stroke," NASB, NIV; "smallest point," NLT; "tiny stroke," NET; "dot," RSV; BAGD, 428; BDAG, 540). Jesus' point is that the Law will not get one slight alteration. Exactly what this means has been debated. Most likely Jesus is affirming that the Law will accomplish all it was designed to do, but only in light of the kingdom's coming. [*keraia*]

16:18 Commits adultery (*moicheuei*). Jesus points to an example of the fact that the kingdom brings the same ethic as the Law by using the example of a marriage and divorce. A vow broken in divorce and remarriage leads to adultery, since the original vow is not honored. Jesus' point is not a detailed exposition on marriage and divorce but simply underscoring the integrity of the marriage vow and that nothing about the change of eras nor the kingdom's coming has changed that kind of a commitment. [*moicheuō*]

16:19 Purple (*porphyran*). This probably refers to outer clothes and reflects the fine dyed clothes of the very wealthy ("splendidly clothed," NLT; BAGD, 694; BDAG, 855). [*porphyra*]

16:20 Covered with sores (*eilkōmenos*). This refers to surface ulcers and abscesses ("filled with sores," RSV; BAGD, 251; BDAG, 318). Later Judaism taught that to depend on food from another, be ruled by a wife, or to have a body full of sores was to have no life (*b Besa* 32b). [*elkoō*]

16:21 Dogs (*kynes*). This term refers to a wild, undomesticated dog, which was an unclean animal (BAGD, 461; BDAG, 579). [*kuōn*]

16:22 Abraham's bosom (*eis ton kolpon Abraam*). This is a reference to the patriarch's welcoming of the righteous ("Abraham's side," NET; NIV, "Abraham's bosom," RSV, NASB; "with Abraham," NLT; 4 Macc. 13:17; TDNT 3:825-26). [*Abraam + kolpos*]

16:23 Hades (*hadē*). Hades is the place of the dead that is the equivalent to the OT Sheol ("hades," NASB, RSV; "hell," NIV, NET; "the place of the dead," NLT; Ps. 16:10; 86:13). By the time of the NT it is reserved for where the unrighteous are found. [*hadēs*]

16:26 Chasm (*chasma*). This term indicates an impassable gulf exists between the righteous and judged, so that there is no way to move from the place of the blessed to that of the judged. The final judgment is permanent. This is the only use of this term in the NT. [*chasma*]

16:29 Moses and the prophets (*Mōusea kai tous prophētas*). This reference to the Scriptures is a way of saying that all one needs to know about how to avoid judgment is in the Scriptures of old. In all likelihood what the rich man is suffering from is his lack of compassion for those in need, whom he could have helped. He did not love his needy neighbor. Such compassion is urged throughout these writings (Deut. 14:28-29; Isa. 3:14-15; Amos 2:6-8; Mic. 2:1-2; Zech. 7:9-10; Bock, 1375). [*Mōusēs + prophētēs*]

17:1 Enticement to unbelief (*skandala*). This is Luke's only use of this term, which Paul often uses to mean, to cause to stumble ("temptations to sin," RSV, NIV, NLT—is probably too broad; "stumbling blocks," NASB—merely renders the figure; "Temptations to commit apostasy," NET—is more precise; Rom. 9:33;

11:9; 1 Cor. 1:23; Gal. 5:11; EDNT 3:249). In the Lucan context it refers to the inevitable enticement to lead disciples away from belief. It is a warning of the fate of those who are Jesus' opponents. [*skandalon*]

17:2 Millstone (*mylikos*). This is the only use of this term in the NT. It refers to the heavy stone that was part of a grinding mill. To place it around a neck and toss one into the sea meant certain death. Thus, it is a way of picturing judgment. [*mylikos*]

17:4 Seven times (*heptakis*). This number is designed to express that as often as forgiveness is requested, it should be given. In the parallel, Matthew 18:22, this is expressed as seventy times seven, a number one would not keep counting. [*heptakis*]

17:6 Sycamine tree (*tē sykaminō*). This sycamine tree (RSV), probably a black mulberry (NET; "mulberry," NASB; NLT, NIV), has one of the most extensive root systems of any tree in the area (BAGD, 776; BDAG, 955). Jesus' point is not that one needs a certain amount of faith, but merely the presence of faith can accomplish amazing things. [*sykaminos*]

17:10 Unworthy (*achreioi*). This term can mean "useless" (Matt. 25:30) or "unworthy" ("undeserving," NET; "unworthy," NASB; NIV, RSV; 2 Sam. 6:22; BAGD, 128; BDAG, 160,2). The sense of "useless" seems unlikely in this context where service is present. The point is that their function is such that praise is not required, as duty should produce faithfulness. [*achreios*]

17:14 Priests (*tois hiereusin*). Jesus' instruction means that they will be healed, as the priests were to check and see that the leprosy was gone (Lev. 13:19; 14:1-11). By obeying the instruction to go, the lepers would show their trust. [*hiereus*]

17:18 Foreigner (*allogenēs*). This is the NT's only use of this term. It refers to the Samaritan who was the only one among ten people who was appreciative to Jesus of his healing. The remark again suggests how those outside of Israel are more spiritually sensitive to Jesus than those in Israel (Luke 7:9). [*allogenēs*]

17:20 Signs (*paratērēseōs*). This is another term used only here in the NT ("signs," NASB, NIV, NET, RSV; "with careful observation," NIV—is a poor rendering, missing the apocalyptic force of sign completely and putting the stress on the observer, not the indicator). It probably refers to some cosmic or heavenly sign. It was believed that such an indicator would accompany the kingdom's coming. Jesus denies that there will be any need to hunt to see the kingdom's coming. The major reason he gives is in the next verse. The kingdom is already present with him. Another reason is given in the rest of the discourse. When the Son of Man comes in power, it will be obvious. There will be no need to hunt for the arrival of the kingdom in its full power. [*paratērēsis*]

17:21 In your midst (*entos hymōn*). This is one of the most important expressions in Luke on the kingdom. Its meaning is debated. Some argue that it means "within you," as the phrase can be rendered this way (NIV; Ps. 39:4 [38:4 LXX]). The problem with this rendering is that Jesus is speaking to the Pharisees. They hardly seem to be likely recipients of such a word. Secondly, no where else is the kingdom said to be in anyone. The other options are "within your grasp," "in your presence," "among you" (NLT), or "in your midst" (NET, NASB; "in the midst of you," RSV). All of these other options render the same idea— Jesus brings the kingdom and presents it

before them now. The point of "within your grasp" is that one does not need to hunt for the kingdom, but only embrace it (BAGD, 269; BDAG, 340, 1). The point of "in your presence" is that Jesus himself represents the presence of the kingdom. Either way, Jesus is highlighting the current availability of the kingdom through him and his message, so that no looking for signs is required to find it (Bock, 2:1415-18). Either sub-meaning ("in your grasp" or "in your midst") is possible here. One other point is that the kingdom is spoken here as present now, not as a future thing, given the use of the present tense verb *estin*. In vv. 22-37, the kingdom's coming in full power in the future is discussed. Those later verses shift the time frame in view to the kingdom's future completion. [*entos*]

17:24 Lightning (*hē astrapē*). Jesus points out how the future coming of the Son of Man will be as visible and sudden as lightning flashing in the sky (BAGD, 118; BDAG, 146). [*astrapē*]

17:25 Must suffer (*dei . . . pathein*). Jesus notes that before the Son of Man returns his suffering must take place. Thus, the kingdom cannot come in fullness until this suffering takes place. Note the use of "must" (*dei*). This is Luke's favorite word for the divine plan (see Luke 2:49). Luke uses this verb *paschō* for suffering six times in his Gospel (9:22; 13:2; 22:15; 24:26). [*dei, paschō*]

17:26-29 Noah, Lot (*Nōe, Lōt*). These two figures depict two of the most catastrophic judgments of the OT (Gen. 6–7; 18–19). Jesus says that the return will be like those days when people were simply living and then judgment came in full force. [*Nōe, Lōt*]

17:31 Not come down (*mē katabatō*). This judgment is so devastating that there will not be time to recover anything ("go down," NIV, NASB; "go into," NLT; "come down,"

NET, RSV). There is only time to flee. Jesus is painting a picture of just how devastating the judgment is. [*katabainō*]

17:33 Life (*psychēn*). This verse, using the term for soul as representative of the life ("life," NET, RSV, NASB, NIV, NLT), is very much like Luke 9:24, where this image was also present. To look out for one's self interest will lead to death. To lose one's life by identifying with God will bring life. [*psychē*]

17:34-35 Will be taken (*paralēmphthēsetai*). This verb in the two examples of two sleeping together and the women grinding points to a separation that comes at the judgment the Son of Man brings. The fact that the stress is on judgment means there is no rapture in view here. The comparison to Noah and Lot shows the emphasis on judgment, as does the reference to vultures in v. 37. Though it is debated whether those taken are taken in judgment or to be delivered, those who are taken do picture those taken away for salvation just as Noah and Lot left the scene of the judgment. It is those left behind who are the gathering place for the vultures (on the alternative view, those taken are taken to a place where the vultures gather). [*paralambanō*]

17:37 Where (*pou*). This interrogative is also debated as to its force. Do the disciples ask, where are those people taken? In which case, the vultures picture the place of death to which the judgment takes them. Or is the question, where will these things take place? In which case, Jesus' answer is where you see the vultures, there is where it happens. The judgment will be that visible. The point of Jesus' reply in this latter more likely sense is that the issue of the locale is not as important as the certainty and finality of this judgment. [*pou*]

18:1 Do not lose heart (*egkakein*). This term

means "to become weary," but with an activity in view our idiom of not giving up or losing heart is a good rendering ("not lose heart," NASB, RSV, NIV; "not give up," NIV; NLT; BAGD, 215; BDAG, 272; 2 Cor. 4:1, 16; Eph. 3:13). The parable illustrates that we should not give up praying for God's justice and vindication to come, the topic of 17:22-37. This is Luke's only use of this verb. [*egkakeō*]

18:3 Widow (*chēra*). A widow in the ancient world might not always be elderly, as most people only lived into their thirties. Luke loves to discuss widows and show how they are cared for, mentioning them 12 out of 26 NT uses (nine times in Luke). They are always portrayed sympathetically. Here the woman asks for a judge to come to her defense in a legal matter. The cultural assumption is that the only way she can get justice is through legal protection. [*chēra*]

18:5 Wear me out (*hypōpiazē*). This term literally means to strike in the face, "to beat someone black and blue" (TDNT, 9:450, n. 88; EDNT 3:409). Figuratively, like its use here, it refers to wearing someone out. The persistence of the woman brings the judge's response. We should pray for God's justice like that. [*hypōpiazō*]

18:7 Vindicate (*ekdikēsin*). This term shows the subject of the parable. If an unjust judge will respond, how much more will a righteous God vindicate his elect saints from injustice ("give justice," NET, NLT; "bring about justice," NASB; "get justice," NIV; "vindicate," RSV). This term looks to God judging the unrighteous (Ps. 149:7 LXX; Mic. 5:15; 1 Macc. 3:15; 7:9, 24, 38). The next verse assures the saints that God's vindication will come quickly. [*ekdikēsis*]

18:8 Find faith (*heurēsei tēn pistin*). There is a tension in this verse, for however quickly

God's vindication comes, there will be enough delay that some will not have faith. This is why Jesus raises the question of whether the Son of Man will find faith when he does return. To hold to faith will require endurance (Luke 8:15). [*heuriskō + pistis*]

18:11 I thank you (*heucharistō*). The Pharisee begins a praise psalm, where the petitioner thanks God for something done on the petitioner's behalf. But the Pharisee distorts the psalm's form when he prays about how great he is in comparison to others. Jesus holds such arrogance up as an example not to follow. [*heucharisteō*]

18:13 Be merciful (*hilasthēti*). The request for mercy is really a request that God expiate his sins, that his just wrath be appeased in his mercy (EDNT, 2:185). This verb shows up in Hebrews 2:17 of Jesus' high priestly work to expiate sin. God in his grace and mercy will act to atone for sin. This expressed humility before God of a need for forgiveness is what Jesus commends in v. 14 as making this man justified. So in this parable, the tax collector's humble prayer was heard, making him an example of how to pray and how to see oneself before God. [*hilaskomai*]

18:15 Infant (*brephē*). These are toddlers or smaller ("little ones," NET; "babies," NASB, NIV; "little children," NLT; "infants," RSV). They are children who could be read to from Scripture (2 Tim. 3:15). It can also designate a newborn or even a baby in the womb (Luke 1:41, 44; 2:12). Here it is small children that are meant. [*brephos*]

18:16-17 Children/child (*paidia/paidion*). Here another general term for child is used. The comparison probably centers on a child's dependence (Ps. 131:2; Luke 9:47-48). [*paidion*]

18:18 To inherit eternal life (*zōēn aiōnion klēronomēsō*). This exact phrase appeared in Luke 10:25 to set up the parable of the Good Samaritan. See that discussion where the expression means to be saved into the world to come. [*zōē + klēronomeō*]

18:19 Good (*agathon/agathos*). The retort by Jesus about only God being good is much discussed. What the man intended as a way to compliment Jesus and possibly butter him up, Jesus took as an opportunity to respond and make it clear that the man's question was a serious one. The man should not say things, take the matter too lightly, or assume too much. More important than any respect the man might have for a teacher is an appreciation he needs to have for God's uniqueness. [*agathos*]

18:22 Sell all (*panta . . . pōlēson*). This request is unique to this scene. In it Jesus is seeking to expose the rich man's commitment to his wealth and his lack of interest in helping others, like the poor. In Luke 19, Zacchaeus is another rich man who does not sell all but has salvation because he now has become generous and just with his goods. Jesus' promise to the man who sells all is that he will have treasure in heaven, so the remark probes which riches the man prefers. [*pōleō*]

18:24 Hard (*dyskolōs*). This adverbial term speaks of how difficult something can be (BAGD, 209; BDAG, 265). For example, the related adjectival term was used in the church fathers of how difficult it is to keep commandments (*Hermes, Mandates* 12, 4, 6). [*dyskolōs*]

18:25 Eye (*trēmatos*). This term is only used here in the NT (also in the parallel of Matt. 19:24). It refers to an opening or hole in something (BAGD, 826; BDAG, 1015). A variant reading in Matthew uses a term (*trypēma*) that means "something which is bored," suggesting that the needle was made of wood. A needle was one of the smallest items a person in Israel dealt with regularly. Jesus is really saying that it is impossible for a rich man to be saved on his own. [*trēma*]

18:27 Possible (*dynata*). Jesus' answer that God can make possible the impossible is designed to respond to the shock that the rich cannot get to heaven on their own, for the belief was that wealth was a sign of blessing. In fact, this belief explains the question that produced this answer, "Then who can be saved?" If it is not the rich, then who is it? Jesus replies that people get saved because God does it. [*dynatos*]

18:28-29 Left (*aphentes/aphēken*). Peter's speaking of leaving home and family is seeking reassurance that he has done the right thing and has done what Jesus asked of the rich man. Jesus does reassure him that those who make such a sacrifice for the kingdom are blessed now and receive eternal life in the age to come. Thus, the answer to the rich man's question in 18:18 is really found ultimately here in 18:29-30, since the eternal life the man asks about there is present as a blessing here. [*aphiēmi*]

18:30 Eternal life (*zōēn aiōnion*). The same phrase as appears in 18:18. See the discussion in 18:28-29. [*zōē* + *aiōnios*]

18:32 Shamefully treated (*hybristhēsetai*). This detail is part of the approaching events Jesus predicts will take place in Jerusalem (one of seven in vv. 32-33) and is unique to Luke's version. This detail is not verbally noted when the passion itself is narrated, as the narrative as a whole reflects its reality ("mistreated," NASB; "insult him," NIV; "treated shamefully," NLT; "insolently mistreated," NET; "shamefully mistreated," RSV; BAGD,

831). It is OT and Jewish language of what the scoffer does to the righteous innocent (Zeph. 3:11-12; conceptually, Ps. 94:2-7 [93:207 LXX] and Sir. 10:6-18). This passage is one of the most detailed predictions of what awaits Jesus in Jerusalem. [*hybrizō*]

18:34 Did not grasp (*ouk eginōskon*). This final description of the disciples' lack of understanding or knowledge suggests what other Synoptics make clear. They did not grasp how the suffering Jesus predicts could be possible, nor how it could fit into God's plan for who they believed Jesus to be ("did not grasp," RSV, NET; "did not comprehend," NASB; "did not know what he was talking about," NIV; "failed to grasp what he was talking about," NLT). One of the earlier parallels in Mark 8:32 and Matthew 16:22 shows that what Jesus said was understood, but it was rejected as not being applicable to Jesus. So also at this point, they did not see how what Jesus said could fit with his messiahship. They did not know how this could work. [*ginōskō*]

18:38 Son of David (*huie Dauid*). This title shows how insightful the blind man was. He understood Jesus as the regal Son of David, who also had the power to heal the blind, a sign of the arrival of the era of promise (Luke 7:22-23). The miracle sets the table for Jesus' entry into Jerusalem as the hoped for king. It also stands in contrast to the rich man, who had all the world could offer but saw nothing. [*huios* + *Dauid*]

18:42 Receive your sight (*anablepson*). This verb is used three times in this scene out of its seven uses in Luke's Gospel. Jesus is the only one in the Bible who gives sight to the blind. This is a work attributed only to God and is promised in association with the promised new era in the OT (Exod. 4:11; Ps. 146:8; Isa. 29:18; 35:5; 42:7). Jesus brings light to the blind of the world (John 9). [*anablepō*]

19:2 Chief tax collector (*architelōnēs*). Zacchaeus was in charge of a group of tax collectors who bid for the right to collect the tax and administered it. This meant that he would get a cut of all his workers' commissions, making him a very wealthy, and a very unpopular, man. This is the only use of this term in the NT. On tax collectors, see Luke 3:12. [*architelōnēs*]

19:4 Sycamore (*sykomorean*). This is probably a fig-mulberry tree, that is, a sycamore-fig tree (BAGD, 776; BDAG, 955). It has a short trunk and long, wide, lateral branches like a short oak tree. This is the only use of this term in the NT. [*sykomorea*]

19:7 Sinner (*hamartōlō*). Once again there is a complaint about Jesus hanging out with sinners (Luke 5:27-32; 7:30-35; 15:1; 18:10-14). This led to their murmuring and Jesus' defense of pursuing sinners. [*hamartōlos*]

19:8 Fourfold (*tetraploun*). This fourfold (RSV) restitution for fraud and extortion accepts the double penalty of the OT for rustlers ("four times," NASB, NIV, NLT, NET; Exod. 22:1; 2 Sam. 12:6). So Zacchaeus was taking full responsibility for his actions, including accepting the penalty for those actions. In addition, to give away half one's goods was more than the proverbial 20 percent that was considered generous by later Jewish standards (*b Ketub* 50a). This is the only NT use of this term. [*tetraplous*]

19:9 Son of Abraham (*huios Abraam*). Zacchaeus' heart and response receives a commendation from Jesus. The pronouncement of a beatitude makes him a true and exemplary Son of Abraham. He represented the best of the progeny of the patriarch. [*huios + Abraam*]

19:10 To seek (*zētēsai*). Here it is Jesus' initiative in saving the lost that is underscored. Just as he took the initiative with Zacchaeus, so he does with sinners in general. This type of saying is a mission statement summarizing Jesus' ministry. It is also an example of what Luke wants his readers to do. Zacchaeus' seeking of Jesus in v. 3 had met with Jesus seeking him out and saving him according to v. 10 [*zēteō*]

19:11 Immediately (*parachrēma*). The use of this term (RSV; NASB, NET) to describe the kingdom is speaking of the full arrival of kingdom promise ("at once," NIV; "right away," NLT). The disciples thought that Jesus was going to bring the victorious and ruling kingdom upon coming into Jerusalem. The parable was designed to correct that misunderstanding. Luke likes this term, as 16 of the 18 NT uses are in Luke–Acts. [*parachrēma*]

19:12 To receive (*labein*). The image of receiving a kingdom (NASB, NET, RSV) on the departure pictures how the kingdom's decisive authority is put in place after Jesus' death ("to have himself appointed king," [NIV] puts too much stress on the king's own work, removing the passive idea; "to be crowned king," [NLT] is a better summary rendering). The idea is repeated in v. 15. [*lambanō*]

19:13 Ten minas (*mnas*). The parable discusses ten servants given equal benefits ("ten minas," NET, NASB, NIV; "ten pounds," RSV, NLT). A mina equaled 100 drachma or about four months wage for an average worker (BAGD, 524; BDAG, 654). It was a modest sum in ancient terms. Though ten servants are in view here, Jesus simplifies the parable later by mentioning the response of only three of them. All nine NT uses of this term are found in this parable. [*mna*]

19:14 Hated (*emisoun*). The description of the citizens who hate the king brings to mind the Jews who have rejected Jesus from the start. The imperfect tense here speaks of an ongoing hatred. The detail parallels how the Jews did not want Archelaus to rule over them in 6 B.C., adding a point to the story that the audience could compare to previous history (Josephus, *Antiquities* 17.213-18). [*miseō*]

19:17 Authority (*exousian*). The reward of authority (NASB; NET; RSV) appears to picture a responsibility in the kingdom to come ("take charge of," NIV; "be governor of," NLT). The image implies that there is still a role for believers in the era to come and that faithfulness is rewarded. [*exousia*]

19:21, 22 Severe (*austēros*). This term severe (RSV; NET) refers to someone who is strict, exacting (NASB), or hard (NIV, NLT), even harsh. The term is only used twice in the NT, both in this parable (2 Macc. 14:30; MM, 93). The remark shows that even though the servant was given responsibility, he lacked a positive relationship to the master. [*austēros*]

19:26 Will be taken away (*arthēsetai*). This explanation is for the third servant who is an "odd man out." He ends up with absolutely nothing according to the parable. The meaning of this is debated. Some argue he has no reward in the era to come, since that is the point of the mina imagery. However, the explanation indicates the man ended up with nothing and that he had no real relationship to the master. So he is judged, as the similar parable in Matthew 25:30, where he is cast into outer darkness and where there is weeping and gnashing of teeth, a figure describing total despair at total rejection. [*airō*]

19:27 Slay (*katasphaxate*). The execution of the citizens who did not want the ruler pictures the judgment of those rejecting Jesus ("slay,"

RSV; NASB; "slaughter," NET; "kill," NIV; "execute," NLT). It is a graphic term, meaning to slaughter someone (BAGD, 419; BDAG, 528). This is the only use of this term in the NT. [*katasphazō*]

19:31, 34 Need (*chreian*). This refers to the custom of *angaria*, where a major figure uses an animal or lodging on the basis of need ("has need of," RSV; NASB; "needs," NET; NLT; NIV). Such rights were often extended to rabbinic figures (Bock, 1549-1550). [*chreia*]

19:36 Garments (*ta himatia*). This action of respect is only noted in one other biblical text, 2 Kings 9:13 ("cloaks," NET; NIV, "garments," RSV; NLT; "coats," NASB). Other Gospels note the tie to Zechariah 9:9 in Jesus' riding of the animal (Matt. 21:5; John 12:15). [*himation*]

19:38 The King (*ho basileus*). This is the only term added to the citation of Ps. 118:26 in the first half of the note of praise. Jesus is presented by the disciples as the hoped for Messiah. This is the first of five times Jesus is noted as king or charged as such in this Gospel (Luke 23:2, 3, 37, 38). [*basileus*]

19:40 Stones would cry out (*hoi lithoi kraxousin*). The crying out of something is a way of saying creation will speak if everyone else is silent. So Abel's blood cries out in Genesis 4:10 and Jerusalem's stones cry out in Habakkuk 2:11. The remark is an absolute refusal to rebuke the disciples as some Pharisees request. Jesus accepts the praise. [*lithos* + *krazō*]

19:41 He wept (*eklausen*). This is the only place in the Synoptic Gospels where Jesus weeps ("began to cry," NLT). He also weeps for Lazarus in John 11:33. [*klaiō*]

19:43 Your enemies (*hoi echthroi*). This reference to enemies and siege predicts what the

Romans will do to Jerusalem in A.D. 70 as a judgment for the covenantal unfaithfulness of rejection of the Messiah. The language of the verse conceptually recalls the OT prophets' announcements of exile, as the idea of "days coming" suggests, as well as the descriptions of suffering and defeat (Jer. 7:32-34; Ps. 137: 9; Jer. 6:6-21; 8:18-22; Isa. 29: 1-4; Nah. 3:10). The description includes the prediction of the temple's destruction, as noted in v. 44 [echthros]

19:44 Visitation (episkopēs). This term (RSV, NET, NASB) gives the reason for the judgment. They missed the visit of God through the promised King ("time of God's coming," NIV; "rejected the opportunity God offered," NLT). The language of the visit is important in Luke with the use of the related verb in Luke 1:68, 78 and 7:16. [episkopē]

19:46 House of prayer (oikos proseuchēs). Jesus uses Isaiah 56:7 and Jeremiah 7:11 to explain what the temple, God's house, should be and what it has become. It was to be a place of prayer (Isa), but it has become a den of robbers (Jer). The allusion is to the fact that the money-changers have come into the holy space of the temple and made it common, even though they were providing a convenience of changing the currency for the temple tax and making available pure sacrificial animals for travelling pilgrims. The money-changers were not price gouging, but had just been moved into the temple area to sell these items. Previously they had done so outside the boundaries of the temple. Jesus challenges the move and raises the issue of his authority to challenge the leadership on how the temple operates. As such, he acts as a king with prophetic authority who is cleansing the city of her sin, as was hoped would happen at the end in a new temple (Antiquities 18.85-87; Jewish War 6.283-85; 1 Enoch 24–25). [oikos]

19:47 Destroy (apolesai). The temple incident was a direct challenge to the way the leadership oversaw the worship of the nation. The leaders now knew Jesus had to be stopped and sought to remove him ("destroy," NASB; RSV; "assassinate," NET; "kill," NIV, NLT). This is the first use of this verb in Luke that refers to the leaders' desire to eliminate Jesus. [apollymi]

19:48 Hung on/upon (exekremato). This is the only use of this term in the NT. It is a graphic description of the drawing power of Jesus' teaching. They hung on his teaching. The leaders knew they could not seize Jesus publically. His popularity made it too risky. [ekkremannymi]

20:2 Authority (exousia). The temple incident caused the leadership to challenge Jesus' credentials to cleanse the temple as he had. The issue of the source of Jesus' authority is central to everything that takes place from this point on until Jesus is crucified. [exousia]

20:4 From heaven was or from men (ex ouranou ēn ex anthrōpōn). This question has been rendered here literally to show the Greek word order with the verb next to "from heaven." Jesus' question is whether the source of John's work was from God or from man. The source of Jesus' actions is a key to the debates over him in the last week of his life. Now the word order in which the question is placed favors the idea that it was from heaven, since that option precedes the verb. The question places the leadership in a dilemma, which they fully appreciate (vv. 5-6), leading to their opting not to answer the question. Anyone reading Luke knows the answer to the question, especially when recalling Luke 3. The leadership really was challenging Jesus' right as an untrained teacher to do what he did in places like the temple, where they had the civil authority.

Jesus' authority was not rooted in human appointment, however. So "John" is the perfect counter reply. [ex]

20:9 Vineyard (*ampelōna*). This term was used in the OT to describe Israel in her role as the home of God's people (Isa. 5; Luke 13:6). This term is used six times in this parable. This represents six of the seven Lucan uses of the image. Jesus' parable builds off of this imagery and makes it more complex. The tenants represent those who are responsible for the care of the vineyard to make sure it is fruitful. So the tenants are the leadership (20:19). Their failure to answer the previous question led to this story that God would replace them as stewards over God's people. [*ampelōn*]

20:13 My beloved Son (*ton huion mou ton agapēton*). This description of Jesus echoes what was said of him at his baptism with John in Luke 3:22, providing another link to the previous controversy over John the Baptist ("my own dear son," NET; "my beloved son," RSV, NASB; "my son, whom I love," NIV; "my cherished son," NLT). [*huios + agapētos*]

20:14 The tenants (*hoi geōrgoi*). The tenants often inherited the land they worked, if the owner had no heirs upon dying. These tenants hope for this result from the removal of the son. Unfortunately, the detail illustrates the hardness of heart in sin, for who would make heirs out of the murderers of one's own son? Luke 20:16 indicates what will happen to the murderers. [*geōrgos*]

20:16 Others (*allois*). Stewardship for God's people will fall into other, more effective hands. Jesus' own disciples are initially meant here. However, eventually this looks to the inclusion of Gentiles among those who lead and shepherd God's people. [*allos*]

20:17, 18 Stone (*lithon*). The stone referred to here alludes to Ps. 118:22. It pictures a king rejected by many, who nonetheless is lifted up and exalted by God in victory. Jesus portrays himself as this figure in fulfillment of Scripture. As Luke's Gospel often does, scriptural fulfillment is uttered and noted by the participants in the narrative. In Luke 20:18, the point of the proverb is whether the stone falls on the pot or the pot on the stone, it is bad news for the pot! To reject the stone is to face judgment. [*lithos*]

20:20 Who pretended (*hypokrinomenous*). The term for pretended is the verbal form of the word from which we also get our word "hypocrite." The translation "pretend" is good here as they are appearing one way, but really are acting from other motives. This is the only use of this verb in the NT [*hypokrinomai*]

Governor (*hēgemonos*). The Jews did not have legal authority to execute someone. Only the Romans could do that. So to remove Jesus they had to get Pilate's approval eventually. The hope was that a political charge could make the matter referable to him. [*hēgemōn*]

20:22 Tribute (*phoron*). The question surrounded the tax (NIV; NLT; NASB) given to Rome ("tribute," NET; RSV). The hope was that either possible answer would get Jesus into trouble. He had two bad options. (1) He could affirm the tax, angering those Israelites who did not want to be under Rome. This would also express a lack of allegiance to God's rule and favor toward the nation. He would lose popularity in Israel. (2) He could deny paying the tax and make a political challenge to Rome, making him vulnerable to a charge before Pilate. It seems they expected the latter answer. The leadership will lie about the answer before Pilate in Luke 23:2, which is the only other use of the term in Luke. [*phoros*]

20:23 Craftiness (*panourgian*). This term expresses an element of deceit as its other uses show ("trickery," NASB; NLT; "duplicity," NIV; "deceit," NET; "craftiness," RSV); 2 Cor. 4:2; 11:3—of the serpent in the garden; Eph. 4:14). [*panourgia*]

20:24 Coin (*dēnarion*). The reference is actually to a Roman denarius (NASB, NIV, NET), which had Caesar's picture on it ("coin," RSV; "Roman coin," NLT). It was what an average worker would get paid in a day. The fact that they had the coin already shows that the leaders live with and accept the currency of the day as part of their life. Jesus' reply simply indicates that Caesar should be honored as the government and so should God be honored with a proper heart response to him. He takes their either-or question and makes it a both-and. [*dēnarion*]

20:27 Sadducees (*Saddoukaiōn*). This group comprised mostly wealthy priests and was the most powerful group within Judaism in Jesus' day. They held most of the major seats on the key council. They not only denied the resurrection, but also only regarded the Pentateuch as key to Scripture. They also did not believe in angels or the afterlife (Josephus, *Antiquities* 18.16-17). As a result, their question about resurrection is supposed to show the ridiculous nature of that belief. They were comfortable with Rome as they had an understanding about how they could work together. This is the only time in Luke's Gospel that they are mentioned by name. They show up five times in Acts (4:1; 5:17; 23:6, 7, 8), once in Mark (12:18), seven times in Matthew (3;7; 16:1, 6, 11, 12; 22:23, 34), and do not appear in John. [*Saddoukaios*]

20:28 Must take the wife (*labē ho adelphos*

autou tēn gynaika). This verse refers to the practice of levirate marriage. In this custom a childless marriage is taken up by a brother to provide a line of descent for the brother ("must take the wife," RSV; "must marry the wife," NASB; "must marry the widow," NIV, NLT; NET; Deut. 25:5; Ruth 4:1-12). The question's force emerges from the fact that when this woman dies she will have seven husbands (v. 33). So the force of the question is, how can a woman have seven husbands in the afterlife, if she is only allowed one in this life? How could she care for *all* of them at once! [*lambanō* + *gynē*]

20:35 Neither marry or are given in marriage (*oute gamousin oute gamizontai*). Jesus' reply is that the afterlife, which he affirms, is not like life on earth in terms of social relationships. There is no marriage or giving in marriage there. So the question loses its force and actually shows an ignorance of what the afterlife is like. [*gameō, gamizō*]

20:36 Like angels (*isangeloi*). Jesus' explanation argues that those who are resurrected get glorified bodies like angels have (NASB, NIV, NLT) and will live eternally ("equal to angels," NET, RSV—in bodily form is the point). This new form of existence renders marriage unnecessary. This is the only use of this term in the NT. [*isangelos*]

20:37 Moses (*Mōusēs*). The appeal to Moses is for the Sadducees who only accept the Pentateuch as authoritative. Using Exodus 3, Jesus argues that if God is the God of the living (v. 38) and is the God of Abraham, Isaac, and Jacob during the time of Moses, who lived long after them, then the patriarchs must be raised. The reply met with acceptance of some, probably of the Pharisees (v. 39), who did believe in resurrection. [*Mōusēs*]

20:42 Lord (*kyrios/kyriō*). Jesus' question is based on a word play about Ps. 110:1 and the divine title of Lord. In the original Hebrew, the reference to God and to David's Lord would be distinguishable. However, both Hebrew (the language of the OT) and Aramaic (the language spoken at this time) could create similar word plays based around words with similar sounds or terms, as appear here in Greek. The title, Lord, is used as a term of respect for either divinity (Gen. 2:8; Isa. 40:5) or for some significant human figure of authority (husband, Gen. 18:12; father, Gen. 31:35; owner, Exod. 21:29; a king, 1 Sam. 26:23; 2 Sam. 1:14, 16; BAGD, 458-60; BDAG, 576-579, II; Spicq, 2:341-52, who details Greek usage with numerous examples). It is a common way to refer to God in the Greek OT (See the careful discussion in EDNT, 2:328-331, especially section 7 on p. 330). In the NT, it can refer to an owner of something (Matt. 20:8), to a husband (1 Pet. 3:6), to God (Rom. 10:9), or to rulers (Acts 25:26). Here Jesus raises a dilemma. How can David, as the ancestor in a society where paternity is respected, call his son "Lord," acknowledging the authority of the descendant? The question is only posed. It is not answered, but its thrust is that the Messiah's more important designation is as Lord, not as Son of David (v. 44). The implications of this point are not spelled out here, but emerge in Luke 22:69 and Acts 2:30-36, where we see that the Lord spoken of is one who can go directly into God's presence and sit at his right hand, exercising his mediatorial authority. As such, this passage is an important one for understanding who the Messiah is and, as a result, who Jesus is. [*kyrios*]

Right Hand (*dexiōn*). This reference to God's right hand is a way of expressing protection, power, and authority (Jer. 22:24, 30). It means that one is at the locale of God's power and blessing (Ps. 16:8, 11; 17:7; 45:9 [45:10 MT]). The passage affirms the close relationship that exists between God and his promised regal representative. [*dexios*]

20:46 Robes (*stolais*). This term describes the long, flowing, fancy robes that the scribes wore. They often reached to the floor and were decorated with attention-grabbing fringe (*Antiquities* 3.151; 11. 80–describes priestly robes). Luke 15:22 used the term to describe the robe given to the prodigal on his return. Jesus rebukes the ostentatiousness that is reflected in the scribes' efforts to draw attention. [*stolē*]

20:47 Long prayers (*makra proseuchontai*). Jesus often taught that public prayers should be crisp and to the point (Matt. 6:1-13; Luke 11:2-4). Prayer should not be done to draw attention to oneself. [*proseuchomai*]

21:1 Treasury (*gazophylakion*). This is probably one of the 13 treasury receptacles located about the temple ("collection box," NLT; "offering box," NET; *m Shek* 2.1; 6.1, 5). These were shaped in the form of trumpets (BAGD, 149; BDAG, 186). [*gazophylakion*]

21:2 Coins (*lepta*). These copper coins were the smallest currency in use. Each one was worth about one-100th of a denarius, or one one-100th of an average worker's daily wage, about seven minutes of their work! In other words, this was not very much money at all, like a few pennies (NLT renders the term as "pennies"). [*lepton*]

Poor (*penichran*). This is not the normal term for poor. It is only used here in the NT. It refers to someone who is needy (BAGD 642; BDAG, 795; Exod. 22:25 [22:24 LXX]); Prov. 28:15; 29:7). The irony is that it is the needy person who is giving so much proportionally. [*penichros*]

21:4 Living (*bion*). In a powerful figure Jesus notes that by tossing in the two coins out of her poverty, she has given "all her life" ("all she had to live on," NASB, NIV; "everything she has," NLT; "all the living," RSV; "everything she had," NET) Her gift is pleasing to God for it came with self sacrifice. [*bios*]

21:5 Adorned (*kekosmētai*). The second temple was in the process of being refurbished by Herod as part of a national reconstruction program. It took 80 years to complete and was in progress when Jesus lived. Many nations sent gifts to help with the décor. Tacitas, the Roman historian, called the temple "immensely opulent" (*History* 5.8). This is what the disciples marvelled at in their comments. [*kosmeō*]

21:6 One stone upon another (*lithos epi lithō*). Jesus predicts that the great temple will one day lie in a heap, the object of judgment. He already noted this for Jerusalem in 19:41-44. Now he makes it clear that there will be no "stone upon stone" at the temple as well. The city will be totally overrun. This took place in A.D. 70. [*lithos*]

21:7 Sign (*sēmeion*). The two questions the disciples ask in Luke inquire about the timing of this catastrophic event and whether there will be any warning or heavenly indicator that this is about to take place. An implication in the question, made more explicit in Matthew's account, is that such a catastrophic event must signal the decisive coming of God in judgment and Jesus' coming as well, though they do not yet appreciate it as a return by Jesus. (They do not yet understand the resurrection to come, so they assume in Matthew that the coming involves Jesus in this life—a coming in decisive judgment at the end of time, whenever and whatever that is.) The disciples were right to think that such a temple judgment indicated a key act of God. So Jesus' reply deals with both the temple's demise in A.D.

70 and the powerful, final return of God in judgment at the end, as one event mirrors the other. This mirroring of two events— what is sometimes called a typological prophetic reading, or a pattern-prophetic reading, of history—would not have been clear to the disciples when Jesus gave the speech. It was only when A.D. 70 did not also bring the final return that it would become clear A.D. 70 was meant to mirror (or give a pattern for) what the end would be like. [*sēmeion*]

21:8 Not led astray (*me planēthēte*). Jesus warns that many messianic pretenders will appear to whom the disciples are to give no heed. To follow them is to be led astray, pursuing a false path ("not misled," NASB; "not deceived," NIV; "don't let anyone mislead you," NLT; "not led astray," RSV, NET; BAGD, 665; BDAG, 822, 2Bd). Such claimants are not to be followed. [*planaō*]

21:9 The end will not be at once (*ouk eutheōs to telos*). The end here refers to the time when the Son of Man returns to earth to judge and vindicate his saints. Luke's version of this discourse has the most time markers of any of the versions. Here Jesus notes that when messianic claimants multiply and wars and tumults come that disciples should not be terrified or think that the end has come. For the end will not come immediately at that time ("the end does not follow immediately," NASB; "end will not come right away," NIV; "end won't follow immediately," "end will not be at once," RSV; "end will not come at once," NET). This is the only verse in Luke where this term carries this sense. In contrast, Luke 1:33 noted how the rule of God through Jesus will have no end. [*telos*]

21:11 Terrors (*phobētra*). This term appears only here in the NT. In the OT it describes something that is horrible to see ("terrors,"

NASB; RSV; "fearful events," NIV; "terrifying things," NLT; "terrifying sights," NET; Isa. 19:17; BAGD, 863; BDAG, 1062). It is part of the description of the cosmic chaos that comes before the end, as nations line up against each other, famines and pestilence comes, and great signs accompany these terrors. Jesus is describing how unstable the creation becomes before the return, signaling the need for the return. The passage's mood recalls the OT and its descriptions of judgment and exile (Jer. 4:13-22; 14:12; 21:6-7; Ezek. 14:21). [*phobētron*]

21:12 Before all of this (*pro de toutōn*). Now Jesus notes how the things he will describe in vv. 12-24 come before the things preceding the end. Thus the persecution and fall of Jerusalem precede the end, and lead into a time known as the "times of the Gentiles." After that, the Son of Man returns. So Jesus is telling the story backwards coming back toward the present time at this point. [*pro*]

Delivering you over (*paradidontes*). Jesus describes the approaching persecution to come for disciples starting with the synagogues ("delivering you up to," RSV; "delivering you to," NASB, NIV; "be dragged into synagogues," NLT; "handing you over to," NET). This same verb is used of how Jewish leadership delivered over Jesus (Luke 9:44). [*paradidōmi*]

21:13 Testimony (*martyrion*). This explains the purpose of the persecution, to witness to Jesus ("testimony," NASB, RSB; "being witnesses," NIV; "to tell them about me," NLT; "serve as witnesses," NET). How this worked can be seen in the early chapters of Acts, like Peter's arrest in Acts 4 or Paul's defense speeches in Acts 22–26. [*martyrion*]

21:14 To answer (*apologēthēnai*). This term means to give a reply in defense or in response to a situation ("how to make your defense," NET; "to defend yourselves," NASB; "how you will defend yourselves," NIV; "how to answer," NLT, RSV; Acts 19:33; 24:10; 25:8; 26:1, 2, 24). [*apologeomai*]

21:15 Wisdom (*sophian*). Jesus promises that he will supply the replies needed. This is an indirect way to speak of the work of the Spirit (Matt. 10:19-20; Mark 13:11). [*sophia*]

21:18 Hair of your head (*thrix ek tēs kephalēs*). In v. 16 Jesus noted how some of the disciples will be put to death, so this expression is figurative. It means that, whatever happens to them physically, absolutely nothing will happen to them spiritually. God will protect and vindicate them. [*thrix*]

21:19 Endurance (*hypomonē*). The only other use of this word in Luke's Gospel was in Luke 8:15, where it described how the good soil bears fruit from the seed. Here endurance leads to preservation of the soul ("endurance," NASB, NET; RSV; "by standing firm," NLT, NIV). Jesus explains the benefits of disciples hanging in there during persecution. [*hypomonē*]

21:20 Her desolation (*hē erēmōsis autēs*). This description of the scene differs slightly from the parallels in Matthew 24:15 and Mark 13:14, which speak of the "abomination of desolation," an allusion to the desecration of the temple. Here Jesus describes the desolation of the city of Jerusalem that is a part of the destruction in A.D. 70 ("her desolation," NET, NASB; "its desolation," NIV, RSV; "its destruction," NLT), but that event itself pictures and is a type of what the end is like, when the temple is desecrated in the way Daniel 9:27 describes. The three synoptic texts are the only verses in which this word appears in the NT. [*erēmōsis*]

21:22 Vengeance (*ekdikēseōs*). The expression

"days of vengeance" (RSV, NLT, NASB, NET; "time of punishment," NIV) indicates that the city is an object of divine judgment at this time and that it is better not to be there when it is under siege. This fulfills what Scripture said would happen for covenantal unfaithfulness and what Jesus predicts in Luke 19:41-44 (see v. 24). It also is like what God will do in the end when the Son of Man does come. As v. 23 suggests, it will be a terrible time of distress. [*ekdikēsis*]

21:24 Times of the Gentiles (*kairoi ethnōn*). This expression indicates that when Israel is overrun in judgment that the following period will be a time when Gentiles dominate in the world ("times of the Gentiles," RSV, NIV, NASB, NET; "age of the Gentiles," NLT). The remark implies that this situation will not continue forever and that the return of the Son of Man, which Jesus describes next, will reverse it. This suggests that Israel's fate will change at that time, something that is also suggested in Luke 13:35. [*kairos* + *ethnos*]

21:25 Distress (*synochē*). This term normally refers to being chained but can refer to psychological distress (Job 30:3; BAGD, 791, 2; BDAG, 974, 2). So there is distress at all the cosmic signs taking place ("distress," NET; RSV; "dismay," NASB; "anguish," NIV; "turmoil," NLT; Isa. 13:9-10; 24:18-20; 34:4; Ezek. 32:7-8; Joel 2:10 are signs texts). [*synochē*]

21:26 Shaken (*saleuthēsontai*). This term is used of reeds shaken by the wind (Luke 7:24) or an earth shaken by earthquakes (Ps. 82:5; BAGD, 740; BDAG, 911). Here the image is of heavenly bodies being rattled— a prospect that brings fear to those who see it ("shaken," RSV, NIV, NET, NASB; "broken up," NLT). [*saleuō*]

21:27 Cloud (*nephelē*). This term is part of the citation of Daniel 7:13, where the Son of Man rides the clouds and receives judgment authority from the Ancient of Days. In the OT, only God or the gods ride clouds (Exod. 14:20; Num. 10:34; Ps. 104:3; Isa. 19:1). So there is an implicit claim of heavenly authority in this image. [*nephelē*]

21:28 Redemption (*hē apolytrōsis*). Such heavenly signs and the return of the Son of Man mean that the consummation of salvation is coming (1 Enoch 51:2). This is Luke's only use of this noun ("redemption," NASB; NIV, RSV, NET; "salvation," NLT). Redemption is a way of describing one freed through a ransom or a payment made (EDNT 1:138). [*apolytrōsis*]

21:31 These things (*tauta*). This is a reference back to the various signs coming before the Son of Man's return ("the events I have described," NLT), as that return is the "end" from the perspective of the discourse. So Jesus says that everything from false claimants of being the Messiah to persecution to the overrunning of Jerusalem point to the approach of the end's arrival. [*outos*]

21:32 This generation (*hē genea*). The meaning of this term in this passage is much debated. It seems clear that it does not refer to the generation of Jesus' time, for the Son of Man did not come in their lifetime. Among the options is that the term has an ethical force, referring either to this righteous or wicked generation, depending on whether it is intended positively or negatively. In this case, it is either a reassurance that the righteous will survive or that the wicked will be judged. Another option is that the term is temporal and refers to the fact that once the events of the end start, it will all take place within a generation (For all of these views, plus a few more, see Bock 2:1688-1692). It is hard to know which sense is present here. Most likely is the negative ethical view (wicked generation) or the idea that once the end starts it will be completed in a generation. [*genea*]

21:34 Approach suddenly (*epistē eph hymas aiphnidios*). The verb used here speaks of a "sudden" approach of the end ("close down upon you," NET; "catch you unaware," NLT; "close on you," NIV; "come on you," NASB; "come upon you," RSV). This verb often carries negative connotations of an approach of misfortune (BAGD, 330; BDAG, 418, 2; Wis. 6:8; 19:1; 1 Thess. 5:3). So here the warning is that those who do not keep watch may meet with misfortune when the return does come, by not being ready for it. [*ephistēmi*]

21:35 Trap (*pagis*). A trap is a snare ("trap," NET; NLT, NIV, NASB; "snare," RSV; BAGD, 602; BDAG, 747, 1; the syntax causes the term sometimes to show up in v. 34 in the English). Jesus' point is that being unprepared for the end is like walking suddenly into a trap. It is unexpected and undesirable. [*pagis*]

22:1 Passover (*pascha*). This feast celebrates the deliverance of the nation in the Exodus (Exod. 12–13). It leads directly into the week-long feast of Unleavened Bread, so that the two often shared the same name (*Antiquities* 3.294). This was one of the pilgrim feasts in the Jewish calendar when the population of Jerusalem swelled with celebrants who traveled to the temple to observe the feast. [*pascha*]

22:3 Satan (*Satanas*). This is the first explicit reappearance of Satan since the temptations in Luke 4:1-13. [*Satan/Satanas*]

22:6 Opportunity (*eukairian*). This word is made up of two parts that simply mean a "good" or "appropriate" + "time." The only two uses of this word in the NT are in this scene (Matt. 26:16). [*eukairia*]

22:7 Passover (*pascha*). Luke and the other Synoptic Gospels are pretty clear that this was a passover meal. This would be a four-course meal, corresponding to the four cups of wine, to commemorate the Exodus (*m Pesah* 10). Thus, the later scene in the Synoptics clearly is a summary of the key features of the meal, which lasted for some time. [*pascha*]

22:11 Guest room (*katalyma*). The only other use of this term, outside the parallel in Mark 14:14, is in Luke 2:7, where it describes the lack of a room for Joseph and Mary during Jesus' birth. Jerusalem's population could triple with pilgrims during this feast time (Bock, 1952). [*katalyma*]

22:16 It (*auto*). The first use of this pronoun in this verse alludes back to the Passover meal. Jesus tells the disciples this is the last such meal he will have until things are fulfilled in the kingdom, a remark which seems to anticipate such a meal in the future. Jesus says the same thing about the cup in 22:18. [*autos*]

22:19 For you (*hyper hymōn*). This is the one place in Luke's Gospel where Jesus' death is explicitly explained as being a substitutionary work. The preposition *hyper* indicates this, especially in a context where the background is the Passover sacrifice. Acts 20:28 will explain that Jesus' death "purchased" the church through Jesus' blood. The presence of Luke 22:19b-20 in Luke is sometimes questioned because of its absence in certain manuscripts of Luke, but it is likely that it was a part of Luke's Gospel (Bock, 1721-22). [*hyper*]
  Remembrance (*anamnēsin*). This term turns the supper into something that is to be regularly commemorated. This term is rare in the NT, appearing also in 1 Corinthians 11:24-25 twice, where the Lord's table is discussed and in Hebrews 10:3 (TDNT 4:678, 682). The meal is to recall Jesus' act of sacrifice and provision. First Corinthians 10:16 calls the meal "a

participation," that is a sharing in (*koinōnia*) the blood of Christ. This Pauline passage probably expresses the idea that the meal represents a corporate affirmation of sharing in the covenant Jesus has established. It means identifying with him. [*anamnēsis*]

22:20 New Covenant (*hē kainē diathēkē*). Jesus' death as expressed in the cup points to his shed blood and the inauguration of the New Covenant with its promise of forgiveness. It also points to God's work from within the heart through the Spirit (Jer. 31:31-33; Ezek. 34:23-26). It is Jesus' way of saying that the promise of hope laid out in the OT has come through Jesus' work on the cross. [*kainē* + *diathēkē*]

22:22 Determined (*hōrismenon*). The betrayal of Jesus, the Son of Man, is a part of God's plan that is working itself out ("been determined" NET, NASB, RSV; "has been decreed," NIV; "since it is part of God's plan,' NLT). Luke frequently uses this term in Acts (2:23; 10:42; 11:29; 17:26, 31). There it also underscores events that are a "determined" part of the plan. [*hōrizō*]

22:24 Greatest (*meizōn*). The disciples were still not appreciating what was taking place. They were debating their rank in the kingdom, which they still thought would be coming in fullness soon as a result of what Jesus was doing. In fact, there was some contention (*philoneikai*, BAGD, 860; BDAG, 1058, 2) over the matter at the meal. As a result, Jesus reminds them that disciples should not be like the world. They should not worry about rank. They should see greatness in service. [*megas*]

22:25 Benefactors (*euergetai*). This term is only used here in the NT ("benefactors," NIV, NASB, RSV, NET; "friends," NLT–really does not get the force of this special Greek title;

"considerate patron" might be better). It describes the title leaders and princes liked to have used to indicate their rank and authority (2 Macc. 4:2; 3 Macc. 3:19; Josephus, *Jewish War* 3.459). Jesus contrasts such a desire for title to the service of a disciple. [*euergetēs*]

22:27 One who serves (*ho diakonōn*). Jesus' example of serving is to be followed by his disciples. The term Jesus uses twice in Luke 22:26-27 is the verbal form of the Greek word from which we get our term deacon, which means one who serves. [*diakoneō*]

22:29 Kingdom (*basileian*). Jesus has just rebuked the Twelve for their debate over rank, but graciously appoints them to a share in the kingdom that God has given to Jesus as Son. This remark indicates the benefits Jesus gives to those who have stuck by him as v. 28 notes that these disciples had continued with him in trial. A place in the kingdom means that they will celebrate at the banquet to come. One day they will also sit on 12 thrones and have authority to judge Israel. [*basileia*]

22:30 Table (*trapezēs*). The reference to the table pictures having a place at the banquet celebration of Jesus that in turn represents fellowship in the end time with him as they celebrate the messianic victory. This banquet imagery is quite common in Luke (12:35-37; 13:29; 14:15-24). However, this is the only Lucan text where the image is invoked by picturing fellowship at a table. [*trapeza*]

22:31 Sift (*siniasai*). This is another term which is used only here in the NT. It represents a figurative expression that pictures "taking someone apart" like one sifts and picks apart grain (Amos 9:9). Satan wants to destroy Peter, but Jesus' intercession will keep Peter's failure, expressed in his three denials (22:34), from destroying him. [*siniazō*]

22:32 Turned again (*epistrepsas*). Jesus' remarks assume a short-term failure on Peter's part that will require his turning back ("turned again," NLT, NASB, RSV; "turned back," NET; NIV). However, Jesus gives him a commission to strengthen the brothers when that turning and restoration takes place. Here is an example of "turning" not referring to conversion, as is common in Acts (Acts 3:19; 9:35; 11:21; 14:15; 15:19; 26:18, 20), but to a restoration of a believer in his or her walk. [*epistrephō*]

22:37 Transgressors (*anomōn*). This term refers to the "lawless" and is part of Jesus' citation of Isaiah 53:12, which he sees fulfilled in his death ("transgressors," RSV, NIV, NASB, NET; "rebels," NLT). Jesus' point in the previous verses about taking a purse, bag, and sword is a way of saying that opposition to the disciples will rise to the point that they will need to look out for themselves. The world's rejection of Jesus will lead to his being treated as a criminal and will spill over to them. [*anomos*]

22:38 Swords (*machairai*). The term can refer to a sword or dagger (BAGD, 496; BDAG, 622). The disciples' inventory of two swords is an indication they are ready to fight for Jesus. He simply dismisses their remark. When they use the swords during his arrest he stops them (22:49-50). They still have much to learn. [*machaira*]

22:40, 46 Temptation (*peirasmon*). In this context, the temptation will be to respond improperly to the events tied to Jesus' arrest and death. However, the disciples prove to be too exhausted to be vigilant in prayer. They respond poorly to the arrest. [*peirasmos*]

22:42 Cup (*to potērion*). This is probably a reference to the cup of wrath (Ps. 75:8-9; Isa. 51:17, 19, 22; Jer. 25:15-16; EDNT, 3:142). This is a part of what Jesus will experience as a part of his death. Jesus initially asks if there is another way to go, but ultimately he expresses that his real desire is simply to do God's will. [*potērion*]

22:44 Agony (*agōnia*). Luke 22:43b-44 are part of a textual problem (some question whether they were originally in Luke's gospel), but these verses most likely belong to Luke (Bock, 1763-64). If so, then the text refers to Jesus' agony and pain as he prayerfully prepares for his death (BAGD, 15; BDAG, 17; 2 Macc. 3:14, 16; "in anguish," NIV, NET; "agony," NLT, NASB, RSV, margin). This is the only use of this term in the NT. [*agōnia*]

More earnestly (*ektenesteron*). This term shows up in two other passages in the NT (Acts 12:5; 1 Pet. 1:22). In Acts it also describes intensity of prayer; while in 1 Pet. it portrays an intense love (BDAG, 310; BAGD, 245). In Luke it shows the intensity of Jesus' prayer. [*ektenoōs*]

Blood (*haimatos*). The text does not indicate that Jesus sweat blood, but that his sweat was like drops of blood. The detail does indicate the intensity of the prayer. [*haima*]

22:48 Son of Man (*ton huion tou anthrōpou*). Jesus' use of this title at this point is important. The Son of Man looked back to Daniel 7:9-14 as Jesus' use of it in Luke 21:27 indicates. Thus Judas is betraying the one to whom God has given judgment authority. [*huios + anthrōpos*]

22:52 Robber (*lēstēn*). This is the term used to describe the bandits who injured the Samaritan in Jesus' parable (Luke 10:30, 36; "bandit," NET). The term is also used of revolutionaries in Josephus (*Jewish War* 2.253-54; "Am I leading a rebellion?" NIV). It describes someone who will freely use violence ("robber," NASB, RSV; "criminal,"

NLT; BAGD, 473; BDAG, 594, 1). Its meaning here is probably broad and generic, so robber or criminal makes sense. In the Greek sentence this term is thrown forward for emphasis. [*lēstēs*]

22:53 The power of <u>darkness</u> (*hē exousia tou skotous*). Jesus connects the action of those arresting him with the force of evil, characterized as darkness ("power of darkness," NET; NASB, RSV, NLT; "when darkness reigns," NIV). So the presence of Satan is in view. This figurative use of darkness appeared in Luke 1:79, where people were said to be living in darkness. It also appeared in 11:35, where it refers to the lack of moral uprightness in one's character. [*skotos*]

22:55 Courtyard (*aulēs*). Many Roman style homes were built around a courtyard in the middle of the home. It appears this home belonged to Caiaphas and Annas. [*aulē*]

22:56 Servant girl (*paidiskē*). This term refers to a young maid (RSV, "slave girl," NET; "servant girl," NASB, NIV, NLT) who serves in the household. She identifies him after staring at him. She would have been one of the lower ranking figures in the home. This term is only used here and in 12:45 in Luke. [*paidiskē*]

22:59 Galilean (*Galilaios*). The parallel accounts note that it was Peter's accent that gave him away as being from the same region as Jesus (Matt. 26:73). [*Galilaios*]

22:62 Wept (*eklausen*). This term is often used for the weeping of grief over the dead (Luke 8:52; John 11:31, 33: "wept," RSV, NIV, NASB, NET; "crying" NLT). Here it is used of Peter's pain for having denied the Lord just as Jesus had predicted. [*klaiō*]

22:65 Reviling (*blasphēmountes*). This term is

strong. It is also used to refer to blaspheming. These soldiers are insulting Jesus in their version of blind man's bluff. Luke uses a term that depicts their actions as insulting ("blaspheming," NASB; "insulting things," NIV; "terrible insults," NLT; "reviling him," RSV, NET). The term is also used to describe how one of the criminals on the cross addresses Jesus (23:39). Luke never uses the term to describe what Jesus has said, even though the parallels in Matthew 26:65 (using this verb) and Mark 14:64 (using the noun) note that this is the high priest's opinion of Jesus' testimony. [*blasphēmeō*]

22:66 Day (*hēmera*). The examination of Jesus has now extended through the night and into the early morning ("daybreak," NIV, NLT; "day came," RSV, NET; "when it was day," NASB). [*hēmera*]

Council (*synedrion*). This is Luke's only use of this term. It refers to what is often called the Sanhedrin, a group of the 71 major Jewish leaders (*m Sanh* 1.6 alluding to Num. 11:16). It is Israel's highest court of appeal. [*synedrion*]

22:67 Christ (*Christos*). The leadership needs a political charge to take to Rome in order to get an execution, since the Romans did not allow them to execute a criminal. This question is seeking to see if Jesus sees himself as a King ("Christ," NASB, NIV, NET, RSV; "Messiah," NLT), a claim that the Romans would be sensitive about and to which they would respond. [*Christos*]

22:68 Not answer (*mē apokrithēte*). Jesus alludes back to the dispute over his authority and that of John the Baptist (Luke 20:1-8). He reminds them that they did not believe nor answer him then. [*apokrinomai*]

22:69 Son of Man (*ho huios tou anthrōpou*). This important title comes from Daniel 7 and describes a human who rides the clouds like God. The Son of Man comes into the presence of the Ancient of Days to receive judgment authority (see Luke 5:24). So Jesus is claiming to be able to go directly into God's presence and be seated by him with authority ultimately to judge. In effect, Jesus says that the council is on trial! His claim to be able to sit at God's side is seen as blasphemous by the council, as the high priest tearing his robes in the parallels to this scene shows (Matt. 26:65; Mark 14:63). For them, God's glory is so unique; no one can sit with God. The claim has implications about Jesus' person which the leadership understands but rejects. In effect, Jesus gives the testimony that sends himself to the cross (Luke 22:71). [*huios + anthrōpos*]

22:70 Son of God (*ho huios tou theos*). This seeks to confirm Jesus' remark and carries both regal overtones (2 Sam. 7:14) and perhaps even more. [*huios + theos*]

You say (*legete*). Jesus' reply is positive but indirect, suggesting that he does not view the title in quite the way they ask about it. It may be that he is rejecting the threatening political implications they want to make out of the title when they go to Rome (Luke 23:2). [*legō*]

23:1 Pilate (*Pilaton*). Pilate was the Roman governor in Judea from A.D. 26-36. He was responsible for collecting taxes and keeping the peace, allowing no power to rise up to challenge Roman interests in Judea. [*Pilatos*]

23:2 Perverting (*diastrephonta*). This is the first of three charges the leadership brings before Pilate. It is the most general charge, that Jesus perverts or misleads the Jewish nation ("misleading our nation," NASB, NET; "subverting our nation," NIV; "leading our people to ruin," NLT; "perverting our nation," BAGD, 189, 2; BDAG, 237, 3). It is the charge of least relevance to the Roman

ruler. So they will specify the charges in the two claims that follow. [*diastrephō*]

Forbidding (*kōluonta*). This is the second charge, that Jesus prohibited the payment of taxes to Rome, the collection of which was Pilate's responsibility ("forbidding," NASB; NET, RSV; "opposes payment of taxes," NIV; "telling them not to pay their taxes," NLT). It is a lie, given what Jesus said in Luke 20:20-26. [*kōluō*]

Saying (*legonta*). The third charge is that Jesus claims to be the Christ, a king, a rival to Caesar ("saying," NASB, RSV; "claims to be," NIV; "claiming," NLT, NET). Thus the leadership took the claim of Luke 22:69 and turned it into a political charge. [*legō*]

23:3 You have said so (*sy legeis*). This idiom means, "Yes, but not in the sense you mean." "It is as you say," as NASB, NIV render, and "You are right in saying that I am," as NLT translates, lacks the appropriate ambiguity in the reply. "You say so," as the NET, and "you have said so," both correctly suggest Jesus demurs slightly. [*legō*]

23:4 No crime (*ouden . . . aition*). Pilate makes the first of several declarations of Jesus' innocence in Luke 23 ("no crime," RSV; "no reason for accusation," NET; "no guilt," NASB; "no basis for a charge," NIV; "nothing wrong," NLT; vv. 14-15, 22). [*aitios*]

23:5 Incites (*anaseiei*). This term refers to stirring up trouble ("stirs up," NASB, NIV; RSV; "causing riots," NLT; "incites," NET). It is used only here and in Mark 15:11 (BAGD, 60; BDAG, 71). [*anaseiō*]

23:7 Herod (*Hērōdou/Hērōdēn*). This ruler of Idumean and Israelite ancestry was the tetrarch appointed by the Romans to help rule in Galilee and Perea (BAGD, 348; BDAG, 439, 2). Pilate was passing the buck and also using the opportunity to affirm Herod's authority, an act that brought the two rulers closer together after some hard times (see 23:12 below). [*Hērōdēs*]

23:8 Sign (*sēmeion*). Herod wanted to see a miracle (NIV, NLT), which Luke calls a sign (RSV, NASB, NET). [*sēmeion*]

23:11 Shining apparel (*esthēta lampran*). These bright (white) clothes serve to picture a wealthy person of power and are part of the mocking of Jesus ("gorgeous robe," NASB; "elegant robe," NIV; royal robe," NLT; "elegant clothes," NET; "gorgeous apparel," RSV; Acts 12:21; EDNT 2:58). [*esthēs*]

23:12 Enmity (*echthra*). The enmity (RSV) was the result of insensitive acts that Pilate engaged in against the Jews when he first became governor. For example, he brought shields with images on them into Jerusalem as a reminder to the Jews that they were under Roman rule (Philo, *Embassy to Gaius* 38.299-305; Josephus, *Antiquities* 18.55-59). Caesar chastised Pilate for this act. Such actions led Herod and Pilate to be "enemies" (So NIV, NASB, NET, NLT). [*echthra*]

23:15 Nothing deserving death (*ouden axion thanatou*). Here Pilate reports that Herod also found Jesus innocent ("nothing deserving death," RSV, NET; NASB; ""nothing to deserve death," NIV; "nothing . . . calls for the death penalty," NLT). All of these notes of innocence turn Jesus into an "innocent sufferer" or a "righteous sufferer," a role often described in the Psalms. [*oudeis*]

23:16 Chastise (*paideusas*). Pilate recommends beating Jesus with a whip to discourage him, but the leadership refuses this suggestion. The term used here means chastise or punish when it has a negative connotation (Lev. 26:18), but refers to a flogging in this legal context ("flogged," NET, NLT;

"punish," NIV, NASB; "chastise," RSV). The two uses in the Gospel of this term are in this passage (Luke 23:22). [*paideuō*]

23:18 They cried out (*anekragon*). The "they" refers back to v. 13, where chief priests, rulers and people are gathered. It is "they" who cry out for Barabbas ("cried out," NIV, NASB, RSV; "shouted out," NET; "a mighty roar rose," NLT). The other two uses of the verb in Luke involve the crying out of demons (4:33; 8:28). [*anakrazō*]

23:19 Insurrection (*stasin*). The only two uses of this term in Luke involve the description of Barabbas (Luke 23:25). But the issue of conflict represented by the term is noted numerous times in Acts, sometimes involving debate and other times violence (Acts 15:2; 23:7—debate [quarrel, Prov.. 17:14]; Acts 19:40; 23:10—riot). [*stasis*]

23:21 Crucify (*staurou*). The crowd urges Pilate to exercise his authority to execute. The expression as a repeated double imperative is emphatic. [*stauroō*]

23:27 Bewailed (*ekoptonto*). This term is graphic. It refers to "beating their breasts in grief" (Luke 8:52; Zech. 7:5; BAGD, 444, 2). These women appear to be genuinely regretful of what is taking place ("mourning," NET; NASB; "mourned," NIV; "grief stricken," NLT; "bewailed," RSV). Such mourning at a death scene is not unusual in Jewish contexts. [*koptō*]

23:29 Barren (*hai steirai*). This verse expresses the reference to the blessed barren (NIV, NASB, NET, RSV; "childless," NLT) in three distinct figures (barren, unopened womb, breasts that do not nurse). The description is a reminder that the nation is under judgment for what is taking place. That which is normally seen as a sign of a judgment is better than normal signs of blessedness like child-bearing, because of the difficult times to come. [*steira*]

23:30 Fall (*pesete*). This is the first of two figures in the verse from Hosea 10:8. The desire that an avalanche cover them shows how horrific the judgment will be. They just want to die. The call for hills to cover them makes the same point in a synonymous, parallel line. [*piptō*]

23:31 Green (*hygrō*). Jesus refers to himself as living ("green") wood. The term refers to "moist" and thus living, green wood (Judg. 16:7-8; BAGD, 832; BDAG, 1023). He notes that if living wood is treated this way, then what will happen when dead ("dry") wood is judged? That is why the women must mourn for themselves, for the death of Jesus points out the presence of "dead" wood by those who have rejected him. [*hygros*]

23:34 They do not know (*ou . . . oidasin*). This prayer for forgiveness in light of the people's ignorance is not an excuse for their responsibility, nor does it mean they did not have an understanding of what Jesus' claims had been. What Jesus means is that they did not understand what they really were doing. The people were acting out of a desire to execute someone they thought had blasphemed, but, in reality, Jesus was who he claimed. The fact that Jesus' death made potential provision for those who executed him and that there remains hope for Israel's response in the future means that this prayer was heard. There is some question whether this verse was textually originally in Luke (thus some translations have it in the margin). However, it seems slightly more likely, given the parallelism with Stephen's remarks in Acts 7 that it should be included (Bock, 2:1867-68). [*oida*]
  Garments (*himatia*). The casting of lots for Jesus' clothes is a description that echoes Ps.

22:18, where a righteous sufferer suffers a similar type of fate. Jesus fulfills that text ("garments," RSV, NASB; "clothing," NET; "clothes," NIV, NLT). [*himation*]

23:35 Christ (*christos*). This verse along with 23:39 show that the focus of the opponents' attention is on Jesus as king and Messiah ("Christ," NIV, NET, RSV, NASB; "Messiah," NLT). The irony of the verse is that God will save Jesus from the cross through resurrection, just as Jesus saved others. The Greek hints at this irony in using a first class condition in the "if" clause. This means that the remark about the Christ, indicates that Jesus is the Christ despite the mockers' sarcasm "If you are the Christ (and we present it as so), then save yourself." This is a literary touch where the author's opinion is encased in the mockers' words. In the original setting, it was likely that Aramaic, not Greek, was used, so the discussion is already in translation. Greek has a first class construction, which Aramaic does not. The same type of first class construction takes place again with the mocking in 23:37. Mocking of Jesus as the Christ is repeated by one of the criminals in 23:39. [*christos*]

23:36 Vinegar (*oxos*). This is a wine-vinegar diluted with water, which was a common drink for soldiers and field hands ("vinegar," RSV, NIV; "sour wine," NET; NLT, NASB; EDNT 2:523; Mark 15:36; Matt. 27:48; John 19:29-30). [*oxos*]

23:37-38 King (*basileus*). The inscription, known as the *titulus*, contained a summary of the charge for which Jesus was executed. It was the messianic claim to be another king that the Romans made as the decisive charge. Luke has used this description of Jesus in Luke 19:38, 23:2-3, 37. It is always on the lips of others. [*basileus*]

23:39 Railed (*eblasphēmei*). The term for the derisive criminal's remarks means to slander or even to blaspheme ("railed," NET, RSV; "was hurling abuse," NASB; "hurled insults," NIV; "scoffed," NLT). Thus Luke suggests that this mocking was untrue and offensive, just as in 22:65. [*blasphēmeō*]

23:41 Nothing wrong (*ouden atopon*). The other thief comes to Jesus' defense and declares Jesus' innocence. This term means to do something morally wrong (BAGD, 120, 2; BDAG, 149, 2). The second thief denies Jesus has performed such action. Luke only uses the term in his Gospel here to describe Jesus' innocence. [*atopos*]

23:42 Kingdom (*basileian*). The responsive thief sees Jesus as the king, despite his crucifixion and asks to be in his kingdom, a step of real faith as they hang dying. The thief hopes to be present in Jesus' future reign, which must suppose he accepts a resurrection one day. Jesus will give him more than he asks for by noting a different timing. [*basileia*]

23:43 Today (*sēmeron*). Jesus tells the thief that entry into the kingdom will not have to wait, but will take place this very day for the man. Luke uses one of his favorite terms, "today," to highlight the point. This is the last of this Gospel's 11 uses of this term. [*sēmeron*]

Paradise (*paradeisō*). This term appears only three times in the NT (2 Cor. 12:4; Rev. 2:7). It is another way to refer to heaven and God's presence (Isa. 51:3; Ezek. 28:13; 31:8; 1 Enoch 17–19). [*paradeisos*]

23:44 Hour (*hōra/hōras*). Hours were counted from sunrise, so the sixth to ninth hour is about noon to three in the afternoon (NET, NLT note the time this latter way). The cosmic sign of unusual darkness sug-

gests judgment is present. [*hōra*]

23:45 Curtain (*katapetasma*). There is discussion as to which curtain is meant ("curtain," NET, NIV, RSV; "veil," NASB, NLT). This term is used of both the curtain that separates the Holy of Holies (Lev. 21:23) and the one that separates the temple from the outer court (Exod. 26:37). It is hard to be sure which is meant, though the tearing of the outer curtain would be a more public event. Either way, the point is that access to God has been opened up. God is emerging from his temple (Acts 7:45-50). [*katapetasma*]

23:46 Spirit (*pneuma*). Jesus dies citing Ps. 31:5, a psalm of trust in the goodness of God. He commits the care of himself to the Father. [*pneuma*]

23:47 Innocent/Righteous (*dikaios*). The two translations given for this term are both possible here ("innocent," NASB, RSV, NLT, NET; "righteous," NIV). Innocence would underscore the theme that has been present throughout Luke 23 and is slightly more likely. Righteous would also mean that Jesus did no wrong and is implied in the remark that Jesus is innocent. So the term depicts Jesus' innocence either way. [*dikaios*]

23:49 Saw (*horōsai*). This note indicates that the events described had eye-witnesses ("saw," RSV, NET; "watching," NIV, NLT; "seeing," NASB). The fact that women are portrayed as the witnesses means this final scene's details were not fabricated, for the testimony of women was normally not well received. One making up such an account would not entrust it culturally to the word of these women. Thus, the account takes an unusual cultural angle to make the point that these Galilean women saw this event. [*horaō*]

23:51 Had not consented (*ouk . . . sygkatateth-*

eimenos). As at the beginning of Luke, it is pious people who respond to God's will as the pious and righteous Joseph "had not agreed" (NLT) with the council about sending Jesus on to his death. The term literally means "to put down the same vote as" (BAGD, 773; BDAG, 951). This is the only time the term appears in the NT. If the perfect participle is read, and that seems the more likely reading, then the conclusion to disagree is presented as fairly firm. [*sygkatatithēmi*]

23:53 Hewn (*laxeutō*). This tomb appears to have been "cut" (NET, NASB, NIV) into a rock face and would normally have an entrance of about a yard's height ("hewn," RSV; "carved out," NLT). The locale was probably just to the north of Jerusalem. This is another term used only here in the NT. [*laxeutos*]

23:54 Preparation (*paraskeuēs*). This is the day before the Sabbath, when everyone prepares everything for the day of rest. So it is Friday (John 19:42; BAGD, 622; BDAG, 771). [*paraskeuē*]

23:56 Spices and ointments (*arōmata kai myra*). Jews did not embalm the body at death, so the "spices and ointments" (RSV, NLT) served to cover the stench of a dead body ("spices and perfumes," NASB; NIV; "aromatic oils and perfumes," NET; TDNT 4:801; 7:458). The entire activity reflects their care and devotion to Jesus. [*arōma, myron*]

24:2 Rolled away (*apokekylismenon*). The stone over the tomb often would have been placed in a channel cut in front of the entrance. However, sometimes there is no channel. We do not know what was the case here. However, when the women arrived the entrance was open. [*apokyliō*]

24:4 Perplexed (*aporeisthai*). Clearly the women had not anticipated a resurrection. Now the empty tomb left them pondering what was going on ("perplexed," RSV, NASB, NET; "wondering," NIV; "puzzled," NLT). The term used here is quite vivid. It is used of Herod's state of mind upon hearing about Jesus after executing John (Mark 6:20). It is also used of the disciples' reaction when Jesus announces that he will be betrayed by one of them (John 13:22) or Festus' uncertainty about how to proceed with Paul (Acts 25:20). [*aporeō*]

24:5 Living (*zōnta*). Here is the first declaration in Luke that Jesus is alive. He is among the "living" (RSV, NIV, NET, NASB; "who is alive," NLT). He is not in a tomb among the dead. The term is often used to describe one brought back from the dead (3 Kgdms. 17:23 [= 1 Kings]; Matt. 9:18; Acts 9:41; Acts 1:3; BAGD, 336, 1b; BDAG, 425, 1b). [*zaō*]

24:7 Must (*dei*). Luke uses his favorite term for the plan of God here and recalls utterances that stretch back to Luke 9:22. On this term, see Luke 2:49. [*dei*]

24:11 Idle tale (*lēros*). This is a strong term and is the only time the word is used in the NT. It refers to nonsense or empty talk ("pure nonsense," NET; "idle tale," RSV; 4 Macc. 5:11; "nonsense," NASB, NIV, NLT; *Jewish War* 3.405; BAGD, 473; BDAG, 594). Women were not normally trusted as witnesses in the ancient world. Here the crowd thinks that these women are hysterical and beside themselves in grief. Only Peter, who dashes to the tomb, wishes to check out their report. The fact that the account is based initially on women's reports shows that this event is not fabricated. No one in the ancient world would make up such an important account by appealing to the testimony of women. [*lēros*]

24:12 Wondering (*thaumazōn*)—There is some debate whether this verse is a part of Luke, but the manuscript evidence is for its inclusion (the RSV has it in the margin). In the verse, Peter runs to the tomb and leaves "wondering" (NIV, NET, NLT, RSV) about what has taken place (NASB has "marvelling," which may be too strong and positive a rendering). The term used here always suggests an element of surprise at what has taken place (Luke 1:21, 63; 4:22; 11:38). So the term is not so much one of faith as amazement that the tomb was empty. Nonetheless, Peter's run to check things out and his past experience with Jesus' predictions means that he is beginning to understand what is taking place, even though he does not yet fully grasp things. Luke 24:34 indicates Peter came to a fuller understanding later in the day. [*thaumazō*]

24:16 From recognizing (*mē epignōnai*). Luke does not explain how they could not recognize Jesus. It is clear that though Jesus is raised bodily, that body has a different quality than normal flesh. These two will not figure out who Jesus is until much later (24:31). The timing is partly seen as a divine work, as their eyes were kept from recognizing him now, but will be opened when they recognize him later. [*epiginōskō*]

24:18 Visitor (*paroikeis*). This is a vivid term. It means to inhabit a place as a stranger (BAGD, 628, 1a; BDAG, 779, 1). So, in effect, they are asking, "Are you the only one who is such a stranger in Jerusalem that you do not know what took place there?" The question drips with irony. Most translations opt for a description of Jesus as a "visitor" here (NET, RSV, NIV, NASB), but that may be too soft (NLT has "only person in Jerusalem"). Jesus was not nearly as out of the information loop as they suggest. [*paroikeō*]

24:19 Prophet (*prophētēs*). The function of prophet was the starting point for understanding Jesus. He taught and performed the works of God. So the two disciples start here in explaining their hopes surrounding Jesus, hopes now seemingly dashed. [*prophētēs*]

24:21 To redeem (*lytrousthai*). This is a way of describing Jesus as the hoped for Messiah ("redeem," NASB, NET, RSV, NIV; "rescue," NLT). Their hope had been that he would deliver Israel as the hymns in Luke 1:46-55, 69-79 declared. The verb pictures a rescue out of one situation into another. This verb is used only three times in the NT (Titus 2:14; 1 Pet. 1:18). [*lytroō*]

24:23 Vision (*optasian*). This summary of the women's report is part of what tells us that those who announced Jesus' resurrection to the women were angels. It also suggests that what the women saw, no one else at the tomb would have seen. This term for a "vision" appears only four times in the NT (Luke 1:22; Acts 26:19; 2 Cor. 12:1). [*optasia*]

24:24 Did not see (*ouk eidon*). Their report ends on an uncertain note (NLT omits this point). Their desire to see him means that they would not be affirming what had taken place until evidence that Jesus was alive was provided by a demonstration of his presence. [*horaō eidon*]

24:25 Slow (*bradeis*). Their hesitation to believe earns the two disciples a rebuke from Jesus. He calls them "slow of heart" (or dull of heart) to believe all the prophets have spoken (RSV, NET, NIV, NASB; NLT has "you find it so hard to believe," giving the force of the figure; BAGD, 147; BDAG, 183). What has taken place is a realization of things predicted in the Scriptures. [*bradys*]

24:26 Glory (*doxan*). Jesus declares that both

his suffering and his entry into glory, when Jesus was exalted and welcomed by God himself, were always a part of the plan noted for the Christ. Luke uses one of his favorite terms (*dei*) to point to the necessity of what has taken place. This "must" be. [*doxa*]

24:27 Interpreted (*diermēneusen*). This is the Gospel's only use of this verb. Jesus explains the whole of Scripture in light of this plan ("interpreted," RSV, NET; "explained," NASB, NIV; "quoted passages," NLT—is a little too vague as it lacks the note of explanation intended here). Many of the texts used within Luke–Acts to explain Jesus' person and work from the OT may have been revealed at this time, especially texts used for the first time in Acts. [*diermēneuō*]

24:31 Vanished (*aphantos*). This term is part of an idiom that literally reads "he became invisible from them" ("Vanished," RSV, NET; NASB; "disappeared," NIV, NLT; BAGD, 124; BDAG, 155). This "becoming invisible" means he vanished. It is this element that suggests that Jesus' existence after the resurrection has taken on new qualities he did not have in this life. [*aphantos*]

24:32 Burn (*kaiomenē*). This term normally refers to lighting a lamp, which gives off a burning light. This is the only use of this term with a figurative meaning in the NT ("burn," NET, RSV; "burning," NASB, NIV; "feel strangely warm," NLT). To speak of hearts burning is to speak of being moved by something. [*kaiō*]

24:37 Spirit (*pneuma*). The disciples were not expecting to see Jesus, even after he had appeared to many. So when he did appear, they were surprised and thought that it was some type of spirit ("spirit," NASB, RSV, NET; "ghost," NIV NLT). [*pneuma*]

24:38 Troubled (*tetaragmenoi*). This term describes someone who is disturbed or unsettled by something ("troubled," RSV, NASB; "frightened," NET, NIV; "terribly frightened," NLT; BAGD, 805; BDAG, 990, 2). The appearance was troubling to the disciples and their heart response was such that they just could not initially accept that this was the risen Jesus. The frankness with which these accounts portray the disciples' slowness to accept the resurrection speaks to their veracity. Even after some discussion, their reaction is mixed as they have joy, but still do not believe (24:41). Only when he takes a meal of baked fish do they accept the fact that a risen Jesus is speaking (24:42). [*tarassō*]

24:39 Flesh and bones (*sarka kai ostea*). Jesus' point is that he still has the structure of body he had when he was alive, even though he is raised and its characteristics are different than when he was alive ("flesh and bones," NASB, RSV, NIV, NET; "bodies," NLT). Jesus' point is that the marks of crucifixion show he is not a mere spirit. This is Luke's only use of the term for bones. [*sarx, osteon*]

24:44 Must (*dei*). As in Luke 24:7, the carrying out of the divine plan is again underscored with this term. These things "must" take place. Now the reference point is not an utterance of Jesus, but the Scripture itself, referred to as "Moses, the prophets, and the Psalms," a designation that has shown up in the Dead Sea Scrolls as a reference to Scripture (epilogue to 4QMMT, line 10). [*dei*]

24:46 To suffer (*pathein*). This is the first of three infinitives in vv. 46-47 that summarize the plan of God as it pertains to Jesus' work. First, there is the suffering, which Jesus has constantly set before the disciples as the way he would go (Luke 9:22; 17:25; 22:15; 24:26). Acts will pick up this theme (Acts 1:3; 3:18; 17:3). [*paschō*]

Rise (*anastēnai*). The second element of the plan involved God's raising Jesus from the dead. The passive form of the infinitive suggests that God raised Jesus. The Father's work of power is an act of vindication on behalf of Jesus. This hope is defended from Scripture in Acts 2:25-31 and 13:32-35. [*anistēmi*]

24:47 Will be preached (*kērychthēnai*). The preaching of God's plan to the nations with a call to repentance for the forgiveness of sins is also something that comes from the scriptural hope. Here the activity of what will become the early church is seen to fall within the plan. Of course, the appeal to this preaching as coming in Jesus' name is a theme Acts will pick up (Acts 2:38; 3:6, 16; 4:7, 10, 12; 5:28; 9:14-16; 22:16; 26:9). Here is one of the themes that links Luke to Acts as a single narrative. [*kēryssō*]

24:48 Witnesses (*martyres*). Here is a term that will also become important in Acts (Acts 1:8, 22: 2:32; 3:15; 5:32; 10:39, 41; 13:31, 22:15, 20; 26:16). Those who have seen the Lord and his work can now testify to him as witnesses of what God has done. [*martys*]

24:49 Promise (*epangelian*). The reference to the Father's "promise" (RSV, NASB) looks back to the promised Spirit that John the Baptist first mentioned in Luke 3:15-17 and that Jesus will note in Acts 1:4-5 ("has promised," NET, NIV; "promised," NLT). In the verse the term is a noun and looks to a specific promise from God. The Spirit is the enablement for witness that is also grounded in God's power. It includes his promise to wash and indwell them, as noted in Jeremiah 31:31-33 and Ezek. 36:23-27. [*epangelia*]

Power (*dynamin*). What Jesus will send to them is "power from on high," a reference to the Spirit which invokes New Covenant overtones (see John 6:45 and his upper room dis-

course about the Paraclete). It is power and enablement that the Spirit supplies (Acts 1:5, 8; 2:17-21, 30-36). When the Spirit comes in Acts 2, the disciples are enabled to begin their witness. Thus, this remark ties back to the mission mentioned in 24:47 of preaching to the nations. [*dynamis*]

24:51 Was taken up (*anephereto*). The language says Jesus "was taken up" (NET, NIV, NLT; "was carried up," RSV, NASB; BAGD, 63, 1; BDAG, 75, 1). This is the only place where it refers to being taken up into heaven. The fact that Jesus blesses them here makes this text one of the few places where Jesus functions like a priest in Luke. [*anapherō*]

24:52 Joy (*charas*). This mood also matches the mood of joy that started the Gospel in Luke 1–2 and that runs throughout Luke (Luke 1:14; 2:10; 8:13; 10:17; 15:7, 10; 24:41). They were thrilled about what God was doing and that they had the honor to share in it. [*chara*]

24:53 Temple (*hierō*). The Gospel story in Luke ends where it started—in the temple, in Jerusalem. The disciples obediently and joyously await the Spirit, who will come in Acts 2. That book tells the rest of Luke's story about Jesus' work (Acts 1:1). [*hieron*]

JOHN

W. Hall Harris

1:1 In the beginning (*archē*). The Greek reader of John's Gospel might assume this term referred to a basic concept in Greek philosophy. In Aristotle's terminology the question was, "What is the 'beginning' (same Greek word as here) and what is the origin of the things that are made?" (cf. BAGD 112, "the first cause"). But for John, the words are not primarily an allusion to Greek philosophy; but a conscious allusion to the opening of Gen. 1:1, "In the beginning God created the heavens and the earth." Opening his Gospel this way the evangelist signals that Jesus is about to embark on a new creation. [*archē*]

The Word (*logos*). Before the creation, the "Word" already existed. This is John's term for the preincarnate Christ; after John 1:14 the Word is identified as Jesus of Nazareth (LN 33.100; TDNT 4:129). Although Philo used the term *logos* over 1,400 times in his extant writings, it is unlikely that John's use is connected to, or depends on, Philo's. Even in John's Gospel the term is used after 1:14 with a variety of meanings. But John's theology consistently drives toward the conclusion that Jesus, the incarnate Word, is just as much God as God the Father. The construction in John 1:1c does not equate the Word with the person of God the Father; rather it equates the essence of the Word with that of God: "what God was, the Word was" (REB). [*logos*]

1:2 With God (*pros*). The preposition *pros* often implies not just proximity or direction, but interrelationships (LN 89.112). Here it can have the meaning "in company with" (BDAG 875). [*pros*]

1:3 All things were created (*egeneto*). The Greek verb *ginomai* means "to come into existence" here (BDAG 197). In connection with the phrase "in the beginning" in v. 1 this alludes to the universe's creation (cf. Gen. 1:1). [*ginomai*]

1:4 Life (*zōē*). This is a very important concept in the fourth Gospel. John uses this word 37 times, 17 of which occur in combination with *aiōnios* ("eternal"). In all the uses outside the prologue (1:1-18) it is clear from context that "eternal life" is meant. The two uses here in 1:4, if they do not refer to "eternal life" as well, would be the only exceptions. See also the discussion of "eternal life" at 17:2. [*zōē*]

The light (*phōs*). Light/darkness imagery is a favorite motif of John. Prior to the discovery of the Dead Sea Scrolls it was sometimes suggested that John was indebted to second-century Gnosticism for the contrast between light and darkness (and thus that John's Gospel was not written until mid-second century A.D.). After the discovery of the *War Scroll* (1QM) from Qumran, however, it became

261

apparent that light/darkness imagery was prevalent among separatist Jewish sectarian groups like those at Qumran in the second century B.C. So the concept has roots in ancient Josephus expression as well. [*phōs*]

1:5 The <u>darkness</u> (*skotia*). "Darkness" in John's Gospel does not usually refer to people or a group of people, but to the evil environment in which people find themselves (3:19; 8:12; 12:35). For John, darkness is not something that seeks to "understand" the light, but represents the forces of evil, which seek to "overcome" it. It includes everything that is at enmity with God, whether earthly or demonic (BDAG 932). [*skotia*]

Has not <u>overcome</u> (*katelaben*). The verb is not easy to translate. Many English versions see the term, which can mean "to seize" or "to grasp" to refer figuratively to "grasping with the mind," and translate something like "has not understood" (NIV) or "did not comprehend" (NASB). Others focus on the conflict between light and darkness and translate "has not overcome" (RSV). The term here probably carries a deliberate double meaning for the evangelist, since "darkness" is not normally used in John in reference to people, yet people are introduced in the following verses. This double meaning is hard to convey in an English translation (but cf. NET— "the darkness has not mastered it"—the English verb "to master" is used in both sorts of contexts, as "he mastered his lesson/his opponent"). [*katalambanō*]

1:6 Sent (*apestalmenos*). The Greek term *apostellō* means "to send." In John's usage the term frequently refers to Jesus himself as "sent" by God (although in John 1:6 the referent is John the Baptist). It carries the implication of "sent with full authority" and is related to the noun *apostolos* ("apostle"). When Jesus uses the term to refer to himself in dialogue with both the Jewish religious leaders and with his own disciples, it denotes the full authority of God behind what he says and does (TDNT 1:404). He speaks for God, representing the God who "sent" him. On the other hand, when Jesus speaks of God the Father (rather than himself), he refers to "the One who sent me" (*ho pempsas me*) using a different Greek verb, *pempō*. (This formula is used exclusively by Jesus except for one instance by John the Baptist, 1:33). The difference in usage between the two verbs *apostellō* and *pempō* is important. In general, when Jesus wants to ground his authority in God who sent him and who is therefore responsible for his words and deeds and who guarantees they are true, *apostellō* is used. When Jesus wants to affirm that God the Father participates in his work (through sending him into the world), *pempō* is used. By extension, *apostellō* is used twice of the disciples (4:38; 17:18) who are sent out with Jesus' full authority behind them. [*apostellō* + *pempō*]

1:7 As a <u>witness</u> (*martyrian*). "Witness" (NASB, NIV) or "testimony" (RSV) is also one of the major themes of John's Gospel. The verb *martyreō* occurs 33 times in the fourth Gospel (compared to once in Matthew, once in Luke, and none in Mark) and the noun *martyria* 14 times (none in Matthew, once in Luke, three times in Mark). It refers primarily to confirmation or attestation based on personal knowledge or belief (BDAG 618), much as we would think of a "witness" in a court of law. This witness provides information about a person or an event concerning which the speaker has direct knowledge (LN 33.262). [*martyria*]

To <u>testify</u> (*martyrēsē*). The verb is similar in meaning to the corresponding noun (*marturia*). The relationship can be seen in the pairs of English words "a witness" and "to bear witness" or "testimony" and "to testify." [*martyreō*]

1:9 The world (*kosmon*). The "world," mentioned here for the first time, is an important Johannine concept. Generally, in John, the term does not refer to the totality of creation (the universe) although there are exceptions at 11:9; 17:5, 24; 21:25. Instead, it refers to the world of human beings and their affairs. Even in the following verse "the world" created through the *Logos* is capable of knowing (or not knowing) its Creator. Sometimes in John the term is further qualified as "this world" (8:23; 9:39; 11:9; 12:25, 31; 13:1; 16:11; 18:36) in contrast to the heavenly world, the world above (cf. 8:23; 18:36). In rabbinic thought "the present world" was contrasted with "the world to come." For John, "this world" is contrasted to a world other than this one, already existing—"this world" is the lower world, corresponding to which there is a "world above" (cf. 8:23; 18:36). Jesus appears in John's Gospel not only as the Messiah by whom an eschatological future is anticipated (as in the Synoptic Gospels), but also as an envoy from the heavenly world to this world (6:14; 9:39; 11:27; 16:28). This idea connects to the descent/ascent motif, which appears repeatedly in the fourth Gospel (cf. 1:51). The descent is mentioned in 3:13, the lowest point of which is 12:37 where Jesus is rejected largely by his own people. It is followed by the ascent, which is comprised of both crucifixion (cf. 12:32) and resurrection/exaltation (20:17). The "world" can thus also refer specifically to those people and powers opposed to and hostile toward Jesus (and by extension, rejecting his disciples as well). [*kosmos*]

1:10 Did not know (*egnō*). Here the Greek verb means "to recognize someone for who they claim to be" (BAGD 161). A large part of the irony in John's Gospel results from the fact that "the true light" (i.e., the Word), through whom the world was created, went unrecognized when he came into the world. [*ginōskō*]

1:11 What was his own (*idia*). This expression is neuter gender in Greek ("his own [things]") in contrast with the following phrase, "his own people." Here it can refer to "home" (RSV) or "possessions" (either home—"Israel" or possessions—"messianic office"; BDAG 467; cf. "What was his own," NRSV). [*idios*]

His own people (*hoi idioi*). In the Gospel of John this expression refers to the Jewish people, who were "his (i.e., Jesus') own people." They should have received him, but they did not. This failure to recognize Jesus is part of the irony prevalent in John's Gospel. [*idios*]

Did not receive (*parelabon*). The term looks not at mere recognition in a cognitive sense, but includes the idea of acceptance and welcome (LN 34.53). It implies agreement or approval (BDAG 768). [*paralambanō*]

1:12 Authority (*exousian*). Here the word means "power" in the sense "to exercise the ability or capability to do something" (BAGD 278). Those who believe in Jesus are given the "power" (so RSV, NRSV) to become God's children. The power in this context derives from Jesus himself. [*exousia*]

Children of God (*tekna*). This is John's term for believers as God's "children" (cf. 11:52; also 1 John 3:1, 2, 10; 5:2). It represents a relationship that results from being born "from above" (3:3; cf. also 1 John 2:29; 3:9), that is, born spiritually. John consistently distinguishes between believers as "children" (*teknia*) and Jesus himself as God's "son" (*huios*) in a unique sense. John never uses *huios* of believers, as Paul does (TDNT 5:653). [*teknon*]

To those who believe in (*pisteuousin*). The verb *pisteuō* occurs 98 times in John's Gospel (compared to 11 times in Matthew, 14 times in Mark, and nine times in Luke). The corresponding noun form *pistis* is never used at all in John; some have suggested this was because the noun was in use in some pre-gnostic sects and this caused the evangelist to avoid using it. The verb is used in four major ways in the Gospel of John: (1) of believing facts, reports, etc., 12 times; (2) of believing people (or the Scriptures), 19 times; (3) of believing "in" Christ, 36 times; (4) used absolutely without any person or object specified, 30 times. This leaves one instance, 2:24, where Jesus refused to "entrust" himself to certain individuals. Of these categories, the most significant is the third, where the verb is used with the preposition *eis* and the accusative case. This construction refers to trust in Christ, as opposed to mere intellectual assent, and approaches the Pauline formula "in Christ" (*en Christō*). Some interpreters have held that John used this formula when he wanted to indicate genuine faith as opposed to false profession (the instances where the verb *pisteuō* is used with the simple dative). However, it is more likely that John's distinction lies not with genuine faith versus mere false profession, but with the content of what is believed about Jesus, as indicated by the context (e.g., "Son of God," "king of Israel" in 1:49; "Son of Man" in 9:35; "the Christ, the Son of God who comes into the world" in 11:27). A number of people throughout the fourth Gospel apparently "believed" in Jesus as the Messiah (2:23; 8:31) while defining "Messiah" according to their own presuppositions (political deliverer, military leader, king; cf. 6:15). [*pisteuō*]

1:13 Born (*egennēthēsan*). The image of physical birth is used here to describe the origin of the "children of God." The following clauses explain that this birth is not physical but spiritual, the result of a supernatural process. The metaphor is bold because the Greek verb *gennaō* is commonly used of the male parent's action in the reproductive process (BAGD 155); in the classical literature it is used only rarely of the mother bearing a child (LS 162). Reference to the male role is

further implied by inclusion of the preposition *ek* ("from, of"), cf. BDAG 193. So God initiates the birth. [*gennaō*]

Not of blood (*haimatōn*). The word "blood" is plural in the Greek text, and this has been seen as a problem by many interpreters. At least some sources in antiquity imply that blood was thought of as being important in the development of the fetus during its time in the womb (cf. Wis. 7:1, "in the womb of a mother I was molded into flesh, within the period of ten months, compacted with blood, from the seed of a man and the pleasure of marriage"). Here in John 1:13 the plural term may imply the action of both parents. It may also refer (in non-technical terms) to the "genetic" contribution of both parents, and so be equivalent to "human descent" (BAGD 22). [*haima*]

1:14 Flesh (*sarx*). This term does not carry with it overtones of sinfulness here (as it often does in Paul's writings). For John *sarx* refers to the physical nature in its weakness and humility. The evangelist's statement that "the Word became flesh" constitutes the most concise formulation of the incarnation in the NT. John 1:1 makes it clear that the Word was fully God, but 1:14 makes it clear that the Word was also fully human (cf. CEV "became a human being"; NLT "Became human"). A docetic interpretation (i.e., Jesus only appeared to be human) is completely ruled out here. [*sarx*]

Lived (*eskēnōsen*). The word translated "lived" (literally, "took up residence," BDAG 929) alludes to the OT tabernacle, where the *Shekinah*, the visible glory of God's presence, stayed (cf. Exod. 33:7-10). This divine glory can now be seen in Jesus. See also John 2:19-21. [*skēnoō*]

Glory (*doxan*). This is another significant term in John's Gospel. One might assume the term means "radiance" or "splendor," one of its basic meanings, but this does not exhaust the term's meaning in the fourth Gospel (TDNT 2:249). For John, Jesus' "glory" is connected to his exaltation achieved through the cross (cf. 12:23-24). Thus when Jesus undergoes his passion, he can say, "God is glorified in him" (13:31). Likewise Jesus can repeatedly pray for his "glorification" (12:28; 13:31-32; 17:1, 4-5). The statement here (1:14) is not a general one, but is made by the evangelist in the first person (cf. the testimony in 21:24). Ultimately Jesus' "glory" can be seen only through faith ("glory" is linked to belief in him in 2:11; cf. also 11:40). [*doxa*]

The one and only (*monogenous*). The Greek term may also be translated "the unique one." Although older English versions translated the term as "only begotten" (KJV, NASB), such a rendering is misleading because it appears to express a metaphysical relationship. In Greek the word could be used of an only child, a son (Luke 7:12; 9:38) or a daughter (Luke 8:42). The term was also used to describe something unique (the only one of its kind) such as the mythological Phoenix bird (1 Clement 25:2). It was used of Isaac (Heb. 11:17 and also Josephus, *Ant.* 1.13.1 [1.222]) who was not Abraham's only son but was one of a kind because he was the child of promise. In this sense the word is reserved for Jesus alone in John's writings. Although for John all Christians are "children of God" (*tekna theou*), Jesus is God's Son in a unique, one-of-a-kind sense ("the one and only," NIV, NET). The word always means this in John (1:14, 18; 3:16, 18). The unique character of the relationship between the Father and the Son is one of the important, repeated themes of John's Gospel. [*monogenēs*]

Truth (*alētheias*). The relevant OT background is Exod. 34:6, because vv. 17-18 compares the incarnation of the Word with God's revelation to Moses on Mount Sinai. Vocabulary differences between the Greek version of Exod. 34:6 and John's expression here indicate, however, that John's usage should

determine the meaning of the terms involved. Among other things, this explains why attempts to equate the Greek word for "truth" (*alētheia*) with the OT concept of "faithfulness" (*'emet*) do not work in the fourth Gospel. The point of contact between John 1:14 and Exod. 34:6 is God's revelation of himself to Moses in the giving of the law at Sinai, and in the incarnation of the Word in John. Contrary to Greek philosophical ideas, "truth" in John is personal, not intellectual, and is acquired through God's revelation. It is not abstract, but has been individually revealed in history. For John, Jesus is the final revelation of God (1:18), so it should come as no surprise that Jesus is also described as "truth" itself (14:6). It is highly ironic when Pilate, at Jesus' trial, asks (perhaps sarcastically) "What is truth?" because by this time the reader of the fourth Gospel will know that "truth" is personal, relational, and incarnate, that is, Jesus himself. When Pilate asks the question, "truth" in person, incarnate, is standing there before him. Likewise, God is also "true" (3:33) and the source of "truth" (8:40). The Holy Spirit is also referred to as the "Spirit of truth" (15:26) in a context where the Spirit guides the disciples into the "truth" (16:13). Jesus' disciples are expected to "practice the truth" (3:21), which means to "live it out," and to worship the Father "in spirit and in truth" (4:23-24). [*alētheia*]

1:15 He was before me (*prōtos*). Literally, "he was first of me." Most commentators agree this phrase should be understood in a temporal sense, "he existed before me." However, the Word was not just "prior" to John the Baptist, but was "first" in an absolute sense (cf. 1:1). In the fourth Gospel, John the Baptist always shows remarkable deference to Jesus. [*prōtos*]

1:16 From his fullness (*plērōmatos*). The Greek noun *plērōma* echoes the adjective *plērēs* ("full") in v. 14. Although the noun is a favorite word of Paul it occurs only here in John's Gospel. In context it refers to the incarnate Word, in whom the "fullness" of God's "grace" is present, and who then supplies an accumulation of grace to believers (TDNT 6:302). [*plērōma*]

Grace upon grace (*charin . . . charitos*). The meaning of this phrase is difficult. It could be (1) love (= grace) under the new covenant in place of love (= grace) under the Sinai covenant, thus, replacement; (2) grace corresponding to grace, thus correspondence; (3) grace "on top of" grace, thus accumulation. The most commonly held view is (3) in one sense or another. Accumulation is probably the idea. The background for the statement may be Exod. 33:13, "If I have found grace in your sight, let me know your ways, that I may know you, so that I may find grace in your sight." The Greek OT of Exod. 33 uses the word *charis* for "grace," the same term used by John. This sense is also supported by a usage in Philo, *Posterity* 43 (145). [*charis*]

1:17 The law (*nomos*). This refers to the Mosaic Law, the old covenant given at Sinai. In Jewish sources the Law was regarded as God's gift (Josephus, *Ant.* 3.8.10 [3.223]; *Pirqe Abot* 1.1; *Sifre Deut.* 31:4 §305). [*nomos*]

Truth (*alētheia*). "Grace" and "truth" are related, as in 1:14. [*alētheia*]

1:18 The only one (*monogenēs*). See the discussion in 1:14. [*monogenēs*]

Has made him known (*exēgēsato*). The verb means "to explain, to reveal" or even "to set forth in great detail, expound" (BDAG 349). This is the Greek term from which the English word "exegesis" (an explanation or interpretation of a text) is derived. Although some have argued against the meaning "explain" here based on the absence of a direct object in the Greek text (TDNT 2:908), direct objects were frequently omitted in

Koine Greek when clear from the context. John's point here is that Jesus, the Word become incarnate (1:14), has fully "explained" (or revealed) what God is like (Cf. NASB). As Jesus said to Philip in John 14:9, "The one who has seen me has seen the Father." [*exēgeomai*]

1:19 Testimony (*martyria*). John the Baptist's "testimony" about Jesus appears to take place over three days: day one, John's testimony about his own role is largely negative (1:19-28); day two, John gives positive testimony about who Jesus is (1:29-34); day three, John sends his own disciples to follow Jesus (1:35-40). See the discussion at 1:7. [*martyria*]

The Jews (*Ioudaioi*). In the Gospel of John the term may refer to (1) the entire Jewish people; (2) the residents of Jerusalem and the surrounding territory; (3) the Jewish religious leaders in Jerusalem; or (4) all those who were hostile to Jesus. Here the referent is the Jewish leaders in Jerusalem. Some recent translations have attempted to give a more nuanced rendering in context (cf. "the leaders in Jerusalem" [CEV]; "the Jewish authorities in Jerusalem" [TEV]; "the Jewish leaders" [NLT, NET]). Cf. TDNT 3:377. [*Ioudaios*]

1:20 Confessed (*hōmologēsin*). The verb means "to confess or acknowledge something," normally in a public setting (BDAG 708). It is particularly important in John's Gospel in contexts relating to Jesus' identity as Messiah (cf. 9:22). The opposite of this term is used in the next clause, "deny" (*ērnēsato*). [*homologeō + arneomai*]

The Christ (*Christos*). The Greek word was originally an adjective ("anointed"), developing in the Greek OT (LXX) into a substantive ("an anointed one"), and then into a technical generic term ("the anointed one"). During the intertestamental period it developed still further into a technical term referring to the hoped-for anointed one, a specific individual. However, there was no uniform all-encom-

passing Jewish expectation of a single eschatological figure in the first century A.D. A
majority of the Jewish people expected the
Messiah. But some pseudepigraphical books
describe God's intervention without mentioning an anointed Davidic king (in parts of *1
Enoch*, for example, the figure of the Son of
Man, not the Messiah, embodies the expectations of the author). Jewish Essenes at
Qumran seem to have expected three figures:
a prophet, a priestly Messiah, and a royal
Messiah. Since John the Baptist was operating
in an area not too far from the Essene center at
Qumran on the Dead Sea, it is not surprising
the authorities in Jerusalem were curious as to
who he was. [*Christos*]

1:21 Elijah (*Ēlias*). In Mal. 4:5 it is said that
Elijah would be the precursor of the Messiah.
John the Baptist's denial here, however,
seems at odds with Jesus' own statements in
Matt. 11:14 (cf. Mark 9:13, Matt. 17:12) that
John the Baptist *was* Elijah. According to
Gregory the Great, John was not Elijah, but
exercised toward Jesus the *function* of Elijah
by preparing his way. But that explanation
avoids the difficulty, since in John's Gospel
the question from the Jewish authorities concerns precisely his function. Clearly John was
not Elijah personally (reincarnated), so Bible
students have to wrestle with what Jesus
intended by the identification. Mark 6:14-16
and 8:28 indicate both the people and Herod
distinguished between John the Baptist and
Elijah, probably reflecting the Baptist's own
perspective on the matter. [*Ēlias*]

The prophet (*prophētēs*). This is a reference to the "prophet like Moses" of Deut.
18:15, by this time an eschatological figure in
popular belief. Acts 3:22 identifies Jesus as
this prophet. [*prophētēs*]

1:23 Make straight (*euthynate*). This verb, part
of a quotation from Isa. 40:3, means "to make
straight" or "to cause something to be in a

straight or direct line" (BDAG 406). Here it
constitutes a call to prepare through repentance for the Lord's arrival on the scene, and
is thus to be taken figuratively (cf. *T. Sim.* 5:2).
The term refers in some classical contexts to
steering a ship on a straight course (LN 54.21;
cf. Jas 3:4). [*euthynō*]

1:24 Had been sent (*apestalmenoi*). See 1:6.
Here the term describes the delegation of
priests and Levites "sent" by the Jewish religious leaders in Jerusalem (v. 19) to interview
John the Baptist and determine who he was.
The verb *apostellō* implies that these representatives carried the full authority of the
Jewish authorities (specified as "Pharisees"
here) who sent them. [*apostellō*]

From the Pharisees (*Pharisaiōn*). Pharisees
were members of one of the key, influential
religious and political parties of Judaism of
Jesus' time. There were many more Pharisees
than Sadducees; according to Josephus, there
were more than 6,000 Pharisees at about this
time (*Ant.* 17.2.4 [17.42]), although the
Sadducees had the key posts of power.
Pharisees disagreed with Sadducees on certain doctrines and patterns of behavior. The
Pharisees were strict and zealous adherents
to the Mosaic Law of the OT and to numerous
additional traditions such as angels and bodily resurrection (TDNT 9:11-46; LN 11.49).
[*Pharisaios*]

1:25 Baptizing (*baptizeis*). This verb is used
by Josephus (*J. W.* 3.8.5 [3.368]) to refer to the
"sinking" of a ship. The fourth Gospel does
not present John's baptism as one for repentance as the Synoptic Gospels do (cf. Matt.
3:11; Luke 3:3; Mark 1:4). Instead, the sole
emphasis in John's Gospel is on the identification of Jesus as the Messiah; the Baptist
says "in order that he might be revealed to
Israel, I came baptizing with water" (v. 31).
[*baptizō*]

1:26 With water (*hydati*). John mentions, like Matthew and Luke, that John the Baptist baptized "with water." However, unlike the synoptic accounts, John does not mention that the "one who comes after" him (v. 27) will baptize with the Holy Spirit (Matt. 3:11; Mark 1:8; Luke 3:16) and with fire (Matt. 3:11; Luke 3:16). [*hydōr*]

Whom you do not know (*oidate*; also vv. 31, 33.) The sense here is "know about" (BAGD 555) or "recognize" (NET), much the same as 1:10, although the Greek verb was *ginōskō* there. This interchange of similar terms is typical for John and is done for stylistic reasons. [*oida*]

1:27 Worthy (*axios*). John the Baptist saw himself as not "worthy" even to untie the sandal strap of the Messiah. Originally the term referred to "balancing the beam of the scales," and therefore "equivalent" or "of equal worth" (TDNT 1:379). In the fourth Gospel John the Baptist consistently deferred to Jesus as the Messiah. [*axios*]

The strap of his sandal (*himanta*). In the first century Greek and Jewish cultures people usually went around barefoot or else wore sandals. The term *himantos* refers to the leather "strap" (NET) or "thong" (NASB, NRSV) used to bind a sandal to the foot (cf. LN 6.20). Unbinding the sandals was considered one of the least worthy tasks of a slave in first-century Jewish culture (TDNT 5:310; cf. Mark 1:7; Luke 3:16; Acts 13:25), and John the Baptist did not consider himself "worthy" to do even that for Jesus, despite the fact that John himself was a prophet. [*himas*]

1:28 Bethany (*Bēthania*). This refers to a place on the east side of the Jordan River where John the Baptist was said to be baptizing (BDAG 174). The general region would have been Perea, a territory controlled by Herod Antipas. It is not to be confused with the village near Jerusalem, which was the home of Mary, Martha, and Lazarus (cf. 11:1, 18; 12:1). [*Bēthania*]

1:29 The Lamb of God (*amnos*). The background to the imagery of Jesus as the "Lamb of God" is highly debated. (1) In Jewish apocalyptic literature there is the figure of a conquering Lamb who will destroy evil in the world (*T. Jos.* 19:8; *1 Enoch* 90:38), and this imagery is repeated in Rev. 7:17 and 17:14. This fits well with John the Baptist's preaching in the Synoptic Gospels (Matt. 3:12; Luke 3:17). But the words used for "lamb" in John's Gospel and Revelation are different: John 1:29 uses *amnos* while Rev. 7:17 and 17:14 use *arnion*. Furthermore the descriptive phrase "who takes away the sin of the world" does not really fit an apocalyptic picture, but seems to fit better with the concepts of sacrifice and redemption. (2) Others have seen the lamb imagery here as drawn from the "Suffering Servant" (Isa. 53:7): "Like a lamb that is led to the slaughter, and like a sheep that is silent before its shearers, he did not open his mouth." This text is applied to Jesus in Acts 8:32, and the second section of Isaiah (chapters 40-55), where all the "servant songs" occur, is associated in the NT with John the Baptist (cf. John 1:23 and Isa. 40:3). Furthermore, Jesus is related to the "suffering servant" elsewhere in the fourth Gospel (12:38, cf. Isa. 53:1). Yet there are also differences: the Lamb in John 1:29 is said to "take away" the sin of the world, while the suffering servant in Isa. 53:11 "bears" or "carries" the sins of many. Early Christians would probably not have drawn a sharp distinction, however, as to whether Jesus by his death took away sin or took it on himself. (3) Finally, others have seen the "Lamb of God" here as an allusion to the Passover lamb. Unlike the mention of the lamb in the "servant songs" in Isaiah, where the lamb is merely an isolated, incidental element, the Passover lamb was a real lamb. Passover symbolism is present in the Gospel of John, especially in relation to Jesus' death. Jesus' condemnation occurs at noon on the day before the Passover (19:14), at the very time the priests were beginning to slaughter the Passover lambs in the temple. While he was on the cross, "hyssop" was used to give Jesus a sponge of wine (19:29), and hyssop was also used to smear the blood of the Passover lamb on the doorposts in Exod. 12:22. Furthermore, John 19:36 sees a fulfillment of Scripture in that none of Jesus' bones were broken, and according to Exod. 12:46 no bone of the Passover lamb was to be broken. Some have insisted that the Passover lamb was not a sacrifice *per se*. But by Jesus' time the sacrificial context had probably begun to merge with the symbol of deliverance, which the Passover lamb represented (cf. 1 Cor. 5:7). The slaughtering of the Passover lambs in the temple court probably furthered this. It is true that the Greek OT uses a different Greek word (*probaton*) for the Passover lamb, but the difference in terminology is not decisive. In conclusion, the imagery of the Passover lamb is probably behind the statement here in John 1:29, although the suffering servant motif may not be completely excluded. [*amnos*]

Takes away (*airōn*). Here the verb means "to take away" or "to remove" (BDAG 29). The same verb occurs in the Greek OT (1 Sam. 15:25; 25:28) with the meaning of pardoning sin or removing guilt. Here Christ "carries sin away," a thought not far removed from "bearing it on himself." The lamb imagery here also contributes to the picture of atonement drawn from the Jewish sacrificial system. [*airō*]

Sin (*hamartian*). In two passages in 1 John there is a precise definition of "sin" that also fits the concept in the fourth Gospel. First John 3:4 states that "the one who practices sin also practices lawlessness, and sin is lawlessness." First John 5:17 affirms that "all unrighteousness is sin." Sin for John contradicts what is right (i.e., it is unrighteousness) and violates God's will, so that it is lawlessness. It

comes from opposition to God (and by extension, from opposition to Jesus and his teaching in the fourth Gospel). It is expressed as sins against one's neighbor or brother (cf. 1 John 3:12, where Cain, who murdered his brother Abel, is the prototype). For John, sin involves guilt (9:41) and thus causes separation from God (9:31). The person who refuses to acknowledge Jesus' identity (summed up in the expression "I am") remains in his sin and dies in his sin (8:24). In 1 John 3:5 the plural of "sins" is used, which focuses more on sinful acts, while the singular "sin" here looks more at a sinful condition. [*hamartia*]

World (*kosmos*). Here the "world" is the world of people, that is, "humanity" or the human race. First John 2:2 has a similar statement about the extent of atonement. See the discussion at 1:9. [*kosmos*]

1:30 Was before me (*prōtos*). See 1:15. [*prōtos*]

1:31 Revealed (*phanerōthē*). In the fourth Gospel the purpose of John the Baptist's baptizing consisted of revealing to Israel the one who was to come after him, the Messiah. See 1:25. [*phaneroō*]

1:32 Descending (*katabainon*; also v. 33). The verb means "to come down" or "descend" (BAGD 408). Geographically it is used of leaving Jerusalem (because it was thought of as the highest point in the land) or of going "down" to the lower elevations around the Sea of Galilee, the Jordan Valley, and the Dead Sea. The major uses of the term refer to the descent of the Spirit on Jesus at his baptism (here and v. 33), to the ascent and descent of angels on the Son of Man (1:51), and to the descent from heaven of the Son of Man himself (3:13; 6:33). Jesus also calls himself the "bread" that "came down" from heaven (6:41). [*katabainō*]

Remained (*emeinen*). (also v. 33) The Greek verb *menō* is a favorite Johannine word, used 40 times in the Gospel of John and 27 times in the Johannine Epistles, against 118 times total in the NT. The general significance of the verb *menō* for John is to express the permanent nature of the relationship between the Father and the Son, and between the Son and the believer ("an inward, enduring personal communion," BAGD 504). As such the term in John is similar to the Pauline concept of being "in Christ" (*en Christō*; cf. TDNT 4:576). Here the use of the word implies that Jesus permanently possesses the Holy Spirit, unlike OT kings and judges on whom the Spirit came temporarily for enablement to accomplish specific actions. Because the Spirit "remains" on Jesus, he will dispense the Spirit to others. Note also the allusion to Isa. 42:1, "Behold my Servant . . . my Chosen One in whom my soul delights. I have put my Spirit upon him." [*menō*]

1:33 The one who <u>sent</u> me (*pempsas*). See 1:6. The verb *pempō* usually occurs on the lips of Jesus in the Gospel of John; this is the only exception. Here the speaker is John the Baptist. Consistent with Jesus' usage of this term, the reference points to God's participation in John's baptizing work. [*pempō*]

The one who <u>baptizes</u> (*baptizōn*). Like the Synoptic Gospels, John presents Jesus as the one who would "baptize" people with the Holy Spirit (Matt. 3:11; Mark 1:8; Luke 3:16). See also 1:25. [*baptizō*]

1:34 Have testified (*memartyrēka*). Here the term means "have borne witness" (RSV, NASB). See the discussion at 1:7. [*martyreō*]

The <u>Son</u> of God (*huios*). John's Gospel puts this concept at the very center of its christology. The expression "Son of God" (shortened occasionally to "Son") occurs 29 times. The phrase occurs in the very purpose statement of the fourth Gospel (20:31). The concept "Son of God" in the Gospel of John involves preexistence, beginning with 1:1, 14,

18 and mentioned later in 8:56-58; 17:5, 24. The Son of God is "sent" into the world by the Father (3:17; 10:36; 17:18), and the Son has both come "from" the Father (3:31; 6:33, 38, 41, 42) and is going back to the Father (13:1, 3; 14:28; 16:28; 20:17). As such, the Son reflects the Father's "glory" (1:14; 14:7, 9-11). As Son of God, Jesus exhibits perfect obedience to his Father (4:34; 5:30; 6:38; 7:28; 8:29), shares the "work" of the Father (5:17, 19; 9:4; 10:32, 37), is in relationship with the Father (14:13, 16; 16:15), is loved by the Father (3:35; 5:20; 10:17; 17:23), and in turn loves the Father (14:31). All of this indicates that Jesus as "Son of God" is completely unique (note the use of the term "*monogenēs*" in 1:14, 18; 3:16). This is further indicated by John's restriction of the term *huios* ("son") to Jesus alone; believers are called God's "children" but never his "sons" (as Paul often does). Finally, belief in Jesus as the "Son of God" is what people are called on to do, and their response to him will determine their eternal destiny (3:17-21, 36; 5:24; 11:26-27). [*huios*]

1:36 The <u>Lamb</u> of God (*amnos*). See the discussion at 1:29. [*amnos*]

1:38 Staying (*meneis*; also twice in v. 39). Here the verb *menō* does not have its "typical" Johannine sense (see 1:32), but simply means to remain in the same place over a period of time (LN 85.55). Such usage proves that for John the term has not completely passed over into a "technical term" (all usages the same without regard to context). Each use must be contextually determined. [*menō*]

1:39 About the <u>tenth</u> hour (*dekatē*). There has been some interpretive debate over whether the "tenth hour" was to be reckoned from midnight or from 6 A.M. It was sometimes argued that Roman reckoning started at midnight, making this a reference to 10 A.M. But the evidence for starting at midnight is slim:

only authorities used the reckoning to measure legal time (for contracts, official documents, etc.); otherwise the Romans reckoned from 6 A.M. (Roman sundials are marked VI, not XII, for noon). In the Passover account in the Gospel of John, the "sixth hour" is on the eve of the Passover (19:42), and this can refer only to noon, not 6 A.M. So the time here would be around 4 P.M. It is thus possible that Andrew and the unnamed disciple spent the night in the same house where Jesus was staying. Middle Eastern hospitality would have dictated that they were asked to do so. [*dekatos*]

1:41 He found . . . we have found (*heuriskei . . . heurēkamen*). (Also in vv. 43, 45) The Greek verb can refer to something found through purposeful search or to something found unexpectedly (BDAG 411). Both meanings are illustrated here: Andrew's search for his brother was deliberate, while their discovery of the Messiah appears accidental. By the time Andrew found his brother, he was convinced Jesus was the Messiah. Apparently he learned this during his short stay with Jesus (1:39). [*heuriskō*]

The Messiah (*Messian*). Both the Greek term *Christos* and the Hebrew and Aramaic term transliterated in Greek as *Messias* mean "the anointed one" (LN 53.82). If John was writing primarily to Jews (as some scholars insist), they would have been Hellenistic Jews, since the evangelist consistently translates Aramaic and/or Hebrew terms into Greek (most Jews living outside of Palestine spoke Greek). [*Messias*]

Christ (*Christos*). See the discussion at 1:20. [*Christos*]

1:42 Cephas (*Kēphas*). Only John among the four evangelists gives the Greek transliteration of the Galilean Aramaic form of Simon's new name, *Qepha* (the equivalent Greek form is *Petros*). Both the Aramaic and Greek forms mean "Rock" (LN 93.211). Neither *Petros* in Greek nor *Qepha* in Aramaic is a normal proper name; it is more like a nickname. The change of name from "Simon" to "Cephas" is indicative of the key role he will play. [*Kēphas*]

1:43 He wanted to depart (*exelthein*). The referent is Jesus, although no explanation is given for why he wanted to set out for Galilee at this point. Probably he wanted to attend the wedding feast at Cana (about a two-day trip). [*exerchomai*]

1:44 Bethsaida (*Bēthsaida*). Although the evangelist thought of this town as in Galilee (cf. 12:21), Bethsaida was technically in Gaulanitis, the territory of Philip the Tetrarch, across from Herod's Galilee. It is possible there were two places named Bethsaida, one in Gaulanitis and one in Galilee, but the usage by the evangelist may simply reflect popular imprecision. Locally Bethsaida was considered part of Galilee, even though it was just east of the Jordan River. This territory was heavily Gentile (which may explain why Andrew and Philip, who were from Bethsaida, both have Gentile names). The fishing industry was prominent there. [*Bēthsaida*]

1:45 Nathanael (*Nathanaēl*). Traditionally identified with Bartholomew (although John never describes him as such), he appears here after Philip, just as in all lists of the Twelve except the one in Acts 1:13, Bartholomew follows Philip (BAGD 532). Also, the Aramaic *Bar-tolmai* means "son of Tolmai," the surname, so the man almost certainly had another name. [*Nathanaēl*]

In the law (*nomō*). Technically "the law" referred to the Pentateuch, the first five books of the OT, also known as the five books of Moses. Since "Moses" is mentioned as writing about the Messiah "in the law," that is the meaning here. Although an expression like "the law and the prophets" became a common way of referring to the entire OT, "the prophets" (*hoi prophētai*) are mentioned separately here, referring specifically to the prophetic books of the OT. The messianic prophecy alluded to here could have been Deut. 18:15-18. [*nomos + prophētēs*]

Nazareth (*Nazaret*). Nazareth was relatively small and obscure, located only about four miles from the large city of Sepphoris, which rivaled Tiberias (cf. 6:23) in importance. Both larger cities possessed significant Hellenistic influence. How much this culture influenced Jesus is not clear. [*Nazaret*]

1:46 Good (*agathon*). The term, when used of people, means one meeting a high standard of worth and merit (BDAG 3). [*agathos*]

1:47 Deceit (*dolos*). Jesus was probably making a wordplay on "Israelite" and "deceit," since in the OT Israel (that is, Jacob) was known for his "deceit" (Gen. 27:35; 31:26). [*dolos*]

1:48 Know (*ginōskeis*). On one level Nathanael's question meant "How are you acquainted with me?" (cf. 1:10). But when Jesus replied that he had seen Nathanael "under the fig tree" he was demonstrating supernatural knowledge, since he knew precisely *which* tree Nathanael had been sitting under. [*ginōskō*]

1:49 The Son of God (*huios*). Nathanael's confession here ("You are the Son of God; you are the King of Israel") is best understood as identifying Jesus as the Messiah. It has strong allusions to Ps. 2:6-7, a well-known messianic psalm. What Nathanael's exact understanding was at this point is hard to determine, but "Son of God" was a designation for the Davidic king in the OT, and Nathanael places it in parallel with "King of Israel" here. See discussion of the title "Son of God" at 1:34. [*huios*]

1:50 Believe (*pisteueis*). What Nathanael had presumably just "believed" was that Jesus was the Messiah, since he just used two messianic titles, "Son of God" and "King of Israel." For discussion of *pisteuō* ("believe"), see 1:12. [*pisteuō*]

1:51 Angels . . . ascending . . . descending (*angelous . . . anabainontas . . . katabainontas*). "Angels" as supernatural beings appear often in the Bible as God's messengers, and the presence of the Messiah on earth now marks the beginning of new comings and goings between heaven and earth. The Son of Man attended by angels signifies his union with God (cf. TDNT 1:84). Jesus as the revealer of heavenly things is another important theme of John's Gospel (cf. 3:12-13). Jesus' words here may also be a deliberate allusion to Gen. 28:12 ("Jacob's ladder"), where angels also ascended and descended. Nathanael, the "true" Israelite, would be the beneficiary of this new revelation that Jesus would bring. See discussion of "descending" at 1:32. [*angelos + anabainō + katabainō*]

The Son of Man (*huion . . . anthrōpou*). The title "Son of Man" is used 13 times in John's Gospel. It is associated especially with the themes of crucifixion (3:14; 8:28), revelation (6:27, 53), and eschatological authority (5:27; 9:39). The title as used in the Gospel of John has as its background the Son of Man figure who appears before the "Ancient of Days" in Dan. 7:13-14 and is granted universal ruling authority. Thus, for the evangelist, the emphasis in this title is not at all on Jesus' humanity (as is commonly supposed), but on his heavenly origin and divinely-granted authority to rule. [*huios + anthrōpos*]

2:1 The third day (*tritē*). This is probably a reference to the "third day" after the last recorded events, the call of Philip and Nathanael (1:43-51). [*tritos*]

A wedding (*gamos*). A Jewish wedding in

the first century lasted for seven days, and large numbers of people would be invited. These were joyous occasions, and the food, drink, and festivities could put quite a strain on the host's financial resources. [*gamos*]

Cana (*Kana*). Cana in Galilee was not a well-known place. It is mentioned in the NT only here and in John 4:46 and 21:2. Josephus (*Life* 16 [86]) stated that he once had his quarters there. The probable location is either Khirbet Cana, eight miles north of Nazareth, or Khirbet Kenna, four miles northeast of Nazareth. [*Kana*]

2:2 Invited (*eklēthē*). The Greek verb *kaleō* is used of invitations to weddings elsewhere in the NT (Matt. 22:3; Luke 14:8; Rev. 19:9) and also in secular literature (Diodorus Siculus 4.70.3), as well as indicating invitations to other kinds of social gatherings like sacrificial meals (1 Cor. 10:27, cf. BDAG 503). Since Jesus' mother, Jesus himself, and his disciples were invited, either the bride or groom (or both) were probably either friends or relatives of Jesus' family. The attitude of Mary in approaching Jesus and asking him to do something when the wine ran out also suggests some sort of familial obligations were involved. [*kaleō*]

2:3 The mother of Jesus (*mētēr*). (Also in v. 1) Mary, the mother of Jesus, is never mentioned by name in the Gospel of John. The connection between Mary and the "beloved disciple" at the foot of the cross (19:26-27) may explain this silence, if the "beloved disciple" is John, son of Zebedee, the author of the fourth Gospel. None of his immediate family members are mentioned by name in John's Gospel. [*mētēr*]

2:4 Woman (*gynai*). This was Jesus' normal polite way of addressing women (Matt. 15:28; Luke 13:12; John 4:21; 8:10; 19:26; 20:15). However, it is unusual for a son to address his

mother with this term. The custom in both Hebrew (or Aramaic) and Greek would be for a son to use a qualifying adjective or a title. What significance should be attached to Jesus' usage? It probably indicates that a new relationship now existed between Jesus and his mother once he had set out on his public ministry. He was no longer or primarily only her son but the "Son of Man." This is also suggested by Jesus' use of the same term in John 19:26 from the cross as he gave his mother into the care of the beloved disciple. [*gynē*]

My hour (*hōra*). The Greek word *hōra* (literally, "hour"; cf. NIV, NLT, NET "time") has special significance in John's Gospel (2:4; 4:21, 23; 5:25, 28, 29; 7:30; 8:20; 12:23, 27; 13:1; 16:25; 17:1). It frequently refers to the particular period in Jesus' life when he was to depart from this world and return to the Father (13:1), the "hour" when the Son of Man is glorified (17:1). This is accomplished through his suffering, death, resurrection (and ascension, though this last element is not emphasized by John). John 7:30 and 8:20 imply that Jesus' arrest and death are included in the "hour." John 12:23 and 17:1, refer to the Son's glorification and imply that the resurrection and ascension are included. Here in John 2:4 Jesus' remark to his mother indicates that the time for this self-revelation has not yet arrived; his identity as Messiah is not ready to be made public. [*hōra*]

2:6 Stone water jars (*hydriai*). The term *hydria* describes a container for water (LN 6.127, BDAG 1023; KJV, NASB, NLT "waterpots"). These jars held water for Jewish purification rituals. Jars made of stone were not as likely to contract ceremonial uncleanness as jars made from materials like clay. [*hydria*]

Ceremonial washing (*katharismon*). The most common act of ceremonial cleansing under the OT Levitical system was washing the hands; this took place before grace at meals (TDNT 3:421). The concept of purity is a significant motif in John's Gospel (3:25; 13:10-11; 15:2-3); the disciples are clean because of their association with Jesus (15:3). [*katharismos*]

Two or three **measures** (*metrētas*). KJV, "two or three firkens"; most modern translations convert to "gallons." A "measure" (*metrētēs*) was approximately nine gallons, so each of the jars held 18-27 gallons of water; the total amount of liquid contained by six of these jars would have been between 108 and 162 gallons. [*metrētēs*]

2:7 To the top (*anō*). When filling a container this term means to fill it to the top or brim (BDAG 92). [*anō*]

2:8 Draw (*antlēsate*). The Greek verb is used generally of drawing water from a container or a well (LN 47.1). Some classical uses refer to bailing out bilge water or bailing out a ship (LS 82). Based on the usage of the term some interpreters have insisted the water drawn here was taken from a well rather than from the stone water jars mentioned in v. 6, but there is nothing inherent in the Greek verb that implies well water, and the context strongly implies the water was taken from the water jars. [*antleō*]

The **chief steward** (*tō architriklinō*). (Also twice in the following verse) Traditionally this individual has been regarded as the head servant or "chief steward" (NRSV) in charge of all the servants at a banquet or feast (LN 46.7, BAGD 113). Some have understood this to be the "master of ceremonies" (NLT) at the wedding, however (like a modern toastmaster). [*architriklinos*]

2:9 That had become (*gegenēmenon*). No extensive description of the miracle is given, but the simple report that the water in the jars "had become" wine. John typically does not focus on the miracles themselves, but on their significance for those who observe them. [*ginomai*]

2:10 The good wine (*kalon*). (Twice in this verse) This word refers to the quality of the wine Jesus produced at the wedding feast: "good, fine, precious." In contrast with the inferior wine mentioned here it could have a superlative nuance, "best." The inferior wine usually was served later at wedding feasts. [*kalos*]

2:11 Signs (*sēmeion*). This key term in John's Gospel, occurring 17 times (cf. KJV "miracles; NIV, NET "miraculous signs"), is used to describe miraculous events performed by Jesus that point to something even greater (LN 33.477). These "signs" singled out by the evangelist for special mention point ultimately to Jesus' identity. The term only applies to Jesus in the fourth Gospel (it is even specifically pointed out that John the Baptist performed no "sign" in 10:41). In addition the term describes certain specific "sign-miracles" (the number of which is often stated to be seven, but lists differ as to which incidents are involved). The term is also used to refer to "signs" performed by Jesus in a general sense (2:23; 3:2; 6:2, 26; 9:16). Sometimes there is even summary mention of the great number of "signs" performed (11:47; 12:37; 20:30). In general, the sign-miracles in John's Gospel are the kinds of miracles anticipated with the coming of the messianic age (cf. Isa. 35:5, also Matt. 11:5; Luke 7:22). Miracles in the fourth Gospel labeled specifically as "signs" are the water changed to wine at the wedding in Cana of Galilee (here in 2:11), the healing of the nobleman's son (also at Cana, 4:54), the feeding of the 5,000 (6:14), and the raising of Lazarus (12:18). The "signs" mentioned in a general sense in 9:16 are also connected to the healing of the man born blind in 9:1-7. The healing of the paralytic at Bethesda in 5:2-9 is probably also to be included as an example of "the signs he performed on those who were sick" (6:2). Various suggestions have been made to bring the total number of "sign-miracles" specifically discussed in John's Gospel up to seven, the most prominent of which are Jesus walking on the sea (6:16-21) or the cleansing of the temple (2:14-22). All these "signs" point to Jesus' identity (cf. 3:2), but the last of them (the raising of Lazarus in 11:1-44) prepares the way for the passion narrative and foreshadows (and invites comparison with) Jesus' own resurrection. Although not described by John as one of the "sign-miracles," the resurrection of Jesus functions similarly to the previous signs in that it leads those who understand its significance to believe (20:8). [*sēmeion*]

Glory (*doxan*). The sign miracle of changing the water into wine is said to reveal Jesus' "glory," which is connected here to the disciples' faith. See 1:14 for this term. [*doxa*]

Believed (*episteusan*). This is the first time Jesus' disciples are said to "believe" in him. No specific mention is made of what the disciples believed about Jesus at this point, but presumably, based on Andrew's statement (1:41) and Nathanael's (1:49), they believed Jesus to be the Messiah. For discussion of *pisteuō* ("believe"), see 1:12. [*pisteuō*]

2:12 Capernaum (*Kapharnaoum*). This was a town on the shore of the Sea of Galilee, the exact location of which is still debated (BDAG 537). Although John's Gospel gives no details of what Jesus said or did there, it is clear from the Synoptic Gospels that Capernaum was a center of Jesus' Galilean ministry and could even be called "his own town" (Matt. 9:1). The royal official whose son Jesus healed (John 4:46-54) was from Capernaum. He may have heard Jesus speak there or heard about him from one of his disciples. [*Kapharnaoum*]

His brothers (*adelphoi*). Traditionally there have been three ways of understanding the

term "brothers" here: (1) The view of Epiphanius, that they were children of Joseph by a former marriage; (2) Jerome's view, that they were cousins; and (3) the view of Helvidius, that these were children of Joseph and Mary after the birth of Jesus. The last view is preferred because it is the most natural way to understand the phrase. [*adelphos*]

2:13 The Passover (*pascha*). This was the major Jewish festival celebrated on the 14th of the month Nisan, which continued to the 15th and was immediately followed by the Feast of Unleavened Bread, which ran from the 15th to the 21st of Nisan (BAGD 633). This is the first of three (and possibly four) Passovers mentioned in John's Gospel. If we assume the Passovers are mentioned in the fourth Gospel in chronological order, this would be the first of Jesus' public ministry. Another Passover is in 6:4, and still another Passover is mentioned in 11:55; 12:1; 13:1; 18:28, 39; 19:14 (all referring to the same one). Some interpreters think John 5:1 also refers to a Passover, in which case it would be the second and 6:4 the third of Jesus' public ministry. [*pascha*]

2:14 The temple (*hierō*). (Also in v. 15) In the NT this term refers (with the exception of Acts 19:27) to the temple in Jerusalem, including the entire temple precinct with its buildings, courts, and storerooms (LN 7.16). The merchants would have been located in the Court of the Gentiles rather than inside the main temple building, so many recent translations use an expression like "the temple courts" (NIV, NET) or "the temple area" (NAB, NLT). [*hieron*]

The money changers (*kermatistas*). The corresponding verb *kermatizō* is found frequently in the secular papyri with the meaning "to change money" (BDAG 541). Because Roman denarii and Attic drachmas carried imperial Roman portraits, which were considered idolatrous by the Jews, these coins could not be used to pay the half-shekel temple tax. The "money changers" exchanged these coins for legal Tyrian coinage at a small profit. [*kermatistēs*]

2:15 A whip of cords (*phragellion*). The term is a Latin loanword (*flagellum*). It refers to a "whip" or "lash" (KJV, NASB "scourge"), which could consist of either a single thong or multiple thongs, with or without weighted stone or metal tips on the ends (LN 6.26, BAGD 865). In the form used by the Roman authorities to administer floggings or scourgings it was an instrument of torture, but it is highly unlikely that the device made by Jesus here was so complicated or dangerous. John says it was made of "cords," and it was intended to be used more like a cattle prod, rather than to administer punishment. [*phragellion*]

The money changers (*kollybistōn*). This is a different Greek word for "money changers" than the one in the previous verse. However, there is no appreciable difference in meaning. This illustrates the evangelist's love of stylistic variation. [*kollybistēs*]

2:16 Take ... away (*arate*). Here the verb means "to remove, carry off, take away" in a literal sense (LN 15.203), referring specifically to the live pigeons being sold as sacrifices. [*airō*]

A marketplace (*oikon emporiou*). Literally, "a house of merchants" (BAGD 257, "market-house"; KJV "an house of merchandise': RSV "a house of trade"). On the surface level this refers to the activity of the merchants and money changers in the temple area. In John's Gospel this also constitutes an allusion to the prophecy of Zech. 14:21, where the Hebrew word often translated "Canaanite" may also be translated "merchant" or "trader." Read in this light, Zech. 14:21 states that in "that day" (referring to the day of the Lord, at the establishment of the messianic kingdom) there would be no "merchant" in the house of the Lord. This is consistent with Jesus' words and actions on the occasion, which suggest he was fulfilling messianic expectations when he cleared the temple of merchants. His disciples would appreciate this significance as they had just witnessed the miracle of the water turned to wine at the wedding in Cana with all its messianic implications. [*emporion*]

2:17 Remembered (*emnēsthēsan*). Unlike v. 22, where it is specifically said the disciples "remembered" what Jesus had said after his resurrection, it is not clear here whether they remembered the quotation from Ps. 69:10 at the time or after the resurrection. [*mimnēskomai*]

Zeal (*zēlos*). The word can be used in a bad sense to refer to jealousy or envy, but here it is used in a good sense to refer to "deep devotion" or "earnest concern" (BAGD 337, LN 25.46; cf. NLT, NET "passion"). It refers to Jesus' devotion to the sanctity of his Father's house, the temple. [*zēlos*]

Will consume (*kataphagetai*). Here there is another wordplay. At one level the verb can mean "eat up" (KJV "Hath eaten me up") or "devour" (NET; cf. LN 23.11) and even now in English we can speak of a person "consumed" with a goal, purpose, or idea (NIV, NRSV "will consume me"). On this level Jesus was totally "consumed" with zeal for his Father's house. On another level, the verb can mean "consumed" in the sense of "totally destroyed" (LN 20.45, cf. Rev. 11:5), and in this sense Jesus was "consumed" by his zeal for the temple, because it led the Jewish religious authorities to engineer his crucifixion at the hands of the Romans. In light of the following remarks about "destroying" the temple in v. 19, this is the ultimate meaning of the phrase here. [*katesthiō*]

2:18 The Jews (*Ioudaioi*). See 1:19. Here and in

v. 20 the term refers to the authorities, the Jewish leaders in Jerusalem. [*Ioudaios*]

Sign (*sēmeion*). See 2:11. This is not necessarily John's usual meaning for the term *sēmeion* because it is used here by Jesus' opponents, who demanded a "sign" of divine authentication in light of his actions in clearing the merchants out of the temple. Whether in the view of the authorities this constituted a request for a miracle is not entirely clear. Jesus never obliged such a demand. However (ironically) the only "sign" the Jewish leadership in Jerusalem will get is the one predicted by Jesus in 2:19, his crucifixion, death, burial, and resurrection. Cf. the "sign of Jonah" in the Synoptic Gospels (Matt. 12:39-40; Luke 11:29-32). [*sēmeion*]

2:19 Destroy (*lysate*). The verb means "to reduce something by violence into its components," i.e., "to destroy" (BDAG 607). It is imperative mood, but this is more than a simple conditional imperative ("if you destroy"). Its force is more like the ironical challenge found in the OT prophets (Amos 4:4; Isa. 8:9): "Go ahead and do this and see what happens!" [*lyō*]

Temple (*naon*). (Also in vv. 20, 21) Again there is a wordplay here based on a double referent. At one level this refers to the building in Jerusalem where the conversation is taking place. It is sometimes argued that there is a distinction between the term *naos*, which refers to the sanctuary itself, and *hieron*, a more general term referring to the entire temple precincts. This distinction is unlikely for two reasons: (1) There is overlap in the NT between the two terms with no real distinction between them (TDNT 4.882); (2) John's love of stylistic variation, his exchange of essentially synonymous terms, should also cause such a distinction to be suspect. At the second level in this context, the "temple" refers to Jesus' own physical body (v. 21), which will be "destroyed" by

his death and "rebuilt" by his resurrection. The two referents for the "temple" here make possible another example of the "misunderstood statement" in John's Gospel, since the Jewish religious authorities understand the remark to refer to the actual temple building (v. 20), while the evangelist, in an explanatory comment, points out that the real referent was Jesus' body (vv. 21-22). [*naos*]

2:20 Forty-six years (*etesin*). According to Josephus (*Ant.* 15.11.1 [15.380]), Herod's decree to begin on this temple was issued in the 18th year of Herod the Great's reign, which would have been around 19 B.C. (Although debated, the date given in the *Antiquities* is probably more accurate than the date given in *J. W.* 1.21.1 [1.401]). [*etos*]

2:22 Remembered (*emnēsthēsan*). This refers to something the disciples "remembered" after Jesus' resurrection. Note that the evangelist is writing this from a post-resurrection point of view. See also v. 17. [*mimnēskomai*]

Believed (*episteusan*). Here the content of what the disciples believed is specified: the Scripture (probably a reference to Ps. 69:9, quoted in John 2:17) and the word Jesus spoke, referring to his statement about destroying and rebuilding the temple, which the evangelist explains in v. 21 as a reference to Jesus' own body (i.e., his death and resurrection). For discussion of *pisteuō* ("believe"), see 1:12. [*pisteuō*]

2:23 Believed (*episteusan*). Here the belief of the "many" is based on their seeing the miraculous signs Jesus performed. This connection with signs suggests they believed Jesus to be the Messiah, a belief which was not incorrect, but for the evangelist was inadequate, since John's Gospel begins (1:1, 18) and ends (20:28) with the affirmation that Jesus is God. [*pisteuō*]

2:24 Would not entrust (*episteuen*). The Greek verb translated "would not entrust" here (NIV, NRSV, NET; Greek *pisteuō*) is the same one translated "believed" in the previous verse. Again, this is a reflective insight added by the evangelist (cf. v. 22). It serves as a transition to the interview with Nicodemus, and as a comment on the general public response to Jesus' ministry at this time. While these people might be believers, they had imperfectly understood Jesus' message and ministry. The real issue here is not the genuineness of these individuals' faith (as the question is often framed) but its object and extent. The author does not elaborate, but it seems likely that these people had seen the signs and (correctly) interpreted their messianic significance. But the plan they envisioned was not God's plan, which involved the Messiah's death and resurrection. It was probably this factor in particular that Jesus was not willing to entrust to them. The crowds in their exuberance may have been ready to try to make Jesus king (cf. 6:15), yet in no way could they have accepted such a painful revelation about his true destiny. In fact, Jesus had not even fully and openly entrusted himself to his own disciples at this point, so that in 14:9 he could still say to Philip, "How long have you been with me and have not known me?" Thus the individuals described here had believed in Jesus as Messiah, but the concept of Messiah they had believed in was their own, not that of Jesus. [*pisteuō*]

3:1 A ruler of the Jews (*archōn*). This word denotes a member of the Sanhedrin, the highest legal, legislative, and judicial body among the Jews in the first century A.D. (BAGD 113; NRSV "a leader of the Jews"; NIV, NET "a member of the Jewish ruling council"). [*archōn*]

3:2 At night (*nyktos*). The term refers to the period of darkness between sunset and sunrise (BDAG 682). Perhaps Nicodemus came to meet with Jesus "at night" because he feared public association with him, or he wanted a lengthy discussion without interruptions. The evangelist gives no explanation for the timing. But the time noted is significant in terms of the light-darkness motif (cf. John 9:4; 11:10; 13:30; 19:39; 21:3). Out of the darkness of his life and religiosity Nicodemus came to the Light of the world. John probably had multiple meanings or associations in mind here, as is frequently the case. [*nyx*]

A teacher (*didaskalos*). The term *didaskalos* describes a religious teacher and in many contexts corresponds to the title "Rabbi," which is used here by Nicodemus to address Jesus (BAGD 191). [*didaskalos*]

Signs (*sēmeia*). See 2:11. The mention of "signs" also forms a link with John 2:23-25. These people in Jerusalem apparently believed Jesus to be the Messiah because of the signs he had performed. Nicodemus had apparently seen them too. But for Nicodemus all the signs meant was that Jesus was a great teacher sent from God. His approach to Jesus was therefore well-intentioned but theologically inadequate. Unlike the common people (whose loyalty to Jesus would later prove fickle when he failed to fulfill their messianic expectations), Nicodemus had failed to grasp the messianic implications of the miraculous signs. [*sēmeion*]

3:3 Born (*gennēthē*). (Also in vv. 4, 5, 6, 7, 8) The verb refers to spiritual birth, although Nicodemus misunderstood and thought it referred to a second physical birth. See the discussion at 1:13. [*gennaō*]

From above (*anōthen*). The Greek term *anōthen* has a double meaning. The word may mean "again" (LN 67.55; KJV, NASB, NIV, NLT) or "from above" (BAGD 77, LN 84.13; NRSV, NET). Such double meanings are common in the fourth Gospel, although it is lost in almost all English translations. John uses *anōthen* five times in all (3:3, 7, 31; 8:23; 19:11). In the last three cases the context makes clear that it means "from above." Here the primary meaning intended by Jesus is the same, although Nicodemus apparently understood the other meaning, "again," which explains his reply, "How can a man be born when he is old? He can't enter his mother's womb a second time and be born, can he?" The Gospel of John frequently uses the "misunderstood statement" to surface a particularly important point. Jesus says something that is misunderstood by the disciples or (as here) by someone else, which in turn gives Jesus the opportunity to explain more fully what he really meant. [*anōthen*]

The **kingdom** of God (*basileian*). (Also in v. 5) John uses the word "kingdom" (*basileia*) only five times (3:3, 5; 18:36 [3 times]). Only here (vv. 3, 5) is it qualified with the phrase "of God." The fact that John does not stress the concept of the "kingdom of God" does not mean it is absent from his theology, however. For Nicodemus, the phrase "kingdom of God" would surely have called to mind the messianic kingdom, which the Messiah was supposed to usher in. But the point Nicodemus had missed was that Jesus, the Messiah, was speaking with him (cf. 4:26). [*basileia*]

3:5 Water and Spirit (*hydatos . . . pneumatos*). As is often the case in John's Gospel, the problem with these terms is determining the referents. "Water," for example, is often understood as a reference to water baptism. The Greek word *pneuma* ("Spirit") could be understood as "spirit/Spirit" or as "wind." In the context both of these elements are connected with Jesus' statement about being "born from above." Isa. 44:3-5 and Ezek. 37:9-10 are underlying OT passages that combine water and wind as symbols of the

Spirit of God working among people to give life. Both occur in contexts treating Israel's future restoration as a nation prior to establishing the kingdom. It is therefore appropriate that Jesus should raise them in a conversation with Nicodemus about entering God's kingdom. In other words, both water and wind were figures (based on OT passages, which as a teacher Nicodemus should have known) that represent the Spirit's regenerating work in people's lives. [*hydōr + pneuma*]

3:6 Flesh . . . spirit (*sarx . . . pneuma*). For John the term *sarx* emphasizes merely a creature's weakness and mortality. It is a neutral term, not necessarily sinful as in Paul's writings (BAGD 744). Here the point is that whatever is born of physical heritage is physical (cf. 4:23-24). Likewise, whatever is born as a result of the Spirit's work (in other words, "born from above") is spiritual. [*sarx + pneuma*]

3:8 The wind (*pneuma*). Again the physical realm illustrates the spiritual realm, although the force is heightened by the wordplay here on wind/spirit (see 3:5). By the end of the verse, however, the referent of the final occurrence of *pneumatos* is the Holy Spirit. [*pneuma*]

3:10 The teacher of Israel (*didaskalos*). See 3:2. Jesus' description of Nicodemus as "the teacher of Israel" here is filled with irony. The question Jesus asked implies that Nicodemus had enough information at his disposal from the OT Scriptures to understand the necessity of being born from above by the Spirit's regenerating work. Isa. 44:3-5 and Ezek. 37:9-10 are passages Nicodemus should have known. Another significant passage is Prov.. 30:4-5. [*didaskalos*]

3:11 We know (*oidamen*). Here firsthand knowledge is indicated (cf. the eyewitness testimony in 1 John 1:2). [*oida*]

We testify (*martyroumen*). See the discussion at 1:7. [*martyreō*]

Testimony (*martyrian*). Earlier John the Baptist had given his testimony; here the testimony (KJV, NASB "witness") is that of Jesus. It is remarkably similar to the words of 1 John 1:2: "And we have seen and testify and report to you the eternal life which was with the Father and was revealed to us." See the discussion of both noun and verb at 1:7. [*martyria*]

3:12 Earthly things . . . heavenly things (*epigeia . . . epourania*). Clearly in the context "earthly things" are in contrast to "heavenly things" (cf. BAGD 290). What are these "earthly things"? It makes the most sense to take this as a reference to the things Jesus has just said (and is about to say, vv. 13-15). If so, then "earthly things" are not necessarily strictly physical things, but are called "earthly" because they take place on earth, in contrast to things like v. 16, which take place in heaven. Some have also added that the things are called "earthly" because physical analogies (birth, wind, water) are used to describe them. That may be so, but it still seems more likely that Jesus calls these things "earthly" because they happen on earth. When he heard about these things Nicodemus did not "believe," and he would not believe after hearing "heavenly things" either, unless he first believed in the "earthly" (which included the necessity of a Spirit's regenerating work from above). Nicodemus obviously "believed" something about Jesus ("you are a teacher come from God," v. 2) or he would not have inquired further. Jesus, however, judged this belief to be inadequate. [*epigeios + epouranios*]

3:13 Has ascended . . . descended (*anabebēken . . . katabas*). The perfect tense verb in Greek appears to look at a past completed event. If these are the words of the evangelist, there is not a problem, because he looks back on Jesus' ascension from the perspective of writing the Gospel. If the words are assigned to Jesus, they are somewhat harder to explain. It is important to note the similarities between this verse and 1:51, though here the ascent and descent is accomplished by the Son himself rather than by angels. The story of Jacob in Gen. 28 appears to be the background for 1:51. Jacob's vision highlights the freedom of communication and relationship between God and humankind, which is also a major theme of John's Gospel. In both Gen. 28 and John 1:51 this communication is mediated through angels, but here in 3:13 it is mediated through the Son of Man. As such it simply points out that no one from earth has ever "gone up" to heaven and "come down" again. The Son, who has come down from heaven, is the only one who has been there. This stresses Jesus' heavenly origin and also authenticates his authority to talk about "heavenly" things. [*anabainō + katabainō*]

The Son of Man (*huios . . . anthrōpou*). (Also in v. 14) Here again the title "Son of Man" looks at Jesus as one who has been given regal authority. [*huios + anthrōpos*]

3:14 Lifted up . . . lifted up (*hypsōsen . . . hypsōthēnai*). The verb means "to lift or raise something spatially" (BDAG 1045). The analogy is drawn between the bronze serpent that Moses "lifted up" on the pole in the desert (Num. 21:5-9) and the Son of Man being "lifted up," which is ultimately a prediction of Jesus' crucifixion (cf. John 12:32). Wis. 16:6-7 (in a midrash on Num. 21:9ff.) states, "They . . . had a symbol of salvation to remind them of the precept of your law. For he who turned to it was saved, not by what he saw, but by you, the Savior of all." In the Gospel of John the concept of Jesus being "lifted up" refers to one continuing action of ascent, beginning with the cross but ending

John

with Jesus' exaltation at the Father's right hand. [*hypsoō*]

The serpent (*opsin*). The Greek term is a general one that may refer to any kind of "snake" (LN 4.52; NIV, NLT). Here it refers to the bronze serpent lifted up by Moses in Num. 21:9. Just as looking up at the bronze serpent healed the Israelite, so looking to Christ crucified and exalted can save the believer (cf. John 6:40). Cf. TDNT 5:581. [*ophis*]

3:15 Everyone who believes (*pisteuōn*). (Also in v. 16) Here in both instances the verb "believe" is used in the sense of "exercise faith in, put one's trust in." The Israelite in the wilderness who was stricken by the plague (Num. 21:9) had to look to the bronze serpent to be healed; this "looking" constituted an act of faith, just as "believing" in Jesus did. [*pisteuō*]

Eternal life (*zōēn*). (Also in v. 16) This is the first occurrence of the formula "eternal life" in John's Gospel, although "life" in 1:4 is to be understood in the same way even though not qualified by the adjective "eternal." See the discussions of the term at 1:4 and 17:2. [*zōē*]

3:16 For God so loved (*houtōs*). The Greek adverb *houtōs* can refer to the degree or extent to which something is done, or (more frequently) to the manner in which something is done (BAGD 597-98). Though frequently understood as a statement about *how much* God loved the world, it is likely in context that manner is also involved (cf. NET, "For this is the way God loved the world"). This is not to say that the degree or extent of God's love is excluded here; it would be perfectly in keeping with John's tendency to employ double meanings to see a reference here both to the extent of God's love and the manner in which it is expressed. [*houtōs*]

The world (*ton kosmon*). (Also twice in v.

17 and once in v. 19) Here the "world" is the world of people, that is, "humanity" or the human race. As in 1:29, there is no indication whatsoever in the context that the referent of "the world" here should be limited only to certain individuals, such as the elect (cf. 1 John 2:2). [*kosmos*]

His one and only Son (*monogenē*). See the discussion of "one and only" in 1:14 and the summary discussion of the title "Son" at 1:34. [*monogenēs* + *huios*]

Perish (*apolētai*). In the middle voice the verb *apollymi* can mean either "perish, die" or "be lost" (BAGD 95). Both these meanings occur in John's Gospel, the first here in 3:16 (also 10:28; 17:12) and the second in 6:12. It is typical for John (who frequently expresses things in an "either/or" framework) to express only two alternatives, as here: "perish" or "have eternal life." [*apollymi*]

3:17 Did not send (*apesteilen*). See 1:6. Jesus was "sent" by the Father on a mission, and that mission was the world's salvation. The verb *apostellō* here implies that Jesus was sent with God's full authority to carry out that mission. [*apostellō*]

To condemn (*krinē*). The Greek verb *krinō* generally refers to the passing of a sentence, "to judge." In John this prerogative belongs to God, but has been handed over to the Son (5:22, 30). Here the focus is on the negative outcome of judgment, "to condemn" (also in the following verse). [*krinō*]

Should be saved (*sōthē*). The verb here refers to God's salvation (LN 21.27). John uses this verb only six times (here, 5:34; 10:9; 11:12; 12:27; 12:47). Two of these (11:12, 12:27) have nothing to do with theological salvation. As for the remaining four instances, the object of "saving" is the "world" (here and in 12:47), "the Jews" in 5:34, and "anyone" in 10:9 (although the words are directed to "some of the Pharisees" in 9:40, and this dialogue is a continuation of that). In two of these contexts (here and 12:47) the concept of "being judged" (i.e., "condemned") is linked as the alternative to "being saved." For John, the concept of "being saved" essentially means "attaining salvation," or in John's preferred terms, "attaining eternal life." [*sōzō*]

3:18 Is not condemned (*krinetai*). (Twice in this verse) The believer escapes "condemnation," but the person who refuses to believe "has been condemned already" (NET; NIV, "stands condemned already"). For John, judgment (i.e., when a negative outcome is in view, "condemnation") is not something that is confined to the distant future, but happens when a person refuses to believe in Jesus Christ in the present. On the scale of "already—not yet," John places almost all the emphasis on the "already." See also the previous verse. [*krinō*]

3:19 The judgment (*krisis*). The noun "judgment" (KJV "condemnation"; NIV "verdict"; NET "basis for judging"; Greek *krisis*) is related to the verb "to judge" (*krinō*) in vv. 17, 18. Rather than being portrayed as an eschatological event in the future (as in the Synoptic Gospels), "judgment" for John is something that is occurring in the present. The coming of Jesus as the "Light" (cf. 1:9; 8:12) into the world provokes this "judgment," because individuals are forced to "choose up sides" for or against him. This is expressed in vv. 20-21 as either "hating the light" and "refusing to come to the light" (which results in condemnation), or as "doing what is true" and "coming to the light," in which case the person does not undergo "judgment" (i.e., "condemnation," v. 18). One's eternal destiny is decided by one's response to Jesus Christ, and for John there is no middle ground whatsoever [*krisis* + *krinō*]

Evil (*ponēra*). The Greek term can refer to that which is morally corrupt and evil, or "wicked" (LN 88.110). In this context, how-

ever, "evil" is defined by one's reaction to "light" and "darkness." People do "evil" deeds because they have rejected the "light" (that is, Jesus himself). In this sense what is "evil" is anything that is against the mission of the Son (3:17) who comes into the "world" to "save" it (TDNT 6:557). [*ponēros*]

3:20 Evil (*phaula*). Another Greek term is translated "evil" here, which pertains to moral corruption, "bad, evil" (LN 88.116) or even "worthless" (BAGD 854). However, in typical Johannine fashion, it is essentially synonymous in context with the term *ponēros* in the previous verse. [*phaulos*]

So that it may be manifested (*phanerōthē*). The verb means "to cause something to become visible," that is, "to reveal or expose publicly" (BDAG 1048; NRSV "so that it may be clearly seen"; NET "so that it may be plainly evident"). The evildoer hates the light because he does not want his evil deeds to be exposed to public scrutiny. [*phaneroō*]

3:21 The truth (*alētheian*). Literally, the person who "practices the truth" (NASB, NET, NIV "lives by the truth") comes to the light. [*alētheia*]

3:22 Judean territory (*gēn*). In the narrative as it stands, Jesus has already been in "Judean territory" (NET), that is, Jerusalem. It is possible that the Judean rural districts (NIV, NRSV "the Judean countryside") are in view, although the phrase "after these things" in the verse specifies an indefinite amount of time, so that there could have been intervening events. [*gē*]

3:23 Aenon . . . Salim (*Ainōn . . . Saleim*). The exact locations of these places are unknown. Three possibilities have been suggested: (1) in Perea, which is in Transjordan (cf. John 1:28). Perea is just across the Jordan River from Judea. (2) In the northern Jordan Valley, on the west bank some eight miles south of Scythopolis. With the Jordan River so close, however, the reference to abundant water (John 3:23) seems superfluous. (3) Samaria has also been suggested—there is a town called Salim four miles east of Shechem, and eight miles northeast of Salim is modern Ainun. In the general vicinity are many springs of water. In any case, the evangelist almost certainly had in mind real places, even if their exact location is uncertain. [*Ainōn + Saleim*]

3:25 A disagreement (*zētēsis*). The term here refers to a "dispute" (NET) or "argument" (BDAG 429; NIV, CEV, NLT). The nature of this disagreement is not described and is impossible to determine with any degree of certainty. It is possible (though far from certain) that it concerned Jesus' authority to overturn Jewish ceremonial laws regarding purification, since the subject of the "disagreement" is specified as "ceremonial washing" (cf. 2:6). [*zētēsis*]

3:28 I have been <u>sent</u> (*apestalmenos*). See 1:6, where John the Baptist is described as a man "sent" from God to testify (i.e., bear witness) to the light (i.e., Jesus Christ). That is precisely what John the Baptist is doing here. God's full authority is behind John as forerunner of the Messiah. [*apostellō*]

3:29 The <u>friend</u> **of the bridegroom** (*philos*). In many respects the "friend of the bridegroom" was similar to a best man at a wedding. A Jewish wedding lasted for seven days (cf. Judg. 14:12; Tob 8:20); on the evening of the first day the marriage was contracted in the course of a formal meal. After this the newly married couple went to the bridal chamber to consummate their marriage, superintended by the "friend of the bridegroom." The reference to "the bridegroom's voice" in this verse probably alludes to the call for the "friend of

the bridegroom" to collect the blood-stained linen that was the sign of the bride's virginity, a practice based on Deut. 22:13-21. Thus John 3:29 is a metaphor drawn from common everyday life of the period. It is more debated whether John's symbolism goes beyond this to regard Jesus as the heavenly "Bridegroom" of the church, the bride of Christ (cf. 2 Cor. 11:2; Eph. 5:25). [*philos*]

3:31 From above (*anōthen*). See 3:3. This expression constitutes a lexical link to Jesus' words to Nicodemus about the necessity of being born "from above" (i.e., a spiritual birth). Here John the Baptist is saying essentially the same thing Jesus said to Nicodemus about the need for a spiritual birth. The contrast between "earth" and "heaven" (again, the imagery of "above" and "below") is also present here. [*anōthen*]

3:32 Testimony (*martyrian*). (Also in v. 33) See the discussion at 1:7. [*martyria*]

3:33 Has certified (*esphragisen*). The Greek verb, literally "to seal," means to demonstrate the truth or validity of something by providing authentic proof (LN 28.53; NIV, NRSV "has certified"; NET "has confirmed clearly"). What is certified is that God is "true," an adjective that when referred to persons means "truthful, righteous, honest" (BAGD 36). The adjective is related to the noun *alētheia* (see 1:14 for discussion). [*sphragizō + alēthēs*]

3:34 Has sent (*apesteilen*). See 1:6. Here the referent is Jesus, although the speaker is either John the Baptist or the evangelist (the latter is more likely; this seems to be a summary statement). Jesus was sent with the full authority of the Father behind him. [*apostellō*]

    The <u>words</u> (*rhēmata*). Here the term refers to the content of Jesus' teaching (BAGD 735). In 4:41 the term *logos* means essentially the same. Frequently an attempt is made to distinguish between the "spoken word" (*rhēma*) and the "written word" (*logos*), but this should not be pressed, because in John the terms often overlap (LN 33.98). [*rhēma* + *logos*]

Not by **measure** (*metrou*). The expression means "without measure" (BAGD 515). Jesus is contrasted with the OT prophets. A later Jewish midrash, *Lev. Rab.* 15:2, states, "The Holy Spirit rested on the prophets by measure." [*metron*]

3:35 In his hand (*cheiri*). For the Father to give "all things" into the Son's "hand" [= power; BAGD 880] means that the Father gives the Son universal sovereignty (cf. Dan. 7:13-14). [*cheir*]

3:36 The one who rejects (*apeithōn*). The verb can mean "disobey" (NRSV), but in this context refers to the refusal to believe in the Son. It can be used of either Jews or Gentiles, and is virtually synonymous with *apistia*, "faithless, unbelieving" (TDNT 6:11). [*apeitheō*]

Will not **see** (*opsetai*). The person who rejects the Son will not "see" (i.e., experience; BDAG 719) eternal life. [*horaō*]

Wrath (*orgē*). This is not a frequent theme in the fourth Gospel, but it is clearly present here (TDNT 5:422). The term parallels Paul's usage: God's (righteous) anger directed against sinners. A deliberate refusal to "obey" the Son (i.e., in this context, "believe in" the Son) leaves an individual subject to God's wrath. [*orgē*]

4:1 Knew (*egnō*). Here it is not clear how Jesus "knew" this. In other contexts supernatural knowledge on the part of Jesus is often involved, as in 2:25; 5:6; 6:15. However, someone else could have informed Jesus that the Pharisees had heard about his success. (*ginōskō*)

Disciples (*mathētas*). A "disciple" was a follower who was also a pupil. The noun is related to the Greek verb *manthanō*, "to learn."

Rabbis in first century Judaism typically collected followers as students. In the fourth Gospel we see John the Baptist doing this (1:35), and Jesus' opponents are described as "disciples of Moses" (9:28) even though no personal relationship was involved. Rather a chain of tradition could be traced back to the one regarded as "teacher" (TDNT 4:443). John 4:1 and 6:60 both imply that Jesus had a large following beyond the Twelve. A characteristic seems to be that these people followed Jesus around (6:66). Finally, John in his Gospel does not refer to the Twelve as "apostles," but "disciples." The motivation for this may have been the evangelist's preference to use the related verb *apostellō* ("to send") for Jesus and his mission from the Father. The disciples of Jesus inherit this mission after his return to the Father (17:18). The effect of this choice of terminology is to minimize the distinction between the Twelve and believers in general, all of whom are "disciples" of Jesus. [*mathētēs*]

4:2 Was not baptizing (*ebaptizen*). The evangelist goes out of his way to make the point here that Jesus himself was not baptizing people with water the way John the Baptist was. See 1:25 and 1:33. [*baptizō*]

4:4 It was necessary (*edei*). With the imperfect form of the impersonal verb *dei* in both direct and indirect discourse there may be only logical necessity (LN 71.34). The verb *dierchomai* means "to travel through" a region or territory (BDAG 244). Here, however, travel through Samaria was not geographically necessary (or customary). Jewish travelers normally went east of Samaria up the Jordan valley to avoid setting foot in "unclean" Samaritan territory. In John's Gospel this impersonal verb typically indicates divine necessity: that is, God's will or plan (3:7, 14, 30; 4:4, 20, 24; 9:4; 10:16; 12:34; 20:9). [*dei* + *dierchomai*]

4:5 Sychar (*Sychar*). This town was somewhere in the vicinity of Shechem. In recent times it has often been identified with the village of Askar, about a mile northeast of Jacob's well at the southeast foot of Mt. Ebal. Jerome (*Quaest. in Gen.* 66.6), however, considered the name to be a corrupt form of *Sychem*, that is, Shechem (BAGD 795), and excavations appear to indicate that Jerome was right (BDAG 979). Nearby was the "piece of land" (*chōrion*) that Jacob gave to his son Joseph (BDAG 1095). [*Sychar* + *chōrion*]

4:6 Jacob's well (*pēgē*). This Greek term could be used to describe a spring of water that flowed by itself (cf. Rev. 8:10), a natural source of water like an artesian well. Here, however, it is used to describe a well with a constant flow of water (one that was available year round). Such a well consisted of a shaft at the bottom of which was a pool of water, and there was often a low stone wall around the edge of the shaft (LN 7.57). Since there is also another term for a "well" or "cistern" used in the passage (*phrear* in vv. 11, 12), it is often suggested that the evangelist was distinguishing between the two terms. Thus he was comparing the source of the "living water" Jesus promised the woman to a "free-flowing well" that provided an inexhaustible supply. In comparison to this, Jacob's well became a mere "cistern." This may be so, but the evangelist's love of stylistic variation may mean there is no difference in meaning. [*pēgē* + *phrear*]

Having become weary (*kekopiakōs*). The statement is theologically important because in John's Gospel, which so often emphasizes Christ's deity (cf. 1:1), the remark reflects Jesus' humanity (NRSV "tired out by his journey"; NET "since he was tired from the journey"). [*kopiaō*]

The sixth hour (*hōra*). This is probably noon. See 1:39 for further discussion of time in the fourth Gospel. [*hōra*]

4:9 Have no dealings with (*synchrōntai*). The verb *synchraomai* generally means "to have association with," implying spatial proximity and/or joint activity (BAGD 775, LN 34.1; NIV "do not associate with"). Some scholars see a reference here to the use of common dishes, drinking vessels, or utensils (NRSV "do not share things in common with the Samaritans"; NET "use nothing in common with the Samaritans"). Since there was an assumption among many Jews that Samaritans were ceremonially unclean, a Jew would contract this uncleanness by using a drinking vessel after a Samaritan. [*synchraomai*]

Samaritans (*Samaritais*). The Samaritans were descendants of two groups: (1) the remnant of native Israelites who were not deported after the fall of the Northern Kingdom in 722 B.C., and (2) foreign colonists brought in from Babylonia and Media by the Assyrian conquerors to settle the land with inhabitants who would be loyal to Assyria. Theological disagreement existed between the Samaritans and the Jews because the Samaritans recognized only the first five books of the OT (the Pentateuch) and refused to worship at the Jerusalem temple. After the exile to Babylon the Samaritans obstructed the Jewish rebuilding of Jerusalem. In the second century B.C. the Samaritans helped the Syrians in their wars against the Jews. In 128 B.C. the Jewish high priest retaliated burning the Samaritan sanctuary on Mount Gerazim. [*Samaritēs*]

4:10 The gift of God (*dōrean*). This term refers to something given or transferred freely from one person to another, "a gift" (BDAG 266). Jesus offers the woman "living water," which symbolically refers to the Holy Spirit (cf. 7:38-39). Thus the "gift" here is also to be understood as the Spirit. [*dōrea*]

Living water (*hydōr zōn*). (Also in v. 11.) The word translated "living" (*zōn*) is used in the Greek OT to describe flowing water from a spring in contrast to water in a cistern (Gen. 26:19; Lev. 14:5; Zech. 14:8). In contrast, stagnant water would be called "dead water" (*hydōr nekron*, BAGD 337). Jesus was referring to a different kind of water entirely, however: in John's Gospel "water" is frequently a symbolic image of the Holy Spirit (cf. 7:38-39). The double meaning leads to the woman's misunderstanding in the following verse—she thought Jesus was referring to some unknown source of drinkable water, which would render unnecessary her frequent trips to Jacob's well. [*hydōr + zaō*]

4:11 Sir (*kyrie*). The Greek term *kyrios* means both "Sir" (as a form of polite address) and "Lord," depending on the context. In this passage there is probably a gradual transition from one meaning to the other as the woman's respect for Jesus increases (cf. 4:15, 19). [*kyrios*]

    The **well** (*phrear*). (Also in v. 12) See the discussion on "well" at 4:6. [*phrear*]

4:14 Springing up (*halloumenou*). The verb *hallomai* is used of quick movement (like jumping or leaping) on the part of living beings, and by extension, of the quick movement of inanimate things (BAGD 39). This is the only time it is applied to the action of water (RSV, NIV "welling up"; NRSV "gushing up"). In the Greek OT, however, this verb is used to describe the "Spirit of God" as it falls upon Samson and Saul (Judg. 14:6, 19; 15:14; 1 Sam. 10:6, 10; Isa. 35:6). In John's Gospel water is a frequent symbol for the Holy Spirit (cf. 7:38-39). Finally, the outpouring of the Holy Spirit was a sign of messianic days (Joel 2:28-29; Isa. 44:3-5; Ezek. 39:29). [*hallomai*]

4:17 Well have you said (*kalōs*). This Greek adverb means "correctly" or "accurately" (LN 72.12). There is a possible implication of the thing referred to being commendable, in which case Jesus was telling the woman her

admission was to be commended. [*kalōs*]

4:18 Truly (*alēthes*). The term in this context means "true" as related to a fact or statement. Jesus affirmed that what the woman had told him was true (BAGD 36). [*alēthēs*]

4:19 I perceive (*theōrō*). The Greek verb means to come to an understanding of something: "notice, perceive, observe," etc. (BDAG 454), which in contemporary English is expressed as "I see" (NRSV, NET). The woman's observation that Jesus was a "prophet" was based on Jesus' comment that she had had five husbands and was currently living with someone who was not her husband (vv. 17-18). The woman saw Jesus' knowledge of her past and present situation as supernatural, since Jesus as a Jewish stranger could not possibly have known the information about her through normal means. [*theōreō + prophētēs*]

4:20 This mountain (*orei*). (Also in v. 21) This refers to Mt. Gerazim, where the Samaritan shrine was located. A temple built there by the Samaritans in the 4th century B.C. was destroyed by John Hyrcanus when he captured Shechem and the surrounding country in 128 B.C., but sacrifices continued to be offered there. According to Samaritan tradition, Mt. Gerazim (rather than the temple mount in Jerusalem) was Mt. Moriah (Gen. 22:2) and the place God chose for his name to reside (Deut. 12:5). This dispute led to this question. [*oros*]

4:21 Believe me (*pisteue*). Here the verb simply means "believe that I am telling you the truth," or "believe that what I say is true." [*pisteuō*]

    Woman (*gynai*). This is a polite form of address (BAGD 168). See also 2:4. [*gynē*]

4:22 Salvation (*sōtēria*). The term is used here

in a theological sense and is the only time this noun appears in the fourth Gospel. The statement "salvation is from the Jews" is made in contrast to Samaritans (TDNT 3:377). It means that salvation begins with those who have been up to this point the covenant community of God, and proceeds outward from there, to the Samaritans (cf. 4:42) and ultimately to the world (cf. 3:17). [sōtēria]

4:23 An hour (hōra). In context this does not refer specifically to Jesus' "hour" (see 2:4), but it is related. This refers to the "hour" (i.e. time, NIV, NLT, NET) when it will be possible to worship the Father without the need of a localized temple. This is the sort of worship that will be possible under the "new" covenant, which Jesus is about to usher in. [hōra]

True worshipers (alēthinoi). Note how the woman was concerned about *where* people ought to worship, while Jesus focuses on *what sort* of people ("true worshipers") ought to worship, and *who* they ought to worship ("the Father"). [alēthinos]

Spirit (pneumati). (Also in v. 24) The term here does not refer directly to the Holy Spirit, but more generally to the "spiritual realm" as opposed to the physical realm. In the following verse the same term refers to God as a spiritual being as opposed to a being that can be perceived by the physical senses (BAGD 675). Nevertheless, because God is a spiritual being, human beings, to worship him truly, must possess the Holy Spirit and worship in the power the Holy Spirit provides. Worshiping "in spirit and truth" (v. 24) means to worship in the empowerment the Spirit provides. The phrase "spirit and truth" thus is a metonymy (a figure of speech where one thing represents another) for genuinely worshiping God, who himself is spirit, with this empowerment. [pneuma]

4:25 Christ (Christos). (Also in v. 29) Here the term "Messiah" (Messias) is translated as "Christ" for the benefit of John's readers. See the discussion at 1:20. [Christos]

4:26 I am (egō eimi). Here there is an understood predicate, "I am [he]." Jesus was identifying himself to the woman as the one she had just spoken about, the Messiah. Some interpreters see more in the expression, however, and believe the evangelist intends an allusion to Exod. 3:14, the OT text where Yahweh revealed his name to Moses as "I am." John uses "I am" frequently in his Gospel, but it is important to note whether or not a predicate is present, as in "I am the door" (10:7), "I am the Good Shepherd" (10:11), "I am the way, the truth, and the life" (14:6), etc. There are at least three instances, all in chapter 8, where a reference to Exod. 3:14 is probably present (8:24, 28, 58), with the last of these being clear in context ("Before Abraham was, I am"). [egō + eimi]

4:27 They marveled (ethaumazon). BAGD 352 has "be surprised that" (followed by indirect discourse). The context, however, calls for slightly stronger wording (cf. NET, "they were shocked because he was speaking with a woman"). In ancient Jewish culture, a man often did not address women in public. [thaumazō]

4:28 Water jar (hydrian). See 2:6. No volume is specified for the woman's "water jar" (BDAG 1023) nor is the material noted (it was probably made of clay, however). In her excitement to tell her fellow villagers that a stranger claiming to be the Messiah had turned up at Jacob's well, the woman left the jar behind. For the evangelist, this is also symbolic: no jar would be needed to contain the "living water," which Jesus had offered her. [hydria]

4:29 Perhaps (*mēti*). (RSV, NLT "Can this be"; NIV "Could this be"; NET "Surely he can't be") This word, an interrogative particle, normally is used in questions that expect a negative answer (BAGD 520; LN 69.16). This should not be taken as an indication the woman did not believe, however. The form of the question may be explained by her expecting to receive strong opposition to a claim that Jesus was the Messiah. [*mēti*]

4:32 Food (*brōsin*). This term could refer to various kinds of food like meat offered to idols (1 Cor. 8:4), bread (2 Cor. 9:10), or even grass as "food" for sheep, in a non-biblical papyrus document (BAGD 148). [*brōsis*]

4:34 Food (*brōma*). The term can refer to literal food (BDAG 184) although it is different from the term describing the "provisions" (*trophē*) the disciples had gone into town to purchase (v. 8) and the "food" (*brōsis*) Jesus had just mentioned (v. 32). Here Jesus was referring to spiritual nourishment that was derived from doing and completing God's will and work. The evangelist has now used three different terms for food in these verses, illustrating his love of stylistic variation. There is little significant difference between them. [*brōma* + *trophē* + *brōsis*]

The one who sent me (*pempsantos*). See 1:6 for the nuance of this verb used by Jesus. Since the Father's "work" is mentioned in the next clause, it is easy to see how Jesus here views himself as participating in it. In fact, he will invite the disciples to participate in that work too, since they will have the opportunity to testify to the Samaritans who had come out from the town of Sychar to find out who Jesus was. [*pempō*]

To finish (*teleiōsō*). The "work" the Father had sent the Son to "complete" (NRSV, NET) or "finish" (KJV, NIV) was the salvation of the world (3:17), and it would be "finished" on the cross (19:28, 30). [*teleioō*]

4:35 Lift up your eyes (*eparate*). This idiom has OT roots (cf. Gen. 13:10; 1 Chron. 21:16; BAGD 281) and refers figuratively to "raising" the eyes to reflect on something. [*epairō*]

4:36 Wages (*misthon*). This term may refer to "pay" (NET) or "wages" (NIV, NRSV) earned by a worker—and thus deserved (LN 57.173). It may also refer to recompense for good or evil deeds done by an individual, in the sense of "reward" (LN 38.14). Here the term is being used figuratively by Jesus to describe the reward of those who labor in bringing people to him, in this case the Samaritans (TDNT 4:699). [*misthos*]

Fruit (*karpon*). In its literal sense the term refers to produce from plants or trees (LN 3.33) or to the "harvest" (CEV) or "crop" (NIV) that results (LN 43.15). Here the term is used figuratively for the reaped "spiritual crop." While in other contexts this may include moral virtues or character qualities in the life of the disciple (cf. 15:2), here it refers to potential converts from among the approaching Samaritans. See also 15:16. [*karpos*]

4:39 Believed (*episteusan*). (Also in vv. 41, 42) Here the meaning of the expression is the same as in 3:15, 16, 18, "exercise faith in, put one's trust in." However, the specific content of the Samaritan's "belief" in Jesus is specified in v. 42—they believed him to be the "Savior of the world." This certainly represents an advance over Nicodemus ("a teacher come from God," 3:2), but it also surpasses the disciples' own belief at this point, which centered around Jesus as the Jewish Messiah. The Samaritan's concept of who Jesus is extends beyond Judaism to "the world" (cf. 3:17). [*pisteuō*]

4:41 His word (*logon*). The point is that the Samaritans believed in Jesus on account of what he said ("his word," i.e., "message," NLT) without the need of miraculous signs. In this regard they were more receptive to

Jesus' message and mission than his own people, the Jews, were (cf. 1:11). [*logos*]

4:42 Your word (*lalian*). This refers to what the woman told the villagers, as opposed to Jesus' "message" (v. 41). [*lalia*]
   The **Savior of the world** (*sōtēr*). The term "savior" has its normal sense of "deliverer, preserver, rescuer" (BAGD 800; LN 21.22). Yet here there is irony in the Samaritan's declaration that Jesus was indeed "the Savior of the world," in comparison to John's prologue (1:11—"he came to his own, and his own did not receive him"). The Samaritans, whom the Jews regarded as Gentiles, proclaimed him "the Savior of the world." The Samaritans represent the entire world (TDNT 7:1016). They correctly saw Jesus as more than the Jewish Messiah. [*sōtēr*]

4:44 His own country (*patridi*). John's Gospel clearly identifies Jesus with Galilee (1:46) and does not even mention his Judean birth. [*patris*]

4:45 Welcomed (*edexanto*). This verb means to "receive" someone (NASB), particularly with friendliness or openness, like one would "welcome" a guest (LN 34.53; NIV, NRSV). This reception among the Galileans contrasts with Jesus' reception in Judea (Jerusalem). [*dechomai*]

4:46 Cana (*Kana*). See 2:1. Not only the location, but the mention of the first sign miracle, the water turned to wine, serves notice to the reader that Jesus' Galilean ministry has come full circle, and we are ready to move on to something new (cf. 4:54). [*Kana*]
   Nobleman (*basilikos*). (Also in v. 49) Although this term could describe a relative of the Herodian family, more likely it refers to a "royal official" (BAGD 136; NIV, NRSV, NET). He would have been a servant

of Herod, tetrarch of Galilee (who was popularly called a king, cf. Matt. 14:9; Mark 6:14-29). Capernaum was a border town, where many administrative officials lived. [*basilikos*]

4:47 Heal (*iasētai*). The verb means "to restore someone to health after a physical sickness or disease" (BDAG 465). The nobleman's son was "about to die"; the boy was at the point of death, and his father was desperate enough to make a journey of some 20 miles in an attempt to get help for him. The condition is not noted here, but v. 52 says that "the fever" left him. [*iaomai*]

4:48 Signs (*sēmeia*). The term refers to miracles. See the discussion at 2:11. [*sēmeion*]
   Wonders (*terata*). Josephus uses this term to describe a wide variety of events that point to God's ultimate sovereignty: storms (*J. W.* 4.4.5 [4.287]), phenomena in the heavens (*J. W.* 6.5.3 [6.288]), and a strange event in the temple (*J. W.* 6.5.3 [6.292]) are all described using this word. The combination "signs and wonders" frequently occurs in Acts (4:30; 5:12; 14:3; 15:12). [*teras*]
   Will not believe (*pisteusēte*). Here belief in Jesus is tied to miraculous signs. Jesus is speaking not just to the nobleman but the crowd, since the verbs "see" and "believe" are second person plural. [*pisteuō*]

4:49 Child (*paidion*). This is another term for "child" that can be used even of a newborn infant as well as older children, usually below the age of puberty (BAGD 604, LN 9.42). Earlier the nobleman's "son" had been mentioned (v. 47). [*paidion*]

4:50 Believed (*episteusen*). Here the content of what the nobleman believed is specified as "the word that Jesus spoke to him," referring to his son's recovery. When Jesus told the nobleman his son would recover, he believed it. [*pisteuō*]

4:51 Going down (*katabainontos*). This participle, which means "descending" (LN 15.107; TDNT 1:522), accurately describes the route the nobleman would have followed from Cana back to Capernaum. The road led east across the Galilean hills and then descended to the Sea of Galilee, more than one day's journey of some 20 miles. This indicates John's familiarity with Palestinian geography. [*katabainō*]

4:52 Began to improve (*kompsoteron*). This expression can be translated "began to improve" (BAGD 443; NET) or "got better" (LN 23.135; NIV, CEV). [*kompsoteron*]

The fever (*pyretos*). This term simply refers to a fever, presumably a high one. There is no other indication in the context of the precise nature of the boy's ailment (TDNT 6:958). [*pyretos*]

4:53 He believed (*episteusen*). The expression means the same as in 1:12, 3:15, 16, 18, "exercise faith in, put one's trust in." [*pisteuō*]

His whole household (*oikia*). Here the Greek term *oikix* does not refer to the building, but to the family of relatives by both descent and marriage, as well as slaves and servants, living in the same household (LN 10.8; BAGD 557; BDAG 695, 2). It is the concept of an extended family. [*oikia*]

4:54 Sign (*sēmeion*). See the discussion at 2:11. [*sēmeion*]

5:1 A feast (*heortē*). A textual variant here reads "the feast." The variant would almost certainly refer to Passover, but the preferred reading ("a feast") probably refers to some other feast. The incidental note in 5:3 that the sick were lying outside in the porticoes of the pool also supports a feast other than Passover because Passover falls near the end of winter

and the weather would not have been warm. Likewise, the feast of tabernacles is not likely because it forms the central setting for John 7 (where there are many contextual indications that this particular feast is in view). This leaves Pentecost as the feast most likely referred to here. At some time prior to this, Pentecost in the Jewish tradition (reflected in Jewish intertestamental literature and later post-Christian rabbinic writings) became identified with the giving of the Law to Moses on Mt. Sinai. Such an association might explain Jesus' reference to Moses in John 5:45-46. However, for the evangelist, the really important fact was that the healing involves a Sabbath. That is what provoked controversy with the Jewish religious leaders in 5:16-47. [*heortē*]

5:2 The Sheep Gate (*probatikē*). The traditional understanding of a reference to the Sheep Gate near the temple in the north city wall of Jerusalem is probably correct (BDAG 865). [*probatikos*]

A pool (*kolymbēthra*). The "pool" is generally assumed to be the double pool now called the pool of St. Anne, near the temple mount. The two pools were trapezoidal in shape, 165 feet wide at one end and 220 feet wide at the other, with a combined length of 315 feet, divided by a central partition. There were rows of columns on all four sides and on the central partition, forming the "five porticoes" mentioned here. Stairways at the corners permitted descent to the pools. [*kolymbēthra*]

Hebrew (*Hebraisti*). John uses this term five times, here and in 19:13, 17, 20, and 20:16. It literally means "in Hebrew," but the words described by this term in the fourth Gospel are Aramaic. It is worth noting that Josephus did not always distinguish between Hebrew and Aramaic in his use of the related term *Hebraios* (TDNT 3:374) and apparently John did not do so either. Thus some modern translations render the phrase "in Aramaic" (NIV, NET). [*Hebraisti*]

Bethesda / Bethzatha (*Bēthesda / Bēthzatha*). A textual variant produces different forms of the pool's name. Both may refer to the same location, one (*Bēthesda*) a Greek rendering (KJV, NIV, NLT, NET) and the other (*Bēthzatha*) a translation of the Aramaic intensive plural form of the same (RSV, NRSV, CEV). If so, this would be a rare instance in which both textual traditions are correct. [*Bēthesda, Bēthzatha*]

Porticoes (*stoas*). These "covered colonnades" (NIV) or "covered walkways" (NET) were open on one side (to the side facing the pool). People could stand, sit, or walk protected from the weather or heat (LN 7.40). [*stoa*]

5:3 Paralyzed (*xērōn*). This is a figurative use of the word, which literally means "dry, withered." When referring to human beings it describes arms or legs as "shrunken, withered, or wasted," and thus "paralyzed" (LN 23.173). [*xēros*]

5:6 Knowing (*gnous*). Supernatural knowledge on the part of Jesus (cf. 2:25) is implied here, though not demanded by this statement. Jesus could also have obtained the information from his disciples or from bystanders. [*ginōskō*]

Well (*hygiēs*). (Also in vv. 9, 11, 14, 15) This term refers to a state of wellness in contrast to sickness (LN 23.129). Jesus was offering the paralytic (the "one who was sick," v. 7) the opportunity to escape from his physical disability and be restored to a state of health. [*hygiēs*]

5:7 Sir (*kyrie*). See 4:11. This use involves polite address. The paralytic who was healed by Jesus never acknowledged him as Lord—instead, he reported Jesus to the authorities. [*kyrios*]

Troubled (*tarachthē*). Here the verb is used in a literal sense to refer to the "stirring" of the water in the pool (BDAG 990; NRSV, NLT, NET). John also uses the word figuratively to describe inner turmoil or agitation (cf. 11:33). [*tarassō*]

5:8 Pallet (*krabatton*). (Also in vv. 9, 10, 11) The term refers to a relatively lightweight and small "mat" (NIV, NRSV, NET) or "pallet" (RSV, NASB) on which a person could lie down (LN 6.107, BAGD 447). In some cases these mats would be sturdy enough to be used as stretchers to carry an invalid (Mark 2:4) although that is probably not the case here. This was probably a reed or cloth mat that could be easily rolled up and carried. [*krabattos*]

5:9 The Sabbath (*sabbaton*). The temporal note "it was the Sabbath" is significant because the timing produced the confrontation. [*sabbaton*]

5:10 The Jews (*Ioudaiou*). See 1:19. Here the term refers to the Jewish religious authorities in Jerusalem, since they are concerned with maintaining the Sabbath ordinance. [*Ioudaios*]

5:13 Had withdrawn (*exeneusen*). The verb means "to withdraw quietly, to slip out," in the sense of leaving a place without being noticed (LN 15.60). This was made easier in the present case because there was a crowd present. [*ekneuō*]

5:14 Worse (*cheiron*). The Greek term refers to something that is even less satisfactory than what preceded (LN 65.29). Probably this does not mean the man would be stricken with an even more severe ailment. It is more likely Jesus was alluding to what would happen at the man's judgment (cf. v. 29), which could be "worse" than any physical disability by far. [*cheirōn*]

5:16 Were persecuting (*ediōkon*). The verb can mean "to pursue" but in this context it refers to the act of oppressing or "harassing" one (NLT), with the implication that this activity is organized and deliberate (LN 39.45). By v. 18 the evangelist says the Jewish religious leaders were so violently opposed to Jesus that they were trying to "kill" him. [*diōkō*]

5:17 Working (*ergazetai*). The verb means "to perform work, to labor by expending effort" (LN 42.41). Used of God, it implies that he is a living, active, creative God, whose various "works" are described in his interventions in human history in the OT (TDNT 2:640). Since human beings were born on the Sabbath and died on the Sabbath, the Jewish authorities in Jesus' day understood God to be working on the Sabbath because only God could give life, and only God could deal with people in judgment. But this Sabbath privilege was peculiar to God alone, and in claiming the right to heal on the Sabbath Jesus was claiming to share in a divine privilege, "thus making himself equal with God" (5:18). This explains the violence of the reaction to Jesus' statement, "My Father is working until now, and I am working." [*ergazomai*]

5:18 Equal (*ison*). The term can refer to something "equal" in number, size, quality, or characteristics (BAGD 381; LN 58.33). Equality with God was an implication of Jesus' claim to be "working" on the Sabbath just as his Father was "working." This labor amounted to "breaking" the Sabbath, since the Sabbath rest ordinance was not observed. The Jewish authorities in Jerusalem reacted violently to this claim seeking to kill Jesus. See also 5:17. [*isos*]

5:19 These things (*tauta*). The problem with this term concerns its referent. What are the "things" that the Son sees the Father doing and does likewise? Probably this refers to the same activities that the rabbis saw as legitimate works of God on the Sabbath (see 5:17). The Father grants life on the Sabbath, and so does Jesus. But just as the Father grants physical life on the Sabbath, the Son grants spiritual life (cf. 5:21). Just as the Father judges those who die on the Sabbath, so Jesus determines the destiny of people on the Sabbath (cf. 5:22-23). Not only has this power been granted to Jesus in the present, it will be his in the future as well. In 5:28 not only the spiritually dead but also the physically dead are in view. [*houtos*]

5:20 Loves (*philei*). This verb describes the love the Father has for the Son, an indication that this verb for John does not describe a lesser kind of love than the verb *agapaō* (cf. 21:15). If anything, the love described by the verb used here is one based on interpersonal relationship (LN 25.33). In view of John's tendency to use synonyms interchangeably, though, it is probably best not to make too much of the choice of verb. See also the discussion at 11:5. [*phileō*]

5:21 Makes them alive (*zōopoiei*). In classical Greek this verb could be used of the birth of animals or of the growth of plants (TDNT 2:874). Here it is used of the Father and the Son granting people spiritual life. In the case of the Father it is connected with the resurrection of the dead and thus is similar to the verb *egeirō*. When the Son is said to "make alive" whoever he wishes, it is in the sense of granting "eternal life" to them in the present (cf. v. 24). [*zōopoieō*]

5:23 May honor (*timōsi*). Here Jesus is claiming that he as the Son is due the same "honor" given to the Father, based on the authority the Father gives him to "judge" (v. 22). People are therefore under the same obligation to the Son as they are to the Father. This also shows the Son's equality with the Father. [*timaō*]

Who sent (*pempsanta*). (Also in v. 24) The two occurrences here imply the Father's participation in the Son's work, so that failure to honor the Son is also a failure to honor the Father who "sent" him. [*pempō*]

5:24 Who believes (*pisteuōn*). Here the meaning of the expression could be the same as in 3:15, 16, 18, "exercise faith in, put one's trust in," although the preposition *eis* ("in") is not used with the verb here. The object specified here is "the one who sent me," referring to the Father (v. 23), but one could argue that "what the Father testifies about me" is what is implied. [*pisteuō*]

Judgment (*krisin*). Here "judgment" (NRSV) in the sense of a negative outcome, "condemnation" (KJV), is in view. The person who responds in faith to the Son ("hears my word and believes him who sent me") gains "eternal life," escapes condemnation ("will never be condemned" CEV, NLT), and has "passed over" from death to life (see the following discussion). [*krisis*]

Has passed over (*metabebēken*). The verb means "to transfer over or pass over from one place to another" (cf. 13:1). It can refer to changing one's residence (Luke 10:7). It can also be used of objects like a mountain (Matt. 17:20). John uses the term here to refer to a change of state or condition (BDAG 638; "crossed over from death to life," NIV; NET). The person who "believes" in Jesus has "transferred over" from the state of spiritual "death" to the state of spiritual (i.e., eternal) "life." The perfect tense looks at a past action with results existing at the time of writing. This is consistent with John's concept of "eternal life," which begins not in the world to come, but in the present, at the time of belief (i.e., conversion). [*metabainō + zōē*]

5:25 An hour (*hōra*). Cf. 4:23. The term refers here to an indefinite future "time" (NIV,

NET) when "the dead" will be raised in a general resurrection at the "last day" (cf. 11:24). Although some interpreters argue that this statement is fulfilled with Lazarus (11:44), the verb "will hear" is plural in this verse, and v. 28 states that "all" who are in the tombs will come out. Although much of the eschatology in John's Gospel can be described as "realized" (i.e., already fulfilled in the present), this verse and vv. 28-29 clearly cannot refer to the present time. [*hōra*]

Will live (*zēsousin*). This verb could refer to coming to life physically or spiritually. If one understands the "hour" in v. 25 and v. 28 to be the same "hour," then this refers to the general resurrection of the dead, since that is clearly what v. 28 refers to. If one understands two different "hours" in vv. 25 and 28, then v. 25 could refer to those spiritually "dead" people who "hear" the Son's voice and respond in faith, receiving eternal life ("will live"). [*zaō*]

5:26 Has life (*zōēn*). Here "life" refers to eternal life, possessed by the Father and the Son, and available to believers. [*zōē*]

5:27 Authority (*exousian*). The term is used of the possibility or freedom of action given by a king or government, conferring authority or permission on groups or individuals (TDNT 2:562). Here it refers to the "authority" given to the Son by the Father; it is connected to the "Son of Man" concept, which in the fourth Gospel is drawn from the imagery in Dan. 7:13-14, where judgment "authority" is transferred to the Son of Man in relation to God's kingdom. [*exousia*]

Judgment (*krisin*). (Also in v. 29) Here "judgment" is connected both to Jesus' identity as the Son of Man and to the future "judgment," which takes place at the general resurrection of the dead (vv. 28-29). The "resurrection of judgment" in v. 29 refers to a resurrection leading to condemnation. [*krisis*]

5:28 The tombs (*mnēmeiois*). Although this term could refer to monuments to the dead, some of which also served as "tombs" (LN 7.76), it could also refer simply to "graves" (LN 7.75). The term is used in 11:17, 31 for Lazarus's "tomb," which is described in 11:38 as a cave with a stone in front of it to seal it. [*mnēmeion*]

5:29 Evil (*phaula*). See 3:20. This entire section has many connections to 3:17-21. [*phaulos*]

5:30 Judge . . . judgment (*krinō . . . krisis*). See the discussion at 3:19. Although the Father had "given all judgment" to the Son (v. 22) and had "given him authority to carry out judgment" (v. 27), Jesus still indicated here that he does nothing on his own authority, but seeks the will of the Father who sent him. The unity of the Father and Son is emphasized. [*krinō + krisis*]

5:32 Another (*allos*). The problem with this term is the referent—is it John the Baptist, or God the Father? In the nearer context (v. 33) it would seem to be the Baptist. However, v. 34 appears to indicate that Jesus did not receive testimony from human beings. It is probably better to see the referent as God the Father, with v. 32 being explained by v. 37. This makes the comments about John the Baptist in vv. 33-36 a parenthetical digression. [*allos*]

5:34 May be saved (*sōthēte*). The object of "saving" here is "the Jews" (cf. vv. 18-19). For John, the concept of "being saved" essentially means "attaining salvation," or in John's preferred terms, "having eternal life." See the discussion at 3:17. [*sōzō*]

5:35 A lamp (*lychnos*). Sir. 48:1 states that the word of Elijah was "a flame like a torch." Because of the connection between John the Baptist and Elijah (see John 1:21), it was natural for Jesus to apply this description to John. [*lychnos*]

5:36 The works (*erga*). Here the plural "works" (NET "deeds") refers to the sign miracles that Jesus performs and which testify to his identity. However, the use of the verb *teleioō* here (usually translated "accomplish," "complete," or "finish") suggests a connection to the "one work" the Father gave Jesus to do, the mission of providing salvation for the world (3:17), which would ultimately necessitate Jesus going to the cross (cf. 17:4). [*ergon + teleioō*]

5:37 Who sent (*pempsas*). (Also in the following verse) See the discussion at 1:6. Here a different verb for "to send" than *apostellō* is used. This verb usually implies the Father's participation in the works of the "sent" one, Jesus, who tells his hearers they have neither "heard his [= God's] voice nor seen his form." The reader of the fourth Gospel will remember that Jesus is himself the complete and full revelation of God (1:18; cf. also 14:9). [*pempō*]

His form (*eidos*). The statement "You have neither heard his voice nor seen his 'form'" recalls Num. 12:8 (the Greek text of John is virtually identical to the OT Greek translation of Num. 12). This refers to God's "form," or outward appearance ("seen him face to face," CEV, NLT). The statement fits the general point made in John that Jesus is the outward and visible revelation of the Father (1:18; 14:9). [*eidos*]

5:38 Residing (*menonta*). For Jesus to say to his opponents that they did not have God's word "residing" in them ("abiding" NASB; NRSV; NIV "nor does his word dwell in you") says that they utterly reject God, his revelation in the Scriptures (v. 39), and ultimately his revelation in Jesus himself, whom the Father "sent" (v. 36). [*menō*]

Do not believe (*pisteuete*). Here the object of the verb "believe" is specified as "the one whom that one [i.e., the Father] sent," referring to Jesus himself. In context, the issue is whether the hearers will "come" to Jesus or not (v. 40). [*pisteuō*]

5:39 Search (*eraunate*). The verb emphasizes the diligence of the investigation or search, to seek out information by careful inquiry (LN 27.34). See also TDNT 2:655-57. [*eraunaō*]

Eternal life (*zōēn*). (Also in the following verse) Note the following examples from the rabbinic tractate *Pirqe Abot* ("The Sayings of the Fathers"): *Pirqe Abot* 2:8, "he who has acquired the words of the law has acquired for himself the life of the world to come"; *Pirqe Abot* 6:7, "Great is the law for it gives to those who practice it life in this world and in the world to come." The reader of John's Gospel would, of course, recognize what the current Jewish authorities did not—that Jesus himself (not the Torah) is the true source of eternal life (cf. the dialogue with Nicodemus in 3:1-15 and the dialogue with the Samaritan woman in 4:7-26). [*zōē*]

5:41 Glory (*doxan*). Here and in v. 44 "glory" is used in the sense of "praise" or "honor" from men, a usage different from the general meaning of the term in the fourth Gospel (TDNT 2:248). See 1:14 for a summary of the meaning of this term. [*doxa*]

5:43 Receive (*lambanete*). (Also in v. 44) Here is the fulfillment of what was stated in the prologue to John's Gospel: "he came to his own, and his own did not 'receive' him" (1:11). The two verbs are not identical; *paralambanō* is used in 1:11 and *lambanō* here, but they are related, and *lambanō* is used in 1:12. "Receiving" Jesus and "believing" in him (v. 44) are also related here, as they are in 1:12. [*lambanō*]

5:44 Believe (*pisteusai*). Here the meaning of the expression is the same as in 3:15, 16, 18, "exercise faith in, put one's trust in." "Believe" in v. 44 is parallel to "receive" in v. 43, just as it is in 1:12, and both refer to a faith response to Jesus. [*pisteuō*]

Seek (*zēteite*). Here Jesus accuses his opponents of not "seeking" the "glory" that comes from God. The reference to "glory" recalls 1:14, "and we beheld his 'glory'— 'glory' as of the one and only from the Father, full of grace and truth." The verb has a range of meaning in John's Gospel: "look for in order to find the whereabouts of someone or something that has been lost" (6:24, 26; 7:34, 36), "seek for someone or something without knowing where to find it" (18:4, 7), "investigate, examine, deliberate (on the facts)" (16:19), "investigate" (as a legal term, perhaps in 8:50b and 11:56), "seek" in the sense of desire or try to obtain (5:44; 7:18; 8:50a), or with an interrogative pronoun in a question (1:38; 4:27). Other combinations with infinitives occur in 5:18 and 7:1. Uses that involve other people "seeking" Jesus are especially significant, because in the case of his opponents (as here), there will come a time when they will want to find Jesus but will not be able to (7:34). [*zēteō*]

5:45 Condemn (*katēgorēsō*). Ironically, the final condemnation will come from Moses, even though Moses is the one the Jewish authorities have trusted ("hoped"). There is widespread evidence that first-century Jews looked on Moses as their intercessor (Philo, *Life of Moses* 2.166; *T. Moses* 11.17). In Josephus, Moses speaks of himself and God as "vilified" by the rebellious Israelites, but says both he and God will not cease their efforts on the Israelites' behalf (*Ant.* 3.13 [3.298]). Somewhat later Samaritan texts like *Memar Marqah* 4.10 also speak of Moses' intercessory role. So Jesus is saying that Moses would no longer intercede for the Jewish people; rather due to their rejection of Jesus as God's Messiah, Moses would "condemn." [katēgoreō]

Hoped (ēlpikate). The verb means "to put one's hope in someone or something" (BAGD 252). Here the Jewish religious leaders have "put their hope" in Moses. This is very similar and in contrast to John's concept of "trusting in" (pisteuō) Jesus Christ. [elpizō]

5:46 Believed ... would believe (episteuete ... episteuete). (Also twice in the following verse) Here what is believed is specified as "Moses," meaning "what Moses wrote about the Messiah" (cf. 1:45; see also the following verse, "his writings"). The person who really believed Moses would also believe what Jesus said ("believe me"). What is not believed in the following verse is Jesus' "words." [pisteuō]

5:47 Writings (grammasin). The first five books of the OT were traditionally considered to be the writings of Moses. What Moses wrote was being contrasted with what Jesus said ("my words"). [gramma]

6:1 Tiberias (Tiberiados). This is another name for the Sea (or Lake) of Galilee (BAGD 815; LN 93.597). In the NT only John refers to the Sea of Galilee by this name (cf. 21:1), but this is correct local usage. In the mid-20s Herod Antipas enlarged and enhanced the town of Tiberias on the southwestern shore of the lake, naming it in honor of Tiberius Caesar. After this time the name came into use for the lake itself. [Tiberias]

6:2 The signs (sēmeia). This is a reference to other "signs" not mentioned elsewhere by John (cf. 21:25). See the discussion of this term at 2:11. [sēmeion]

6:3 The mountain (oros). This term may refer to a relatively high elevation of land compared to a "hill" (LN 1.46). It may also refer

to "hill country" or higher, rougher ground (TDNT 5.484; "went up into the hills," NLT). In this case it may refer to the high country east of the Sea of Galilee (known generally today as the Golan Heights). [oros]

6:6 Testing (peirazōn). The verb is used here of "testing" something to discover its nature or character (BDAG 792). When used of God or Jesus "testing" people, it generally has a favorable sense, in that people are given the opportunity to prove themselves faithful. The illustration has often been used of an automobile manufacturer "testing" its own vehicles. When Ford puts Ford cars to the test, the hope is that they will successfully pass the test. [peirazō]

6:7 Two hundred denarii (dēnariōn). Since the "denarius" was a Roman silver coin worth about a day's wage for a laborer (BAGD 179; LN 6.75), "two hundred" would be an amount worth about eight months' wages. [dēnarion]

6:9 Barley loaves (krithinous). These were loaves made from barley flour. They recall 2 Kings 4:42-44, where Elisha multiplied barley loaves. These, along with the two small fish, were basic dietary staples of the time for ordinary people. [krithinos]

Fish (opsaria). The usual meaning of this word is a small morsel of food eaten with bread, but in some contexts it is clear the word means "fish." (LN 5.16) In the account of the feeding of the 5,000 only John uses this term to describe the "two fish." Matthew, Mark, and Luke all use the word ichthys. [opsarion]

6:10 Sit down (anapesein). This verb means "to be in a reclining position while eating" (LN 17.23). In this ancient context, where there was no formal meal and no table, the term refers to sitting down on the ground. [anapiptō]

Grass (*chortos*). The presence of so much "grass" may well represent an eyewitness recollection. The term refers to green grass of a field or meadow (BAGD 884). [*chortos*]

Five thousand (*pentakischilioi*). The number given here probably did not include the women and children present, but adult males only. See the parallel in Matt. 14:21. [*pentakischilioi*]

6:11 Having given thanks (*eucharistēsas*). This reflects a typical Jewish blessing before a meal (BAGD 328). [*eucharisteō*]

He distributed (*diedōken*). The verb means "to divide up among various parties, to distribute" (BDAG 227). It is used elsewhere of "dividing up" the spoils after an attack on a palace (Luke 11:22). [*diadidōmi*]

6:12 Be lost (*apolētai*). Here the verb *apollymi* means "be lost" (BAGD 95). This refers to the "fragments" of the "barley loaves" gathered up by the Twelve after people had "eaten their fill" (*eneplēsthēsan*). John makes no further mention of the "fish," presumably because the following "Bread of Life" discourse is based on the "bread" imagery in the present passage. [*apollymi*]

6:14 The prophet (*prophētēs*). The referent is the "prophet like Moses" of Deut. 18:15, by this time an eschatological figure in popular belief (See 1:21). Acts 3:22 identifies Jesus as this prophet. [*prophētēs*]

6:15 Knowing (*gnous*). Once again this verb is used with the implication of supernatural knowledge (cf. 2:25; 5:6). [*ginōskō*]

Seize (*harpazein*). The verb has the idea of grabbing or seizing someone or something by force (LN 18.4). After the miracle of the feeding of the 5,000, the crowds were so convinced that Jesus was the Messiah that they were prepared "to take him by force" (NLT) to make him king. From John's perspective

this effort was misguided, reflecting popular messianic expectations but failing to recognize the true nature of Jesus' mission (cf. 3:17; 18:36). [*harpazō*]

King (*basilea*). The nature of Jesus' kingship will become an issue again in the passion narrative of John's Gospel (18:33 ff.). [*basileus*]

Withdrew (*anechōrēsen*). This verb means "to move away from a location," implying a considerable distance (LN 15.53). Jesus, knowing that his "hour" had not yet come, "withdrew again up the mountainside alone." The ministry of miracles in Galilee, concluding with this last public miracle in Galilee recorded by John, aroused such a popular response that there was danger of an uprising. This would have provided the authorities with an excuse to arrest Jesus. Since the time for arrest (Jesus' "hour") had not yet arrived, he moved away from the crowds to forestall this. Furthermore, the Galileans' volatile reaction to the signs prepares for and foreshadows the misunderstanding of the miracle itself, including the misunderstanding of Jesus' explanation (John 6:22-71). [*anachōreō*]

6:17 Got aboard (*embantes*). They "embark" in a boat (LN 15.95). The "boat" used by the disciples here was probably a fishing boat (see Luke 5:7). [*embainō*]

Dark (*skotia*). John states it was "already dark" and Jesus had not yet come to them when the disciples got into the boat to cross the lake to Capernaum. The element of darkness adds to the suspense and the storm's sinister nature, but for the evangelist it may represent more. In light of the frequent use of light/darkness imagery in John's Gospel, the situation here finds the disciples "in the dark" without Jesus. [*skotia*]

6:18 Rose up (*diegeireto*). The literal meaning of the verb is to "wake up" someone who is asleep (BAGD 193), but by figurative extension it refers to a body of water becoming "stirred up" (NASB) or rough with wind and waves (NLT "the sea grew very rough"). John adds that "a strong wind was blowing," so that conditions were rapidly deteriorating on the lake. [*diegeirō*]

6:19 Having rowed (*elēlakotes*). The verb means "to be driven along" or "moved by force" (LN 15.161) and can refer to a ship "driven along" by the wind (BAGD 248). However, in some contexts as here the verb means "to row a ship or boat by means of oars." [*elaunō*]

Three or four miles (*stadious*). Literally, "twenty-five or thirty stades." A "stade" is a unit of linear measure equal to about 607 feet (BAGD 764). The distance the disciples had rowed was thus about three to three-and-a-half miles. Since the Sea of Galilee at its widest point is seven miles by 12 miles, they were approximately in the middle of the lake. [*stadion*]

6:20 It is I (*egō eimi*). On one level this statement can be read as simple identification (cf. 4:26), but on another level, Jesus is the one who bears the divine Name (cf. Exod. 3:14). For the evangelist the account of Jesus walking on the sea takes on the character of a theophany, not unlike the Transfiguration recorded in the Synoptic Gospels (Mark 9:1-8 and parallels). To the disciples in the boat (probably the Twelve, cf. 6:67), not to the crowds, Jesus revealed that he was much more than a political Messiah. Who he was could be summed up by the revealing phrase "I am." [*egō + eimi*]

6:22 Boat (*ploiarion*). This word can describe a small ship, boat, or skiff (BAGD 673). The form is diminutive, but in some contexts this need not imply a particularly small boat (LN 6.42). [*ploiarion*]

6:24 Seeking (*zētountes*). (Also in v. 26) People "seeking" Jesus is another theme in John's Gospel. See the discussion of this verb at 5:44. [*zēteō*]

6:26 Were filled (*echortasthēte*). This verb means to eat until one is completely satisfied (LN 23.15; NRSV "you ate your fill of the loaves"). The incident referred to is recorded in 6:12, but there a different Greek word is used. Once again this illustrates the evangelist's fondness for stylistic variation. [*chortazō*]

6:27 Which perishes (*apollymenēn*). The verb in reference to things can mean "be lost, pass away, be ruined" (BAGD 95). In *Shepherd of Hermas*, Mandate 5.1.5, it is used to describe spoiled honey. Here the term may refer to "food that spoils" (NIV), but in context the focus is more on the temporary nature of this kind of food ("food that disappears," NET). [*apollymi*]

The Son of Man (*huios . . . anthrōpou*). Here the title "Son of Man" looks at Jesus as one who has been given regal authority, but related to the authority given the "one like a Son of Man" in Dan. 7:13. This is to be seen in contrast to the authority of a mere earthly king, which is what the crowds were wanting to bestow on Jesus in the immediately preceding context (6:15). See the discussion at 1:51. [*huios + anthrōpos*]

Has sealed (*esphragisen*). The Greek verb, literally "to seal," means to demonstrate the truth or validity of something by providing authentic proof (LN 28.53). Here Jesus is the referent; the Father has put his "seal of approval" on him (NIV, NET). This includes, but is not limited to, the "sign miracles" that Jesus had been performing (v. 26). [*sphragizō*]

6:28 The works of God (*erga*). Here the plural "works," spoken by the crowd, is a response to Jesus' comment in v. 27, "Do not 'work' for the food which perishes but for the food which endures to eternal life." Although the crowd's question may refer indirectly to the sign miracles that Jesus has been performing, it is more likely the crowd thought there was some "work" Jesus was telling them to do. This is confirmed by Jesus' statement in the next verse, where he defines the "work" (now singular) of God as "to believe in the one whom he has sent." [*ergon*]

6:29 Sent (*apesteilen*). Here the term implies God's full authority behind Jesus' words and works. In light of the "works" that Jesus does, which are authenticated by God, the one "work" for his hearers to do is "believe" in him, that is, "in the one God sent." See the discussion at 1:6. [*apostellō*]

6:30 Sign (*sēmeion*). The crowd responded to Jesus' statement about believing in the one God had sent by demanding a "sign," especially something like the manna God provided for the Israelites in the wilderness. See the discussion of this term at 2:11. [*sēmeion*]
    Believe (*pisteusōmen*). Here the verb occurs without the preposition *eis* ("in") with "you" (referring to Jesus) as its object. The implied object of belief is "what you say about yourself," that is, "what you claim yourself to be." [*pisteuō*]

6:31 The manna (*to manna*). This Greek word is found in classical literature from the time of Hippocrates (5th century B.C.) to refer to a "morsel, grain, crumb," especially of incense (TDNT 4:462). Probably because it was so similar in sound to the Hebrew term, it was used by the Greek OT to translate it in a number of verses like Num. 11:6, 9; Deut. 8:3, 16. So it came to be used for the OT manna by ancient Jewish writers like Philo and Josephus, so that was the commonly used term for the Hebrew word. [*manna*]
    Bread from heaven (*arton*). (Also in vv. 32)

The word "bread" can refer to bread in particular or "food" in general (cf. Matt. 6:11) since bread was the most important food (BAGD 110). This forms part of a quotation from Ps. 78:24, which refers to the giving of manna in the wilderness (cf. Exod. 16:35). The manna is referred to as "bread" (i.e., "food, a source of sustenance"), and it came "from heaven" (ie, from God). It was physical food miraculously (i.e., spiritually) provided. [*artos*]

6:32 The true bread from heaven (*alēthinon*). Here the meaning could be more like "genuine," but Jesus as truth incarnate and the revealer of God himself is not excluded in the context. By the time we get to the following verse, the "bread of God" is Jesus himself, who gives "life" to the world. [*alēthinos*]

6:33 Comes down (*katabainōn*). The major uses of this verb all involve Jesus. It refers to the descent of the Spirit on Jesus at his baptism (1:32-33), to the ascent and descent of angels on the Son of Man (1:51), and to the descent from heaven of the Son of Man himself (3:13; 6:33). Here Jesus calls himself the "bread," which "comes down from heaven." [*katabainō*]
    Life (*zōēn*). Here the term refers to "eternal life." Unlike the manna in the OT, which provided physical nourishment for God's people in the wilderness, the "bread of God" Jesus refers to here that "comes down from heaven" was capable of imparting eternal "life." [*zōē*]

6:34 This bread (*arton*). See 6:31-32. The crowd listening to Jesus understood that he was promising some kind of "heavenly bread," probably like the manna provided in the wilderness. Once again Jesus was speaking on a spiritual level of himself as the "bread from heaven," but the hearers misunderstood. [*artos*]

6:35 I am (*egō eimi*). This is one of the "I am" statements with a predicate. Here Jesus identified himself as "the bread of life," an image associated with ideas of sustenance ("will never hunger") and the provision of manna in the wilderness during the Exodus. See also 4:26. [*egō + eimi + artos*]

The one who comes to me (*erchomenos*). The expression "comes to me" is a frequent one in John's Gospel for responding to Jesus in faith (6:37, 44, 45). [*erchomai*]

The one who believes in me (*pisteuōn*). The parallelism between this phrase and the earlier phrase "the one who comes to me" indicates that for John these phrases are virtually equivalent. Both refer to a positive response to Jesus (cf. John 3:17-21). The negative statement, indicating refusal to believe, is found in the following verse. [*pisteuō*]

Shall never thirst (*dipsēsei*). This expression recalls the promise of "living water" Jesus made to the Samaritan woman (4:13-14). Images of both "hungering" and "thirsting" are woven into the Bread of Life remarks to refer to spiritual hunger and thirst, which Jesus alone fills. [*dipsaō*]

Ever (*pōpote*). This adverb adds intensity, normally to a negative statement (BDAG 900). It means "ever, at any time." The implication is that this action will never happen. [*pōpote*]

6:37 I will not cast out (*ekbalō*). Since "the one who comes to me" refers to the person who "comes" to Jesus in faith (cf. 3:21, 6:45) Jesus here promises that he will not reject ("cast out" RSV, NASB; NIV, NRSV "will never drive away"; NLT "will never reject") such an individual. [*ekballō*]

6:38 I have come down (*katabebēka*). Here Jesus speaks plainly of himself as having "come down from heaven." See the summary at v. 33 above. [*katabainō*]

6:39 Lose (*apolesō*). Here the verb *apollymi* can mean either "perish, die" or "be lost" (BAGD 95). Both these meanings occur in John's Gospel, the first in 3:16; 10:28; 17:12 and the second in 6:12. Here the meaning "perish, die" is indicated because the context deals with being "raised up at the last day," an eschatological event. [*apollymi*]

Raise ... up (*anastēsō*). The verb means to cause someone to live again who has died (LN 23.94). In the background of this saying is the first century Jewish belief in a general resurrection of the dead, which would take place "at the last day" and be followed by judgment, which assigned one's eternal destiny (Dan. 12:2). Such a belief was held by the Pharisees and most other groups, except the Sadducees, who denied the resurrection. This belief is reflected in Martha's statement in 11:24 where the same verb is used. [*anistēmi*]

The last day (*eschatē*). This refers to the "day of the Lord," when God would raise the dead for judgment, transform the present world, and inaugurate his eternal kingdom (cf. TDNT 2:697). [*eschatos*]

6:40 Beholds (*theōrōn*). The verb means "to be a spectator, to look at, to observe, to perceive" (BAGD 360). The participle here refers to the person who "beholds the Son" (NASB) not just physically, but with spiritual insight, discerning his identity and mission (NIV "everyone who looks to the Son"). Note that here the result (having "eternal life" and being raised up "at the last day") is produced by "beholding" the Son and "believing" in him. Cf. John 6:54 where an identical result is produced by eating Jesus' "flesh" and drinking his "blood." This suggests that the phrase in 6:54 ("eats my flesh and drinks my blood") is to be understood in terms of the earlier phrase here ("beholds the Son and believes in him"). [*theōreō*]

6:41 The Jews (*Ioudaioi*). See 1:19. Here the referent should probably be restricted to those Jews who were hostile to Jesus, since the "crowd" mentioned in 6:22-24 was almost all Jewish (note they addressed Jesus as "Rabbi" in 6:25). [*Ioudaios*]

I am (*egō eimi*). See the discussions at 6:35 and 4:26. [*egō + eimi*]

6:42 I have come down (*katabebēka*). Here Jesus' opponents repeat his claim to have "come down from heaven." See the discussion of this verb at v. 33. [*katabainō*]

6:44 To come to me (*elthein*). This expression means responding to Jesus in faith. See 6:35, where "comes to me" and "believes in me" are virtually interchangeable. [*erchomai*]

Who sent (*pempsas*). See the discussion at 1:6. The use of this term here implies the Father's participation, which is precisely the subject under discussion. [*pempō*]

Draws (*elkysē*). The basic meaning of the verb is "to tug" or "to draw" (with a material object specified, cf. 18:10; 21:6, 11). The word is even used once of magnetic attraction (TDNT 2:503; BAGD 251). In this context it speaks of a supernatural attraction of some sort, but whether it is binding or irresistible is not mentioned (cf. CEV "Makes them want to come"). There is a parallel with 6:65 where Jesus says that no one can come to him unless the Father has permitted it. This parallels the citations from Isaiah by the evangelist to reflect the spiritual blindness of the Jewish leaders (cf. 9:41; 12:39-40). [*elkyō*]

6:45 The prophets (*prophētais*). This phrase refers to the section of the OT known as "the prophets" (BAGD 723). The quotation is actually from Isa. 54:13. [*prophētēs*]

Comes to me (*erchetai*). The expression "comes to" Jesus refers to a personal response of faith in him. See 6:35, 44. [*erchomai*]

6:46 Has seen (*heōraken*). This statement that no one "has seen the Father" recalls 1:18 in the prologue to John's Gospel. [*horaō*]

6:47 The one who believes (*pisteuōn*). Here the meaning of the expression is the same as in 3:15, 16, 18, "exercise faith in, put one's trust in." As in 3:16, the "one who believes" has "eternal life." [*pisteuō + zōē*]

6:48 The bread of life (*artos*). See 6:32-33 where Jesus describes himself as the "bread of God, the one who comes down from heaven and gives life to the world." The phrase here is a condensed version of the earlier one. The point is that Jesus is the source of spiritual sustenance, and personal appropriation of him by faith results in eternal life. [*artos*]

6:51 Of the world (*kosmou*). Here the "world" refers to people, that is, "humanity" or the human race. This is also in keeping with God's "love" for the "world" in giving his Son (3:16). See a similar statement about the atonement's extent in 1 John 2:2. See also John 1:9. [*kosmos*]

My flesh (*sarx*). Since *sarx* in John's Gospel is related to the incarnation (1:14), what Jesus means here is that he will give up his life (i.e., his physical body will be crucified). This is the "living bread," and one must partake of it by faith in order to "live forever," an expression that means "experience eternal life." [*sarx*]

6:52 His flesh (*sarka*). (Also in vv. 51 and 53) Once again Jesus' opponents understood him literally (on the physical level rather than the spiritual level) and thought that by speaking about giving them his "flesh" to "eat," he was talking about some form of cannibalism, which would have been especially abhorrent to a Jew. What they failed to see was that the "eating" meant personal appropriation by faith, rather than the consuming of physical food. [*sarx*]

6:53 Drink ... blood (*piēte ... haima*). Now the "drinking" of "blood" is added to the image, another action that would be especially abhorrent to a Jew. It was forbidden in the OT to drink the blood of animal sacrifices (Lev. 17:10, 14; Deut. 12:23; Gen. 9:4). In calling for a personal response by faith in him, including reference to his sacrificial death, Jesus was using terms designed to be particularly repugnant to the Jewish religious leaders (cf. v. 52). [*pinō + haima*]

6:54 The one who eats (*trōgōn*). The Greek word here translated "eats" (LN 23.3) when used of animals may mean "gnaw, nibble, munch, eat (audibly)" (BAGD 829). The Greek term is a different one than the word translated "eat" (*esthiō*) in 6:52, 53; it may simply reflect a preference for one form over the other on the evangelist's part rather than an attempt to express a slightly more graphic meaning (John loves stylistic variation, and the original discourse was probably in Aramaic rather than Greek, so the evangelist may be paraphrasing what Jesus said). If there is a difference in meaning, the word used here (*trōgō*) is the more graphic and vivid of the two ("gnaw" or "chew"). Cf. also TDNT 8:236. [*trōgō*]
  Eternal life (*zōēn*). Here the outcome of "eating" Jesus' "flesh" and "drinking" his "blood" is twofold: the person who does this "has eternal life," which is realized now (the "already"), and Jesus will "raise him up at the last day," which is future (the "not yet"). This outcome, both the "already" and the "not yet," is expressed identically in 6:40, but the response that brings about the outcome is stated there as "every one who beholds the Son and believes in him." This places "beholds the Son and believes in him" in tandem with the phrase here, "eats my flesh and drinks my blood." Since both phrases pro-

duce the same outcome, John has simply exchanged the imagery of "beholding the Son and believing in him" (which speaks of personal appropriation by faith) with the alternative of "eating Jesus' flesh and drinking his blood," which also speaks of personal appropriation by faith. For John the terminology is essentially interchangeable. See also the discussions of the term "life" at 1:4 and 17:2. [*zōē*]

6:56 Resides (*menei*). Now there is further interchange of imagery: in 6:54 eating Jesus' "flesh" and drinking his "blood" produces the twofold outcome of having "eternal life" and the promise of being "raised up at the last day." Here the same process of eating Jesus' "flesh" and drinking his "blood" leads to a relationship of mutual indwelling ("resides in me, and I in him"; CEV "you are one with me, and I am one with you"). The phrases that describe personal appropriation by faith ("eat ... flesh and drink ... blood") remain the same here, but the outcomes have changed. This is another example of John's use of interchangeable imagery. For John (and for Jesus) the concepts of "attaining eternal life" and of "residing in Jesus" are virtually interchangeable. Note, however, that the "not yet" portion, being "raised up at the last day," is no longer mentioned here. That is because the outcome "resides in me, and I in him," covers *both* the "already" and the "not yet." This is similar to Jesus' statement to Martha in 11:26, "the one who lives [i.e., possesses eternal life] and believes in me will never die [now or in the future]." See the discussion of the verb "reside" at 1:32. [*menō*]

6:57 The one who eats (*trōgōn*). Here the translation "consumes" is more appropriate than simply "eats" (NET; cf. NIV "feeds on me") because it is the internalization of Jesus by the individual that is in view. [*trōgō*]

6:58 Will live forever (*zēsei*). This expression means "will experience eternal life" (cf. 11:26). The expression also occurs at 6:51, 57. [*zaō*]

6:59 Synagogue (*synagōgē*). The word denotes a place for Jewish prayer and worship, with recognized leadership (cf. Luke 8:41). Though there was only one temple in Jerusalem, many synagogues existed in various places (LN 7.20). Though the origin of the synagogue is not clear, it seems to have arisen in the post-exilic community during the intertestamental period. A town could establish a synagogue if there were a minimum of ten men. In normative Judaism of the NT period, the OT Scriptures were read and discussed in the synagogue by the men who were present (the process is described in the Mishnah, *m. Megilla* 3-4; *m. Berakot* 2). [*synagōgē*]

6:60 Hard (*sklēros*). The Greek term literally means "hard," with a figurative use meaning "hard, harsh, unpleasant, difficult" (BAGD 756). This could mean "hard to understand" (CEV; NET) or "hard to accept" (NIV, NRSV, NLT). [*sklēros*]

Able to hear it (*akouein*). The Greek verb *akouō* could imply hearing with obedience here (LN 36.14). It could also emphasize the acceptance of what Jesus had just said (i.e., "Who can accept what he has said?" NIV, NRSV, NLT). However, since the context contains several replies by those in the crowd that suggest uncertainty or confusion over the meaning of what Jesus had said (6:42; 6:52), the meaning "understand" is probably to be preferred here (CEV, NET). [*akouō*]

6:61 Knowing (*eidōs*). Here Jesus' supernatural knowledge is implied, as in 2:25; 5:6; 6:15, but the Greek verb is different (again indicating stylistic variation by the evangelist). [*oida*]

Cause . . . to stumble (*skandalizei*). In this context the verb means "to be offended" (NET) or "to take offense at some action" (RSV; LN 25.180). It may signal a crisis in the disciples' faith (TDNT 7:357). Some of Jesus' disciples had taken offense at his teaching (perhaps the graphic imagery of "eating his flesh" and "drinking his blood"). Jesus now warned them that even worse cause for stumbling was to come—his upcoming crucifixion (vv. 61-62). [*skandalizō*]

6:62 Ascending (*anabainonta*). Jesus' "ascending" in John's Gospel is to be accomplished through the cross, the first stage in Jesus' return to the Father. John describes Jesus' departure from this world and his return to the Father as one continuous movement from cross to resurrection to ascension, ending where he was "before" (cf. 1:1). See the discussions at 1:32, 1:51, and 3:13. [*anabainō*]

6:63 Gives life (*zōopoioun*). Here this verb is used of the granting of spiritual life to people. This work is attributed to the "Spirit" here, while the Father and Son give life in 5:21. [*zōopoieō*]

The flesh (*sarx*). This term also occurs in 6:51, 52, 53, 54, 55. Here it does not refer to Jesus' "flesh," which is given for the life of the world, but to humanity in all its frailness and weakness (cf. 1:14). Human effort and human nature are of absolutely no benefit ("profits nothing") in obtaining spiritual (i.e., eternal) life. Instead, this life can only be obtained by hearing and obeying Jesus' "words" (i.e., his teaching). [*sarx*]

6:64 Knew (*ēdei*). Jesus' supernatural knowledge is implied using this Greek verb in 6:61. Here the knowledge is clearly supernatural because it involves a future action. [*oida*]

Who would betray (*paradōsōn*). This verb means to turn a person over to the control of someone else, either because the person is guilty of a crime and should be punished, or because the person is an innocent party being handed over to enemies who will victimize them (LN 37.111). This is the first of 15 occurrences in the Gospel of John, many of which are to Judas Iscariot as Jesus' betrayer, as here. [*paradidōmi*]

6:65 To <u>come</u> to me (*elthein*). Again the phrase refers to a personal response to Jesus in faith (NIV "has enabled him"; NLT "brings them to me"; NET "has allowed him to come"). See the discussion of this phrase at 6:35. It also occurs in vv. 44, 45. [*erchomai*]

Has been granted (*dedomenon*). Somehow the Father "grants" to people to respond to Jesus in personal faith. The mechanism for how this happens is never explained in John's Gospel. It remains in the background but is never elaborated (cf. 6:44). [*didōmi*]

6:67 The <u>twelve</u> (*dōdeka*). (Also in v. 70) This expression is used frequently in Matthew for Jesus' closest followers (Matt. 10:1, 5; 11:1; 20:17; 26:14). John uses it only here and in 6:70, 71 and 20:24 to refer to the disciples. In both Matthew and John the term is used when the emphasis is on the close relationship to Jesus (TDNT 2:327). [*dōdeka*]

6:68 Eternal <u>life</u> (*zōēs*). Here it is Jesus' "words" that produce "eternal life." This means, in essence, that Jesus' teaching leads to eternal life (something the Gospel of John has repeatedly emphasized). See the discussions of the term "life" at 1:4 and 17:2. [*zōē*]

6:69 Have believed (*pepisteukamen*). Here the object or content of the disciples' faith is specified. They have "believed" that Jesus is the "Holy One of God." [*pisteuō*]

The <u>Holy One</u> of God (*hagios*). This is the response of Peter on behalf of the Twelve, when Jesus questioned them concerning

their loyalty to him. The confession here differs considerably from the synoptic accounts (Matt. 16:16; Mark 8:29; Luke 9:20) and concerns the disciples' personal allegiance to Jesus, in contrast to those other disciples who had just deserted him (6:66). Yet the confession is more than just an acknowledgment that Jesus was the Messiah. Since God the Father is called "Holy Father" in 17:11, the association of this title with Jesus puts him at the side of God (TDNT 1:102). [*hagios*]

6:70 Choose (*exelexamēn*). Here Jesus speaks of having "chosen" the "Twelve," yet there is specific reference to one of them, Judas, who would betray him (v. 71). As later in 13:18, Jesus' choosing of all the Twelve, including the betrayer, is portrayed as deliberate and with complete knowledge of what would happen. [*eklegomai*]

Devil (*diabolos*). Although typically translated as an indefinite noun in English ("a devil"; NASB, NIV, NRSV, NLT), the word *diabolos* (as opposed to *daimonion*) in the NT is monadic (i.e., one-of-a-kind, cf. 1 Pet. 5:8; Rev. 20:2), with the meaning "the devil" (D. B. Wallace, *Greek Grammar Beyond the Basics*, 249; cf. NET). There is no significant difference in the NT between *Satanas* and *diabolos* (TDNT 2:79). Naturally, when Jesus referred to Judas as "the devil," he was speaking figuratively, as he often did. [*diabolos*]

6:71 Iscariot (*Iskariōtou*). This is the first time that "Judas, son of Simon Iscariot" is mentioned in the fourth Gospel. At least half a dozen explanations for the name "Iscariot" have been proposed, but it is probably transliterated Hebrew meaning "man of Kerioth," referring to his place of origin (LN 93.181). [*Iskariōtēs*]

To <u>betray</u> him (*paradidonai*). Judas is immediately identified (as in Matt. 10:4, Mark 3:19, and Luke 6:16) as the one who would "betray" Jesus. [*paradidōmi*]

7:1 The Jews (*Ioudaioi*). See 1:19. Here the referent is restricted to the Jewish religious authorities or leaders who were Jesus' primary opponents. [*Ioudaios*]

Were seeking (*ezētoun*). In other cases John uses this verb for people who are "seeking" Jesus (6:24), while here the Jewish leaders were "seeking" (i.e., attempting) to kill him. [*zēteō*]

7:2 The feast of tabernacles (*skēnopēgia*). The Greek term (used only here in the NT) means "the setting up of a tent or hut" (TDNT 7.390). This feast was an annual event that began on 15th Tisri (approximately October) and was both a harvest festival and a commemoration of the days after Israel left bondage in Egypt when they lived in tents. To celebrate the feast, huts were constructed of leafy branches of trees, either on the flat roofs of their houses or in the courtyards. This is the only NT use, though it appears nine times in the Greek OT. In Jewish literature it is a technical term for the feast. The only known exception to the meaning of "tent" in classical literature appears where Aristotle referred to the building of nests by swallows in *Hist. Animalium* 9.7. [*skēnopēgia*]

7:3 Depart from here (*metabēthi*). The verb means "to transfer over or pass over from one place to another" (BDAG 638; NIV, NRSV, NET "leave here"). Here it refers literally to Jesus leaving Galilee and going to Judea. Elsewhere in John's Gospel it pictures Jesus' departure from "this world" and return to the Father (13:1) and to the transfer from spiritual death to spiritual (i.e., eternal) life when a person believes in Jesus. [*metabainō*]

Your works (*erga*). This term refers to miraculous deeds, like *sēmeion*, but these are mere miracles, not signs. Jesus' brothers, who said this, did not yet believe in him (7:5). It is possible to see these words as a suggestion that Jesus try to win back the disciples who had deserted him (cf. 6:66). More likely,

given the following verse, is to take the words as advice that if Jesus was going to put forward messianic claims (i.e., by performing miracles), he should do so in Jerusalem. [*ergon*]

7:4 In secret (*kryptō*). This term means "secretly" or "hidden" here (BAGD 454). It stands in contrast with the following term "openly." [*kryptos*]

Openly (*parrēsia*). The basic meaning of the first part of v. 4 is, "if you are going to perform signs to authenticate yourself as Messiah, you should do them in Jerusalem." Mainstream Jewish apocalyptic tradition held that the Messiah would appear at Jerusalem. [*parrēsia*]

Reveal yourself (*phanerōson*). This verb means "to make known, reveal" clearly and in some detail (LN 28.36; NRSV, NIV, NET "show yourself to the world"). Jesus' brothers were urging Jesus to demonstrate clearly his identity as Messiah. His brothers were obviously aware of messianic claims related to Jesus, although they themselves had not believed in him at this point (v. 5). [*phaneroō*]

To the world (*kosmō*). The use of this term is like John 4:42, where the Samaritans proclaimed Jesus to be the Savior of "the world," that is, the world of people or the human race. [*kosmos*]

7:5 Did not believe in him (*episteuon*). Apparently Jesus' brothers did eventually come to believe in him (cf. Acts 1:14). Here the meaning is probably that they were still refusing to "exercise faith in him" (cf. 3:15, 16, 18), although it is possible to understand this statement to mean Jesus' brothers did not believe him to be the Messiah. [*pisteuō*]

7:6 My time (*kairos*). Here the Greek word *kairos* means the same as the word *hōra* ("hour") used elsewhere (cf. 2:4) in John's Gospel (LN 67.1). Jesus again referred to the time of his return to the Father, characterized by his death, resurrection, and exaltation (what John calls "glorification"). This use of synonymous terms is another example of stylistic variation. In contrast to this, Jesus said his brothers' "time" was "always ready" (*hetiomos*, BDAG 401). [*kairos*]

7:7 The world (*kosmos*). Here the "world" refers to not all of humanity, but specifically to those people and powers in opposition to Jesus and hostile to him. Hatred of the world for both Jesus and his disciples is a frequent theme in the Gospel of John (cf. 15:18-25). [*kosmos*]

7:8 Go up (*anabēte*). One always speaks of going "up" to Jerusalem in Jewish idiom, regardless of the direction from which one came (NASB, NET). This was because Jerusalem was identified by the Jews with Mt. Zion in the OT, so that altitude rather than direction was the issue. [*anabainō*]

My time (*kairos*). See 7:6. Although the Greek word here is *kairos*, it parallels John's use of *hōra* ("hour") elsewhere in the fourth Gospel as a reference to the time appointed for Jesus by the Father for his death, resurrection, and glorification—in short, his return to the Father. [*kairos*]

7:10 In secret (*kryptō*). This term normally means "secretly" or "hidden" (cf. 7:4), but here it means "privately" (BAGD 454; RSV "in private"). When Jesus does get to Jerusalem (v. 14), he makes no attempt to remain hidden (in fact, he makes himself quite conspicuous). This suggests the phrase "in secret" here does not mean "covertly," but that Jesus did not accompany the main body of pilgrims going to Jerusalem for the feast (cf. v. 8), perhaps to avoid a premature "triumphal entry" scene. [*kryptos*]

7:11 The Jews (*Ioudaioi*). See 1:19. As in 7:1,

the referent is restricted here to the Jewish authorities who were Jesus' primary opponents. [*Ioudaios*]

Were seeking (*ezētoun*). See 5:44. In light of the use of this term in other contexts to refer to "seeking" Jesus in a positive sense, the negative use here is ironic. [*zēteō*]

he (*ekeinos*). Literally, "that one," referring to Jesus. In 1 John this pronoun is consistently used as a reference to Jesus as distinguished from God the Father, but this is not the case in the Gospel of John (see 9:12). [*ekeinos*]

7:12 The people (*ochlois*). (twice) As opposed to the Jewish religious authorities mentioned in both the preceding and following verse, this term refers to the "common people" (NET). [*ochlos*]

7:15 Were marveling (*ethaumazon*). This verb means "to wonder or marvel at some event or object" (LN 25.213; NIV "were amazed'; NRSV, NET "were astonished"; NLT "were surprised"). Whether the reaction is positive or negative depends on the context. Here the term describes the Jewish religious leaders' reaction to Jesus' public teaching in the temple; it probably bordered on incredulity. [*thaumazō*]

Know letters (*grammata*). The expression "letters" here refers to elementary knowledge like reading and writing (BAGD 165). This accusation may not have been strictly true, since Jesus probably attended a local synagogue school as a boy. [*gramma*]

Not having been taught (*memathēkōs*). The term means "to gain knowledge or skill by instruction" (BDAG 615), often through formal education (NET "has never had formal education"). In the context of his debate with the Jewish religious leaders, this refers to the fact that Jesus was not a disciple of a particular rabbi (cf. Paul in Acts 22:3) and lacked advanced instruction in the Mosaic Law under a recognized rabbi. Ironically, when the Jewish leaders came face to face with the Word-become-flesh—the preexistent *Logos*, Creator of the universe, and divine Wisdom personified—they treated him as an untaught, unlearned person without the formal qualifications to be a teacher. [*manthanō*]

7:18 Glory (*doxan*). As in 5:41, 44, "glory" is used in the sense of "praise" or "honor" from men, a usage different from the general meaning of the term in the fourth Gospel (TDNT 2:248). See 1:14 for a summary of the meaning of this term. [*doxa*]

7:19 The law (*nomon*). This term refers to the Mosaic Law, the core of Jewish belief found in the OT (1:17). [*nomos*]

7:20 The crowd (*ochlos*). See 7:12. Many of the crowd, if they had just arrived from surrounding districts for the feast, probably were not aware of any plot against Jesus. The plot was on the part of "the Jews," which in this context refers to the Jewish religious leaders (cf. 7:1, 11, 13, 15). John distinguishes between the leadership and the populace in terms of their responses to Jesus. [*ochlos*]

You have a demon (*daimonion*). This is the first time in John's Gospel that the charge of demon possession is made against Jesus. It is possible, because demon-possessed people were thought of as behaving insanely, that the expression here does not actually constitute a charge of demon possession (Jesus does not comment on the charge at all, but only mentions the anger of his accusers in the following verse). It may be that Jesus' comment about seeking to kill him was viewed by the crowd as crazy behavior, and that is what provoked this charge. There is a possibility, though, that behind this comment by the crowd is the suggestion that Jesus was a false prophet (since such were thought to be connected with demonic spirits). [*daimonion*]

7:21 One work (*ergon*). The "one work" ("one deed"; RSV, NASB) refers to the last previous public miracle in Jerusalem recorded by John, the Sabbath healing of the paralyzed man at Bethesda in 5:1-9 (NIV, NET "one miracle"). It was after this miracle that the Jewish leaders began trying to kill Jesus (cf. 5:18), although there it was probably an unplanned emotional response as opposed to an organized plot. [*ergon*]

7:22 Circumcision (*peritomēn*). (Also found in the following verse.) Although this could refer to the circumcision of adult male proselytes, it primarily refers to the Jewish practice of circumcising male infants on the eighth day after birth (cf. Phil. 3:5). [*peritomē*]

7:23 Is not broken (*lythē*). The Rabbis counted 248 parts to a man's body. In the Talmud (*b. Yoma* 85b) R. Eleazar ben Azariah (ca. A.D. 100) stated, "If circumcision, which attaches to one only of the 248 members of the human body, suspends the Sabbath, how much more shall the saving of the whole body suspend the Sabbath?" So absolutely binding did rabbinic Judaism regard the command of Lev. 12:3 to circumcise on the eighth day, that in the Mishnah *m. Shabbat* 18.3; 19.1, 2, and *m. Nedarim* 3.11 all hold that the command to circumcise overrides the command to observe the Sabbath. [*lyō*]

Well (*hygiē*). This term refers to a state of wellness in contrast to sickness (LN 23.129). Jesus was referring to the paralytic he had healed at the pool of Bethesda (see 5:6). [*hygiēs*]

7:24 According to appearance (*opsin*). A "judgment" based on outward form or "external appearance" (NET) alone would not be accurate (LN 30.14). [*opsis*]

7:25 Seeking (*zētousin*). Here again the verb is used of "attempting" or "trying" to kill

Jesus (see 7:1). At this point Jerusalem's residents are clearly distinguished from the Jewish religious leaders who are viewed as Jesus' main opponents in John. They also are distinguished from the pilgrims who had come into the city for the feast (v. 20). [*zēteō*]

7:26 The rulers (*archontes*). Since the crowd is speaking here (cf. 7:25), the Jewish leaders are referred to here as "the rulers," although in 7:1, 11, 13, 15 they are called simply "the Jews." Some people who had heard Jesus were so impressed with his teaching that they began to infer from the inactivity of the opposing Jewish leaders a tacit acknowledgment of Jesus' messianic claims. Once again the evangelist distinguishes carefully between the Jewish leadership and the populace. [*archōn*]

7:27 Where . . . from (*pothen*). (Twice in this verse and once in 7:28) The Greek term refers here to one's place of origin (BAGD 680). Since Jesus in his public ministry was known as a Galilean from Nazareth, this is probably what the crowd refers to here. John assumes, however, that the reader knows where Jesus was really from, since he tells the reader in the first verse of the fourth Gospel, John 1:1, "the Word was with God," and in 1:14, "the Word became flesh." Thus John does not even bother to answer the crowd's objection at this point. [*pothen*]

7:29 From him (*par'*). The preposition *para* ("from") followed by the Greek genitive case has the local sense preserved here and can be used of one person sending another (BAGD 609; cf. John 6:46, 9:16, 33; 17:7). However, this does not necessarily imply metaphysical origin in essence or eternal generation, but is a general reference to origin. [*para*]

Sent me (*apesteilan*). The verb used here is different from the one in v. 28 and means "sent with full authority." [*apostellō*]

7:30 Seeking (*ezētoun*). Here it is the crowd that is trying to seize Jesus (cf. v. 25). This is apparently different from the attempted arrest by the Jewish leaders mentioned in v. 32. [*zēteō*]

His hour (*hōra*). Jesus' "hour" ("time" NIV, NLT, NET) had not yet arrived. Again this is given as the reason none of Jesus' opponents were able to "seize" him (i.e., arrest him). [*hōra*]

7:31 The crowd (*ochlou*). (Also found in the following verse.) Again the "crowd" (both residents of Jerusalem and festal pilgrims) is distinguished from the Jewish religious leaders who opposed Jesus. [*ochlos*]

Signs (*sēmeia*). See the discussion at 2:11. The "signs" (NASB, NRSV; "miraculous signs" NIV, NLT, NET) mentioned here by the crowd apparently include other miracles not mentioned by John. Even though many of these people "believed in him" because of the signs, there is no indication in context that their belief was not genuine. For John, it is better to believe on the basis of miracles than not to believe at all (cf. 10:37-38; 20:29). However, the connection with "signs" suggests that what these people "believed" was that Jesus was the Messiah. Since messianic expectations differed, this was not necessarily an adequate confession; John's Gospel begins (1:1, 18) and ends (20:28) with the affirmation that Jesus Christ is God (cf. 2:23). [*sēmeion*]

7:32 Sent (*apesteilan*). Here the officers were dispatched with the authority of the chief priests and Pharisees to "seize" (i.e., arrest or take into custody) Jesus. [*apostellō*]

The chief priests and Pharisees (*archiereis . . . Pharisaioi*). This phrase is a comprehensive term for the groups represented in the ruling council, the Sanhedrin (cf. John 7:45; 11:47; 18:3; Acts 5:21, 27). See also the discussion of "Pharisees" at 1:24. [*archiereus + Pharisaios*]

Officers (*hypēretas*). Literally, "servants." The "officers" (NASB, NET) of the Sanhedrin (cf. John 19:6) should be distinguished from the Levites serving as temple police (perhaps mentioned in John 7:30, 44). Even when performing "police" duties such as here, the officers of the Sanhedrin are doing so only as part of their general tasks (TDNT 8:540). Although frequently translated here as "temple guards" (NIV, NLT) or "temple police" (NRSV), the group mentioned here were representatives of the chief priests and Pharisees whose activity was not limited to the temple area. [*hypēretēs*]

7:33 The one who sent me (*pempsanta*). Jesus speaks here of his return ("I am going") to the Father. This is going to take place in only a short while ("a little longer"). [*pempō*]

7:35 The Jews (*Ioudaioi*). See 1:19. The term probably refers more generally to those Jews who were hostile to Jesus, since the leaders are mentioned separately in this context (7:32, 45). [*Ioudaios*]

The **dispersion** (*diasporan*). The Greek term *diaspora* ("the Dispersion," NASB, NRSV; "the Jewish people dispersed among the Greeks," NET) is used in the Greek OT as a technical term referring to those Jews not living in Palestine, but "dispersed" or scattered among the Gentiles (TDNT 2:98; BAGD 188). They are referred to as "Greeks" here. [*diaspora*]

7:37 The great [day] (*megalē*). From Deut. 16:13 it appears that the feast went on for seven days. However, Lev. 23:36 refers to an eighth day, mentioned separately from the seven. It is not entirely clear whether the seventh or eighth day was the climax of the feast, called here "the last day of the feast, the great one." Since according to the Mishnah (*m. Sukka* 4.1) the ceremonies with water and lights did not continue after the seventh day,

it is more likely that the seventh day of the feast is meant. [*megas*]

Thirsts (*dipsa*). See the discussion at 6:35 where "thirst" is related to "hunger," both of which are metaphors for spiritual hunger and thirst (rather than physical appetites). Jesus' statement here also recalls the offer of "living water" to the Samaritan woman (4:13-14). Jesus was inviting those who had a spiritual "thirst" to come to him and be satisfied. [*dipsaō*]

Let him come to me (*erchesthō*). See the repeated uses of this phrase in 6:35, 44, 45, 65. In 6:35 the phrase "come to me" is in parallel with "believes in me" (as here) and means virtually the same thing. [*erchomai*]

Let him drink (*pinetō*). Jesus' offer to the Samaritan woman at Jacob's well is again recalled here (4:13-14). The concept of "drinking" the Spirit is not unique to John's Gospel; it is also found in 1 Cor. 12:13. [*pinō*]

7:38 His belly (*koilias*). The term *koilia* can refer literally to the complete digestive apparatus (stomach and intestines), to the womb, or more generally to the hidden inner recesses of the human body (BAGD 437). In this context it is often understood to refer figuratively to the innermost being of the individual believer (NRSV, "out of the believer's heart"; NIV, "from within him"), from which the "rivers of living water" (explained in the following verse as the Holy Spirit) flow forth to others. However, it is difficult to find Johannine parallels that make the believer the source of living water for someone else (neither 4:14 nor 14:12 are really parallel). The Gospel of John repeatedly makes Jesus himself the source of the living water (4:10), which is a way of referring to the Spirit (14:16; 20:22). The symbolism of John 19:34 is a deliberate allusion to what is predicted here. [*koilia*]

Living water (*hydatos*). The expression here recalls Jesus' offer to the Samaritan woman (4:10). The "living water" Jesus offered there and here is explained in the following verse as a metaphor for the Holy Spirit. [*hydōr*]

7:39 The Spirit (*pneumatos*). The imagery of living water in John's Gospel refers to the Holy Spirit, as this verse makes clear. [*pneuma*]

Not yet (*oudepō*). The entire phrase reads literally, "For the Spirit was not yet, because Jesus was not yet glorified." This adverb does not mean that the Holy Spirit did not yet exist; most translations supply the verb "given" in English to prevent this misunderstanding (cf. KJV, NASB, NIV, NLT, NET). John's phrase reflects time expressed from a human standpoint (cf. BDAG 735) and has nothing to do with the preexistence of the third Person of the Godhead. The meaning of the statement is that the era of the Holy Spirit had not yet arrived at the time Jesus was speaking—the Spirit was not yet at work in the lives of the disciples (as would later be the case) because Jesus had not yet returned to his Father (cf. Acts 19:2). [*oudepō*]

Glorified (*edoxasthē*). Jesus' "glorification" here refers to his exaltation when he returned to the Father, which he would accomplish through the cross. [*doxazō*]

7:40 The crowd (*ochlou*). Here some of the "crowd" speak up again. They were last mentioned at v. 31. [*ochlos*]

The prophet (*prophētēs*). The referent here is the "prophet like Moses" of Deut. 18:15, by this time an eschatological figure in popular belief. Acts 3:22 identifies Jesus as this prophet. [*prophētēs*]

7:42 From the seed of David (*spermatos*). This verse is particularly ironic because it was true of Jesus. He was a "descendant of David" (NET; cf. NIV "will come from David's family") and had been born in Bethlehem (neither of which are mentioned in the Gospel of John). It appears the evangelist was at least aware that accounts of Jesus' birth were common knowledge, so that the reader of the fourth Gospel would see these statements by the crowd as truly ironic. [*sperma*]

7:44 To seize him (*piasai*). Here it was certain members of the crowd rather than officers sent by the chief priests and Pharisees who wanted to "seize" ("arrest" NRSV) Jesus. The verb has the idea of grabbing or seizing someone or something by force (LN 18.4). [*piazō*]

7:46 No one ever (*oudepote*). This adverb negates an indefinite period of time (BDAG 735). Obviously the officers of the chief priests and Pharisees were deeply impressed by what Jesus said. [*oudepote*]

7:48 Believed in him (*episteusen*). Here the meaning of the expression is best understood as "believed him to be the Messiah" even though no object is specified and the preposition *eis* ("in") is used with the verb. The issue for the Jewish religious leadership was whether Jesus was in fact the Messiah or not (cf. 1:19-20). [*pisteuō*]

7:49 This crowd (*ochlos*). Here the Jewish religious leaders take a very disparaging view of the crowd's opinion that Jesus was the Messiah (cf. 7:40, where the crowd had identified Jesus as "the prophet"). [*ochlos*]

Accursed (*eparatoi*). The term used here does not mean that the Jewish religious leaders were calling down a curse on the crowd, but that as far as the leaders were concerned the crowd already stood accursed (CEV, "these people who don't know the Law are under God's curse anyway"). They were already condemned and under God's judgment, or at least under the immediate threat of that judgment (LN 33.475). This scorn for the common people and their theological insight reflected the scribes' attitude toward the unlearned (TDNT 1:451). [*eparatos*]

7:51 Our law (*nomon*). This is a reference to the Mosaic Law, mentioned last in 7:23. [*nomos*]

Judge (*krinei*). Here the meaning is "condemn" (NIV, NET) since in the context a negative outcome to the process of "judging" is anticipated. [*krinō*]

7:52 Search (*eraunēson*). This verb refers to a careful, thorough effort to learn something through diligent inquiry (BDAG 389; NIV "Look into it"; NET "Investigate carefully"). Here it refers to the OT Scriptures, which the Jewish religious leaders invited Nicodemus to search. [*eraunaō*]

8:1 The Mount of Olives (*oros*). This is a hill running north to south, just under two miles long, lying east of Jerusalem across the Kidron Valley. It took its name from the large number of olive trees that grew on it (LN 3.9). [*oros*]

8:3 The scribes (*grammateis*). In the NT the term refers to experts in the Law of Moses (BDAG 206; NLT "Teachers of religious law"), who are often grouped with the "chief priests" or the Pharisees. [*grammateus*]

The Pharisees (*Pharisaioi*). The motivation for the action of the scribes and Pharisees here was probably not a real concern for the Mosaic Law, since v. 6 says they were "testing" Jesus. Rather, they were looking for an accusation against him. [*Pharisaios*]

8:4 Caught in the act (*autophōrō*). The term refers to thieves, evildoers, and especially adulterers caught in the act (BAGD 124). [*autophōros*]

8:5 In the law (*nomō*). The accusers themselves misrepresented the Mosaic Law, which states that in the case of adultery, *both* the man and woman must be put to death (Lev. 20:10; Deut. 22:22). Here Jesus' opponents mention only the woman (in the Greek

text the pronoun "such" [*toiautas*] is feminine and refers only to the woman). [*nomos*]

8:6 Testing (*peirazontes*). The verb is used here to refer to a process that is designed to entrap someone through an inquiry (BDAG 793; NIV "They were using this question as a trap"). This usage is fairly common in the Synoptic Gospels, referring to attempts by Jesus' opponents to trap him in some statement that could be used against him. This is the only example of such usage in John. As Bible translations note, it is disputed on the basis of ancient manuscript evidence whether this section of John's Gospel (7:53-8:11) is original to John. [*peirazō*]

Wrote (*kategraphen*). The Greek verb *katagraphō* may indicate only the action of writing on the ground by Jesus. However, in the overall context of Jesus' response to the accusation against the woman, it can also be interpreted as implying that what Jesus wrote was a counter-accusation against the accusers (LN 33.63). The context gives no clue as to the content of what Jesus wrote. Why then bother to mention in the narrative that Jesus wrote at all? Probably the act of writing itself was regarded as a symbolic act. In Exod. 31:18 the first set of stone tablets were inscribed by God's "finger," and here it is specifically mentioned that Jesus "wrote with his finger." Jesus wrote here with the same authority as God originally wrote. [*katagraphō*]

8:7 The one . . . without sin (*anamartētos*). Since "sin" for John involves the violation of God's will and constitutes lawlessness, to be "without sin" here would mean that the hearers had perfectly obeyed God's law and never transgressed his will. This was impossible, and the hearers knew it, since all of them were sinners just as the woman they had accused. [*anamartētos*]

8:10 Condemn (*katekrinen*). (Also in the following verse) This is not the usual verb used for "condemn" in John's Gospel. The usual term is simply *krinō* (cf. 3:19). The meaning of the verb here is somewhat intensified: "to condemn someone as definitely guilty and subject to punishment" (LN 56.31). [*katakrinō*]

8:12 I am (*egō eimi*). See the discussion at 4:26. The expression occurs twice in this section (here and in v. 18). In both instances it is simply an emphatic way of affirming the assertion. But these two uses foreshadow the use of the same phrase in 8:24, 58, where the expression is used in an absolute sense and represents a claim to deity (cf. v. 59). [*egō + eimi*]

8:14 From where (*pothen*). (Twice in this verse.) See 7:27. The ignorance of the religious authorities concerning Jesus' origin works on two levels at once. First, they thought Jesus came from Galilee, although he really came from Bethlehem in Judea. Second, they did not know that he came from heaven, from the Father, and he would return there. [*pothen*]

I am going (*hypagō*). (Twice in this verse) Jesus is going back to heaven, to the Father who sent him. He will get there through the cross. [*hypagō*]

8:15 Judge (*krinete*). (Twice in this verse and once in the following verse.) It is clear (even in the following verse) that Jesus did judge. However, he did not practice the same kind of judgment the Pharisees did when they tried to condemn people. Jesus did not come to judge the world but to save it (John 3:17). Nevertheless, and not contradictory to this, Jesus' coming into the world did bring judgment, because it forced people to make a choice. Would they accept Jesus or reject him? Would they come to the light or shrink back into the darkness? As they responded to

Jesus, so were they judged (so John 3:19-21). One's response to Jesus determines one's eternal destiny. [*krinō*]

According to the flesh (*sarka*). Here the meaning is "you judge according to outward things, by externals" (BAGD 744; NIV, NRSV "by human standards"; NET "by outward appearances"). [*sarx*]

8:16 My judgment (*krisis*). Jesus' "judgment" is not based on externals, but is true, because he and the Father participate together in the judgment. [*krisis*]

The Father who sent me (*pempsas*). See 1:6. Here Jesus and the Father who "sent" him both participate together in the judgment. [*pempō*]

8:17 Your law (*nomō*). This refers to the Mosaic Law. The passage Jesus referred to was Deut. 17:6. [*nomos*]

8:19 If you knew me (*ēdeite*). Jesus' response is based on his identity with the Father (cf. John 1:18; 14:9). Here is another example of the misunderstood statement in John's Gospel. The Pharisees understood this as a reference to Jesus' earthly father, while Jesus was really speaking of his heavenly Father. The Son, for John, is the only way to know the Father (cf. 1:18; 14:6). [*oida*]

8:20 The treasury (*gazophylakiō*). The Greek term can be translated "treasury" (NASB, NRSV) or "treasure room" in this context, referring to the rooms in the Jerusalem temple courts, which were used for storage (LN 7.33). Here, however, it is more likely that the term refers to the collection boxes or receptacles themselves, which were located near the Court of Women (BAGD 149; NIV, "near the place where the offerings were put"; NET "near the offering box"). These were used to collect freewill offerings and were mentioned by Josephus (*J. W.* 5.5.2 [5.200], 6.5.2 [6.282];

Ant. 19.6.1 [19.294]) and in 1 Macc. 14:49 and 2 Macc. 3:6, 24, 28, 40 (cf. Mark 12:41; Luke 21:1). [*gazophylakion*]

His **hour** (*hōra*). Once again Jesus' enemies were powerless to "seize" (i.e., arrest) him, because his "hour" (NIV, NLT, NET "time") had not yet arrived. [*hōra*]

8:21 I am going (*hypagō*). (Twice in this verse.) Jesus was "going" back to the Father. See 7:34. [*hypagō*]

You will die in your sins (*apothaneisthe . . . hamartiais*). The expression "die in your sins" is similar to an expression found in the Greek OT at Ezek. 3:18, 20 and Prov. 24:11. To die with one's sin unrepented and unatoned would be the ultimate disaster to befall a person. Jesus' warning here is stern but to the point. [*apothnēskō + hamartia*]

8:22 The Jews (*Ioudaioi*). See 1:19. Here the phrase refers to the Jewish religious leaders in Jerusalem. The Pharisees had begun this line of questioning in 8:13, and since then there has been no clear change in the identity of Jesus' opponents. [*Ioudaios*]

8:23 From below . . . from above (*katō . . . anō*). Jesus is the one who has come down from heaven "above," to enable people to be born "from above" (cf. 3:3) and thus to possess eternal life. The contrast here is between heaven, where Jesus is from, and earth "below," where his opponents are from (BDAG 535). [*katō + anō*]

This world (*kosmou*). Here the term is further qualified as "this world," which stands in contrast to the heavenly world, the world "above." [*kosmos*]

8:24 Your sins (*hamartiais*). (Twice in this verse.) See 8:21 and the discussion at 1:29. Vv. 24-30 explain the urgency of Jesus' insistence that when he goes away, there will be no other possibility of delivering them from sin.

When Jesus is "lifted up" (8:28) in crucifixion, resurrection, and exaltation, he will draw all people to himself (cf. 12:32), and in that moment it will be clear to those who have eyes to see that he truly bears the divine name and has the power of raising people, both physically and spiritually, from the dead. But if his hearers refuse to believe then there is no other way (cf. 14:6) that leads to the Father above, and such people will go to their graves permanently separated from the gift and the Giver of eternal life. [*hamartia*]

Believe (*pisteusēte*). On one level the meaning of the expression is the same as in 3:15, 16, 18, "exercise faith in, put one's trust in." On another level this can be understood to mean "believe that I am [the Messiah]." In context, forgiveness of sins is a major theme, so the object of belief here would be that Jesus was someone who had the authority to forgive sins. On still another level, as the reader of the fourth Gospel would recognize by now, Jesus is not "just" the Jewish Messiah, but is God incarnate (cf. 1:1, 18). It is possible here to read Jesus' self identification using the phrase "I am" as absolute (see the following entry). [*pisteuō*]

I am (*egō eimi*). See the discussion at 4:26. There is an implied predicate nominative here ("the Christ"—RSV; "the one I claim to be"— NIV) following the "I am" statement. What Jesus' hearers probably had to acknowledge was that he is the Messiah (cf. 20:31). Some interpreters, however, take this phrase as written in Greek (without any predicate) and similar in force to 8:28 as non-predicated (i.e., absolute). If so, it alludes to the name for God in Exod. 3:14 ("I am"), so that Jesus was identifying himself as God. [*egō + eimi*]

8:25 The beginning (*archēn*). The expression probably refers here to the "beginning" of Jesus' public ministry. Some, however, have taken the expression as an idiom meaning "at all" so that the entire response by Jesus is a rhetorical question, "Why do I even talk to you at all?" (BAGD 112; NRSV). [*archē*]

8:26 To judge (*krinein*). Here the meaning of the verb could be "to condemn" (NRSV; NLT) although Jesus could be speaking merely of "rendering judgment." [*krinō*]

8:27 They did not understand (*egnōsan*). Again the evangelist's comment, intended for the benefit of the reader, reveals a post-resurrection awareness. The disciples did not understand until after the resurrection that Jesus was discussing his special relationship to the Father, who sent him as an envoy and was going to take him back after he died. This is one of several such notes in John (see John 2:22). [*ginōskō*]

8:28 Have lifted up (*hypsōsēte*). Here Jesus is referring to his crucifixion, with the verb "lifted up" referring to the cross. See the discussion at 3:14. [*hypsoō*]

    You will know (*gnōsesthe*). Here, in contrast to v. 24, "belief" has been replaced by "knowledge." When the Son of Man is "lifted up" (i.e., on the cross), his identity will be clear for all to see. [*ginōskō*]

    I am (*egō eimi*). See the discussions at 4:26 and especially 8:24. [*egō + eimi*]

8:29 The things that are pleasing (*aresta*). This term refers here to things that are pleasing or satisfying to God (BDAG 130). In the secular papyri the term is used to describe the quality of goods ("acceptable," TDNT 1:456). [*arestos*]

8:30 Believed in him (*episteusan*). The content of what these people believed is not specified, but it is likely in context that they believed Jesus to be the Messiah. [*pisteuō*]

8:31 The Jews (*Ioudaious*). See 1:19. Here the phrase refers to the Jewish people in Jerusalem who had been listening to Jesus' teaching in the temple and had believed his claim to be the Messiah. Certainly some of the Jewish religious leaders may have been included in this group (cf. 8:22), although there is nothing in the immediate context that specifies the group's exact composition. In what sense did these people trust Jesus? They had believed his messianic claims (v. 25), which he had spoken to them from the beginning. But they had insisted on believing Jesus to be the type of Messiah *they* had anticipated—chiefly political. This is suggested by their refusal to admit that anyone had ever enslaved them (v. 33) in spite of the Roman occupation (not to mention the Babylonian captivity). [*Ioudaios*]

    Who had believed in him (*pepisteukotas*). Again, as in the previous verse, the content of what these people "believed" is not specified, but it probably means these Jewish listeners believed Jesus to be the Messiah. As soon as Jesus began to discuss the need to "continue" (or "remain") in his word in order to become his disciples and the need for them to become "free" from their enslavement to sin, however, they turned on him. Eventually they sought to kill him (v. 59). [*pisteuō*]

8:32 The truth (*alētheian*). (Twice in this verse) The statement "you will know the truth, and the truth will make you free" is often taken as referring to truth in the philosophical (or absolute) sense, or in the intellectual sense, or even (as the Jewish people who heard it here apparently understood it) in a politically, liberating sense. In the context of John's Gospel (particularly in light of the Prologue) this must refer to truth about Jesus' person and work. He is the truth, and relating to that truth saves. [*alētheia*]

    Will make you free (*eleutherōsei*). The hearers were currently in a state of slavery from which they needed to be freed (cf. v. 33, "we have never been enslaved to anyone").

Though they would not acknowledge it, they were enslaved to sin. [*eleutheroō*]

8:33 Descendants of Abraham (*sperma*). Jesus' opponents claimed kinship with Abraham as the basis for their privileged position (see Luke 3:8). Given that they are addressing Jesus who is the true Seed of Abraham, this is highly ironic. [*sperma*]

8:34 The one who practices sin (*hamartian*). See 8:21, 24, and the discussion at 1:29. The Greek construction is more emphatic than simply "everyone who sins." Repeated, continuous action is stressed (NET "everyone who practices sin"). The one whose life is characterized by repeated, continuous sin is enslaved to sin. To break free from this slavery requires God's intervention. Although the statement is true at the general level, in particular the sin of the Jewish religious authorities, repeatedly emphasized in the fourth Gospel, is their sin of constant unbelief. The Greek present tense here looks at the continuing refusal of the Jewish leaders to acknowledge who Jesus is, in spite of mounting evidence. [*hamartia*]

8:35 Does not remain (*menei*). (Twice in this verse) The one who is a "slave" has no familial relationship, and thus no permanent place in the household (NIV, "has no permanent place in the family"; NRSV "does not have a permanent place in the household"). [*menō*]

    Forever (*aiōna*). (Twice) Jesus' point is that, in contrast to the slave, a son, as a descendant or blood relative, will always be guaranteed a place in the family ("remains forever"). [*aiōn*]

8:36 The son (*huios*). The referent here can be understood as "any son," a continuation of the generic illustration begun in the previous verse (cf. NET). However, some interpreters (and translations, cf. RSV, NASB, NIV) have

understood this as a direct reference to Jesus himself ("the Son"). If the illustration is generic, the point is that the "son" of the household has authority to "free" someone in the household who is a slave. If Jesus is the referent here, he, as God's Son has authority to free those in the household who are enslaved to sin (i.e., in this context, his hearers). [*huios*]

8:37 Has no place (*chōrei*). The basic idea of the Greek term is something making progress or headway where resistance is involved (BAGD 889; NET "my teaching makes no progress among you"). Negated here the term means that Jesus' word makes no headway. [*chōreō*]

8:39 Children of Abraham (*tekna*). The term here does not refer to Jesus' opponents as physical descendants of Abraham (which they claimed to be, cf. vv. 33, 37), but as Abraham's spiritual descendants (which they were not). The issue was an inner similarity of nature with Abraham, which these people lacked (BAGD 808). The "deeds of Abraham" ultimately refers to his faith in God—again, something absent in Jesus' present hearers. [*teknon*]

8:41 The deeds of your father (*erga*). See v. 44, where this statement will be clarified. Since the "father" of Jesus' opponents is the devil, the "deeds" refer to "murder," which the devil had done "from the beginning." [*ergon*]

    We were not born (*gegennēmetha*). See 1:12. The statement "We were not born of immorality" is ironic here, because Jesus' opponents were implying that it was not themselves but Jesus who was the product of an illicit relationship (NIV "We are not illegitimate children"; NLT "We were not born out of wedlock"). This indicates they did not know Jesus' true origin and were not aware of the supernatural events surrounding his birth, but it may also indicate the timing of Jesus' birth was unusual. The evangelist does not even bother to refute the opponents' suggestion but lets it stand, assuming his readers will know the true story. [*gennaō*]

8:42 Have gone out (*exēlthon*). (NIV, NRSV "came from God") Several times in John's Gospel Jesus' affirmation of his identity and mission take the form "I have gone out from God" (here, 16:27, and 17:8; 13:3 is not spoken by Jesus but is otherwise similar). Here this is combined with the assertion that the Father "sent" Jesus. [*exerchomai*]

8:43 My speech (*lalian*). Here is a wordplay that is ironic: Jesus' opponents cannot understand his "speech" ("what I am saying" NASB, NLT, NET) because they cannot "hear" (i.e., accept and respond to) his "word" (RSV). The term "speech" refers here to Jesus' characteristic message (BDAG 583). This is one more misunderstanding in a long series of misunderstandings in John 8 (vv. 19, 22, 25, 33). [*lalia*]

Hear (*akouein*). The negated term does not refer to literal deafness here, but an inability to listen and accept something (LN 31.56). [*akouō*]

8:44 You are from your father (*ek*). The Greek preposition *ek* in this context emphasizes the idea of source or origin (LN 89.3; BAGD 234). Jesus said his opponents were the devil's very offspring (a statement which would certainly infuriate them). [*ek*]

The devil (*diabolou*). Here the referent of this term is clearly Satan (cf. BAGD 182). [*diabolos*]

A murderer (*anthrōpoktonos*). This rare term refers to a "murderer." The phrase "from the beginning" does not refer to Cain's murder of Abel here, but to the devil as the one who brought death into the world by deceiving

Adam (BDAG 81). The devil is the destroyer of the life God created. The term is used figuratively in 1 John 3:15 of someone who hates his fellow Christian. [*anthrōpoktonos*]

The lie (*pseudos*). The devil also denies the truth that God reveals. In particular the expression here, accompanied by the Greek article, could be a specific reference to "the" lie, a denial of the person and work of Christ himself, ultimately to be propounded by the Antichrist (cf. 1 John 2:21-23). [*pseudos*]

8:45 Do not believe me (*pisteuete*). (Also in the following verse) Here "believe me" means "believe what I am telling you" (cf. 4:21), stated in v. 40 as "the truth which I heard from God." The context is more concerned with believing Jesus' words, particularly in regard to their enslavement to sin (v. 34). [*pisteuō*]

8:46 Convicts me (*elenchei*). The context here involves confrontation and suggests a forensic meaning, "proves me guilty of sin" (NIV, NET) See also the discussion at 16:8. [*elenchō*]

Sin (*hamartias*). "Sin" for John is a violation of God's will that causes guilt and separation from God. Jesus, who was one with the Father (17:22), could therefore never be "convicted" of "sin." [*hamartia*]

8:48 Have a demon (*daimonion*). (Also in the following verse; NIV "demon-possessed"; NLT, NET "possessed by a demon") It is not entirely clear what is meant by the charge. It is possible that "Samaritan" refers to a heretic, in which case the meaning is "You are a heretic and are possessed by a demon." Since the dual charge gets only one reply (8:49), the two phrases might be interchangeable. Two Samaritans often connected with this passage are Simon Magus (Acts 8:14-24) and in later traditions Dositheus (noted in Justin, *Apology* 26:1, 4-5). They claimed to be sons of God, were regarded as mad, that is, possessed by demons. See also John 10:20, where the concepts of demon possession and insanity are linked. [*daimonion*]

8:49 Honor (*timō*). In answer to the "demon" charge, Jesus replied that he "honored" the Father. This is achieved through his obedience to carry out the Father's will (vv. 42, 55). [*timaō*]

8:50 Seeks . . . judges (*zētō . . . krinōn*). (Twice in this verse) Although some have taken the sense of "seek" to be "investigate" in the second occurrence in this verse, in the sense of conducting a legal inquiry or investigation, it makes good sense to see the meaning of both instances of "seek" in the verse to be the same. Jesus does not "seek" his own "glory" (but rather seeks the Father's glory); on the other hand the Father "seeks" Jesus' "glory" and will maintain it by judging (i.e., condemning) those who reject Jesus' message and mission (cf. TDNT 2:892). [*zēteō + krinō*]

8:51 Keep (*tērēsē*). (Also in the following verse) The verb means "to keep, observe, fulfill, pay attention to" (especially in the Greek OT in contexts involving law or teaching; 1 Sam. 15:11). Here the object is not the Mosaic Law but Jesus' "word" (BAGD 815; LN 36.19; NLT, NET "obeys my teaching"). [*tēreō*]
  See (*theōrēsē*). Here the verb means to experience an event (LN 90.79). Those who "keep" Jesus' words will not experience death "forever." They have passed from death to life (cf. 5:24). For John, eternal life begins in the present and extends into the world to come. [*theōreō*]

8:52 The prophets (*prophētai*). (Also in the following verse) This refers to the OT prophets, all of whom had died. [*prophētēs*]
  Taste (*geusētai*). The figurative use here means "to experience" (LN 90.78). [*geuomai*]

8:54 Glorify (*doxasō*). (Twice in this verse) Here

the verb "glorify" and the noun "glory" both refer to "honor" or "praise" (cf. 5:41, 44; 7:18) in the first instance. In the second instance ("it is my Father who glorifies me") there is a wordplay that can also be understood to refer to God's "exaltation" of Jesus, which takes place through the cross. [*doxazō + doxa*]

8:55 I keep (*tērō*). Here God's "word" is kept (BAGD 815; LN 36.19). See also 8:51. [*tēreō*]

8:56 My day (*hēmeran*). The term *hēmera* ("day") here refers to the day of the definitive revelation of Jesus' glory (TDNT 2:951). For John, Jesus' glorification occurs on the cross, so the Messiah's upcoming sacrificial death would be involved. It is still difficult to make the connection to Abraham, however. In what sense did Abraham "see" Jesus' "day," since the past tenses ("rejoiced," "saw") appear to refer to something that occurred during the patriarch's lifetime? Gen. Rab. 44:25ff. (cf. 59:6) states that Rabbi Akiba, in a debate with Rabbi Johanan ben Zakkai, held that Abraham had been shown not only this world but the world to come (which would include the days of the Messiah). More likely, though, Gen. 22:13-15 lies behind Jesus' words here. This passage, known to Jewish rabbis as the *Akedah* ("Binding"), tells of Abraham finding the ram that would replace his own son Isaac on the altar of sacrifice—an occasion of certain rejoicing. In God's provision of the ram to die in place of Isaac, Abraham "saw" the sacrifice of God's own Son, who died for the entire world (John 3:16; 1 John 2:1-2). [*hēmera*]

8:58 I am (*egō eimi*). Here the phrase "I am" is a clear allusion to Exod. 3:14 and therefore a claim to deity. It was understood as such by the Jewish religious authorities, as their response in the following verse shows. They "picked up stones to throw at him" (8:59) for what they considered blasphemy, that is, defaming God by claiming divine preroga-tives. [*egō + eimi*]

8:59 Hid himself (*ekrybē*). The verb means "to hide" in a context like this, although the exact nature of the "hiding" is not clear. Following the "I am" statement in v. 58 and the attempt to stone Jesus in the present verse, the evangelist tells us Jesus "hid him-self," without describing how. Whether or not he employed supernatural means to veil himself from his enemies here, it is clear that he could escape from them whenever he wanted. Ultimately this points to Jesus' sovereignty over the situation. [*kryptō*]

9:1 From birth (*genetēs*). Although this par-ticular phrase does not occur anywhere else in the NT, it is good Greek for "from the time of birth." In light of the placement of this account in the narrative, the evangelist is apparently suggesting that this man is repre-sentative of all humanity. People are not by nature receptive to the light (1:5, 10), but are spiritually blind from birth. It is the role of Jesus as the Light who comes into the world to enlighten everyone (cf. 1:9). [*genetē*]

9:2 Who sinned (*hēmarten*). This question by Jesus' disciples assumes that sin (regardless of who committed it) was the cause of the man's blindness. This was a common belief in Judaism. The rabbis used Ezek. 18:20 to prove there was no death without sin, and Ps. 89:32 to prove there was no punishment without guilt (cf. the Talmud, *b. Shab.* 55a). Since the man was born blind, the disciples assumed the sin must have been on the part of his par-ents or during his time in the womb. *Song Rabbah* 1:41 (a later rabbinic work) states that when a pregnant woman worshiped in a pagan temple, the unborn child also commit-ted idolatry. This is one example of how, in rabbinic Jewish thought, an unborn child was capable of sinning. Jesus pointed out in the

following verse, however, that individual sin was *not* the cause of the man's blindness. [*hamartia*]

9:3 The works of God (*erga*). See 5:36, where the "works" of God are those sign miracles that bear witness to who Jesus is. Here the meaning is the same: "works" in the plural refers to the miracles for which Jesus was by now well-known. [*ergon*]

May be revealed (*phanerōthē*). This verb means "to make known, reveal" clearly and in some detail (LN 28.36; RSV "made mani-fest"; NIV "be displayed"). The main point is that God's "works" (and through them, the Son of God who does them) are to be "revealed" (cf. 9:16, 31). [*phaneroō*]

9:4 It is necessary (*dei*). In John's Gospel this impersonal verb typically indicates divine necessity, that is, God's will or plan (3:7, 14, 30; 4:4, 20, 24; 9:4; 10:16; 12:34; 20:9). [*dei*]

Night (*nyx*). Here the contrast is between "day" and "night," that is (figuratively), between the conditions of "light" and "dark-ness" (BDAG 682). For John, in view of the identification of Jesus as the Light of the world (8:12; 9:5), "night" involves the depar-ture of Jesus from the world. That departure is approaching (cf. 7:34; 8:21-23), the Light will soon be withdrawn, and darkness will reign for a time—but not forever (cf. 1:5, 10). See also the discussion at 3:2. [*nyx*]

9:5 The world (*kosmō*). (Twice in this verse.) World here means not so much a place as where "humanity" is (v. 4). See the discus-sion at 1:9. [*kosmos*]

The light (*phōs*). Jesus' statement "I am the light of the world" connects the present account with 8:12. Here (more clearly than in 8:12) it is clear that the evangelist did not see Jesus' statement as a metaphysical definition of the person of Jesus, but a description of his *effect* on the world, forcing everyone to decide whether to "come to the light" or to remain in darkness (cf. John 3:19-21). See the discussion at 1:4. [*phōs*]

9:6 Clay (*pēlon*). The term refers here to moistened earth of a clay-like consistency (LN 2.18; NIV, NRSV, NLT, NET, "mud"). In other contexts (e.g., Rom. 9:21) the same term can refer to potter's clay. It was also found in both magical formulae and medical prescriptions (TDNT 6:118), suggesting Jesus' superiority to both magic and medicine. For Jesus to make the clay was work, and thus, for the authorities, a violation of the Sabbath (cf. 9:14; also, in the Mishnah, *m. Shabbat* 7:2 prohibited kneading on the Sabbath). [*pēlos*]

Spittle (*ptysmatos*). Saliva (NIV, NRSV, NLT, NET) was occasionally used as a healing agent in pagan cultures (BAGD 727), so at the popular level it might have been viewed that way here. Note how the Greek word sounds like what is described. [*ptysma*]

Anointed (*epechrisen*). The verb means to rub on or smear on substances like salve or oil (LN 47.15; NIV "put it on"; NRSV "spread the mud on"; NET "smeared the mud on"), so it was an appropriate way to describe the placing of mud on the man's eyes. [*epichriō*]

9:7 The pool of Siloam (*kolymbēthran*). This described an obviously well known pool in Jesus' day. Josephus describes a "fountain" called Siloam (*J. W.* 5.4.2 [5.145]), but it is not entirely certain whether he was referring to the Lower (or Old) Pool or the nearby Upper Pool, which is the modern Pool of Siloam. [*kolymbēthra + Silōam*]

"Sent" (*apestalmenos*). The pool's name in Hebrew is *shiloah* from the Hebrew verb "to send." In Gen. 49:10 the somewhat obscure *shiloh* was interpreted as a messianic reference by later Jewish tradition, (*Gen. Rab* 98.13; 99.10) and some have argued for a lexical connection between the two names (although this is doubtful). However, the water that was poured out at the altar during the feast of tabernacles was drawn from the pool of Siloam. Why does John as evangelist comment on the name of the pool? In John's Gospel the concept of "sending" is important. The Father "sent" the Son, and the Son "sent" the man born blind to the pool. The name of the pool is applicable to the man's situation, but also to Jesus himself, who was "sent" from heaven. See 1:6. [*apostellō*]

9:9 I am he (*egō eimi*). Here the statement is simply the man's acknowledgement that he was the same individual who used to beg. This is an indication that John has not made the phrase into a technical term that always refers to Jesus' deity. [*egō + eimi*]

9:11 That one (*ekeinos*). See 7:11. It is clear that this demonstrative pronoun is not a technical term for Jesus in the fourth Gospel (as it is in 1 John), since throughout chap. 9 it is used to refer to the man born blind. [*ekeinos*]

Received sight (*aneblepsa*). The verb was used in classical Greek with the same meaning it has here: "gain sight" or "regain sight" (BAGD 50; NIV "and then I could see"; NET "and was able to see"). Whether one's sight is regained or is gained for the first time must be determined from the context. Here the man was clearly stated to be blind from birth (v. 1). [*anablepō*]

9:14 Sabbath (*sabbaton*). (Also in v. 16) See 5:9, where a similar note is given to alert the reader that it was the Sabbath. Here again Jesus had done something to cause controversy by performing work on the Sabbath. [*sabbaton*]

9:16 Keep (*tērei*). Here the verb refers to "observing" the Sabbath (NRSV, NET). The Jewish religious leaders considered the work involved in making the mud as a Sabbath violation. See also 8:51. [*tēreō*]

A sinner (*hamartōlos*). Although the meaning of the term is "a person who commits sin," John never uses this word to refer to people in general or individuals in particular. It is used only of Jesus, and only by his opponents as an accusation against him. [*hamartōlos*]

A division (*schisma*). Although some of the Jewish religious leaders assumed automatically that since he broke the Sabbath, Jesus could not be from God, others were troubled by the obvious facts: How could a man who was a "sinner" perform such miraculous signs? This created a "division" among them, but the account proceeds on the premise of the first group, that a man who broke the Sabbath could not be from God. [*schisma*]

9:17 A prophet (*prophētēs*). See 1:21. Here, since the word *prophētēs* is not accompanied by the Greek article, and since in his initial reply in 9:11-12 the man born blind showed no particular insight into Jesus' true identity, the term probably does *not* refer to *the* prophet of Deut. 18:15, but merely to a divinely endowed person working miracles. The Pharisees had put the man on the spot, and he felt compelled to say something about Jesus, but still didn't have a clear conception of who Jesus was. So he labeled him a "prophet" (cf. 4:19). [*prophētēs*]

9:18 The Jews (*Ioudaioi*). See 1:19. Here the phrase refers to the Jewish religious leaders, notably the Pharisees, mentioned in 9:13, 15, 16. [*Ioudaios*]

Did not believe (*episteusan*). Here the content of what was not "believed" is specified in the context of "that he had been blind." At this point the Jewish religious leaders had not turned to open hostility. Instead, the dilemma represented in v. 16 was real: a man who was good enough to perform such a miracle would not have performed it on the Sabbath.

So the Jewish leaders assumed there had been a mistake, probably in the man's story. The next step, therefore, was to interrogate the man's parents; perhaps the man had not really been born blind after all. [*pisteuō*]

Called (*ephōnēsan*). Here the verb means "summoned" (LN 33.307) in the sense of calling the parents in for an inquiry (NLT "called in"; NIV "sent for"). [*phōneō*]

9:21 He is of age (*hēlikian*). (Also in v. 23) As an idiom this refers to the age of legal maturity (NET "he is a mature adult"). The word has this meaning frequently in the secular Greek papyri (BDAG 436). [*ēlikia*]

9:22 Put out of the synagogue (*aposynagōgos*). The term is used in the NT only by John and refers to excommunication from the Jewish synagogue (LN 11.46; BAGD 100; NLT, "expelled from the synagogue"). As used by John to describe what was done to one who "confesses" that Jesus was the Messiah, it is dismissed as anachronistic by some and nonhistorical by others. In later Jewish practice there were at least two forms of excommunication: a temporary ban for 30 days, and a permanent ban. But whether these distinctions applied in NT times is far from certain (TDNT 7:848). There is no substantial evidence for a formal ban on Christians until after the time John's Gospel could possibly have been written. Therefore this may refer to some form of excommunication adopted as a contingency to deal with those who were proclaiming Jesus to be the Messiah. If so, there is no other record of the procedure than the three occurrences in John (9:22; 12:42; 16:2). It could well have been local, limited to the area around Jerusalem. [*aposynagōgos*]

9:24 They called (*ephōnēsan*). See 9:18. Deciding that their interrogation of the man's parents was fruitless, the Pharisees recalled (NIV, NET "summoned") the man himself for further questioning. [*phōneō*]

Glory (*doxan*). The expression "Give glory to God" is an idiom meaning "Admit the truth" (cf. Josh. 7:19). [*doxa*]

9:28 They reviled (*eloidorēsan*). When pressed further, the man stuck to his story, and the Jewish religious leaders were reduced to mocking him (NIV "hurled insults at him"; NET "heaped insults on him"). By v. 34 the argument had become completely *ad hominem*. [*loidoreō*]

9:29 Where he is from (*pothen*). The Greek term refers to one's place of origin (BAGD 680). Once again the debate centers over Jesus' place of origin. See also the discussion at 7:27. [*pothen*]

9:30 A marvel (*thaumaston*). The term means "a wonder, marvel, something remarkable" (BAGD 352). The man who received sight used it as more of an exclamation here, however: "What a marvelous thing!" (NIV "Now that is remarkable!"; NRSV "Here is an astonishing thing!"; NET "This is a remarkable thing"). Again John's tendency to include wordplays may be present here, because the real "marvel" is the miraculous healing of the man's eyes. Yet the man himself uses the term in an ironic way to describe the lack of knowledge on the part of the Jewish religious leaders who opposed Jesus. Although they were reluctant to acknowledge that Jesus really came from God (cf. however, Nicodemus in 3:2), the man who received his sight was convinced that Jesus had come "from God" (v. 33). [*thaumastos*]

9:31 Sinners (*hamartōlōn*). By implication this is an accusation against Jesus. See the discussion of this term at 9:16. [*hamartōlos*]

A worshiper of God (*theosebēs*). The word literally means "a fearer of God," and by extension, since "fear" and "reverence" are often related, "a worshiper of God" (NIV "the godly man"; NET "if anyone is devout"). This particular attitude toward God is explained in the next clause as being evidenced by one who "does his will" (i.e., "obeys him"). This is a prerequisite to being "heard" by God—to having one's prayers answered (cf. TDNT 3:126). [*theosebēs*]

9:32 From eternity past (*aiōnos*). Although in places the expression can simply mean "from of old, from antiquity," there are also instances where it refers to "the beginning," i.e., of the world (cf. Josephus, *J. W.* 5.10.5 [5.442]). That is the meaning in context here (NRSV "Never since the world began"; NET "Never before"). Such a miracle had never been heard of before. [*aiōn*]

9:33 From God (*para*). The preposition *para* ("from") followed by the Greek genitive case carries the local sense and can be used of one person sending another (BAGD 609). [*para*]

9:34 You were born completely in sin (*hamartiais . . . holos*). The Greek term *holos* here looks at the completeness of the man's sinfulness (LN 78.44; NIV "were steeped in sin at birth"; NET "were born completely in sinfulness"). This is probably a Johannine idiom, since it occurs elsewhere (John 13:10, *katharos holos*). The point of this insult is that the man who had received sight had not previously adhered rigorously to all the conventional requirements of the OT law as interpreted by the Pharisees (LN 88.118). Thus in their view he had no right to instruct them about Jesus, so they "threw him out." [*holos + hamartia*]

9:35 Finding him (*heurōn*). Jesus took the initiative in "finding" the man whom he had healed, since the man apparently did not yet know who Jesus was. [*heuriskō*]

Do you believe in (*pisteueis*). Here and in the next verse the meaning of the expression is the same as in 3:15, 16, 18, "exercise faith in, put one's trust in." The content of what is to be believed is specified as "the Son of Man," an allusion to Dan. 7:13 and the figure there who is given universal sovereignty. [*pisteuō* + *huios* + *anthrōpos*]

9:38 He worshiped him (*prosekynēsen*). The verb *proskyneō* is used in 4:20-25 of worshiping God, and again with the same sense in 12:20. Assuming the authenticity of 9:38-39a (some of the earliest and most important NT manuscripts lack these verses) this is the only place in John's Gospel where anyone is said to have worshiped Jesus using this term. As such, these words form the climax of this story, but they may represent an addition by a later copyist. [*proskyneō*]

9:39 Judgment (*krima*). This term is basically synonymous with the other noun for "judgment" in John's Gospel, *krisis* (LN 56.30). Jesus' statement here creates a contradiction, but only a superficial one, with the mission statement in 3:17. There Jesus' mission was to save the world; he did not come with the mission of condemning it. But (as 3:19-21 explains, along with the example here) by the very fact of the Light coming into the world, "judgment" is provoked. As people respond to Jesus, so are they judged. Light necessitates a choice (to come to the Light or to remain in the darkness), and this choice is one's judgment. [*krima*]

This world (*kosmon*). Here the term is qualified as "this world," which stands in contrast to the heavenly world, the world "above," a world other than this one, already existing. [*kosmos*]

9:41 Have sin (*hamartian*). This construction also occurs in John 15:22, 24, 19:11, and 1 John 1:8. In John's usage "sin" is a condi-

tion or characteristic quality (BAGD 43). A wrong action has been committed or a wrong attitude exists, resulting in a state of "sin" (cf. NIV; NET "be guilty of sin"). [*hamartia*]

Remains (*menei*). See 1:32. The blind man received physical sight, and this led him to spiritual sight as well. The Pharisees, who claimed to possess spiritual sight (v. 40), were spiritually blinded. The reader might recall Jesus' words to Nicodemus (3:10), "Are you the teacher of Israel and do not understand these things?" Put another way, to receive Jesus was to receive the light of the world, while to reject him was to reject the light, close one's eyes, and "become blind" (v. 39). This is the serious sin of which Jesus had warned before (8:21-24). Such blindness was incurable because they had rejected the only cure that exists (cf. 12:39-41). [*menō*]

10:1 The door (*thyras*). (Also in v. 2) Here the term refers to the literal "door" to the sheepfold (BDAG 462). Jesus will later use this term figuratively to refer to himself as the opening that permits the passage of his followers, "the sheep," (vv. 7, 9). [*thyra*]

The fold of the sheep (*aulēn*). The Greek term *aulē* refers to a walled enclosure, either the courtyard of a house or an enclosure for livestock like "sheep" as here (LN 7.56, BAGD 121; NIV "sheep pen"). There was more than one type of sheepfold in use in Palestine in Jesus' day. This one seems to be a courtyard in front of a house, surrounded by a stone wall (often topped with briars for protection). Sheep were kept inside at night, particularly during the colder winter months, and taken out during the day to pasture. [*aulē*]

A thief (*kleptēs*). As far back as Homer, this term meant "someone who steals" or "embezzles secretly and craftily" (TDNT 3:754). In the Greek OT the related verb described one of the chief sins, along with murder, adultery, and bearing false witness (Jer. 7:9). Here Jesus describes "all those who came before him" (v 8) claiming to be rulers or leaders of the community, like the Herodians and Pharisees. The imagery would not have been missed by them. [*kleptēs*]

A robber (*lēstēs*). Whereas the "thief" stole primarily by stealth, the "robber" stole primarily by violent assault. The term here means "robber, highwayman, bandit" (BAGD 473). [*lēstēs*]

10:3 The doorkeeper (*thyrōros*). The term describes the person who guards the entrance door of a house or building (LN 46.8; KJV "porter"; NIV "watchman"; NRSV, NLT "gatekeeper"). It could refer to either a man or a woman (BAGD 366), although the masculine form is used here. There have been many suggestions as to who the "doorkeeper" in the parable represents, but none are convincing. More likely there are details in the parable that are necessary as part of the overall picture but without symbolic significance. [*thyrōros*]

Leads them **out** (*exagei*). The verb means to "bring out" or "lead out" someone or some animate thing (BAGD 271). It has been suggested that there was more than one flock in the fold (perhaps indicated by the presence of the "doorkeeper," since only the larger sheepfolds would have a guard). When it was time to pasture the sheep, each shepherd called his own flock and separated the sheep. Against such an interpretation, however, the Gospel of John never mentions distinctions among the sheep in this fold. Although there are other sheep to be brought in (10:16), they are to be "one flock" with "one shepherd." [*exagō*]

10:4 He puts forth (*ekbalē*). Here the verb does not have the connotation of force as it frequently does elsewhere ("throw out"), but refers simply to causing someone or something (here sheep) to move from one location to another (BDAG 299; NIV, NRSV "has brought out"; CEV "has led out"). [*ekballō*]

10:5 Will flee (*pheuxontai*). When a "stranger" attempts to take the sheep out of the fold, they will not follow him because they do not recognize his voice. In fact, the sheep will "flee" from him. The verb means "to run away from" (LN 15.61; NIV, NET). [*pheugō*]

10:6 This figure of speech (*paroimian*). The Greek word *paroimia* (used again in 16:25, 29) refers to a fairly short narrative that has symbolic meaning (NIV, NRSV "figure of speech"; NLT "illustration"; NET "parable"). This term does not occur in the Synoptic Gospels, where *parabolē* ("parable") is used instead. Nevertheless, the two terms are similar in meaning (LN 33.15, TDNT 5:856). [*paroimia*]

10:7 The door of the sheep (*thyra*). Here the statement is unusual; the reader might have expected Jesus to say, "I am the Shepherd of the sheep." The meaning is clarified in v. 9: Jesus is the "door" (NIV, NRSV "gate") through which the sheep pass as they go in and out of the fold (BDAG 462). [*thyra*]

10:8 All . . . **before me** (*pantes*). The referent of this phrase is somewhat difficult, since the most obvious one would be Jesus' predecessors, the prophets and saints of the OT. But Jesus could hardly be saying this about them; his attitude toward such people is clear in 5:46 and 8:56. The use of the present tense ("all who came before me are thieves and robbers") provides a contextual clue: "all who came before me" refers to the Jewish religious leaders of Jesus' own day, who came in the "darkness" before the "Light." [*pas*]

10:9 He will be saved (*sōthēsetai*). The verb

here refers to "anyone" (although the words are directed to "some of the Pharisees" in 9:40, and this dialogue is a continuation of that). For John, "being saved" essentially means in John's preferred terms, "attaining eternal life." [sōzō]

Will go in and **go out** (*eiseleusetai . . . exeleusetai*). In other contexts this phrase is an idiom for living or conducting oneself in relationship to some community (cf. Acts 1:21; also Num. 27:17; 2 Chron. 1:10). Here Jesus' words may well look forward to the new covenant community of believers. In Luke 9:4 both these verbs occur in the context of the safety and security provided by a given household for the disciples (cf. BAGD 233). [*eiserchomai + exerchomai*]

Will find pasture (*nomēn*). The term refers in non-biblical texts to a place of "grazing land," and to the opportunity for foraging that such land provides (BDAG 675). In Ezek. 34:13-14 "pasture" refers to the mountain heights of Israel after the nation's restoration and the establishment of God's kingdom. Jesus himself is the means of entry into the kingdom. [*nomē*]

10:10 Destroy (*apolesē*). Here the verb means "to ruin, destroy, or cause the destruction of something or someone" (cf. LN 20.31). Ultimately Jesus' mission (cf. 3:16-17) stands in stark contrast to the purposes and activities of those who have preceded him. [*apollymi*]

Abundantly (*perisson*). The word means "extraordinary in amount, abundant, profuse" (BDAG 805; NIV "have it to the full"; NLT "in all its fullness"). What is emphasized here is the overflowing quality of the eternal life that Jesus came to give (cf. Rom. 5:20). [*perissos*]

10:11 The good shepherd (*poimēn*). (Twice in this verse) Here the metaphor changes: Jesus, who in vv. 7-10 was the Door, now becomes the Shepherd. Compare Ezek. 34:11-12,

where *Yahweh* himself is the Shepherd who replaces inadequate shepherds of the nation. At the least, Jesus' metaphor of himself as the Shepherd would constitute a messianic claim. At the strongest, it would amount to an identification with God himself—a claim to deity. [*poimēn*]

Lays down (*tithēsin*). (Also in vv. 15, 17, 18) In John's writings this verb frequently refers to Jesus' act of "laying down his life," which took place on the cross (BAGD 816). It has this meaning in John 10:11, 15, 17, 18; 13:37; 15:13, and 1 John 3:16. It is also used of Jesus "laying aside" his outer clothing in John 13:4, which may well represent the same thing, since the ultimate significance of the footwashing that follows is Jesus' sacrificial death for his disciples. [*tithēmi*]

For (*hyper*). (Also in v. 15) The Greek preposition *hyper* followed by the genitive case can mean "for the benefit of," but in some contexts relating to the death of Christ it goes beyond this to imply atonement (TDNT 8:510) and even substitution. Jesus speaks openly of his death on behalf of others twice in this section (vv. 11, 15). When he says the good shepherd lays down his life for the sheep, Jesus is speaking very specifically. He has his own death on the cross in view. For a literal shepherd with a real flock of sheep, the death of the shepherd would spell disaster for the sheep, but here it results in life for them. [*hyper*]

10:12 The hired worker (*misthōtos*). (Also in the following verse) This term is found in Plato, *Politicus* 290a, referring to a "day laborer" (TDNT 4:695). The focus is on work done for pay (LN 57.174; NIV, NRSV, NLT, NET "hired hand"). A worker who was simply paid to do a job would have no interest in the sheep and would not risk his life for them. When they were threatened, he would run away. [*misthōtos*]

Snatches (*harpazei*). This Greek verb has the idea of seizing something by force and dragging it off (BAGD 109). Since in this context a "wolf" scatters the flock as a result, the meaning "attacks" is preferable (LN 39.49; NIV, CEV, NLT, NET). [*harpazō*]

10:13 Does not care (*melei*). The verb means "to be especially concerned about something," with the implication of some degree of apprehension (LN 25.233). A hired worker lacks such concern for the sheep. [*melō*]

10:14 Know (*ginōskō*). (Twice in this verse and twice in the following verse) Here the verb emphasizes the personal nature of the relationship between Christ (the Good Shepherd) and the believer ("my own"), which in turn is modeled after the relationship between the Father and the Son (v. 15). The term implies a personal fellowship here (TDNT 1:711). [*ginōskō*]

10:15 I lay down (*tithēmi*). See the discussion at 10:11, where the same phrase, "lay down . . . life for the sheep" occurs. In v. 11 it is the "Good Shepherd" who lays down his life, while here Jesus uses the first person ("I lay down my life for the sheep"). [*tithēmi*]

10:16 Other sheep (*probata*). The language is clearly figurative; Jesus does not mean he owns other livestock, but that there are other people to be brought into the kingdom. The "other sheep" here are almost certainly the Gentiles—Jesus' mission to the Samaritans was highlighted already in John 4:4-42. Such an emphasis also recalls the mission of the Son in John 3:16-17, which was to save the world, not just Israel. Such an emphasis would be particularly appropriate if the evangelist were writing to a non-Palestinian and primarily non-Jewish audience. [*probaton*]

This **fold** (*aulēs*). See 10:1. Here the sheepfold is not a literal one; Jesus is speaking of bringing other "sheep" (people) in who do not belong to this "fold." The fold is the kingdom. Initially it was to consist of Jewish people, but others (Gentiles) are to be brought into the "one flock," foreshadowing the Jewish and Gentile unity of the church (cf. Eph. 2:14-18). [*aulē*]

It is necessary (*dei*). In John's Gospel this impersonal verb typically indicates divine necessity, that is, God's will or plan (3:7, 14, 30; 4:4, 20, 24; 9:4; 10:16; 12:34; 20:9). [*dei*]

One flock (*poimnē*). This is a figurative reference to the church, comprised of Jewish believers and Gentile believers ("this fold"). For John, the unity of the flock is not a given, naturally existing unity, but a unity Jesus created, the end result of Jesus' work (cf. Eph. 2:15). [*poimnē*]

One shepherd (*poimēn*). The "one shepherd" refers to Jesus himself. [*poimēn*]

10:18 No one takes it away (*airei*). Here Jesus explains that his death is voluntary. He could not possibly be harmed if it were not permitted (cf. 19:11). [*airō*]

Authority (*exousian*). (Twice in this verse) Here Jesus says that the "authority" to "lay down" (i.e., give up, surrender) his life has been given to him by the Father. While "authority" here could mean something like "authorization" (i.e., Jesus had the Father's "permission") to do this, the term *exousia* here means something like "inherent authority" or "inherent power," so that ultimately this refers to Jesus' "right to act" in this regard (KJV, NRSV "power"). BAGD 277 renders the phrase here "have the right to lay it down" (so NLT). This fits with the previous clause, "No one takes it from me, but I lay it down of my own accord." [*exousia*]

This commandment (*entolēn*). This is the Father's "commandment" regarding the "laying down" and "taking up" of his life again. Later Jesus will speak of the "work" given him by the Father to accomplish, which will refer to the same thing (17:4). [*entolē*]

10:19 A division (*schisma*). See 9:16. In 10:6 the response of the listeners had been lack of understanding. This time it was "division." These verses recall previous occasions in John's Gospel where there was division over Jesus (7:12, 25-27, 31, 40-41; 9:16). [*schisma*]

10:20 Is insane (*mainetai*). See also 8:48. The Greek term here refers to insanity, not anger, so that the person is behaving in a completely irrational manner (LN 30:24; NIV "raving mad"; NLT "crazy"; NET "has lost his mind"). Such a person has lost control of himself (BAGD 486). So the leaders claim about Jesus (cf. TDNT 4:361). [*mainomai*]

10:22 The feast of the dedication (*enkainia*). This is a reference to Hanukkah. The Greek name for this feast, *enkainia*, literally means "renewal" and was used to translate "Hanukkah," which means "dedication" (cf. BAGD 215). In the Greek OT this noun (and its related verb) was the standard term used to refer to the consecration of the altar of the tabernacle (Num. 7:10-11), the altar of Solomon's temple (1 Kings 8:63; 2 Chron. 7:5) and the altar of the second temple (Ezra 6:16). The feast of Hanukkah itself celebrated the victories of 165-164 B.C. when Judas Maccabeus drove out the Syrians, rebuilt the altar, and rededicated the temple in Jerusalem on 25 Kislev (1 Macc. 4:41-61). See also Josephus, Ant. 12.7.6 (12.325). [*enkainia*]

Winter (*cheimōn*). The feast of the dedication (Hanukkah) began on 25 Kislev, in November-December of the modern Gregorian calendar. [*cheimōn*]

10:23 The portico of Solomon (*stoa*). See 5:2. A "portico" was a covered walkway formed by rows of columns supporting a roof (LN 7.40). It was usually open on one side. The "portico of Solomon" (so NRSV, NET; NIV, NLT "Solomon's Colonnade") was located in the temple complex, with the open side fac-

ing in toward the temple proper (BAGD 759). [*stoa*]

10:24 The Jews (*Ioudaioi*). The question the Jewish leaders asked Jesus ("Are you the Christ?") is the same their representatives asked John the Baptist earlier (1:19-34). [*Ioudaios*]

Keep us **in suspense** (*tēn psychēn hēmōn aireis*). The Greek phrase literally means, "How long will you take away our life?" This is an idiom meaning "to keep someone in suspense" so that they cannot come to a conclusion about something (LN 30.36, BAGD 24; NIV, NRSV, NLT, NET). The basic question the Jewish religious leaders were asking was whether Jesus was indeed the Messiah. [*airō*]

Plainly (*parrēsia*). This is another idiom. The term means "with boldness," but this refers to something done in a clear or publicly evident manner (LN 28.29). The Jewish religious leaders were pressing Jesus to make a public declaration if he was the Messiah. [*parrēsia*]

10:25 Do not believe (*pisteuete*). In context what is not "believed" here is that Jesus was the Messiah (note the question Jesus was asked in the previous verse). [*pisteuō*]

The works (*erga*). Like John 5:36 the plural "works" is used to describe the miraculous works that Jesus has been doing, which "testify" to his identity. [*ergon*]

10:27 And I know them (*ginōskō*). Here the personal nature of the relationship between Jesus as the Shepherd and his followers as "sheep" is indicated, as in 10:14. [*ginōskō*]

10:28 Will never perish (*apolōntai*). Here the verb *apollymi* means "perish, die" (BAGD 95). See 3:16, where "perish" or have "eternal life," are also contrasted. [*apollymi*]

No one **will snatch** them (*harpasei*). (Also

in the following verse) The evangelist does not specify who might try to "snatch away" those who belong to Jesus, but the implication is that the forces of evil are actively at work. The verb *harpazō* is used of "grabbing" or "snatching violently" (BDAG 134). Jesus assures believers that this attempt will not succeed. [*harpazō*]

10:29 Greater than all (*meizon*). This statement gives added assurance to the believer. Because the Father is "greater" still, those in the flock are completely secure, kept by the Father's power. [*megas*]

10:30 Are one (*hen*). The Greek word *hen* ("one") is neuter, not masculine, so the assertion is not that Jesus and the Father are one person, but one "thing." Identity of the two persons is not what is asserted, but essential unity (unity of essence). Jesus' unity with the Father also provides the transition to the second phase of Jesus' self-revelation at the feast of the dedication, his identity as the Son of God (vv. 32-39). [*heis*]

10:32 Many good works (*erga*). See 5:36 and also 10:25. Here Jesus refers to the miracles he has performed "from the Father," which point to his identity as God's Son (NIV "many great miracles"; NLT "many things to help the people"; NET "many good deeds"). [*ergon*]

10:33 Blasphemy (*blasphēmias*). In general the term refers to defaming or reviling others, speaking against them so as to damage their reputation (LN 33.400). With reference to God, one way in which this could be done was by claiming some sort of equality with God. First-century Jews would have regarded any such claim to be blasphemy because it demeaned the reputation of God. That is the case here. This is the first time the official charge of "blasphemy" is made against Jesus in the fourth Gospel, although

it was implied in John 8:59. [*blasphēmia*]

Make yourself God (*theon*). See 5:18, where a similar idea is expressed. Jesus' opponents charged that he was only a man, but made himself out to be God. [*theos*]

10:34 Your law (*nomō*). The quotation is from Ps. 82:6. Technically the Psalms are not part of the OT "law" (a term that usually applied to the five books of Moses), but occasionally (as here) the term "law" was applied to the entire OT. [*nomos*]

You are gods (*theoi*). Ps. 82:6 was understood in rabbinic Judaism as an attack on unjust judges who, though they have been given the title "gods" because they exercise judgment (a quasi-divine function), are mortal and will die like other men. The argument here is often seen as follows: if it was an OT practice to refer to men like the judges as "gods," and that was not blasphemy, then why object when this term is applied to Jesus? This really does not fit the context, however, since according to this interpretation Jesus was not making any claim for deity (comparing himself to an OT judge) and would therefore not be subject to the charge of blasphemy. Instead, what is actually happening here is a common form of rabbinic argument, arguing from the lesser to the greater. The reason the OT judges could be called "gods" is because they were vehicles of the word of God (cf. John 10:35). But granting that premise, Jesus deserved to be called God much more than they, since he is the Word incarnate (John 1:14), the one whom the Father sanctified and sent into the world to save the world (3:17; 10:36). This Gospel's prologue points to this interpretation. [*theos*]

10:35 Cannot be broken (*lythēnai*). Here Jesus did not explain what was meant by "broken," but it is clear from the context. Jesus' argument depended on the exact word used in Ps.

82:6. If any other word than "gods" had been used in the psalm, his argument would have been meaningless. Since the OT Scriptures did use this word in Ps. 82:6, the argument is binding, because the Scriptures cannot be "broken" in the sense of being shown to be in error (NRSV "cannot be annulled"; NLT "cannot be altered"). [*lyō*]

10:36 Sanctified (*hēgiasen*). The verb means "to include a person in the inner circle of what is holy," in the sense of "consecrate, dedicate, sanctify" (BDAG 10). Here it is related to the Father's "sending" of Jesus into the world to save the world (cf. 3:17). The Son was "dedicated" or "set apart" (NIV, NET) for this task. [*hagiazō*]

10:37 The works (*erga*). See 5:36; also 10:25, 32. Jesus said that the "works" (NET "deeds") he did should indicate whether he was truly from the Father or not. If the Jewish religious authorities could not believe in him, it would be better to believe in the works he did than not to believe at all. [*ergon*]

Do not believe me (*pisteuete*). (Also twice in the following verse) Here the content of what the Jewish religious leaders were supposed to "believe" about Jesus is specified in the following verse: "the Father is in me and I am in the Father." With the close identification between Jesus and the Father asserted here, a further step is being taken in Jesus' claims, which now go beyond simply being the Jewish Messiah. What he was claiming bordered on equality with God, a claim Jesus had advanced before (cf. 5:18). However, it should come as no surprise to the reader of the fourth Gospel (cf. 1:1, 18; 5:18; 8:58). [*pisteuō*]

10:38 Know and understand (*gnōte . . . ginōskēte*). Here the verb means "recognize" or "acknowledge" and is used twice for emphasis. What is "known" here is Jesus' unity with the Father (TDNT 1:711). [*ginōskō*]

10:39 To seize him (*piasai*). The Greek verb can either mean "to arrest" (LN 37.110) or "to seize, capture, grasp" (LN 18.3). In context it is not entirely clear whether the authorities were simply trying to arrest Jesus (NRSV, NLT), or were renewing their attempt to kill him (cf. 10:31) by seizing him (NIV, NET) and taking him out to be stoned. [*piazō*]

He departed (*exēlthen*). Regardless of the authorities' intentions, Jesus escaped their clutches. It is not clear, however, whether Jesus' escape should be understood as a miracle; the text gives little indication and even less description. Perhaps it is enough to say that until his "hour" came, Jesus was completely safe from human hands. His enemies were powerless to touch him until they were permitted to do so. See also 8:59. [*exerchomai*]

10:40 Beyond the Jordan (*Iordanou*). This refers to a place on the eastern side of the Jordan River. In 1:28 the place where John the Baptist was baptizing was called "Bethany beyond the Jordan." Perhaps the evangelist does not mention the name of the place here to avoid confusion with the other Bethany, the village near Jerusalem that was the home of Mary, Martha, and Lazarus, mentioned in 11:1. However, for the attentive reader, it does produce a curious effect: Jesus was in Bethany (the place beyond the Jordan) when he heard that Lazarus was sick in Bethany (the village near Jerusalem). [*Iordanēs*]

11:1 Sick (*asthenōn*). (Also in the following verse) This verb refers to bodily weakness of an unspecified type (BAGD 115). John uses the verb to describe the condition of the nobleman's son in 4:46 who was at the point of death. The participle from this verb describes the paralytic at the pool of Bethesda (5:7). [*astheneō*]

11:2 Who anointed (*aleipsasa*). It is surprising that the evangelist identifies Mary here as "the one who anointed the Lord with ointment and wiped his feet with her hair," since that event is not mentioned until 12:3. Some have seen this as evidence of dislocation of material or evidence of preexisting sources in the fourth Gospel, but many see it as an indication that John expected his readers already to be familiar with the story of Mary's anointing of Jesus. [*aleiphō*]

With ointment (*myrō*). The term refers to "ointment" (RSV, NASB) or "perfumed oil" (NET; LN 6.205, TDNT 4:800), although the preparation was often made from myrrh (our English word derives from the Greek word myron). [*myron*]

11:3 Sent (*apesteilan*). Here the term refers to sending a message about Lazarus's condition and is not directly connected with the uses of the same verb that refer to Jesus (see discussion at 1:6). We are not told that Martha and Mary asked him specifically to come, perhaps because they realized the danger involved for Jesus to come so near to Jerusalem (cf. v. 8). But it is clear that this was a request for some help, though the nature of that help was not specified. [*apostellō*]

11:4 Sickness (*astheneia*). The exact nature of the "sickness" is not specified. However, Johannine double-meanings abound here: "death" would not be the end of the matter, but Lazarus was going to die. Ultimately his death and resurrection would lead to the death and resurrection of the Son of God (11:45-53). In John's Gospel the "trigger event" that precipitates Jesus' arrest, trials, and crucifixion is the raising of Lazarus. [*astheneia*]

May be glorified (*doxasthē*). There is a wordplay here between the terms "glory" (referring to God's "glory"—that is, the "praise" that comes to him for the miracle of the raising of Lazarus), and the "glorification" of the Son of God, which is not praise that comes to him for this miracle, but refers

instead to his own crucifixion, resurrection, and return to the Father that the miracle precipitates. Note the response of the Jewish authorities in 11:47-53. Jesus' "glorification" in John is consistently portrayed as his return to the Father, which is accomplished through his arrest, trials, crucifixion, burial, and resurrection (see 1:14) [*doxa* + *doxazō*]

11:5 Loved (*ēgapa*). John's Gospel uses two different Greek verbs for love, *agapaō* and *phileō*. It is sometimes asserted that the first of these relates to divine love and the second to human love, but this is mistaken, because both verbs can, depending on the context, express the total range of loving relations between people, between people and God, and between God and Jesus (LN 25.43). The "disciple whom Jesus loved" is described using both *agapaō* (13:23) and *phileō* (20:2). An example of *phileō* referring to the love between the Father and the Son can be found in 5:20, and this can hardly refer to human love. Sometimes the alternation between these verbs is more stylistic in nature, simply to avoid repetition (21:15-17). In contexts where there is a distinction between the terms, *phileō* expresses love or affection based on close personal relationship, while *agapaō* focuses more on love or affection based on deep appreciation and/or high regard. In this context, then, if there is any distinction to be made, it would mean that Jesus "regarded Martha and her sister and Lazarus highly" (v. 5). [*agapaō*]

11:6 He remained (*emeinen*). Here the verb simply means "to remain in a given location" (NIV, NLT "stayed where he was"). There is no indication in the narrative why Jesus, when he heard that Lazarus was "sick," chose to wait two days longer before departing for Bethany. Some interpreters have speculated that Jesus intentionally waited for Lazarus to die, or that Lazarus was already dead when the message reached him, but he chose to delay to make the resurrection more miraculous. However, it is probably best to understand this simply as an indication that Jesus' timing was always deliberate and in God's will. [*menō*]

11:8 The Jews (*Ioudaioi*). Here the phrase refers to the Jewish religious authorities who had just been trying to stone Jesus for blasphemy (cf. 1:19; 10:31). [*Ioudaios*]

11:9 The light (*phōs*). (Also in the following verse.) On the surface "the light of this world" refers to the sun, but the reader of John will recall Jesus' statement, "I am the light of the world," in 8:12 and understand the phrase figuratively of Jesus himself. There is only a limited time left ("Are there not 12 hours in a day?") until the Light will be withdrawn (i.e., until Jesus leaves to return to the Father who sent him). The person who walks around in the dark will "stumble" (i.e., trip and fall; cf. the departure of Judas in 13:30). [*phōs*]

This **world** (*kosmou*). Here the term refers on one level to the physical world, but on another level to the world of human beings, who are being challenged either to come to the light (i.e., Jesus himself) or remain in the darkness (cf. 3:19-21). [*kosmos*]

11:11 Has fallen asleep (*kekoimētai*). The Greek verb *koimaō* literally means "sleep" (LN 23.66, BAGD 437) but also occurs in both secular Greek literature and the Bible as a euphemism for death when referring to believers (Gen. 47:30; Deut. 31:16; Isa. 14:8; 43:17; Acts 7:60; 13:36; 1 Cor. 7:39; 11:30; 15:6, 51; 1 Thess.. 4:14; 2 Pet. 3:4). This metaphorical usage by its very nature emphasizes the hope of resurrection. Believers will one day "wake up" out of death. Here, the term refers to Lazarus's physical death, although the disciples misunderstood and thought Jesus

was speaking of actual sleep (cf. v. 13) from which he would "awaken" Lazarus. [*koimaō*]

11:12 He will recover (*sōthēsetai*). Here the verb *sōzō* has nothing to do with theological salvation, but only with physical recovery from an illness (NIV "will get better"; NRSV "will be all right"). See the discussion at 3:17. [*sōzō*]

11:14 Plainly (*parrēsia*). Jesus' clear and open statement to the disciples that Lazarus had died is best understood as another example of his supernatural knowledge (cf. 2:25; 4:18), since the message only said that Lazarus was sick. See also 10:24. [*parrēsia*]

11:15 That you may believe (*pisteusēte*). It is necessary to understand the disciples' belief here in a developmental sense, because there are numerous previous references to the disciples' faith in the Gospel of John, notably 2:11. The disciples' concept of who Jesus really was is continually being expanded and challenged. They are undergoing spiritual growth. The climax is reached in Thomas's confession in 20:28 that Jesus is Lord and God. [*pisteuō*]

11:16 Didymus (*Didymos*). The other name associated with Thomas literally means "twin" (BDAG 242), which probably indicates he had a twin brother (otherwise unnamed). One gets the impression from Thomas's statement here that he is something of a pessimist resigned to his fate. Yet his dedicated loyalty to Jesus and determination to accompany him at all costs is commendable. In addition, the reader should not overlook the contrast between this statement and Thomas's confession in 20:28, which forms the climax of John. Certainly Thomas's concept of who Jesus was had changed dramatically between the present verse and 20:28. [*Didymos*]

11:17 <u>Four</u> days (*tessaras*). There is no description of the journey itself. When Jesus arrived, Lazarus had been in the tomb "four days" already. He had died shortly before that. Common practice was to bury people immediately after they died (cf. Ananias and Sapphira in Acts 5:6, 10). There is some later evidence (early third century) of a rabbinic belief that the soul hovered near the body of the deceased for three days, hoping to be able to return to the body. But the fourth day it saw the beginning of decomposition and finally departed (*Lev. Rab.* 18:1). If this tradition is as old as the first century, it might suggest the significance of the four days. After this time Lazarus's resurrection would be a first-order miracle, an unequivocal demonstration of God's power. However, the tradition might not be this early, and the evangelist does not mention any symbolic significance regarding the four days in the context. [*tessares*]

11:18 One and three-quarter <u>miles</u> (*stadiōn*). Literally, "fifteen *stades*." A *stade* is a unit of linear measure equal to about 607 feet (BAGD 764). Here the distance would be about one and three quarter miles. [*stadion*]

11:19 The <u>Jews</u> (*Ioudaiōn*). See 1:19. Here the phrase appears to refer to residents of Jerusalem in general since the Jewish religious authorities are specifically mentioned in 11:45-46. The people here would have been Lazarus's friends or relatives who had come out to "console" them, that is, to offer condolences. [*Ioudaios*]

11:20 She <u>met</u> him (*hypēntēsen*). As in the familiar incident in Luke 10:38-42, we again find Martha occupied with the responsibilities of hospitality. She is the one who went out to "meet" Jesus, while Mary stayed in the house. [*hypantaō*]

11:23 Will rise again (*anastēsetai*). (Also in the following verse) Jesus' statement that Lazarus would "rise again" is another misunderstood statement in the fourth Gospel. Martha apparently understood Jesus to be referring to the general resurrection at the end of the age. However, as Jesus went on to point out in 11:25-26, Martha's understanding of a resurrection at the end of the age was inadequate for the present situation, because the gift of life that conquers death was a present reality in Jesus. This is consistent with John's perspective on eternal life. It is not only a future reality (as in the Synoptic Gospels) but something to be experienced in the present as well (the "already" in the "already—not yet" framework of the NT). [*anistēmi*]

11:25 The <u>resurrection</u> (*anastasis*). Jesus' statement "I am the resurrection and the life" is the direct answer to Martha's profession of v. 24. While not excluding the final (future) resurrection, it indicates the present realization of what she expected to see on the last day. [*anastasis*]

The <u>life</u> (*zōē*). Jesus does not simply say that he gives resurrection and life, but that he is resurrection and life. In him the life of the age to come, after the resurrection, is already present and available. This is "eternal life." See the discussions of the term at 1:4 and 17:2. [*zōē*]

Will live (*zēsetai*). Although some have understood this as a reference to (resurrected) physical life, it is more consistent with John's usage everywhere else to see this as a reference to eternal life. Those who believe in Jesus, even if they die physically, will live spiritually. [*zaō*]

11:26 Everyone who <u>lives</u> (*zōn*). This is best understood as a reference to eternal life already possessed by the believer. [*zaō*]

Will never <u>die</u> (*apothanē*). Since believers do continue to experience physical death, this is more likely a reference to spiritual death. The negation (translated "never") is literally "will not possibly . . . for ever" and is the strongest possible negation in Koiné Greek. [*apothnēskō*]

Believe this (*pisteueis*). Here the content of belief is specified as "this," referring to Jesus' statement in vv. 25-26. Jesus was asking Martha if she believed what he had just said. [*pisteuō*]

11:27 I have believed (*pepisteuka*). Here the content of what Martha believed is given as "that you are the Christ, the Son of God, who comes into the world." This confession is essentially similar to the purpose statement for John's Gospel (20:31). So in what respect is Martha's "confession" here different from what the evangelist wants the reader of his Gospel to believe? In between the two "confessions" (here and 20:31) is the statement by Thomas, "my Lord and my God" (20:28), which affirms Christ's deity using terms the Greek OT used to translate *Yahweh* and *Elohim*. Thus it is reasonable to think that the final affirmation (20:31) involves an understanding that Jesus is God incarnate (which should come as no surprise to John's readers given statements in the prologue [cf. 1:1, 14, 18]). [*pisteuō*]

11:28 The teacher (*didaskalos*). This is a title frequently used for Jesus. See 3:2. [*didaskalos*]

11:31 To weep (*klausē*). This verb means "to weep, wail," with emphasis on the noise accompanying the weeping (LN 25.138; NIV "to mourn"). In some cases this may involve ritual mourning and even professional mourners. Here the observers thought Mary was going to Lazarus's tomb to offer public lament. [*klaiō*]

11:33 He was deeply moved in spirit (*enebrimēsato*). This Greek verb indicates a strong display of emotion (BAGD 254), often with indignation implied (LN 25.56; NLT "was moved with indignation"). In the Greek OT the verb and its cognates are used to describe indignation (Dan. 11:30; cf. Mark 14:5). Jesus displayed this reaction to the afflicted in Matt. 9:30 and Mark 1:43. He was not angry at the afflicted, but because he was face-to-face with the manifestations of Satan's realm of evil. Here the idea is similar. The realm of Satan was represented by physical death. [*embrimaomai*]

Troubled (*etaraxen*). The verb *tarassō* means "to cause acute emotional distress or turbulence" (LN 25.244; NET "greatly distressed") or "to stir up, disturb, unsettle, throw into confusion" (BAGD 805). It occurs in contexts similar to those of *enebrimēsato*. John uses it in 14:1, 27 to describe the disciples' reaction to Jesus' announcement of his imminent death, and in 13:21 the verb describes Jesus' reaction to Judas's betrayal. [*tarassō*]

11:35 Wept (*edakrysen*). The Greek verb used here of Jesus (*dakryō*) is different from the verb used in v. 33 for Mary and the Jews' weeping (*klaiō*). The latter term refers to loud public wailing and cries of lament, while *dakryō* means "to shed tears" (LN 25.137) and refers to quiet grief. [*dakryō*]

11:36 Loved (*ephilei*). In the present context, the people who observed Jesus weeping assumed that it was due to his personal affection for Lazarus. (*phileō*)

11:38 To the tomb (*mnēmeion*). Lazarus's "tomb" is described here as a "cave" with a "stone" placed upon it. Such a cave used for burial may have been artificially enlarged. Many such tombs have been excavated in the Jerusalem area. [*mnēmeion*]

11:39 Take away (*arate*). (Also in v. 41) The

verb means "to carry off, remove" or in some contexts "to lift up" (Rev. 10:5). However, it is unlikely here that the meaning was to "lift up and carry away" the stone that sealed Lazarus's tomb, because such stones typically would be rolled along in a track or groove. [*airō*]

He smells (*ozei*). This verb means "to stink" (LN 79.47). After "four days" the body is decomposing and the burial spices and ointments would not mask the odor. [*ozō*]

Four days (*tetartaios*). See 11:17, although a different Greek phrase was used there. Although all the details of the miracle itself are not given, the details that are mentioned are important. Given the time period of "four days" and the fact that decomposition had already begun, the narrative leaves no doubt that Lazarus had really died. [*tetartaios*]

11:40 If you believe (*pisteusēs*). Here the meaning of the expression is difficult to pin down, because no specific content is specified. The meaning could be the same as in 3:15, 16, 18, "exercise faith in, put one's trust in," although given Martha's confession in v. 27, she presumably "believed" in Jesus in this sense already. Another possibility is that Jesus meant "believe that I am" [he], that is, God incarnate (cf. 8:24, 28, 58). [*pisteuō*]

The glory of God (*doxan*). The revelation of God's "glory" is the miracle's primary purpose. This statement recalls Jesus' words when he heard about Lazarus's illness (v. 4). [*doxa*]

11:41 Lifted up his eyes (*ēren . . . anō*). This idiom, which means "looking up," has OT roots (cf. Gen. 13:10; 1 Chron. 21:16; cf. BAGD 281). This was probably a common posture in prayer. Jesus did this when he prayed in 17:1, and the tax collector in Luke 18:13 did not feel worthy to do this. [*airō* + *anō*]

11:42 That they may believe (*pisteusōsin*). Here the content of what is to be "believed" is specified as "that you [= God] sent me." [*pisteuō*]

You sent me (*apesteilas*). In this context the issue before the crowd is whether Jesus operated with God's authority and power. [*apostellō*]

11:43 He shouted (*ekraugasen*). The Greek verb refers to a loud cry or scream (LN 33.83). Here it is combined with the phrase "with a loud voice" to reinforce it (TDNT 3:901). Jesus' purpose was probably to ensure that everyone could hear what he said (cf. 11:41-42). [*kraugazō*]

11:44 With wrappings (*keiriais*). The term refers to the "binding material" (something like the strapping material used to web couches; NRSV, NET "strips of cloth"; NIV "strips of linen") that was wrapped around a corpse in preparation for burial (BDAG 538). [*keiria*]

With a facecloth (*soudariō*). The Greek word *soudarion* (NLT "headcloth") is a Latin loanword (*sudarium*). It refers to a small cloth used to wipe off perspiration, similar to a modern handkerchief (BAGD 759). This item is not mentioned in connection with Jesus' burial (19:40), but is mentioned as being in his tomb (20:7). Since it is also mentioned here, it was probably customary. Some speculate that it was wrapped under the chin and tied on top of the head to prevent the mouth of the corpse from falling open (Brown 2:986), but this is not certain. [*soudarion*]

Unbind him (*lysate*). There is a potential double meaning here, since on one level the verb means "to untie" (LN 18.18; NLT, NET "unwrap"), referring to the actual strips of cloth in which Lazarus's body was wrapped for burial. However, the same verb occurs in Luke 13:16 to describe the healing of a woman who had been disabled for 18 years

(BAGD 483). So it is probable that the evangelist thought of Lazarus as being "released" from death itself. The text gives no description of how Lazarus came out of the tomb. Was he completely wrapped in strips of cloth? The evangelist had no concern for such details. Of more significance in comparison to Jesus' own resurrection, where the graveclothes were left behind (20:6-7), is that Lazarus brought his graveclothes out of the tomb with him, since he would need them again. [*lyō*]

11:45 Believed in him (*episteusan*). The response to the raising of Lazarus was mixed. Many of those Jews from Jerusalem who witnessed it "believed in him," which presumably means "believed Jesus to be the Messiah," although this is not explicitly stated. Others, however, went directly to the Pharisees and reported the things Jesus had done. In the context there is little doubt they did so out of hostility to Jesus. Once again Jesus' activity provokes people to "choose up sides" (cf. 3:19-21). [*pisteuō*]

11:47 The Sanhedrin (*synedrion*). The word refers to the highest legal, legislative, and judicial body among the Jews of the first century (NRSV, NET "the council"; NLT "the high council"; NIV "the Sanhedrin"). According to the Mishnah (*m. Sanh.* 1:6) it was composed of 71 men, that is, 70 members and the high priest as president (TDNT 7:863). Under the Roman occupation of Palestine the death sentence could only be handed down by the procurator (John 18:31). The present verse contains the only use of the term in John's Gospel, and the only singular usage without the Greek article in the NT. This probably refers to an informal meeting rather than the official Sanhedrin, since Caiaphas in 11:49 is referred to as "one of them" while in the official Sanhedrin he, as high priest, would have presided over the assembly. They informally discussed what to do about Jesus and his activities. [*synedrion*]

11:48 Will believe in him (*pisteusousin*). Whenever the Jewish religious leaders are involved in discussions of who Jesus is, the issue is typically whether he is the Messiah or not. [*pisteuō*]

Our **place** (*topon*). In context the referent is the temple in Jerusalem. [*topos*]

11:49 High priest (*archiereus*). (Also in v. 51) John's Gospel is sometimes accused of inaccuracy, since in OT times the high priesthood was a lifetime office rather than an annual one. However, Roman governors had the power to depose the high priest (although such removal did not necessarily impact their influence, cf. 18:13). The statement can also be read to mean that during "that year" of which the evangelist spoke, Caiaphas was high priest. [*archiereus*]

11:50 It is expedient for you (*sympherei*). The verb means "to be advantageous or beneficial" and can mean "is better" where a contrast is stated or implied (BDAG 960; NIV, NRSV "it is better for you"; NET "it is more to your advantage"). Caiaphas was no doubt expressing a common sense statement of political expediency. Yet at the same time he was unconsciously echoing a saying of Jesus himself (Mark 10:45). Caiaphas was right—the death of Jesus *would* save the nation from destruction. Yet Caiaphas could not suspect that Jesus would die not for the political entity of Israel, but for the true people of God, and that he would save them not from physical destruction, but from eternal destruction (cf. 3:16-17). The understanding of Caiaphas's words, in a sense that he could not have imagined at the time he uttered them, surfaces an important point. It shows how John understood that words and actions could be invested retrospectively with a meaning not consciously intended or understood by those present at the time. [*sympherō*]

For the people (*hyper*). See the discussion at 10:11. The meaning for Caiaphas was "for the benefit of," but given the earlier usage at 10:11 the reader will see that substitution ("in place of") is ironically meant. [*hyper*]

Should not perish (*apolētai*). See 3:16, where the same verb is used. There is high irony here, because Caiaphas was ready to destroy Jesus in order to prevent the entire Jewish nation from being destroyed, yet God had "given" his Son so that whoever believed in him would not "be destroyed" but have eternal life. [*apollymi*]

11:51 He prophesied (*eprophēteusen*). This represents an "unconscious" prophecy on Caiaphas's part, but in the view of the evangelist, a prophecy nonetheless. [*prophēteuō*]

11:52 Scattered abroad (*dieskorpismena*). With this statement John affirms that Jesus' mission was broader than to the Jewish nation alone (cf. 4:42; 10:16). Ultimately the mission on which the Son was sent is the salvation of the "world" (3:17). [*diaskorpizō*]

Gathered into one (*synagagē*). There are echoes of Pauline concepts here in the stress on the unity of believing Jews and Gentiles (cf. Eph. 2:14-22). See also Jesus' prayer in 17:21. [*synagō*]

11:53 They took counsel (*ebouleusanto*). At this point there is the beginning of a formal plot to "kill" Jesus. The verb "took counsel" looks at the planning necessary to take a certain course of action (LN 30.56) and could be translated "plotted" (NIV) or "planned together" (NET). [*bouleuō*]

11:54 Openly (*parrēsia*). Jesus was no longer going around teaching and speaking publicly due to increased opposition from the Jewish religious leaders. [*parrēsia*]

Ephraim (*Ephraim*). The exact location of this town is unknown, although many have suggested it refers to the present town of Et-Taiyibeh, identified with ancient Ophrah (Josh. 18:23) or Ephron (Josh. 15:9). If this is correct, the location would be about 12 to 15 miles northeast of Jerusalem. [*Ephraim*]

11:55 The Jewish Passover (*pascha*). This is the final Passover of Jesus' public ministry. [*pascha*]

To purify themselves (*hagnisōsin*). It was necessary for pilgrims "to cleanse themselves ritually" (NET) in order to be ceremonially clean so they could observe the Passover (LN 53.50). [*hagnizō*]

11:57 The chief priests and the Pharisees (*archiereis . . . Pharisaioi*). In their desperation the Jewish religious leaders, in their need for intelligence regarding the whereabouts of Jesus, now gave orders for anyone who knew where he was to "report" the information to them, so they could "seize" (i.e., arrest) Jesus. [*archiereus* + *Pharisaios*]

12:2 A dinner (*deipnon*). This term refers to the main meal of the day (KJV, RSV, NASB "supper"); it could refer to an everyday meal, to a formal meal with guests ("feast, formal dinner"), or even to a cultic meal like the Passover (BDAG 215). [*deipnon*]

One of those reclining at table (*anakeimenōn*). In the NT the verb *anakeimai* occurs only in the sense of "reclining at table" (cf. Matt. 9:10; 22:10, 11; 26:7, 20; Mark 14:18; 16:14; Luke 22:27; John 6:11; 12:2; 13:23, 28). In the first century in both middle eastern and Mediterranean culture men did not typically eat meals sitting on chairs around a table. Instead, they lay on cushions on their left side (to leave the right hand free for eating) with their head closest to the low table and the feet pointing away. Women, children, and slaves, however, usually ate standing or in other ways

(TDNT 3:654). While the verbs *anakeimai* and *katakeimai* became generalized in meaning to denote simply the eating of a meal without specifying the exact reclining position of those eating (LN 23.21, cf. BAGD 55), it was considered essential to recline at the Passover meal since the reclining position signified the status of the Israelites after the Exodus as freemen rather than slaves. [*anakeimai*]

12:3 A pound (*litran*). The term refers to a Roman "pound," which weighed 12 ounces (LN 86.4). BAGD 475 gives the metric equivalent as 327.45 grams, which is probably too exact. Ancient sources give weights that vary between 325 and 340 grams. [*litra*]

Pure nard (*nardou*). "Nard" (KJV "spikenard") was an extremely fragrant oil made from the root and head (or "spike") of the nard plant (genus *Valerianna*) from northern India. Because this had to be imported it was enormously expensive. The exact meaning of the adjective *pistikēs* ("pure") is difficult to determine. It is frequently understood as deriving from *pistis* and referring to the purity of the oil of nard (so LN 79.97; NIV, NRSV, NET "pure nard"), but more likely it is something like a brand name, "pistic nard," the precise significance of which is unknown. [*nardos*]

The fragrance (*osmēs*). On one level this comment by the evangelist suggests the recollection of an eyewitness. There may be more to the statement, however. In the later rabbinic literature, *Eccl. Rab.* 7.1.1 states, "The fragrance of good oil is diffused from the bedroom to the dining hall, but a good name is diffused from one end of the world to the other." If this saying were as old as the first century, it might be the evangelist's way of indicating Mary's act of devotion to the Lord would be spoken of throughout the entire world (cf. Mark 14:9). [*osmē*]

12:4 To betray (*paradidonai*). See 6:71. Again the evangelist writes from a post-resurrection point of view, giving information that an eyewitness would not have known. [*paradidōmi*]

12:5 Three hundred denarii (*dēnariōn*). See 6:7. Here the amount ("three hundred") would have exceeded what a common laborer could earn in an entire year, taking into account Sabbaths and feast days when no work was done. [*dēnarion*]

12:6 A thief (*kleptēs*). This parenthetical note by the evangelist is one of the indications in the Gospels that Judas was of bad character even before he betrayed Jesus. However, the comment may also be intended as a narrative link between the frustrated greed of Judas and his subsequent decision to betray Jesus for money. See also the discussion of this term at 10:1. [*kleptēs*]

The money box (*glōssokomon*). This term originally described the case or box for the mouthpiece of a flute, then came to refer to a case or container for anything (BAGD 162). In the Greek OT the term is used in 2 Chron. 24:8, 10 for a collection box for money. LN 6.143 notes that the Greek expression may be understood as an idiom, and some modern translations paraphrase this as "common fund" (NJB) or "common purse" (REB, NRSV). [*glōssokomon*]

12:7 Let her keep it (*tērēsē*). Here the verb *tēreō* means "to reserve or preserve" something for a definite purpose or a suitable time (BAGD 814). [*tēreō*]

The day of my burial (*entaphiasmou*). The term can refer to the preparations necessary for burial, or to the burial itself (BDAG 339). This incident, along with the references to Judas in the context, foreshadows the passion narrative of John 18–19. Mary's action in anointing Jesus' feet was interpreted by Jesus himself as preparation for his "burial." Normally one would not anoint the feet of a living person but the head (cf. Mark 14:3), but one could anoint the feet of a corpse to prepare it for burial. Mary had thus performed (unconsciously) a prophetic or symbolic act—one Jesus understood, but at the time, the disciples almost certainly did not. [*entaphiasmos*]

12:9 The Jews (*Ioudaiōn*). See 1:19. These residents of Jerusalem had heard by now about Jesus' raising of Lazarus and were curious to see both of them. [*Ioudaios*]

12:10 To kill (*apokteinōsin*). Apparently the plot to kill Lazarus never got beyond the planning stage, since the evangelist makes no further mention of it. [*apokteinō*]

12:11 The Jews (*Ioudaiōn*). See 1:19. Here the phrase refers primarily to those residents of Jerusalem who had heard about Lazarus's resurrection (cf. v. 9) and as a result were believing Jesus to be the Messiah. [*Ioudaios*]

12:13 Branches of palm trees (*baia . . . phoinikōn*). Since the word *baion* by itself was a technical term for "palm branch," the genitive phrase *tōn phoinikōn* ("of palm trees") is somewhat redundant. It may have been added as an additional clarification for readers of John's Gospel not familiar with the term *baion* (LN 3.53). The date palm was common in Palestine at the time and was often depicted on coins (BAGD 864). The Mosaic Law stated that "branches of palm trees" were to be used to celebrate the feast of tabernacles (Lev. 23:40). [*baion + phoinix*]

To meet him (*hypantēsin*). When the crowd of pilgrims who were coming to Jerusalem for the Passover (cf. 11:55) heard that Jesus was also coming to Jerusalem, they hurried out to "meet him." By this time Jesus' reputation was well known. [*hypantēsis*]

Were shouting (*ekraugazon*). An ingressive force for the imperfect tense ("began to

shout" NASB, NET) is indicated by the context (see John 11:43). [*kraugazō*]

Hosanna (*hōsanna*). The expression literally meant in both Hebrew and Aramaic "O Lord, save [us]" (cf. Ps. 118:25-26). By the first century it was probably a familiar liturgical expression of praise on the order of "Hail to the king" (TDNT 9:684; NLT "Praise God!"). Here it refers to the messianic King upon his entry into Jerusalem. For Gentile converts to Christianity who had no Jewish background, however, the term probably had much the same meaning as it currently has in English (LN 33.364). In words familiar to every Jew in the first century the evangelist is indicating that at this point messianic expectations are now at the point of realization. [*hōsanna*]

The king of Israel (*basileus*). The qualifying phrase "the king of Israel" is added by the evangelist (it is not part of the quotation from Ps. 118:25-26) to explain for his readers who "the one who comes in the name of the Lord" is. See also John 1:49, where the phrase occurs in parallel with "Son of God." [*basileus*]

12:14 A young donkey (*onarion*). John does not include the detailed accounts of finding the donkey recorded in the Synoptic Gospels. He does, however, see this as a fulfillment of Scripture, which he indicates by quoting Zech. 9:9. [*onarion*]

12:15 Daughter of Zion (*Siōn*). The phrase is an idiomatic way to refer to the inhabitants of Jerusalem (LN 11.66; cf. Matt. 21:5; CEV "people of Jerusalem") drawn from Zech. 9:9. The concept is also found in the OT in Lam. 2:1 and refers partly to Jerusalem itself and partly to the people living in it (TDNT 7:308). [*Siōn*]

12:16 At first (*prōton*). This is another note by the evangelist to inform the reader that Jesus' disciples did not at first associate the prophecy from Zech. 9:9 with the events as they happened. This association came with the later post-resurrection insight the Holy Spirit provided to the disciples after Jesus' return to the Father. Note the similarity with 2:22, which follows another allusion to a prophecy from Zechariah (14:21). [*prōtos*]

Was glorified (*edoxasthē*). Jesus' "glorification" here refers to his exaltation when he returned to the Father, which he would accomplish through the cross. See 1:14. [*doxazō*]

12:19 The world (*kosmos*). Here the response of the Jewish religious authorities is one of pessimism. Their statement is hyperbole, but it is warranted by the diverse groups of people who have joined the multitudes welcoming Jesus at the triumphal entry (cf. vv. 12, 17, 18). See 1:9. [*kosmos*]

12:20 Some Greeks (*Hellēnes*). The term could refer in the broad sense to persons who lived under the influence of Greek culture, but it also could describe "God-fearers" who were Gentiles favorably inclined to Judaism (BAGD 252). Proselytes in the full technical sense would probably not be called "Greeks" any longer. Many God-fearing Gentiles came to worship at the major Jewish feasts without being full proselytes. In the context, John's quotation of Zech. 9:9 in the preceding material (v. 15) becomes even more significant because of this incident and the way Jesus responded to it. According to Zech. 9:10, Messiah would proclaim peace to the Gentiles, and here they come (representatively, of course). Jesus had already said that he had other sheep from a different fold (10:16) and that he would lay down his life for them (10:17). The appearance of these Gentiles wanting to see Jesus indicates that it is now time for him to lay down his life. The hour of his glorification (his return to the Father through death, resurrection, and exaltation) has come at last (vv. 23, 27-28). Jesus then went on to speak about his death (v. 24, 32-33). The arrival of Jesus' "hour" is so important that John never actually mentions whether the Greeks got to see Jesus or not. [*Hellēn*]

12:21 Philip (*Philippō*). (Also twice in the following verse) Philip is first mentioned in John's Gospel in 1:43. It is possible the Greeks who wanted to see Jesus approached Philip because of his Greek name, though it was not unusual for Jews from border areas to have Greek names during this period. The name means "fond of horses" (LS 862). [*Philippos*]

12:23 The hour has come (*hōra*). The phrase here recalls all the previous references to Jesus' "hour" (NLT, NET "time") in the Gospel of John. See the discussion of the term at 2:4. [*hōra*]

The Son of Man (*huios . . . anthrōpou*). "Son of Man" looks at Jesus as one who has been given regal authority according to the imagery of Dan. 7:13. See 1:51. [*huios + anthrōpos*]

Be glorified (*doxasthē*). Jesus' path to glorification lies through the cross, and it lies just ahead. There is no doubt, in light of the following verse, that Jesus is referring to his death here. See 1:14. [*doxazō*]

12:24 Remains (*menei*). Here the verb simply describes something (a grain of wheat) that remains in the state or condition in which it was found (BAGD 504). See 1:32. [*menō*]

Fruit (*karpon*). The saying here is proverbial in nature; a seed planted in the ground will bear "fruit." However, in this context the statement ultimately refers to Jesus himself in his death and resurrection, and the "fruit" is converts for the kingdom (NLT, "a plentiful harvest of new lives"). See 4:36 and especially 15:16. [*karpos*]

12:25 Loses it (*apollyei*). Here the verb *apollymi* means "lose" (BAGD 95). Paradoxically the person who tries to preserve his life will "lose" it, while the person who "hates his life" in the present world will preserve it. [*apollymi*]

This world (*kosmō*). Here the term is further qualified as "this world," which stands in contrast to the heavenly world, the world "above." It is possible to see in the contrast here the more typical rabbinic distinction between "this world" as the present world and "the world to come," where one receives "eternal life," so that the distinction is sequential. This is not the usual distinction in the fourth Gospel, however, since "eternal life" is something believers possess in the present (5:24). See 1:9. [*kosmos*]

12:26 Serves me (*diakonē*). (Twice in this verse) The person who "serves" Jesus is the one who gives up his claim to life in the present world out of love for, and allegiance to, Jesus. To "serve" Jesus is in effect to "hate" one's own life. In the last part of v. 26 Jesus made it clear that such a person will be "where" he is, participating in his glory, and will receive "honor" from the Father. This is what Jesus' servants will receive for following him. [*diakoneō*]

Will honor (*timēsei*). The one who serves Jesus will be "honored" by the Father. The statement "he must follow me" carries the implication of following Jesus even to the cross, that is, the sacrifice of life itself. Such a person will "be where he (Jesus) is," and thus participate in Jesus' glory. See 5:23. [*timaō*]

12:27 Is troubled (*tetaraktai*). This verb refers to acute emotional or mental distress (LN 25.244; CEV, NLT "deeply troubled"; NET "greatly distressed"). As Jesus contemplated the "hour" of his suffering and death, he described his internal distress, which (however severe) did not deter him from completing the Father's work. [*tarassō*]

Save me (*sōson*). The term in context refers to Jesus' "deliverance" from the hour of his suffering and death (BAGD 798; NET "deliver me"). This is a hypothetical question, because Jesus went on to state that it was for "this very hour" that he had come. His sacrificial death had always remained the primary purpose of his mission (cf. 3:16-17). Now, faced with the completion of that mission, would he ask the Father to spare him from it? The expected answer, of course, is no. [*sōzō*]

This hour (*hōras*). (Twice in this verse) The "hour" to which Jesus had come here was the "hour" of his departure (i.e., death) and return to the Father (CEV, "keep me from this time of suffering"; NLT, "save me from what lies ahead"). See 2:4. [*hōra*]

12:28 Glorify (*doxason*). (Three times in this verse) There is a wordplay on this verb. Jesus' prayer for God's name to be "glorified" (i.e., "praised" or "honored," cf. 5:41, 44; 7:18) would ultimately be answered in Jesus' exaltation (i.e., "glorification") when he returned to the Father, which he would accomplish through the cross. A similar wordplay occurs in 11:4. [*doxazō*]

12:29 An angel (*angelos*). See 1:51. In popular belief this may represent a euphemism for God himself having spoken. [*angelos*]

12:31 The judgment (*krisis*). See 3:19, where "judgment" is provoked by the coming of the Light into the world, which forces people to choose between the Light (Jesus, cf. 8:12) and the darkness. [*krisis*]

The ruler of this world (*archōn*). The referent here is Satan, described as "the ruler of this world" (KJV, NIV, NLT "the prince of this world"). On the phrase "this world," see 1:9. [*archōn + kosmos*]

Will be cast out (*ekblēthēsetai*). The Greek verb means "to drive out, expel, throw out," more or less forcibly (BAGD 237). The statement refers to Satan's loss of authority over the world, in principle rather than in fact at this point, since 1 John 5:19 states that the whole world (still) lies in the power of the evil one. In an absolute sense the declaration is proleptic, as the coming of Jesus' "hour" marks the end of Satan's domain and his defeat, even though that defeat has not been ultimately worked out in history yet, but awaits the consummation of the age. [*ekballō*]

12:32 Will draw (*elkysō*). The specific nature of this "attraction" is not described. See 6:44. [*elkyō*]

12:33 Signifying (*sēmainōn*). This is an explanatory note by the evangelist (RSV, NIV "to show"; NASB, NRSV, NLT "to indicate"). The words "lifted up from the earth" in v. 32 are explained as a reference to Jesus' crucifixion. [*sēmainō*]

12:34 The law (*nomou*). This refers to the Mosaic Law. The passage alluded to is probably Ps. 89:35-37, although other passages that have been suggested are Ps. 110:4, Isa. 9:7, Ezek. 37:25, and Dan. 7:14. None of these are in the Pentateuch, but in common usage "law" could refer to the entire OT (LN 33.56; cf. Jesus' usage in John 10:34). Ps. 89:36-37 refers to David's "seed" remaining forever, and later in the same psalm v. 51 speaks of the "anointed" (Messiah). The psalm was interpreted messianically in both the NT (Acts 13:22; Rev. 1:5; 3:14) and in the rabbinic literature (*Gen. Rab.* 97). [*nomos*]

Remains (*menei*). The statement by the crowd reflects the popular belief that Messiah, once he came, would stay forever. See the discussion at 1:32. [*menō*]

It is necessary (*dei*). In John's Gospel this impersonal verb typically indicates divine necessity, that is, God's will or plan (3:7, 14, 30; 4:4, 20, 24; 9:4; 10:16; 12:34; 20:9). [*dei*]

The Son of Man (*huion . . . anthrōpou*). (Twice in this verse) The question "Who is this Son of Man?" presents the crowd's dilemma. If Jesus (whom many of them believed to be the Messiah, as the triumphal entry into Jerusalem showed) identified himself with the Son of Man who was to be "taken up" or "taken away," how could this be reconciled with their belief that Messiah, when he came, would remain forever? Now the Son of Man imagery here corresponds closely to the Son of Man in Dan. 7:13-14, who is taken up in the clouds and presented before the Ancient of Days (a clear exaltation and enthronement motif) and given a kingdom. This Jesus is about to fulfill through his glorification-exaltation through the cross. [*huios* + *anthrōpos*]

To be lifted up (*hypsōthēnai*). The crowd did not understand "lifted up" (v. 32) as a reference to crucifixion, but John's readers certainly would in light of v. 33. [*hypsoō*]

12:35 The light (*phōs*). The noun *phōs* occurs five times in vv. 35-36. The phrase "yet a little time" recalls 7:33, and the ideas are similar, since Jesus is speaking here (as he was there) of his physical presence in the world. The reference to "light" recalls 8:12, where Jesus identified himself as the Light of the world, and especially 3:19-21, where the judgment consists of the Light (i.e., Jesus) coming into the world and provoking a response from men to come either to the light or shrink back into darkness. Here the same imagery is amplified, because we are reminded that Light is in the world only for a limited time (i.e., there is a limited time in which to respond to the light, or as here, by "walking in that light"). Those who refuse or delay will be "overtaken" by the darkness, which is coming after the light is taken away. The person who tries to walk in the darkness is unable to see and thus "does not know where he is going." [*phōs*]

Overtake you (*katalabē*). See 1:5. Here the

term means "overtake, come upon, seize with hostile intent" (BAGD 413). The warning works on two different levels. To the Jewish people in Jerusalem to whom Jesus spoke, the warning reminded them that there was only a little time left to accept Jesus as Messiah. To John's readers Jesus' words warn that there is a finite, limited time in which each individual has opportunity to respond to the Light (Jesus). After that comes "darkness." The response to Jesus decisively determines one's fate for eternity. [*katalambanō*]

12:36 Believe in the light (*pisteuete . . . phōs*). Here it becomes clear that Jesus was speaking of himself under the imagery of "the light." His hearers were exhorted to "believe in the light," which referred to placing their faith in him. Thus the meaning matches John 3:15, 16, 18, "exercise faith in, put one's trust in." The refusal to "believe" in Jesus in the following verse would mean the same. [*pisteuō + phōs*]

Sons of light (*huioi phōtos*). The expression "sons of . . ." is a Semitic idiom that refers to persons of a class or kind, characterized in some way by the genitive-case word or phrase that follows (LN 9.4, BAGD 834). The phrase "sons of light" refers to men and women (KJV, NRSV "children of light"; CEV, NLT "children of the light") to whom the truth of God has been revealed and who are therefore living according to this truth— thus, "people of God" (cf. Luke 16:8; Eph. 5:8; 1 Thess.. 5:5). [*huios + phōs*]

He hid himself (*ekrybē*). Once again Jesus demonstrated his ability to "hide himself" from his enemies at will. [*kryptō*]

12:38 Might be fulfilled (*plērōthē*). The unbelief of the Jewish religious leaders and many of the people fulfills remarks by Isaiah (6:10; 53:1). This response of unbelief, resulting in the rejection of Jesus, has been a recurring theme, foreshadowed in John 1:11. [*plēroō*]

Who has believed (*episteusen*). In the context of the OT quotation, the content of what is "believed" is given as "our report." [*pisteuō*]

The arm of the Lord (*brachiōn*). The expression "arm of" (an extension of the figure "hand of") refers to "power of" (LN 76.3). Thus here the referent is God's activity and power (cf. NLT), which has been revealed in the sign miracles Jesus has performed (cf. v. 37). [*brachiōn*]

12:39 They were not able to believe (*pisteuein*). The unbelief of Jesus' opponents is viewed here as God's judgment, supported by the quotation from Isa. 6:10. This same OT passage is used elsewhere in the NT to explain Jewish unbelief (Paul's final words in Acts 28:26-27; also Rom. 11:8 using Isa. 29:10). [*pisteuō*]

12:40 He has blinded (*tetyphlōken*). All of the statements from Isa. 6:10 are viewed by the evangelist as constituting God's judgment on Jesus' opponents: they were spiritually "blinded," their hearts were "hardened," rendering them incapable of "seeing" and "understanding" spiritually "lest they turn" (i.e., repent). [*typhloō*]

Turn (*straphōsin*). Here the verb means to "turn, change inwardly, be converted" (BAGD 771). The idea is one of turning back to God (as indicated by their response to Jesus; KJV, NASB "and be converted"). [*strephō*]

12:41 His glory (*doxan*). The "glory" that Isaiah saw in Isa. 6:3 was the glory of *Yahweh* (typically translated as "Lord" in most English versions of the OT). Here John speaks of the prophet Isaiah seeing the glory of Christ (since the next clause, "and spoke about him," must refer to Christ rather than *Yahweh*). Given the statements in 1:1 and 1:14 in the prologue to John's Gospel, the evangelist probably had no difficulty applying this OT text to Christ. [*doxa*]

12:42 Believed in him (*episteusan*). Having said that the Jewish religious leaders persisted in their unbelief, John now adds as a clarification that some of them in fact "believed in him." The Greek phrase *homōs mentoi* functions as a strong adversative ("nevertheless"). These were "rulers," a term which probably indicates members of the Sanhedrin (cf. Nicodemus in 3:1 and 7:50; Mark 15:43 of Joseph of Arimathea, and Luke 18:18 of another). On account of "the Pharisees" these individuals were not willing to admit their faith in Jesus publicly. Here the content of what was believed by these leaders is not specified, but is probably best understood as "believed in him as the Messiah." The same penalty for "believing in him" mentioned here, being "put out of the synagogue," was connected in 9:22 to the confession that Jesus was the Messiah ("Christ"). [*pisteuō*]

12:43 The glory (*doxan*). (Twice in this verse) Here "glory" has the meaning "praise" (cf. 5:41, 44; 7:18). These members of the Sanhedrin were more interested in getting praise from others than from God. There is also in the context the reference to Jesus' own "glory" (v. 41) and its connection with God's glory. Their mistaken priorities make them seek the wrong glory. [*doxa*]

12:44 Cried out (*ekraxen*). The verb can refer to a scream or shriek, but here it means "call out in a loud voice" in an attempt to communicate something (BDAG 563; NET "shouted out"). [*krazō*]

12:45 The one beholding me (*theōrōn*). (Twice in this verse.) See 6:40. To "behold" the Son is to "behold" the Father who sent him (cf. 1:18, and Jesus' reply to Philip in 14:9). [*theōreō*]

12:46 A light (*phōs*). Once again there is the contrasting imagery of "light" and "darkness." On Jesus' identification of himself as the "Light of the world," see 8:12 and 9:5. There are also connections to 3:16-21, where Jesus as the "Light" provokes judgment, because the way a person responds to Jesus determines that individual's destiny. But as here, the purpose of Jesus as the Light coming into the world was not to condemn the world but to save it. [*phōs*]

12:47 My words (*rhēmatōn*). The Greek term here refers to the "sayings" (RSV, NASB) of Jesus, including the "I am" statements in the fourth Gospel, like "I am the bread" (6:41), "I am the light of the world" (8:12), "I am the door" (10:7, 9), "I am the good shepherd" (10:11), "I am the resurrection and the life" (11:25), and "I am the way, the truth, and the life" (14:6). [*rhēma*]

Does not keep (*phylaxē*). Here the meaning is "obey" (LN 36.19; CEV, NLT, NET), and this is similar to 8:51, except that the verb is different (*tēreō* in 8:51). [*phylassō*]

But to save (*sōsō*). The object of "saving" is the "world" (here as in 3:17). In both of these contexts (here and 3:17) the concept of "being judged" (i.e., "condemned") is linked as the alternative to "being saved," that is, "attaining eternal life." [*sōzō*]

12:48 The one who rejects me (*athetōn*). See 3:36. The phrase is a strong one, referring to the person who deliberately rejects Jesus. The polarization, which is such a significant characteristic of the fourth Gospel, is present again here. A person either accepts Jesus, placing one's faith in him, or rejects him utterly, leading to eternal ruin. [*atheteō*]

Has one who judges him (*krinonta*). (Twice in this verse.) Here Jesus says that his "word" will "judge" the one who rejects him. See 3:19. [*krinō*]

At the last day (*eschatē*). This refers to the "day of the Lord" (NLT, "the day of judgment") when God would raise the dead for judgment, transform the present world, and inaugurate his eternal kingdom (cf. TDNT 2:697). [*eschatos*]

12:50 Eternal life (*zōē*). Significantly, Jesus did not say here that "keeping" or "obeying" the Father's "commandment" leads to eternal life, but that the "commandment" itself *is* eternal life. This is the commandment concerning what Jesus was to say (v. 49) that the Father gave him. Jesus' words and works that resulted from the Father's commandment are the source of eternal life in the world. With this statement Jesus' public ministry comes to a close. Nothing more is recorded in John's Gospel of anything said by Jesus to the people at large. The remaining material in John concerns mainly Jesus' words to his disciples in the Upper Room in preparation for his departure and return to the Father, and the account of his trials, crucifixion, and resurrection. [*entolē* + *zōē*]

13:1 Knowing (*eidōs*). (Also in v. 3) Again Jesus' knowledge of the situation and of his mission and destiny are clearly expressed. For Jesus, not one of these incidents happened by accident, nor did any of them take him by surprise. This verb is also used for such supernatural knowledge on Jesus' part in 6:61, 64. [*oida*]

His hour (*hōra*). This was the "hour" (NIV, CEV, NET "time") of Jesus' return to the Father. See 2:4. [*hōra*]

That he should depart (*metabē*). The verb means "to transfer over or pass over from one place to another" (BDAG 638). Here it refers to Jesus' departure from "this world" and return to the Father. See 5:24. [*metabainō*]

Having loved (*agapēsas*). The use of the verb *agapaō* here may be intended to suggest to the reader a link to 3:16-17. God "loved" the world and "sent" his Son; now the Son "loves" his own, the disciples, whom he has chosen. [*agapaō*]

To the end (*telos*). This term forms a literary link with John 19:30 (not apparent in some translations, cf. NIV, NLT "showed . . . the full extent of his love"), when Jesus says his final words from the cross, "It is ended" (the noun and verb are cognate: that is, they share the same root-form). The full extent ("end") of Jesus' love for his disciples is not merely seen in his humble service to them in washing their feet (the most common interpretation of the passage). The full extent of Jesus' love for the disciples is demonstrated in his sacrificial death for them on the cross. The footwashing episode becomes a prophetic act, an acting out beforehand of his death on their behalf. The message for the disciples was that they were to love one another like Jesus loved them— not just in humble, self-effacing service, but in their willingness to die for one another (cf. 1 John 3:16). [*telos*]

13:2 Dinner (*deipnou*). (Also in v. 4) See 12:2; cf. NASB, NRSV, NLT "supper"; NIV, CEV, NET "the evening meal." According to John's Gospel this meal took place on the eve of the Passover (which began at sundown, around 6:00 P.M., on Thursday); Passover would begin at sundown on Friday. The Synoptic Gospels appear to portray this Last Supper as a Passover meal (although John does not). It may be that Jesus celebrated the Passover according to a different calendar, although there is no easy solution to this problem. [*deipnon*]

Put into the heart (*beblēkotos*). Cf. NIV, "prompted"; NLT "enticed." This action must be read in light of 13:27, and appears to refer to a preliminary idea or plan. [*ballō*]

13:4 Laid aside (*tithēsin*). (NIV, NRSV, NLT "took off"; NET "removed.") Since this verb is frequently used by John to refer to Jesus "laying down" his life on the cross (10:11, 15, 17, 18, 13:37, 15:13), it has been suggested that the "outer garment" Jesus laid aside here symbolized his laying aside his life. This is in keeping with the significance of the footwashing as developed by John. [*tithēmi*]

A towel (*lention*). (Also in the following verse) The Greek word *lention* is a loanword from Latin (*lentium*) and refers to a piece of cloth used for drying (LN 6.161). The term also occurs in the rabbinic literature (BAGD 471). This would have been a piece of linen cloth, long enough for Jesus to wrap it around his waist and of sufficient length to wipe the disciples' feet. [*lention*]

He girded himself (*diezōsen*). (Also in the following verse) The verb means to "tuck up" a garment by wrapping a belt or piece of cloth around it, or to tie such a belt or piece of cloth around the waist (LN 49:14; NIV, NLT "wrapped . . . around"; NRSV, NET "tied . . . around"). [*diazōnnymi*]

13:5 Began to wash (*niptein*). The verb is used of washing, usually parts of the body like hands or feet (BAGD 540). A first-century host in the Middle East was expected to provide water for washing the feet of his guests, since the feet would become dusty with travel. (Streets in Jerusalem, however, were generally kept very clean.) Washing the feet of someone else was a task for a menial servant; a host would never perform this action for his guests. [*niptō*]

13:6 Do you wash (*su . . . nipteis*). See the previous verse. Peter was not about to allow Jesus to perform this menial task for him, so he protested (v. 8). [*niptō*]

13:7 After these things (*meta*). Jesus made it clear to Peter that what he was doing Peter would not understand at the time, but he would later (the Greek expression *meta tauta* refers to an indefinite period of time, BDAG 638; NIV, NRSV "later"; NLT "someday"). Peter would come to understand the signifi-

cance of what Jesus had done (cf. 12:16). Again, this reflects the post-resurrection insight that all the disciples would receive after Jesus had been raised from death. [*meta*]

13:8 Have no share with me (*meros*). The term can indicate a "share" (KJV, NASB, NIV "part") in a person (as here) or in a thing (the tree of life [Rev. 22:19], the lake of fire [Rev. 21:8], or the resurrection [Rev. 20:6]). If Peter did not allow Jesus to wash his feet, he would have no participatory interest in Jesus. In other words, Peter would be an outsider. [*meros*]

13:10 The one who has bathed (*leloumenos*). In this particular context bathing refers to the ceremonial washing that Jesus and the disciples would have undertaken prior to the meal. Jesus applied this "bath" symbolically to refer to the spiritual cleansing of the disciples. [*louō*]

To wash (*nipsasthai*). In this context the verb has a deeper significance than the literal washing of the disciples' feet might indicate. Verse 10 implies a cleansing from sin is in view. [*niptō*]

Clean (*katharos*). (Twice in this verse and once in the following verse) A common understanding of the passage sees the "bath" as one's initial cleansing from sin, which leaves only lesser, partial cleansings from sin after conversion. This seems doubtful, however, because Jesus stated the disciples were "completely clean" except for Judas (vv. 10, 11). What they needed was to have their feet washed by Jesus. In the context of John's Gospel, the footwashing signifies not only an example of humble service, but also Jesus' sacrificial death on the cross. What the disciples needed to accept (as represented by their allowing Jesus to wash their feet) was this act of self-sacrifice on the part of their master. This makes Peter's initial rejection of the act of humiliation by his Master all the more significant. It also explains Jesus' harsh reply to Peter (v. 8; cf. Matt. 16:21-23). [*katharos*]

13:11 He knew (*ēdei*). This statement is very similar to 6:64, with the same reference to the betrayer. Here the knowledge is clearly supernatural because it involves a future action. [*oida*]

13:12 Resumed his place (*anepesen*). At one level this verb refers to Jesus resuming his place at the meal after the footwashing. At another level, since the footwashing represents his humiliation in going to the cross, we have an acting out of the so-called *kenosis* (or self-emptying) passage in Phil. 2:6-11, with "resuming his place" equalling the exaltation of Phil. 2:9-11. [*anapiptō*]

What I have done for you (*pepoiēka*). Jesus was asking the disciples if they understood the significance of his actions in washing their feet. Ultimately he has set them an example, not just of humble service, but of sacrificial love to the point of death. They did not understand this at the time, but would understand later, after the resurrection (v. 7; cf. 1 John 3:16). [*poieō*]

13:14 If I . . . have washed (*enipsa*). (Twice in this verse.) See the discussion at 13:5. [*niptō*]

You ought (*opheilete*). Compare 1 John 3:16, where the followers of Jesus "ought" (same verb as here) to "lay down their lives for one another." [*opheilō*]

13:15 An example (*hypodeigma*). The term refers to an "example" or "model," "a definite prototype" (TDNT 2:33, LN 58.59). The example Jesus has given is one of self-sacrifice up to the point of death (cf. 15:13; see also v. 10 above). [*hypodeigma*]

13:16 The slave (*doulos*). See 8:34. Again Jesus used an illustration from everyday life, that of "slave" and "master." The disciples are not

greater than Jesus himself, so if he has set them an example, they should be willing to die for one another (cf. 1 John 3:16). [*doulos*]

13:18 I have chosen (*exelexamēn*). In particular Jesus is speaking of the Twelve here, including the betrayer, Judas. Jesus' "choosing" of Judas as one of his disciples is portrayed here as deliberate and with the full knowledge that Judas would betray him. [*eklegomai*]

May be fulfilled (*plērōthē*). Here again, as in 12:38, the words of the Scripture, Ps. 41:9, are seen to be "fulfilled" in the betrayal of Jesus by Judas. [*plēroō*]

Has lifted up his heel (*epēren*). This expression occurs in a quotation from Ps. 41:9. Its precise meaning is somewhat debated (BAGD 727, "raise one's heel against someone for a malicious kick"; LN 8.52, "denoting antagonism and opposition"). In any case the phrase refers to betrayal by a close associate (CEV, NLT, NET "has turned against me"). [*epairō*]

13:19 That you may believe (*pisteusēte*). Jesus says he is telling the disciples about his betrayal "before it happens" so that when it happens they may "believe." Here the content of what the disciples were to "believe" is specified: "that I am [he]." Some argue for a non-predicated use of *egō eimi* here (Brown 2:555), in which case the content of the disciples' belief would be "that Jesus was God incarnate," identified with the "I am" of Exod. 3:14. In the present situation this is more likely (cf. 14:9). [*pisteuō*]

13:20 The one who receives (*lambanōn*). (Four times in this verse.) The verb means "to accept, receive, come to believe" in the sense of believing in something and acting accordingly (LN 31.50; NIV, NET "accepts"; CEV, NLT "welcomes"). This recalls 1:12 in the prologue. [*lambanō*]

13:21 He was troubled in spirit (*etarachthē*). This verb was used in 12:27 to describe Jesus' reaction to the coming of his "hour." Jesus was completely in control of the situation (cf. 13:3), yet he was not emotionally oblivious to what was coming upon him. See 11:33. [*tarassō*]

13:22 Uncertain (*aporoumenoi*). The Greek verb means "to be in perplexity, with the implication of serious anxiety" (LN 32.9; NASB, NIV "at a loss"; NET "worried and perplexed"). Here the disciples were completely at a loss to understand what Jesus meant. [*aporeō*]

13:23 Was reclining in the bosom (*anakeimenos*). See 12:2. People taking part in such a meal would have reclined on the left side, with the left arm supporting their body and leaving the right hand and arm free for use in eating. The disciple to the right of Jesus would have his head immediately in front of Jesus and could be described as "reclining next to him (NIV, NRSV)." [*anakeimai*]

Whom Jesus loved (*ēgapa*). This is the "beloved disciple." This individual is also mentioned in 19:26; 20:2; 21:7; and 21:20. The later references seem to indicate that this disciple stood in a very close relationship to Jesus. When combined with the omission of all reference in the fourth Gospel to John son of Zebedee, it is most likely that the "beloved disciple" should be understood as referring to him. See the discussion of the verb "loved" at 11:5. [*agapaō*]

13:24 Gestured (*neuei*). The verb means to signal someone using part of one's body, especially the head or the hands (LN 33.485; RSV "beckoned"; NASB, NET "gestured"; NIV, NRSV, NLT "motioned"). It is not clear where Peter was located in relation to Jesus, but it was far enough away that a gesture of some sort was necessary. [*neuō*]

13:26 The morsel (*psōmion*). (Twice in this verse and once in the following verse and v. 30.) This was a small piece of bread broken off from a loaf (BAGD 894, LN 5.4; NIV, NRSV, NET "this piece of bread"). [*psōmion*]

13:27 Satan (*Satanas*). This is the only time in John's Gospel that Satan is mentioned by name. Judas had already come under satanic influence prior to the meal (v. 2; cf. also Luke 22:3). The statement here probably marks the end of the process that had begun earlier. [*Satan/Satanas*]

13:30 It was night (*nyx*). See 3:2. Here the phrase is more than just a time indicator; it recalls all the light/darkness imagery of the fourth Gospel, starting with the prologue (1:5). With the departure of Judas setting in motion the betrayal, arrest, trials, crucifixion, and death of Jesus, daytime was over and "night" had come (John 9:5; 11:9-10; 12:35-36). Judas had become one of those who walked at night and stumbled, because the light was not in him (11:10). [*nyx*]

13:31 Is . . . glorified (*edoxasthē*). (Twice in this verse and three times in the following verse.) This is a repetition of the statement Jesus made in 12:23, but there is no contradiction. The coming of the Greeks marked the beginning of Jesus' "glorification," but the departure of Judas to betray Jesus actually inaugurated the process of Jesus' return to the Father. [*doxazō*]

13:32 Immediately (*euthys*). The "glorification" of Jesus, his return to the Father via the cross, was imminent at this point. [*euthys*]

13:33 Little children (*teknia*). This is the diminutive form of *teknon*, which is similar in meaning (cf. 1:12), but has the additional nuance of endearment (NLT "dear children"; cf. 1 John 2:1, 12, 28; 3:7, 18; 4:4; 5:21). [*teknion*]

The **Jews** (*Ioudaiois*). See 1:19. Jesus' statement is an allusion to comments he made in 8:21. There (cf. 8:22) as here the referent was primarily the Jewish religious authorities. [*Ioudaios*]

13:34 A new commandment (*entolēn*). By labeling this a "new commandment" Jesus was connecting it with the ten commandments given by God to Israel at Sinai, which was a covenant setting. That Jesus' followers love one another characterizes the new covenant. [*entolē*]

That you love one another (*agapate*). (Twice in this verse.) The "love" Jesus has showed for his disciples effected their salvation, since he laid down his life for them. This they could not duplicate, but they could follow his example of sacrificial service to one another, even to death if necessary. [*agapaō*]

13:35 Disciples (*mathētai*). The sign by which Jesus' disciples will be recognized by the "world" is their sacrificial love for one another, a love that had been modeled for them by Jesus when he "laid down his life" for them. Jesus' expectation was that all his disciples would behave this way toward one another (cf. 1 John 3:16). [*mathētēs*]

13:36 Follow (*akolouthēsai*). (Twice here and once in the following verse.) The verb literally means "to follow after," and can refer to those who accompany someone else, or even to those who follow Jesus (BAGD 31). Jesus is speaking of the road to the cross, and tells Peter he cannot now follow his Master in death, but he will follow later (cf. 21:18-19). [*akol.outheō*]

13:37 I will lay down (*thēsō*). (Also in the following verse.) See 10:11, where Jesus used the same expression, "lay down his life," to refer to his own sacrificial death on the cross.

Peter was not yet ready to follow this path on behalf of his Lord, but one day he would be ("afterward," v. 36; cf. 21:18). Instead, before this can happen, Peter would deny Jesus three times (for the fulfillment of this prediction, see 18:27). Ironically, as the reader of John well knows, it was not Peter who was about to die for Jesus, but Jesus who was about to die for Peter. [*tithēmi*]

13:38 Deny me (*arnēsē*). Here is Jesus' prediction of Peter's threefold denial. Given Peter's rash promise to "lay down his life" for Jesus (v. 37), this becomes ironic. [*arneomai*]

14:1 Do not let . . . be troubled (*tarassesthō*). See 11:33. The same Greek verb is used to describe Jesus' own state in 11:33; 12:27; and 13:21. Here Jesus is looking ahead to the events of the evening and the next day—his arrest, trials, crucifixion, and death, which will cause his disciples extreme emotional distress (NET "be distressed"). [*tarassō*]

Believe in (*pisteuete*). (Twice here) It is difficult to know whether to read the two occurrences of the verb *pisteuō* in this verse as indicatives ("you believe") or imperatives ("believe"). According to form, both uses may be either. It is probably best to see the first as indicative ("you believe in God") and the second as imperative ("believe also in me"). The disciples' faith in him as Messiah and Lord would be cast into doubt by coming events, and so Jesus moved from affirming their faith in God to exhorting them to have faith in him. [*pisteuō*]

14:2 My Father's house (*oikia*). Although frequently understood as a reference to heaven, the only other place in John's Gospel where the phrase "my Father's house" occurs is in 2:16, where it refers to the temple. Then in 2:19-22 the evangelist reinterpreted the temple as Jesus' body, which was to be "destroyed" in death and "rebuilt" in resurrection after three days. See next entry. [*oikia*]

Many dwelling places (*monai*). The word *monē* means "a dwelling place" or "residence" (LN 85.76; NIV, NLT "many rooms"). It occurs only twice in the NT, here and in v. 23. Both BAGD (527) and TDNT (4:579) take the referent of the term to be "heavenly" dwelling places, the most common interpretation. The cognate verb *menō* is a crucial term in Johannine theology (see discussion at 1:32). It frequently refers to the mutual indwelling of the Father and the Son in the believer. With this understanding the "dwelling place" Jesus has "gone away to prepare" refers to Jesus himself, and his "return" refers not to the second coming but to his return in resurrection after his death. This is consistent with John's emphasis on the present reality of eternal life (5:24, 7:38-39) and on the possibility of worshiping the Father "in Spirit and in truth" (4:21-24) in the present age. [*monē*]

14:3 Where I am (*hopou*). Jesus' statement "I will come again" is true on more than one level. Although usually understood to refer to Jesus' return for believers at his second coming, it more likely refers to his return to the disciples after his resurrection and the possibility of residing "in" him (cf. 14:2). At that time Jesus will be with the Father. [*hopou*]

14:4 The way (*hodon*). (Also in the following verse.) The term in its literal sense refers to a path or roadway, but the usage here is figurative (cf. BAGD 553). Jesus was going back to the Father, and the "way" he was going was via the cross (Jesus had mentioned this before [12:32]. His disciples did not understand this at the time [12:33]). As far as the disciples were concerned, the "way" back to the Father would be through Jesus but without appreciating the cross. Jesus is now correcting this misunderstanding. [*hodos*]

14:6 I am (*egō eimi*). See the discussion at 4:26.

The context suggests the three predicates here ("way," "truth," and "life") are not all parallel. The following statement, "no one comes to the Father except through me," appears to relate mainly to the first predicate, "I am the way." The second and third explain the first: "I am the way, namely, the truth and the life." [*egō + eimi*]

The way (*hodos*). See 14:4. Here the term refers to the "roadway" to God, and is similar to Jesus' statement in 10:7, 9, "I am the door." Jesus is the means of access to the Father. [*hodos*]

The truth (*alētheia*). This is related to Jesus' statement in 8:31-32, "You will know the truth, and the truth will make you free." Freedom from sin was the main point in the context of 8:34-36. [*alētheia*]

The life (*zōē*). This statement is like 11:25, where Jesus said, "I am the resurrection and the life." Jesus came to offer eternal life in abundance (10:10; cf. 3:5-8). [*zōē*]

14:7 If you had known me (*egnōkate*). Although there is a textual variant here, the best reading results in a first class conditional sentence in Greek: Assuming that the disciples have known Jesus, they will know the Father. This fits better with the following statement, "from the present time you know him and have seen him" (cf. 1:18). [*ginōskō*]

14:8 Show us (*deixon*). (Also in the following verse.) It is clear from Philip's request that he (if not all the disciples) had misunderstood Jesus' statement in v. 7. In what sense could they have seen the Father? [*deiknymi*]

14:9 You do not know me (*egnōkas*). See v. 7. In another example of the misunderstood statement in John's Gospel, Philip's request gave Jesus the opportunity to explain once more his relationship to the Father. Because Jesus and the Father are one (cf. 10:30), Jesus could say, "the one who has seen me has seen the Father (cf. 1:18). [*ginōskō*]

14:10 Do you not believe that (*pisteueis*). Here the content of what is believed is specified as "that I am in the Father and the Father in me." The form of the question in Greek expects the answer "yes." The mutual interrelationship between the Father and the Son is something that Jesus expected even his opponents to recognize (cf. 10:38). The mutual interrelationship of the Father and the Son expressed here and in the following verse points to Jesus' deity (cf. 1:1, 18). [*pisteuō*]

Residing in me (*menōn*). The verb speaks of the mutual relationship of the Father with the Son. See 1:32. [*menō*]

His works (*erga*). See 5:36. Here these "works" (NET "miraculous deeds") refer to the sign miracles Jesus had been performing (cf. v. 12), which were designed to direct unbelievers to faith in him, and to undergird the faith of those who were already his followers. [*ergon*]

14:11 Believe me that (*pisteuete*). In the first part of v. 11 Jesus appealed to the disciples to believe in the permanent interrelationship he has with the Father, based on his "words." In the next part of the verse he calls on them to believe because of his "works." [*pisteuō*]

Believe because of the works themselves (*erga . . . pisteuete*). See v. 10. The sign miracles Jesus had been performing were to serve as a basis for belief (cf. 2:11). [*pisteuō + ergon*]

14:12 Greater than these (*meizona*). It is sometimes assumed that the "works" Jesus speaks of here refer to "more powerful miracles" than those he performed himself. However, when one examines the miraculous deeds performed by the apostles in the Book of Acts, these do not appear to have surpassed the miracles of Jesus either in scope or in number. It is more likely that the "works" that surpassed those of Jesus refer

to the conversions described in the second chapter of Acts under the ministry of Peter. On the day of Pentecost probably more people were added to the church than had become followers of Jesus in the entire time of his earthly ministry. After that, the message went forth not only in Judea, Samaria, and Galilee, but to the farthest parts of the known world. [*megas + ergon*]

14:13 May be glorified (*doxasthē*). The verb *doxazō* ("to glorify") is used here in the sense of "to be praised" or "honored," a usage different from the general meaning of the term in the fourth Gospel to refer to Jesus' own "glorification" through the cross (TDNT 2:248). Here the Father will be "glorified" in what the Son does. [*doxazō*]

14:15 My commandments (*entolas*). A close parallel can be found in 1 John 5:3, "For this is the love of God, that we keep his commandments." The verse here provides the transition between the promises of answered prayer that Jesus made to his disciples in vv. 13-14 and the promise of the Holy Spirit, which is introduced in v. 16. Obedience is the proof of genuine love. [*entolē*]

14:16 Another Advocate (*paraklēton*). The word *allon* ("another") implies that an "advocate" (KJV, "Comforter"; RSV, NIV, NLT "Counselor"; NASB "Helper") has been with the disciples already. Here it is best to understand this as a reference to Jesus himself, since the "other advocate" is coming when he departs. First John 2:1 presents Jesus as a *paraklētos* (same Greek word) in his role as intercessor in heaven. Here the implication is that Jesus has been a *paraklētos* to the disciples in his earthly ministry as well. Much is often made of the meaning of the Greek word *allos*, that it means "another of a similar kind." Not all commentators agree on such a sharp distinction between the words *allos* and *heteros* in this context. But it does appear that Jesus, although he is not directly spoken of as a *paraklētos* in the fourth Gospel, had generally performed actions for his disciples that a *paraklētos* would perform. The Greek word *paraklētos* (often transliterated "Paraclete") is difficult to translate. No single English word matches the range of meaning of the Greek term. Various possibilities are "comforter," "counselor," "helper," "encourager," "mediator," or "advocate" (LN 12.19). The term "advocate" (NRSV, NET) has more forensic overtones, but in 16:5-11 a forensic context is certainly present (cf. LS 597). Furthermore, the secular Greek usage from the fourth century B.C. onward consists primarily of legal advocacy, as in "helper in court" (TDNT 5:800). The same usage is consistently found in Philo (TDNT 5:802). The meaning in the only NT passage outside the Gospel of John, 1 John 2:1, is clearly "advocate." In the present verse the question remains how strictly the legal usage is adhered to, but "advocate" is certainly within the range of meaning here. [*paraklētos*]

14:17 The Spirit of truth (*pneuma . . . alētheias*). Here Jesus describes the "Advocate" as "the Spirit of truth." According to 16:13 it is the Spirit who will reveal truth to the disciples after Jesus' departure, so the genitive construction here is probably descriptive of a characteristic: it is the Spirit who is characterized by truth, who communicates it to the disciples. [*pneuma* + *alētheia*]

The **world** (*kosmos*). "The world" will not be able to receive the Spirit, although the disciples will. This indicates that Jesus' disciples are no longer "of the world" (cf. 17:6, 9). [*kosmos*]

Resides with you (*menei*). There was a sense in which the Holy Spirit (the "Spirit of truth") was already "with" the disciples, but after Jesus returned to the Father, the Spirit would be "in" them. This indicates a change in the relationship the disciples would have with the Spirit, a change initiated by the

departure of Jesus (cf. 16:7). See 1:32. [*menō*]

14:18 Leave you desolate (*orphanous*). The term refers to someone deprived of some relationship, and can refer to an "orphan". Here it refers to the condition of being without the aid and comfort of someone who was an associate and friend (BDAG 725; NASB, NIV, NLT, NET "as orphans"). Already in 14:3 Jesus spoke of "going away" and "coming again" to his disciples. This refers not only to his second coming, but to his return to the disciples after the resurrection. Here it is more likely that Jesus' post-resurrection appearances to the disciples are primarily in view, since Jesus speaks in the following verse of the disciples "seeing" him after the world can "see" him no longer. A number of commentators, however, have taken the present verse as a reference to the Holy Spirit's coming, since this has been the topic of the preceding verses. In spite of this, vv. 19-20 appear to contain references to Jesus' appearances to the disciples after his resurrection ("a little while," "in that day"). This is another example of Johannine double meaning, so that Jesus "returns" to his disciples in one sense in his post-resurrection appearances to them, and in another sense with the indwelling presence of the "other Advocate" (cf. vv. 16-17). [*orphanos*]

14:19 The world (*kosmos*). Here again the "world" is the world of people, but in particular those who are hostile to Jesus and his disciples. These people will not "see" Jesus any longer after his death and resurrection, but the disciples will "see" him (a reference to Jesus' post-resurrection appearances, cf. Acts 10:41). [*kosmos*]

14:20 In that day (*hēmera*). Again, determining the referent is problematic. "That day" could be a reference to the second coming. But the statement in v. 19 that the world will not "see" Jesus, does not fit that event. It is better to take this as a reference to the post-resurrection appearances of Jesus to his disciples (which allows the phrase "a little while" in v. 19 to be taken literally; NLT "When I am raised to life again"). Compare the statement in Acts 10:40-41: "God made him manifest, not to all the people, but to us who were chosen as witnesses." [*hēmera*]

I am in my Father (*en*). The mutual relationship of Jesus and the Father is now extended to believers: "and you in me and I in you." See 14:10. [*en*]

14:21 Keeps them (*tērōn*). Here "keep" means "obey" (LN 36.19; NIV, NLT, NET), referring to Jesus' "commandments." Note that the context here is discipleship; obedience becomes the proof of one's love for Jesus. [*tēreō*]

I will manifest myself (*emphanisō*). (Also in the following verse.) Jesus' self-revelation to those who obey his "commandments" is explained in v. 23 as the mutual indwelling of the Father and the Son in the believer. [*emphanizō*]

14:22 To the world (*kosmō*). The disciples apparently still expected at this point that Jesus was going to reveal his identity as Messiah to the world at large. Even on the night before Jesus' crucifixion, his disciples still did not understand what lay ahead. [*kosmos*]

14:23 He will keep (*tērēsei*). (Also in the following verse.) Here the verb means "to keep, observe, fulfill, pay attention to" (especially in the Greek OT involving law or teaching; NIV, NET "obey"). Here the object is Jesus' "word" (BAGD 815; LN 36.19), while in v. 21 it was Jesus' "commandments." The two are probably interchangeable. [*tēreō*]

We will come to him (*eleusometha*). This refers to both Jesus and the Father. This promise is not completely fulfilled by Jesus'

post-resurrection appearances to the disciples, particularly as there is no indication of indwelling ("take up residence" or "make our home"; NLT "and live with them"; NET "and take up residence with him") with regard to the post-resurrection appearances. This promise is fulfilled with the coming of the Holy Spirit. [*erchomai*]

14:25 While remaining with you (*menōn*). Here the participle refers to Jesus "remaining" with the disciples, a reference to his time with them during his earthly ministry. [*menō*]

14:26 The Advocate (*paraklētos*). Here the "advocate" Jesus had spoken of earlier (v. 16) is specifically identified as "the Holy Spirit." [*paraklētos*]

Will send (*pempsei*). Jesus has frequently used this verb of the Father who "sent" him, but now uses it of the Father "sending" the Holy Spirit in his name. See 1:6. [*pempō*]

Will teach you all things and bring to your remembrance all things (*didaxei . . . hupomnēsei*). The ministries of the Spirit/Paraclete are twofold: teach and bring to memory. "All things" does not mean "all knowledge in the universe." Some have taken it to mean "all you will ever need to know," but in conjunction with the following phrase "all things I have said to you" it is much more likely that the Spirit's teaching ministry is not intended to reveal exhaustive truth, but rather the full significance of what Jesus did and said while with the disciples. In this sense, the second clause ("remind you of all things I have said to you," BDAG 1039; NIV, NRSV, NLT) is explanatory and qualifies the first clause ("will teach you all things"). [*didaskō + hypomimnēskō*]

14:27 Peace (*eirēnēn*). (Twice) Jesus uses this term to greet his disciples after his resurrection (20:19, 21, 26). The term reflects the Hebrew term *shalom* as a farewell greeting

(BAGD 227). Ultimately Jesus is referring to the indwelling of the Spirit/Paraclete whose presence after Jesus' departure and return to the Father will remain with and comfort them. [*eirēnē*]

The **world** (*kosmos*). The world's "peace" is different from the "peace" provided by Jesus, so there is an element of hostility here. This is escalated by the reference to the "ruler of this world" (i.e., Satan) in v. 30. [*kosmos*]

Be troubled (*tarassesthō*). The verb *tarassō* means "to cause acute emotional distress or turbulence" (LN 25.244; NET "be distressed") or "to stir up, disturb, unsettle, throw into confusion" (BAGD 805). Jesus refers here to the disciples' emotional turmoil at his "departure" (v. 28), which will take place shortly when he is crucified. [*tarassō*]

14:28 You would have rejoiced (*echarēte*). The term means "to rejoice, be glad, enjoy a state of happiness and well-being" (LN 25.125). But why should the disciples have reacted this way? They should do so because Jesus was on the way to the Father who would glorify him (17:4-5). Jesus' departure now signified that the Father's work was completed (cf. 19:30). Now Jesus would be glorified with the glory he had with the Father before the creation (17:5). This should cause rejoicing by the disciples because when Jesus was glorified he promised to glorify his disciples as well (17:22). [*chairō*]

Greater than I (*meizōn*). This statement has caused much christological and trinitarian debate. By the fact that Jesus compares himself to the Father, his divine nature is taken for granted. There have been two orthodox interpretations to the phrase: (1) The Son is eternally generated while the Father is not (so Origen, Tertullian, Athanasius, Hilary, and others). (2) As man, the incarnate Son was less than the Father (so Cyril of Alexandria, Ambrose, Augustine). For John, the second explanation is more likely. [*megas*]

14:29 You may believe (*pisteusēte*). The statement here does not mean the disciples had not "believed" prior to this time—over and over the evangelist has affirmed that they had (cf. 2:11). Rather, when the disciples see these things happen, their level of trust in Jesus would increase and expand. Thomas's confession in 20:28 is representative of this increased understanding of who Jesus is (cf. 13:19). [*pisteuō*]

14:30 The ruler of this world (*archōn*). See 12:31, where a similar phrase refers to Satan. The soldiers, officers, and Judas (in particular) who were coming to arrest Jesus represented the evil one's coming. In light of the statement in 13:27 that Satan "entered into" Judas Iscariot, the evangelist can say that the coming of Judas represents Satan's coming. [*archōn + kosmos*]

14:31 The world (*kosmos*). World is used in a more neutral sense here, of people who (even if they remain in "the world") are capable of recognizing Jesus' love for the Father, despite the mention of Satan earlier. [*kosmos*]

15:1 I am (*egō eimi*). This is another of the "I am" statements that occur with predicates (cf. 6:35, 48; 8:12; 10:7, 9; 10:11, 14; 11:25; 14:6). Only here and later in v. 5 is there additional development of the affirmation by further predication: "my Father is the gardener" (v. 1) and "you are the branches" (v. 5). Thus these two statements do not relate to Jesus' identity alone, but to his relationship to the Father and to the disciples. [*egō + eimi*]

The true vine (*ampelos*). In the context of first century Palestine, the term refers to a "grapevine" (BDAG 54). Numerous OT passages refer to Israel as a vine (Ps. 80:8-16; Isa. 5:1-7; Jer. 2:21; Ezek. 15:1-8; 17:5-10; 19:10-14; Hos. 10:1). The vine was symbolic of Israel, used on coins issued by the Maccabees. The OT passages that use this imagery typically regard Israel as faithless to *Yahweh* and/or the object of severe punishment. Ezek. 15:1-8 speaks of the worthlessness of wood from a vine; a branch cut from a vine was worthless except to be burned as fuel. Jesus' description of himself as the "true vine" here is to be seen against the OT background, but it differs significantly. It represents new imagery, apparently original with Jesus. The vine imagery in John 15:1-8 emphasizes fruitfulness in the Christian life. Such fruitfulness results not from human achievement, but from one's position in Christ. Jesus is not just giving the disciples comforting advice, but calling them to difficult, faithful service. [*ampelos*]

The **vinedresser** (*geōrgos*). Although the term can mean "farmer" in general terms (BDAG 196), it can refer to someone who assigns agricultural work on a contractual basis, like a "tenant farmer" or "vinedresser" (RSV, NASB; cf. NRSV "vinegrower"; NIV, NLT, NET "gardener"). Here, of course, it refers to God ("my Father"). [*geōrgos*]

15:2 He takes it away (*airei*). The Greek verb *airō* can mean "lift up, take up, pick up" (John 5:8-12; 8:59) or "take away, remove" (John 11:39; 16:22; 17:5; cf. BAGD 24) or even "destroy" (LN 20.43, cf. John 11:48). In context the meaning "take away, remove" fits better, especially in the light of v. 6, which describes worthless branches as being "thrown out," an image incompatible with restoration. One option, therefore, would be to understand the branches that are taken away (v. 2) and thrown out (v. 6) as believers who forfeit their salvation because of unfruitfulness. However, many see this interpretation as encountering problems with John's teaching on the security of the believer, especially John 10:28-29. This leaves two basic ways of understanding Jesus' statement about removal of branches: (1) These statements may refer to an unfaithful (disobedient) Christian, who is judged at the judgment seat of Christ "through fire" (cf. 1

Cor. 3:11-15). In this case the "removal" of 15:2 may refer (in an extreme case) to that Christian's physical death. (2) These statements may refer to someone who was never a genuine believer in the first place (e.g., Judas and the withdrawing Jews of 6:66), in which case 15:6 refers to eternal judgment. In either instance it is clear that 15:6 refers to the fires of judgment (cf. OT imagery in Ps. 80:16 and Ezek. 15:1-8). But view (1) requires the phrase be understood in terms of the judgment of believers at Christ's judgment seat. This concept is absent in John, because the believer does not come under judgment in the Gospel: note especially 3:18, 5:24, and 5:29. The first reference (3:18) is especially important because it occurs in the context of 3:16-21, a key section to which John repeatedly alludes. A similar image to this one is used by John the Baptist in Matt. 3:10, "And the ax is already laid at the root of the trees; every tree therefore that does not bear good fruit is cut down and thrown into the fire." Since this is addressed to the Pharisees and Sadducees who were coming to John for baptism, it almost certainly represents a call to initial repentance. More importantly, however, the imagery of being cast into the fire constitutes a reference to eternal judgment. The Matthean imagery is much nearer to the Johannine imagery in 15:6 than the Pauline concept of the judgment seat of Christ (a judgment for believers) mentioned above. The use of the Greek verb *menō* in 15:6 also supports view (2). When used of the relationship between Jesus and the disciple and/or Jesus and the Father, abiding emphasizes the permanence of the relationship (John 6:56; 8:31; 8:35; 14:10). The prototypical branch who has not remained is Judas, who departed in 13:30. He did not bear fruit, and is now in the realm of darkness, a mere tool of Satan. His eternal destiny, being cast into the fire of eternal judgment, is still to come. So it is most likely that the branches who do not bear fruit and are taken away and burned are false believers—those who profess to belong to Jesus but do not really belong to him. In John, the primary example of this is Judas. [*airō*]

Bearing fruit (*karpon*). (Twice) Many interpret the imagery of "fruit" here and in 15:4, 5 in terms of good deeds or character qualities, relating it to passages like Matt. 3:8 and 7:20; Rom. 6:22; and Gal. 5:22. One must remember, however, that for John, to have eternal life at all is to bear fruit, while one who does not bear fruit shows that he does not have the life (or, as in John 8:41, conduct is the clue to paternity; see also 1 John 4:20). [*karpos*]

He prunes it (*kathairei*). There is a word-play here, since the verb *kathairō* can mean both "cleanse, make clean" (LN 79.49) and "prune, take away, cut off" (LN 43.12). There is also a wordplay (not reproducible in English) between *airō* and *kathairō* in this verse. Branches that are entirely unproductive are "cut off," while branches that are productive are "pruned" to bear more fruit. While the Father's purpose in cleansing his people is clear, the precise means he uses is not obvious, though the following verse sheds some additional light on this. [*kathairō*]

15:3 Clean (*katharoi*). See 13:10, which is the only other place in John's Gospel where the phrase "you are clean already" occurs. There Jesus had used it of the disciples being cleansed from sin. This further confirms the meaning of 15:2, 6 (see above), since Judas was specifically excluded from the cleansing of 13:10 ("but not all of you"). [*katharos*]

15:4 Reside (*meinate*). (Three times) Although some interpreters have taken the statement as an imperative of command ("Reside in me, and see that I reside in you"), the evangelist has used a conditional imperative before (2:19) and that is more likely here: "If you reside in me, then I also will reside in you." Relationship between Jesus

and the disciples is reciprocal. [*menō*]

To bear fruit (*karpon*). See 15:2. The disciples would produce no "fruit" from themselves if they did not remain in their relationship to Jesus, because the eternal life that leads to fruit originates with Jesus. He is the source of the disciples' productivity. [*karpos*]

15:6 They are burned (*kaietai*). The person who does not "reside" in Jesus is "thrown out" like a "branch" and "dries up." The primary agricultural metaphor in vv. 1-8 supplies the imagery. A branch cut off from the vine will "dry up" because its source of nourishment and sustenance is cut off. Again, the primary example of a "branch" that did not "reside" in the vine is Judas Iscariot, who had departed in 13:30. The verb in the passive voice, *kaietai*, means "to be burned up, to be consumed by fire" (BAGD 396). The evangelist does not tell who it is who does the gathering and throwing into the fire. Although it is sometimes claimed that realized eschatology is so prevalent in the fourth Gospel that no references to final eschatology appear at all, the fate of these branches seems to point to the opposite. The imagery is that of eschatological judgment, and recalls some of the OT vine imagery that involved divine rejection and judgment of disobedient Israel (Ezek. 15:4-6; 19:12). [*kaiō*]

15:7 If you reside (*meinēte*). (Twice) This recalls 14:13-14, where the disciples were promised that if they asked anything in Jesus' name it would be done for them. That thought and this one are quite similar, since here it is conditioned on the disciples "remaining" in Jesus and his words "remaining" in them. The first phrase refers to the genuineness of the disciples' relationship with Jesus. The second use refers to their obedience. When both of these qualifications are met, the disciples would be asking in Jesus' name, and therefore according to his will. [*menō*]

15:8 Is glorified (*edoxasthē*). Here the Father is "glorified" when the disciples produce abundant fruit. Just as Jesus had done the works that he had seen the Father doing (5:19-29), so also would his disciples. [*doxazō*]

My **disciples** (*mathētai*). If sacrificial love toward one another is the mark of Jesus' disciple, then "bearing fruit" is the proof. Jesus' expectation here is clear: all his disciples, as long as they are attached to the "vine," are going to bear "much fruit." [*mathētēs*]

15:9 Reside (*meinate*). (Also twice in the following verse.) The disciples are to "reside" in Jesus' "love." This will be demonstrated by their "keeping" his commandments (see the following verse.) just as Jesus "kept" his Father's commandments. [*menō*]

15:10 Commandments (*entolas*). (Twice) See 15:12, where the plural "commandments" will be reduced to a single "commandment" to "love one another," an echo of 13:34-35 where "love" was the distinguishing characteristic of the disciple of Jesus. [*entolē*]

15:11 Joy (*chara*). The theme of "joy" will be resumed again at greater length in 16:20-24. Here it is said to be "made full" (so NASB; NIV, NRSV, NET "may be complete"; cf. 3:29). [*chara*]

15:12 My commandment (*entolē*). Here the plural "commandments" of 15:10 have been reduced to a singular "commandment." This refers to the "new" commandment of 13:34, and it is repeated in 15:17 below. The love the disciples are expected to have for one another is compared to Jesus' love for them. This love was illustrated in 13:1-20 with the washing of the disciples' feet, introduced by the statement in 13:1 that Jesus loved them

"to the end," as his death will show. The disciples' love for one another must extend to the point of a self-sacrificial willingness to die for one another if necessary. Jesus introduces the theme of his sacrificial death in the next verse. In both 10:18 and 14:31 Jesus spoke of his death on the cross as a "commandment" he had received from his Father, which links the concepts of "commandment" and "love" in the same way they are linked here. [*entolē*]

15:13 Lay down (*thē*). Although often understood as a general statement, in the context this must refer primarily to Jesus' own death on the cross for his followers, whom he goes on in the next verse to describe as "friends." This is the same way the expression is used by Jesus himself in 10:11, 15, 17, 18. Some have questioned whether love for enemies is not greater than love for friends, but that is not the point here, since at the time Jesus was speaking these words, only his "friends" were present (Judas had departed already, cf. 13:30). [*tithēmi*]

15:14 You are my friends (*philoi*). Some have understood the term "friends" here to refer to a smaller group within Christianity as a whole, perhaps only the apostles who were present when Jesus spoke these words. This has sometimes been supported by comparing it to the small group of associates and advisors to the Roman emperor who were known as "Friends of the Emperor." Others have taken this to refer only to those Christians who as disciples are obedient to Jesus. Either way, the result is to create a sort of "inner circle" of Christians who are more privileged than mere "believers" or average Christians. However, it is clear that Jesus' words must be addressed to all true Christians, not just some narrower category of more highly committed believers, because Jesus' sacrificial death, which is his act of love toward his "friends" (v. 13), applies to all Christians equally (cf. 13:1). [*philos*]

What I command you (*entellomai*). What Jesus had "commanded" his disciples was to "love one another" the way he had "loved" them, which had been acted out in the foot-washing in 13:1-20 and referred to his death on the cross for them. [*entellomai*]

15:16 I chose you (*exelexamēn*). (Twice in this verse.) The assertion that Christians are "chosen" by God is a frequent NT theme (Rom. 8:33; Eph. 1:4-6; Col. 3:12; 1 Pet. 2:4). Jesus told the Twelve in John 6:70 and 13:18 that he chose them, and 15:27 makes it clear that Jesus in the immediate context addressed those who have been with him from the beginning. In John's Gospel the Twelve, as Jesus' closest and most committed followers, are presented as the models for all Christians, both in terms of their election and in terms of their mission. [*eklegomai*]

Appointed you (*ethēka*). The term means "to appoint someone to a particular task, to assign" (BDAG 1004). Jesus had "assigned" the disciples the task of "going and bearing fruit." [*tithēmi*]

Bear fruit (*karpon*). (Twice in this verse.) See also 15:2. Here the purpose for which the disciples were "appointed" is reiterated: They are to "go and bear fruit, fruit that remains." The introduction of the concept of "going" at this point suggests strongly that the "fruit" in the passage is more than just character qualities in the disciples' own lives, but involves "fruit" in the lives of others, i.e., converts to Christianity. There is a mission involved (cf. 4:36). The idea that the fruit is permanent relates back to vv. 7-8, as does the reference to asking the Father in Jesus' name. As the imagery of the vine and the branches develops in chapter 15, the "fruit" that the branches produce shifts in emphasis from character qualities in the disciples' own lives (vv. 2, 4, 5) to the idea of a mission that affects

the lives of others (here in v. 16). The point of transition is the reference to "fruit" in v. 8. [*karpos*]

Remain (*menē*). Here the "fruit" will "remain." (NIV, NRSV, NLT "will last"). This implies the fruit's permanent rather than transitory nature. [*menō*]

15:18 Hates (*misei*). (Twice in this verse and once in the following verse.) For John, "hate" is the opposite of "love," which is to be the distinguishing characteristic of the disciple (13:34-35). A similar theme is foreshadowed in John 7:7, namely, the world's hatred for Jesus (and for his disciples as well, because of their likeness to him). [*miseō*]

15:19 Would love (*ephilei*). Here the sense is more like "the world would befriend its own." See the discussion at 11:5. [*phileō*]

I chose you (*exelexamēn*). Two themes are brought together here. (1) Unlike his opponents, Jesus is "not of this world" (8:23). (2) Jesus "chose" and "appointed" the disciples (15:16). Now Jesus links these two ideas by telling the disciples he has "chosen" them "out of the world." While the disciples will still be "in" the world after Jesus has departed, they will not belong to it (cf. 17:15-16). The same theme occurs in 1 John 4:5-6. See also 13:18. [*eklegomai*]

15:20 A slave (*doulos*). Jesus now recalled an earlier statement to the disciples made in 13:16. As the master has been treated, so will the slaves (KJV, RSV, NIV, NLT "servant") be treated. If the world had "persecuted" Jesus, it would certainly persecute the disciples, too. If the world had "obeyed" Jesus' word, it would obey the disciples' word. These statements imply that the disciples were to carry on Jesus' ministry after his departure and return to the Father. They would continue to spread the message Jesus himself had taught. They also would encounter the same response that he did. [*doulos*]

15:21 The one who sent me (*pempsanta*). As usual in John's Gospel, this expression refers to God the Father with special reference to his participation in the words and works of Jesus. In the final analysis it is the world's ignorance of God that causes people to respond to Jesus and his disciples as they do. See the discussion at 1:6. [*pempō*]

15:22 They would not have sin (*hamartian*). Jesus describes the world's guilt (NIV, NET "be guilty of sin"). He came to these people with words (v. 22) and sign miracles (v. 24), and yet they remained obstinate in unbelief, a sin which was without excuse. Jesus is not saying here that if he had not come and spoken to these people, they would be sinless. Rather, he is saying that if he had not come and spoken to them they would not be guilty of the sin of rejecting him and the Father. For John, rejecting Jesus is the ultimate sin for which there can be no forgiveness, because the one who has committed this sin has at the same time rejected the only cure that exists. See 9:41 [*hamartia*]

15:24 The works (*erga*). In particular, for John, these "works" refer to the sign miracles Jesus had performed, which testified to who he was (NLT "miraculous signs"; NET "miraculous deeds"). See the discussion at 5:36. [*ergon*]

15:25 Their law (*nomō*). As in 10:34 and 12:34, here "law" refers broadly to the entire OT, since the Scripture quoted is from Ps. 35:19 or Ps. 69:4. The latter is more likely the source, since this particular Psalm is referenced elsewhere in John's Gospel (2:17; 19:29). In both instances the contexts involve Jesus' suffering and death. [*nomos*]

15:26 The Advocate (*paraklētos*). See 14:16. The world had rejected Jesus (and the Father who sent him), even though it had heard his words and seen his works. But when Jesus departs from the world he will not leave the world without a continuing witness. In fact, there will be more than one: the Spirit/Paraclete whom Jesus would send will continue to testify about him, and the disciples will also continue to testify to the world (v. 27). [*paraklētos*]

I will send (*pempsō*). See 14:16 and 14:26, where Jesus said the Father would "send" the Spirit/Paraclete. Now Jesus spoke of sending the Spirit/Paraclete himself. This points to the close union between the Father and the Son. The two are so closely identified that this degree of interchange is possible. [*pempō*]

The Spirit of truth (*pneuma . . . alētheias*). This refers to the Holy Spirit. See 14:17. [*pneuma + alētheia*]

Proceeds (*ekporeuetai*). (NIV, NET "goes out from"; NRSV, CEV "comes from.") This statement probably does not say much about the eternal procession of the Holy Spirit, since the context is not concerned with the eternal mutual interrelationships of the three Persons of the Trinity, but with the continuation of the Son's mission once he had departed from the world. The Greek preposition *para* (translated "from" here) indicates relationship rather than source. The same preposition is used in 1:1 ("the Word was with God") and in 16:27 and 17:8 to describe the mission of the Son. [*ekporeuomai*]

15:27 From the beginning (*archēs*). This refers to the "beginning" of Jesus' public ministry. [*archē*]

16:1 So that you may not be caused to stumble (*skandalisthēte*). See 6:61. Here and again in v. 4 Jesus gave his purpose for telling his disciples about coming persecution—so that when it occurs, the disciples would not "fall away" (so RSV, NLT, NET;

NIV "go astray"; cf. BAGD 752). In this context "falling away" refers to the confusion and doubt that the disciples would experience when such persecution began. Jesus warned the disciples that they would face persecution and even martyrdom as they sought to carry on his mission in the world after his departure to the Father. This material has parallels in the Olivet Discourse (Matt. 24:3-25:46). [*skandalizō*]

16:2 Who kills you (*apokteinas*). Such opposition to the disciples would materialize later. The stoning of Stephen (Acts 7:58-60) and the killing of James, John's brother, by Herod Agrippa I (Acts 12:2-3) are notable examples. Persecution and killing of Jesus' disciples is also predicted in Matt. 24:9; Mark 13:12; and Luke 21:12-17. [*apokteinō*]

Service (*latreian*). The word here virtually refers to sacrifice (NRSV "worship"), since it is used in connection with the verb *prospherō* ("to bring, to offer"; TDNT 4:65). The hatred of the world for Jesus' disciples will be so great that the people who kill the disciples will think they are offering service to God in what amounts to a sacrifice. [*latreia + prospherō*]

16:3 They do not know (*egnōsan*). Ignorance of Jesus and ignorance of the Father are linked in 8:19. The world's ignorance of the Father appears in 8:55; 15:21; and 17:25. [*ginōskō*]

16:4 Their hour (*hōra*). This does not refer to Jesus' "hour" but to the "hour" of all those in the world who hate Jesus' disciples. Jesus is referring to the "time" (NIV, NET), after his departure, when his disciples will be persecuted for their testimony about him. See 2:4. [*hōra*]

You may remember (*mnēmoneuēte*). Jesus did not want his disciples to be taken by surprise when the time of persecution arrived. [*mnēmoneuō*]

From the beginning (*archēs*). Here the expression means "at the first," that is, from the "beginning" of Jesus' time with the disciples. See also 15:27. [*archē*]

16:5 To the one who sent me (*pempsanta*). The theme of Jesus' impending departure and return to the Father who "sent" him is resumed, as it likewise is in vv. 10, 17, and 28. [*pempō*]

16:6 Grief (*lypē*). The term here refers to a state of mental pain or anxiety: "sadness" (NET), "sorrow" (NASB, NRSV), "grief" (NIV; cf. LN 25.273). Jesus said that this had come over the disciples because he had just spoken to them about the persecutions they were going to experience (15:18-25; 16:1-4). [*lypē*]

16:7 The truth (*alētheian*). Here the idiom means "I tell you for certain," but with the typical Johannine flair for wordplay, it can also be taken in a literal sense: when Jesus said, "I tell you the truth," he was really doing so. See 1:14. [*alētheia*]

It is profitable for you (*sympherei*). Jesus' disciples must have seen his talk of departure (v. 5) as a disaster for themselves, and the mention of persecution (v. 6) added to their grief. The statement here resumes an earlier comment (14:28) that the disciples should rejoice because Jesus was going to the Father. Later Jesus states that when he is glorified, he will glorify them, too (17:22). Here Jesus tells the disciples it is to their "advantage" (NRSV, NET) if he goes away because unless he does, the Spirit/Paraclete will not come to them. [*sympherō*]

I will send him (*pempsō*). As the Father "sent" the Son, the Son promises to "send" the Spirit/Paraclete. See 1:6. [*pempō*]

16:8 He will convict (*elenxei*). See 3:20, 8:46. The verb *elenchō* has a range of meaning: "bring to light, expose"; "demonstrate, prove"; "convict, convince"; "reprove, correct"; "punish" (BAGD 249). Some of the meanings like "punish" may be ruled out in this context, but it is very difficult to decide between some of the other possibilities. Here the verb is often understood to mean "convince" in the sense that the Spirit/Paraclete will "convince" (RSV, NLT) or "convict" (NASB, NIV) the world concerning Jesus, so that at least some will repent. However, the verb does not necessarily imply the conversion or reform of the "convicted" party, so that the meaning here is much more like a legal sense, where "conviction" of the accused does not imply repentance or even acknowledgment of guilt. This can also be seen in 14:17, where the "world" cannot receive the Paraclete, and in 3:20, where the evildoer refuses to come to the light, lest his evil deeds be "exposed." Although the meaning "prove guilty" would fit the context here, it does not fit the context as well in the second and third assertions of vv. 10, 11. This led Brown (2:705) to suggest a more general sense for *elenchō* here, "prove wrong." But it is more likely there is a developmental aspect to the meaning, which shifts from "prove guilty" in the initial statement here to "prove wrong" (NRSV, NET) in the understood repetitions of the statement in vv. 10-11. [*elenchō*]

Concerning sin (*hamartias*). (Also in the following verse.) See 1:29. [*hamartia*]

Concerning righteousness (*dikaiosynēs*). (Also in v. 10) This term, although common in Paul's writings, occurs in John's Gospel only here and in v. 10. It is commonly assumed to mean "forensic justification" here as it frequently does in Paul, in which case it would pertain to "the world"—those people convicted to repent of their sins by the Spirit/Paraclete and who are then "justified." However, the clause which follows here is important in determining the contextual meaning of the term—the "righteousness" here has to do with Jesus' return to the Father

and his absence from the disciples. It is more likely here that the term refers to Jesus' own "righteousness" (in the sense of "vindication"), which is exemplified in his glorification as he returns to the Father (v. 10). Jesus' claim to be one with the Father, repeatedly rejected by his opponents who labeled him a deceiver, a sinner, and a blasphemer (5:18; 7:12; 9:24; 10:33) is "vindicated" by his resurrection and return to the Father. In Jesus' vindication, his followers are vindicated as well, but their vindication derives from his. [*dikaiosynē*]

Concerning judgment (*kriseōs*). (Also in v. 11) See 3:19. [*krisis*]

16:11 The ruler of this world (*archōn*). The referent here is Satan. See 12:31, 14:30. [*archōn*]

Is judged (*kekritai*). Jesus' glorification, his vindication, constitutes a "judgment" on Satan (NRSV, NET "has been condemned"; NIV "stands condemned"). This does not mean that Satan does not continue to be active in the world and to exercise some power over it, since the judgment is not immediately executed. But his judgment is certain. See 3:19. [*krinō*]

16:13 He will guide you (*hodēgēsei*). The verb can refer to guiding someone to a destination, although here it has the idea of the Spirit assisting someone to acquire desired information or knowledge (BDAG 690). [*hodēgeō*]

All the truth (*alētheia*). What Jesus had said in 8:31-32 ("you will know the truth, and the truth will make you free") will ultimately be realized in the Spirit's ongoing ministry to the disciples after Jesus has returned to the Father. [*alētheia*]

He will declare to you (*anangelei*). This verb means to provide information, possibly in considerable detail (LN 33.197; NASB "will disclose"; NIV, NET "will tell"). The things the Holy Spirit will reveal to the disciples do not originate from him ("he will not speak from himself"), but consist of things he has "heard." The point here concerns the *source* of the things the Spirit will reveal to the disciples, and does not specifically exclude originality of content. [*anangellō*]

Things to come (*erchomena*). Part at least of what the Spirit will reveal to the disciples will concern "things to come" (not just fuller implications of Jesus' previous sayings). This would seem to indicate that some new revelation is involved in terms of content. But the Spirit is not the source of these things—Jesus himself is the source (v. 14), and he will continue to speak to his followers through the Spirit. This text does not address whether these words apply (1) to all Christians throughout all ages, or (2) only to the apostles, or (3) to all Christians but only before the death of the last apostle. Different modern commentators will answer that question differently. Since in the context of the Farewell Discourse (John 13:31-17:26) Jesus was preparing the remaining 11 disciples to carry on his ministry after his departure, it is more likely that these statements should be specifically related only to them. For instance, in giving the Book of Revelation the Spirit speaks through an apostle to the church today of things still to come. One implication of this is that a doctrine, to be authentic, does not have to be traced all the way back to Jesus in person. All that is required is the authority of an apostle. [*erchomai*]

16:14 Will glorify (*doxasei*). It is important to note that the Holy Spirit's ministry will not draw attention to himself, but will "glorify" Jesus. The verb *doxazō* ("to glorify") is used here in the sense of "to praise" or "to honor" (see 14:13). See 1:14. [*doxazō*]

16:16 A little while (*mikron*). (Also twice in the following verse, once in v. 18, and twice

in v. 19) This refers to the short period of time between Jesus' death and burial, when the disciples would "see [him] no longer," and his resurrection, after which they would see him again. [*mikros*]

16:19 Jesus knew (*egnō*). Supernatural knowledge on Jesus' part of what the disciples were thinking is possible but not necessary here. Given the disciples' confused statements recorded in the preceding verses, it was probably obvious to Jesus that they wanted to ask him what he meant. See 2:25; 5:6; 6:15 for similar uses of this verb where supernatural knowledge on Jesus' part may be implied. [*ginōskō*]

16:20 You will weep (*klausete*). Here Jesus contrasted the disciples' response to his crucifixion with that of the unbelieving world. [*klaiō*]

The world (*kosmos*). The "world" of "humanity" is in opposition to the disciples and hostile to them, as indicated by the opposite reactions to Jesus' death and resurrection here on the part of the disciples and the "world." [*kosmos*]

Joy (*charan*). See 15:11, where "joy" is described as "fulfilled." Once Jesus has returned to his disciples after his resurrection, their "grief" will become "joy." [*chara*]

16:21 Is in labor (*tiktē*). Jesus now compares the disciples' situation to a woman's "grief" in childbirth. Just as the woman experiences real pain and anguish, so the disciples will also undergo real anguish at Jesus' crucifixion. But once the child is born, the mother's anguish is "turned into joy," and the past "suffering" is gone. The same goes for the disciples after Jesus' resurrection and reappearance. They will forget the anguish experienced at his death. [*tiktō*]

16:22 Will take away (*airei*). The idea of permanence attached to the disciples' "joy" suggests more than just their joy in recognizing that Jesus has overcome death (20:20). They will also experience the Paraclete's permanent presence as a result of Jesus' departure (cf. 14:17). [*airō*]

16:25 In figures of speech (*paroimiais*). (Twice in this verse.) The meaning is essentially the same as in 10:6. In the preceding context of the Farewell Discourse Jesus had certainly used obscure language and imagery (13:8-11, 16; 15:1-17; and 16:21 are all examples). In his post-resurrection appearances, Jesus will speak "openly" of the Father to his disciples. [*paroimia*]

16:26 In my name (*onomati*). The theme of the disciples asking the Father directly is resumed from vv. 23-24. The reason for this is given in v. 27. [*onoma*]

16:27 Loves (*philei*). (Twice in this verse.) Since God is the subject here, there may be little difference in the use of the verb *phileō* for love as opposed to *agapaō*. See 11:5. [*phileō*]
    Have believed that (*pepisteukate*). Here the content of what the disciples "have believed" is that Jesus "came from God." This statement is repeated in v. 30. Jesus affirmed that his remaining disciples (Judas departed in 13:30) had believed in his heavenly origin. "From God" implies not only the "place" from which Jesus had come, but that he was acting on God's behalf as God's designated emissary with God's full authority. [*pisteuō*]

16:28 Am going to the Father (*poreuomai*). This phrase (cf. 14:12, 28) is a summary of the entire fourth Gospel. It summarizes the earthly career of the Word made flesh, Jesus of Nazareth. His mission to be Savior of the world involved a sending from the Father culminating in his departure from the world

and return to him (via the cross). [*poreuomai*]

16:29 Figures of speech (*paroimian*). Jesus' disciples now affirmed that he was speaking "openly" and not in "obscure figures of speech" (NET; NLT "parables"). However, even at this point, the disciples did not understand about the crucifixion and resurrection, as Jesus points out. [*paroimia*]

16:31 Do you now believe (*pisteuete*). Jesus now questioned the disciples' belief (that he had come "from God," v. 30) by predicting they would abandon him when he was arrested, tried, and crucified. Their belief in him would be renewed after the resurrection (cf. 20:19-23). [*pisteuō*]

16:33 I have overcome (*nenikēka*). The verb means "to be victorious over, to conquer, to win a victory over" (LN 39.57). What is "conquered" (NRSV, NET) here is "the world," which in this context refers to the sum total of everything opposed to God (BAGD 539). The triumphant note here recalls 1:5, "the light shines in the darkness, and the darkness has not overcome it" (although a different Greek verb is used in 1:5, *katalambanō*). [*nikaō*]

17:1 The hour (*hōra*). Jesus had stated before that his "hour" had come, both in 12:23 when some Greeks sought to speak to him, and in 13:1 just before he washed the disciples' feet. The "hour" is best understood as a period of "time" (NIV, NLT, NET) starting at the end of Jesus' public ministry and extending through the passion week, ending with Jesus' return to the Father through death, resurrection, and exaltation. The "hour" begins with the occurrence of the first events that lead to Jesus' death. [*hōra*]
    Glorify (*doxason*). (Twice in this verse.) Again there is a wordplay on this verb. Jesus' prayer to be "glorified" would be answered in his exaltation (which John describes as his

"glorification") when he returned to the Father, which Jesus would accomplish through the cross. On the other hand, the Son would "glorify" the Father in the sense of bringing praise or honor to God (cf. 5:41, 44; 7:18). A similar wordplay occurs in 11:4 and 12:28. [*doxazō*]

17:2 Authority (*exousian*). Here the term refers to the "authority" to judge (cf. 5:27), since the next phrase makes it clear that Jesus does not give eternal life to everyone, but only to those whom the Father has "given" him. This is "authority" that the Father has delegated to the Son (cf. BDAG 353). [*exousia*]

Eternal life (*zōēn*). (Also in the following verse.) Here Jesus defines "eternal life," although it is worked into the prayer in such a way that many interpreters regard it as a parenthetical comment by the evangelist. It does not refer simply to unending life in the sense of prolonged duration. Rather, it refers to a quality of life that is derived from a relationship with God. Here attaining "eternal life" is defined as being in relationship with the Father, the one true God, and Jesus Christ whom the Father sent. The only way to receive this life is through the Son (14:6). Although some have argued that the verb *ginōskō* ("know") here is evidence of gnostic influence in John, there is a crucial difference: for John this knowledge is not intellectual, but relational. It involves being in relationship. [*zōē*]

17:4 I have glorified you (*edoxasa*). Jesus had "glorified" the Father while he was on earth by obeying the Father and finishing his "work" (see below), thus bringing praise or honor to God (cf. 5:41, 44; 7:18; 17:1). [*doxazō*]

By completing (*teleiōsas*). The notion of Jesus being sent on a mission into the world has been mentioned before in John's Gospel, notably in 3:17. It was alluded to in the previous verse here. The "completion" of the

"work" the Father had sent the Son to accomplish was mentioned by Jesus in 4:34 and 5:36. [*teleioō*]

The work (*ergon*). The "work" the Father sent the Son to complete involved the Son's mission as Savior of the world (3:17; 4:42). However, this was to be accomplished specifically through Jesus' sacrificial death on the cross (implied by the reference to the Father "giving" the Son in 3:16). Jesus' last words from the cross in 19:30 were "It is finished" (= "completed"). [*ergon*]

17:5 Glorify me (*doxason*). The meaning here parallels 17:1. The addition of the phrase "in your presence" makes it clear that Jesus' exaltation through the cross is in view. [*doxazō*]

Before the world was (*pro*). This statement strongly asserts the preexistence of Christ, and alludes to 1:1, 14. [*pro*]

17:6 Your name (*onoma*). The Father's "name" will be mentioned again in 17:11, 12, and 26, but it is not often mentioned elsewhere in the fourth Gospel (only in 5:43; 10:25; 12:28). In one sense the name represents the person (cf. 1:12). Thus Jesus, in saying that he has "made known" the Father's name, says that he has fully revealed who God is and what he is like (cf. 1:18 and 14:9). But in John's Gospel Jesus himself is identified with God repeatedly (10:30; 14:11; etc.) and nowhere is this more apparent than in Jesus' absolute uses of the phrase *egō eimi* without a predicate (8:24; 8:28; 8:58; and possibly 13:19). The Father's name that Jesus has made known is thus the divine Name revealed to Moses (Exod. 3:14). [*onoma*]

They have kept (*tetērēkan*). In 8:55 Jesus said that he "kept" his Father's word, but this is the one time in the fourth Gospel that the disciples are said to have "kept" (NIV, CEV, NET "obeyed") it. [*tēreō*]

17:8 They received (*elabon*). The verb means

"to accept, receive, come to believe" in the sense of believing in something and acting accordingly (LN 31.50; NIV, NLT, NET "accepted"). This recalls 1:12 in the prologue. [*lambanō*]

I came from you (*para*). Several times in John's Gospel Jesus' affirmation of his identity and mission take the form "I have gone out from God" (8:42; 16:27; and here; 13:3 is not spoken by Jesus, but is otherwise similar). [*para*]

They have believed (*episteusan*). Here, as in 16:27, the disciples are said to have believed that God "sent" Jesus (on the term "sent," *apesteilas*, see 1:6). [*pisteuō* + *apostellō*]

17:9 Not concerning the world (*kosmou*). Jesus now specified that his prayer was for the disciples, not for those in "the world." Here the "world" is "humanity," as distinguished from Jesus' followers who were no longer "of the world" (15:19). [*kosmos*]

17:10 I am glorified (*dedoxasmai*). Here Jesus could speak of being "glorified" in the disciples in light of what he had already said in vv. 7-8. The disciples now understand that he had come from the Father and been sent by the Father. Jesus would, of course, be "glorified" by the disciples further after the resurrection, as they carried on his ministry after his departure and return to the Father. [*doxazō*]

17:11 In the world (*kosmō*). (Twice in this verse.) At this point Jesus' departure from the world is so near that he can speak of himself as no longer "in the world." In doing so he contrasts his own situation with that of the disciples, who are still "in the world." [*kosmos*]

Keep them (*tērēson*). Here the verb means "to keep" in the sense of keeping the disciples unharmed or unmoved (BAGD 815; NIV "protect them"; NET "keep them safe"). This is Jesus' prayer for the Father to protect the disciples while he departs and returns to

the Father (v. 13). [*tēreō*]

They may be one just as we are (*hen*). See 10:30, where Jesus had stated that he and the Father were one. Now, in his prayer for the disciples on the eve of his departure, Jesus prays for that unity to extend to the disciples as well. [*heis*]

17:12 I have guarded (*ephylaxa*). The verb means to take careful measures to protect or guard someone or something (BDAG 1068; NIV "kept them safe"; NET "watched over them"). This recalls the Good Shepherd imagery of 10:14 and especially 10:27-30. [*phylassō*]

Is lost (*apōleto*). Here the verb *apollymi* can mean either "perish, die" or "be lost" (BAGD 95). Both these meanings occur in John's Gospel, the first here (also 3:16; 10:28) and the second in 6:12. Here one meaning ("lost") leads to the other ("perish, die"), since the imagery here recalls the Good Shepherd of 10:7-18. [*apollymi*]

The son of perdition (*apōleias*). See 12:36. Here the idiom means "one appointed for destruction," (NIV "doomed to destruction"; NLT "headed for destruction"; NET "destined for destruction") and refers to Judas Iscariot. The same phrase is used in 2 Thess.. 2:3 to refer to the man through whom Satan acts to rebel against God in the last days. In John's Gospel Judas is clearly a tool of Satan. He is described as "the devil" in 6:70. In 13:2 Satan put into Judas's heart the idea of betraying Jesus, and in 13:27 Satan himself entered Judas. Immediately following this, Judas left Jesus' and the disciples' company to enter into the realm of darkness (13:30). [*apōleia*]

Fulfilled (*plērōthē*). The statement here seems to indicate that the OT Scriptures predicted Judas's betrayal and defection. The exact passage is not specified here, but Ps. 41:9 is quoted by Jesus in 13:18 with reference to the traitor, so it is highly probable that Ps. 41:9 is the passage alluded to here. [*plēroō*]

17:14 I am not of the <u>world</u> (*kosmou*). (Also in v. 16) In v. 11 Jesus said he was no longer "in the world." The statement points to both origin and allegiance. Jesus was not "of the world" because he came from heaven on a mission from the Father (3:17). The disciples were not "of the world" because their allegiance was to Jesus (cf. also 18:36). [*kosmos*]

17:15 That you <u>keep</u> them (*tērēsēs*). See v. 11. Jesus did not pray for the Father to "take" the disciples "out of the world," but that the Father would "protect them" (NIV; CEV, NLT, NET "keep them safe") from the "evil one" while they remained in the world. [*tēreō*]

    The evil one (*ponērou*). This phrase refers to the devil (BDAG 851). While the Greek noun is genitive singular and therefore could be either neuter ("that which is evil") or masculine ("the evil one"), the frequent use of the masculine in 1 John 2:13-14; 3:12; and 5:18-19 suggests the masculine is present here. Jesus is praying for his disciples to be protected from Satan. [*ponēros*]

17:17 <u>Sanctify</u> them (*hagiason*). The Greek verb *hagiazō* is used here in its normal sense. Disciples are consecrated or set apart to God (LN 53.44, BAGD 8, TDNT 1:111; NET "Set them apart"). [*hagiazō*]

    Truth (*alētheia*). (Twice in this verse and once in v. 19) The disciples operate in the sphere of "the truth." The idea of "practicing" the truth was introduced in 3:21. In 8:32 Jesus told some of his hearers that if they continued in his word they would "truly" be his disciples, and they would know the "truth," and the truth would make them free. The disciples with Jesus here, during his Farewell Discourse, have continued in his word (except for Judas Iscariot) and they do "know the truth" about who Jesus is and

why he has come into the world (17:8). Therefore Jesus can ask the Father to set them apart just as he himself is set apart, so that they might carry on his mission in the world after his departure. See also the discussion at 1:14. [*alētheia*]

17:18 Into the <u>world</u> (*kosmon*). (Twice in this verse.) Jesus now compared the mission on which he was sending the disciples to his own mission "into the world," the mission on which he was "sent" by the Father. The nature of the prayer in chapter 17 as a consecratory prayer for the disciples can now be seen: Jesus was setting them apart for the work he had called them to do. The disciples were, in a sense, being commissioned for their task. [*kosmos*]

17:19 I <u>sanctify</u> myself (*hagiazō*). See v. 17. Here Jesus refers to "consecrating himself" (RSV), a topic introduced already in 10:36 where Jesus referred to himself as "the one whom the Father sanctified and sent into the world." This is spoken of as something already accomplished. Here, however, it is something Jesus does for his disciples. This suggests a reference to his impending death on the cross. There is in fact a wordplay here, based on slightly different meanings for the Greek verb *hagiazō* ("dedicate, consecrate, set apart," cf. v. 17). In 10:36 (in reference to Jesus), 17:17 and 19 (to the disciples), this verb means to "set apart" for a task, in the sense that OT prophets (cf. Jer. 1:5) and priests (Exod. 40:13; Lev. 8:30; 2 Chron. 5:11) were "consecrated" or "set apart" to perform the tasks to which God appointed them. But when Jesus speaks of "setting himself apart" (NET; cf. NLT "give myself entirely to you") on behalf of the disciples here, the meaning is closer to the consecration of a sacrificial animal (Deut. 15:19). Jesus was "setting himself apart" to do the Father's will, that is, to go to the cross on behalf of the disciples (and all believers). [*hagiazō*]

17:20 Those who <u>believe</u> in me (*pisteuontōn*). Although the Greek participle here is present tense, in context it must carry a futuristic force. The disciples whom Jesus is leaving will carry on his ministry. In doing so, others will come to believe in him. This will include not only Jewish Christians, but other Gentile Christians who are "not of this fold" (10:16). Thus Jesus' prayer for unity is most appropriate in light of the probability that most of John's readers are Gentiles (much like Paul stresses unity between Jewish and Gentile Christians in Eph. 2:14-22). [*pisteuō*]

17:21 All may be <u>one</u> (*hen*). The model for the unity among believers is the unity between the Father and the Son, a unity of essence that allows for diversity of persons. [*heis*]
   May believe (*pisteuē*). Here the content of what "the world" (cf. 1:9 for a discussion of *kosmos*) is to "believe" is "that you [= the Father] have sent me [= Jesus]." The Father authenticates Jesus' words and works, and his "glory" (vv. 22, 24) is being revealed. [*pisteuō*]

17:22 The <u>glory</u> (*doxan*). (Also in v. 24) The "glory" that belongs to Jesus he now passes on to his disciples, who will share in it. Jesus is "glorified" in the disciples (v. 10), and they will see Jesus' "glory" (v. 24). Paul expresses a very similar thought in 2 Cor. 3:18 (TDNT 2:251). [*doxa*]

17:23 May be <u>completed</u> into one (*teteleiōmenoi*). Jesus' gift of "glory" to believers (v. 22a) results in their unity (vv. 22b, 23a) with the ultimate result of confronting "the world" again with Jesus' claims (v. 23b). [*teleioō*]

17:24 <u>Where</u> I am (*hopou*). Since Jesus and the Father are "one" (v. 21), Jesus could be described as "with the Father." [*hopou*]
   Before the <u>foundation</u> of the world

(*katabolēs*). This refers to the "creation of the world" (NIV, NET) when Jesus possessed "glory" with the Father before creation (cf. 1:1-3) and before his incarnation (1:14). [*katabolē*]

17:25 The <u>world</u> (*kosmos*). The "world" is the world of people, used in a negative sense similar to 1:10: "he was in the world, and the world was made through him, and the world did not know him." [*kosmos*]

18:1 The Kidron <u>Valley</u> (*cheimarrou*). The Greek word *cheimarros* can refer to a *wadi*, a ravine or valley normally dry but flowing with water either in the rainy (winter) season or from melting snow coming from higher elevations (LN 1.77). Here the term refers to the narrow valley itself just outside Jerusalem rather than the stream at the bottom of it (LN 1.52). This ravine, known today as Wadi en-Nar, begins to the north of Jerusalem, passes the temple mount and the Mount of Olives and goes on through the wilderness of Judea to end up at the Dead Sea. It is dry most times, filled with water only during periods in the rainy season. [*cheimarros*]
   A garden (*kēpos*). The "garden" (NIV "olive grove"; NET "orchard") is unnamed in John, but it is Gethsemane (Matt. 26:36; Mark 14:32). [*kēpos*]

18:3 The <u>cohort</u> (*speiran*). The Greek word *speira* is a technical term referring to a unit of soldiers nominally 600 strong, that is, one-tenth of a legion (BAGD 761). It is the standard Greek translation of the Latin term *cohors*, and thus is normally translated "cohort" (NASB). A cohort would normally be under the command of a "chiliarch" ("commanding officer," v. 12). Because it seems unlikely that an entire cohort would be sent out to arrest a single individual, some have suggested the term here refers to a smaller unit known as a "maniple," a force of 200 (NIV, NRSV "a detachment"). But the use of the term here does not necessarily mean the entire cohort was sent out, but only that the cohort was tasked to make the arrest (cf. LN 55.9). (Likewise, saying that the fire department put out the fire does not necessarily mean that every firefighter was on the scene at the time.) The Roman soldiers mentioned here must be responding to Pilate's orders to accompany the chief priests' officers and Pharisees, since they would have been under the prefect's direct command. It is not difficult to understand why Pilate wished to help the Jewish authorities. With many pilgrims in Jerusalem for the Passover, the Romans would have been especially nervous about any prospective uprising. No doubt the chief priests and Pharisees told Pilate that this Jesus was claiming to be the Messiah—or in terms Pilate would understand, king of Israel. [*speira*]

The officers (*hypēretas*). These "officers" had made an unsuccessful attempt to arrest Jesus already (7:32-44) and had been roundly criticized for their failure to do so (7:45-49). This may well explain the reason the Jewish leaders had made sure Roman soldiers accompanied these officers on this occasion. No more mistakes were to be tolerated. [*hypēretēs*]

Lanterns (*phanōn*). Although the Greek word *phanos* in earlier usage referred to a torch, by NT times it was used primarily to identify a lamp for outdoor use with some kind of protection from wind and weather (LN 6.103, BAGD 853). Although the mention of "lanterns and torches" suggests eyewitness detail, in connection with the light/darkness motif of John's Gospel it is a vivid reminder that night (darkness) has come at last (cf. 9:4, 13:30). [*phanos*]

Torches (*lampadōn*). Here the term is used for a "torch," as it is frequently used by classical Greek authors. In other contexts the word could refer to a lamp with a wick and a place for oil, but in an outdoor setting in conjunction with the term *phanos*, a torch is meant (BDAG 585). [*lampas*]

Weapons (*hoplōn*). The word could be used of a "tool," but in a context involving soldiers it refers to a "weapon." Defensive weapons (like shields) would be included as well as offensive ones like swords (BDAG 716). [*hoplon*]

18:4 Knowing (*eidōs*). Jesus' knowledge of future events is in view here. It has been mentioned before, using this verb in 6:6 and 13:1. Supernatural knowledge on Jesus' part using this verb may also be implied in 6:61, 64; 13:11. [*oida*]

18:5 Who betrayed him (*paradidous*). The evangelist inserts here a parenthetical note that Judas, "the one who betrayed him" (18:2; cf. 6:71), was standing with the group of soldiers and officers of the chief priests. Although many commentators have considered this an awkward insertion, in fact it heightens considerably the dramatic effect of the response to Jesus' self-identification in the following verse. It has the added effect of informing the reader that along with the others, the betrayer himself ironically falls down at Jesus' feet (v. 6). [*paradidōmi*]

18:6 I am (*egō eimi*). (Also in v. 8) Here it is difficult to know how much significance to see in the expression "I am," since on one level there is an implied predicate here, and the phrase amounts to a self-identification by Jesus: "I am [he]." Jesus answers the statement that "Jesus of Nazareth" was the one sought by the group for arrest. However, for the reader of the fourth Gospel, Jesus made this affirmation of his identity using a formula that had occurred before, in 8:24, 28, and 58. Jesus had applied to himself the divine name of Exod. 3:14, "I AM." Therefore on another level this event functions as something of a theophany, which caused his enemies to recoil and prostrate themselves before him. This serves as a vivid reminder to John's reader that even in this dark hour, Jesus held ultimate power over his enemies and the powers of darkness. It was his own choice to submit to arrest. See also the discussion at 4:26. [*egō + eimi*]

18:8 Let these go (*hypagein*). With this request to release the disciples, Jesus demonstrated that even in the hour of his betrayal and arrest, he still protected and cared for his followers, while giving himself up on their behalf. By handing himself over to his enemies, Jesus secured the disciples' freedom. From John's perspective, Jesus was acting out beforehand what he would actually do for his followers when he went to the cross. [*hypagō*]

18:9 May be fulfilled (*plērōthē*). The evangelist uses this formula here and again in 18:32 to refer to Jesus' words. Elsewhere in John's Gospel the verb describes the NT fulfillment of OT Scripture (12:38, 13:18, 15:25, 17:12, 19:24, 36). [*plēroō*]

    I did not lose one of them (*apōlesa*). Although there are some similarities to 6:39, the closest parallel is 17:12, where the betrayer, Judas, is specifically excluded. Jesus refers to his genuine disciples here. [*apollymi*]

18:10 A sword (*machairan*). (Also in the following verse.) This term describes a short sword, much like a dagger. These were widely known and used in the Greek world. The term is as old as Homer and was used of a weapon since the time of Herodotus in the fifth century B.C. (TDNT 4:524). It would typically be carried in a sheath hung from the belt. [*machaira*]

    His right ear (*ōtarion*). The same Greek term, a double diminutive, is used in Mark 14:47 to describe what was "cut off." This may indicate only part of the right ear was severed. [*ōtarion*]

18:11 The sheath (*thēkēn*). This term is used in the classical Greek literature and in Josephus (*Ant.* 8.10.4 [8.264]; 16.7.1 [16.181]) to refer to a "grave," but the other meaning, a "sheath" for a sword, is also found in Josephus (*Ant.* 7.11.7 [7.284]) and applies here (BDAG 455). [*thēkē*]

    The cup (*potērion*). The cup is also mentioned in Gethsemane in the synoptic accounts (Matt. 26:39; Mark 14:36; Luke 22:42). In the synoptic accounts it is mentioned in Jesus' prayer. This occurrence would certainly complement the synoptic accounts if Jesus had only finished praying about this shortly before the appearance of Judas with the soldiers and officers. Only here in John's Gospel is it specifically said that the cup is given to Jesus to drink by the Father, but again this is consistent with the synoptic mention of the cup in Jesus' prayer—it is the cup of suffering that Jesus is about to experience. [*potērion*]

18:12 The commanding officer (*chiliarchos*). The Greek term literally describes the "commander of a thousand," but it was used as the standard translation of the Latin *tribunus militum* or *tribunus militare*, the military tribune who commanded a cohort of 600 soldiers (BAGD 881, LN 55.15). [*chiliarchos*]

    Bound him (*edēsan*). Jesus' "binding" is a detail not related by the Synoptics. Everything in John's account suggests Jesus accompanied his captors willingly. The evangelist may be alluding to another willing victim, Isaac, who allowed himself to be "bound" to the altar (Gen. 22:9). [*deō*]

18:15 Another disciple (*mathētēs*). Many interpreters have identified this unnamed "other disciple" with the "beloved disciple," that is, John son of Zebedee. Mainly this is done because the phrase "the other disciple" that occurs here is also used to describe the "beloved disciple" in 20:2, 3, 4, and 8. Peter is also closely associated with the beloved disciple in 13:23-26; 20:2-10; 21:7; and 21:20-23. [*mathētēs*]

Was known to the high priest (*gnōstos*). (Also in the following verse.) Some have objected to the identification of the "other disciple" in this verse as John, son of Zebedee because of the statement that this disciple "was known to the high priest." How could the uneducated son of an obscure Galilean fisherman be known to such a powerful and influential family in Jerusalem? But the common attitude concerning the disciples' low social status and lack of formal education may be a misconception. Zebedee is portrayed in Mark 1:20 as a man wealthy enough to have hired servants, and Mark 10:35-45 presents both of Zebedee's sons as concerned about status and prestige. John's mother appears in the same light in Matt. 20:20-28. Contact with the high priest's family in Jerusalem might not be so unlikely in such circumstances. There is also a statement in Eusebius, quoting Polycrates, that John, son of Zebedee was a priest (*Hist. eccl.* 3.31.3). [*gnōstos*]

18:17 The slave girl who attended the door (*thyrōros*). The term describes a person who stands and guards the door into a house or building (LN 46.8). The word can be used of a man or a woman, though here it is specified that this was a slave girl (*paidiskē*). [*thyrōros*]

I am not (*ouk eimi*). This phrase stands in contrast to the phrase "I am" by which Jesus identified himself in 18:6, 8. [*eimi*]

18:18 A charcoal fire (*anthrakian*). Charcoal fires do not give off a great deal of light. The fire was there because it was "cold." Peter's action in "warming himself" with the slaves and officers was probably not as dangerous as some have supposed, because it would have been difficult to recognize him as one of Jesus' followers in the dim, shadowy courtyard. [*anthrakia*]

18:19 Concerning his disciples (*mathētōn*). True to what is known about Annas's character, he was more interested in how many followers Jesus had managed to collect than in the truth or falsity of his "teaching," since the question about the "disciples" comes first. [*mathētēs*]

18:20 Openly (*parrēsia*). This statement does not mean that Jesus' teaching was clear (cf. 10:24), but simply that Jesus made his messianic claims openly, not "in secret." [*parrēsia*]

To the world (*kosmō*). Here, as in 7:4, the phrase means essentially "in public," or "to the world at large." There Jesus' brothers had urged him to reveal himself "to the world." [*kosmos*]

All the Jews (*Ioudaioi*). See 1:19. Here the phrase appears to refer to the Jewish people generally, since for them the synagogues and temple courts in Jerusalem were important public gathering places. [*Ioudaios*]

18:22 Struck (*rapisma*). Literally, "gave a slap." The term can describe a blow with a club, rod, whip, or a slap with the hand (BAGD 734). A slap in the face is clearly indicated in Matt. 5:39, and is almost certainly what is meant here (NRSV, NLT, NET "struck . . . on the face"). [*rapisma*]

18:23 Wrongly (*kakōs*). Jesus knew that according to the law he was entitled to have witnesses (Deut. 17:6; 19:15), and he had done nothing wrong in insisting that the law be followed. [*kakōs*]

Testify (*martyrēson*). Here the verb means "specify what the wrong was," or "give proof of the wrong" (BAGD 492; NLT "you must give evidence for it"). [*martyreō*]

18:24 Sent him (*apesteilen*). This is irony. Here it is not the Father who "sent" Jesus (cf. 1:6) to save the world (3:17), but Annas who "sent" him to Caiaphas for trial. [*apostellō*]

18:26 A relative (*syngenēs*). This term describes a relative, someone from the same extended family (LN 10.6). This person was related to Malchus, the "high priest's slave" whose "ear" Peter had cut off in the garden of Gethsemane (cf. v. 10). This presented more of a problem for Peter because here was someone who might be able to identify him positively. This provoked Peter's third and final denial of Jesus. [*syngenēs*]

18:27 Denied it (*ērnēsato*). See 13:38, where Jesus predicted Peter's denials. No indication is given here of Peter's emotional state at this third denial (as in Matt. 26:74; Mark 14:71), or that he remembered that Jesus had foretold the denials (Matt. 26:75; Mark 14:71; Luke 22:61), or the bitter remorse Peter felt afterwards (Matt. 26:75; Mark 14:72; Luke 22:62). [*arneomai*]

A rooster crowed (*alektōr ephōnēsen*). See 13:38. It is more likely that this refers to an actual rooster crowing, although a number of scholars have suggested this was a technical term for the trumpet call, which ended the third watch of the night (midnight to 3 A.M.), known in Latin as the *gallicinium* (translated into Greek as *alektorophonia*, a term used in Matt. 26:34 and Mark 13:35). In this case Jesus would have prophesied the exact time at which Peter's denials took place (Bernard, 2:604). In any event a natural cockcrow would have occurred at approximately 3 A.M. in Palestine at this time of year (March-April). [*alektōr* + *phōneō*]

18:28 The praetorium (*praitōrion*). (Twice in this verse.) The Greek term is a Latin loanword that refers to the Roman governor's official residence (LN 7.7; NRSV "Pilate's headquarters"; NET "the Roman governor's residence"). In Palestine the governor's permanent residence was in Caesarea (cf. Acts 23:33-35). He also had a residence in Jerusalem, which he normally occupied only during principal feasts or times of political unrest. The building's location is uncertain. It is either (1) the fortress or tower of Antonia, on the east hill north of the temple area, the traditional location of the Roman praetorium since the twelfth century, or (2) the palace of Herod on the west hill near the present Jaffa Gate. [*praitōrion*]

So that they would not be defiled (*mianthōsin*). It is not precisely clear what type of ceremonial defilement (NIV "uncleanness") was in view here. Acts 10:28 states that it was "unlawful" for a Jew to associate with or visit a Gentile, but how defilement occurred is not specified. Some have thought John to be in error here about the statement concerning the eating of the Passover on the next day, since the type of ceremonial impurity the Jewish leaders would have incurred here could be removed by a bath at the end of the day. But this requires knowledge of the defilement's exact nature. For example, if it involved contact with a corpse, defilement would have lasted seven days (Num. 19:11). [*miainō*]

18:29 What accusation (*katēgorian*). Since Pilate has cooperated with them by providing Roman soldiers to aid in Jesus' arrest, the Jewish leaders were probably expecting Pilate to grant them permission to carry out the death sentence on Jesus (the Jewish authorities were not permitted to exercise capital punishment under the Roman occupation without official Roman permission, cf. v. 31). They must have been somewhat surprised to hear Pilate's question "What accusation (NIV, CEV "What charges") do you bring against this man?" because it indicated that he was going to try the prisoner himself. Thus Pilate was regarding Jesus' trial before Caiaphas and the Sanhedrin as only an inquiry and their verdict as merely an accusation. [*katēgoria*]

18:30 An evildoer (*kakon poiōn*). The Jewish religious leaders responded to Pilate's question with a statement that Jesus was an "evildoer" (NIV, NRSV, NLT, NET "a criminal") without noting a specific crime. [*kakos + poieō*]

Handed him over (*paredōkamen*). This verb has repeatedly been used to describe Judas as the betrayer of Jesus (6:64, 71; 12:4; 13:2, 11, 21; 18:2, 5; 21:20). Here, however, it is used of the Jewish religious authorities who "handed Jesus over" to Pilate. [*paradidōmi*]

18:31 Judge him (*krinate*). The verb obviously means "pass sentence on" or even "condemn," since the Jewish religious leaders replied that they were not permitted to carry out a capital sentence. [*krinō*]

According to your law (*nomon*). This refers to the Mosaic Law. Pilate, as the chief representative of Rome in a troubled area, was probably in Jerusalem for the Passover because of the danger of an uprising (his main residence was in Caesarea, cf. Acts 23:35). At this time, on the eve of the feast, he would have been a busy and perhaps even a worried man. It is not surprising that he offered to hand Jesus back over to the Jewish authorities to pass judgment on him. Pilate possibly realized when no specific charge was mentioned that he was dealing with an internal dispute over some religious matter, in which he would have had little interest. As far as John is concerned, though, this points out who was really responsible for Jesus' death. The Roman governor would have had nothing to do with it if he had not been pressured by the Jewish religious authorities, on whom the real responsibility rested. [*nomos*]

We are not permitted to put anyone to death (*exestin*). The historical background behind this statement is difficult to reconstruct. Scholars are divided over whether this statement in John's Gospel accurately reflects the judicial situation between the Jewish authorities and the Romans in first-century Palestine. It appears that the Roman governor may have given the Jewish authorities permission to carry out capital punishment for specific offenses if some of them were religious (the death penalty for Gentiles caught trespassing in the inner courts of the Jerusalem temple, for example). It is also noted that the Jewish authorities did in fact carry out a number of executions, some of them specifically pertaining to Christians (e.g., Stephen, according to Acts 7:58-60, and James the Just, who was stoned to death in the 60s according to Josephus, *Ant.* 20.9.1 [20.200]). But Stephen's death may be explained as the result of "mob violence" rather than a formal execution, and as Josephus goes on to point out, James was executed in the period between two Roman governors, and the high priest at the time was subsequently punished for the action. Overall it appears likely that the Romans kept very close control of the death penalty for fear that in the hands of rebellious locals such power could be used to eliminate factions favorable or useful to Rome. A province as troubled as Judea would not likely have been excepted from this. [*exestin*]

18:32 Fulfilled (*plērōthē*). The "word" of Jesus that is fulfilled here must be recorded in 12:32, because 12:33 contains exactly the same explanatory phrase ("signifying by what sort of death he was about to die") found here. [*pleroō*]

18:33 The King of the Jews (*basileus*). It is difficult to know what Pilate's attitude was when he asked Jesus this question. Some have understood the remark to be sarcastic or incredulous as the Roman governor looked at this lowly and humble prisoner. Others have thought Pilate was impressed by Jesus' regal disposition and dignity, so that the question was sincere. Later it is apparent that Pilate considered Jesus innocent (v. 38) and therefore probably also harmless, so an attitude of incredulity is most likely, but there are no clear contextual clues. [*basileus*]

18:35 Am I a Jew (*Ioudaios*). Many have read in Pilate's reply the Roman contempt for the Jewish people. Some of that may well be present, but strictly speaking, all Pilate affirmed was that he, as a Roman, had no firsthand knowledge of Jewish customs or belief. What he knew about Jesus must have come from the Jewish authorities. [*Ioudaios*]

18:36 My kingdom (*basileia*). (Three times) Jesus qualified his answer to make it clear to Pilate that he was no political revolutionary. See "kingdom" at 3:3. [*basileia*]

Would fight (*ēgōnizonto*). The absence of military resistance by Jesus' "servants" (his disciples) should indicate to Pilate that Jesus' "kingdom" was not "from here," i.e., from "this world." Actually Peter did try to resist (18:10-11), but Jesus ordered him to stop. [*agōnizomai*]

To the Jews (*Ioudaiois*). Here the expression refers to the Jewish religious leaders, specifically the members of the Sanhedrin (cf. 11:49-50). [*Ioudaios*]

18:37 I was born (*gegennēmai*). Here Jesus is referring to his physical birth, the means by which he came "into the world." On the phrase "come into the world" see 1:9, where the "true light, that enlightens everyone, was coming into the world." [*gennaō + erchomai + kosmos*]

The truth (*alētheia*). (Twice here and once in the following verse.) See 1:14. With his reply in the following verse, "What is truth?" Pilate dismissed the matter. Pilate's attitude at this point, as in v. 33, is not clear. The evangelist has not given enough information in the narrative to be sure. However, within the narrative, Pilate's question serves to make

the reader reflect on what "truth" is, and that answer had already been given in the narrative (14:6). When Pilate asked the question, "What is truth?" he had "truth" (personal, relational revelation from God, i.e., Jesus himself) standing right before him. [*alētheia*]

18:38 No cause (*aitian*). This is a technical legal term for the grounds for an accusation in court (LN 56.4; cf. NET). Pilate by using this term indicated he found no grounds for accusing Jesus of any crime. Luke also points to Pilate saying Jesus was innocent (Luke 23:4). [*aitios*]

18:39 That I release (*apolysō*). (Twice) Pilate offered to release Jesus, reminding the Jewish authorities about their "custom" that he "release" one prisoner for them at the Passover. There is no evidence outside the Bible alluding to such a customary practice. It is, however, also mentioned in Matt. 27:15 (described as a practice of the Roman governor) and in Mark 15:6 (described as a practice of Pilate). This may explain the lack of extrabiblical references to the practice—it was not a permanent one acknowledged by all Roman governors of Palestine, but one peculiar to Pilate as a means of appeasement, intended to promote better relations with his subjects. Such a limited meaning is certainly consistent with the statement here. [*apolyō*]

18:40 Barabbas (*Barabban*). The name "Barabbas" in Aramaic means "son of *abba*," that is, "son of the father." Presumably the man had another name (it may even have been Jesus, according to a textual variant in Matt. 27:16, although this is uncertain). For the evangelist the name "Barabbas" had ironic significance. The crowd was asking for the release of a man called Barabbas, "son of the father," while Jesus, who was truly the Son of the Father, was condemned to die in his place. [*Barabbas*]

A robber (*lēstēs*). It is possible that Barabbas was merely a "robber" or highwayman, but it is more likely given the use of the Greek term *lēstēs* in Josephus and other early sources, that he was a guerrilla warrior or revolutionary leader (Brown, 2:857; TDNT 4:258; NIV "had taken part in a rebellion"; CEV "was a terrorist"; NET "was a revolutionary"). The same Greek term was used a number of times by Josephus (*J. W.* 2.13.2-3 [2.253-54]) to describe the revolutionaries or guerrilla fighters who, from mixed motives of nationalism and greed, kept the rural districts of Judea in constant turmoil in the first century. [*lēstēs*]

19:1 Scourged him (*emastigōsen*). The Greek verb refers to the beating given to those condemned to death (BAGD 495; NIV, NRSV "had him flogged"). The verb should be read as causative ("had him scourged"): Pilate did not administer the scourging himself, but ordered his officers to do so. A Roman governor would not administer such a punishment in person. The choice of wording by the evangelist here may allude to Isa. 50:6, "I gave my back to those who scourge me." Three forms of corporal punishment were employed by the Romans, in increasing degree of severity: *fustigatio* ("beating"), *flagellatio* ("flogging"), and *verberatio* ("severe flogging, scourging"). The first could occasionally be a punishment in itself, but according to Roman law the more severe forms were a part of the capital sentence as a prelude to crucifixion. The most severe of the three is present here, indicated by the Greek verb *mastigoō*. It was carried out with a whip that had fragments of bone or pieces of metal bound into the tips, which could rip the victim's body open or cut muscle and sinew to the bone. The number of strokes was not prescribed; it continued until the flesh hung down in bloody shreds (TDNT 4:516). [*mastigoō*]

19:2 A crown of thorns (*stephanon*). (Also in v. 5) The Greek term describes a wreath or garland made of either leaves or precious metals beaten or molded to resemble leaves (LN 6.192). The crown mentioned here, however, was made of some thorny material. It has traditionally been regarded as an additional instrument of torture, but more likely the purpose of the thorns was not to inflict more suffering but to imitate the spikes of the "radiant corona," a type of crown portrayed on rulers' heads on many coins from this period. The spikes on this type of crown represented rays of light pointing outward (the best modern illustration is the crown on the head of the Statue of Liberty in New York harbor). [*stephanos*]

A purple robe (*porphyroun*). (Also in v. 5) The word refers to cloth that had been dyed reddish-purple with a dye made from a type of shellfish, from which the name was taken (BDAG 855). The purple color indicated royal status and was a further mockery of Jesus in addition to the crown of thorns. Roman officers wore a purple outer cloak (cf. Matt. 27:28, called here a "robe"), which was a sign of their authority. [*porphyra*]

19:3 Hail (*chaire*). The greeting used by the soldiers, "Hail, King of the Jews," mocks Jesus based on the standard salutation for the emperor, "*Ave, Caesar*" ("Hail to Caesar"). [*chairō*]

19:4 No cause (*aitian*). See 18:38. Pilate declared Jesus innocent a second time. [*aitios*]

19:5 Behold the man (*idou*). The Greek particle *idou* serves to draw attention to what follows."Look!" (LN 91.13). Pilate may have meant no more than "Here is the accused!" or in a more contemptuous way, "Here is your king!" Others, however, have taken Pilate's statement as intended to evoke pity from

Jesus' accusers: "Look at this poor fellow!" For the evangelist, however, Pilate's words constitute an unconscious allusion to Zech. 6:12, "Look, here is the man whose name is the Branch." In this case, Pilate (unknowingly and ironically) presented Jesus to the nation under a messianic title. [*idou*]

19:6 Crucify (*staurōson*). (Three times) Crucifixion was the cruelest form of punishment practiced by the Romans. Roman citizens could not normally be crucified. It was reserved for the worst crimes like treason and evasion of due process in a capital case. The Roman historian Cicero called it "a cruel and disgusting penalty" (*Against Verres* [*In Verrum*] 2.5.63-66 [163-70]). Josephus called it the worst of deaths (*J. W.* 7.6.4 [7.203]). [*stauroō*]

Take him (*labete*). Was Pilate really offering a serious alternative to the Jewish leaders who wanted Jesus crucified? Was he offering them an exception to the statement in 18:31 that the Jewish authorities did not have the power to carry out a death penalty? Although a few scholars have suggested that the situation was so far out of control at this point that Pilate really was telling the chief priests they could go ahead and crucify a man he had found to be innocent, this seems highly unlikely. Far more probable is that Pilate's statement is given out of frustration and sarcasm. The context supports this, since the Jewish authorities make no attempt to seize Jesus and crucify him; rather, they continue to pester Pilate to order Jesus' crucifixion. [*lambanō*]

Find no cause (*aitian*). See 18:38. This is the third time Pilate declared Jesus innocent. [*aitios*]

19:7 The Jews (*Ioudaioi*). See 1:19. Here in context the term refers specifically to the chief priests and their officers, mentioned in the preceding verse. These are the same ones who brought Jesus from Caiaphas's house to Pilate in the first place. They remained out- side the praetorium so as not to incur ceremonial defilement (18:28). [*Ioudaios*]

We have a law (*nomon*). (Twice) See 18:31 where Pilate refers to "your law." The "law" the Jewish leaders referred to was not the entire Mosaic Law, but Lev. 24:16 in particular, the law against blasphemy. [*nomos*]

19:8 He was more afraid (*ephobēthē*). Pilate's fear of Jesus was not sufficient to overcome his fear of being denounced by the Jewish religious authorities (see v. 12 below). [*phobeō*]

19:9 Where are you from (*pothen*). The reader of John's Gospel already knows the answer to this question—Jesus is from God. This creates a heightened sense of irony here. [*pothen*]

19:10 Authority (*exousian*). (Twice and once in the following verse.) Pilate reminded Jesus that he bears the *imperium*, the imperial power of Rome, on behalf of Caesar. In contrast to this, the reader of John's Gospel will remember that Jesus has been granted "authority" by his Father that surpasses that of the Roman emperor (cf. 5:27). [*exousia*]

19:11 It was given to you from above (*anōthen*). The expression means "from heaven," that is, "from God," but the alert reader of John's Gospel will recall 3:3 and Jesus' conversation with Nicodemus. [*anōthen*]

The one who betrayed me to you (*paradous*). This appears to be a reference to Judas at first (cf. 6:71), yet Judas did not deliver Jesus up to Pilate but to the Jewish authorities. The singular participle may be a reference to Caiaphas, who as high priest was representative of all the Jewish authorities, or it may be a generic singular referring to all the Jewish authorities directly. [*paradidōmi*]

The greater sin (*meizona*). Because Pilate had no authority over Jesus except what had been given to him from God, the one who handed Jesus over to Pilate was guilty of "greater sin." This does not absolve Pilate of all guilt. It simply means his guilt was less than those who handed Jesus over to him, because he was not acting against Jesus out of deliberate hatred or calculated malice like the Jewish authorities. [*megas + hamartia*]

19:12 Was seeking (*ezētei*). Here the verb means "trying" or "attempting." See 7:1 for similar usage, which also shows how ironic this instance is. The Jewish religious leaders had been "seeking" to kill Jesus, and now the Roman governor Pilate is "seeking" to release him! [*zēteō*]

The Jews (*Ioudaioi*). See 1:19. Here in context the term refers specifically to the chief priests and their officers, as in v. 7 above. [*Ioudaios*]

Friend of Caesar (*philos*). The expression "friend of Caesar" could have a more general meaning, referring merely to a person loyal to the Roman emperor, or it could have a technical sense, as a title bestowed by the emperor for loyal service (BAGD 395). Some have argued that the technical sense (a formal title) was not in use before the time of the Emperor Vespasian (A.D. 69-79). But there appears to be significant evidence for much earlier usage as a title. Assuming the formal title "Friend of the Emperor" was in use in the early part of the first century, what is the probability that it had been bestowed on Pilate? Pilate belonged to the equestrian order, which designated lower nobility as opposed to senatorial rank. As such he would have been eligible to receive such an honor. It also appears that a powerful political figure, Sejanus, was his patron in Rome. Sejanus had considerable influence with the Emperor Tiberius. The historian Tacitus quoted Marcus Terentius in his defense before the Senate as saying that close friendship with Sejanus "was in every case a powerful recommendation to the Emperor's friendship" (*Annals* 6.8). Thus it is possible Pilate held the title "Friend of the Emperor." If so, the Jewish authorities were putting significant psychological pressure on Pilate to convict and execute Jesus. They had finally specified the charge against Jesus as treason ("Everyone who makes himself to be king"). If Pilate now failed to convict Jesus, the Jewish authorities could complain to Rome that Pilate had released a traitor. Such a complaint would have carried more weight with Pilate than one might at first suppose because Pilate's record as governor was not entirely above reproach. Furthermore, Tiberius, who lived away from Rome on the island of Capri, was known for his suspicious nature, especially toward rivals or those who posed a political threat. Finally, Sejanus, Pilate's patron in Rome, came under suspicion of plotting to seize the imperial succession for himself, and was deposed in October of A.D. 31. It may even have been to Sejanus that Pilate owed his appointment in Judea. If Jesus' trial was taking place after Sejanus's death, Pilate would now have been in a very delicate position politically. [The two most common suggested dates for Jesus' death are A.D. 30 and 33.] The Jewish authorities used Pilate's loyalty as leverage against him. Even if Jesus' trial was taking place before the fall of Sejanus the accusation of supporting or releasing a traitor would have been viewed very seriously by Tiberius. Whether or not the Jewish religious leaders knew how powerful their veiled threat to Pilate was, it had the desired effect. Pilate went directly to the judgment seat to pronounce his verdict. [*philos*]

19:13 The judgment seat (*bēmatos*). The "judgment seat" was typically a raised platform mounted by steps and usually furnished with a seat. It was used by government officials in addressing an assembly or making official pronouncements, often judicial in nature (LN 7.63, BAGD 140). [*bēma*]

The Pavement (*Lithostrōton*). The Greek term may mean either "stone pavement" or "mosaic." It is something of a generic term. It was used in the Greek OT in 2 Chron. 7:3 to describe the pavement of Solomon's temple. Here either meaning is possible (BAGD 474). The precise location of this place is still uncertain, although a paved court on the lower level of the Fortress Antonia has been suggested (it is unclear whether this particular paved area was laid prior to A.D. 135). [*lithostrōtos*]

In Hebrew (*Hebraisti*). (Also in vv. 17, 20) This refers to the Aramaic language rather than Hebrew (NIV, CET, NET). See 5:2. [*Hebraisti*]

Gabbatha (*Gabbatha*). The evangelist does not say that *Gabbatha* is the Aramaic translation for the Greek term *Lithostrōton*. He simply points out that in Aramaic the place had another name. A number of meanings have been suggested for the name, but the most likely is "elevated place." It is possible that this was a term used by the common people for the judgment seat itself, which always stood on a raised platform. [*Gabbatha*]

19:14 The day of preparation of the Passover (*paraskeuē*). The Greek term *paraskeuē* ("day of preparation") appears in all four of the Gospels as a description of the day on which Jesus died. It could refer to any Friday as the day of preparation for the Sabbath (Saturday), and this is the way the Synoptic Gospels use the term (Matt. 27:62; Mark 15:42; Luke 23:54). John, however, specifies in addition that this was not only the day of preparation for the Sabbath, but also the day of preparation for the Passover, so that the Sabbath on the following day was the Passover (cf. v. 31). [*paraskeuē*]

About the sixth hour (*hektos*). See 1:39. When the time note "about the sixth hour" (NRSV, CEV, NLT, NET "about noon") is combined with the day, "the day of prepara-

tion for the Passover," it becomes apparent that Jesus was going to die on the cross at the very time the Passover lambs were being slaughtered in the temple courts. Exod. 12:6 required the Passover lamb to be kept alive until the 14th Nisan, the eve of the Passover, and then slaughtered by the head of the household at twilight (literally, in the Greek OT, "between the two evenings"). By the first century the slaughtering was no longer done by the heads of households, but by the priests in the temple courts. But so many lambs were needed for the tens of thousands of pilgrims who came to Jerusalem to celebrate the Passover (some estimates exceed 100,000 pilgrims) that the slaughter could not be completed during the evening. Therefore the rabbis redefined "between the two evenings" as beginning at noon, when the sun began to sink toward the horizon. Thus the priests had the entire afternoon of 14th Nisan in which to complete the slaughter of the Passover lambs. According to John's Gospel, this was the very time Jesus was dying on the cross. [*hektos*]

The Jews (*Ioudaiois*). See 1:19. Here in context the term refers specifically to the chief priests and their officers, as in vv. 7, 12 above. [*Ioudaios*]

19:16 He handed him over to them (*paredōken*). Jesus, who has been "handed over" to Pilate by the chief priests (18:35), is now "handed over" to the Jewish religious leaders. Since the crucifixion was carried out by a squad of Roman soldiers, the statement here is figurative. Jesus was "handed over" to the Jewish religious leaders in the sense that they finally got their wish as far as Jesus was concerned. He was sentenced to die by the Roman governor. [*paradidōmi*]

19:17 Carrying (*bastazōn*). The Greek verb is used of carrying or bearing a relatively heavy or burdensome object (LN 15.188). As was customary practice in Roman crucifixions, the condemned prisoner was made to "carry" his own cross. [*bastazō*] **His own cross** (*stauron*). This was probably only the crossbeam, called in Latin the *patibulum*, since the upright beam usually remained in the ground at the place of execution. According to Matt. 27:32 (= Mark 15:21) the soldiers forced Simon to take the cross. Luke 23:26 states the cross was placed on Simon so that it might be carried behind Jesus. A reasonable explanation of John's statement is that Jesus started out carrying his cross until he was no longer able to do so, at which point Simon was forced to take over. [*stauros*]

Place of a Skull (*Kraniou*). The Greek word means *kranion* means "a skull," but in the NT it is used only for the hill where Jesus was crucified (LN 8.11). According to v. 20 this place was outside the city. The Latin equivalent to the Greek *kranion* is *calvaria*. Thus the English word "Calvary" is a transliteration from Latin rather than a NT place name (cf. Luke 23:33 KJV). [*kranion*]

19:18 They crucified him (*estaurōsan*). See v. 6. The evangelist did not elaborate on the details of the crucifixion. For first century readers this would not have been necessary. [*stauroō*]

19:19 A title (*titlon*). (Also in the following verse.) It was customary to place a placard or "notice" (NIV, NET, NRSV, NASB "an inscription"; NLT "a sign") on the cross of the charge for which the criminal was executed (BAGD 820). The Greek verbs "wrote" and "placed" should be understood as causatives, since Pilate would not have performed this action in person. He ordered it to be done. [*titlos*]

On the cross (*staurou*). See v. 17. John says merely that the notice was "on the cross." Luke 23:38 states the inscription was placed "over him." Matt. 27:37 says it was placed

over Jesus' head. [*stauros*]

The King of the Jews (*basileus*). See 18:33. This inscription is an important detail, because it shows that Jesus was executed for claiming to be a king. From the point of view of Pilate and the executioners, it was probably intended to be ironic, since Pilate had already stated three times that he found Jesus innocent of any crime (18:38; 19:4, 6). Pilate's motivation in writing "The King of the Jews" on the notice is not easy to determine. He may have meant this as a final mockery of Jesus, but Pilate's earlier mockery seemed to be motivated by a desire to gain pity from the Jewish authorities in order to have Jesus released. More likely Pilate saw this as a subtle way of getting back at the Jewish authorities who pressured him into executing a man he considered to be innocent. For the evangelist, the notice was certainly ironic. Jesus really was "the King of the Jews," but was largely rejected by his own people (cf. 1:11). [*basileus*]

19:20 Many of the Jews (*Ioudaiōn*). See 1:19. Here the phrase refers to the residents of Jerusalem in general. The religious leaders are singled out in the following verse. [*Ioudaios*]

19:21 The chief priests of the Jews (*archiereis . . . Ioudaiōn*). See vv. 6-7. Nowhere else in John's Gospel are the two expressions "the chief priests" and "the Jews" combined. Earlier in v. 15 the chief priests were called merely *archiereis* ("chief priests"). Set next to the remark about the inscription, this is probably another example of Johannine irony. They failed to respond to "the King of the Jews." [*archiereus + Ioudaios*]

19:23 The soldiers (*stratiōtai*). (Twice and once in the following verse.) See 18:3; 19:2. The Gospel of John is the only one of the four Gospels to specify the number of soldiers involved in the crucifixion. This was a *quaternion*, a squad of four Roman soldiers. It was accepted Roman practice for the soldiers who performed a crucifixion to divide the possessions of the condemned person among themselves. [*stratiōtēs*]

The tunic (*chitōna*). (Twice) This was a long garment (NASB, NRSV, NET "tunic"; NLT "robe") worn under the cloak next to the skin (LN 6.176; NIV "undergarment") by both men and women (BAGD 882). [*chitōn*]

Seamless (*araphos*). This term describes a garment without a seam (LN 48.6). John states it was woven "from top to bottom." Many attempts have been made to guess the symbolic significance of this statement, such as the seamless tunic representing Jesus' priesthood, or representing the unity of all believers, but the evangelist does not elaborate. As far as the narrative is concerned, the point of the tunic being seamless is that the soldiers decided not to rip it apart into four shares, but to cast lots for it as a whole, thus fulfilling Scripture. [*araphos*]

19:24 Cast lots (*lachōmen*). They used marked pebbles or broken pottery pieces (LN 30.104; NLT, NET "throw dice"). [*lanchanō*]

19:28 Knowing (*eidōs*). Jesus' supernatural knowledge is in view. Cf. 6:61, 64; 13:1, 11. [*oida*]

Completed (*tetelestai*). The Father's work for Jesus was now "finished" (NRSV, NLT; cf. 17:4). [*teleō*]

To fulfill the Scripture (*teleiōthē*). The Greek verb *teleiōthē* ("fulfill") is a wordplay on the previous verb *tetelestai* ("it is completed"). The Scripture mentioned here is probably Ps. 69:21, "They also gave me gall for my food, and for my thirst they gave me vinegar to drink." Also suggested is Ps. 22:15, "My tongue cleaves to the roof of my mouth, and you [God] lay me in the dust of death." Ps. 22:1 reads "My God, my God, why have you

forsaken me?," a statement Jesus made from the cross, found in both Matt. 27:46 and Mark 15:34. [*teleioō*]

I thirst (*dipsō*). In light of the connection in the fourth Gospel between thirst and the living water that Jesus offers (cf. 4:13-15), it is highly ironic that here Jesus himself, the source of that living water, expresses his thirst. And since 7:39 associates the living water with the Holy Spirit, Jesus' statement here amounts to an admission that at this point he has been forsaken by God (cf. Ps. 22:1; Matt. 27:46; Mark 15:34). [*dipsaō*]

19:29 Sour wine (*oxous*). (Twice, once in the following verse.) The "sour wine" (NASB, NRSV, NLT, NET; NIV "wine vinegar") was known in Latin as *posca*, and referred to cheap vinegar wine diluted heavily with water. It was the drink of slaves and soldiers, and was relatively effective in quenching thirst (BAGD 574, LN 6.201). It was probably there for the soldiers who had carried out the crucifixion (TDNT 5:288). [*oxos*]

On hyssop (*hyssōpō*). The Greek term *hyssōpos* refers to a small aromatic bush, the exact identification of which is uncertain. The hyssop used to lift the wet sponge may have been a form of reed (the Greek term *kalamos* is used in Matt. 27:48 and Mark 15:36). The biblical name "hyssop" can refer to several different species of plant (at least 18 different plants have been suggested). Since hyssop was used in the OT for Passover purification rituals (Exod. 12:22) these associations may be more important for John than the type of plant employed. [*hyssōpos*]

19:30 It is finished (*tetelestai*). Many of the themes of the fourth Gospel are summed up here. Jesus indicated with this statement that the Father's work was now finished (17:4). He had obediently fulfilled his Father's will (18:11). [*teleō*]

Handed over the spirit (*paredōken*). Jesus

is portrayed in John as in control of events up until the very end. He voluntarily gave up his life at this point (cf. 10:18). [*paradidōmi*]

19:31 That their legs might be broken (*kateagōsin*). (Also in vv. 32, 33) The verb means "to break or shatter (a rigid object)" (LN 19.35). The Jewish authorities, because it was the day of preparation for the Sabbath (and the Passover, cf. v. 14), requested Pilate to order the legs of the three crucified men to be broken. This would hasten their deaths, since a person who was crucified needed to push upward with the legs in order to breathe. The practice of breaking the legs of crucified victims was known in Latin as *crurifragium*, and was done with a heavy mallet. Once dead, the bodies could be removed before the beginning of the Sabbath at 6 P.M. This was based on the law of Deut. 21:22-23 and Josh. 8:29 that specified that the bodies of executed criminals who had been hanged on a tree should not remain there overnight. According to Josephus this law was interpreted in the first century to apply to the bodies of those who had been crucified (*J. W.* 4.5.2 [4.317]). Philo of Alexandria also mentions that on occasion, especially at festivals, the bodies were taken down and given to relatives to bury (*Flaccus* 10 [83]). The normal Roman practice would have been to leave the bodies on the crosses to serve as a warning to other would-be offenders. [*katagnymi*]

19:34 Pierced (*enyxen*). The Greek verb *nyssō* ("pierce, stab") can indicate a range of actions from a slight prod to a mortal wound (cf. LN 19.15). However, if it was obvious to the soldiers that Jesus was already dead, it is unlikely one of them would have tried to inflict a wound. More likely one of the soldiers gave an exploratory stab with a spear to see if the body would jerk. If not, the vic-

tim was really dead. The thrust was hard enough to penetrate Jesus' side, however, since the evangelist goes on to state that "blood and water flowed out immediately." [*nyssō*]

With a spear (*lonchē*). The term can refer to a "spear" or "lance," although there is classical support for the meaning "spear point," referring specifically to the metal tip of a wooden lance or spear (BDAG 601), which may be more likely here. [*lonchē*]

Blood and water (*haima . . . hydōr*). The "blood and water" that flowed from Jesus' side as a result of the spear thrust is probably to be connected with statements in 1 John 5:6-8; both passages have "water," "blood," and "testimony" in common. In 1 John 5:7 the Spirit is mentioned as the source of the testimony, while here the testimony comes from one of the disciples (v. 35). The connection between the Spirit and the living water with Jesus' statement of thirst just before he died in the preceding context has already been noted (v. 28). For John, the "water" that flowed from Jesus' side was a symbolic reference to the Holy Spirit, who could now be given because Jesus was glorified (cf. 7:39). Jesus had now departed and returned to that glory that he had with the Father before the creation of the world (cf. 17:5). The mention of "blood" recalls the Passover lamb as a sacrificial victim. Later references to sacrificial procedures in the Mishnah appear to support this—*m. Pesahim* 5:3, 5 states that the sacrificial animal's blood should not be allowed to congeal, but should flow forth at death so that it could be used for sprinkling, and *m. Tamid* 4:2 actually specifies that the priest is to pierce the heart of the sacrificial victim and cause the blood to come forth. [*haima* + *hydōr*]

19:35 Has testified (*memartyrēken*). This statement confirms that this crucifixion account consisted of eyewitness "testimony."

However great the theological symbolism narrated, they actually occurred and were not composed simply to make a theological point. [*martyreō*]

19:36 Not a bone of him will be broken (*syntribēsetai*). This phrase is a quotation from Exod. 12:10 (in the Greek OT); Exod. 12:46; Num. 9:12; and Ps. 34:20. The first is the closest in form to the quotation here. Jesus' death fulfills this text. [*syntribō*]

19:37 Whom they have pierced (*exekentēsan*). This phrase is a quotation from Zech. 12:10, but Zechariah's entire context connects with events surrounding the crucifixion. In the first part of Zech. 12:10 the "Spirit of grace and of supplication" is poured out on the house of David and the inhabitants of Jerusalem. In Zech. 13:1 *Yahweh* (typically rendered as "Lord" in the OT) says, "In that day a fountain will be opened for the house of David and for the inhabitants of Jerusalem, for sin and for impurity." John may well have seen the blood flowing from Jesus' pierced side as the connection here, since the shedding of the sacrificial victim's blood represents cleansing from sin. Although the Jewish authorities and the Roman soldiers certainly "looked on the one whom they had pierced" as he hung on the cross, John may have an allusion to the second coming in mind too, since that is clearly the context of Zech. 12–14. Those responsible for Jesus' crucifixion will "look upon him" in another way when he returns to judge (Rev. 1:7). [*ekkenteō*]

19:39 A mixture of myrrh (*smyrnēs*). The Greek word *smyrna* referred to the resinous gum of the shrub *Balamodendron myrrha*. It was a principal ingredient used in preparing a corpse for burial (BAGD 758, LN 6.208). [*smyrna*]

Aloes (*aloēs*). The Greek word *aloē* (directly taken over into English) refers to the aromatic resin of a plant similar to a lily, used for preparing a corpse for burial (LN 6.209). [*aloē*]

About a hundred pounds (*litras*). Since a Roman "pound" weighed about 12 ounces, this would be about 75 pounds of spices (NIV, CEV, NLT, NET). [*litra*]

19:40 In linen cloths (*othoniois*). The Greek term *othonion* refers to "strips of linen cloth" (NET; LN 6.154; the term in 11:44 is a different one). Since the term used here is both plural and a diminutive, it has caused a considerable debate among NT scholars because it appears to contradict the Synoptic Gospels, which mention a *sindōn* (Matt. 27:59), a large single piece of linen cloth. If the word here is understood to refer to smaller cloth strips, like bandages, there would be a difference, but diminutive forms often lack their diminutive force in Koiné Greek (BDF §111.3), so there would not be any difference (CEV, "a linen cloth"; NLT, "a long linen cloth"). [*othonion*]

The spices (*arōmatōn*). This Greek word is a more general term referring to the aromatic oils, spices, and herbs used in preparing a corpse for burial (LN 6.207). Since the Jews did not practice embalming in either the Egyptian or the modern sense, these aromatic materials were used to cover the stench of decay and slow the body's decomposition. [*arōma*]

19:41 A new tomb (*mnēmeion*). (Also in the following verse.) This was probably a cave, perhaps enlarged artificially, with a low entrance (about three feet high) and a stone rolled across the entrance to seal the tomb. Many such tombs have been excavated around Jerusalem. [*mnēmeion*]

20:1 Early, while it was still dark (*prōi skotias*). This statement appears to conflict with Mark 16:1-2, which states that when the women came to the tomb, the sun had already risen. There are several possible, non-contradictory explanations for this. It may be that the tomb and the pathway to it were still in darkness for a short while after the sun had actually risen. Some have thought that John's note refers to the time Mary departed from her house, while Mark's refers to the time the women actually arrived at the tomb. [*prōi* + *skotia*]

The **stone** (*lithon*). This would have been a disk-shaped "stone" that rolled in a groove. Some of these were large enough to require several men to roll them away from the entrance. [*lithos*]

20:2 She ran (*trechei*). When Mary found the stone removed, she "ran" to inform Peter and the beloved disciple. John's narrative does not mention that Mary was in the company of other women when she went to the tomb, but this is suggested by the plural verb in her report to Peter and the other disciple, "We do not know where they have placed him." [*trechō*]

20:4 Ran ahead (*proedramen*). The Greek verb means "to run ahead" (BAGD 722), "to run in front of, to run ahead of" (LN 15.235), "to outrun" (LS 703; RSV, NIV, NRSV, NLT). The "other disciple" (the "disciple whom Jesus loved," v. 2) outran Peter and so arrived at the tomb first. This verse has been a significant factor in depictions of John, son of Zebedee as a young man (especially when combined with traditions that he wrote last of all the four evangelists and lived into the reign of Domitian). But this verse does not actually say anything about John's age, nor is age always directly related to running speed. [*protrechō*]

20:5 Bending over to look (*parakypsas*). The Greek verb means "to bend over or stoop down," with the implication of looking at or into something more closely (LN 17:31). In most cases the entrance, as evidenced in

tombs excavated near Jerusalem, is less than three feet high, so that an adult would have to bend down and practically crawl inside. Presumably by the time the beloved disciple reached the tomb there was enough light to penetrate the low opening and illuminate the interior so that he could see the strips of linen cloth lying there. [*parakyptō*]

20:7 The faceclothoth (*soudarion*). A "facecloth" was not mentioned in connection with Jesus' burial in 19:40, but was probably customary and therefore assumed. [*soudarion*]

Rolled up in a place by itself (*entetyligmenon*). The Greek participle here means "folded up" (BAGD 270; NIV, NLT), "rolled up, made into a roll" (LN 79.120; NRSV, CET, NET). The precise implication of this term has been disputed. Some interpreters have sought to prove that when the disciples saw the graveclothes, they were still arranged just as they had been when they were wrapped around Jesus' body (so that when the resurrection took place the resurrected body of Jesus passed through them without rearranging or disturbing them). In this case the description of the facecloth as being "rolled up" does not refer to its being folded, but collapsed in the shape it had when wrapped around Jesus' head. In spite of this reconstruction's intriguing nature, it is more likely that the phrase should be understood to mean the cloth was separated from the other graveclothes and rolled or folded up. This is consistent with the different conclusions reached by Peter and the other disciple (vv. 8-10). All that the condition of the graveclothes indicated was that the body of Jesus had not been stolen by grave robbers, since anyone who had come to remove the body (whether the Jewish authorities or anyone else) would not have bothered to unwrap it. And even if one could imagine that they had done so (perhaps to search for valuables such as rings or jewelry buried with the corpse), they would certainly not have bothered to take the time to roll up or fold the facecloth and leave it in a different place in the tomb. [*entylissō*]

20:8 He saw and believed (*episteusen*). What is the understood object of the verb *pisteuō* here? The subject is the beloved disciple, but what did he "believe" (since v. 7 describes what he saw)? Some have suggested that what he believed was Mary Magdalene's report that the body had been stolen (v. 2). But this could hardly be the case. Due to the way the entire scene is narrated, such a trivial conclusion would amount to an anticlimax. It is true that the plural "they" in the following verse applies to both Peter and the beloved disciple, and this appears to be a difficulty if one understands that what the beloved disciple "believed" here was Jesus' resurrection. However, the following verse simply says Peter and the other disciple did not understand the Scripture concerning the resurrection. Thus it appears that John intends his readers to understand that when the beloved disciple entered the tomb after Peter and saw the state of the graveclothes, he believed in the resurrection. [*pisteuō*]

20:9 To rise from the dead (*anastēnai*). John does not mention what specific Scripture is in mind (neither did Paul in 1 Cor. 15:4). Messiah's resurrection in general terms may have been seen by the earliest Christians in Isa. 53:10-12 and Ps. 16:10. Specific references to resurrection may have been tied to Jonah 1:17 and Hos. 6:2 because they mention "the third day." [*anistēmi*]

20:12 Two angels (*angelous*). See 1:51. The "angels" themselves do not play a major role in John's account of Jesus' resurrection. They did not explain the significance of the empty tomb, but simply asked Mary the reason why she was weeping (v. 13). [*angelos*]

20:13 Woman (*gynai*). (Also v. 15) This was a polite form of address (BAGD 168). [*gynē*]

20:15 The gardener (*kēpouros*). The text gives no clue what it was that led Mary to conclude that she was speaking with the gardener. Perhaps it was the only logical conclusion under the circumstances. John does not describe what Jesus looked like or how he was dressed. Some have seen this latter point as a difficulty since he left all the graveclothes in the tomb, but this is not necessarily a problem. The two angels who had appeared in the tomb were both clothed in white, and it is reasonable to suppose that the resurrected Jesus' appearance was similar. [*kēpouros*]

20:16 In Hebrew (*Hebraisti*). This is the Aramaic language rather than Hebrew (NIV, CEV, NET). [*Hebraisti*]

Rabboni (*rabbouni*). This is an Aramaic word (transliterated into Greek) meaning "my teacher" (an honorific title for a teacher of the Jewish Scriptures). See LN 33.247. [*rabbouni*]

20:17 Do not touch me (*haptou*). The verb can refer to close contact generally, but can also mean "cling to" in the sense of holding on to someone (BDAG 126; NASB, NLT). This is a prohibition stated with a present imperative. In a specific instance like this one the aorist imperative would normally be used (while the present imperative is more frequent in general commands and prohibitions). The nuance of the present imperative in a specific instance could be "Stop touching me," with the implication that Mary already was. [*haptō*]

Ascended (*anabebēka*). (Twice) The reason Jesus gave why Mary should stop holding on to him is that he had not yet "ascended" to the Father. Many fanciful explanations have been given as to why Jesus should say this, particularly as he invites Thomas to touch his wounds later (20:27). The verb here is different, however. Mary was apparently more intent on "clinging" to Jesus (see the preceding discussion). By virtue of his resurrection, however, Jesus had entered into a new dimension of relationship with all of his followers. It was not appropriate that Mary should cling on to him. [*anabainō*]

20:18 Proclaiming (*angellousa*). The verb means "to announce" something to someone (BDAG 8; NASB). John does not record how the disciples reacted to Mary's announcement that she had seen the risen Lord. Mark 16:9-11 (part of the longer, disputed ending of Mark) says that when Mary announced this, the disciples refused to believe it. Given the content of her message, such a response is not surprising (see Luke 24:11). [*angellō*]

20:19 The doors being shut (*kekleismenōn*). The Greek verb *kleiō* means "to shut, lock, bar" (BAGD 434). Since in the present context the doors were shut because of fear of the Jewish authorities, "lock" or "bar" would be implied (NIV, NRSV, NLT, NET). The significance of this statement is sometimes debated. It is often understood to mean that Jesus, when he entered the room where the disciples were gathered, passed through closed doors. This may well be the case, but the text does not affirm this *per se*. It is possible to assume that the doors swung open of their own accord before him, or that he simply "materialized" in the middle of the room without passing through doors or walls at all. John's point here is not the precise details, but that the closed doors were no obstacle at all to the resurrected Jesus. [*kleiō*]

    Peace (*eirēnē*). (Also in v. 21) This was a common Jewish greeting. [*eirēnē*]

20:20 Rejoiced (*echarēsan*). This was a fulfillment of Jesus' words to the disciples in the Farewell Discourse (16:20-22) that they would have sorrow while the world rejoiced,

but that their sorrow would be turned to lasting joy when they saw him again. [*chairō*]

20:21 As the Father has sent me, I send you (*apestalken . . . pempō*). This is essentially Jesus' "commissioning" of the disciples in the fourth Gospel, similar to Matt. 28:19-20. Here both verbs for "sending" occur together in the same verse. See 1:6. [*apostellō* + *pempō*]

20:22 He breathed (*enephysēsen*). The use of the Greek verb *emphysaō* to describe the action of Jesus here recalls Gen. 2:7 in the Greek OT, where "the Lord God formed man out of the dust of the ground, and breathed into his nostrils the breath of life, and man became a living being." This time, however, it is Jesus who is breathing the breath/Spirit (same Greek word) of eternal life, life from above, into his disciples (cf. 3:3-10). Furthermore, there is the imagery of Ezek. 37:1-14, the prophecy concerning the resurrection of the dry bones. In Ezek. 37:9 the "Son of Man" is told to prophesy to the "wind/breath/Spirit" (same Hebrew word; also same Greek word in the Greek OT) to come and breathe on the corpses so that they will live again. In Ezek. 37:14 the Lord promised, "I will put my Spirit within you, and you will come to life, and I will place you in your own land." In terms of ultimate fulfillment the prophecies in Ezek. 37 look at the regeneration of Israel immediately prior to the establishment of the messianic kingdom. However, the evangelist saw in what Jesus did for the disciples here a partial and symbolic fulfillment of Ezekiel's prophecy, much as Peter made use of the prophecy of Joel 2:28-32 in his sermon on the day of Pentecost (Acts 2:17-21). What then did Jesus do for his disciples here? In light of the symbolism of the new creation, as well as the regeneration symbolism from Ezek. 37, Jesus at this point "breathed" into the disciples the "breath" of eternal life. This would have come in the form of the Holy Spirit, who was to indwell them. The promise of the Spirit to come had been given in John 7:37-39. Jesus was now glorified, so the Spirit could be given. What then is the relationship of this incident to the account of the Holy Spirit's coming in Acts 2? It is probably best to view these as two separate events that had two somewhat different purposes. Here in John 20:22 it was eternal life itself that was given, while the power of the Spirit would be given later, on the day of Pentecost (Acts 2). At that time the disciples would be granted power to witness and to carry out the mission Jesus had given them. Finally, it is important to remember that in the historical unfolding of God's program for the church, these events were significant and unique in establishing the foundations of the new era. [*emphysaō*]

20:23 If you retain (*kratēte*). (Twice) In this context the verb means "to hold, to keep, to cause to continue" (LN 13.34) or "to retain" (BAGD 448). The closest parallel to the statement here is found in Matt. 16:19, 18:18. This probably does not refer to apostolic "power" to "forgive" or "retain" the sins of individuals (as it is sometimes understood, NIV "if you do not forgive them"; NLT "If you refuse to forgive them"), but to the power of proclaiming this forgiveness that Jesus entrusted to his disciples. This is consistent with the notion that the disciples were to carry on Jesus' ministry after he departed from this world and returned to the Father, a repeated theme of the Farewell Discourse (15:27, 16:1-4, 17:18). [*krateō*]

20:25 I will not believe (*pisteusō*). What Thomas was refusing to "believe" here was that Jesus had risen from the dead, as reported by his fellow disciples. The narrative's dramatic tension is heightened when Thomas, seeing for himself the risen Jesus, believes *more* than just the

resurrection (see 20:28). [*pisteuō*]

20:27 Do not be unbelieving but believing (*apistos . . . pistos*). Although these are adjectives rather than verbs, the meaning is essentially the same as the verb "believe" in 3:15, 16, 18, "exercise faith in, put one's trust in." [*apistos + pistos*]

20:28 My Lord and my God (*kurios . . . theos*). Thomas's words have been variously understood: (1) as subjects with the complement omitted ("My Lord and my God [has risen from the dead]"), (2) as predicate nominatives ("[You are] my Lord and my God," CEV), or (3) as vocatives ("My Lord and my God!"). The second option is more likely, because the context here appears confessional. Thomas's statement, while it may have been an exclamation, does in fact confess the faith that he had previously lacked. Jesus responded to Thomas's statement as if it were a confession (v. 29). With Thomas's proclamation here, it is difficult to see how any more profound analysis of Jesus' person could be given. It echoes 1:1 and 1:14 together: the Word was God, and the Word became flesh (Jesus of Nazareth). The Gospel of John opened with many other titles for Jesus: Lamb of God (1:29, 36), Son of God (1:34, 49), Rabbi (1:38), Messiah (1:41), King of Israel (1:49), and Son of Man (1:51). Now the climax is reached with Thomas's declaration, "My Lord and my God." The reader has come full circle from 1:1, where John had affirmed who Jesus is, to 20:28, where the last of the disciples has come to the full realization of who Jesus is. What Jesus has predicted in 8:28 had now happened: "When you lift up the Son of Man, then you will know that I am [he]" (Greek "I am"). By being "lifted up" in crucifixion (which led in turn to his death, resurrection, and exaltation with the Father) Jesus had revealed his true identity as both Lord (*kyrios*, used by the

Greek OT to translate *Yahweh*) and God (*theos*, used by the Greek OT to translate *Elohim*). [*kyrios* + *theos*]

20:29 Do you believe (*pepisteukas*). (Twice) Here the unexpressed object of belief is Jesus' resurrection (cf. 20:25). [*pisteuō*]

20:30 Signs (*sēmeia*). The evangelist mentions many other "miraculous signs" (NIV, NLT, NET) performed by Jesus in the presence of the disciples, which are not written in the Gospel of John. One can only speculate what these other signs are. John says they were performed in the presence of the disciples, which emphasizes again their role as witnesses (cf. 15:27). The point here is that the evangelist acknowledges that he has been selective in his use of material. He has chosen to record those incidents from Jesus' life and ministry that supported his purpose in writing this Gospel. Much that might be of tremendous interest, but which does not directly contribute to that purpose in writing, has been omitted. [*sēmeion*]

    In this book (*bibliō*). Here "this book" refers to the Gospel of John itself. [*biblion*]

20:31 That you may believe (*pisteusēte*). (Twice) This verse is the purpose statement for the Gospel of John. Although it may seem clear on the surface, there has been much debate over whether John was writing primarily for an audience of unbelievers, with purely evangelistic emphasis (NRSV, "so that you may come to believe"; CEV, "so that you will put your faith in"), or whether he envisioned an audience of believers, whose faith he wishes to strengthen. There are several important points to the discussion: (1) In the immediate context (20:30), the other signs spoken of by the author were performed in the presence of the disciples. (2) In the case of the first of these signs, at Cana, the author makes a point of the effect the miracle had on

the disciples (2:11). (3) If the primary thrust of the fourth Gospel is toward unbelievers, it is difficult to see why so much material in chapters 13-17 (the last meal and Farewell Discourse, concluding with Jesus' prayer for the disciples), all of which deals almost exclusively with the disciples, is included. (4) The disciples themselves were repeatedly said to have believed in Jesus throughout the Gospel of John, beginning with 2:11, yet they still needed to believe after the resurrection (if the experience of Thomas in 20:27-28 is any indication). (5) The Gospel of John appears to be written with the assumption that the readers are familiar with the basic story (or perhaps with one or more of the Synoptic Gospels, although this is less certain). Thus no account of the birth of Jesus is given at all. Although he is identified as being from Nazareth, the words of the Pharisees and chief priests to Nicodemus (7:52) are almost certainly to be taken as ironic, assuming John's reader knows where Jesus was really from. Likewise, when Mary is identified in 11:2 as the one who anointed Jesus' feet with the ointment, it is apparently assumed that the readers are already familiar with the story, since the incident referred to in 11:2 is not actually mentioned in the narrative until 12:3. However, all these considerations must be set over against the clear statement of purpose in the present verse, 20:31, which seems to have significant evangelistic emphasis. In addition to this there is the repeated emphasis on "witness" throughout the fourth Gospel (the witness of John the Baptist in 1:7, 8, 15, 32, 34, and 5:33; the Samaritan woman in 4:39; Jesus' own witness, along with that of the Father who sent him, in 8:14, 18, 37; the witness of the disciples themselves in 15:27; and finally the witness of the author himself in 19:35 and 21:24). In light of all the evidence, it seems best to say that John wrote with a dual purpose: to witness to unbelievers concerning

Jesus, so that they might come to believe in him and have eternal life, and to strengthen the faith of those who were already believers, by deepening and expanding their understanding of who Jesus is. [*pisteuō*]

The **Christ** (*Christos*). See the discussion at 1:20. [*Christos*]

The **Son** of God (*huios*). See the summary discussion of the title "Son of God" at 1:34. [*huios*]

Life (*zōēn*). Here the meaning is "eternal life." See 1:4 and 17:2. [*zōē*]

21:1 Revealed himself (*ephanerōsen*). (Twice) This verb means "to make known, reveal" clearly and in some detail (LN 28.36). Here it describes Jesus revealing himself to his disciples in one of his post-resurrection appearances. [*phaneroō*]

21:3 I am going fishing (*halieuein*). The verb means "to catch fish," whether with a line or with a net (LN 44.7). Fishing was often done at night on the Sea of Galilee so that the catch could be sold the next morning. Although some interpreters have read into Peter's actions a permanent return to his old profession, nothing narratively suggests that. Peter had seen the risen Lord along with the other disciples (20:19-20). The disciples had even been given a sort of "commissioning" with a general statement of purpose (20:21). Yet none of this dictates that Peter had given up on his calling or was discouraged because he had denied the Lord. [*halieuō*]

21:5 Children (*paidia*). This is a term for "child" that can be used even of a newborn infant as well as older children, usually below the age of puberty (BAGD 604, LN 9.42). It is somewhat unusual here in that Jesus' followers are typically referred to by the terms *teknon* (cf. 1:12) or *teknion* (cf. 13:33) elsewhere in John's Gospel. [*paidion*]

Fish (*prosphagion*). This Greek word is somewhat unusual. In Hellenistic Greek it described a side dish to be eaten with bread (BAGD 719) but in some contexts was the equivalent of the Greek word *opson* ("fish"). In this context, fish in general are clearly meant. [*prosphagion*]

21:6 The net (*diktyon*). (Also in vv. 8, 11) This is a NT general term for a fishing net (cf. Matt. 4:20). This would have been a net pulled between two boats to trap fish in between. [*diktyon*]

They could not **pull** it **in** (*helkysai*). The verb's basic meaning is to "pull" or "draw" (TDNT 2:503; NASB, NIV, NRSV "haul . . . in"; NLT "draw in"; NET "pull . . . in"). Here it refers to the net overloaded with fish. This is the same verb used in 6:44 to describe the "drawing" of people to Jesus by the Father (without detailed explanation). [*helkyō*]

21:7 He girded his outer garment (*diezōsato*). The verb means to "tuck up" or "tuck in" a garment (NET) by wrapping a belt or piece of cloth around it, or to tie such a belt or piece of cloth around the waist (LN 49:14). [*diazōnnymi*]

For he was **naked** (*gymnos*). The Greek word *gymnos* can refer to complete nudity (Mark 14:52), or to being scantily clad (LN 49.22). The meaning "without an outer garment" is found in Aristophanes (*Nubes* 498) in the fourth century B.C. (TDNT 1:773). Scantily clad is usually the way the word is understood here, since it is widely recognized that nudity would have been offensive to Jews. It would thus mean something like "stripped for work" (RSV, NASB, NLT) that is, with one's outer clothing removed, so that Peter was wearing either a loincloth or a loose-fitting tunic (a long shirt-like garment worn under a cloak). Believing himself inadequately clad to greet the Lord, Peter then threw his outer garment around himself and dived into the sea. Barrett (580-81) offered the explanation that a greeting was a religious act and could not be performed unless one was fully clothed. However, this still leaves the improbable picture of a person with much experience around the water putting *on* his outer garment before plunging in. Much more likely is Brown's suggestion (2:1072) that the Greek verb *diazōnnymi* ("girded himself") does not mean putting the outer clothing on, but tying the clothing around oneself (see 13:4-5 of Jesus tying the towel around himself). In this case Peter being "naked" could mean that he was naked underneath his tunic or outer garment and thus could not take it off before jumping into the water. But he did pause to tuck it up and tie it with a rope or girdle before jumping in, to allow his legs more movement. Thus the clause that states Peter was naked is explanatory (note "for"), giving the reason why Peter stopped to gird up his garment rather than taking it off. [*gymnos*]

21:8 Two hundred cubits (*pēchōn*). The Greek term *pēchys* ("cubit") describes a measure of length about 18 inches (BAGD 657). The distance is about 100 yards. [*pēchys*]
  Dragging (*syrontes*). This is a different Greek verb meaning "to pull, drag, draw" from the one used in v. 6 (LN 15.212; NIV "towing") and exhibits John's love of stylistic variation. [*syrō*]

21:9 A charcoal fire (*anthrakian*). This describes a fire that has burned down to the coals. This detail in the narrative may simply be an eyewitness reminiscence, but it may also be deliberately intended to recall the "charcoal fire" in the high priest's courtyard (18:18) where Peter was warming himself as he betrayed Jesus. This link is significant because the primary purpose of the dialogue that follows between Peter and Jesus is Peter's restoration after his denials. Peter is clearly the focus of the narrative here. [*anthrakia*]
  Fish (*opsarion*). (Also in the following

verse.) The usual meaning of this word is a small morsel of food eaten with bread, but in some contexts it means "fish" (LN 5.16). [*opsarion*]

21:11 Large fish (*ichthyōn*). This is the third Greek term for "fish" in the passage (also in vv. 6, 8; cf. vv. 5, 9 where different Greek words are used). According to BAGD 384 it is frequently used to describe fish as food (Matt. 7:10; 14:17, 19; 15:36; 17:27; Mark 6:38, 41, 43; Luke 5:6, 9; 9:13, 16; 11:11; 24:42; John 21:6, 8, 11). The number of "large fish" in the net, 153, has been the subject of much speculation. Although many symbolic interpretations have been proposed (many seeing "unity" in the fact that the net was not torn), the text itself gives no clue as to the significance of the number. The detail given here is more likely indicative of an eyewitness recalling the scene. [*ichthys*]

21:15 More than these (*toutōn*). Most likely "these" refers to the other disciples, meaning "Do you love me more than these other disciples do?" (CEV "more than the others do"; NET "more than these do") There is irony here: Peter had boasted in 13:37, "I will lay down my life for you." The Synoptic Gospels present Peter as boasting even more explicitly of his loyalty to Jesus ("Even if they all fall away, I will not," Matt. 26:33; Mark 14:29). Thus the semantic force of what Jesus asks Peter here amounts to something like "Now, after you have denied me three times, as I told you that you would, can you still affirm that you love me more than these other disciples do?" [*houtos*]
  I love you (*philō*). (Also once in v. 16 and three times in v. 17) This is the second Greek word for "love" used in the passage. Although at the popular level a distinction is frequently made between the two terms, with *phileō* indicating mere "human" love or natural affection, and *agapaō* indicating a

higher, "divine" love, it is very unlikely that John is making any distinction in the terms here. (1) The evangelist has a habit of introducing stylistic variations in repeated material without any significant difference in meaning (compare, for example, 3:3 with 3:5, and 7:34 with 13:33). An examination of the uses of the two Greek verbs *agapaō* and *phileō* in John indicates a general interchangeability between the two. Both terms are used of God's love for people (3:16; 16:27), of the Father's love for the Son (3:35; 5:20), of Jesus' love for people (11:3, 5), of the love of human beings for one another (13:34; 15:19), and of the love of people for Jesus (8:42; 16:27). (2) If the original conversation between Jesus and Peter took place in Aramaic (as is probable), there would not have been any difference expressed because both Aramaic and Hebrew have only one basic word for love. In the Greek OT both verbs, *agapaō* and *phileō*, are used to translate the same Hebrew word for love (although *agapaō* is more frequent). Also, the Syriac version of the NT uses only one verb to translate both Greek verbs in vv. 15-17 (Syriac is very similar to Palestinian Aramaic). (3) Peter's answers to the questions asked with *agapaō* are "yes" even though he answers with *phileō*. If he is being asked to love Jesus on a "higher" or "more spiritual" level, his answers give no indication of this. One would be forced to conclude (in order to consistently maintain a distinction between the two Greek verbs) that Jesus finally conceded defeat and accepted only the "lower" form of love from Peter. It is much more likely that the interchange between the two Greek verbs here is a mere stylistic variation, consistent with his use of minor variations elsewhere. [*phileō*]

My lambs (*arnia*). The difference between this word and the word for "sheep" in vv. 16-17 is probably more stylistic variation on the evangelist's part. [*arnion*]

21:16 Shepherd (*poimaine*). It is sometimes pointed out that the verb used in the previous verse and again in v. 17 ("feed") describes a more restricted activity, that of feeding animals, while this verb refers to guiding and protecting the flock as well as feeding it. This may be true, but taken comprehensively both terms form a general description of pastoral care. Again we are probably dealing with stylistic variation here on the part of the evangelist. [*poimainō*]

21:18 You girded yourself (*ezōnnues*). This verb refers to dressing oneself (NIV, CEV). It literally means "to tie with a belt," the last item of clothing to be put on, but figuratively refers to the entire process of dressing (LN 49.8). [*zōnnuō*]

You will stretch out your hands (*ekteneis*). The verb is used of laying out anchors from a ship (Acts 27:30), but is found in Epictetus (3.26.22) as a comparison to one who is crucified (BDAG 310). An allusion to crucifixion is probably the meaning here. [*ekteinō*]

Another will gird you (*zōsei*). Again, the verb means "to tie with a belt," and could typically refer to dressing, but in the context the wordplay results in the meaning "will tie you up" (NET), referring to Peter being tied up and led off to execution. Early church tradition holds that Peter was crucified in Rome under Nero around A.D. 64 (Tertullian, *Scorpiace* 15). [*zōnnymi*]

21:19 He would glorify (*doxasei*). Here the expression "glorify God" almost certainly indicates martyrdom (cf. 1 Pet. 4:16). The parallelism of this phrase to similar phrases in 12:33 and 18:32, which describe Jesus' own death by crucifixion, have led many interpreters to suggest that Jesus was predicting not only martyrdom for Peter, but crucifixion. This appears to be confirmed by the phrase "stretch out your hands" in the previous verse. Some have objected that if that phrase did indeed refer to crucifixion, the order of events in v. 18 is wrong, because the "binding" and "leading where one does not wish to go" should precede the "stretching out" of the hands on the cross. However, Brown (2:1108) sees this as a deliberate reversal of the normal order to emphasize the stretching out of the hands. Another possible explanation is that Roman practice typically involved stretching out and tying the condemned prisoner's hands to the crossbeam (known in Latin as the *patibulum*) and forcing him to carry it to the place of execution (the upright beam normally stayed in the ground and was reused). See also 17:1. [*doxazō*]

21:20 The one who betrays you (*paradidous*). This recalls the incident at the Last Supper in 13:25 where this disciple asked Jesus about the betrayer. [*paradidōmi*]

21:22 To remain (*menein*). (Also the next verse.) "To remain" means "to remain alive," or to continue to live (BAGD 504; NIV, NLT). John 21:23 explains, "that this disciple would not die." [*menō*]

Until I come (*erchomai*). (Also the next verse.) This would be a clear reference to Jesus' second coming (NIV, NLT "return"; NET "come back"), since this conversation takes place after Jesus' resurrection. [*erchomai*]

21:24 Who has written (*grapsas*). This appears to refer to the Gospel of John itself, with the possible exception of v. 24, which may be a parenthetical attestation by other witnesses. The first person singular resumes in v. 25, however, so the first person plural "we" here may simply be an inclusive way of referring to the readers. [*graphō*]

21:25 The world (*kosmon*). The term refers to the present physical "world." [*kosmos*]

The books that would be written (*biblia*). See 20:30. The evangelist concludes the Gospel of John with a note about his selectivity of material. He has not attempted to write an exhaustive account of Jesus' words and works, for that would not be possible. The statement "the world could not contain the books that would be written" is hyperbole, and as such has some similarity to the conclusion of the book of Ecclesiastes (12:9-12). As it turns out, the statement seems more true of the fourth Gospel itself, which with the passing of every year is the subject of an ever-lengthening list of books, articles, and commentaries. The statement here serves as a final reminder that our knowledge of Jesus, no matter how well-attested it may be, is still partial. Everything Jesus said and did in his three and one-half years of earthly ministry is not known. This supports the major theme of John's Gospel, however: Jesus is repeatedly identified as God, and although he may be truly known on the basis of his self-disclosure, he can never be known exhaustively. There is far more to know about Jesus than could ever be written down or known. On this appropriate note John's Gospel ends. [*biblion*]

ENGLISH INDEX

A

Abba; Mark 14:36

Aboard; John 6:17

Abomination; Matt. 24:15; Mark 13:14; Luke 16:15

Above; John 3:3; 8:23

Abraham; Matt. 3:9; Luke 3:8, 34; John 8:33. See also Children of Abraham; Son of Abraham

Abraham's bosom; Luke 16:22

Abundantly; John 10:10

Abuse; Luke 6:28

Abyss; Luke 8:31

Acceptable; Luke 4:24

Acceptable year of the Lord; Luke 4:19

Accompany; Mark 16:17

Accomplished; Luke 1:1

Accursed; John 7:49

Accusation; John 18:29

Adam; Luke 3:38

Adorned; Luke 21:5

Adultery; Luke 16:18

Advanced; Luke 1:7

Advocate; John 14:16, 26; 15:26

Aenon; John 3:23

Affliction; Mark 5:29

Afraid; Luke 12:4-5; John 19:8

After; John 13:7

Against you; Matt. 18:15

Agony; Luke 22:44

Agree; Matt. 18:19

Alert; Matt. 24:42; Mark 13:33

Alike; Luke 14:18

Alive; John 5:21

All before me; John 10:8

Alms; Matt. 6:2; Luke 11:41

Aloes; John 19:39

Already; Matt. 3:10

Amazed; Luke 2:47; 4:36

Angels; Matt. 1:20; 18:10; 22:30; 25:41; Luke 20:36; John 1:51; 12:29; 20:12

Anger; Matt. 18:34

Angry; Matt. 5:22

Anoint; Mark 14:8; Luke 4:18; John 9:6; 11:2

Another; John 5:32

Answer; Luke 21:14; 22:68

Anxious; Matt. 6:25

Apart from; Matt. 10:29

Apostles; Matt. 10:2; Luke 6:13

Apparel; Luke 23:11

Appearance; John 7:24

Appoint; John 15:16

Approach; Matt. 26:45; Luke 21:34

Argument; Luke 9:46-47

Arm of the Lord; John 12:38

As he said; Matt. 28:6

Bond; Mark 7:35

Bone; Luke 24:39; John 19:36

Book; Matt. 1:1; John 20:30; 21:25

Booths; Luke 9:33

Born; John 1:13; 3:3; 8:41; 18:37

Bound; John 18:12

Branches; John 12:13

Bread; Luke 6:4; John 6:31, 32, 34. See also Sacred bread; True bread from heaven

Bread of life; John 6:48

Breathed; John 20:22

Bridegroom; Matt. 9:15; Luke 5:34

Bring to; John 14:26

Broke; Mark 14:3

Broken; John 7:23; 10:35; 19:31, 36

Brother; Matt. 5:22; 22:24; 28:10; John 2:12

Build; Luke 11:47-48

Burial; John 12:7

Burn; Luke 24:32; John 15:6

Burned their city; Matt. 22:7

Bury; Matt. 8:21; Luke 9:59

Bushel; Mark 4:21

C

Caesar; Matt. 22:17

Calf; Luke 15:27

Call; Luke 5:32; John 9:18, 24

Camel's hair; Mark 1:6

Can; Luke 6:39

Cana; John 2:1; 4:46

Canaanite; Matt. 15:22

Capernaum; Luke 4:23; John 2:12

Care; Luke 10:40; John 10:13

Carpenter; Mark 6:3

Carrying; John 19:17

Cast; Luke 6:22

Cast lots; John 19:24

Cast out; John 6:37; 12:31

Catch; Luke 11:54

Catching men; Luke 5:10

Caught in the act; John 8:4

Cause; Matt. 19:3; John 18:38; 19:4, 6

Cause to sin; Matt. 18:6

Cause to stumble; John 6:61

Cent; Matt. 5:26

Centurion; Matt. 8:5; Mark 15:39; Luke 7:2

Cephas; John 1:42

Ceremonial washing; John 2:6

Certificate of divorce; Matt. 5:31; 19:7

Certified; John 3:33

Charcoal fire; John 18:18; 21:9

Charge; Matt. 27:37

Chasm; Luke 16:26

Chastise; Luke 23:16

Chief priest; Matt. 2:4; Mark 11:27; John 7:32; 19:21

Chief steward; John 2:8; 11:57

Child; Mark 10:15; John 4:49

Children; Matt. 18:3; Luke 9:48; 11:7; 13:34; 18:16-17; John 13:33; 21:5

Children of Abraham; John 8:39

Children of God; John 1:12

Choose; John 6:70; 15:16, 19

Chosen; Matt. 22:14; Luke 1:9; 9:35; John 13:18

Christ; Matt. 1:1; Mark 1:1; 8:29; Luke 3:15; 4:41; 9:20; 22:67; 23:35; John 1:20, 41; 4:25; 20:31

Church; Matt. 16:18; 18:17

Circumcision; Luke 1:59; 2:21; John 7:22

Cities of Israel; Matt. 10:23

City of David; Luke 2:4

Clay; John 9:6

Clean; Mark 7:19; John 13:10; 15:3

Cleanse; Matt. 8:2

Clear; Matt. 6:22

Cloak; Matt. 14:36; Mark 10:50

Clothing; Matt. 3:4

Cloud; Mark 9:7; Luke 9:34; 21:27

Cohort; John 18:3

Coin; Luke 20:24; 21:2

Colt; Mark 11:2

Come; Matt. 24:3, 27; John 14:23; 21:22

Come all; Matt. 11:28

Come down; Luke 17:31; John 6:38, 42

Come near; Luke 10:9, 11

Come to me; John 6:44, 45, 65; 7:37

Come upon; Luke 11:20

Comes; John 6:35

Comes down; John 6:33

Comforted; Matt. 5:4

Coming one; Matt. 11:3

Command; Luke 8:25; John 15:14

Commanding officer; John 18:12

Commandment; Matt. 5:19; 15:3; John 10:18; 13:34; 14:15; 15:10, 12

Company of soldiers; Mark 15:16

Compassion; Matt. 9:36; 18:27; 20:34; Mark 6:34; 8:2; 9:22; Luke 7:13

Compel; Mark 1:12; Luke 14:23

Compile; Luke 1:1

Complete; John 17:4, 23; 19:28

Completely; John 9:34

Conceive; Luke 1:31

Condemn; John 3:17, 18; 5:45; 8:10

Confess; John 1:20

Consented; Luke 23:51

Consolation of Israel; Luke 2:25

Consume; John 2:17

Contempt; Mark 9:12

Convert; Matt. 23:15

Convict; John 8:46; 16:8

Copper coin; Mark 12:42

Cor; Luke 16:7

Corban; Mark 7:11

Cornerstone; Mark 12:10

Council; Matt. 10:17; Mark 13:9; Luke 22:66

Counsel; John 11:53

Country; John 4:44

Courtyard; Luke 22:55

Covenant; Matt. 26:28; Mark 14:24; Luke 1:72

Covetousness; Luke 12:15

Craftiness; Luke 20:23

Created; John 1:3

Creation; Mark 16:15

Credit; Luke 6:32-34

Crime; Luke 23:4

Cross; Mark 8:34; Luke 9:23; John 19:17, 19

Crowd; Matt. 4:25; 15:32; John 7:20, 31, 40, 49

Crowed; John 18:27

Crown; Matt. 27:29

Crown of thorns; John 19:2

Crucify; Matt. 26:2; Mark 15:13; Luke 23:21; John 19:6, 18

Cry out; Mark 15:34; Luke 19:40; 23:18; John 12:44

Cubit; Luke 12:25; John 21:8

Cup; Mark 14:36; Luke 22:42; John 18:11

Curse; Mark 14:71

Curtain; Luke 23:45

Cut him to pieces; Luke 12:46

Cut short; Matt. 24:22

D

Daily; Matt. 6:11

Dark; John 6:17; 20:1

Darkness; Matt. 4:16; 8:12; Luke 22:53; John 1:5

Daughter; Mark 5:34

Daughter of Zion; John 12:15

David. See City of David; House of David; Of David; Seed of David; Son of David; Throne of David

Dawned; Matt. 4:16

Day; Luke 22:66; John 8:56; 14:20

Temple; Matt. 26:61; Luke 24:53; John 2:14, 19

Temple tax; Matt. 17:24

Temporary; Matt. 13:21; Mark 4:17

Tempt; Matt. 4:1; Luke 4:2, 12

Temptation; Matt. 6:13; Luke 11:4; 22:40, 46

Tempter; Matt. 4:3

Tenant; Matt. 21:33; Luke 20:14

Tenant farmers; Mark 12:1

Tender mercy; Luke 1:78

Tenth hour; John 1:39

Territory; John 3:22

Terrors; Luke 21:11

Test; Matt. 4:7; Mark 10:2

Testify; John 1:7, 34; 3:11; 18:23; 19:35

Testimony; Mark 1:44; Luke 5:14; 21:13; John 1:19; 3:11, 32

Testing; John 6:6; 8:6

Tetrarch; Matt. 14:1; Luke 3:1

Thank you; Luke 18:11

Thanks; John 6:11

That one; John 9:11

That servant; Luke 12:43, 45, 47

Theirs; Matt. 5:2

There; Matt. 18:20

These; John 21:15

These things; Luke 21:31

Thief; John 10:1; 12:6

Things; Matt. 11:27; Luke 5:26; 21:31; John 3:12; 5:19; 16:13

Thinks; Luke 8:18

Third day; Matt. 20:3; John 2:1

Thirst; John 6:35; 7:37; 19:28

Thorns; Luke 8:7; John 19:2

Those around him; Mark 4:10

Those who are outside; Mark 4:11

Thought; Matt. 1:19; Luke 9:46-47

Throne; Matt. 19:28

Throne of David; Luke 1:32

Tiberias; John 6:1

Time; Matt. 25:19; John 7:6, 8

Times; Luke 21:24

Timid; Mark 4:40

Tithe; Matt. 23:23; Luke 11:42

Title; John 19:19

Today; Luke 2:11; 4:21; 23:43

Told; Luke 2:20

Tolerable; Luke 10:12, 14

Tomb; Matt. 27:52, 60; John 5:28; 11:38; 19:41

Top; John 2:7

Torch; John 18:3

Torment; Mark 5:7; Luke 8:28

Torn; Matt. 27:51; Mark 15:38

Torn apart; Mark 1:10

Touch; John 20:17

Towel; John 13:4

Tower; Luke 14:28

Tradition; Matt. 15:2; Mark 7:3

Train; Matt. 13:52

Transfigured; Matt. 17:2; Mark 9:2

Transgressors; Luke 22:37

Trap; Mark 12:13; Luke 21:35

Treasure; Matt. 6:19

Treasury; Luke 21:1; John 8:20

Trees. See Fig tree; Good tree; Palm trees; Sycamine tree

Treat him; Matt. 18:17

Trespasses; Matt. 6:14

Tribulation; Matt. 24:21; Mark 13:19

Tribute; Luke 20:22

Trouble; Matt. 6:34

Troubled; Luke 24:38; John 5:7; 11:33; 12:27; 13:21; 14:1, 27

True; Luke 16:11

True bread from heaven; John 6:32

True worshipers; John 4:23

Truly; Mark 3:28; John 4:18

GREEK TRANSLITERATION INDEX

Anachōreō; John 6:15

Anaginōskō; Matt. 21:16; 24:15

Anagkazō; Luke 14:23

Anaideia; Luke 11:8

Anaitios; Matt. 12:7

Anakeimai; John 12:2l; 13:23

Anaklinō; Matt. 8:11; Luke 13:29

Anakrazō; Luke 23:18

Anamartētos; John 8:7

Anamnēsis; Luke 22:19

Anangellō; John 16:13

Anapauō; Matt. 11:28

Anapherō; Luke 24:51

Anapiptō; John 6:10; 13:12

Anaseiō; Mark 15:11; Luke 23:5

Anastasis; Matt. 22:23; Luke 2:34; John 11:25

Anatellō; Matt. 4:16

Anathematizō; Mark 14:71

Anatolē; Luke 1:78

Anektos; Luke 10:12, 14

Anēr; Matt. 7:26

Aneu; Matt. 10:29

Angellō; John 20:18

Angelos; Matt. 1:20; 18:10; 22:30; 25:41; Luke 7:27; John 1:51; 12:29; 20:12

Anistēmi; Luke 24:46; John 6:39; 11:23; 20:9

Anō; John 2:7; 8:23; 11:41

Anoia; Luke 6:11

Anoigō; Luke 3:21

Anomia; Matt. 13:41; 24:12

Anomos; Luke 22:37

Anōthen; John 3:3, 31; 19:11

Anthistēmi; Matt. 5:39

Anthrakia; John 18:18; 21:9

Anthrōpoktonos; John 8:44

Anthrōpos; Matt. 5:16; 8:20; 20:18; Mark 2:14; 13:26; Luke 5:24; 22:48, 69; John 1:51; 3:13; 6:27; 9:35; 12:23, 34

Anti; Mark 10:45

Antleō; John 2:8

Apairō; Luke 5:35

Aparneomai; Matt. 26:34; Mark 8:34; 14:30

Apechō; Mark 14:41

Apeitheō; John 3:36

Aphantos; Luke 24:31

Aphesis; Matt. 26:28; Mark 1:4; Luke 1:77; 3:3

Aphiēmi; Matt. 9:6; 12:32; 19:27; Mark 1:18; Luke 5:20; 7:47; 13:35; 18:28, 29

Aphistēmi; Luke 8:13

Aphorizō; Matt. 13:49; 25:32

Aphrōn; Luke 12:20

Apistia; Mark 6:6

Apistos; Luke 9:41; John 20:27

Apneomai; Matt. 10:33

Apo; Luke 14:18

Apodekatoō; Matt. 23:23; Luke 11:42

Apodidōmi; Matt. 22:21; Mark 12:17

Apodokimazō; Mark 8:31

Apographō; Luke 2:1

Apokalypsis; Luke 2:32

Apokalyptō; Matt. 11:25

Apokathistanō; Matt. 17:11

Apokathistano-; Mark 9:12

Apokathistēmi; Matt. 17:11; Mark 8:25; 9:12

Apokrinomai; Luke 22:68

Apokteinō; John 12:10; 16:2

Apokyliō; Luke 24:2

Apōleia; John 17:12

Apologeomai; Luke 21:14

Apollymi; Matt. 10:6, 28, 39; 12:14; 18:14; Luke 9:24; 13:3, 5; 19:47; John 3:16; 6:12, 27, 39; 10:10, 28; 11:50; 12:25; 17:12; 18:9

Apolyō; Matt. 1:19; Luke 6:37; John 18:39

Apolytrōsis; Luke 21:28

Aporeō; Luke 24:4; John 13:22

Apostasion; Matt. 5:31; 19:7

Ekpeirazō; Matt. 4:7; Luke 4:12

Ekplēssō; Luke 2:48

Ekporeuomai; John 15:26

E

Ean; Matt. 22:9

Ecclēsia; Matt. 16:18

Echidna; Matt. 23:33; Luke 3:7

Echō; Luke 9:58

Echthra; Luke 23:12

Echthros; Luke 1:74; 19:43

Ēdē; Matt. 3:10

Egkakeō; Luke 18:1

Egō; Matt. 26:40; Luke 12:17-19; John 4:26; 6:20, 35, 41; 8:12, 24, 28, 58; 9:9; 14:6; 15:1; 18:6

Ei; Luke 7:39; 13:9

Eidon; Mark 15:32; Luke 24:24

Eidos; John 5:37

Eimi; Matt. 18:17, 20; John 4:26; 6:20, 35, 41; 8:12, 24, 28, 58; 9:9; 14:6; 15:1; 18:6, 17

Eipon; Matt. 1:22; 5:21; 10:27; 23:39; 26:25; 28:6

Eirēnē; Matt. 10:13, 34; Luke 1:79; 10:5; 14:32; John 14:27; 20:19

Eirēnopoios; Matt. 5:9

Eis; Matt. 18:15; Luke 14:18

Eiserchomai; Matt. 23:13; Mark 9:47; John 10:9

Ek; John 8:44

Ekatontarchēs; Luke 7:2

Ekballō; Mark 1:12; Luke 6:22; John 6:37; 10:4; 12:31

Ekdikēsis; Luke 18:7; 21:22

Ekei; Matt. 18:20

Ekeinos; Luke 12:43, 45, 47; John 7:11; 9:11

Ekkenteō; John 19:37

Ekklēsia; Matt. 18:17

Ekkremannymi; Luke 19:48

Eklegomai; Luke 9:35; John 6:70; 13:18; 15:16, 19

Eklektos; Matt. 22:14; Mark 13:20

Ekneuō; John 5:13

Ekteinō; John 21:18

Ekthambeō; Mark 14:33

Ektinassō; Mark 6:11

Ektenoōs; Luke 22:44

Ekzēteō; Luke 11:50

Elachistos; Matt. 25:40

Elaia; Matt. 21:2

Elaion; Matt. 25:8; Luke 10:34

Elaunō; John 6:19

Eleēmōn; Matt. 5:7

Eleēmosynē; Matt. 6:2; Luke 11:41

Eleeō; Matt. 5:7; 18:33

Elenchō; John 16:8

Elenxō; Matt. 18:15

Eleos; Matt. 9:13; Luke 1:50, 72; 10:37

Eleutheroō; John 8:32

Eleutheros; Matt. 17:26

Ēlias; Matt. 11:14; 17:3; Luke 4:25; 9:19; John 1:21

Ēlikia; John 9:21

Elkoō; Luke 16:20

Elkyō; John 6:44; 12:32

Elpizō; Matt. 12:21; John 5:45

Embainō; John 6:17

Embrimaomai; Matt. 9:30; Mark 1:43; John 11:33

Emmanuoēl; Matt. 1:23

Empaizō; Mark 15:20; Luke 14:29

Emphanizō; John 14:21

Emphysaō; John 20:22

Empimprēmi; Matt. 22:7

Emporion; John 2:16

En; John 14:20

Endreuō; Luke 11:54

Endyma; Matt. 3:4; 22:11

Hypsistos; Mark 5:7; Luke 1:32
Hypsoō; John 3:14; 8:28; 12:34
Hyssōpos; John 19:29

I

Iakōb; Luke 1:33
Iaomai; Luke 9:2; John 4:47
Iatros; Luke 5:31
Ichthys; John 21:11
Idios; John 1:11
Idou; John 19:5
Iēsous; Matt. 1:1; Luke 8:39
Iōnas; Matt. 12:39
Iōta; Matt. 5:18
Ioudaia; Luke 4:44
Ioudaios; Matt. 2:2; 28:15
Isangelos; Luke 20:36
Ischyros; Luke 11:22
Iskariōtēs; John 6:71
Isos; John 5:18
Israel; Matt. 2:6
Israēl; Matt. 9:33; 10:6, 23; 15:31; Luke 1:54, 80

K

Kain; Luke 22:20
Kaiō; Luke 24:32; John 15:6
Kairos; Matt. 8:29; 16:3; Luke 21:24; John 7:6, 8
Kaisar; Matt. 22:17
Kakia; Matt. 6:34
Kakopoieō; Luke 6:9
Kakos; Matt. 21:41; John 18:30
Kakōs; John 18:23
Kaleō; Matt. 22:3; Luke 5:32; 14:16; John 2:2
Kalos; Matt. 13:23; 26:10; John 2:10
Kalōs; John 4:17
Kamēlos; Mark 1:6
Kana; John 2:1; 4:46
Kananaios; Matt. 15:22

Kapharnaoum; Luke 4:23; John 2:12
Kardia; Matt. 5:8; 6:21
Karpos; Matt. 3:8; 7:16; 21:34; Luke 3:9; John 4:36; 12:24; 15:2, 4, 16
Kartharizō; Mark 7:19
Katabainō; Luke 17:31; John 1:32, 51; 3:13; 4:51; 6:33, 38, 42
Katabolē; John 17:24
Katagnymi; John 19:31
Katagraphō; John 8:6
Katakrinō; John 8:10
Katalambanō; John 1:5; 12:35
Katalyma; Mark 14:14; Luke 2:7; 22:11
Katanoeō; Matt. 7:3
Katapetasma; Luke 23:45
Katartizō; Luke 6:40
Kataskēnoō; Luke 13:19
Kataskeuazō; Luke 1:17
Katasphazō; Luke 19:27
Katēcheō; Luke 1:4
Katēgoreō; John 5:45
Katēgoria; John 18:29
Katesthiō; John 2:17
Kathairō; John 15:2
Katharismos; Luke 2:22; John 2:6
Katharizō; Matt. 8:2
Katharos; Matt. 5:8; John 13:10; 15:3
Kathedra; Matt. 23:2
Kathēgētēs; Matt. 23:10
Kathēmai; Matt. 24:3; Mark 14:62; Luke 8:35
Katheudō; Matt. 9:24; Mark 5:39; Luke 8:52
Kathexēs; Luke 1:3
Kathistēmi; Matt. 24:47
Kathizō; Matt. 5:1
Kathōs; Matt. 28:6
Katō; John 8:23
Katoikeō; Matt. 23:21
Keiria; John 11:44

Lambanō; Luke 19:12; John 5:43; 13:20; 17:8; 19:6

Lampas; John 18:3

Lambanō; Luke 20:28

Lanchanō; Luke 1:9; John 19:24

Laos; Matt. 1:21; 27:25; Luke 2:31

Latreuō; Matt. 4:10; Luke 1:74; 4:8

Laxeutos; Luke 23:53

Legiōn; Mark 5:9; Luke 8:30

Legō; Matt. 1:22; 5:21; 10:27; 27:11; Mark 15:2; Luke 9:21; 22:70; 23:2, 3

Lention; John 13:4

Lepra; Luke 5:12

Lepros; Mark 1:40

Lepton; Mark 12:42; Luke 12:59; 21:2

Lēros; Luke 24:11

Lēstēs; Matt. 27:38; Mark 11:17; 14:48; Luke 22:52; John 10:1; 18:40

Leukos; Luke 9:29

Libanos; Matt. 2:11

Limnē; Luke 8:23

Lithos; Matt. 21:42; Luke 19:40; 20:17, 18; 21:6; John 20:1

Lithostōtos; John 19:13

Litra; John 12:3; 19:39

Logos; Matt. 8:16; 13:19; 18:23; 24:35; Mark 4:14; Luke 8:11; John 1:1; 3:34; 4:41

Loidoreō; John 9:28

Lonchē; John 19:34

Lordanēs; John 10:40

Lōt; Luke 17:26-29

Loudaios; Mark 15:2; John 1:19; 2:18; 5:10; 6:41; 7:1, 11, 35; 8:22, 31; 9:18; 10:24; 11:8, 19; 12:9, 11; 13:33; 18:20, 35, 36; 19:7, 12, 14, 20, 21

Louō; John 13:10

Luchnos; Luke 8:16

Luō; Luke 13:15, 16

Lychnos; Luke 11:33-34, 36; John 5:35

Lykos; Matt. 10:16

Lyō; Matt. 16:19; 18:17; John 2:19; 7:23; 10:35; 11:44

Lyp; John 16:6

Lypeō; Matt. 17:23

Lytron; Matt. 20:28; Mark 10:45

Lytroō; Luke 24:21

Lytrōsis; Luke 1:68; 2:38

M

Machaira; Matt. 10:34; 26:51-52; Luke 22:38; John 18:10

Magos; Matt. 2:1

Mainomai; John 10:20

Makarios; Matt. 5:2

Makran; Mark 12:34

Makrothen; Mark 8:3

Mamōnas; Matt. 6:24; Luke 16:9, 11, 13

Manna; John 6:31

Manthanō; John 7:15

Martyreō; John 1:7, 34; 3:11; 18:23; 19:35

Martyria; John 1:19; 3:11, 32

Martyrion; Mark 1:44; Luke 5:14; 21:13

Martys; Matt. 18:16; Luke 24:48

Mastigoō; Matt. 10:17; John 19:1

Mastix; Mark 5:29

Mathētēs; Matt. 5:1; 10:24; Mark 2:15; John 4:1; 13:35; 15:8; 18:15, 19

Mathēteuō; Matt. 13:52; 28:19

Maththaios; Matt. 9:9

Mechri; Luke 16:16

Megaleiotēs; Luke 9:43

Megalynō; Luke 1:46

Megas; Matt. 20:25; 22:36; Luke 1:15; 22:24; John 7:37; 10:29; 14:12, 28; 19:11

Megistan; Mark 6:21

Melei; Luke 10:40

Melō; John 10:13

Menō; Luke 8:27; John 1:32, 38; 5:38; 6:56;
8:35; 9:41; 11:6; 12:24, 34; 14:10, 17, 25;
15:4, 7, 9, 16; 21:22

Merimna; Mark 4:19

Merimnaō; Matt. 6:25

Meris; Luke 10:42

Meros; John 13:8

Messias; John 1:41

Meta; Matt. 26:40; Mark 5:18; John 13:7

Metabainō; Matt. 8:34; John 5:24; 7:3; 13:1

Metamelomai; Matt. 27:3

Metamorphō; Matt. 17:2

Metamorphoō; Mark 9:2

Metanoeō; Matt. 3:2; Luke 15:7

Metanoia; Matt. 3:8; Mark 1:4; Luke 3:3

Mētēr; John 2:3

Mēti; Mark 14:19; Luke 6:39; John 4:29

Metrētēs; John 2:6

Metron; Luke 6:38; John 3:34

Miainō; John 18:28

Mignymi; Luke 13:1

Mikros; Matt. 10:42; 11:11; 18:6; Mark 9:42;
John 16:16

Mimnēskomai; John 2:17, 22

Miseō; Luke 14:26; 19:14; John 15:18

Misthos; Matt. 5:12; 10:41; 20:8; Luke 6:35;
10:7; John 4:36

Misthōtos; John 10:12

Mna; Luke 19:13

Mnēmeion; Matt. 27:52, 60; Luke 11:44;
John 5:28; 11:38; 19:41

Mnēmoneuō; John 16:4

Mnēmosynon; Mark 14:9

Mnēsteuō; Matt. 1:18; Luke 2:5

Modios; Mark 4:21

Mogilalos; Mark 7:32

Moicheuō; Luke 16:18

Monē; John 14:2

Monogenēs; John 1:14, 18; 3:16

Mōros; Matt. 7:26; 23:17; 25:2

Moschos; Luke 15:27

Mōusēs; Matt. 23:3; Luke 16:29; 20:37

Mōysēs; Matt. 17:3

Mylikos; Luke 17:2

Mylos; Mark 9:42

Myrizō; Mark 14:8

Myron; Matt. 26:7; Luke 7:37; 23:56;
John 11:2

Mystērion; Matt. 13:11; Mark 4:11;
Luke 8:10

N

Naiman; Luke 4:27

Naos; Matt. 26:61; John 2:19

Nardos; Mark 14:3; John 12:3

Natham; Luke 3:31

Nathanaēl; John 1:45

Nazaret; John 1:45

Nazōraios; Matt. 2:23

Neaniskos; Mark 16:5

Nekros; Matt. 8:22

Nephelē; Mark 9:7; Luke 9:34; 21:27

Nēpios; Matt. 11:25; Luke 10:21

Nēsteuō; Matt. 4:2; 6:16; Mark 2:18;
Luke 5:33

Neuō; John 13:24

Nikaō; John 16:33

Niptō; John 13:5, 6, 10, 14

Nōe; Luke 17:26-29

Noeō; Matt. 24:15

Nomē; John 10:9

Nomikos; Matt. 2:35

Nomizō; Luke 3:23

Nomos; Matt. 5:17; John 1:17, 45; 7:19, 51;
8:5, 17; 10:34; 12:34; 15:25; 18:31; 19:7

Nymphios; Matt. 9:15; Luke 5:34

Nyn; Luke 1:49

Nyssō; John 19:34

Nyx; John 3:2; 9:4; 13:30

O

Ochlos; Matt. 4:25; 15:32; Luke 3:10; John 7:12, 20, 31, 40, 49

Ōdin; Mark 13:8

Oida; Matt. 25:12; Luke 4:34; 23:34; John 1:26; 3:11; 6:61, 64; 8:19; 13:1, 11; 18:4; 19:28

Oikia; Matt. 10:12; John 4:53; 14:2

Oikodomeō; Luke 11:47-48

Oikonomia; Luke 16:2

Oikos; Matt. 21:13; Luke 19:46

Oiktirmōn; Luke 6:36

Oinopotēs; Luke 7:34

Oinos; Luke 10:34

Oknēros; Matt. 25:26

Oligopistia; Matt. 17:20

Oligopistos; Matt. 8:26

Oligos; Matt. 25:21

Omnuō; Matt. 5:36; 23:16

Onarion; John 12:14

Oneidizō; Mark 16:14

Oneidos; Luke 1:25

Onikos; Mark 9:42

Onoma; Luke 6:22; 10:20; John 16:26; 17:6

Opheilēma; Matt. 6:12

Opheilō; Luke 11:4; John 13:14

Ophis; John 3:14

Ophthalmos; Matt. 20:15; Mark 7:22

Opos; Matt. 5:1

Opsarion; John 6:9; 21:9

Opsis; John 7:24

Optasia; Luke 1:22; 24:23

Orgē; Matt. 3:7; Luke 3:7; John 3:36

Orgizō; Matt. 5:22; 18:34

Ornis; Luke 13:34

Oros; Matt. 21:1; 28:16; Mark 11:23; John 4:20; 6:3; 8:1

Orphanos; John 14:18

Osmē; John 12:3

Osphys; Luke 12:35

Osteon; Luke 24:39

Ōtarion; John 18:10

Othonion; John 19:40

Ou; Matt. 12:2

Ouai; Matt. 11:21; 23:13; Mark 13:17; 14:21; Luke 6:24

Ouchi; Luke 4:22; 6:39

Oude; Mark 5:3

Oudeis; Mark 5:3; Luke 23:15

Oudepō; John 7:39

Oudepote; John 7:46

Ouketi; Mark 5:3

Oupanos; Matt. 3:16

Ouranos; Matt. 3:2; 19:12

Outos; Matt. 23:36; 24:34; Luke 21:31

Oxos; Mark 15:36; Luke 23:36; John 19:29

Ozō; John 11:39

P

Pagideuō; Matt. 22:15

Pagis; Luke 21:35

Paideuō; Luke 23:16

Paidion; Matt. 18:3; Mark 10:15; Luke 9:48; 11:7; 18:16-17; John 4:49; 21:5

Paidiskē; Mark 14:66; Luke 22:56

Pais; Matt. 12:18

Palingenesia; Matt. 19:28

Panourgia; Luke 20:23

Para; Mark 3:21; John 7:29; 9:33; 17:8

Parabolē; Matt. 13:3; Mark 3:23; 4:2; Luke 5:36

Parachrēma; Luke 19:11

Paradeisos; Luke 23:43

Paradidōmi; Matt. 25:14; 26:16; Mark 3:19; 9:31; 14:10; 15:1; Luke 1:2; 9:44; 21:12; John 6:64, 71; 12:4; 18:5, 30; 19:11, 16, 30; 21:20

Paradosis; Matt. 15:2; Mark 7:3

Paradoxos; Luke 5:26

Parakaleō; Matt. 5:4

Parakathezomai; Luke 10:39

Paraklēsis; Luke 2:25

Paraklētos; John 14:16, 26; 15:26

Parakoloutheō; Mark 16:17; Luke 1:3

Parakouō; Mark 5:36

Parakyptō; John 20:5

Paralambanō; Matt. 24:40; Luke 17:34-35; John 1:11

Paralytikos; Matt. 4:24; Mark 2:3

Paraptōma; Matt. 6:14

Paraskeuē; Mark 15:42; Luke 23:54; John 19:14

Paratēreō; Luke 6:7; 14:1

Paratērēsis; Luke 17:20

Pareimi; Matt. 26:50

Parerchomai; Mark 6:48; 13:30

Paroikeō; Luke 24:18

Paroimia; John 10:6; 16:25, 29

Parousia; Matt. 24:3, 27

Parrēsia; John 7:4; 10:24; 11:14, 54; 18:20

Parthenos; Matt. 1:23; Luke 1:27

Pas; Matt. 11:27, 28; 24:9; 28:18, 20; John 10:8

Pascha; Matt. 26:19; Mark 14:1; Luke 22:1, 7; John 2:13; 11:55

Paschō; Luke 9:22; 17:25; 24:46

Patassō; Matt. 26:31

Patēr; Matt. 5:16; 24:36; Luke 11:2

Patris; Mark 6:1; John 4:44

Pēchys; John 21:8

Pēgē; John 4:6

Peirasmos; Matt. 6:13; Luke 11:4; 22:40, 46

Peirazō; Matt. 4:1, 3; Mark 10:2; Luke 4:2; John 6:6; 8:6

Pēlos; John 9:6

Pempō; John 1:6, 33; 4:34; 5:23, 37; 6:44; 7:33; 8:16; 14:26; 15:21, 26; 16:5, 7; 20:21

Penichros; Luke 21:2

Pentakischilioi; John 6:10

Pentēkonta; Luke 16:6

Pentheō; Matt. 5:4

Peri; Mark 4:10

Perissos; John 10:10

Peristera; Matt. 3:16; Luke 2:24

Peritemeō; Luke 1:59

Peritemnō; Luke 2:21

Peritomē; John 7:22

Petra; Matt. 16:18

Petros; Matt. 4:18

Phaneroō; John 1:31; 3:20; 7:4; 9:3; 21:1

Phanos; John 18:3

Pharisaios; Matt. 3:7; 16:12; Mark 2:16; 7:5; Luke 5:17; 7:36; John 1:24; 7:32; 8:3; 11:57

Phaulos; John 3:20; 5:29

Phēmē; Luke 4:14

Pheugō; Matt. 26:56; Mark 16:8; John 10:5

Phileō; John 5:20; 11:36; 15:19; 16:27; 21:15

Philippos; John 12:21

Philos; Matt. 11:19; John 3:29; 15:14; 19:12

Phimoō; Mark 4:39; Luke 4:35

Phobeō; Matt. 1:20; 14:27; John 19:8

Phobeō; Luke 12:4-5

Phobētron; Luke 21:11

Phoinix; John 12:13

Phōneō; John 9:18, 24; 18:27

Phoros; Luke 20:22

Phortizō; Luke 11:46

Phōs; Matt. 4:16; 5:14; Luke 2:32; John 1:4; 9:5; 11:9; 12:35, 36, 46

Phragellion; John 2:15

Phragelloō; Mark 15:15

Phrear; John 4:6, 11

Phronimos; Matt. 7:24; 25:4; Luke 12:42

Phthanō; Matt. 12:28; Luke 11:20

Phylakē; Mark 6:48; Luke 12:38

Phylaktērion; Matt. 23:5

Phylassō; Luke 11:28; John 12:47; 17:12

Proskairos; Matt. 13:21; Mark 4:17

Proskyneō; Matt. 2:2; 28:9; Luke 4:7; John 9:38

Prosōpon; Matt. 18:10; Mark 12:14; Luke 9:51

Prosphagion; John 21:5

Prospherō; John 16:2

Prothesis; Mark 2:26; Luke 6:4

Prōtokathedria; Mark 12:39

Prōtoklisia; Luke 14:8

Prōtos; Matt. 20:8; Mark 6:21; 7:27; John 1:15, 30; 12:16

Protrechō; John 20:4

Psēphizō; Luke 14:28

Pseudomartyria; Matt. 26:59

Pseudoprophētēs; Matt. 7:15; Luke 6:26

Pseudos; John 8:44

Psōmion; John 13:26

Psychē; Matt. 10:28; Mark 8:35; Luke 12:22; 17:33

Ptōchos; Matt. 5:2; Luke 4:18; 6:20; 14:21

Ptōma; Mark 15:45

Ptōsis; Luke 2:34

Ptuon; Luke 3:17

Ptysma; John 9:6

Pygmē; Mark 7:3

Pylē; Matt. 16:18

Pyr; Matt. 3:12; 25:41; Luke 3:9; 9:54; 12:49

Pyretos; John 4:52

R

Rabbi; Matt. 23:7

Rabbouni; Mark 10:51; John 20:16

Rapisma; John 18:22

Rhama; Matt. 2:18

Rhaphis; Mark 10:25

Rhēma; Matt. 4:4; Luke 1:37-38; 5:5; John 3:34; 12:47

Rhomphaia; Luke 2:35

Rhysis; Mark 5:25; Luke 8:43

S

Sabbaton; Mark 2:24; Luke 4:16; 6:1; 13:14; John 5:9; 9:14

Saddoukaios; Matt. 3:7; 16:12; Mark 12:18; Luke 20:27

Saleim; John 3:23

Saleuō; Luke 21:26

Samaritēs; Luke 10:29; John 4:9

Sapros; Luke 6:43

Sarepta; Luke 4:26

Sarx; Matt. 19:5; Luke 24:39; John 1:14; 3:6; 6:51, 52, 63; 8:15

Satan; Matt. 4:10; 16:23; Luke 10:17

Satanas; Matt. 16:23; Mark 1:13; Luke 22:3; John 13:27

Saton; Luke 13:21

Schisma; John 9:16; 10:19

Schizō; Matt. 27:51; Mark 1:10; 15:38

Selēniazomai; Matt. 4:24

Sēmainō; John 12:33

Sēmeion; Matt. 16:3; Mark 8:11; 13:4; Luke 2:34; 11:29; 21:7; 23:8; John 2:11, 18; 3:2; 4:48, 54; 6:2, 30; 7:31; 20:30

Sēmeron; Luke 2:11; 4:21; 23:43

Sikera; Luke 1:15

Silōam; John 9:7

Simōn; Matt. 4:18

Sinapi; Matt. 13:31; Mark 4:31

Sindōn; Mark 14:51

Siniazō; Luke 22:31

Siōn; John 12:15

Siōpaō; Luke 1:20

Skandalizō; Matt. 11:6; 18:6; Mark 4:17; 14:27; Luke 7:23; John 6:61; 16:1

Skandalon; Matt. 16:23; 18:7; Luke 17:1

Skēnē; Matt. 17:4; Mark 9:5; Luke 9:33

Skēnoō; John 1:14

Skēnopēgia; John 7:2

Skirtaō; Luke 1:41

Sklērokardia; Matt. 19:8; Mark 10:5

Tarassō; Luke 24:38; John 5:7; 11:33; 12:27; 13:21; 14:1, 27

Teknion; John 13:33

Teknon; Luke 13:34; John 1:12; 8:39

Tektōn; Mark 6:3

Teleioō; John 4:34; 5:36; 17:4, 23; 19:28

Teleios; Matt. 5:48; 19:21

Teleiōsis; Luke 1:45

Teleō; John 19:28, 30

Teleuteō; Matt. 9:18

Telōnēs; Matt. 18:17; Mark 2:15; Luke 3:12

Telōnion; Mark 2:14; Luke 5:27

Telos; Luke 21:9; John 13:1

Teras; John 4:48

Tēreō; Matt. 28:20; John 8:51, 55; 9:16; 12:7; 14:21, 23; 17:6, 11, 15

Tessares; John 11:17

Tesserakonta; Matt. 4:2

Tetartaios; John 11:39

Tetartos; Mark 6:48

Tetraarchēs; Matt. 14:1

Tetraplous; Luke 19:8

Tetraarcheō; Luke 3:1

Tetrarchēs; Matt. 14:1

Thambos; Luke 4:36

Thanatos; Matt. 4:16; Luke 1:79

Thaptō; Matt. 8:21; Luke 9:59

Thaumastos; John 9:30

Thaumazō; Luke 1:21; 2:33; 7:9; 24:12; John 4:27; 7:15

Theaomai; Matt. 6:1; 23:5

Thēkē; John 18:11

Thelēma; Mark 3:35

Thelō; Matt. 20:14

Thēnskō; Luke 8:49

Theōreō; John 4:19; 6:40; 8:51; 12:45

Theos; Matt. 15:31; 19:24; 21:43; Mark 1:1; 3:11, 35; Luke 22:70; John 10:33, 34; 20:28

Theosebēs; John 9:31

Therapeuō; Matt. 4:23

Thēreuō; Luke 11:54

Therismos; Matt. 9:37; Luke 10:2

Thēsauros; Matt. 6:19

Thlipsis; Matt. 24:21; Mark 13:19

Thorybos; Mark 14:2

Thrēneo; Luke 7:32

Thrix; Mark 1:6; Luke 21:18

Thronos; Matt. 19:28

Thymiama; Luke 1:10

Thumos; Luke 4:28

Thygatēr; Mark 5:34

Thyra; John 10:1, 7

Thyrōros; John 10:3; 18:17

Tis; Luke 4:34

Tiberias; John 6:1

Tiktō; John 16:21

Timaō; John 5:23; 8:49; 12:26

Tithēmi; John 10:11, 15; 13:4, 37; 15:13, 16

Titlos; John 19:19

Topos; John 11:48

Trachēlos; Luke 15:20

Trapeza; Luke 22:30

Trechō; John 20:2

Trēma; Luke 18:25

Tritos; John 2:1

Trōgō; John 6:54, 57

Trophē; John 4:34

Trugōn; Luke 2:24

Trymalia; Mark 10:25

Typhloō; John 12:40

X

Xērainō; Mark 3:1; 9:18

Xēros; John 5:3

Z

Zacharias; Matt. 23:35